Human Resource Management

Human Resource Management

Sixth Edition

David A. DeCenzo
Towson University

Stephen P. Robbins
San Diego State University

John Wiley & Sons, Inc.

New York   Chichester   Weinheim   Brisbane   Toronto   Singapore

EDITOR	Ellen Ford
MARKETING MANAGER	Carlise Paulson
SENIOR PRODUCTION EDITOR	Kelly Tavares
COVER DESIGNER	Karin Kincheloe
PHOTO EDITOR	Jennifer Atkins
ILLUSTRATION EDITOR	Jaime Perea
ILLUSTRATION STUDIO	Wellington Studio
TEXT DESIGNER	Meryl Sussman Levavi/Digitext, Inc.
COVER ART	Diana Ong, "A Crowd," 1940/SuperStock, Inc.

This book was set in Garamond Light by Progressive Information Technologies and printed and bound by Van Hoffman Press. The cover was printed by Phoenix Color.

This book is printed on acid-free paper. ∞

Library of Congress Cataloging in Publication Data:
DeCenzo, David A.
   Human resource management : concepts and applications/ David A.
DeCenzo, Stephen P. Robbins. -- 6th ed.
     p.   cm.
   Includes index.
   ISBN 0-471-29989-8 (alk. paper)
   1. Personnel management.   I. Robbins, Stephen P., 1943-   .
II. Title.
HF5549.D396   1999
658.3--dc21
                                           98-40473
                                             CIP

Printed in the United States of America

10 9 8 7 6 5 4 3 2 1

Preface

Welcome to the sixth edition of our *Human Resource Management* text. We're glad you're taking the time to read this preface and getting to know this book better. We'll use this section to address three important things: (1) what this book is about, (2) the important in-text learning aids, and (3) who, besides the authors named on the cover, were instrumental in the book's development.

ABOUT-THE-BOOK

When we revised the book for the fifth edition, we made some major changes. We downsized the book, eliminated material that at the time we felt was courageous, added a heavy dose of pedagogy to make the book more "student-friendly," and brought the book to market in paperback. We took some risks, bucking the "market" to some extent, and kept our fingers crossed that we had made the correct decisions. Well, we are happy to report that thanks to you and countless others, the fifth edition was a resounding success. The market accepted our changes, students appreciated the effort to provide them good learning tools, and most everyone was appreciative of the book being in paperback. We knew for the sixth edition that we'd have to continue with this tradition, offer our readers more, and once again produce a market-leading product.

We started this process by going back to our users—and even sought advice from those who hadn't chosen us as their HRM text. What we got was plenty of advice—and a lot of very good suggestions. We looked hard at our research, and made the changes that clearly will make this edition of HRM even better than the last. For this information, and to those who provided it, we are grateful. So what did we do?

We began with a set of goals—to once again produce a text that addressed the most critical issues in human resource management (HRM). We also continued with our tradition of achieving a delicate balance between basic HRM functions, and the new world of HRM. Moreover, in a dynamic field like HRM, a completely updated research base is a must. You want to know, after all, the current state of the field. We have undertaken an extensive literature review to include hundreds of 1996, 1997, and 1998 citations from business periodicals and academic journals in this text. For example, you'll find some of the latest information on sexual harassment in Chapter 3, as well as the effect of the Internet on such HRM activities as recruiting (Chapter 6 and the Appendix).

Probably one of the major elements of this new edition is the addition of more pedagogy. Through the efforts of Connie Sitterly, international consultant, trainer, author, founder and owner of Management Training Specialists, and pro-

This product has been developed based upon the Human Resources body of knowledge as defined by the Human Resource Certification Institute (HRCI), an affiliate at the Society for Human Resource Management (SHRM)

fessor at Texas Woman's University (an individual who brings years of entrepreneurial, training and development, and academic experience to this project), we've included learning aids and assessments that will assist the readers in understanding themselves better, and gaining skills that will be invaluable in their future career endeavors.

LEARNING AIDS

Our experience has led us to conclude that a text becomes highly readable when the writing is straightforward and conversational, the topics flow logically, and the authors make extensive use of examples to illustrate concepts. These factors guided us in developing this text as a highly effective learning tool. Previous text users have regularly commented on how clearly our books present ideas. We think this one, too, is written in a clear, lively, concise, and conversational style. Furthermore, our classroom experience tells us that students remember and understand concepts and practices most clearly when they are illustrated through examples. So we've used a wealth of examples to clarify ideas.

Each chapter of this book is organized to provide clarity and continuity. Each begins with *Learning Objectives,* which identify specifically what the reader should gain after reading the chapter. Within the chapters themselves, we address and highlight the most important current issues with features such as *Workplace Issues,* boxed articles that bring to light the most current topics and issues in the workplace today; end-of-chapter *Summary* sections, which relate chapter material specifically to the learning objectives; and *Key Terms* in each chapter, which are highlighted in the text and defined in the *Glossary* of the book.

Have you had students tell you that they read the assignments and thought they understood the material, but still didn't do well on the exam? Well, we have both had this experience and know that many students have, too. In fact, much of the feedback we got from users of the fifth edition was extremely positive on this point. So we've continued the *Testing Your Understanding* questions at the end of each chapter. These questions are designed to assist readers in determining if they understood the chapter material. In most cases, questions link directly to the learning objectives. We've answered each of these questions for readers. These questions have been specifically written to challenge your critical thinking, and generally require some application from the chapter's content. We close out each chapter with an *Experiential Exercise,* a *Web Wise Exercise,* and a *Case Application*. Roll-Plays and Field Assignments encourage students to think and act as an HRM professional, and encourage working in group situations.

Supporting Material

This book is supported by a comprehensive learning package that helps instructors create a motivating environment and provides students with additional instruments for understanding and reviewing major concepts.

The *Instructor's Resource Guide* developed by Vicki Kaman, Colorado State University, provides many useful items, including sample syllabi, learning objectives, key concepts, chapter overview, chapter outline, lecture suggestions, review and discussion questions, media resources, and the additional case per chapter.

The *Test Bank,* developed by Trudy Somers, Towson University, consists of approximately 1800 multiple-choice, true/false, and completion questions categorized by level of difficulty, text-page reference, and learning objective being tested. The Test Bank is available in paper form and in a computerized version called MICROTEST.

▶ A set of full-color PowerPoint slides visually highlights key concepts and figures found in the text.

▶ Video selections from the popular and highly regarded business news program *Nightly Business Report* bring to life the topics and issues of HRM by highlighting actual stories of companies and the HRM issues they face.

▶ Wiley and the Dow Jones Company have teamed up to offer an exciting new way to extend your textbook beyond the walls of the classroom—the *Business Extra Program*—comprised of *The On-Line Business Survival Guide for Management*—which includes a special password for Wiley's *Business Extra* Web site through which you and your students get instant access to a wealth of current articles as well as a special offer for the *Wall Street Journal Interactive Edition. The On-Line Business Survival Guide for Management* can be packaged with the text.

ACKNOWLEDGMENTS

Getting a finished book into a reader's hands requires the work of many people. The authors do their part by efficiently developing an outline, thoroughly researching topics, and accurately keyboarding sentences into their computers. We would like to recognize just a few of the people who contributed to this text.

First of all are our reviewers. As we previously mentioned, the reviewers for the sixth edition were fantastic. They gave us great feedback and provided some insight to us. The book you have before you is a much better learning tool because of our reviewers' insights. We only hope that you can see how your comments influenced us—even though not every suggestion was possible to implement. Specifically, we wish to recognize reviewers from this edition as well as reviewers of previous editions: Dennis Middlemist, Colorado State University; John McClendon, Temple University; John A. Lust, Illinois State University; Fraya Wagner-Marsh, Eastern Michigan University; Andrew Klein, Keller Graduate School of Management; Jack Kondrasuk, University of Portland; Howard Stanger, Buffalo State College; Alison Barber, Michigan State University; Judy Weisinger, Northeastern University; Arthur Worthington, Richard Stockton College; Claudia Harris, North Carolina Central University; and Sam Hazen, Tarleton State University.

A book doesn't simply appear automatically on bookstore shelves. It gets there through the combined efforts of many people. For us, this is the outstanding publishing team at John Wiley & Sons, consisting of Ellen Ford, our editor; Carlise Paulson, Marketing Manager; Kelly Tavares, Senior Production Editor; and Karin Kincheloe, Senior Designer. We also thank Trudy Somers for her work in the "Testing Your Understanding" questions, and the Test Bank and to Vicki Kaman for the work on the Instructor's Resource Manual.

Clearly, we owe a special debt of gratitude to Connie Sitterly. Connie, your work was fabulous, right on target with us, and turned around in unbelievably record time. There is no doubt that our continued success with HRM, sixth edition will be directly related to your fine efforts. And we hope that this is the start of a long-term association with us and future editions of HRM.

Last, we want to acknowledge a few people individually. For Dave, I wish again to thank my family who never appear to tire of my maniacal writing efforts. To my wife, Terri, and my four quickly growing kids—Mark, Meredith, Gabriella, and Natalie—you are the guiding lights of my life.

For Steve, I would like to acknowledge the support of my wife, Laura. Thanks, honey, for understanding the weird life of a writer.

DAVE DECENZO
STEVE ROBBINS

David A. DeCenzo received his Ph.D. from West Virginia University. He is an Associate Dean and Professor of Management at Towson University. His major teaching and research interests focus on the general areas of human resource management, management, and organizational behavior. He has published articles in such journals as Harvard Business Review, Business Horizons, Risk Management, Hospital topics, and Performance and Instruction.

Dr. DeCenzo has spent his recent years writing textbooks. His books include Human Resource Management, 6th edition (1999) with Stephen Robbins; Fundamentals of Management, 2nd edition (1998) with Stephen Robbins; Human Relations (1997); Essentials of Labor Relations (1992) with Molly Bowers; and Employee Benefits (1990) with Stephen Holoviak, all published by Prentice Hall. These books are used widely at colleges and universities in the U.S., as well as schools throughout the world.

Dr. DeCenzo also has industry experience as a corporate trainer, and has served as a consultant to a number of companies, including G&K Services, Inc., Moen, Inc., HealthCare Strategies, Inc., AlliedSignal Technical Services Corporation, First National Bank of Maryland, Teledyne/Landis Machine Company, Blue Cross & Blue Shield of Maryland, the Tnemec Company, the James River Corporation, Packaging Division, and the Managerial and Professional Society of Baltimore.

In Dr. DeCenzo's other life, he participates in raising his four children (Mark, Meredith, Gabriella, and Natalie) with his wife, Terri. He isn't setting any world record times, but does plenty of "running" around.

Stephen P. Robbins received his Ph.D. from the University of Arizona. He previously worked for the Shell Oil Company and Reynolds Metals Company. Since completing his graduate studies, Dr. Robbins has taught at the University of Nebraska at Omaha, Concordia University in Montreal, the University of Baltimore, Southern Illinois University at Edwardsville, and San Diego State University. Dr. Robbins' research interests have focused on conflict, power, and politics in organizations, as well as the development of effective interpersonal skills. His articles on these and other topics have appeared in such journals as Business Horizons, the California Management Review, Business and Economic Perspectives, International Management, Management Review, Canadian Personnel and Industrial Relations, and the Journal of Management Education.

In recent years, Dr. Robbins has been spending most of his professional time writing textbooks. These include Management, 6th edition (1999) with Mary Coulter, Organizational Behavior, 8th edition (1998); Supervision Today! 2nd edition, (1998) with David DeCenzo; Managing Today! (1997); Essentials of Organizational Behavior, 5th edition (1997); Training in InterPersonal Skills, 2nd edition, (1996) with Philip Hunsaker; and Organization Theory, 3rd edition (1990), all published by Prentice Hall. These books are used at more than a thousand U.S. colleges and universities, as well as hundreds of schools throughout Canada, Latin America, Australia, New Zealand, Asia, Scandinavia, and Europe.

In Dr. Robbins' "other life," he participates in masters' track competition. Since turning 50 in 1993, he has set numerous indoor and outdoor world sprint records. He's also won gold medals in World Veteran Games in 100m, 200m, and 400m. In 1995, Robbins was named the year's outstanding age-40-and-over male track and field athlete by the Masters Track and Field Committee of USA Track & Field, the national governing body for athletes in the United States.

To: **Our Readers**

From: **Dave DeCenzo and Steve Robbins**

Subject: **How to get the most out of this text**

All authors of a textbook generally include a preface that describes why they wrote the book and what's unique about it, and then thank a lot of people for the role they played in getting the book completed. Well, we're no different; we did that, too. But it has become crystal-clear to us that two things are common about a book's preface. First, it's usually written for the professor, especially one who's considering selecting the book. Second, students don't read the preface. That's unfortunate because it often includes information that students would find useful.

As authors, we do listen to our customers. And many of ours have told us that they'd enjoy some input from us. So, we've written this memo. Our purpose is to provide you with our ideas about the book, how it was put together, and more importantly, how you can use it to better understand the field of HRM—and do better in this class!

This book was written to provide you with the foundations of HRM. Whether you intend to work in HRM or not, most of these elements will affect you at some point in your career. How? Take, for example, the performance appraisal. Although you might not currently be in a position to evaluate another individual's work performance, if you are working, you're more than likely to have your performance appraised. For that matter, each time you take an exam in a class, your performance is being evaluated. Consequently, it's important for you to have an understanding of how it should work, and the potential problems that may exist.

We began Part I of this book with an emphasis on providing you with an overview of HRM, its approach, and its cast of characters. From there, we move to more global issues surrounding the HRM function. The environment in which HRM operates is changing rapidly, so we want you to get a feel for what is happening in the business world today and what implications it presents for HRM. Next, we need to turn our attention to the laws that affect HRM activities. Much of how HRM operates is guided by legislation and court decisions that prohibit practices that adversely affect certain groups of people. Without a good understanding of these laws, an organization's performance can suffer, and the organization can be vulnerable to costly lawsuits. Part I ends with a discussion of several areas designed to get the maximum effort from workers.

Parts II through V provide coverage of the fundamental activities that exist in HRM. Part II explores the staffing function, with discussions on employment recruiting, and selection. Part III addresses means for socializing, training, and developing employees. Part IV looks at how organizations evaluate, pay, and reward its employees. Then, in Part V, we look at ways for management to keep their high-performing employees, and the rights employees have.

Much of the discussion in Part II through V reflects typical activities in an organization that is not unionized. When a union is present, however, many of these practices might need modification to comply with another set of laws. As such, we reserved the final chapter for dealing with labor—management relations.

While we are confident that completing the 16 chapters contained in the book will provide the fundamentals of HRM, a text has to offer more. It should not only cover topics (we hope, in an interesting and lively way), it should also assist in the learning process. It should be written in such a way that you can understand it, it keeps your attention, and it provides you an opportunity for feedback. We think we've met each of these goals. Of course, only you can be the judge of our claim. But let's look at how we arrived at our conclusion.

To be understandable and lively means that we need to communicate with you. We make every attempt in this text to have it sound as if we were in front of your class speaking with you. Writing style is important to us. We use examples whenever possible—real companies, so you can see that what we talk about is happening in the "real world." In the past, people using our books have indicated that our writing style does help hold their attention. But the communication connection, albeit critical, is only half of the equation. The ultimate tests for you are: Does the book help you do well on exams? Does it help prepare you for a job?

We start every chapter with learning objectives. We view these as the critical learning points. They present a logic flow from which the material will be presented. If you can explain what is proposed in each learning objective, you'll be on the right track to understanding the material. But memory sometimes fools us. We read the material, think we understand it, see how the summaries directly tie the learning objectives together, then take the exam and receive a grade that is not reflective of "what we knew we knew." We have given a lot of thought to that issue, and think we've come up with something that will help—putting a feedback test in the book! Let's explain.

The typical textbook ends each chapter with a set of review questions. Unfortunately, your tests rarely look much like the review questions. Exams, for the most part, frequently emphasize multiple-choice exams. So we've replaced the review questions with a set of test questions. These questions are actual questions that we've used to test our students' understanding of the material. If you can correctly answer these questions, then you're one step closer to enhancing your understanding of HRM. Recognize, of course, that these are only a learning aid. They help you to learn but don't replace careful reading or intensive studying. And don't assume that getting a question right means you fully understand the concept covered. Why? Because any set of multiple-choice questions can only test a limited range of information. So don't let correct answers lull you into a sense of false security. If you miss a question or don't fully understand why you got the correct response, go back to the material in the chapter and reread the material.

Learning, however, goes beyond just passing a test. It also means preparing yourself to perform successfully in tomorrow's organizations. You'll find that organizations today require their employees to work more closely together than at any time in the past. Call it teams, horizontal organizational structures, matrix management, or the like, the fact remains that your success will depend on how well you work closely with others. To help model this group concept for you, we have included class exercises in this text. Each of these experiential learning efforts is designed to highlight a particular topic in the text and give you an opportunity to work in groups to solve the issue at hand.

One last thing before we close: What can you take out of this course and use in the future? Many business leaders have complained about how business schools train their graduates. Although business schools have made many positive accomplishments, one critical component appears lacking—practical skills. The skills you need to succeed in today's business environment are increasing. You must be able to communicate (both verbally and in a written format), think creatively, make good and timely decisions, plan effectively, and deal with people. In HRM, we have an opportunity to build our skills bank. As you go through this text, you'll find a dozen or more practical skills that you can use on your job. We hope you give them special attention, practice them often, and add them to your repertoire.

If you'd like to tell us how we might improve the next edition of this book, we encourage you to write Dave DeCenzo at the College of Business and Economics, Towson University, Towson, Maryland 21252-0001; or e-mail him at ddecenzo@saber.towson.edu.

Brief Contents

Contents

xv

This book is dedicated to
Meredith, who has taught
many the true meaning of
strength, and who has shown
that up hill battles can
be conquered with faith,
support, and the passion to
laugh again.

1. Fundamentals of Human Resource Management

LEARNING OBJECTIVES

After reading this chapter, you will be able to:

1. Define management and identify its primary functions.
2. Describe the importance of human resource management.
3. Explain what is meant by the term human resource management.
4. Identify the environmental influences affecting human resource management.
5. Characterize how management practices affect human resource management.
6. Discuss the effect of labor unions on human resource management.
7. Outline the components and the goals of the staffing, training, and development functions.
8. List the components and goals of the motivation and the maintenance functions of human resource management.
9. Outline the major activities in the employment, training and development, compensation and benefits, and employee relations departments of human resource management.
10. Explain how human resource management practices differ in small businesses and in an international setting.

"*Good* afternoon, staff," said Chris Thompson, vice president of human resource management (HRM). "As you know, it's time once again for us to take a look at where we've been, and what issues need addressing as we continue to support this organization's strategic directions. Even though we meet weekly to discuss day-to-day activities, I feel it's necessary for us to have these planning sessions to reassess how we are helping this organization achieve its goals. So, now that you have settled in, let me start by giving you my 'state-of-HRM' recap.

"We have been providing a first-class service to our clients. Over the past couple of years, we have worked hard to put in place many of the programs that have truly aided this company. For example, we now have our family-friendly benefits program fully functioning. In its first year alone, we were able to cut recruiting costs by more than 33 percent. We've done this in part through our Intranet access to our HR systems. We were also one of the first in the area to implement a detailed policy on employee monitoring—keeping informed on employee activities. But a policy alone wouldn't suffice. We effectively enlightened each employee of this organization about the policy and what is unacceptable behavior. We have helped design training programs that support senior management's continuous improvement program. And let me remind you of these findings just released by our president. Through these efforts, productivity has improved more than 11 percent in the past twelve months. Much of this productivity increase has been attributable to our changing emphasis from specialized jobs to ones that have a more employee-involved, team approach. We'll need to continue to assist organizational members, and ourselves, in how to effectively work as teams. Although I could go on about our accomplishments, we cannot take the position that we've succeeded. On the contrary, there are new challenges ahead. Let me address some of the more important issues facing us over the next few years.[1]

"Organizations have evolved tremendously over the past decade. Change is no longer something that occurs in a controlled fashion. Rather, it is constantly before us, as we deal with the uncertainty brought about by a dynamic world. As such, we all learn how to become more flexible in dealing with the changes that will arise. We must assist others in taking active roles in managing the change, as opposed to sitting back and helping them react to it. This means that we've got to retrain ourselves and others in terms of effective managerial skills and competencies such as project management and team building.

Chris Thomson meets with his staff discussing a variety of HRM practices. Their work as a department is to help the organization achieve its strategic goals by helping organizational members deal with such issues as globalization, rightsizing, changing skill levels, continuous improvements, technological advancements, and work-force diversity.

"Closely aligned with these new job requirements will be our continued effort toward enhancing the skill levels of our workers. Today's jobs are more complex and require significant interaction with sophisticated technology. We must ensure that we have the right people for those jobs, which, in most cases, will require us to continuously train and upgrade our employees' skills. But keep in mind this will not be an easy task; all employees are not alike—either in skill level or in their backgrounds. Thus, we need to pay more attention to the diversity that exists in the work force. What do I mean by attention to diversity? By and large, I think that it means recognizing and respecting differences in people. We have employees from all walks of life. Accordingly, we need to be more sensitive to each person's background and their needs. In doing so, we can capitalize on their strengths they bring to us. Consequently, we must advocate more acceptance of one another in the organization as we work toward achieving our common goals by valuing differences as well as similarities.

"In closing, let's not forget the continuing legislation that we face. Each day we make decisions that may be reviewed or questioned by people external to our organization. We must ensure that our HRM practices do not adversely affect any one group. We must give all employees an equal chance to realize their potential and fulfill their career dreams. When that happens, the organization can only benefit. But we can only do this by continuing to have in place effective HRM practices."

INTRODUCTION

When you reflect for a moment on Chris's comments, it is important to note that achieving organizational goals cannot be done without human resources. What is Exxon without its employees? A lot of buildings, expensive equipment, and some impressive bank balances. Similarly, if you removed the employees from such varied organizations as the Chicago Bulls basketball team, Federal Express, Los Angeles City government, or Nokia, what would you have left? Not much. It's people—not buildings, the equipment, or brand names—that make a company.[2]

This point is one that many of us take for granted. When you think about the millions of organizations that provide us with goods and services, any one or more of which will probably employ you during your lifetime, how often do you explicitly consider that these organizations depend on people to make them operate? Only under unusual circumstances, such as when you get put on hold for an hour on a company's toll-free customer-service line or when a major corporation is sued for a discriminatory HRM practice, do you recognize the important role that employees play in making organizations work. But how did these people come to be employees in their organizations? How were they selected? Why do they come to work on a regular basis? How do they know what to do on their jobs? How does management know if the employees are performing adequately? And if they are not, what can be done about it? Will today's employees be adequately prepared for the technologically advanced work the organization will require of them in the years ahead? What happens in an organization if a union is present?

These are some of the many questions whose answers lie in the subject of the foundations of human resource management. Yet the field of HRM is not

It's people, not buildings . . . that make a company.

one that exists in isolation. Rather, it's part of the larger field of management. So, before we attempt to understand how an organization should manage its human resources, let's briefly review the essentials of management.

The Essentials of Management

Management is the process of efficiently achieving the objectives of the organization with and through people. To achieve its objective, management typically requires the coordination of several vital components that we call functions. The primary functions of management that are required are **planning**[3] (e.g., establishing goals), **organizing** (i.e., determining what activities need to be completed to accomplish those goals), **leading** (i.e., ensuring that the right people are on the job with appropriate skills, and motivating them to levels of high productivity), and **controlling** (i.e., monitoring activities to ensure that goals are met). When these four functions operate in a coordinated fashion, we can say that the organization is heading in the correct direction toward achieving its objectives. Common to any effort to achieve objectives are three elements: goals, limited resources, and people.

In any discussion of management, one must recognize the importance of setting goals. Goals are necessary because activities undertaken in an organization must be directed toward some end. For instance, your goal in taking this class is to build a foundation of understanding HRM, and obviously, to pass the class. There is considerable truth in the observation, "If you don't know where you are going, any road will take you there." The established goals may not be explicit, but where there are no goals, there is no need for managers.

Limited resources are a fact of organizational life. Economic resources, by definition, are scarce; therefore, the manager is responsible for their allocation. This requires not only that managers be effective in achieving the established goals, but that they be efficient in doing so. Managers, then, are concerned with the attainment of goals, which makes them effective, and with the best allocation of scarce resources, which makes them efficient.

The need for two or more people is the third and last requisite for management. It is with and through people that managers perform their work. Daniel Defoe's legendary Robinson Crusoe could not become a manager until Friday's arrival.

In summary, managers are those who work with and through other people, allocating resources, in the effort to achieve goals. They perform their tasks through four critical activities—planning, organizing, leading, and controlling.

The Importance of Human Resource Management

Prior to the mid-1960s,[4] personnel departments in organizations were often perceived as the "health and happiness" crews.[5] Their primary job activities involved planning company picnics, scheduling vacations, enrolling workers for health-care coverage, and planning retirement parties. That has certainly changed during the past three decades.

Federal and state laws have placed many new requirements concerning hiring and employment practices on employers. Jobs have also changed. They have become more technical and require employees with greater skills. Furthermore, job boundaries are becoming blurred. In the past, a worker performed a job in a specific department, working on particular job tasks with others who did similar jobs. Today's workers are just as likely, however, to find themselves working on project teams with various people from across the organization. Others may do the majority of their work at home—and rarely see any of their coworkers. And, of course, global competition has increased the importance of organizations improving the productivity of their work force. This has resulted in the need for HRM specialists trained in psychology, sociology, organization and work design, and law.[6] Federal legislation requires organizations to hire the best-qualified candidate without regard to race, religion, color, sex, disability, or national origin—and someone has to ensure that this is done. Employees need to be trained to function effectively within the organization—and again, someone has to oversee this. Furthermore, once hired and trained, the organization has to provide for the continuing personal development of each employee. Practices are needed to ensure that these employees maintain their productive affiliation with the organization. The work environment must be structured to induce workers to stay with the organization, while simultaneously attracting new applicants. Of course, the "someones" we refer to, those responsible for carrying out these activities, are human resource professionals.

Today, professionals in the human resources area are important elements in the success of any organization. Their jobs require a new level of sophistication that is unprecedented in human resource management.[7] Not surprisingly, their status in the organization has also been elevated.[8] Even the name has changed. Although the terms *personnel* and *human resource management* are frequently used interchangeably, it is important to note that the two connote quite different aspects.[9] Once a single individual heading the personnel function, today the human resource department head may be a vice president sitting on executive boards and participating in the development of the overall organizational strategy (see "Meet Nancy Howell").[10]

The Strategic Nature   Many companies today recognize the importance of people in meeting their goals. HRM must therefore balance two primary responsibilities—that of "being a strategic business partner and representative of employees."[11] For instance, at the Gannett Company (Publishers) and Nevada Federal Credit Union, employees are viewed as having a critical role in creating greater business success.[12] In return, these employees have needs to be met. Consequently, when major decisions affecting the organization and its people are made by the company's executives, HR typically is present to facilitate the employees' side of the business.

> **HRM must be a strategic partner and the employees' representative simultaneously.**

Clearly HRM has a significant role in today's organization. HRM must be forward thinking. They must not simply react to what "management" states. Rather they must take the lead in assisting management with the "people" component of the organization. Moreover, employees of an organization can assist it in gaining and maintaining a competitive advantage. Attracting and keeping such employees require HRM to have policies and practices that such employees desire. Being a strategic partner also involves supporting the business strategy. This means analyzing organizational designs, the culture, and performance systems—and recommending and implementing changes where necessary.[13]

NANCY HOWELL

Vice President and Corporate Human Resources
Manager of INSpire Insurance

Nancy Howell knows how to network, not only with people but with the latest technology as well. Nancy is vice president and corporate human resources manager of INSpire Insurance Solutions. Headquartered in Fort Worth, Texas, INSpire offers the most comprehensive and reliable integrated technology, systems and policy and claims administration to property and casualty companies in the industry throughout North America, South America and Europe. With over 25 years of human resource experience, Ms. Howell has earned the designation of SPHR, the Human Resource Certification Institute's (HRC) distinction as a Senior Professional in Human Resources.

One of her biggest challenges lies in staffing a high-tech environment. Due to the increased demand for highly trained technical employees today, recruiting has become an increasing challenge and a major focus of HR to attract and retain high-tech personnel. Howell has come up with some creative ways to find the right people for INSpire's outsourcing solutions. Her philosophy is that people prefer to work for organizations that are competent, trustworthy, and fun! Believing that a company's

growth and prosperity over the years will be directly tied in to how HR plans work-force strategies she has been creative in finding new and innovative tactics in staffing a rapid-growth company. Since technology is such a major influence in her organization, it was just natural for Howell to turn to the latest technological tools to recruit new employees throughout the United States and abroad.

One of Howell's solutions has been to form an *alliance with local colleges* to recruit computer science majors for a three-year customized program tailored to fit her company's needs. INSpire provides mentors to guide students through their college program, and assist the college in developing coursework which has direct application within the insurance industry. Also provided are internship and work/study opportunities for students. Some of the courses recommended within the INSpire curriculum include COBOL, Visual Basic, C++, and Database Management. Upon graduation, and if they have met the criteria for the job, INSpire will hire them and reimburse their college expenses 100 percent. For the students, this offers an opportunity that alleviates the uncertainty of higher education while ensuring a career path when they graduate. For INSpire, it allows new em-

ployees to make an immediate impact and be ahead of the curve for future challenges.

Videoconferencing has become part of the Human Resources department as a tool for face-to-face interviewing. INSpire, in conjunction with colleges nation-wide, are able to set up interviews with job candidates in order to visit with them "face-to-face" about their career goals. This proves to be helpful not only in the initial stages of the interview process, but for the new employee orientations as well.

Another avenue that Howell feels is becoming extremely critical in locating a strong technology skill base of employees has become the *Internet*. As an extension of the corporate web site, Howell has constructed quick, easily accessible and informative job openings on-line. Once the link is accessed, the potential employee can choose either location of employment or current jobs available. If people want to know more about an individual job, they can just click the link to pull up a complete job description for the position and the job location at any one of INSpire's branches around the country.

How do you keep those valuable employees once they are on board? Howell has always practiced what she preaches: never forget that each employee needs to feel valued and understood. Provide the very best career development programs, compensation and benefit packages, and have a participative management approach. Once employees "buy in" they are more likely to "stay in."

Who says you can't have high touch in a high-tech environment.

HRM Certification Many colleges and universities are also helping to prepare HRM professionals by offering concentrations and majors in the discipline. Additionally, there exists an accreditation process for HRM professionals. The Society for Human Resource Management offers opportunities for individuals to distinguish themselves in the field by achieving a level of proficiency that has been predetermined by the Human Resource Certification Institute as necessary for successful handling of Human Resource Management affairs (see HRM Skills at the end of this chapter).

A CLOSER LOOK AT THE FOUNDATIONS OF HRM

Human resource management is the part of the organization that is concerned with the "people" dimension. HRM can be viewed in one of two ways. First, HRM is a staff, or support, function in the organization. Its role is to provide assistance in HRM matters to line employees, or those directly involved in producing the organization's goods and services. Second, HRM is a function of every manager's job. Whether or not one works in a "formal" HRM department, the fact remains that to effectively manage employees requires all managers to handle the activities we'll describe in this book. That's important to keep in mind!

Every organization is comprised of people. Acquiring their services, developing their skills, motivating them to high levels of performance, and ensuring that they continue to maintain their commitment to the organization are essential to achieving organizational objectives. This is true regardless of the type of organization—government, business, education, health, recreation, or social action. Getting and keeping good people is critical to the success of every organization.

To look at HRM more specifically, we propose that it is an approach consisting of four basic functions: (1) staffing, (2) training and development, (3) motivation, and (4) maintenance. In less academic terms, we might say that HRM is made up of four activities: (1) getting people, (2) preparing them, (3) stimulating them, and (4) keeping them.

When one attempts to piece together an approach for human resource management, many variations and themes may exist. However, when we begin to focus on HRM activities as being subsets of the four functions, a clearer picture arises (see Exhibit 1-1). Let's take a closer look at each component.

The External Influences

The four HRM activities don't exist in isolation. Rather, they are highly affected by what is occurring outside the organization. It is important to recognize these **environmental influences** because any activity undertaken in each of the HRM processes is directly, or indirectly, affected by these external elements. For example, when a company downsizes (sometimes referred to as rightsizing) its work force, does it lay off workers by seniority? If so, are an inordinate number of minority employees affected?

Although any attempt to identify specific influences may prove insufficient, we can categorize them into four general areas—the dynamic environment, governmental legislation, labor unions, and current management practice.

The Dynamic Environment of HRM   It has been stated that the only thing that remains constant during our lifetimes is change (and paying taxes!). We must, therefore, prepare ourselves for events that have a significant effect on our lives. HRM is no different. Many events help shape our field. Some of the more obvious ones include globalization, work-force diversity, changing skill requirements,[14] corporate rightsizing, continuous improvement, reengineering work processes, decentralized work sites, and employee involvement.[15] Although these topics are the primary focus of Chapter 2, let's briefly look at them now.

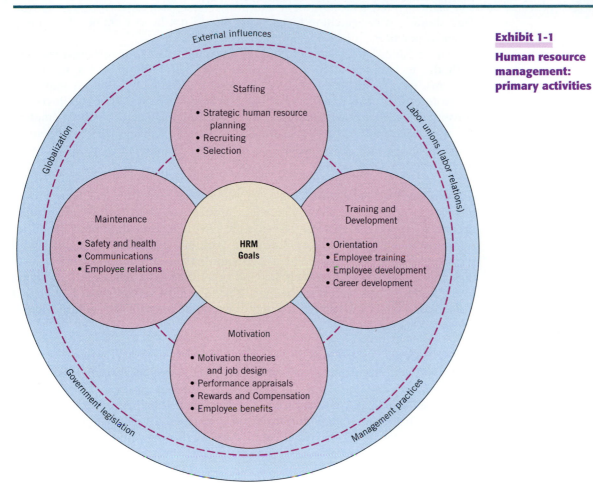

Exhibit 1-1

Human resource management: primary activities

Globalization reflects the worldwide operations of many businesses today. We are no longer bound by continents or societal cultures. Work-force diversity includes the varied backgrounds of employees that are present in our companies today.[16] Homogeneity of employees, and their needs, no longer exist. As Chris Thompson pointed out, our work today is more complex, requiring employees with sophisticated skills. Without them, many employees will lack the basic abilities to successfully perform in tomorrow's organizations.

Corporate rightsizing, continuous improvement, and reengineering all relate to one another. As the world changed, U.S. companies had to compete harder to maintain their leading industrial status. This meant doing things differently. In an effort to become more productive, organizations downsized to create greater efficiency by eliminating certain jobs. Of the jobs and work processes remaining, continuous improvement looks at ways of improving job effectiveness. By continuously improving on methods, techniques, processes, and the like, companies made constant efforts to better what they produce. But what if what they produce, even if it's better, still doesn't satisfy the customer? In those cases, reengineering is necessary. Whereas continuous improvement looks at new and improved ways of producing goods and services, reengineering looks at starting the processes over again from scratch. That is, instead of improving on an existing product, the organization would analyze what should be done and how

Diversity means recognizing and respecting differences in people.

they should do it. Searching for answers would not be constrained by current business practices.[17]

Decentralized work sites are quickly becoming part of many organizations. With the technologies that are available (personal computers, fax machines, modems, etc.), work that was once done on the company premises may now be more cost-effectively handled at the employee's home. Lastly, employee involvement looks at how employees' work lives are changing. Involved employees now have more control over their jobs. Certain activities, like goal setting, were once the sole responsibility of managers. With employee involvement, such an action today permits participation.

Governmental Legislation   Many employees today wishing to take several weeks of unpaid leave to be with their newborn children, and return to their previous job without any loss of seniority, have an easier time making the request. Although some employers may see such an application as negatively affecting the work flow, government legislation has given employees the right to take this leave. Laws supporting this and other employer actions are important to the HRM process. Listed in Exhibit 1-2 are a number of laws that have had a tremendous effect on HRM in organizations. We'll explore this critical area in depth in Chapter 3.

Labor Unions   Labor unions were founded and exist today to assist workers in dealing with the management of an organization. As the certified third-party representative, the union acts on behalf of its members to secure wages, hours, and other terms and conditions of employment. Another critical aspect of unions is that they promote and foster what is called a *grievance procedure,* or a specified process for the resolving of differences between workers and management. In many instances, this process alone constrains management from making unilateral decisions. For instance, a current HRM issue is the debate over employers' ability to terminate employees whenever they want. When a union is present and HRM practices are spelled out in a negotiated agreement, employers cannot fire for unjustified reasons. Because of the complexities involved in operating under the realm of unionization and the special laws that pertain to it, we will defer that discussion until Chapter 16, when we will explore the unique world of labor relations and collective bargaining.

Management Thought   The last area of external influence is current **management thought.** Since the inception of the first personnel departments, management practices have played a major role in promoting today's HRM operations. Much of the emphasis has come from some of the early, and highly regarded, management theorists. Four individuals specifically are regarded as the forerunners of HRM support: Frederick Taylor, Hugo Munsterberg, Mary Parker Follet, and Elton Mayo.

Frederick Taylor, who is often regarded as the father of **scientific management,** developed a set of principles to enhance worker productivity. By systematically studying each job and detailing methods to attain higher productivity levels, Taylor's work was the first sense of today's human resource practices that we see. For instance, Taylor advocated that workers needed appropriate job training and should be screened according to their ability to do the job (a forerunner of skill-based hiring). Hugo Munsterberg and his associates made suggestions to improve methods of employment testing, training, performance

Exhibit 1-2

Relevant Laws Affecting
HRM Practices

Year Enacted	Legislation	Focus of legislation
1866	Civil Rights Act	prohibits discrimination based on race
1931	Davis–Bacon Act	paying prevailing wage rates
1935	Wagner Act	legitimized unions
1938	Fair Labor Standards Act	requires premium pay rates for overtime
1947	Taft–Hartley Act	balanced union power
1959	Landrum–Griffin Act	requires financial disclosure for unions
1963	Equal Pay Act	requires equal pay for equal jobs
1964	Civil Rights Act	prohibits discrimination
1967	Age Discrimination in Employment Act	adds age to protected group status
1970	Occupational Safety and Health Act	protects workers from workplace hazards
1974	Privacy Act	permits employees to review personnel files
1974	Employee Retirement Income and Security Act	protects employee retirement funds
1976	Health Maintenance Organization Act	requires alternative health insurance coverage
1978	Mandatory Retirement Act	raises mandatory retirement age from 65 to 70; uncapped in 1986
1986	Immigration Reform and Control Act	requires verification of citizenship or legal status in the United States
1986	Consolidated Omnibus Budget Reconciliation Act	provides for benefit continuation when laid off
1988	Employment Polygraph Protection Act	prohibits use of polygraphs in most HRM practices
1989	Plant Closing Bill	requires employers to give advance notice to affected employees
1990	Americans with Disabilities Act	prohibits discrimination against those with disabilities
1991	Civil Rights Act	overturns several Supreme Court cases concerning discrimination
1993	Family and Medical Leave Act	permits employees to take unpaid leave for family matters

evaluations, and job efficiency. Mary Parker Follet, a social philosopher, advocated people-oriented organizations. Her writings focused on groups as opposed to the individuals in the organization. Thus, Follet was one of the forerunners of today's teamwork concept and group cohesiveness. But probably the biggest advancement in HRM came from the works of Elton Mayo and his famous Hawthorne studies.

The **Hawthorne studies,** so named because they were conducted at the Hawthorne Plant of Western Electric just outside of Chicago, ran for nearly a decade beginning in the late 1920s. They gave rise to what today is called the *human relations movement.* The researchers found that informal work groups had a significant effect on worker performance. Group standards and sentiments were more important determinants of a worker's output than the wage incentive plan. Results of the Hawthorne studies justified many of the paternalistic programs that Human Resource managers have instituted in their organizations. We can point to the advent of employee benefit offerings, safe and healthy working conditions, and the concern by every manager for human relations as directly stemming from the work of Mayo and his associates at Hawthorne.[18]

In today's organizations, we can see the influence of management practice affecting HRM in a variety of ways. Motivation techniques that have been cited in management literature, as well as W. Edwards Deming's influence on continuous improvement programs to enhance productivity, have made their way into HRM activities. Writers like Tom Peters and Peter Drucker emphasize letting employees have a say in things that affect their work, teams, and reengineering. Implementing these will ultimately require the assistance of HRM professionals.

Now that you have a better picture of what affects this field, let's turn our attention to the functions and activities within HRM.

The Staffing Function

Although recruiting is frequently perceived as the initial step in the staffing function, there are a number of prerequisites. Specifically, before the first job candidate is sought, the HR specialist must embark on employment planning. This area alone has probably fostered the most change in human resource departments during the past fifteen years. We can no longer hire individuals haphazardly. We must have a well-defined reason for needing individuals who possess specific skills, knowledge, and abilities that are directly likened to specific jobs required in the organization. No longer does the HR manager exist in total darkness, or for that matter, in a reactive mode. Not until the mission and strategy of the organization have been fully developed can human resource managers begin to determine the human resource needs.

Specifically, when a company plans strategically, it determines its goals and objectives for a given period of time. These goals and objectives often result in structural changes being made in the organization; that is, these changes foster changes in job requirements, reporting relationships, how individuals are grouped, and the like. As such, these new or revised structures bring with them a host of pivotal jobs. It is these jobs that HRM must be prepared to fill.

As these jobs are analyzed, specific skills, knowledge, and abilities are identified that the job applicant must possess to be successful on the job. This aspect cannot be understated, for herein lies much of the responsibility and success of HRM. Through the job analysis process, HRM identifies the essential qualifications for a particular job. Not only is this sound business acumen, for these jobs are critically linked to the strategic direction of the company, but it is also well within the stated guidelines of **major employment legislation.** Additionally, almost all activities involved in HRM revolve around an accurate description of the job. One cannot recruit without knowledge of the critical skills required, nor can one appropriately set performance standards, pay rates, or invoke disciplinary procedures fairly without this understanding.

Once these critical competencies have been identified, the recruiting process begins. Armed with information from employment planning, we can begin to focus on our prospective candidates. When involved in recruiting, HR specialists should be attempting to achieve two goals. These goals are to obtain an adequate pod of applicants, thereby giving human resources and line managers more choices, while simultaneously providing enough information about the job such that those who are unqualified will not apply. Recruiting, then, becomes an activity designed to locate potentially good applicants, conditioned by

A lot has been written these days about how to motivate the "slackers" among the Generation X members. While many managers are having difficulty maintaining this age group's loyalty, Denise Pagura, owner of Northern Lights Tree Farm in Dublin, Ohio, has not had any difficulty. Simply put, she sets high standards and encourages them to "rise to meet" the challenges. Moreover, she has found that her employees will work long hours and perform physically demanding work so long as she manages the employees properly—giving them the respect they deserve.

the recruiting effort's constraints, the job market, and the need to reach members of under-represented groups like minorities and women.

Once applications have come in, it is time to begin the selection phase. Selection, too, has a dual focus. It attempts to thin out the large set of applications that arrived during the recruiting phase and to select an applicant who will be successful on the job. To achieve this goal, many companies use a variety of steps to assess the applicants. The candidate who successfully completes all steps is typically offered the job, but that is only half of the equation. HRM must also ensure that the good prospects accept the job offer, if made. Accordingly, HRM must communicate a variety of information to the applicant, such as the organization culture, what is expected of employees, and any other information that is pertinent to the candidate's decision-making process.

Once the selection process is completed, the staffing function has come to an end.[19] The goals, then, of the staffing function are to locate competent employees and get them into the organization. When this goal has been reached, it is time for HRM to begin focusing its attention on the employee's training and development.

The Training and Development Function

Whenever HRM embarks on the hiring process, it attempts to search and secure a candidate whom we labeled as the "best" possible candidate. And while HRM professionals pride themselves on being able to determine those who are qualified versus those who are not, the fact remains that few, if any, new employees can truly come into an organization and immediately become fully functioning, 100 percent performers. First, employees need to adapt to their new surroundings. Socialization is a means of bringing about this adaptation. While it may begin informally in the late stages of the hiring process, the thrust of socialization continues for many months after the individual begins working.

During this time, the focus is to orient the new employee to the rules, regulations, and goals of the organization, department, and work unit. Then, as the employee becomes more comfortable with his or her surroundings, more intense training can occur.

Reflection over the past few decades tells us that, depending on the job, employees often take a number of months to adjust to their new organizations and jobs. Does that imply that HRM has not hired properly, or the staffing function goals were not met? On the contrary, it indicates that intricacies and peculiarities involved in each organization's positions result in jobs being tailored to adequately meet organizational needs. Accordingly, HRM plays an important role in shaping this reformulation of new employees so that within a short period of time they, too, will be fully productive. To accomplish this, HRM embarks on four areas in the training and development phase: employee training, employee development, organization development, and career development. It is important to note that employee and career development are more employee centered, whereas employee training is designed to promote competency in the new job. Organization development, on the other hand, focuses on system-wide changes. While each area has a unique focus, all four are critical to the success of the training and development phase. We have summarized these four in Exhibit 1-3.

At the conclusion of the training and development function, HRM attempts to reach the goal of having competent, adapted employees who possess the up-to-date skills, knowledge, and abilities needed to perform their current jobs more successfully. If that is attained, HRM turns its attention to finding ways to motivate these individuals to exert high energy levels.

The Motivation Function

The motivation function is one of the most important, yet probably the least understood, aspects of the HRM process. Why? Because human behavior is complex. Trying to figure out what motivates various employees has long been a concern of behavioral scientists. However, research has given us some important insights into employee motivation.

Exhibit 1-3

Training and Development Activities

Employee training:	Employee training is designed to assist employees in acquiring better skills for their current job. The focus of employee training is on current job-skill requirements.
Employee development:	Employee development is designed to help the organization ensure that it has the necessary talent internally for meeting future human resource needs. The focus of employee development is on a future position within the organization for which the employee requires additional competencies.
Career development:	Career development programs are designed to assist employees in advancing their work lives. The focus of career development is to provide the necessary information and assessment in helping employees realize their career goals. However, career development is the responsibility of the individual, not the organization.
Organization development:	Organization development deals with facilitating system-wide changes in the organization. The focus of organization development is to change the attitudes and values of employees according to new organizational strategic directions.

First of all, one must begin to think of motivation as a multifaceted process—one that has individual, managerial, and organizational implications. Motivation is not just what the employee exhibits, but a collection of environmental issues surrounding the job. It has been proposed that one's performance in an organization is a function of two factors: ability and willingness to do the job.[20] Thus, from a performance perspective, employees need to have the appropriate skills and abilities to adequately do the job. This should have been accomplished in the first two phases of HRM, by correctly defining the requirements of the job, matching applicants to those requirements, and training the new employee on how to do the job. But there is also another concern, which is the job design itself. If jobs are poorly designed, inadequately laid out, or improperly described, employees will perform below their capability. Consequently, HRM must look at the job. Has the latest technology been provided in order to permit maximum efficiency? Is the office setting appropriate (properly lit and adequately ventilated, for example) for the job? Are the necessary tools readily available for employee use? For example, if an employee prints on a laser printer throughout the day, and the printer is networked to a station two floors up, that employee is going to be less productive than one who has a printer on his or her desk. While not trying to belittle the problem with such an example, the point should be clear. Office automation and industrial engineering techniques must be incorporated into the job design. Without such planning, the best intentions of managers to motivate employees may be lost or significantly reduced.

Additionally, many organizations today are recognizing that motivating employees also requires a level of respect between "management" and the workers. This respect can be seen as involving employees in decisions that affect them, listening to employees, and implementing their suggestions where appropriate.

The next step in the motivation process is to understand the implications of motivational theories. Some motivational theories are well known by most practicing managers, but recent motivation research has given us new and more valid theories for understanding what motivates people at work. (We'll look at these issues in Chapter 4.) Performance standards for each employee must also be set. While no easy task, managers must be sure that the performance evaluation system is designed to provide feedback to employees regarding their past performance, while simultaneously addressing any performance weaknesses the employee may have. A link should be established between employee compensation and performance: The compensation and benefit activity in the organization should be adapted to, and coordinated with, a pay-for-performance plan.

Throughout the activities required in the motivation function, the efforts all focus on one primary goal: to have those competent and adapted employees, with up-to-date skills, knowledge, and abilities, exerting high energy levels. Once that is achieved, it is time to turn the HRM focus to the maintenance function.

The Maintenance Function

The last phase of the HRM process is called the **maintenance function.** As the name implies, the objective of this phase is to put into place activities that will help retain productive employees.[21] When one considers how job loyalty of employees has declined in the last decade—brought about in part by management responses to leveraged buyouts, mergers, acquisitions, downsizing, changing family requirements, and increased competition[22]—it is not difficult to see the importance of maintaining employee commitment.[23] To do so requires some basic common sense and some creativity. HRM must work to ensure that the working environment is safe and healthy; caring for employees' well-being has a major effect on their commitment. HRM must also realize that any problem an employee faces in his or her personal life will ultimately be brought into the workplace. Employee assistance programs, such as programs that help individuals deal with stressful life situations, are needed. Such programs provide many benefits to the organization while simultaneously helping the affected employee.[24]

In addition to protecting employees' welfare, it is necessary for HRM to operate appropriate **communications programs** in the organization. Included in such programs is the ability for employees to know what is occurring around them and to vent frustrations. Employee relations programs should be designed to ensure that employees are kept well informed—through e-mail, bulletin boards, town hall meetings, or teleconferencing—and to foster an environment where employee voices are heard. If time and effort are expended in this phase, HRM may be able to achieve its ultimate goal of having competent employees, who have adapted to the organization's culture, with up-to-date skills, knowledge, and abilities, who exert high energy levels, who are now willing to maintain their commitment and loyalty to the company. This process is difficult to implement and maintain, but the rewards should be such that the effort placed in such endeavors is warranted.

HRM Areas

The areas of HRM can take on a number of characteristics. Describing the various permutations and combinations goes well beyond the scope of this book.[25] Yet, in spite of the different configurations, in a typical nonunion HRM department, we generally find four distinct areas: (1) employment, (2) training and development, (3) compensation/benefits, and (4) employee relations. Oftentimes reporting to a vice president of human resources, managers in these four areas have specific accountabilities. Exhibit 1-4 is a simplified organizational representation of HRM areas, with some typical job titles and a sampling of what these job incumbents earn.

Employment   The main thrust of the employment function is to promote the activities of the staffing function. Working in conjunction with position control specialists (either in compensation, in benefits, or in a comptroller's office), the employment department embarks on the process of recruiting new employees.[26] This means correctly advertising the job to ensure that the appropriate skills, knowledge, and abilities are being sought. After sorting through resumes or applications, the employment specialist usually conducts the first weeding-out of candidates who applied but do not meet the job's requirements. The remaining applications are then typically forwarded to the line area for its review. After reviewing the resumes, the line manager may then instruct the employment specialist to interview the selected candidates. In many cases, this initial interview is another step in the hiring process. Understanding what the line manager desires in an employee, the employment specialist begins to further fil-

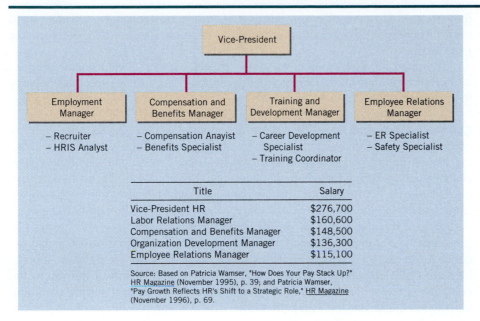

Exhibit 1-4

Sample HRM Organizational Chart (and average salaries of selected HRM positions in large firms.) [In small and medium-sized firms, one individual may perform duties in several areas.]

ter down the list of prospective candidates. During this phase, candidates who appear to "fit" the line area's need typically are scheduled to meet with the line manager for another interview.

It is important to note that the employment specialist's role is not to make the hiring decision, but to coordinate the effort with line management. Once the line area has selected its candidate, the employment specialist usually makes the job offer and handles the routine paperwork associated with hiring an employee.

Training and Development The training and development section of an organization is often responsible for helping employees to maximize their potential. Their focus is to enhance the personal qualities of the employees such that the improvements made will lead to greater organizational productivity.[27] More importantly, the training and development members are often better known as the organization's internal change agents. The role of these change agents, or organizational development specialists, is to help the members of the organization cope with change. Changes that occur in an organization come in many forms. It can be a cultural change where the philosophy, values, and ways of operating are changed by top management. For instance, changing from a production focus of producing whatever the company wants and selling it to the public, to a marketing focus whereby what is produced and sold is contingent on consumer demand, requires a new organizational orientation.[28] A change may also occur in the organization's structure, which can result in layoffs, new job assignments, team involvement, and the like, and again requires new orientations by the organizational members. We may also see changes in procedures or policies where employees must be informed and taught to deal with such occurrences. For instance, a growing concern of companies has been to implement policies to stop sexual harassment from occurring in the organization. Not only must employees understand what constitutes sexual harassment, they must also become more sensitive to issues surrounding a diverse work force. Training and education often leads this charge as the best form of prevention.

Training and development may also include career development activities and employee counseling to make better choices about their careers to achieve their desired goals.

Compensation and Benefits Work in a compensation and benefits area[29] is often described as dealing with the most objective areas of a subjective field. As the name implies, compensation and benefits is concerned with paying employees and administering their benefits package. These tasks are by no means easy ones. First of all, job salaries are not paid on a whim; rather, dollar values assigned to positions come from elaborate investigations and analyses. These investigations run the gamut of simple, logical job rankings (i.e., the position of president of a company should be paid more than the position of a maintenance engineer) to extensive analyses. Once these analyses are finished, job ratings are statistically compared to determine the relative worth of the job to the company. External factors, such as market conditions, limited supply of potential workers, and the like, may affect the overall range of job worth. Additionally, analysis is conducted to ensure that there is internal equity in the compensation system. This means that as job rates are set, they are determined on such dimensions as skill, job responsibility, effort, and accountability—not by personal characteristics that may be suspect under employment law.

On the benefits side of the equation, much change has occurred over the past decade. As benefit offerings to employees have become significantly more costly, the benefits administrator (who may also have the title of risk manager) has the responsibility of piecing together a benefits package that meets the needs of the employees, while simultaneously being cost-effective to the organization. As such, much effort is expended searching for lower-cost products, like health insurance, while concurrently maintaining or improving quality. Additionally, various new products are often reviewed, such as flexible benefits programs and utilization reviews, to help in benefit–cost containment. But benefits should not be viewed solely from a "cost-containment" perspective. Benefits have a strategic nature to them in that they are helpful in attracting and retaining high-quality employees.

The benefits administrator also serves as the resource information officer to employees regarding their benefits. Activities such as helping employees prepare for their retirement, looking for various pay-out options, keeping abreast of recent tax law changes, or helping executives with their perquisites, are conducted.[30] This gives this individual a great deal of responsibility, but also high visibility in the organization.

Employee Relations The final phase in our scheme of HRM operations is the employee relations function. Employee relations (ER) has a number of major accountabilities. Before we go further, however, we must differentiate between employee relations and labor relations. While the two are structurally similar, labor relations involves dealing with labor unions. As such, because other laws apply, some of the techniques in employee relations may not be applicable. For instance, in a unionized setting, a specific grievance procedure might be detailed in the labor–management contract, and might involve the union, management, and the alleged wronged employee. In a nonunion environment, a similar procedure might exist or the grievance might be handled one-on-one. While these may be subtle differences, the fact remains that labor relations requires a different set of competencies and understanding.

In the nonunion setting, however, we see employee relations specialists performing many tasks. As mentioned earlier, one of their key responsibilities is to ensure that open communications permeates the organization. This is done by fostering an environment where employees talk directly to supervisors and settle any differences that may arise. If needed, employee relations representatives intervene to assist in achieving a fair and equitable solution. ER specialists are also intermediaries in helping employees understand the rules. Their primary goal is to ensure that policies and procedures are enforced properly, and to permit a wronged employee a forum to obtain relief. As part of this role, too, comes the disciplinary process. These representatives are in place to ensure that appropriate disciplinary sanctions are used consistently throughout the organization.

In addition to the communications role, the employee relations department is responsible for additional assignments. Typically in such a department, statistics are collected, tabulated, and written up in the company's affirmative action plan documentation. This material is updated frequently and made available to employees on request. Part of their responsibility is to ensure safe and healthy work sites. This may range from casual work inspections to operating nursing stations and coordinating employee-assistance programs. However involved, the premise is the same—to focus on those aspects that help make an employee committed and loyal to the organization through fair and equitable treatment, and by listening to employees.

Lastly, there is the festive side of employee relations. This department is responsible for company outings, company athletic teams, and recreational and recognition programs. Whatever they do under this domain, the goal remains—having programs that benefit the workers and their families to make them feel part of a community.

Conclusion

Although we have presented four generic areas of HRM, we would be remiss not to recognize the changing nature of HRM in today's organizations. As organizations change structures (to reflect global competition and the like), there has been a movement away from centralization of functional areas toward more self-contained units. In companies where strategic business units, or market-driven units dominate,[31] an HRM professional may be assigned to these units to handle all the HRM operations. In fact, it is estimated that on average one HRM specialist serves the needs of one hundred employees.[32] While a headquarters HRM staff remains to coordinate the activities, the HRM representative is expected to perform all the HR functions. Accordingly, the movement toward generalist positions in HRM appears to be on the rise.[33]

Another trend is also closely aligned with the generalist-versus-specialist discussion. That trend is called shared services.[34] In large organizations like Allied Signal and du Pont, companies that are geographically dispersed are finding it more cost-effective to share their HRM services among the divisions. Under **shared services,** each location is staffed by a few generalists who handle routine local matters like recruiting, policy implementation, grievances, employee training, and the like. Specialized services, like organization development and compensation and benefits, are handled by a staff located at a centralized location. Each location, then, shares these services offered by the centralized unit, and uses only what is necessary for the division. As such, each location gets specialized care on an as-needed basis without the cost of having full-time staff.

And then there's one last area to be addressed about the changing nature of HRM. In some organizations, top management has made a decision to outsource some of the work HRM professionals once handled.[35] For example, private staffing agencies may perform the recruiting and selection activities, several consulting firms providing training programs, and yet another financial organization handling the majority of a company's benefits administration. It is our contention that when much of HRM is outsourced, managers and employees still need to understand what the basic HRM issues and activities are. So whether what we will describe in this book is done by you or another company employee, or by someone external to your organization, you need some familiarity with these fundamental HRM practices.

HRM IN A SMALL BUSINESS

The discussion about the four departments of HRM refers to situations where there are sufficient resources available for functional expertise to exist. However, such is not always the case. Take, for instance, the small business operation. In these organizations, the owner–manager oftentimes performs these activities (sure some may be outsourced). In other situations, small-business human resource departments are staffed with one individual, and possibly a full-time secretary. Accordingly, such individuals are forced, by design, to be HRM generalists. Irrespective of the unit's size, the same activities are required in small businesses, but on a smaller scale. These small-business HRM managers must be able to properly perform the four functions of HRM and achieve the same goals that a larger department achieves. The main difference is that they are doing the work themselves without benefit of a specialized staff. There may be a tendency to use outside consultants to assist in HRM activities. For instance, benefit administration may be beyond the capability of the small businessperson. In that case, benefit administration may need to be contracted out. HRM in a small business requires that individuals keep current in the field and legal issues. For example, the Family and Medical Leave Act of 1993 is applicable to those organizations that have fifty or more employees. Accordingly, the small business may be exempt from many laws affecting employment practices. Being aware of this information can save the small business time and money. Before we begin to pity this small business HRM manager, let's look at the benefits from such an arrangement. Often, these individuals feel that they are less constrained in their jobs. That is, the bureaucratic hierarchy that accompanies larger organizations is often absent in the small business. Furthermore, some small-business HRM managers use this arrangement to their advantage. For instance, in recruiting efforts, a selling point to attract a good applicant might be the aspect of freedom from a rigid structure that the small business opportunity offers. Moreover, in some instances, the work may be done off-site—in the employee's home.[36]

HRM IN A GLOBAL MARKETPLACE

As a business grows from a regional to a national one, the human resource management function must take on a new and broader perspective.[37] As a national company expands overseas, first with a sales operation, then to production facilities and fully expanded operations or to international joint ventures, the human resources function must adapt to a changing and far more complex environment.

All the basic functions of domestic HRM are more complex when the organization's employees are located around the world, and additional human resource management activities are often necessary that would be considered invasions of employee privacy in domestic operations. This is necessary partially because of the increased vulnerability and risk of terrorism sometimes experienced by American executives abroad.

When a corporation sends its American employees overseas, that corporation takes on responsibilities that add to the basic HRM functions. For example, the staffing, and training and development functions take on greater emphasis. Not only are organizations concerned about selecting the best employee for the job, they must also be aware of the entire family's needs. Why? Many individuals who take international assignments fail because their spouses or family just can't adjust to the new environment. Furthermore, the relocation and orientation process before departure may take months of foreign language training and should involve not just the employee, but the employee's entire family. Details such as work visas, travel, safety, household moving arrangements, and family issues such as the children's schooling, medical care, and housing, all must be provided for.[38] Administrative services for the expatriate employees also must be available once they are placed in their overseas posts. All these additional functions make international human resource management a very costly undertaking.

Where is one of the world's leading steel mills located. Pennsylvania, Ohio? How about in Mexico. Like many other industries, steel production has truly become a global business. Here these workers at the Lazaro Cardenas steel mill manufacture steel products that will be used in autos, appliances, and construction sectors around the world.

SUMMARY

(These summaries relate to the Learning Objectives identified on p. 1.)

After having read this chapter you should know:

1. Management is the process of efficiently achieving the strategic objectives of the organization with and through people. The four main functions of management are planning, organizing, leading, and controlling. Three factors common to the definition of organizations are goals, limited resources, and people.

2. Human resource management is responsible for the people dimension of the organization. It is responsible for getting competent people, training them, getting them to perform at high effort levels, and providing mechanisms to ensure that these employees maintain their productive affiliation with the organization.

3. Human resource management is comprised of the staffing, development, motivation, and maintenance functions. Each of these functions, however, is affected by external influences.

4. Environmental influences are those factors that affect the functions of HRM. They include the dynamic environment of HRM, government legislation, labor unions, and management thought.

5. Management practices affect HRM in a number of ways. As new ideas or practices develop in the field, they typically have HRM implications. Accordingly, once these practices are implemented, they typically require the support from HRM to operate successfully.

6. Labor unions affect HRM practices in a variety of ways. If a union exists, HRM takes on a different focus—one of labor relations as opposed to employee relations. Additionally, what occurs in the unionized sector frequently affects the activities in organizations where unions are not present.

7. The components of the staffing function include strategic human resource planning, recruiting, and selection. The goal of the staffing function is to locate and secure competent employees. The training and development function includes orientation, employee training, employee development, organization development, and career development. The goal of the development function is to take competent workers, adapt them to the organization, and help them to obtain up-to-date skills, knowledge, and abilities for their job responsibilities.

8. The components of the motivation function include motivation theories, appropriate job design, reward and incentive systems, compensation and benefits. The goal of the motivation function is to take competent, adapted employees, with up-to-date skills, knowledge, and abilities, and provide them with an environment that encourages them to exert high energy levels. The components of the maintenance function include safety and health issues, and employee communications. The goal of the maintenance function is to take competent, adapted employees, with up-to-date skills, knowledge, and abilities, who are exerting high energy levels, to maintain their commitment and loyalty to the organization.

9. The departments of employment, training and development, compensation and benefits, and employee relations support the components of the staffing, training and development, motivation, and maintenance functions respectively.

10. In large HRM operations, individuals perform functions according to their specialization. Such may not be the case with small business HRM practitioners. Instead, they may be the only individuals in the operation, and thus, must operate as HRM generalists. In an international setting, HRM functions become more complex, and typically require additional activities associated with staffing, and training and development.

EXPERIENTIAL EXERCISE:
Getting Acquainted

Beginning a new semester is associated with excitement, but also anxiety. New friends can be made, and new frontiers can be crossed. But one of the more basic issues that face us is what is expected in this class. By now, you probably have received a course syllabus that provides some necessary information about how the class will operate. No doubt this information is important to you and is designed to help you "plan" your semester. But there is another side to that equation—giving your instructor some indication of what you want/expect from the class. Some information can serve a useful purpose for your instructor.[39] To help collect these data, you'll need to answer some questions. First, take out a piece of paper, place your name at the top, then respond to the following:

1. What do I want from this course (other than a passing grade)?

2. Why is this "want" important to me?
3. How does information covered in this course fit into my career plans?
4. What is my greatest challenge in taking this class?

When you have finished answering the questions, team up with several class members (preferably two or three others who you do not already know) and exchange papers. Get acquainted with one another, using the responses to the four questions above as an icebreaker. Then, as your professor goes around the room, introduce your team (each member introduces another team member) and share your group's responses to these questions with the class and your instructor.

WEB-WISE EXERCISES

Search the Web to identify site listings for those organizations that you intend to benchmark before visiting or interviewing their human resources manager.

Recommended sites include:

Hoover's On-line

http://www.hoovers.com/
Search by company name, industry, or geography to get summary information on businesses. Provides links to other sites for further information.

Resources for Business

http://www.aristotle.net/business/buslink.html
This site provides useful access to variety information categories: Markets; corporate Web sites; and publications.

You may want to search for the organization's annual report from the following site:

AT&T's Business Network

http://www.bnet.att.com
Contains searchable databases and links on virtually all business subjects. Includes thousands of industry and marketing analyses, company Web page "Yellow Pages," investor databases including annual reports and regional business resources.

To learn more about major developments in the field of human resources, review the following site and print two updates or summaries for the following site:

Society for Human Resource Management

http://www.shrm.org/
Daily updates and summaries of major developments in the field of human resources

CASE APPLICATION: Family-Friendly Benefits Arrive in Corporate America

What do G.T. Water (Plumbing) Products, Fel-Pro, Mattel Toys, Nike, and Procter & Gamble have in common? They each have recently been cited in *Working Mother* magazine as one of the best one hundred companies for women to work for.[40] In what way? Each company provides special benefits to its employees that benefit working moms. For example, G.T. Water offers all twenty-four of its employees time off from work for family matters. Even though a federal law mandates this for many organizations, G.T. Water is exempt because it has fewer than fifty employees. And Fel-Pro, the Skokie, Illinois, gasket-making company, offers its employees $6,500 in tuition assistance for their children.

Companies today are reacting to new demands placed on them by their diversified work force. Whereas three decades ago, when the work force was predominately male and moms stayed home with their 2.5 kids, today's workers are not that homogeneous. Workers are more likely to be female than male. And whether men are willing to admit it or not, most women still have the greater burden and responsibility for child care. But that doesn't have to mean our companies cannot be responsive to the changing work force.

Accompanying today's diversity is the realization that the way we've treated workers with children in the past, and the benefits we offered them, may no longer meet their current needs. Family life is important to our workers, and in many cases will win out in the decision of career versus family. Fortunately, organizational decision makers today are not looking at the situation as a win–lose proposition. Rather, to attract and keep "good talent" requires companies to strongly compete for those skills. One way to successfully compete is to meet the worker's individualized needs. In the 1990s, this might come in the form of time off from work to "bond" with a newly arrived child, or on-site day-care facilities—something that was virtually nonexistent in the 1960s.

Questions:

1. Do companies have the responsibility to provide special benefits for working moms? Explain your rationale.
2. Suppose you have a work force that is evenly divided—50 percent have children and 50 percent do not. Is providing child-care benefits for half of your work force giving those employees something additional that the other half cannot use? What do

What skills and competencies are necessary for successful performance in HRM? Although it is extremely difficult to pinpoint exactly what competencies will serve you best when dealing with the uncertainties of human behavior, we can turn to the certifying body in HRM for answers. Specifically, the Human Resource Certification Institute (HRCI) suggests that certified HR practitioners must have exposure and an understanding in six specific areas of the field. These include management practices, selection and placement, training and development, compensation and benefits, employee and labor relations, and health, safety, and security.[41] Let's briefly look at each one, and relate these specifically to the part of this book where they are addressed.

Management practices:	As a subset of management, HRM practitioners are required to have a general understanding of the field of management, its history and theories (especially those relating to the behavioral component), and the trends and their implications that exist today. They must also understand the financial aspects of the business, its technology, and the capabilities of organizational members.[42] Specific reference to text: Chapters 1, 2, and 4.
Selection and placement:	HRM practitioners require an understanding of how jobs are filled, the various methods of recruiting candidates, and the selection process. Emphasis in this area is on making good decisions about job candidates that use valid and reliable measures. Specific reference to text: The Staffing Function—Chapters 5, 6, and 7.
Training and development:	For employees to be successful in an organization, they must be trained and developed in the latest technologies and skills relevant to their current and future jobs. This means an understanding of adult learning methodologies, relating training efforts to organizational goals, and evaluating the effort. Specific reference to text: Chapters 8 and 9.
Compensation and benefits:	One of the chief reasons people work is to fulfill needs. Intrinsic or extrinsic aside, one major need is compensation and benefits. Yet, these offerings are probably the most expensive offerings with respect to the employment relationship. As such, the HRM practitioner must understand the intricacies involved in establishing an effective, yet cost-effective compensation and benefits package. Specific reference to text: Chapters 10, 11, and 12.
Employee and labor relations:	Working with employees requires an understanding of what makes employees function. Satisfying monetary needs alone will not have a lasting impact. Employees need to be kept informed and have an avenue in which to raise suggestions or complaints. When the case involves unionized workers, the HRM/labor relations practitioner must understand the various laws that affect the labor–management work relationship. Specific reference to text: Chapters 1, 15, and 16.
Health, safety, and security:	A basic need of individuals is the safety one must feel at the workplace. This means freedom from physical and emotional harm. Mechanisms must be in place to provide a safe work environment for employees. Programs must permit the employee to seek assistance for those things affecting their happiness. Specific reference to text: Chapters 1, 13, and 14.

SOURCE: Raymond B. Weinberg, Robert L. Mathis, and David C. Cherington, *Human Resource Certification Institute Certification Study Guide* (Alexandria, VA: Human Resource Certification Institute, 1991).

you think would be the motivational effect on those employees without children?

3. What role do you see Human Resources playing in promoting, and offering these family-friendly benefits? In which function of HRM would you see this activity having the greatest impact? Explain.

TESTING YOUR UNDERSTANDING

(So how well did you fulfill the learning objectives?)

1. Organizational efficiency is expressed as
   a. planning for long-range goals.

b. making the best use of scarce resources.

c. goal attainment.

d. meeting deadlines.

e. rewarding and recognizing time-saving activities.

2. When a compensation director reports on successful cost containment with a new health-care package, the primary management function being performed is

a. planning.

b. organizing.

c. leading.

d. controlling.

e. delegating.

3. All of the following are typical responsibilities for the human resources management professional except

a. training employees to function effectively within the organization.

b. hiring the best-qualified candidates.

c. establishing working conditions that are conducive to retaining the best workers.

d. providing for continued personal development of employees.

e. evaluating the performance of managerial employees.

4. Which statement is most likely to be true of Chris Thompson, a top-level human resources professional in a large corporation?

a. She would have worked her way up from a clerical job.

b. She would have a narrow and well-defined interest.

c. She would have been vice president of marketing or finance before getting this assignment.

d. She would be aware of the strategic importance people have in the attainment of organizational success.

e. None of the above are true of Chris Thompson.

5. A vice president of human resources of a medium-sized manufacturing firm had to retain a full-time corporate attorney in 1991 after the Americans with Disabilities Act was passed. What external influence most prompted this action?

a. Government legislation.

b. Work force diversity.

c. Labor unions.

d. Management thought.

e. Restructuring the corporation.

6. What point is made in the external influences section of the text?

a. Human resource managers need to be aware of their ability to exert influence outside of their organizations on the surrounding community.

b. Human resource managers need to be aware of external factors because all human resources management activity undertaken is either directly or indirectly influenced by these factors.

c. Human resource management goals affect the motivation function, which affects legislation.

d. Human resource management goals affect the development function, which influences management practices.

e. Human resource management goals affect the staffing and training and development functions, which influence both management practices and labor unions.

7. Elton Mayo's Hawthorne studies have contributed to which current management practices?

a. Informal work groups have a significant effect on worker performance.

b. Wage incentive plans are the most important influence on work group productivity.

c. Employees who receive training for job skills they already possess are less motivated than other employees.

d. Union workers are less productive than nonunion workers.

e. Union workers are more productive than non-union workers.

8. Which one of the following statements best reflects why labor unions were founded?

a. To satisfy a social belonging need in workers.

b. To assist management in hiring and firing workers.

c. To act on behalf of workers to secure favorable terms and conditions of employment.

d. To preserve guild ancestries.

e. To offer an alternative career path for workers.

9. A human resources manager in a medium-sized manufacturing firm sets his pay scale in accordance with local prevailing union rates. Why would she do that if her company is nonunion?

a. Grievance procedures can occur in any organization.

b. It is the influence of the spillover effect.

c. Negotiated agreements are binding by geographical area.

d. Comparable wages are a good way to get his company in the union.

e. He balances the high wages with lower benefits.

10. Which one of the following is best descriptive of the selection process?

a. It assesses probable job success of applicants.

b. It reaches members of under-represented groups, such as minorities and women.

c. It builds a large applicant pool.

d. It provides remedial skill training, when necessary.

e. It matches goals and objectives to structural changes of the organization.

11. System-wide development functions are part of

a. employee orientation.

b. employee training.

c. organization development.

d. career development.

e. employee development.

12. The major objective of the maintenance function is best stated as

a. retaining productive employees.

b. reducing grievance procedures and lawsuits.

c. maintaining recruiting costs.

d. supporting employee wellness centers.

e. keeping pay scales in line with geographical peers.

13. What is the difference between employee relations and labor relations?

a. Labor relations deals with unskilled workers. Employee relations deals with highly skilled, technical workers.

b. Labor relations deals with hourly workers. Employee relations deals with salaried workers.

c. Labor relations deals with manufacturing workers. Employee relations deals with clerical workers.

d. Labor relations deals with unionized workers. Employee relations deals with nonunion workers.

e. Labor relations deals with foreign workers. Employee relations deals with U.S. workers.

14. What are the differences between human resources management in a large and a small business?

a. There is no difference. The activities are the same, just on a grander scale in a larger organization.

b. Small businesses can afford to hire only specialists.

c. Small businesses need only employment department activities, and, therefore, hire only recruiters.

d. Small businesses usually have generalists who perform a variety of HRM tasks.

e. Small businesses do not need any human resources management professionals.

15. How important is human resources management to an organization?

a. Human resources management is expendable—the first functional area to be cut in hard times.

b. Human resources management is important only for social action and public sector organizations.

c. Human resources management is important only for manufacturing sector organizations.

d. Human resources management is important for all organizations that want to get and to keep good people.

e. Human resources management is important only for small companies. Large organizations have professional managers to provide needed support for employees.

16. Mayo's Hawthorne studies contributed which principles to management practices?

a. Informal work groups have a significant effect on worker performance.

b. Wage incentive plans are the most important influence on work group productivity.

c. Employees who receive training for job skills they already possess are less motivated than other employees.

d. Union workers are less productive than nonunion workers.

e. Union workers are more productive than nonunion workers.

17. Marty is a human resources consultant hired by a large manufacturing firm to find out why so many new employees were leaving within their first six months of employment. He suggested a formal orientation program. Why?

a. Marty probably specializes in orientation programs.

b. Orientation helps new employees adapt to their new surroundings.

c. Orientation programs provide a "halo effect" for even the worst organization that usually lasts at least six months.

d. Orientation helps to build the applicant pool.

e. Training is a necessary first step for all employees.

18. Why is the maintenance function important to an organization?

a. Commitment from good employees contributes to organizational success.

b. Most home-based problems an employee faces will not affect job performance.

c. A safe and healthy work environment maintains OSHA standards.

d. Organizational loyalty is an old-fashioned idea.

e. It is not important. Maintenance is the only human resources management function that is optional.

Endnotes

1. Based on *Summarized Results of HRI's 1994 Annual Survey of Issues Impacting Human Resources Management* (St. Petersburg, Fla.: Human Resource Institute, 1994); and Commerce Clearing House, Human Resources Management, Ideas and Trends (May 25, 1994), p. 85.

2. Benjamin Schneder, "The People Make the Place," *Personnel Psychology,* Vol. 40, No. 3 (Autumn 1987), p. 437.

3. For a comprehensive overview of management, see Stephen P. Robbins and David A. DeCenzo, *Fundamentals of Management* (Englewood Cliffs, N.J.: Prentice Hall, 1998), Ch. 1. It is also worth noting that changes in the world of work reveal that these work functions may no longer be just the purview of managers, but instead, be part of every worker's job responsibility.

4. While no specific date is identified regarding the "birth" of personnel departments, the generally accepted inception of

personnel was in the early 1900s in the BF Goodrich Company

5. They were seen as performing relatively unimportant activities. In fact, the personnel department was often seen as an "employee graveyard"—a place to send employees who were past their prime and couldn't do much damage. See also, Vitor M. Marciano, "The Origins of Development of Human Resource Management," *Published in Best Papers Proceedings,* Academy of Management, Dorothy Perrin Moore, Editor (August 6–9, 1995), Vancouver, British Columbia, Canada, pp. 223–227.

6. Rebecca B. Edwards, "Legal Skills Important Part of HR Professional's Tool Kit," *HR News* (May 1996), p. 26; and Vitor M. Marciano, "The Origins and Development of Human Resource Management," Published in Best papers Proceedings, Academy of Management, Dorothy Perrin More, Editor, (August 6–9, 1995), Vancouver, British Columbia, Canada, pp. 223–227.

7. See, for example, Augustine A. Lado and Mary C. Wilson, "Human Resource Systems and Sustained Competitive Advantage: A Competency-Based Perspective," *Academy of Management Review,* Vol. 19, No. 4 (1994), pp. 699–727.

8. Jeffrey Pfeffer, "Producing Sustainable Competitive Advantage Through the Effective Management of People," *Academy of Management Executive,* Vol. 9, No. 1 (1995), p. 55.

9. Ibid., p. 49.

10. Mitchell Lee Marks, "Let's Make a Deal,: *HRMagazine* (April 1997), 125–131; Alan Bush, "The Business of HR Is Business," *HRMagazine* (May 1996), p. 112; Timothy J. Galpin and Patrick Murray, "Connect Human Resource Strategy to the Business Plan," *HRMagazine* (March 1997), pp. 99–104; and David Guest, "Personnel and HRM: Can You Tell the Difference?" *Personnel Management* (January 1989), pp. 48–51.

11. Martha I. Finney, "The Catbert Dilemma: The Human Side of Tough Decisions," *HRMagazine* (February 1997), pp. 70–76; "HR Must Balance Demands of Dual Roles, Ellig Says," *HR News* (July 1996), p. 9.

12. Mike Verespej, "How to Manage Adversity," *Industry Week* (January 1998), p. 24; Russell W. Coff, "Human Assets and Management Dilemmas: Coping with Hazards on the Road to Resource-Based Theory," *Academy of Management Review,* Vol. 22, No. 2 (Summer 1997), pp. 374–402; and Linda Thornburg, "Winners Touch Many Lives," *HRMagazine* (September 1995), pp. 47–55.

13. See, for example, George C. Tokesky and Joanne F. Kornides, "Strategic HR Management Is Vital," *Personal Journal* (December 1994), pp. 115–119; James W. Down, Walter Mardis, Thomas R. Connolly, and Sarah Johnson, "A Strategic Model Emerges," *HR Focus* (June 1997), pp. 22–23; R. Wayne Anderson, "The Future of Human Resources: Forging Ahead or Falling Behind," *Human Resource Management* (Spring 1997), pp. 17–22; Michael Beer, "The Transformation of the Human Resource Function: Resolving the Tension Between a Traditional Administrative and a New Strategic Role," *Human Resource Management* (Spring 1997), pp. 49–56; John E. Delery and D. Harold Doty, "Models of Theorizing in Strategic Human Resource Management: Tests of Universalistic, Contingency, and Configurational Performance Prediction," *Academy of Management Journal* (August 1996), pp. 802–823; Mark A. Huselid, Susan E. Jackson, and Randall S.

Schuler, "Technical and Strategic Human Resource Management Effectiveness as Determinants of Firm Performance," *Academy of Management Journal* (February 1997), pp. 171–188; and Richard Niehaus and Paul M. Swiercz, "Summary of the 1997 HRPS Research Symposium 'Positioning the Human Function for the 21st Century'," *HR: Human Resource Planning* (Fall 1997), pp. 42–54.

14. See, for example, Anne Fisher, "What Labor Shortage?" *Fortune* (June 23, 1997), pp. 154–156; William H. Miller, "Forget 2000! Worry about 2010," *Industry Week* (October 6, 1997), p. 64; and Danny G. Langdon and Kathleen S. Whiteside, "Redefining Jobs and Work in Changing Organizations, *HRMagazine* (May 1996), pp. 97–101.

15. Philip H. Mirvis, "Human Resource Management: Leaders, Laggards, and Followers," *Academy of Management Executive,* Vol. 11, No. 2 (May 1997), pp. 43–56.

16. Robert McGarvey, "X Appeal," *Entrepreneur* (May 1997), pp. 87–89; and Maureen Minehan, "The Aging Baby Boomers," *HRMagazine* (April 1997), p. 208.

17. See, for example, Robert L. Cardy and Gregory H. Dobbins, "Human Resource Management in a Total Quality Organizational Environment: Shifting From a Traditional to a TQHRM Approach," *Journal of Quality Management,* Vol. 1, No. 1 (January 1996), pp. 5–20.

18. Although there has been much criticism of the Hawthorne studies regarding the conclusions they drew, this has in no way diminished the significance of opinions they represent in the development of the field of HRM.

19. Of course we recognize that staffing, as other HRM activities, is continuous, and all functions occur simultaneously. However, for the sake of explanation, we present each function as a linear process.

20. See, for example, Richard Henderson, *Compensation Management: Rewarding Performance,* 7th ed. (Englewood Cliffs, N.J.: Prentice-Hall, 1995).

21. Christopher Gaggiano, "How're You Gonna Keep 'Em down on the Firm?" *Inc.* (January 1998), pp. 71–82.

22. Brian O'Reilly, "The New Deal: What Companies and Employees Owe One Another," *Fortune* (June 13, 1994), pp. 44–52; and Stanley J. Modic, "Is Anyone Loyal Anymore?" *Industry Week* (September 7, 1987), p. 75.

23. For an interesting viewpoint on employee loyalty, see Dominic Bencivenga, "Employers and Workers Come to Terms," *HRMagazine* (June 1997), pp. 91–102.

24. Linda Micco, "Work-Life Policies Enhance Bottom Line," *HR News* (January 1997), p. 2.

25. For a review of the different types of HRM models, see Terrence R. Bishop and Albert S. King, "The Effects of Varying Human Resource Management Models on Perceptions of Human Resource Department Integration In Organizational Management," *Business Journal* (Fall–Spring 1997), pp. 79–85.

26. As we will show in Chapter 5, during a period of downsizing, employment may also be the department handling the layoffs.

27. See, for example, John T. Delaney and Mark A. Huselid, "The Impact of Human Resource Management Practices on Perceptions of Organizational Performance," *Academy of Management Journal,* Vol. 39, No. 4 (August 1996), pp. 949–969; Mark A. Youndt, Scott A. Snell, James W. Dean, Jr.,

and David P. Lepak, "Human Resource Management, Manufacturing Strategy, and Firm, Performance," *Academy of Management Journal,* Vol. 39, No. 4 (August 1996), pp. 836–866; Mark A. Huselid, Susan E. Jackson, and Randall S. Schuler, "Technical and Strategic Human Resource Management Effectiveness as Determinants of Firm Performance," *Academy of Management Journal,* Vol. 40, No. 1 (February 1997), pp. 171–188.

28. See, for example, Nicholas J. Mathys, "Strategic Downsizing: Human Resource Planning Approaches," *Human Resource Planning* (February 1993), pp. 71–86.

29. It should be noted that compensation and benefits may be, in fact, two separate departments. However, for reading flow, we will consider the department as a combined, singular unit.

30. Perquisites, or perks, are special offerings accorded to senior managers in an attempt to attract and retain the best managers possible. We will take a closer look at perks in Chapter 12, "Rewards and Compensation."

31. A strategic business unit, or market-driven unit, refers to a situation whereby these units operate as independent entities in an organization with their own set of strategies and mission.

32. Commerce Clearing House, *Human Resources Management: Ideas and Trends* (August 31, 1994), p. 141. This number represents an 11 percent increase over 1992.

33. Patricia Wamser, "How Does Your Pay Stack Up," *HRMagazine* (November 1995), pp. 41–43.

34. Nicholas J. Mathys, "Strategic Downsizing: Human Resource Planning Approaches," *Human Resource Planning* (February 1993), p. 83.

35. Donna Fenn, "Managing: Do You Need an HR Director," *Inc.* (February 1996), p. 97; and John Mariotti, "Outsourcing Shouldn't Be a Dirty Word," *Industry Week* (September 16, 1996), p. 17.

36. *The Small Business Alliance Quarterly* (Winter 1990), pp. 6–7.

37. Manpower Argus, "More than 100 Million Children Are in Global Workforce," *Employment Trends* (October 1996), p. 4.

38. See, for example, Commerce Clearing House, *Human Resources Management,* 1992 SHRM/CCH Survey (1992), pp. 1–12.

39. The idea for this exercise was derived from Barbara K. Goza, "Graffiti Needs Assessment: Involving Students in the First Class Session," *Journal of Management Education,* Vol. 17, No. 1 [(February 1993), pp. 99–106]. Your authors first used a version of this exercise in their text, *Fundamentals of Management* (Englewood Cliffs, N.J.: Prentice-Hall, 1995), p. 22.

40. Based on the Associated Press article, Robert Naylor, Jr., "Companies Huge and Small Are Cited for Helping Mom," *The Baltimore Sun* (September 14, 1994), pp. D1–2; and Milton Moskowitz and Carol Townsend, "100 Best Companies for Working Mothers: 9th Annual Survey," *Working Mother* (October 1994), pp. 24–68.

41. Martha Finney, "Degrees That Make a Difference," *HRMagazine* (November 1996), pp. 75–82; Barbara Presley Noble, "Retooling the 'People Skills' of Corporate America," *The New York Times* (May 22, 1994), p. F-7; and Linda Thornburg, "Moving HR to the Head Table," *HRMagazine* (August 1994), pp. 50–52.

42. Alice Starcke, "Large-Scale Survey Reveals Views in What It Takes to Succeed in HR," *HR News* (April 1996), p. 2.

2. Human Resource Management in a Changing Environment

LEARNING OBJECTIVES

After reading this chapter, you will be able to:

1. Discuss how the global village affects human resource management practices.
2. Identify the significant changes that have occurred in the composition of the work force.
3. Explain the implications for human resource management of the changing work-force composition.
4. Describe how changing skill requirements affect human resource management.
5. Discuss what is meant by corporate downsizing and identify its effect on human resource management.
6. Explain what is meant by the term continuous improvement initiatives, and identify its goals.
7. Discuss the reengineering phenomena of the 1990s and the role HRM plays in the reengineered organization.
8. Describe the contingent work force and its HRM implications.
9. Explain why work sites may be decentralized and what their implications are for HRM.
10. Define employee involvement and list its critical components.

*M*ost human resource managers understand that for the organization to meet its goals, they must have employees who will be successful performers. Wherever these individuals are, they must be found. And finding the best candidates can be a lengthy process—especially considering that skill shortages in some industries are widespread. In such situations, human resource managers need to get creative, and that's exactly what has happened in compa-

Companies like Sybase, Inc., which specialize in software development, are having difficult times filling job openings in the highly skilled positions. As a result, they've had to resort to creative means to let individuals know that they are hiring, as well as using financial inducements to attract and retain qualified employees.

nies such as Oracle, Informix, Microsoft, and Sybase.[1] Let's see what one company, Sybase, Inc., has had to contend with.

Sybase is an Emeryville, California database software manufacturer. Simply put, Sybase has to "give away the store" to get skilled employees to join the company. That's in part because employment in the software industry has grown nearly 10 percent annually for the past decade—compared to about 2 percent for the general job market. And there's just not enough qualified talent available to fill all the jobs that have been created. So what does Sybase do? Consider these tactics.

Sybase has earmarked nearly $40,000 to advertise that they have positions available. These ads run on local television, as well as in a variety of print media. The company also has spent thousands of dollars on designing and distributing posters that advertise how great a place Sybase is to work. In addition, they have hired a bi-plane to frequently fly over competitors' places of business carrying a banner stating that good paying jobs are available. Current employees, too, are also being enlisted for help. Any employee who refers a job candidate is eligible to win a prize—like a sports vehicle. And if that person is hired, the referring employee can get up to $10,000 as a finder's fee. Candidates, too, can benefit from just listening to what Sybase representatives have to say. Anyone who goes through an employment interview has his or her name entered into a "home-run" drawing. Applicants are eligible to win a large-screen television, a barbecue hammock, 44 pounds of charcoal, 5 cases of beer, and 36 Baby Ruth candy bars!

Many may see Sybase's tactics to attract and retain quality employees as gimmicks. But a company has to be aggressive, especially in a time of skill shortages. For instance, applicants who accept jobs with Sybase get a signing bonus and often receive stock options. In the last few years, several executives received approximately $500,000 in stock options for accepting a position. And today the company is offering options worth close to $5 million to similar level executives.

INTRODUCTION

As we briefly introduced in the last chapter, the world of work is rapidly changing. Even as little as a decade ago, the times were calmer than they are today. But that doesn't mean that ten years ago we didn't experience change. On the contrary, we were then, as we are today, in a state of flux. It's just that today the changes appear to be happening more rapidly.

As part of an organization then, HRM must be prepared to deal with the effects of the changing world of work. For them, this means understanding the implications of globalization, work-force diversity, changing skill requirements, corporate downsizing, continuous improvement initiatives, reengineering, the contingent work force, decentralized work sites, and employee involvement. Let's look at how these changes are affecting HRM goals and practices.

THE GLOBAL VILLAGE AND ITS HRM IMPLICATIONS

Back in 1973, with the first oil embargo, U.S. businesses began to realize the importance that international forces had on profit and loss statements. The world was changing rapidly, with other countries making significant inroads into traditional U.S. markets. Unfortunately, U.S. businesses did not adapt to this changing environment as quickly or adeptly as they should have. The result was that U.S. businesses lost out in world markets and have had to fight much harder to get in. Only by the late 1980s did U.S. businesses begin to get the message. But when they did, they aggressively began to improve production standards, focusing more on quality (we'll look further at this issue later in this chapter) and preparing employees for the global village.[2] It is on this latter point that human resources will have the biggest effect.

What Is the Global Village?

The **global village** is a term that reflects the state of businesses in our world. Business today doesn't have "national" boundaries—it reaches around the world. The rise of multinational and transnational corporations[3] places new requirements on human resource managers. For instance, human resources must ensure that the appropriate mix of employees in terms of knowledge, skills, and cultural adaptability is available to handle global assignments.

In order for human resources to meet this goal, they must train individuals to meet the challenges of the global village. First of all, there must be means for these workers to gain a working knowledge of the language of the country in which they will work. Understanding the language cannot be overstated. There have been too many examples of embarrassing situations and lost business because executives or lower-level managers were unprepared. Product names or marketing strategies have translated poorly in some foreign countries. It has even happened to the president of the United States! For example, in 1992 in Australia, former President George Bush learned the hard way that what signifies the peace sign in the United States translated into an obscenity for the Australian people. Accordingly, before any organization sends any employee overseas, human resources should ensure that the employee can handle the language.[4]

Diversity Awareness a Must in the Workplace

The work force is changing, and anyone not sensitive to diversity issues needs to stop and check his attitude at the door. By the end of the '90s, people of color, white women and immigrants will account for 85% of our labor force. In 1980, blacks made up 10% of the total work force, and by the end of the '90s blacks will make up 12%. Over the next 20 years, U.S. population is expected to grow by 42 million, and African-Americans will account for 22% of that growth.

People are a company's No. 1 asset— not the computers, not the real estate— the people. To waste people is to waste assets, and that is not only bad business, but it is the kind of thinking that today, in our competitive marketplace, will put a business out of business.

Management must realize that equal employment opportunity and affirmative action programs are simply not enough to meet the needs of our changing work force, to improve our workplace culture and environment or to fully utilize the skills of all employees, thereby increasing a company's competitiveness.

To fully maximize the contributions of African-Americans and other people of color, we must commit to voluntarily focus on opportunities to foster mutual respect and understanding. This can be done by valuing our differences, which enrich our workplace. And it should be done not only because it's the law, or because it's morally and ethically the right thing to do or because it makes good business sense, but also because when we open our minds and hearts we feel better about ourselves. And decency is a hard thing to put a price tag on. What can companies and organizations do to facilitate diversity?

▶ Enlist leadership from all levels to accomplish diversity goals.
▶ Identify goals, barriers, obstacles and solutions and develop a plan to meet the goals and overcome the obstacles.
▶ Develop awareness through training, books, videos and articles. Use outside speakers and consultants, as well as internal resources, to determine how to motivate and maximize the skills of a diverse work force.
▶ Establish internally sanctioned employee support systems, networks or groups.
▶ Challenge each employee to question his or her beliefs, assumptions, traditions and how they impact their relationships and decisions.
▶ Modify existing policies or create diversity policies, and communicate them to all current and future hires.
▶ Hold managers accountable and reward them for developing, mentoring or providing awareness training.
▶ Build in accountability through surveys and audits to measure progress as diligently as you would increasing production quotas or maintaining zero loss-time accidents. Then communicate the results and repeat the process. Continuous improvement applies to diversity as well as production.

How are some cutting-edge area companies and organizations rising to such challenges?

▶ Texas Woman's University in Denton has established an Office of Intercultural Services to provide support for students of color. TWU also has helped to support and organize chapters of the National Association of Black Students, National Association of Black Journalists and National Association of Social Workers.
▶ Randy Williams, equal employment opportunity manager at the Federal Aviation Administration, said: "We are well aware of the existence of the glass ceiling for women and minorities. However, we are making significant progress towards shattering the ceiling through our affirmative employment efforts in recruitment, monitoring of supervisory/managerial selections and EEO hiring goals for managers and supervisors. In addition, we have implemented dynamic programs such as Workforce Diversity to facilitate a greater appreciation and acceptance of individual differences."

Unlearning misconceptions and generalizations and allowing for individual differences is only the first step. Floyd Dickens, Jr. and Jacqueline B. Dickens, in their book *The Black Manager*, encourage us to take responsibility for our own attitudes, empower ourselves to make a difference in our organizations, recognize, learn and understand about other cultures, and use the differences to enhance productivity and service.

In supporting diversity, the question is not if or why; the question today is how fast we can move toward a more equitable, productive workplace.

DR. CONNIE SITTERLY, CPCM

Language requirements are also going to extend into communication programs for employees, such as memos and employee handbooks being written in multiple languages. When we go abroad, for instance, searching for people with specific skills, we may be bringing into an organization someone who speaks very little English. Accordingly, we will be required to assist these individuals in learning English as a foreign language—or go even further! That is,

All HRM communications must be sent in multiple languages to assure that all employees can understand the message.

while our foreign-born employees may learn English as a second language, it is advantageous for HRM to assure that any communication provided be understood. To achieve that outcome, companies have moved toward multilingual communications. That is, anything transmitted to employees should appear in more than one language to help the message get through. While there are no hard-and-fast rules in sending such messages, it appears safe to say that such a message should be transmitted in the languages that employees speak to ensure adequate coverage. If that appears to be a major task, think of Digital Equipment Corporation's process. Currently, their Boston factory employs workers from forty-four countries who speak nineteen different languages. To ensure that their messages get across, Digital sends its memos in "English, Chinese, French, Portuguese, Vietnamese, and Haitian Creole."[5]

In addition to the language, human resources must also ensure that workers going overseas understand the host country's culture. All countries have different values, morals, customs, and laws. Accordingly, people going to another country must have exposure to those cultural issues before they can be expected to commence working. It is also equally important for human resource managers to understand how the host society will react to one of these mobile employees. For example, although U.S. laws guard against employers discriminating against individuals on the basis of such factors as race, religion, or sex, similar laws may not exist in other countries. Consequently, cultural considerations are critical to the success of any global business. Although it is not our intent here to provide the scope of cultural issues needed to enable an employee to go to any country, we do want to recognize that some similarities do exist (see Exhibit 2-1). Research findings allow us to group countries according to such cultural variables as status differentiation, societal uncertainty, and assertiveness.[6] These variables indicate a country's means of dealing with its people and how the people see themselves. For example, in an individualistic society like the United States, people are primarily concerned with their own family. On the contrary, in a collective society (the opposite of individualistic) like that in Japan, people care for all individuals who are part of their group. Thus, a strongly individualistic U.S. manager may not work well if sent to a Pacific Rim country where collectivism dominates. Accordingly, flexibility and adaptability are key components for managers going abroad. It will be critical, then, for those in human resources to have an understanding "of the working conditions and social systems globally so that they can counsel management on decisions and issues crossing national frontiers."[7]

HRM must also develop mechanisms that will help multicultural individuals work together. As background, language, custom, or age differences become more prevalent, there are indications that employee conflict will increase. HRM

Exhibit 2-1

Cultural Similarities

Countries That Value Individualism and Acquiring Things	Countries That Value Collectivism and, Relationships and Concern for Others
United States	Japan
Great Britain	Colombia
Australia	Pakistan
Canada	Singapore
Netherlands	Venezuela
New Zealand	Philippines

Meet

PATRICIA GALLUP
Chairman and CEO of PC Connection, Inc.

Patricia Gallup is co-founder, Chairman, and CEO of PC Connection, Inc., a leading direct marketer of brand name computers, software, peripherals, and networking products. She and cofounder David Hall began the Company in 1982 with an $8,000 investment of their personal savings. Until its recent public offering in March 1998, PC Connection had not received outside funding and drove its business growth entirely from internally generated capital and bank borrowings.

An anthropologist by academic training, Gallup spent her college years studying how man uses tools to improve his quality of life. To some that might seem incompatible with her eventual career in high technology. However, most would agree that the computer is the most significant tool man has developed in this millennium.

A 1979 graduate of the University of Connecticut, Gallup received the University's distinguished alumni award in 1994. She has appeared on *Fortune* Magazine's list of top young entrepreneurs, and for the last three years has been named to Working Woman's list of the top 50 women business owners in the United States. In 1997, she was honored as one of the top 50 women entrepreneurs in the world and will again be recognized in 1998. In addition, Gallup is viewed as a trendsetter closer to home, having been named to New Hampshire Edition's list of New Hampshire's Ten Most Powerful Women for four consecutive years.

Gallup has been a driving force in creating a strong corporate culture at PC Connection, a culture built on providing exemplary service to customers. Gallup defines "customer" in the broadest sense, including "traditional" customers (those who buy the Company's products) as well as the Company's vendors whom she also views as an important constituency. Most significantly, she includes the Company's employees, many of whom have been with PC Connection since its inception.

Community and civic involvement has always been a high priority for Gallup. She is a long-time supporter of arts organizations, particularly in the small towns and communities that are home to the Company's 900 employees. For example, under Gallup's leadership, PC Connection has been an ongoing sponsor of the Apple Hill Center for Chamber Music, one of the premier music institutions in New England that provides free chamber music concerts to the public throughout the summer. Additionally, she has been an avid supporter of the Girl Scouts, believing it is important to support organizations that encourage girls to explore the many opportunities that exist for women today. Gallup's interest in the environment and hiking has also benefited many people. The Company is a major contributor to the Monadnock-Sunapee Greenway, one of the longest continuous hiking trails in the state of New Hampshire. In 1991, PC Connection developed a 10-year grant to provide support for the maintenance of the 50-mile long trail. On a more global front, for the past three years, Gallup has accompanied her husband, optometrist Randall K. Minard, to the western highlands of Guatemala where they have established an eye care clinic that serves those in need.

The level of commitment and dedication demonstrated by Gallup as she grew PC Connection into an industry leader has also been exhibited in her support of the communities in which she and her employees live and work. PC Connection's charitable donations have benefited many organizations in New Hampshire and beyond.

must make every effort to acclimate different groups to each other, finding ways to build teams and thus reduce conflict. For instance, at Corning Inc., efforts have been made to assist these issues with respect to African-American and female employees. The purpose of this process is to "identify gender and race issues, find remedial actions, guide program development, and measure results."[8] Such action, however, is not geared to U.S. citizens only;[9] workers from different countries bring with them their own biases toward individuals from other countries, and that also can be problematic. For example, while initiatives have been underway to bring about peace in the Middle East, the dichotomy between Israel and its surrounding Arab neighbors continues. Accordingly, requiring workers from these two areas to work together could create an uneasiness that must be addressed.

Cultural Environments

Understanding cultural environments is critical to the success of an organization's operations, but training employees in these is not the only means of achieving the desired outcomes. Companies like Amadeus Global Travel Distribution, Mars, and Hewlett-Packard are dealing with this issue by hiring nationals in foreign countries in which they operate.[10] What that has meant to these corporations is a ready supply of qualified workers who are well versed in their home country's language and customs. This recruiting has other benefits, too. Because these individuals come from differing backgrounds and are mixed together, there is a spillover training effect: that is, while working closely with one another, individuals informally learn the differences that exist between them and their two cultures. The Mars Company, for example, builds on this informal development by providing formalized training that focuses on the "major differences that lead to problems."[11] But not all employees come from the home country. In Caracas, Venezuela, for example, more than 50,000 Americans are working in the telecom construction industry. Helping them adjust to the Venezuelan culture is critical to their success.

HRM also will be required to train management to be more flexible in its practices. Because tomorrow's workers will come in all different colors, nationalities, and so on, managers will be required to change their ways. This will necessitate managers being trained to recognize differences in workers and to appreciate—even celebrate—those differences. The various requirements of workers because of different cultural backgrounds, customs, work schedules, and the like must all be taken into account.[12] In addition, extensive training to recognize these differences and "change the way [managers] think about people different from themselves"[13] has positive outcomes. Companies like Honeywell, Wang Laboratories, Xerox, and Avon have already begun to formalize this process.[14]

Companies like Levi-Strauss recognize that when searching for areas where work can be performed effectively in the global village, extra efforts sometimes must be made. In Bangladesh, Levi helps fund education programs for members of companies who contract out work for them.

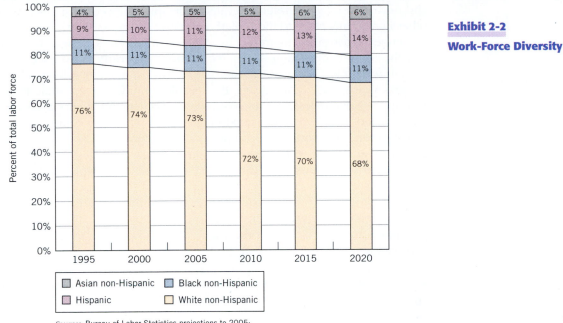

Sources: Bureau of Labor Statistics projections to 2005;
Hudson Institute projections 2010–2020

Exhibit 2-2

Work-Force Diversity

Work-Force Diversity

Fifty years ago, human resource management was considerably simpler because our work force was strikingly homogeneous. In the 1950s, for example, the U.S. work force consisted primarily of white males employed in manufacturing, who had wives who stayed at home, tending to the family's two-plus children. Inasmuch as these workers were alike, personnel's job was certainly easier. Recruiting for these workers was done locally, if in fact, new employees weren't related to a current worker. Because those workers all shared the same interests and needs, personnel's responsibility was to get them in the door, sign them up, tell them about the standardized benefit program, and plan the company's annual Christmas party. Then, when the time came, it was HRM's responsibility to purchase the traditional gold watch, have it engraved, and present it to the employee in a gala event in honor of the employee's retirement. But times have changed. And with these changes have come a new work force, one that by the year 2020 will be characterized as quite diverse (see Exhibit 2-2).[15]

The Work Force of Tomorrow Much of the change that has occurred in the work force is attributed to the passage of federal legislation in the 1960s prohibiting employment discrimination.[16] Based on such laws (we'll look at discrimination legislation in the next chapter), avenues began to open up for minority and female applicants. These two groups have since become the fastest-growing segment in the work force, and accommodating their needs has become a vital responsibility for human resources managers. Furthermore, during this time, birthrates in the United States began to decline. The baby boomer generation had already reached its apex in terms of employment opportunities, which meant that as hiring continued, there were fewer baby boomers left to choose.[17] And as globalization became more pronounced, Hispanic, Asian, and other immigrants came to the United States and sought employment.[18]

Projecting into the future is often an educated guess at best. Trying to predict the exact composition of our **work-force diversity** is no exception, even though we do know it will be made up of "males, females, whites, blacks, Hispanics, Asians, Native Americans, the disabled, homosexuals, straights, and the elderly."[19] Nonetheless, we do have some excellent predictors available to us, the results of which give us a good indication of what is to come. The landmark investigation into work-force composition was conducted by the Hudson Institute and the Department of Labor.[20] Their findings, originally published in 1987, illuminated the changes we can expect over the next two decades. Although there is some debate over the original findings of the Hudson Report, including the Hudson Institute's own sequel to the study, and how rapidly the work-force composition change will occur,[21] three groups in particular are projected to supply significant increases of workers to U.S. firms. These are minorities, women, and immigrants (see Exhibit 2-2).[22]

The Implications for HRM   As women—both natural-born and foreign citizens—become the dominant employees in the work force, HRM will have to change its practices. This means that organizations will need to make concerted efforts to attract and maintain a diversified work force.[23] Like the programs at Xerox, Cigna, duPont, Avon, AT&T, Burger King, Seagram, Allstate, and Levi-Strauss, a good diversity program means having customers looking inside the organization and finding people like them.[24] In these, and other organizations, too, diversity is critically linked to the organization's strategic direction,[25] and oftentimes is tied directly to a manager's yearly performance goals.[26] Where diversity flourishes, the potential benefits from better creativity and decision making, and greater innovation, can be accrued to help increase an organization's competitiveness.

One means of achieving that goal is through the organization's benefits package. This includes HRM offerings that fall under the heading of the family-friendly organization.[27] A **family-friendly organization** is one that has flexible work schedules and provides such employee benefits as child care. Even organizations that use part-time and temporary help personnel have found that family-friendly benefits are needed by these groups to remain committed to the organization, and be productive.[28] We'll look closely at family-friendly organizations in Chapter 12.

In addition to the diversity brought about by gender and nationality, HRM must be aware of the age differences that exist in our work force. Today, there are three distinct groupings.[29] First, there's the mature workers, those born prior to 1946. These workers—the byproduct of the post-Depression era—are security-oriented and have a committed work ethic. Although mature workers had been viewed as the foundation of the work force, they are regarded by the other generational groups as having obsolete skills and being inflexible in their ways. The baby boomers, those born between 1946 and 1964, the largest group in the work force, are regarded as the career climbers—at the right place at the right time. Their careers advanced rapidly as organizational growth during their initial years of employment was unsurpassed. Yet, the view of them is that they are unrealistic in their views and are workaholics. Finally, there's the generation Xers, those born between 1965 and 1975. These twenty-something **baby busters** are bringing a new perspective to the work force—less rule-bound and more self-interest.[30] As a result, they are viewed as being selfish and not willing to play the "corporate game."[31] Consequently, blending the three will require much assistance from HRM. That is, human resource management must train these groups to effectively manage and to deal with one another, and to respect the diversity of views that each offers.[32] In situations like these, a more participative approach to management also appears to work better.[33] For example, companies like the Travelers and the Hartford insurance companies go to great lengths to train their younger managers to deal with older employees; and vice versa. Inasmuch as work attitude conflict is natural, these companies have been successful in keeping problems to a minimum.[34]

Changing Skills Requirements

In any discussion of the changing world of work, the issues of skill requirements must be addressed. As recently as the end of the last century, the United States was primarily an agrarian economy. Our great-grandparents worked the land with sheer brawn, growing food for themselves and those in the community. As the Industrial Revolution continued to introduce machine power, assembly lines, and mass production, workers left the farm, moved to cities, and went to work in factories. For a generation or two, these workers led the United States in becoming the world's leading industrialized nation, producing quality goods in our smokestack industries. But many of these manufacturing jobs have disappeared— replaced by more efficient machines or sent overseas to be done by lower-cost labor. Today, the U.S. economy is essentially driven by service, not manufacturing. Eighty percent of workers are now employed in service-related jobs. In the early years of the next millennium, that number is expected to increase to 88 percent.[35]

What does all this imply about our workers? Segments of our work force are deficient in skills necessary to perform the jobs required in the twenty-first century. The United States as a whole lags behind Singapore, Denmark, Germany, Japan, and Norway in terms of a skilled work force.[36] Some new entrants to the work force simply are not adequately prepared. High-school graduates sometimes lack the necessary reading, writing, and mathematics skills needed to perform today's high-tech jobs.[37] Others in the work force are computer illiterate. Just think of what these deficiencies imply. Imagine tomorrow's aerospace engineers who cannot read a blueprint or explain how wing icing affects lift on an airplane. Or tomorrow's traffic engineer who cannot properly adjust the light sequencing at a busy intersection. Just how bad has it gotten? It is estimated that about 36 percent of all job applicants who are tested for basic reading and math skills fail to pass the tests.[38] In some cases, it is even worse. Take, for example, New York Telephone. The initial step in employment requires one to pass a basic skills test. In a recent evaluation, the company reported that more than 57,000 individuals took the exam that emphasizes reading, math, and reasoning skills. Much to the company's disappointment, only 2,100 applicants passed the test.[39] That's less than 4 percent!

Skill deficiencies translate into significant losses for the organization in terms of poor-quality work and lower productivity, increases in employee accidents, and customer complaints.[40] These losses run into the billions of dollars.[41] This is a major problem that must be addressed, but it is one that cannot be tackled by companies alone. To attack and to begin to correct functional illiteracy will require the resources of companies and government agencies.[42] Human resources will become the hub for providing remedial education. For example, in an effort to acquire potentially productive employees, Aetna Life offers a basic course in clerical and mathematical skills to inner-city residents. Such an attempt was made because the company was experiencing a drastic reduction in clerical applications. Since the program's inception, Aetna reports that all indi-

Skill deficiencies translate into significant losses for the organization.

viduals who have entered this remedial course have moved on to become productive workers for the company.[43] But such programs do not come cheap. A significant portion of the current $80 billion annually spent on employee job training must be targeted to assisting the functionally illiterate. Ford Motor Company currently spends more than $200 million in remedial education.[44]

Corporate Downsizing

The **downsizing** (sometimes referred to as rightsizing, restructuring, retrenchment, or delayering) of corporate America has swept across the country. American companies have worked to become "lean and mean" organizations.[45] As a result of deregulation in certain industries (like the airlines), foreign competition, mergers, and takeovers, organizations have been forced to trim the fat or the inefficiencies from their ranks. Unfortunately, prior to the changes that occurred during the 1980s, American industries enjoyed significant growth—especially in their employee population. However, workers was sometimes hired haphazardly, jobs were frequently ill-defined, and a host of midlevel management positions were created. The cost of such actions were often passed on in terms of "invisible" cost increases—cost increases that consumers took for granted. But changing world economies, increases in inflation at home, and reduced profit levels led in part to the changing corporate America that we see today. In fact, by the mid-1990s, almost all Fortune 500 companies were cutting staff and trimming operations. For example, IBM has cut more than 85,000 jobs, Sears has eliminated 50,000 jobs, and Kodak has trimmed more than 12,000 positions from its organization.[46] And to think that downsizing occurs only in the United States would be incorrect. For example, some of Japan's largest organizations, like Matsushita and Toyota, have had to cut jobs and reassign workers to functions in the organizations that are more productive.[47]

The Rationale Behind Downsizing   Whenever an organization attempts to delayer, it is attempting to create greater efficiency.[48] Efficiency, in part, means getting the same output with fewer inputs: That is the foundation of downsizing. Let's look at this issue more closely. The premise of downsizing is, in part, to reduce the number of workers employed by the organization. While individuals actually producing goods and services have not been immune to layoffs, much of the focus of recent downsizing efforts has been on the management ranks. Companies began exploring just what added value they got from management positions and began to consider what would happen if fewer levels of management existed. What is occurring here is a movement toward a greater span of control to create more efficiencies.

Span of control is the number of employees a manager can effectively and efficiently direct. In the most basic assumption, if a manager can direct the activities of more employees, then that manager is more efficient. Exhibits 2-3 and 2-4 identify two managerial spans of control—one prior to retrenchment and one post-downsizing. In Exhibit 2-3, the span of control is four employees. That means that each manager is directly responsible for four individuals. In this simplified case, there are six layers of management totaling 1,365 managers. There are also 4,096 employees—individuals who produce the goods and services. Realizing that the ratio of managers to employees is not very efficient, this company decides to double the span of control to eight. What happens? Exhibit 2-4 shows the results. After the restructuring, there are now four layers of man-

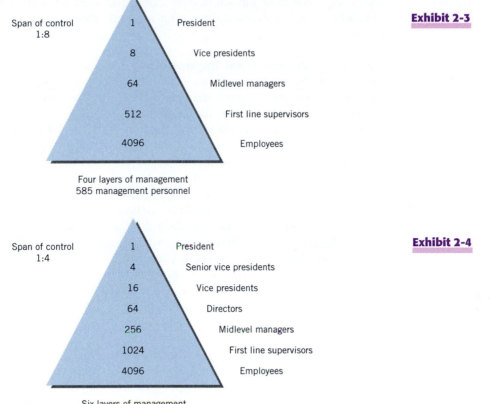

Exhibit 2-3

Span of control
1:8

1 — President

8 — Vice presidents

64 — Midlevel managers

512 — First line supervisors

4096 — Employees

Four layers of management
585 management personnel

Exhibit 2-4

Span of control
1:4

1 — President

4 — Senior vice presidents

16 — Vice presidents

64 — Directors

256 — Midlevel managers

1024 — First line supervisors

4096 — Employees

Six layers of management
1365 management personnel

agement, or 585 managers directing the activities of these same 4,096 employees. What are the savings? By increasing the span of control, the company successfully eliminated two layers of management, eliminating 780 positions. Using an average salary of $45,000.00 per year for all the positions eliminated, this action saved the company more than $35 million in direct pay.[49] For a company that is having financial difficulties, that $35 million provides a significant shot in the arm.

Downsizing raises a number of other issues besides cost savings.[50] First, let's look at the jobs remaining. A job that once required one manager for every four employees has changed overnight. The former manager is now doing the work of two or more people.[51] And although our example above focused only on management levels, downsizing in reality is hitting all levels of employees. Accordingly, it is conceivable that a number of today's workers are doing the jobs of three employees, being expected to "produce" what three employees once did. Consequently, restructuring for downsizing's sake without proper job redesign or training of employees may defeat the purpose of the effort or be counterproductive to the cost savings. Additionally, companies often have downsized without regard to the people dimension of the process. What about the people leaving? What dignity were they afforded in being separated from the company? Were they informed ahead of time, or were they herded into a large auditorium, told their jobs had been eliminated, and escorted out of the building? And what about the surviving employees: How has the company prepared to deal with their anger over friends being dismissed? Their fear that they may be next? Or their job stress from doing the work of several individuals?[52] These effects of corporate restructuring are real issues facing human resource management.

Downsizing and the HRM Implications

So, what should human resource management do to deal with the downsizing of corporate America? In one sense, if they are linked to the strategic direction of the organization, human resources must have input into the downsizing process. HRM must ensure that proper communications occur during this time. They must minimize the negative effects of rumors and ensure that individuals are kept informed with factual data. HRM must also deal with the actual layoff. They must have programs ready to assist the severed workers. For example, employees typically face immediate uncertainties when informed that they're being laid off. Will they receive severance pay? How will health insurance be handled? Will they have any benefits from their retirement plan? Will they receive transition assistance such as help with resumes, or job searches; or retraining? These and similar questions should be anticipated, and responses prepared.

Human resource management is key to the downsizing discussion responsible to its employees. That can be difficult to do when human resource managers are also affected by the retrenchment. They, as with any employee group, are not immune to this corporate action, but they still must maintain their composure in the process.[53]

While organizations attempted to downsize for efficiency's sake, many questions have been raised during the past five years regarding the effectiveness of downsizing. Yes, some company profits soared, but company performance today is not drastically improved over what is was prior to downsizing. In fact, in some organizations, the cuts were so deep that now that economic times have gotten better, they've had to hire some employees back. These new positions are not, however, across the board. Rather, they are in organizations in the service sector and include professional-level, skilled jobs.[54] That is, where it is prudent to hire full-time staff to assist in achieving organizational goals, and where that hiring does not negatively affect an organization's efficiency, then we can expect some of the "lost" jobs returning. But that is only if they are productive positions leading toward organizational goal attainment. For HRM, then, they must work with top management to show this linkage, and then, attract and retain these people.

Continuous Improvement Programs

Continuous improvement programs focus on the long-term well-being of the organization.[55] It's a process whereby an organization focuses on quality and builds a better foundation from which to serve its customers.[56] This oftentimes involves "a company-wide initiative that includes customers and suppliers, supported by top management and implemented in a top-down [manner]."[57] That is, continuous improvement means that a company changes its operations to focus on the customer and to involve workers in matters affecting them.[58]

Under continuous improvement initiatives, companies make constant efforts to better what they produce. Although perfection is an ultimate goal, reality dictates that we never get there. However, companies strive to improve anything that they do, from hiring quality people, to administrative paper-processing, to meeting customer needs.

1. Plan for the long-term future, not for next month or next year.
2. Never be complacent concerning the quality of your product.
3. Establish statistical control over your production processes and require your suppliers to do so as well.
4. Deal with the fewest number of suppliers—the best ones, of course.
5. Find out whether your problems are confined to particular parts of the production process or stem from the overall process itself.
6. Train workers for the job that you are asking them to perform.
7. Raise the quality of your line supervisors.
8. Drive out fear.
9. Encourage departments to work closely together rather than to concentrate on departmental or divisional distinctions.
10. Do not be sucked into adopting strictly numerical goals, including the widely popular formula of "zero defect."
11. Require your workers to do quality work, not just to be at their stations from 9 to 5.
12. Train your employees to understand statistical methods.
13. Train your employees in new skills as the need arises.
14. Make top managers responsible for implementing these principles.

SOURCE: W. Edwards Deming, "Improvement of Quality and Productivity Through Action by Management," *National Productivity Review* (Winter 1981–82), pp. 12–22. Copyright 1981 by Executive Enterprises Inc., 22 West 21st St., New York, NY 10010-6904. Reprinted by permission of John Wiley & Sons, Inc.

Exhibit 2-5

Deming's 14 Points for Improving Organization & Quality

Quality is not a new phenomenon to businesses. In fact, quality concerns date back some fifty years with the pioneering work of W. Edwards Deming. Deming believed that quality could be measured and achieved through a process of statistical controls. These controls were intended to reduce variances in products and achieve a level of uniformity in each one made.[59] That meant, from Deming's perspective, that the 51,084th computer chip produced on an assembly line should have the same quality properties that the first one had. Although Deming's analysis was statistical by nature, he focused on a unique element of quality that was unheard of in those days. His message was that management had more effect on productivity than the actual workers performing their jobs (see Exhibit 2-5). The problems with low productivity, according to Deming, were the fault of management, not the worker.

Deming reinforced this philosophy by developing specific requirements for productivity improvements.[60] For reasons unknown, American businesses rebuked Deming's message. Yet, believing in his concept, Deming took his ideas to Japan, a country then rebuilding after World War II. Japanese productivity prior to Deming's arrival was often shoddy; in fact, during the 1950s and 1960s, "Made in Japan" often meant the product was junk. But with Deming's help, many Japanese companies turned themselves around. By applying his principles, these organizations were able to grow to be the industrial giants they are today. And quality is still at the root of their success!

It took much longer for the management of U.S. organizations to recognize the need for quality. Instead of promoting quality, U.S. management promoted short-term profits as opposed to long-term development. They simply removed themselves from the reality of impending global competition.[61] In other words, they failed to scan the external environment. Not until American consumers turned their buying power to quality products—products that at times cost even more—did these managers begin to address the problem. To help stave off any further erosion of America's competitive nature, continuous improvement emphasis was born.[62] Since that time, similar programs have appeared in almost every organization, private and public—even institutions of higher education.[63]

How successful have these programs been? All indications show progress. For example, at Owens-Corning Fiberglass Corporation's plant in Jackson, Tennessee, the company has salvaged an operation about to go under.[64] Through their improvement efforts, Owens-Corning focused its attention on redefining its goals—both in objectives for the organization and how its work was to be accomplished. The results of this effort led to the production of one quality product, rather than the three that it had in the past. This simplified operation, coupled with the infusion of technology, was able to sustain production at 130 million pounds of fiberglass annually. However, rather than having four layers of management and 540 workers, this same production goal is achieved with one layer of management and 80 employees. For Owens-Corning, this remake at the Jackson plant has fostered a profitable operation—something that had been missing for seven years.

Continuous Improvements Initiatives Today   The focus on continuous process improvements in organizational operations gained momentum in the early 1990s. Unfortunately, such initiatives are not something that can be easily implemented, nor dictated down through the many levels in an organization. Rather, they are likened to an organization-wide development process;[65] that is, the process must be accepted and supported by top management, and driven by collaborative efforts, throughout each segment in the organization.[66]

Every individual must understand what quality means to them on their job and what effort needs to be exerted to achieve the move toward "perfection." These same organizational members must recognize that failing to do so could lead to unsatisfied customers—customers who may take their purchasing power to competitors who do produce quality products and services.[67] And that, too, means knowing just what the customers want. For example, Granite Rock Company is an organization that "produces and sells crushed stone, mixes concrete and asphalt products, and even does some highway paving."[68] There

How have continuous improvement initiatives helped General Motors with the redesign of its Corvette? Through these efforts, the number of parts needed to build the vette decreased more than 34 percent. Moreover, improvement programs implemented also witnessed a decrease in "building time" of 30 percent, resulting in labor savings of nearly $2700 per car.

didn't appear to be a serious need for Granite Rock to change its operations. But its management team, headed by Bruce and Steve Woolpert, wouldn't sit still. They knew that they had to continuously get to know their customers, in terms of what quality meant to them, and convey that to their employees. And do you know what they found? By meeting with customers, they determined that each product line had special customers' needs tied to it. For example, in its concrete operations, customers demanded on-time delivery, which meant that Granite Rock had to be prepared to deliver its products whenever the customer wanted. That, they learned, meant an around-the-clock operation.[69] That customer demand was met, affecting such a change even in a union environment, because it could have meant the difference between success or failure of the business. That's what's important: doing what is necessary to keep the company strong and its people employed.

Do unions understand the necessity for this cooperative effort? Early indications are that they do, for they, too, see the need to continuously improve. This has resulted in unions believing that by supporting continuous improvement efforts, the company recognized the importance of its employees.[70] That translates into training, job security, and other rewards. If the organizations don't keep their customers, the employees don't have jobs!

Is there any doubt about why we need to support continuous process improvement? Total perfection may never be achieved, nor may it be economically feasible to do so. For instance, we wouldn't want to spend $500,000 to get perfection if it cost only $2,000 to correct the defects.[71] Or would we? Nonetheless, not attempting to reach that goal may simply be a bad business decision in today's competitive environment.

HRM Support of Improvement Programs Human resource management plays an important role in the implementation of continuous improvement programs. Whenever an organization embarks on any improvement effort, it is introducing change into the organization. As such, organization development efforts dominate.

Specifically, HRM must prepare individuals for the change. This requires clear and extensive communications of why the change will occur, what is to be expected, and the effects it will have on employees. Improvement efforts may result in changes in work patterns, changes in operations, and even changes in reporting relationships. HRM must avail itself to help the affected employees overcome barriers that may result in resistance to the change, That is, the fear dimension that is often associated with change must be overcome.

Looking for better ways of working oftentimes results in new ways of doing things. Consequently, HRM must be prepared to train employees in these new processes and help them to attain new skills levels that may be associated with the "new, improved" operations.[72]

Reengineering Work Processes for Improved Productivity

Although continuous improvement initiatives are positive starts in many of our organizations, they typically focus on ongoing incremental change. Such action is intuitively appealing—the constant and permanent search to make things better. Yet, many of our companies function in an environment that is dynamic—facing rapid and constant change. As a result, continuous improvement processes may not be in the best interest of the organization. The problem with them is that it may provide a false sense of security.[73] It may give managers a feeling that they're actively doing something positive. Obviously, this is true. But ongoing incremental change avoids facing up to the possibility that what the organization may really need is radical or quantum change. Such drastic change results in the reengineering of the organization.

Reengineering occurs when more than 70 percent of the work processes in an organization are evaluated, and altered.[74] It requires organizational members to rethink what work should be done, how it is to be done, and how to best implement these decisions. That is, reengineering in companies like Federal Express, Bell Atlantic, and Vortex Industries, focuses on simplifying the operations and making them more efficient and more customer focused.[75] As a result, reengineering typically includes three main features: a customer focus, an organizational structure that is production "friendly," and a desire to think about organizational work from scratch. For example, reengineering efforts at Mutual Benefit Life Insurance company focused attention on making its customer insurance applications process more effective. By implementing a new process whereby a case manager has total authority from the time an application is received until the policy is issued, Mutual Benefit has eliminated the work of five separate departments and nineteen different people. Consequently, the application process has decreased from almost one month to as little as four hours.[76] Reengineering efforts, overall, have led to improvements in production quality, speed, innovation, and customer service.[77] Although reengineering efforts may prove worthwhile for organizations, some caution is in order. Reengineering is not a one-time process, and as such is not a quick fix. It should also not be a ploy to simply downsize the organization.[78] Instead, it's a continuous review of the organization's structure and its practices, including how managers manage, to increase productivity and meet organizational objectives.[79] And this last point cannot be ignored. Even James Champy and Michael Hammer, the two individuals credited with introducing corporate America to reengineering, have recognized management's role in all of this. In fact, their chief reason cited for why reengineering efforts fails is management itself.[80] That is, reengineering without changing leadership styles, changing the attitude of workers, involving workers in those things that affect them and their jobs, and building work teams, will not bring about the desired results.

> **Reengineering requires all organizational members to rethink what work should be done.**

Reengineering versus Continuous Improvements

If you've been reading the last few sections closely, you may be asking yourself: Isn't there a contradiction between continuous improvement initiatives and reengineering? On the surface, it may appear so, but consider this. While continuous improvements are necessary for most organizations, they may not always be the right things to do initially. If what you are producing is outdated, or the like, a new, improved version of the product may not be helpful to the company. Rather, in a number of instances, major change is required. After that has occurred, then continually improving it has its rightful place. Let's see how this may be so.[81]

Assume you are the manager responsible for implementing some type of change in your barbeque grill manufacturing process. If you took the continuous improvement approach, your frame of reference would be a kettle drum base made of steel that uses charcoal or propane. Your continuous improvement program may lead you to focus on things like using a different grade of steel for cooking quickness or adjusting the air flow to make the fire burn more efficiently. Of course your grill might be better than you previously made it, but is that enough? Compare your action to that of a competitor who reengineers the process.

To begin, your competitor poses the following question: How does the company design a grill for today's active and environmentally conscious consumer? Starting from scratch, and not being constrained by current manufacturing processes (à la reengineering), the organization completes a redesign with something that looks like a space-age grill—and is electric! That makes this grill ecologically safe! As a result, this grill is quicker and doesn't pollute.

In this contrived example, both companies made progress. But which do you believe made the most progress given the dynamic environment they face? It's a moot point, but it clearly reinforces why companies like Union Carbide, GTE, Thermos, or Mutual Benefit Life opted for reengineering as opposed to incremental change.[82] It is imperative in today's business environment for all managers to consider the challenge of reengineering their organizational processes. Why? Because reengineering can lead to "major gains in cost, service, or time."[83] And it's these kinds of gains that will take companies well into the twenty-first century.

HRM and Reengineering   If we accept the premise that reengineering will change how we do business, it stands to reason that our employees will be directly affected. As such, generating the gains that reengineering offers will not occur unless we address the people issues.

First of all, reengineering may have left employees, at least the survivors, confused and angry. Although a preferred method of "change" would have been to involve employees throughout the process, we need to recognize that reengineering may have left some of our employees frustrated and unsure of what to expect.[84] Long-time work relationships may have been severed—and stress levels may be magnified. Accordingly, HRM must have mechanisms in place for employees to get appropriate answers and direction of what to expect—as well as assistance in dealing with the conflict that may permeate the organization.

Although the emotional aspect is difficult to resolve, for reengineering to generate its benefits, HRM needs to train its employee population. Whether it's a new process, a technology enhancement, working in teams, having more decision-making authority, or the like, our employees are going to need new skills. Consequently, HRM must be in a position to offer the skills training that is necessary in the "new" organization. Even the best process will fail if employees do not have the requisite skills to perform as the process task dictates.

Furthermore, as many components of the organization have been redefined, so too will many of the HRM activities that affect employees. For example, if redesigned work practices have resulted in changes in employee compensation packages (e.g., bonus/incentive pay), such changes need to be communicated to employees. Likewise, performance standards and how employees will be evaluated must also be understood.

The Contingent Work Force

Years ago employment patterns in our organizations were relatively predictable. In good times, when work was plentiful, large numbers of employees were hired. Then as the economy went into a recession and fewer goods were being purchased, companies simply laid off their "surplus" employee population.[85] When the economic picture improved, a new cycle started. But downsizing, restructuring, and reengineering have all changed this management practice. Organizations today often do not have the luxury of hiring lots of individuals when times are good and severing them from organizational service when down times occur. Simply the costs of frequently hiring employees, coupled with increases in unemployment insurance rates (based, in part, on how frequently an employer lays off employees) and the costs associated with separating employees (like severance pay) have required employers to rethink their work population.

In a number of organizations, this dynamic situation has led organizations to employ two types of workers. The first group are the core employees. **Core employees** are workers who hold full-time jobs in organizations. These employees usually provide some essential job tasks—like the chief software designer of a high-tech software development company—that require commitment and permanence in the organization. Employees who hold key core positions enjoy the full slate of employee benefits that typically were provided to full-time employees. Beyond these essential employees are many individuals who "sell" their services to an organization. We collectively call these individuals the contingent work force. **Contingent workers** include individuals who are typically hired for shorter periods of time. They perform specific tasks that often require special job skills, and are employed when an organization is experiencing significant deviations in its work flow. Then, when the special need for them is fulfilled, these workers are let go. But not let go in the traditional layoff sense. Contingent workers have no "full-time" rights in the organization. Consequently, when their project is completed, so, too, may be their affiliation with

Exhibit 2-6

The Contingent Work Force

Part-time Employees:	Part-time employees are those employees who work fewer than forty hours a week. Generally, part-timers are afforded few, if any, employee benefits. Part-time employees are generally a good source of employees for organizations to staff their peak hours. For example, the bank staff that expects its heaviest clientele between 10 A.M. and 2 P.M. may bring in part-time tellers for those four hours. Part-time employees may also be a function of job sharing, where two employees split one full-time job.
Temporary Employees:	Temporary employees, like part-timers are generally employed during peak production periods. Temporary workers also act as fill-ins when some employees are off of work for an extended period of time. For example, a secretarial position may be filled using a "temp" while the secretary is off work during his twelve-week unpaid leave of absence for the birth of his daughter. Temporary workers create a fixed cost to an employer for labor "used" during a specified period.
Contract Workers:	Contract workers, subcontractors, and consultants (may be referred to as freelance individuals) are hired by organizations to work on specific projects. These workers, typically very skilled, perform certain duties for an organization. Often their fee is set in the contract and is paid when the organization receives particular deliverables. Organizations use contract workers because their labor cost is then fixed, and they don't incur any of the costs associated with a full-time employee population. Additionally, some contract arrangements may exist because the contractor can provide virtually the same good or service in a more efficient manner.

the organization. Similarly, because of their status, these workers often do not receive any of the employee benefits that are provided to core workers. Upward to 30 percent of the work force in 1998 was comprised of contingent workers,[86] and that number, given the trends in restructuring and reengineering, is expected to climb to almost 50 percent by the turn of the century.[87] So who makes up the contingency pool? Contingent workers are any individuals who work part-time, as temporaries, or as contract workers (see Exhibit 2-6). And they may hold such diverse jobs as secretaries, accountants, nurses, assembly line workers, lawyers, dentists, computer programmers, engineers, marketing representatives, and human resources professionals. Even some senior management positions are filled with contingent workers.[88]

Are Contingent Workers Throw-Away Workers?

Undoubtedly, since the early 1990s, we have witnessed significant changes in how organizations are staffed. As the changing world of work affects our businesses, reality has indicated that today's organizations simply cannot be efficient if they have surplus employees. The strategic nature of both business and HRM, requires that they both be prepared for "just-in-time" employees. What that means is that organizations must find the proper blend of having a ready supply of skilled workers available when the need arises—not delayed in any manner that might create a serious shortage leading to not meeting the challenge—and not having a surplus pool of workers waiting for something to arise. In order to meet this dual goal, however, organizations must remain flexible in their staffing levels.[89] Contingent workers conveniently fill that void. But at what cost?

Are workers freely becoming contingent workers out of their desire to fulfill personal work, family, lifestyle, or financial needs? Or have individuals been forced into this employment "limbo" as a result of downsizing and the like? The answer to both is unequivocally yes.[90] There are those individuals who prefer the contingent work relationship. This offers workers some of the greatest flexibility in work scheduling—and that's something that workers, especially women, have been requesting from corporate America.[91] With the increasing diversity of the work force, contingent work arrangements permit one to blend family and career goals.[92] Using this logic, we find that contingent positions are, in fact, beneficial to employees.

But we cannot overlook the other side of this issue. Many organizations are using contingent work concepts to save money. Employing contingent workers saves an organization about 40 percent in labor costs, because no benefits are provided. Furthermore, hiring contingent workers protects an organization's core employees from work fluctuations.[93] For instance, Blue Cross and Blue Shield of Rhode Island was able to trim its work force by more than 40 percent over a five-year period without having to lay off one full-timer. To achieve this, some employees are, in fact, being forced into contingent employee roles. For example, a Bank of America employee with more than fourteen years of experience was given a choice: reduce work time to nineteen hours a week and receive no benefits, or be severed from the bank permanently.[94] This employee, given financial responsibilities, took what was minimally available from the bank and looked elsewhere for another part-time job. Unfortunately, individuals in this situation may work forty hours or more each week, for several organizations, and not have the luxury of the benefits package had those forty hours been spent in one organization. And the Bank of America, like other peer institutions, has repeated this process thousands of times. In fact, entering 1995, this organization employed only 19 percent of its work force on a full-time basis.[95] The rest were contingent workers! Simply put, some companies are "dumping" the majority of their full-time work force and replacing it with lower-paid temporaries or contractual workers.[96]

The debate over the use of contingent workers will surely continue. There will always be those who want to be full-time employees, but simply cannot find that opportunity. However, the increasing trend to be lean-and-mean, the increasing competitive nature of business, and the more diverse work force will result in the creation of more temporary jobs. The IRS is paying close attention to this latter activity, though. Failing to withhold payroll taxes or pay social security premiums for temporary workers who are actually working on the company premises for even short durations has led to investigations, and fines and penalties for those companies that have "misclassified" their workers.[97]

HRM Implications of Contingent Workers   When an organization makes its strategic decision to employ a sizable portion of its work force from the contingency ranks, several HRM issues come to the forefront. These include being able to have these "virtual" employees available when needed, providing scheduling options that meet their needs, and making decisions about whether or not benefits will be offered to the contingent work force.[98] No organization can make the transition to a contingent work force without sufficient planning. As such, when these strategic decisions are being made, HRM must be an active partner in the discussions. After all, it is HRM's responsibility to locate and bring into the organization these temporary workers. Just as employment has played an integral role in recruiting full-time employees, so too, will it play a major part in securing needed just-in-time talent.

As temporary workers are brought in, HRM will also have the responsibility of quickly adapting them to the organization. Although orientation for full-time employees is more detailed, the contingent work force, nonetheless, needs to be made aware of the organization's personality. Along this line, too, some training may be required. Even a systems analyst brought in to work on a specific computer programming problem will need to be brought up to speed rather quickly on the uniqueness of the organization's system.

HRM will also have to give some thought to how it will effectively attract quality temporaries. As this becomes the status quo in business, there will be significant competition for the "good" talent. Accordingly, HRM will need to re-examine its compensation philosophy. If temporaries are employed solely as a cost-cutting measure, the pay and benefits offered to contingent workers might be different than those offered to other workers who are used part-time as a result of restructuring and reengineering. HRM, then, will need to begin understanding specifically what these employees want. Is it the flexibility in scheduling, the autonomy these jobs offer, or the control over one's career destiny that such a situation affords individuals that attracts them? Or is it just bad luck, and they are forced into this situation? Understanding the reasons will surely affect the motivation of these workers.[99] For example, Half-Price Books, a Dallas, Texas, book retailer, offers health insurance coverage, retirement, vacation, and sick and holiday pay to its part-time employees. They provide these benefits because they need an ample supply of contingent workers and want to reduce the turnover that often occurs in their industry. By recognizing that many of their workers prefer to work part-time, yet need basic employee benefits, Half-Price Books attracts a higher quality of temporary worker.[100]

Finally, HRM must be prepared to deal with the potential conflict that may arise between core and contingent workers. The core employees may become envious of the higher pay rates and flexibility in scheduling that the contingent workers receive. In the total compensation package, which includes benefits, core employees might earn substantially more money, but these employees may not immediately include the "in-kind" pay (their benefits) in the rate of pay received. For example, paying a training consultant $3,000 for a two-day project management training program might cause some conflict with core HRM trainers although the HRM trainer may not have the time or resources to develop such a program. If the consultant offers twenty-five of these two-day programs over the year, earning $75,000 in consulting fees, a $40,000-a-year company trainer might take offense. Consequently, HRM must ensure that its communication programs anticipate some of these potential conflicts and address them before they become detrimental to the organization—or worse, provide an incentive for core employees to leave!

Decentralized Work Sites

Perkin-Elmer Company, the Norwalk, Connecticut, manufacturer of scientific and laboratory equipment, recently found itself facing a dilemma.[101] It had closed about thirty-five of its sales offices in the United States and made the decision that several hundred of its sales staff employees would work out of their homes. One employee, Wayne Wolinger, took offense!

It wasn't that Wolinger objected to working out of his home. He clearly saw the benefit of being closer to his customers. What he did challenge, however, was the fact that Perkin-Elmer wouldn't compensate him for the costs he would incur by having his office at home. Although the company was setting up the office—furnishings, supplies, and equipment—Wolinger knew his monthly electric bill, insurance premiums, and the like would increase. Simply put, Wolinger wanted to be reimbursed for added expenses. Furthermore, because the company was saving money on warehousing by requiring employees to have spare parts frequently needed by customers at their homes, Wolinger wanted to be compensated for the "lost" space in his house. But company policy was clear—employees were not going to be paid any additional money for working out of their home. As a result, and an inability to reach a satisfactory compromise, Wayne Wolinger was fired.

What happened to Wayne Wolinger may be an extreme case, but one that will surely come to light as more companies move to having workers do their jobs at home. This decentralized work site arrangement has advantages and disadvantages, and will create new issues for HRM.

Work Is Where Your Computer Is   If you go back 150 years in U.S. history, it was not uncommon for workers to be performing their "craft" out of their homes. In fact, most workers performed some tasks, produced a finished product, and took it to a market to sell. But the Industrial Revolution changed all that. Large manufacturing companies drew workers away from rural areas and into the cities. Along with this movement came the traditional job—one that required employees to show up at the company's facility and spend their eight-to-twelve-hour work day.

Downsizing and reengineering is changing all of that again. Jobs as our parents and grandparents knew them are disappearing. And when you factor technological changes that have occurred in the past decade, even where we do our jobs may change. Computers, modems, fax machines, and even the telephone are making decentralized work sites attractive. Why? Several reasons have been cited.[102] Telecommuting capabilities that exist today have made it possible for employees to be located anywhere on the globe.[103] With this potential, employers no longer have to consider locating a business near its work force. For example, if Aetna Insurance in Idaho finds that it is having problems attracting qualified local applicants for its claims-processing jobs, and a pool of qualified workers is available in Colorado Springs, Aetna doesn't need to establish a facility in Colorado. Instead, by providing these employees with computer equipment and appropriate ancillaries, the work can be done hundreds of miles away and then be transmitted to the "home" office.

Telecommuting also offers an opportunity for a business in a high-labor-cost area to have its work done in an area where lower wages prevail. Take the publisher in New York City who finds manuscript editing costs have skyrocketed. By having that work done by a qualified editor in Parkton, West Virginia, the publisher could reduce labor costs. Likewise, not having to provide office space in the city to this editor, given the cost per square foot of real estate in the area, adds to the cost savings.

Decentralized work sites also offer opportunities that may meet the needs of the diversified work force. Those who have family responsibilities, like child care, or those who have disabilities may prefer to work in their homes, rather than travel to the organization's facility. Telecommuting, then, provides the flexibility in work scheduling that many members of the diversified work force desire. Finally, there's some incentive from government agencies for companies to consider these alternative work arrangements. For example, the federal government, in its effort to address environmental concerns in the United States, may

Donald Anderson, pictured with his family, works for Caterpillar Logistics Services, Inc. Part of Donald's job involves managing inventory and parts distribution systems for corporate customers in South America. Obviously, this international work is handled from a central location—Omaha, Nebraska! On a serious note, companies like Caterpillar Logistics have found that lower cost of living areas provide a more family-friendly community for its workers, while simultaneously permitting the company to shave costs. In such instances, this decentralized work site benefits both the employer and the employee.

make state highway funds contingent on the state's ability to reduce traffic congestion in heavily populated areas. One means of achieving that goal is for businesses to receive some incentive, like a tax break, for implementing decentralized work sites. In a similar fashion, state departments of labor may also provide an incentive to businesses to relocate their work activities from more affluent communities to economically depressed areas.[104]

This trend is expected to continue. Currently, about 15 percent of the work force works at home, and that number is expected to rise sharply in the future.[105] And these jobs needn't exist solely in processing or sales type jobs. Instead, telecommuting is affording doctors, lawyers, accountants, service workers, and managers the opportunities to conduct their business directly out of their homes.[106] Of course, as this occurs, it is creating some issues that HRM must deal with.

HRM and Decentralized Work Sites Generally individuals get excited about the opportunities and freedom of working out of their homes. Although there are instances such as those of Wayne Wolinger that must be resolved, many home workers see this work arrangement as a major benefit. For HRM, however, decentralized work sites present a challenge.

Much of that challenge revolves around training managers in how to establish and ensure appropriate work quality and on-time completion. Traditional "face-time" is removed in decentralized work sites, and managers' need to "control" the work will have to change. Instead, there will have to be more employee involvement, allowing workers the discretion to make those decisions that affect them. For instance, although a due date is established for the work assigned to employees, managers must recognize that home workers will work at their own pace. That may mean instead of an individual focusing work efforts over an eight-hour period, the individual may work two hours here, three hours at another time, and another three late at night. The emphasis, then, will be on the final product, not the means by which it is accomplished.

Work at home may also require HRM to rethink its compensation policy. Will it pay workers by the hour, on a salary basis, or by the job performed? More than likely, because certain jobs, like claims processing, can be easily quantified and standards set, pay plans will be in the form of pay for actual work done.

Beyond these issues, HRM must also anticipate potential legal problems that may arise from telecommuting.[107] For example, what if the employee works more than forty hours during the work week. Will that employee be entitled to overtime pay? The answer is yes! As such, decentralized work-site activities will have to be monitored by HRM to ensure that employees are not abusing overtime privileges, and that those workers who rightfully should be paid overtime are compensated.

Because employees in decentralized work sites are full-time employees of an organization, as opposed to contingent workers, it will be the organization's responsibility to ensure the health and safety of the decentralized work site. Equipment provided by the company, for example, that leads to an employee injury or illness is the responsibility of the organization. Although HRM cannot constantly monitor workers in their homes, it must ensure that these workers understand the proper techniques for using the equipment. Additionally, if accidents or injuries occur, employees must understand the regulations for reporting them. Generally that means, for instance, reporting them within forty-eight hours, at which time HRM must investigate immediately.

Employee Involvement

Whenever significant changes occur in an organization, subsequent changes in the way work gets done must also occur. With respect to downsizing, many companies today are requiring their employees to do more, faster, and better, with less. Involving employees means different things to different organizations and people. But by and large, for today's workers to be successful, there are a number of employee involvement concepts that appear to be accepted.[108] These are delegation, participative management, work teams, goal setting, and employer training—the empowering of employees! Let's elaborate on these a bit.

How Organizations Involve Employees   To be successful when facing multiple tasks, often on multiple projects, more employees at all levels will need to delegate some of their activities and responsibilities to other organizational members. This means that employees are going to have to be given certain amounts of authority to make decisions that directly affect their work. Even though delegation was once perceived as something that managers did with lower levels of management, **delegation** will be required at all levels of the organization—in essence, peer delegation, or using influence without authority!

In addition to being required to take on more responsibilities, employees will be expected to make decisions without the benefit of the "tried and true" decisions of the past. And because all these employees are part of the process today, there is more of a need for them to contribute to the decision-making process. In most organizations, the days of autocratic management are over. To facilitate customer demands and fulfill corporate expectations, today's employees need to be more involved. Group decision making enables these employees to have more input into the processes, and greater access to needed information.[109] Such actions are also consistent with work environments that require increased creativity and innovation.

Another phenomenon of involving employees will be an emphasis on **work teams.**[110] The bureaucratic structure of yesterday—where clear lines of authority existed and the chain of command was paramount—is not appropriate for many of today's companies. Workers from different specializations in an organization are increasingly required to work together to successfully complete complex projects. As such, traditional work areas have given way to more of a team effort, building and capitalizing on the various skills and backgrounds that each member brings to the team. Consider, for example, what kind of group it takes to put together a symphony. One musician could not possibly handle the varied instruments—especially playing them at one time. Accordingly, to blend the music of the orchestra, symphonies have string sections, brass instruments, percussions, and the like. At times, however, a musician may cross over these boundaries, like the trombonist who also plays the piano. The basis of these work teams, then, is driven by the tasks at hand. Involving employees allows them an opportunity to focus on the job goals. By giving them more freedom, employees are in a better position to develop the means to achieve the desired ends.

Implications for HRM   Up until now we have addressed some components of employee involvement. For an organization, however, addressing them is not enough. What is needed is demonstrated leadership, as well as supportive management. Additionally, employees need to be trained—and that's where human resource management can make a valuable contribution. Employees expected to delegate, to have decisions participatively handled, to work in teams, or to set goals cannot do so unless they know and understand what it is they are to do. Empowering employees requires extensive training in all aspects of the job. Workers may need to understand how new job design processes. They may need training in interpersonal skills to make participative management and work teams function properly. All in all, we can anticipate much more involvement from HRM in all parts of the organization.

But make no mistake about it. Employee involvement comes at a price. First of all, better control over one's work activities, coupled with better "tools," has been shown to improve productivity.[111] We are doing more with less, but are doing it smarter and more productively. Additionally, as employees see the commitment the organization and HRM have made to them, there is evidence that commitment and loyalty to an organization will increase.[112]

SUMMARY

(This summary relates to the Learning Objectives identified on p. 30.)

After having read this chapter, you should know:

1. Globalization is creating a situation where human resource management must begin to search for mobile and skilled employees capable of successfully performing their job duties in a foreign land. This means that these employees must understand the host country's language, culture, and customs.

2. The work-force composition has changed considerably over the past thirty years. Once characterized as having a dominant number of white males, the work force of the 1990s is comprised of a mixture of women, minorities, immigrants, and white males.

3. The most significant implications for human resource management regarding the changing work-force composition are language and skill deficiencies of available workers, changing management practices to accommodate a diverse work group, dealing with conflict among employees, and providing family-friendly benefits.

4. Changing skill requirements necessitate human resource management to provide extensive training. This training can be in the form of remedial help for those who have skill deficiencies, to specialized training dealing with technology changes.

5. Corporate downsizing is a phenomenon that has swept through U.S. corporations in an effort toward making the organizations more efficient. In many cases, this has meant eliminating layers of management by increasing the span of control. In downsizing, HRM acts as the employees' advocate, communicating all necessary information to affected employees.

6. Continuous improvement seeks to build customer satisfaction through these continuous improvements and employee involvement.

7. Reengineering refers to the radical, quantum change that occurs in the organization. HRM is instrumental in reengineering by preparing employees to deal with the change and training them in new techniques.

8. The contingent work force includes those part-time, temporary, consultants, and contract workers who provide services to organizations on an as-needed basis. The HRM implications of a contingent work force include attracting and retaining skilled contingent workers, adjusting to their special needs, and managing any conflict that may arise between core and contingent workers.

9. Organizations use decentralized work sites because telecommuting arrangements enable organizations to find qualified employees without having to relocate business facilities. Decentralized work sites also provide cost savings to the organization, as well as fulfilling some special needs of a diversified work force. For HRM, decentralized work sites will require training for managers in managing and controlling work, and establishing pay systems to reflect this work arrangement. HRM will also have to monitor the hours home workers spend on the job, as well as ensuring the health and safety of workers in the home office.

10. Employee involvement can be best defined as giving each worker more control over his or her job. To do this requires delegation, participative management, work teams, goal setting, and employee training. If handled properly, involving employees should assist in developing more productive employees who are more loyal and committed to the organization.

EXPERIENTIAL EXERCISE:
Continuous Improvement

Tom has been asked to lead a continuous improvement team to streamline the distribution process and reduce process time by 12 percent within four weeks.

Tom believes that the current distribution process is pretty good and feels that attending more meetings is a waste of team members' time. He also thinks that the team concept is a fad, another name for committees.

How might Tom's thoughts, feelings, and beliefs about teams and continuous improvement impact his actions, reactions, or behaviors as the appointed team leader?

What might be some predictable consequences or results for Tom, his team and employer?

What if Tom is unwilling or unable to change to meet the continuous improvement or team challenges?

What is Tom's responsibility in leading the process improvement team?

How will Tom be accountable?

Explain continuous improvement to Tom, why it is important, and its consequences and benefits to the organization and to Tom.

WEB-WISE EXERCISES

Choose any three from the Web assignments below and print and submit your search findings for class review and discussion.

Inquisit
www.inquist.com
Inquisits notifies you whenever there's news about companies, customers, markets or trends that you have requested it to track.

Assignment: Select and track the changes of two global companies of interest.

CNBC/Dow Jones (business video)
www.cnbcdowjones.com
Live and archived audio, video, and multimedia clips of press conferences, and corporate presentations.

Assignment
Select and review two corporate presentations (minimum of five minutes each) that reflect the concepts noted in the chapter such as global issues, changes, downsizing, quality, continuous improvement, reengineering, diversity, contingent workforce, etc.

Assignment
Learn about resources on Asia Pacific Organizations, business and management development by searching the
Asia Pacific Management Forum
http://www.mcb.co/uk/ampforum/nethome.htm

Assignment
From the site **The Economist**
http://www.economist.com, which is the home page of *The Economist* magazine, select an article on a global human resource issue and print or summarize findings.

Assignment
Select a country that you would like to learn more about their labor markets, industrial production, trade information, commodities, etc. and print findings from the site

Resources for International Economics
http://nmg.clever.net/www/index.html
You may wish to find additional information from these sites:

Resources at Thunderbird (American Graduate School of Management)   http://www.t-bird.edu
or

NLightN
http://www.nlightn.com/index.htm
or

Northern Light
www.nlsearch.com
or

London Times Homepage
http://www.sunday-times.co.uk, which provides excellent coverage of international news events from the *London Times,* including detailed reporting from the European markets.

Assignment
Select a company of interest outside the United States and print findings of your search from the site.

CorporateInformation.com
www.corporateinformation.com

CASE APPLICATION:
Gears, Inc.

Billy Jo Williams is the new plant manager for Gears, Inc., a fifty-year-old, $100 million gear manufacturer.

Stockholders and corporate leadership are unhappy because while other divisions are earning a return of 15 percent, Gears, Inc. has averaged under 3 percent return for the past two years. Changing management has not seemed to improve the results. Gears, Inc.'s number one customer, averaging over 80 percent of sales for Gears, Inc., is so unhappy they have placed Gears, Inc. on probation and have threatened to take their business to a foreign manufacturer due to poor quality and late shipments. In the past six months two mergers of competitors have occurred, which are recognized leaders in quality in the field and would like to expand market share.

Gears, Inc. knows it has problems and pressure to meet the shipments' deadlines, so they have ordered more overtime in order to reach them. Although management recognizes that $3 million in scrapped parts and paying over $15,500 late fines this year indicates quality problems, the new plant manager does not want to release employees from working on their machines in order to attend quality improvement classes available through their Employee Involvement department. Their president, who comments he "doesn't read books" and he doesn't think attending "some soft course on continuous quality improvement" is anything but another reason to get further behind in meeting their schedules. The manufacturing manager says that meeting customers' expectations is enough, don't worry about exceeding expectations or doing more than the minimum required.

1. How would you respond to the president, plant manager, manufacturing manager, and employee involvement coordinator in an upcoming quality issues meeting?
2. What information would you share?
3. What would you be willing to do or provide?
4. What will happen to Gears, Inc. if corrective action is not taken?

TESTING YOUR UNDERSTANDING

How well did you fulfill the learning objectives?

1. The global village has changed the work of the human resources professional. All of the following statements are globalization issues except
   a. training is often provided through the employing organization.
   b. culture sensitization must be provided, often through the employing organization.
   c. conflict reduction techniques may be needed as workers from different countries are combined into work groups.
   d. management training must include how to deal with workers from many different countries.
   e. in U.S. organizations, HR professionals are responsible for screening future employees to make sure they speak English and share American values.

2. Why has work-force diversity changed the work of the human resources professional?
   a. Most human resources professionals are women, and thus, represent a means of correcting past injustices, like pay differences between men and women.
   b. Workers with different backgrounds, values, and expectations have different needs that must be accommodated with different compensation and benefit packages.
   c. Most human resources departments are now also responsible for on-site day-care centers.
   d. Laws require quotas for the employment of all minority groups.
   e. Work-force diversity is not an issue for the human resources professional.

3. What employee-involvement concepts are accepted in today's organizations?
   a. Delegation is a sign of weakness. Employees need to know that the boss is "in charge" to feel secure.
   b. Participative management gives employees more control over the day-to-day activities of their jobs.
   c. Goals should be set by management and clearly spelled out for each employee.
   d. Don't let employee work teams have responsibility for safety or quality. That action leads to suspicion and mistrust.
   e. Employee involvement can be used to increase productivity, but it stifles creativity, and should never be used in a research and development division.

4. Why are human resources departments assuming responsibilities for language training for employees?
   a. Corporate communications may be sent in multiple languages if no single language or group of languages is shared.
   b. The "wrong" word may cause major ill-will if it is interpreted as an insult.
   c. Hiring people with certain skills may necessitate hiring those who don't speak the host company's language.
   d. Global organizations, by definition, require people of different language backgrounds to work together.
   e. Language training is important for all of these reasons.

5. Why are cultural considerations critical to the success of any global business?
   a. Most people want to work with other cultured people.
   c. Making sure that workers in other countries adhere to American values is an important human resources function.

d. Managers must be flexible and adaptable to deal with working conditions and social systems throughout the world.

e. Collective societies stress family values, while individualistic societies stress the work ethic. Therefore, U.S. firms should only do business with organizations in individualistic societies.

f. It is important to place employees only in positions where they will be most comfortable and familiar.

6. What is the best way to help multicultural individuals work together?

a. Assign them major projects with other members of their ethnic group.

b. Pass laws that require them to work together.

c. Make promotions and raises dependent on working together well.

d. Engage in cross-cultural team building activities. Provide training on possible tension-causing areas and, thus, reduce conflict.

e. There is no evidence that multicultural work groups have any more conflicts than single-culture work groups.

7. What changes are causing an increased diversity in the U.S. work force?

a. Most white males are not going to work in the future.

b. Baby boomers have glutted the labor market. No one else will be able to get jobs for decades.

c. Increased globalization and changes in employment laws are bringing more women and racial and ethnic minorities into the labor pool.

d. Work attitudes change as employees get older.

e. Company policies in support of socially responsible activities are increasing.

8. Robin, vice president of human resources for a large, multinational firm headquartered in the United States, is planning major staffing requirements. Today, 80 percent of the employees in the organization are white males, under age 35. Which statement is probably true, based on the projected labor pool profiles for the next two decades?

a. Robin will hire more women in the next decade.

b. The average age of his employees will decrease in the next decade.

c. Hiring will probably be restricted to U.S. citizens.

d. New managers will have to be hired from outside the organization, rather than promoted from within.

e. New managers should be promoted from within.

9. If you were vice president of a major U.S. corporation and could only do one of the following in the next decade, which action would be most responsive to the work-force diversity issue?

a. Offer Chinese language classes. Make sure all company communications are in Mandarin and English.

b. Offer Portuguese language classes. Make sure all company communications are in Portuguese and English.

c. Offer Russian language classes. Make sure all company communications are in Russian and English.

d. Offer French language classes. Make sure all company communications are in French and English.

e. Offer Spanish language classes. Make sure all company communications are in Spanish and English.

10. Why should the director of human resources for Ford Motor Company consider hiring grade-school teachers?

a. Teachers work well with robots on the assembly line.

b. Teachers work well with the Teamsters on the assembly line.

c. Teachers who work for the summer go back to their classrooms and make positive comments about the quality of life on the assembly line to grade-school students, thus reducing the negative image that union workers have with younger people.

d. Over $200 million a year is currently spent in remedial education by Ford Motor Company. Employees on the payroll with grade-school teaching credentials would be a good investment.

e. The mission statement of Ford Motor Company includes a directive to significantly hire from any occupational group that is underemployed.

11. The basis of Deming's pioneering work

a. was created in Japan.

b. is about twenty years old.

c. is that quality can be measured and achieved through a process of statistical controls.

d. is that workers on the line have more control over the quality of work than the production managers.

e. all of these.

12. Considering continuous process improvement activities in organizations, should "zero defects" really be a goal?

a. Yes. Perfection is a reasonable goal.

b. No. 0.1 percent errors can be corrected much more efficiently than they can be prevented.

c. Yes. Most industries find this an attainable goal.

d. No. Current levels of 97 percent accuracy are adequate.

e. Sometimes. For some mistakes, cost benefits cannot be calculated.

13. What's the difference between reengineering and continuous improvement processes?

a. Reengineering involves incremental change focusing on customers while continuous improvement initiatives involves radical change in an effort to redesign the organization.

b. Reengineering involves radical change while continuous improvement initiatives involves incremental change.

c. Reengineering is a function of downsizing and restructuring, while continuous improvement initiatives focuses on making quantum changes in the organizations' operations.

d. Reengineering is the application of the tools Deming taught Japanese businesses, while continuous improvement initiatives deal with statistical control mechanisms.

e. There is no difference between reengineering and continuous improvement initiatives.

14. Contingent workers offer organizations opportunities to smooth out staffing fluctuations. Which one of the following would not be a reason for an organization to hire contingent workers?

a. Reducing labor costs.

b. Existing skill deficiencies in the work force.

c. Promoting family-friendly benefits.

d. Replacing core employees who are not productive.

e. Increasing work-force diversity.

15. Decentralized work sites offer several advantages to organizations and to employees. Which one of the following is not considered an advantage of decentralized work sites?

a. Increased work schedule flexibility.

b. Reduced safety and health regulations.

c. Increased pool of skilled workers.

d. Enhanced job opportunities in depressed areas.

e. All of the above are advantages of decentralized work sites.

16. Why should an organization be wary of moving toward employee involvement? Involved employees have more self-confidence and are less loyal to the organization.

a. Although involved employees are happier employees, they are less productive employees.

b. Employee involvement can't happen overnight. An organization should schedule time to change and implement this kind of change slowly.

c. Control functions are all but eliminated in an employee-involved organization. Accurate performance data are nearly impossible to collect.

d. All of these statements should be concerns for an organization that is contemplating a move toward empowerment.

e. None of these statements should be concerns for an organization that is contemplating a move toward empowerment.

Endnotes

1. Kathy Rebello, "We Humbly Beg You to Take This Job. Please," *Business Week* (June 17, 1996), p. 40.

2. William H. Wagel, "On the Horizon: HR in the 1990s," *Personnel* (January 1990), p. 6.

3. A multinational corporation is an organization that has significant operations in two or more countries. A transnational corporation is one that maintains significant operations in two or more countries simultaneously, and gives each the decision-making authority to operate in the local country.

4. Because of the global nature of work, it is important for students to be bilingual. In terms of gaining employment, those who speak more than one language will have an advantage in the job market.

5. "How America Will Change over the Next 30 Years," *Fortune* (April 23, 1990), p. 167.

6. For a more comprehensive coverage of cultural dimension, see Geert Hofstede, *Cultural Consequences: International Differences in Work-Related Values* (Beverly Hills, Calif.: Sage Publications, 1980).

7. Wagel, p. 17.

8. Stephanie Overman, "Managing the Diverse Work Force," *HRMagazine* (April 1991), p. 31.

9. Bruce W. Nolan, "Racism," *Time* (August 12, 1991), pp. 36–38.

10. *HRMagazine* (January 1991), pp. 40–41.

11. Ibid., p. 40.

12. William H. Wagel, *Personnel* (January 1990), p. 12.

13. "Riding the Tide of Change," *The Wyatt Communicator* (Winter 1991), p. 11.

14. Ibid.

15. Ann Crittenden, "Where Workforce 2000 Went Wrong," *Working Woman* (August 1994), p. 18.

16. Donna Fenn, "Diversity: More Than Just Affirmative Action," *Inc.* (July 1995), p. 93.

17. The baby-boom generation refers to those individuals born between 1946 and 1964.

18. Jonathan A. Degal, "Diversify for Dollars," *HRMagazine* (April 1997), pp. 134–140.

19. Sharon Nelton, "Winning with Diversity," *Nation's Business* (September 12, 1992), p. 18.

20. The Hudson Institute, *Workforce 2000: Work and Workers for the 21st Century* (Indianapolis, Ind.: The Hudson Institute, 1987).

21. Ann Crittenden, "Where Workforce 2000 Went Wrong," p. 18.

22. Richard W. Judy and Carol D'Amico, *Workforce 2020: Work and Workers in the 21st Century* (Indianapolis, IN: Hudson Institute, 1997), p. 109; Betty Holcomb, "No, We're Not Going Home Again," *Working Mother* (November 1994), p. 28. See also James Aley, "Men Ditch the Labor Market," *Fortune* (August 22, 1994), p. 24.

23. Carla Joinson, "Cultural Sensitivity Adds Up to Good Business Sense," *HRMagazine* (November 1995), pp. 82–85.

24. Linda Micco, "Avon, Allstate Honored for Diversity Programs," *HR News* (February 1997), p. 7; Leon Rubis, "Diversity Means Managing the Mix," *HR News* (June 1996), p. 11; "Cigna Lightens Domestic Workload," *HRMagazine* (January 1996), p. 60; and Faye Rice, "How to Make Diversity Pay," *Fortune* (August 8, 1994), p. 79.

25. Gail Robinson and Kathleen Dechant, "Building a Business Case for Diversity," *Academy of Management Executive,* Vol. 11, No. 3 (August 1997), p. 21; Janice R. W. Joplin and Catherine S. Daus, "Challenges of Leading a Diverse Work-force," *Academy of Management Executive,* Vol. 11, No. 3 (August 1997), p. 32; and Alice Starcke and Linda Micco, "Diversity Works Best When Tied to Business Strategies," *HR News* (November 1996), p. 1.

26. Alice Starcke, "Experts: Tie Managers' Pay to Diversity Results," *HR News* (September 1997), p. 12.

27. For a good review of family-friendly companies, see Milton Moskowitz, "100 Best Companies for Working Mothers," *Working Mother* (October 1997), pp. 18–96.

28. Sue Shellenbarger, "Flexible Workers Come under the Umbrella of Family Programs," *The Wall Street Journal* (February 8, 1995), p. B-1.

29. Adapted from C. M. Solomon, "Managing the Baby Busters," *Personnel Journal* (March 1992), p. 56.

30. Ibid. and Anne Fisher, "Readers Sound Off on Gen Xers, Women Bosses, and Various Oddities," *Fortune* (October 13, 1997), p. 191.

31. John Simons, "The Youth Movement," *U.S. News and World Report* (September 23, 1996), pp. 63–70; Hal Lancaster, "You May Call Them Slackers; They Say They're Just Realistic," *The Wall Street Journal* (August 1, 1995), p. B-1; and Suneel Ratan, "Why Busters Hate Boomers," *Fortune* (October 4, 1993), pp. 56–70.

32. Linda Thornburg, "The Age Wave Hits: What Older Workers Want and Need," *HRMagazine* (February 1995), pp. 43–44.

33. Charles E. Cohen, "Managing Older Workers," *Working Woman* (November 1994), pp. 61–62.

34. "Office Hours," *Fortune* (November 5, 1990), p. 184.

35. *The Wyatt Communicator,* p. 11.

36. Jane A. Sasseen, Robert Neff, Shekar Hattangadi, and Silvia Sansoni, "The Winds of Change Blow Everywhere," *Business Week* (October 17, 1994), p. 93.

37. Commerce Clearing House, "Employers to Bear Burden of Adult Literacy," *Human Resources Management: Ideas and Trends* (November 10, 1993), p. 182.

38. Commerce Clearing House, "AMA Surveys: Drug Testing, Basic Skills, and AIDS Policy Benchmarks," *Human Resources Management: Ideas and Trends* (June 8, 1994), p. 97.

39. Stephen P. Robbins, *Management,* 4th ed. (Englewood Cliffs, N.J.: Prentice-Hall, Inc., 1993), p. 370.

40. "Employee Literacy," *Inc.* (August 1992), p. 81.

41. Ibid.

42. Blue Wooldridge and Jennifer Wester, "The Turbulent Environment of Public Personnel Administration: Responding to the Challenge of the Changing Workplace of the Twenty-First Century," *Public Personnel Management,* Vol. 20, No. 2 (Summer 1991), p. 213.

43. *Fortune* (April 23, 1990), p. 176.

44. Ibid.; see also Louis S. Richman, "The New Work Force Builds Itself," *Fortune* (June 27, 1994), pp. 68–69.

45. Although this trend continues, there is a good counterpoint to this activity in Edmund Faltermayer, "Is This Layoff Necessary?" *Fortune* (June 1, 1992), pp. 71–86.

46. "Downsizing—The Toll Keeps Going Up," *U.S. News and World Report* (September 6, 1993), p. 16.

47. Brenton S. Schlender, "Japan's White Collar Blues," *Fortune* (March 12, 1994), pp. 97–104.

48. Joann S. Lublin, "Don't Stop Cutting Staff, Study Suggests," *The Wall Street Journal* (September 27, 1994), p. B-1.

49. We recognize that this number is not an accurate cost savings. In addition, one would have to add in the costs of employee benefits saved and subtract any monies used to "buy people out." The $35 million figure is for illustration purposes only.

50. De'Ann Weimer, "Navistar: Gunning the Engines," *Business Week* (February 2, 1998), pp. 135–138.

51. Anne B. Fisher, "Welcome to the Age of Overwork," *Fortune* (November 30, 1992), p. 64.

52. See Marjorie Armstrong-Stassen and Janina C. Latack, "Coping with Work-Force Reduction: The Effect of Layoff Exposure on Survivors' Reactions," in Jerry L. Wall and Lawrence R. Jauch, eds., *Academy of Management Best Papers Proceedings 1992,* Las Vegas (August 9–12, 1992), pp. 207–12. See also Terence Krell and Robert S. Spich, "A Tentative Model of Lame Duck Situations in Organizations," *Proceedings of the 1992 Conference of the Midwest Society for Human Resources/Industrial Relations* (March 25–27, 1992), pp. 161–75.

53. See, for example, Joann S. Lublin, "The Layoff Industry Learns That the Ax Can Be a Real Grind," *The Wall Street Journal* (November 28, 1994), pp. A-1; A-8.

54. Ibid.; and "A Comeback for Middle Managers," *Fortune* (October 17, 1994), p. 32.

55. Mark Henricks, "Staying Power," *Entrepreneur* (July 1997), p. 70; and Alan C. Fenwick, "Five Easy Lessons: A Primer for Starting a Total Quality Management Program," *Quality Progress,* Vol. 24, No. 12 (December 1991), p. 63.

56. Albert M. Koller, Jr., "TQM: Understanding the Barrier of Total Quality Management," *Manage,* Vol. 42, No. 4 (May 1991), p. 15.

57. Seanna Browder and Andy Reinhardt, "A Fierce Downdraft at Boeing," *Business Week* (January 26, 1998), pp. 34–35; Fenwick, p. 63; and John S. McClenahen, "52 Fiefdoms' No More," *Industry Week* (January 20, 1997), p. 60.

58. David Greising, "Quality: How to Make It Pay," *Business Week* (August 8, 1994), pp. 53–59.

59. See W. Edwards Deming, *Quality Productivity and Competitive Position* (Cambridge, Mass.: MIT Center for Advanced Engineering Study, 1982).

60. See W. Edwards Deming, "Improvement of Quality and Productivity Through Actions of Management," *National Productivity Review* (Winter 1981), pp. 12–22.

61. See, for example, Brian M. Cook, "Quality: The Pioneers Survey the Landscape," *Industry Week* (October 21, 1991), pp. 68–73.

62. Ibid., p. 70.

63. Ibid.; see also Fenwick, p. 64; and David Hughes, "Motorola Nears Quality Benchmark after 12-Year Evolutionary Effort," *Aviation Week and Space Technology* (December 9, 1990), p. 64.

64. Fred R. Bleakley, "How an Outdated Plant Was Made New," *The Wall Street Journal* (October 21, 1994), pp. B-1, B-10. For another view on this topic, see Thomas Y. Choi and Orlando C. Behling, "Top Managers and TQM Success: One More Look After All These Years," *Academy of Management Executive,* Vol. 11, No. 1 (February 1997), pp. 37–46.

65. Joshua Hyatt, "The Zero-Defect CEO," *Inc.* (June 1997), pp. 46–57; and Carla C. Carter, "Seven Basic Quality Tools," *HRMagazine* (January 1992), p. 81.

66. See, for example, Amit Majumdar, Megan Smolenyak, and Nancy Yenche, "Planting the Seeds of TQM," *National Productivity Review* (Autumn 1991), p. 492.

67. Frederick F. Reichheld and W. Earl Sasser, Jr., "Zero Defections: Quality Comes to Services," *Harvard Business Review* (September–October 1990), p. 105.

68. John Case, "The Change Masters," *Inc.* (March 1992), p. 60.

69. Adapted from ibid., p. 61.

70. See Morton Bahr, "Labor and Management–Working Together on Quality," *Journal for Quality and Participation,* Vol. 14, No. 3 (June 1991), pp. 14–17.

71. See, for example, Jay Mathews and Peter Katel, "The Cost of Quality," *Newsweek* (September 7, 1992), pp. 48–49.

72. Edward E. Lawler III, "Total Quality Management and Employee Involvement: Are They Compatible?" *Academy of Management Executive,* Vol. 8, No. 1 (1994), pp. 68–76; and Richard Blackman and Benson Rosen, "Total Quality and Human Resources Management: Lessons Learned from Baldrige Award-Winning Companies," *Academy of Management Executive,* Vol. 7, No. 3 (1993), pp. 49–66.

73. For a good review of the issues surrounding this topic, see A. B. (Rami) Shani and Yoram Mitki, "Reengineering, Total Quality Management, and Sociotechnical Systems Approaches to Organizational Change: Towards an Eclectic Approach?" *Journal of Quality Management,* Vol. 1, No. 1 (January 1996), pp. 131–145.

74. Sandra E. O'Connell, "Reengineering: Ways to Do It with Technology," *HRMagazine* (November 1994), p. 40.

75. See, for example, John Byrne, "Reengineering: What Happened?" *Business Week* (January 30, 1995), p. 16; Benjamin F. Ball, "For ECR to Work, Some Comfortable Practices Must Go," *Advertising Age* (June 6, 1994), p. 28; and Jane A. Sasseen, Robert Neff, Shekar Hattangadi, and Silvia Sansoni, "The Winds of Change Blow Everywhere," *Business Week* (October 17, 1994), pp. 92–94.

76. Nancy K. Austin, "What's Missing from Corporate Cure-Alls," *Working Woman* (September 1994), pp. 16–19.

77. Ibid.

78. John A. Byrne, p. 16.

79. Sandra E. O'Connell, p. 40.

80. John A. Byrne, p. 16.

81. The following story is based on the story of Thermos, appearing in Brian Dumaine, "Payoff from the New Management," *Fortune* (December 13, 1993), pp. 103–104.

82. Thomas A. Stewart, "Reengineering: The Hot New Managing Tool," *Fortune* (August 23, 1993), p. 41.

83. Ibid.

84. Julie Connelly, "Have We Become Mad Dogs in the Office?" *Fortune* (November 28, 1994), p. 197.

85. See, for example, Debra Phillips, "The New Service Boom," *Entrepreneur* (August 1994), pp. 134–140.

86. Ann Crittenden, "Temporary," *Working Woman* (February 1994), p. 32.

87. Jaclyn Fierman, "The Contingency Work Force," *Fortune* (January 24, 1994), p. 32; "BOOM TIMES for Temporary Help Aren't Temporary, Experts Agree," *The Wall Street Journal* (October 25, 1994), p. A-1; and Janet Novack, "Is Lean, Mean?," *Forbes* (August 15, 1994), p. 88.

88. Beth Rogers, "Temporary Help Industry Evolving as It Grows," *HR News* (January 1995), p. 4.

89. See, for instance, Audrey Freedman, "Human Resources Forecast 1995: Contingent Workers," *HRMagazine Supplement* (1994), pp. 13–14.

90. Maggie Mahar, "Part-time: By Choice or by Chance," *Working Woman* (October 1993), p. 20.

91. Ann Crittenden, "Temporary," p. 32.

92. Jaclyn Fierman, "The Contingent Work Force," p. 33.

93. Keith H. Hammonds, Kevin Kelly, and Karen Thurston, "The New World of Work," *Business Week* (October 17, 1994), p. 85.

94. Ann Crittenden, "Temporary," p. 33.

95. Ibid.

96. "Contracting Out White-Collar Jobs Continues to Gain Steam," *The Wall Street Journal* (September 20, 1994), p. A-1.

97. Ani Hadjian, "Hiring Temps Full-Time May Get the IRS On Your Tail," *Fortune* (January 24, 1994), p. 34.

98. For example, see Robert McGarvey, "Temporary Solution," *Entrepreneur* (August 1994), pp. 68–72.

99. See, for example, Leon Rubis, "Benefits Boost Appeal of Temporary Work," *HRMagazine* (January 1995), pp. 54–58; and Anne Murphy, "Do-It-Yourself Job Creation," *Inc.* (January 1994), pp. 36–50.

100. Michael P. Cronin, "The Benefits of Part-Time Work," *Inc.* (December 1994), p. 127.

101. Based on Sue Shellenbarger, "Refusing In-Home Work Costs Him His Job," *The Wall Street Journal* (April 8, 1994), p. B-1.

102. Commerce Clearing House, "Work at Home Increasingly Appealing to Employers, But Legal Pitfalls Abound," *Human Resources Management: Ideas and Trends* (February 16, 1994), pp. 25–26.

103. Sue Shellenbarger, "Telecommuter Profile: Productive, Efficient . . . and a Little Weird," *The Wall Street Journal* (August 23, 1995), p. B-1.

104. Ibid.

105. Thomas Roberts, "Who Are the High-Tech Home Workers?," *Inc. Technology* (1994), p. 31.

106. Ibid.

107. Commerce Clearing House, "Work at Home Increasingly Appealing to Employers, But Legal Pitfalls Abound," *Human Resources Management: Ideas and Trends* (February 16, 1994), pp. 25–26.

108. For a comprehensive overview of empowering employees, see Jay A. Conger and Rabindra N. Kanungo, "The Empowerment Process: Integrating Theory and Practice," *Academy of Management Review,* Vol. 13, No. 3 (July 1988), pp. 471–82.

109. See, for example, Jeffrey Pfeffer, "Producing Sustainable Competitive Advantage Through the Effective Management of People," *Academy of Management Executive,* Vol. 9, No. 1 (1995), pp. 55–72.

110. Keith H. Hammond, Kevin Kelly, and Karen Thurston, "The New World of Work," *Business Week* (October 17, 1994), p. 81.

111. See, for example, Jon L. Pierce, Stephen A. Rubenfeld, and Susan Morgan, "Employee Ownership: A Conceptual Model of Process and Effects," *The Academy of Management Review,* Vol. 16, No. 1 (January 1991), pp. 121–144.

112. Ibid, pp. 136–37; and Brian O'Reilly, "The New Deal: What Companies and Employees Owe One Another," *Fortune* (June 13, 1994), p. 44.

3. Understanding Equal Employment Opportunity

LEARNING OBJECTIVES

After reading this chapter, you will be able to:

1. Identify the groups protected under the Civil Rights Act of 1964, Title VII.
2. Discuss the importance of the Equal Employment Opportunities Act of 1972.
3. Describe affirmative action plans.
4. Define what is meant by the terms *adverse impact, adverse treatment, and protected group members.*
5. Identify the important components of the Americans with Disabilities Act of 1990.
6. Explain the coverage of the Family and Medical Leave Act of 1993.
7. Discuss how a business can protect itself from discrimination charges.
8. Specify the HRM importance of the *Griggs v. Duke Power* case.
9. Define what constitutes sexual harassment in today's organizations.
10. Discuss what is meant by the term *glass ceiling.*

*I*magine you're looking for something to do one evening, and you decide to look in the entertainment section of your local newspaper and "find" a movie. You quickly search the movie reviews and find one that draws your attention. It's a movie about a major corporation led by a middle aged executive, who for fifteen years has helped shape the company into one success story after another. But coupled with that success is a scandal—one that reaches across the seas to the company's headquarters in Sweden. Sound like a movie you've seen? Well, what you are about to see is that this wasn't a movie at all. In fact, it's a story about real-life drama at the Astra USA Company, the Westborough, Massachusetts pharmaceutical company.[1]

At the center of the controversy at Astra was its President and CEO, Lars Bildman. During his reign of control at Astra, Bildman is alleged to have created a culture in the company where, as one manager explained, was for "guys to get drunk and do whatever they could to women." During this time, dozens of women had complained that they were fondled or solicited for sexual favors by some Astra executives. In one instance, a 25-year-old sales rep, attending one of her first sales meetings, ran into a restroom and burst into tears. While in the restroom, this first-year employee recognized two women sales managers and told them what had happened—that the president had groped and tried to kiss her. Seeking some solace from the managers, the sales rep was astounded. All they had to say was "That's the way it is at Astra, and you better get used to it." That's something she just couldn't do!

The Astra case has been one that has garnered a lot of attention. After a six-month investigation by *Business Week* investigative reporters, everything broke loose. What appeared to be the unthinkable was happening—and the "playful" days at Astra were about to end. The story was breaking about what women employees faced—being fondled, solicited for sexual favors, "encouraged" to escort senior executives to bars or dancing clubs, or getting invitations to join the inebriated executives in hotel suites. Female employees at Astra were clearly facing some of the worst employment conditions anyone could. Even many of the males in the organization were amazed. And as one sales rep summed it up, "If ever there was a company where sexual harassment was rampant, this is it." Yet, you'd wonder how this could go on for so long. In many respects, it was easy to see why.

First of all, many of the actions were attributed to the president—the person who set the example in the company. Although he had been described as an excellent executive, he appeared to exhibit another facet of life on the job. He believed that employees should work 8 hours, play 8 hours, and sleep 8 hours. He and some of his executive team made it clear to all employees what mattered most. For example, they encouraged managers to hire "attractive" women. New sales trainees were kept away from family and friends for most of their 15-week initial training—which some described as being like a boot camp. Several evenings a week during this training session, trainees were encouraged to meet with executives in bars, so their social skills could be assessed. Some trainees who didn't exhibit the correct social skills were terminated. Some who gave the "cold shoulder," however, did not see their careers affected. Yet several who "played the game" found that they had better access to top management—and frequently received larger bonuses. Senior management also created the impression in employees' minds that they couldn't fight the deep pockets of the company by complaining or filing suit. Moreover, there was also a great fear of retaliation for "fighting" the company. And in those few instances where some did, company counsel was able to secure settlements in the $20,000–$100,000 range, which included the stipulation that the individual had to keep silent.

This kind of activity, thankfully, cannot continue forever in an organization. At some point in time, the "cover" is shattered. And when it becomes known, it's then time for swift action to take place. When senior officials in Astra's parent company in Sweden heard of the allegations, they immediately went into action. They suspended the president and launched their own investigation. In the end, the president and one of his senior executives were terminated for inappropriate behaviors and abusing their power. Another executive resigned amid the investigation. A fourth, an executive in Sweden, was asked to resign;

Cordelia Webb just couldn't take the harassment any more at Astra. After 2 and ½ years of abuse, she has seen her hair fall out, suffered from severe stomach pains, and scratched her back and chest until the skin was raw. Finally she had to take disability leave. But things didn't stop there; several months later, Astra fired her. She has now taken her case to the EEOC.

not for what he did, but for what he didn't do—notifying his bosses of the actions occurring in Astra USA. And the "violated" employees (all 80 of them) shared in more than a $9 million settlement.[2]

INTRODUCTION

What do Denny's Restaurant, Texaco, Mitsubishi, CBS, and State Farm Insurance have in common? Each has been singled out for practices that allegedly discriminated against minorities or women. In Chapter 1 we introduced the concept of government legislation as it affects employment practices. In this chapter, we will explore this critical influence to provide an understanding of the legislation. Why? Because it is a fact of doing business. Almost every U.S. organization, both public and private, must abide by the guidelines established in the 1964 Civil Rights Act, its subsequent amendment (1972), and other federal laws governing employment practices. Even the United States Congress in early 1995 voted that it, too, would be covered by these same laws! The importance of such legislation cannot be overstated, as these laws permeate all HRM functions in the organization.

Keep in mind that although our discussion will be limited to federal employment legislation, there may also be state or municipal laws that go beyond what the federal government requires. For example, in several states (like California and New Jersey), sexual orientation is considered a "protected class."[3]

While it is impossible to cover all of these laws, HRM managers must know and understand what additional requirements they face.

LAWS AFFECTING DISCRIMINATORY PRACTICES

The beginning of equal employment opportunity is usually attributed to the passage of the 1964 Civil Rights Act. Even though the focus of the activities we will explore in this chapter are rooted in this 1964 act, equal employment's beginning actually goes back more than one hundred years. For instance, Section 1981 of Title 42 of the U.S. Code referred to as the **Civil Rights Act of 1866,** coupled with the Fourteenth Amendment to the Constitution (1868), prohibited discrimination on the basis of race, sex, and national origin. Although these earlier actions have been overshadowed by the 1964 act, they've gained prominence in years past as being the laws that white male workers could use to support claims of reverse discrimination. In such cases, white males used the Civil Rights Act of 1866 and the Fourteenth Amendment to support their argument that minorities were given special treatment in employment decisions that placed the white male at a distinct disadvantage.[4] Under the Civil Rights Act of 1866 employees could sue for racial discrimination.[5] As a result of this act, individuals could also seek punitive and compensatory damages under Section 1981, in addition to the awarding of back pay.[6] However, in 1989, a Supreme Court ruling limited Section 1981 use in discrimination suits in that the law does not cover racial discrimination after a person has been hired.[7] We'll look more at reverse discrimination in our discussion of relevant Supreme Court decisions.

Although earlier attempts were rudimentary in promoting fair employment practices among workers, it was not until the 1960s that earnest emphasis was placed on achieving such a goal. Let's turn our attention, then, to the landmark piece of employment legislation, the Civil Rights Act of 1964.

The Civil Rights Act of 1964

No single piece of legislation in the 1960s had a greater effect on reducing employment discrimination than the Civil Rights Act of 1964. It was divided into a number of parts called Titles—each dealing with a particular facet of discrimination. On college campuses, you may have heard about Title IX issues—usually in the context of what a university spends on both men and women's sports programs. For HRM purposes, however, **Title VII** is especially relevant.

Title VII prohibits discrimination in hiring, compensation, and terms, conditions, or privileges of employment based on race, religion, color, sex, or national origin. Title VII also prohibits retaliation against an individual who files a charge of discrimination, participates in an investigation, or opposes any unlawful practice. Most organizations, both public and private, are bound by the law.[8] The law, however, specifies compliance based on the number of employees in the organization. Essentially, as originally passed in 1964, any organization with twenty-five or more (amended to fifteen or more in 1972) employees is covered.[9] This minimum number of employees serves as a means of protecting, or removing from the law, small, family-owned businesses.[10] The organizations initially covered by the EEO regulations, however, found compliance confusing.

Organizations were faced with relatively new requirements, but detailed guidelines for compliance were lacking. Days of purposefully excluding certain

> **Title VII prohibits discrimination in hiring, compensation, and terms and conditions of employment.**

individuals significantly decreased, yet practices like testing applicants appeared to create the same effect.[11] In an attempt to clarify this procedure, several cases were challenged in the Supreme Court. The outcomes of these cases indicated that any action that had the effect of keeping certain groups of people out of particular jobs was illegal, unless the company could show why a practice was required. The implication of these decisions, for example, was that a company could not hire a maintenance employee using an aptitude test and a high-school diploma requirement unless those criteria could be shown to be directly relevant to the job. In one of these cases, **Griggs v. Duke Power Company** (1971), the company was unable to show job relatedness. Griggs, an applicant for a maintenance job, demonstrated that the power company's tests and degree requirements were unrelated to performance on the job in question. The decision in the *Griggs* case, though, did not mean that specific selection criteria couldn't be used. For instance, in the case of *Washington* v. *Davis* (1967),[12] the Supreme Court held that the use of aptitude tests was permissible. In this case, Davis was an applicant for a position as a metropolitan Washington, D.C., police officer. The police force required all applicants to pass a comprehensive aptitude test. The Supreme Court held that the test measured necessary competencies required to be successful as a police officer.

Even though we began to gain a better understanding of what Congress meant in the writing of Title VII, something was clearly lacking—enforcement mechanisms. By 1972, after realizing that the Civil Rights Act was left much to interpretation, Congress passed an amendment to the act called the Equal Employment Opportunity Act (EEOA). This act was designed to provide a series of amendments to Title VII.[13] Probably the greatest consequence of the EEOA was the granting of enforcement powers to the **Equal Employment Opportunity Commission** (EEOC). The EEOC was granted authority to effectively prohibit all forms of employment discrimination based on race, religion, color, sex, or national origins. The EEOC was given the power to file civil suits (individuals may also file a suit themselves if the EEOC declines to sue) against organizations if it was unable to secure an acceptable resolution of discrimination charges within thirty days. In addition, the EEOA also expanded Title VII coverage to include employees of state and local governments, employees of educational institutions, and employers or labor organizations—as we mentioned earlier, those with fifteen or more employees or members.

Title VII, as it exists today, stipulates that organizations must do more than "just" discontinue discriminatory practices. Enterprises are expected to actively recruit and give preference to minority group members in employment decisions. This action is commonly referred to as **affirmative action.**

Affirmative Action Plans   Affirmative action programs are voluntary programs instituted by an organization to correct past injustices in an employment processes. There were four primary reasons for these plans:

▶ Affirmative action programs were built on the premise that white males made up the majority of workers in our companies.
▶ U.S. companies were still growing and could accommodate more workers.
▶ As a matter of public policy and decency, minorities should be hired to correct past prejudice that has kept them out.
▶ "Legal and social coercion [were] necessary to bring about the change."[14]

What do these imply about affirmative action programs? What affirmative action means is that an organization must take certain steps to show that it is not discriminating. For example, the organization must conduct an analysis of the demographics of its current work force. Similarly, the organization must analyze the composition of the community from which it recruits. If the work force resembles the community for all jobs classifications, then the organization may be demonstrating that its affirmative action program is working. If, however, there are differences, affirmative action also implies that the organization will establish goals and timetables for correcting the imbalance, and have specific plans on how to go about recruiting and retaining protected group members.[15]

In coordinating an EEO program, a few issues arise. First of all, the company must know what the job requires in terms of skills, knowledge, and abilities. Candidates are then evaluated on how well they meet the essential elements of the job. If candidates meet these criteria, then they are essentially qualified, meaning that they should be successful performers of the job. Nowhere under EEO does the federal government require an organization to hire unqualified workers. They do require organizations to actively search for qualified minorities by recruiting from places like predominantly African-American or women's colleges, but they do not force hiring of these individuals under this process. However, as a result of affirmative action programs, an organization should be able to show significant improvements in hiring and promoting women and minorities, or justify why external factors prohibited them from achieving their affirmative-action goals.[16]

Over the past few years, there has been a backlash against affirmative actions programs.[17] Much of the criticism has focused on the realization that affirmative action bases employment decisions on group membership rather than individual performance.[18] This tugs at the heart of fair employment whereby certain groups of individuals [e.g. race, sex, age] are given preferential treatment.[19] As the argument goes, if it was wrong fifty years ago to give "white males" preference for employment, why is it right today to give other individu-

Colgate-Palmolive sees promoting equal access initiatives as benefiting the company and helping to keep it competitive in the future. The company takes individuals like Sydney Sherry, and gives them opportunities to gain skills in all aspects of the job. Sherry, trained as an engineer, has been given opportunities at Colgate-Palmolive to work in marketing, manufacturing, and operations. As she has stated, "Colgate let me do things I had no business doing."

als preference simply because they possess certain traits?[20] Although there has been some movement in a few states to eliminate affirmative action plans, and the issue has been debated in the Congress of the United States, at this point in time, affirmative action plans still exist. And it appears that they will be around for some time.[21]

Irrespective of the controversy surrounding affirmative action plans, throughout much of this discussion we have addressed practices that are designed to assure equal employment opportunity for all individuals. But how do we know if equal employment programs are not operating properly? The answer to that question may lie in the concept of **adverse (disparate) impact.**

Adverse Impact   Adverse impact can be described as any employment consequence that is discriminatory toward employees who are members of a protected group. Protected status categories include race, color, religion, national origin, citizenship status, sex, age 40 and above, pregnancy-related medical conditions, disability, and Vietnam-era veteran military status.

For an example of an adverse impact, we can look at the prior height and weight requirements police departments around the country had years ago. This height requirement was frequently 5′10″ or greater. As such, women who wished to become police officers were unable to. Why? Because the average height of females is shorter than that of males. Accordingly, using this height requirement had the effect of significantly reducing the job opportunities for this group of people. The concept of adverse impact, then, results from a seemingly neutral, even unintentional consequence of an employment practice consequence.[22]

There is another issue that differs from adverse impact, but follows a similar logic. This is called **adverse (disparate) treatment.** Adverse treatment occurs when a member of a protected group receives less favorable outcomes in an employment decision than a nonprotected group member.[23] For example, if a protected group member is evaluated as performing poorly more often, or receives fewer organizational rewards, adverse treatment may have occurred.

The Civil Rights Act of 1964 led the way to change how HRM would function. As the years progressed, other amendments and legislation were passed that extended equal employment opportunity practices to diverse groups. Let's take a look at the more critical of these laws summarized in Exhibit 3-1.

Other Laws Affecting Discrimination Practices

In addition to the Civil Rights Act of 1964, there are a number of other laws and presidential orders that equally affect HRM practices. Specifically, we'll address the Age Discrimination in Employment Act of 1967 (amended in 1978 and 1986), the Pregnancy Discrimination Act of 1978, the Americans with Disabilities Act of 1990, the Family and Medical Leave Act of 1993, and three Executive Orders: 11246, 11375, and 11478.

Age Discrimination in Employment Act of 1967   The **Age Discrimination in Employment Act (ADEA) of 1967** prohibited the widespread practice of requiring workers to retire at the age of 65.[24] It gave protected group status to individuals between the ages of 40 and 65. Since 1967, this act has been amended twice—once in 1978, which raised the mandatory retirement age to 70, and again in 1986, where the upper age limit was removed altogether.[25] As a result, anyone over age 39 is covered by the ADEA.

Exhibit 3-1

Summary of Laws Affecting Discrimination

Civil Rights Act of 1964	Title VII prohibits employment discrimination in hiring, compensation, and terms, conditions, or privileges of employment based on race, religion, color, sex, or national origin.
Executive Order (E.O.) 11246	Prohibits discrimination on the basis of race, religion, color, and national origin, by federal agencies as well as those working under federal contracts.
Executive Order 11375	Added sex-based discrimination to E.O. 11246.
Age Discrimination in Employment Act of 1967	Protects employees 40-65 years of age from discrimination. Later amended to age 70 (1978), then amended (1986) to eliminate the upper age limit altogether.
Executive Order 11478	Amends part of E.O. 11246, states practices in the federal government must be based on merit; also prohibits discrimination based on political affiliation, marital status, or physical handicap.
Equal Employment Opportunity Act of 1972	Granted the enforcement powers for the EEOC.
Vocational Rehabilitation Act of 1973	Prohibits employers who have federal contracts greater than than $2,500 from discriminating against individuals with handicaps, racial minorities, and women.
Vietnam Veterans Readjustment Act of 1974	Provided for equal employment opportunities for Vietnam War veterans. Administered and enforced by the Office of Federal Contract Compliance Programs
Age Discrimination in Employment Act of 1978	Increased mandatory retirement age from 65 to 70. Later amended (1986) to eliminate upper age limit.
Pregnancy Discrimination Act of 1978	Afforded EEO protection to pregnant workers and requires pregnancy to be treated like any other disability.
Americans with Disabilities Act of 1990	Prohibits discrimination against an essentially qualified individual, and requires enterprises to reasonably accommodate individuals.
Civil Rights Act of 1991	Nullified selected Supreme Court decisions. Reinstates burden of proof by employer. Allows for punitive and compensatory damages through jury trials.
Family and Medical Leave Act of 1993	Permits employees in organizations of fifty or more workers to take up to twelve weeks of unpaid leave for family or medical reasons each year.

Of course, there are and have been exceptions to this law. Employees holding certain types of jobs, such as college professors, didn't come under full protection until 1994.[26] Furthermore, other employees—like police and firefighters—may be required to leave their current positions because of strict requirements of the job. For instance, in the airline industry, pilots may not captain a commercial airplane upon reaching the age of 60.[27] Why age 60? That age is a benchmark after which the Federal Aviation Agency believes that medical research can show that the necessary skills to handle an emergency may be lacking, or to significantly decline.[28] Thus, using age 60 as the determining factor, airlines are permitted to remove a pilot at that age for public safety reasons. But that does not mean that they must leave the organization. Should a 60-year-old pilot decide to be a flight engineer or even an airport ticket agent, and if an opening exists, the individual may apply for the job. Failure to allow their retiring pilots to do so is in violation of ADEA.[29]

In applying this act to the workplace, a four-pronged test is typically used to determine if age discrimination has occurred. This test involves proving that one is "a member of a protected group, that adverse employment action was taken, the individual was replaced by a [younger] worker, and the individual was qualified for the job."[30] For example, assume that in an organization's attempt to cut salary costs, it lays off senior employees. Yet, instead of leaving the jobs unfilled, the organization hires recent college graduates who are paid significantly less. This action may be risky and may lead to a charge of discrimination. Should the organization be found guilty of age discrimination, punitive damages up to double the amount of the compensatory amount may be awarded by the courts.[31]

The Pregnancy Discrimination Act of 1978   The **Pregnancy Discrimination Act of 1978** (and supplemented by various state laws) prohibits discrimination based on pregnancy. Under the law, companies may not terminate a female employee for being pregnant, refuse to make an employment decision based on one's pregnancy, or deny insurance coverage to the individual.[32] The law also requires organizations to offer the employee a reasonable period of time off from work. Although no specific time frames are given, the pregnancy leave is typically six to ten weeks.[33] At the end of this leave, the worker is entitled to return to work. If the exact job she left is unavailable, a similar one must be provided.

It is interesting to note that this law is highly contingent on other benefits the company offers. Should the organization not offer health or disability-related (like sick leave) benefits to its employees, it is exempt from this law. However, any type of health or disability insurance offered, no matter how much or how little, requires compliance. For instance, if a company offers a benefit covering 40 percent of the costs associated with any short-term disability, then it must include pregnancy in that coverage.

Closely aligned with the Pregnancy Discrimination Act was an issue of fetal protection. Fetal protection laws, as the name implies, were passed to protect the unborn child from exposure to toxic chemicals. Many of the Fortune 500 companies, like Exxon, General Motors, and DuPont, had policies restricting female employees, pregnant or not, from holding specific jobs.[34] In doing so, fertile females were restricted from these jobs, causing some to lose out on career opportunities.[35] This led to a charge of discrimination. For example, at Johnson Control Inc., the company would not hire fertile females because of the potential for pregnancy abnormalities due to lead exposure from its battery manufacturing. Accordingly, child-bearing females had two choices: become sterile, or don't apply. At issue here was one's right to bear children. Employment at Johnson Control, Inc., required one to give up that freedom.[36] Additionally, medical research in fertility matters shed new light on the issue in that males' exposure to toxic chemicals may also result in fetal abnormalities; yet males were not required to be sterilized as a condition of employment. Accordingly, the Supreme Court ruled in 1991 that fetal protection laws violated Title VII on the basis of sex discrimination and thus must be discontinued.[37]

The Americans with Disabilities Act extends employment protection to most forms of disabilities.

The Americans with Disabilities Act of 1990   The **Americans with Disabilities Act of 1990 (ADA)** extends employment protection to most forms of disability status, including those afflicted with AIDS.[38] It's important, however, to recognize that ADA doesn't protect all forms of disability. For example, some psychiatric disabilities (like pyromania and kleptomania) may disqualify an individual from employment. And while some mental illness advocates have raised concerns, the EEOC and some courts have held that the employer

Years ago, people like Lawrence Scadden would have had difficulty finding a job in many organizations. Blind since age 5, Scadden is the Director of the National Science Foundation's (NSF) program for people with disabilities—a group that funds math and science education programs for students with disabilities. To perform his job effectively and to accommodate his disability, NSF has provided Scadden with a braille typewriter, as well as a sophisticated speech system that interacts with his computer enabling it to talk. The "tools" to accommodate Scadden cost the NSF just over $1,500. More than reasonable given his productivity.

is not held accountable in these special cases.[39] In addition to the extended coverage, companies are further required to make reasonable accommodations to provide a qualified individual access to the job,[40] as well as eliminating any pre-job offer medical exams—unless of course the medical exam is job related.[41] A company may also be required to provide necessary technology to enable an individual to do his or her job. For example, suppose a worker is legally blind. If special "reading" equipment is available and could assist this individual in doing the job, then the company must provide it if that accommodation does not present an undue financial hardship—referred to as a "reasonable accommodation."

The ADA extends its coverage to private companies and all public service organizations like "state and local agencies, restaurants, transportation systems, and communication companies."[42] Compliance with ADA was phased in over four years, with full compliance for companies with fifteen or more employees effective July 26, 1994.[43]

As a final note on this act, it's interesting that contagious diseases, including AIDS, are considered conditions of being disabled. In advancing the decision in the 1987 Supreme Court case of *Arline v. Nassau County*,[44] the ADA views contagious diseases as any other medical disability. With respect to AIDS, there are exceptions that can be implemented, but most of these are rare. In restaurants, for example, the individual may simply be assigned other duties, rather than terminated. Under this law, you must treat the AIDS worker in the same way that you would treat a worker suffering from cancer, and all job actions must be based on job requirements.

The Family and Medical Leave Act of 1993   The **Family and Medical Leave Act** of 1993 (FMLA) originally was proposed to enhance the Pregnancy Discrimination Act to allow leave for childbirth (as well as adoption) to either parent. Initially, this bill was vetoed by then-president George Bush in an at-

Exhibit 3-2

Family and Medical Act

Your Rights
Under The
Family and Medical Leave Act of 1993

FMLA requires covered employers to provide up to 12 weeks of unpaid, job-protected leave to "eligible" employees for certain family and medical reasons. Employees are eligible if they have worked for a covered employer for at least one year, and for 1,250 hours over the previous 12 months, and if there are at least 50 employees within 75 miles.

Reasons For Taking Leave:

Unpaid leave must be granted for *any* of the following reasons:

• to care for the employee's child after birth, or placement for adoption or foster care;

• to care for the employee's spouse, son or daughter, or parent, who has a serious health condition; or

• for a serious health condition that makes the employee unable to perform the employee's job.

At the employee's or employer's option, certain kinds of *paid* leave may be substituted for unpaid leave.

Advance Notice and Medical Certification:

The employee may be required to provide advance leave notice and medical certification. Taking of leave may be denied if requirements are not met.

• The employee ordinarily must provide 30 days advance notice when the leave is "foreseeable."

• An employer may require medical certification to support a request for leave because of a serious health condition, and may require second or third opinions (at the employer's expense) and a fitness for duty report to return to work.

Job Benefits and Protection:

• For the duration of FMLA leave, the employer must maintain the employee's health coverage under any "group health plan."

• Upon return from FMLA leave, most employees must be restored to their original or equivalent positions with equivalent pay, benefits, and other employment terms.

• The use of FMLA leave cannot result in the loss of any employment benefit that accrued prior to the start of an employee's leave.

Unlawful Acts By Employers:

FMLA makes it unlawful for any employer to:

• interfere with, restrain, or deny the exercise of any right provided under FMLA:

• discharge or discriminate against any person for opposing any practice made unlawful by FMLA or for involvement in any proceeding under or relating to FMLA.

Enforcement:

• The U.S. Department of Labor is authorized to investigate and resolve complaints of violations.

• An eligible employee may bring a civil action against an employer for violations.

FMLA does not affect any Federal or State law prohibiting discrimination, or supersede any State or local law or collective bargaining agreement which provides greater family or medical leave rights.

For Additional Information:

Contact the nearest office of the Wage and Hour Division, listed in most telephone directories under U.S. Government, Department of Labor.

U.S. Department of Labor
Employment Standards Administration
Wage and Hour Division
Washington, D.C. 20210

WH Publication 1420
June 1993

U S G.P.O.: 353-606

tempt to let organizations handle this issue through benefit offerings rather than by a federal mandate. The issue was not dropped, however. There was considerable congressional debate, and twelve states enacted legislation related to family leave.[45] As a presidential candidate in the 1992 elections, Bill Clinton promised to support the act. In February 1993, less than a month after being inaugurated, President Clinton signed the act into law—his first law enacted during his presidency!

The Family and Medical Leave Act provides employees in organizations employing fifty or more workers the opportunity to take up to twelve weeks of unpaid leave[46] each year for family matters (like childbirth, or adoption, or for their own illness or to care for a sick family member). These employees are guaranteed their current job, or one equal to it, upon their return. Furthermore, during this period of unpaid leave, employees retain their employer-offered health insurance coverage (see Exhibit 3-2). Currently, about 66 percent of all U.S. workers are covered under FMLA.[47] And it's expected that only about 6 percent of them will opt to take advantage of the law in any given year.[48] This is, in part, because taking the unpaid leave may create financial hardships for the individual.

Surprisingly, a significant percentage of companies are not complying with the act.[49] In these companies, either they are not granting the leaves (15 percent), not guaranteeing the job when the employee returns (9 percent), or are not continuing health benefit coverage during the unpaid leave (10 percent). Some smaller companies, too, are feeling the effects. Entrepreneurs like Ed Sherman, owner of a Hallmark Card shop, feel the law will restrict their growth.[50] Currently employing forty-five individuals, Sherman is exempt from the FMLA. However, adding five more employees mandates his compliance. He's questioning whether growth may be worth the "compliance" costs. On the other hand, Aetna Life and Casualty sees such a law benefitting not only the employee, but also the employer. Over the past few years, in providing similar leave benefits to their employees, the company has saved almost $2 million a year by "reducing employee turnover, and hiring and training costs."[51]

Irrespective of the debate, since its passage, the FMLA has taken on more substance. For example, the Department of Labor has issued guidelines regarding what constitutes a serious health condition.[52] For example, in one case, an employee sued her employer for failing to provide her with FMLA protection to care for her child who was suffering with an ear infection and had to miss school for four days.[53] The court's ruling in this case was that an ear infection was not a serious illness. Moreover, for those employers covered under the FMLA, the Department of Labor implemented certain communication requirements for employers. These requirements went into effect on April 6, 1995 (see Exhibit 3-3).

Relevant Executive Orders   In 1965, President Lyndon Johnson issued Executive Order 11246. This executive order prohibited discrimination on the basis of race, religion, color, or national origin by federal agencies as well as by contractors and subcontractors who worked under federal contracts. This was followed by Executive Order 11375, which added sex-based discrimination to the above criteria. In 1969, President Richard Nixon issued Executive Order 11478 to supersede part of Executive Order 11246. It stated that employment practices in the federal government must be based on merit and must prohibit discrimination based on race, color, religion, sex, national origin, political affiliation, marital status, or physical disability.

Exhibit 3-3

Employer Communication
Requirements Under FMLA

- The FMLA poster must be placed in an easy to see location.
- The employee handbook (or some other form of policy communication mechanism) must state the employee's rights and obligations under FMLA. This is to be reissued to an employee the first time an employee requests leave under FMLA in any given six-month period. The policy must also include:
  - That the leave will be counted against the employee's FMLA leave.
  - An explanation regarding whether or not a medical certification is required; and if it is and the employee fails to provide such information, what consequences the employee may face.
  - An explanation to employees regarding how health insurance premiums are to be paid, if any, to maintain health insurance coverage; and under what circumstances coverage may be discontinued for lack of payment.
  - Information pertaining to medical certification to return to work.
  - An explanation, where appropriate, when the employee's job is considered exempt from FMLA, and the subsequent possibility that returning to one's job may not exist.
  - Information regarding the repayment of employer paid health insurance premiums if the employee does not return to work at the end of the leave period.

SOURCE: Based on material by Marcia Haight, "Final FMLA Rules Require More Communication," *HR News* (March 1995), p. 8.

These orders cover all organizations that have contracts of $10,000 or more with the federal government. Additionally, those organizations with fifty or more employees and/or $50,000 in federal grants must have an active affirmative action program. The **Office of Federal Contract Compliance Program** administers the order's provisions and provides technical assistance.

The Civil Rights Act of 1991

The **Civil Rights Act of 1991** was one of the most hotly debated civil rights laws since the 1964 act. The impetus for this legislation stemmed from a number of Supreme Court decisions in the late 1980s that diminished the effect of the *Griggs* decision. Proponents of the 1964 legislation quickly banded together in an attempt to issue new legislation aimed at restoring the provisions lost in these Supreme Court rulings.

The Civil Rights Act of 1991 prohibits discrimination on the basis of race and prohibits racial harassment on the job; returns the burden of proof that discrimination did not occur back to the employer; reinforces the illegality of employers who make hiring, firing, or promoting decisions on the basis of race, ethnicity, sex, or religion; and permits women and religious minorities to seek punitive damages in intentional discriminatory claims. Additionally, this Act also included the Glass Ceiling Act—establishing the Glass Ceiling Commission whose purpose is to study a variety of management practices in organizations.

What impact did this legislation have on employers? The issue dealing with punitive damages may prove to be the most drastic change to have taken place.[54] For the first time, individuals claiming they have been intentionally discriminated against are able to sue for damages. The amount of these compensatory and punitive charges, however, is prorated based on number of employees in the organization.[55]

GUARDING AGAINST DISCRIMINATION PRACTICES

Facing a number of laws and regulations, it's critical for HRM to implement practices that are nondiscriminatory. Although it is hoped that senior management has established an organizational culture that encourages equal employment opportunity, discrimination does happen.[56] Recall from our earlier discussion that employment discrimination may stem from a decision that is based on factors other than those relevant to the job. Should that occur frequently, the organization may face charges that it discriminates against some members of a protected group. Determining what constitutes discrimination, however, typically requires more than one individual being adversely affected.

Determining Potential Discriminatory Practices

To determine if discrimination possibly occurred, one of four tests can be used. These are the **4/5ths rule,** restricted policies, geographic comparisons, and the McDonnell-Douglas Test.[57] Remember, however, that each of these "tests" is simply an indicator that risky practices may have occurred. It is up to some judicial body to make the final determination.

The 4/5ths Rule   One of the first measures of determining potentially discriminatory practices is to use a rule of thumb called the 4/5th rule. Issued by the EEOC, in its *Uniform Guidelines on Employee Selection Procedures,* the 4/5th rule serves as a basis for determining if an adverse impact has occurred. Of course, the 4/5ths rule is not a definition of discrimination. It is, however, a "practical device to keep the attention of the enforcement agencies on serious discrepancies in hiring and promotion rates, or other employment decisions."[58] Moreover, in applying the 4/5ths rule, the Supreme Court ruled in *Connecticut* v. *Teal* (1984) that decisions in each step of the selection process must conform to the 4/5ths rule.[59]

To see how the 4/5ths rule works, suppose we have two pools of applicants for jobs as management information systems analysts. Our applicants' backgrounds reflect the following: forty applicants are classified in the majority, while fifteen applicants are classified as members of a minority population.[60] After we go through a testing process and an interview, the following number of people are hired: twenty-two majority and eight minority members. Is the organization in compliance? Exhibit 3-4 provides the analysis. In this case, we find that the company is in compliance; that is, the ratio of minority to majority members is 80 percent or greater (the 4/5ths rule). Accordingly, even though fewer minority members were hired, no apparent discrimination has occurred. Exhibit 3-4 also shows the analysis of an organization not in compliance.

Remember, whenever the 4/5ths rule is violated, it only indicates that discrimination *may* have occurred. Should the analysis show that the percentage is less than 80 percent, then more elaborate statistical testing is needed to confirm or reject that there was an adverse impact. That is because many factors can enter in the picture. For instance, if Company A finds a way to keep most minority group members from applying in the first place, it will only have to hire a few of them to meet its 4/5ths rule-of-thumb measure. Conversely, if Company B ac-

Exhibit 3-4 Applying the 4/5ths Rule

In Compliance

Majority Group (MAJ) = 40 applicants			Minority Group (MIN) = 15 applicants			
Item	Number	Percent	Item	Number	Percent	%Min/%Maj
Passed test	30	75%	Passed test	11	73%	73%/75% = 97%
Passed interview	22	73%	Passed interview	8	72%	72%/73% = 98%
Hired	22	100%	Hired	8	100%	100%/100% = 100%
Analysis	22/40 =	55%	Analysis	8/15 =	53%	
Ratio of minority/majority 53%/55% = 96%						

Not in Compliance

Majority Group (MAJ) = 40 applicants			Minority Group (MIN) = 15 applicants			
Item	Number	Percent	Item	Number	Percent	%Min/%Maj
Passed test	30	75%	Passed test	11	73%	73%/75% = 97%
Passed interview	26	86%	Passed interview	4	36%	36%/86% = 41%
Hired	26	100%	Hired	4	100%	100%/100% = 100%
Analysis	26/40 =	65%	Analysis	4/15 =	26%	
Ratio of minority/majority 26%/65% = 40%						

tively seeks numerous minority group applicants and hires more than Company A, it still may not meet the 4/5ths rule.

Restricted Policy   A **restricted policy** infraction occurs whenever an enterprise's HRM activities result in the exclusion of a class of individuals. For instance, assume a company is downsizing and laying off an excessive number of employees who are over age 40. Simultaneously, however, the company is recruiting for selected positions on college campuses only. Because of economic difficulties, this company wants to keep salaries low by hiring people just entering the work force. Those over age 39, who were making higher salaries, are not given the opportunity to even apply for these new jobs. By these actions, a restricted policy has occurred: That is, through its hiring practice (intentional or not), a class of individuals (in this case, those protected by age discrimination legislation) has been excluded from consideration.

Geographical Comparisons   A third means of supporting discriminatory claims is through the use of a geographic comparison. In this instance, the characteristics of the qualified pool of applicants in an organization's hiring market is compared to the characteristics of its employees. If the organization has a proper mix of individuals at all levels in the organization that reflects its recruiting market, then the company is in compliance. Additionally, that compliance may assist in fostering diversity in the organization. The key factor here is the qualified pool according to varying geographic areas.

McDonnell-Douglas Test   Named for the ***McDonnell-Douglas Corp. v. Green*** 1973 Supreme Court case,[61] this test provides a means of establishing a solid case.[62] It has four components that must exist. These are:

1. The individual is a member of a protected group.
2. The individual applied for a job for which he or she was qualified.

3. The individual was rejected.
4. The enterprise, after rejecting this applicant, continued to seek other applicants with similar qualifications.[63]

If these four conditions are met, an allegation of discrimination is supported. It is up to the company to refute the evidence by providing a reason for such action. Should that explanation be acceptable to an investigating body, the protected group member must then prove that the reason used by the company is inappropriate.

If any of the preceding four tests are met, the company might find itself having to defend its practices. In the next section, we'll explain how an enterprise can do that.

Providing a Response to an EEO Charge

If an adverse impact results from the HRM practices in an organization, there are a few remedies for the employer dealing with valid allegations. First, the employer should discontinue the practice. Only after careful study should the practice, or a modified version, be reinstated. However, even if enough evidence exists, an employer may choose to defend its practices. Generally, three defenses can be used when confronted with an allegation. These are job relatedness or business necessity; bona fide occupational qualifications; and seniority systems.

Business Necessity   An organization has the right to operate in a safe and efficient manner. These are business necessities, without which organizational survival could be threatened. A major portion of business necessity involves job relatedness factors, or having the right to expect employees to perform successfully. This means that employees are expected to possess the required skills, knowledge, and abilities needed to perform the essential elements of the job. Job relatedness criteria are substantiated through the validation process. We'll return to this topic in Chapter 6.

Bonafide Occupational Qualifications   The second defense against discriminatory charges is a **bona fide occupational qualification** (BFOQ). Under Title VII, a BFOQ was permitted where such requirements were "reasonably necessary to meet the normal operation of that business or enterprise." As originally worded, BFOQs could be used only to support sex discrimination. Today, BFOQ coverage is extended to other categories covered. BFOQs cannot, however, be used in cases of race or color.

It is important to note that while BFOQs are "legal" exceptions to Title VII, they are very narrowly defined. Simply using a BFOQ as the response to a charge of discrimination is not enough; it must be directly related to the job. Let's look at some examples.

For years, airlines cited BFOQs as the reason for hiring solely female flight attendants.[64] The airlines' position was that most of their passengers were male and preferred to see stewardesses. The courts, however, did not hold the same view. As a result, it is now common to see both sexes today as flight attendants. Using sex as a criterion for a job is difficult to prove. Even the classic washroom attendant case has seen a change: Many fine restaurants have members of the opposite sex working in washroom facilities. As we mentioned earlier, fetal pro-

Meet

INGRID KNOX, AEROSPACE ENGINEER
Federal Aviation Administration

Ms. Knox began her career in Flight Standards as a summer worker. Upon receiving her degree, she joined Airways Facilities as an Electronics Engineer; then transitioned to aerospace engineering in the Rotorcraft Certification Office; and finally moved into Airplane Certification, where she presently certifies large, commuter, and small airplanes. Ms. Knox is one of the few people to have served as Chair of both the Human Relations Committee (HRC) and the Civil Rights Committee (CRC) all in one year.

She has helped resolve tough issues on the HRC such as: no smoking in the office after hours, special parking for car-poolers, possible day care, employees' open forum with management, town hall meeting, differently-abled restroom problems, cafeteria survey, entry through the back door exits, special parking spaces for motorcycles, stamp machine, cafeteria glass doors, suggestion box, and wellness center.

Currently, Ms. Knox is Manager of the Federal Women's Program (FWP), a Federally mandated program developed to enhance the employment and advancement of women in federal agencies. She has been delegated the responsibility of managing the FWP for the FAA Southwest Region. She serves on the Federal Women's Council, helping to provide an annual training program that addresses mentoring for career enhancement, overcoming job burnout, interpersonal communication, coping with transition and change, managing multiple priorities, and community outreach. Ms. Knox's focus is on activities which eliminate barriers, such as sexual harassment and the glass ceiling, by helping to educate women in partnering with management to develop tools that will assist management in measuring their progress. As FWP manager, her focus is on three primary concerns: the development of women, improvement in the work environment of women, underrepresentation of women. She attends Technical Women Organization (TWO) Conferences, Federally Employed Women (FEW) Conferences, and Executive Women in Government (EWIG) meetings as a representative of the FAA's Southwest Region Civil Rights Staff and to support women.

Ms. Knox was a driving force behind the first Rotorcraft Directorate Diversity Statement, identifying to the ACMT the ways a formal statement would encourage the contribution of all employees in an environment where employees never feel harassed or threatened. Her superior achievement toward a model work environment, Equal Employment Opportunity and Diversity activities is clear: She lives the principles and never despairs of making the world a better place.

tection laws as a BFOQ are no longer permissible. However, under certain circumstances sex as a BFOQ has been supported. In a job like modeling, sex can be used as a determining factor.

A religious BFOQ may have similar results. To be an ordained minister in a church, religion may be used as a differentiating factor; but a faculty member doesn't have to be Catholic to teach at a Jesuit college. An organization may refuse to hire individuals whose religious observances fall on days that the enterprise normally operates. And if the organization demonstrates that it cannot reasonably accommodate these religious observances,[65] then a BFOQ may be permissible.[66] But it's getting harder to demonstrate reasonable accommodation. Domino's Pizza, for example, has found that it cannot refuse to hire, or terminate an employee who wears religious clothing—like the Muslim tradition of covering the head with a scarf.[67] HRM managers must understand that some of their "traditional" policies may have to change to reflect the religious diversity of the work force.[68] In terms of national origin, BFOQs become rarer. However, if an organization can show that nationality plays a role in a person's being able to perform successfully on the job, then a BFOQ may prevail.

Our last area of BFOQ is age. With subsequent amendments to the Age Discrimination in Employment Act, age BFOQs are very hard to support. As we mentioned in our discussion of age discrimination, there are times when age

Threase-Mae Jacobs was once told by her employer at a Domino's Pizza location in Colorado that she'd have to leave work or stop wearing her scarf—part of the tradition of her new Muslim religion. After Domino's corporate HR office was notified by the Council on Islamic–American Relations that such action was a discrimination based on religion, Dominos agreed to allow Jacobs to wear the head covering, so long as the scarf she wears is consistent with Domino's colors.

can be used as a determining factor. However, aside from pilots and a select few key management executives in an organization, age as a BFOQ is limited.

Seniority Systems   Finally, the organization's bonafide seniority system can serve as a defense against discrimination charges. So long as employment decisions, like layoffs, are the function of a well-established and consistently applied seniority system, decisions that may adversely affect protected group members may be permissible. However, an organization using seniority as a defense must be able to demonstrate the "appropriateness" of its system.

Although three means are available for organizations to defend themselves, the best approach revolves around job-relatedness. BFOQ and seniority defenses are often subject to great scrutiny, and at times, are limited in their use.

SELECTED RELEVANT SUPREME COURT CASES

In addition to the laws affecting discriminatory practices, HRM must be aware of decisions rendered in the Supreme Court. Many of these cases help to further define HRM practices, or indicate activities that are permissible. While it is impossible to discuss every applicable Supreme Court case, we have chosen a few of the more critical ones for what they have meant to the field.

Cases Concerning Discrimination

Let's return to one of the most important legal rulings affecting selection procedures. In the 1971 *Griggs* v. *Duke Power Company* decision, the U.S. Supreme Court adopted the interpretive guidelines set out under Title VII: That is, tests must fairly measure the knowledge and skills required in a job in order not to discriminate unfairly against minorities. This action, single-handedly, made invalid any employment test or diploma requirement that disqualified African-Americans at a substantially higher rate than whites (even when this was not intended) if this differentiation could not be shown to be job-related. Such action was said to create an adverse (disparate) impact.[69]

The *Griggs* decision had even wider implications. It made illegal most intelligence and conceptual tests used in hiring unless there was direct empirical evidence that the tests employed were valid. This crucial decision placed the burden of proof on the employer. Based on this decision, it was now the responsibility of the employer to provide adequate support that any test used did not discriminate on the basis of non–job-related characteristics. For example, if an employer requires all applicants to take an IQ test, and the results of that test will be used in making the hiring decision, it is the employer's responsibility to prove that individuals with higher scores will outperform on the job those individuals with lower scores. Nothing in the Court's decision, however, precludes the use of testing or measuring procedures. What it did was to place the burden of proof on management to demonstrate, if challenged, that the tests used provided a reasonable measure of job performance.

Although companies began a process of validating these tests, requiring all job applicants to take them raised further questions. In 1975, the Supreme Court decision in the case of *Albemarle Paper Company* v. *Moody* (1975) clarified the methodological requirements for using and validating tests in selection.[70] In the case, four African-American employees challenged their employer's use of tests for selecting candidates from the unskilled labor pool for promotion into skilled jobs. The Court endorsed the EEOC guidelines by noting that Albemarle's selection methodology was defective because:

1. The tests had not been used solely for jobs on which they had previously been validated.
2. The tests were not validated for upper-level jobs alone but were also used for entry-level jobs.
3. Subjective supervisory ratings were used for validating the tests, but the ratings had not been done with care.
4. The tests had been validated on a group of job-experienced white workers, whereas the tests were given to young, inexperienced, and often nonwhite candidates.

In addition to these two landmark cases, other Supreme Court rulings have had an effect on HRM practices. We have identified some of the more important ones and their results in Exhibit 3-5. During the late 1980s, however, we began to see a significant change in the Supreme Court's perception of EEO. One of the most notable cases during this period was *Wards Cove Packing Company* v. *Antonio* (1989).[71] Wards Cove operates two primary salmon canneries in Alaska. The issue in this case stemmed from different hiring practices for two types of jobs. Noncannery jobs that were viewed as unskilled positions were filled by predominately nonwhites (Filipinos and native Alaskans). On the other hand, cannery jobs were seen as skilled administrative/engineering positions and were held by a predominately white group. Based on the ruling handed down in *Griggs* v. *Duke Power,* an adverse (disparate) impact could be shown by the use of statistics (the 4/5ths rule). However, in the decision, the Court ruled that statistics alone could not support evidence of discrimination. Consequently, the burden of proof shifted from the employer to the individual employee.[72]

Case	Ruling
Griggs v. *Duke Power* (1971)	Tests must fairly measure the knowledge or skills required for a job; also validity of tests.
Albemarle Paper Company v. *Moody* (1975)	Clarified requirements for using and validating tests in selection.
Washington v. *Davis* (1976)	Job-related tests are permissible for screening applicants.
Connecticut v. *Teal* (1984)	Requires all steps in a selection process to meet the 4/5ths rule.
Firefighters Local 1784 v. *Stotts* (1984)	Layoffs are permitted by seniority despite effects it may have on minority employees.
Wyant v. *Jackson Board of Education* (1986)	Layoffs of white workers to establish racial or ethnic balances are illegal; however, reaffirmed the use of affirmative action plans to correct racial imbalance.
United States v. *Paradise* (1986)	Quotas may be used to correct significant racial discrimination practices.
Sheetmetal Workers Local 24 v. *EEOC* (1987)	Racial preference could be used in layoff decisions only for those who had been subjected to previous race discrimination.
Johnson v. *Santa Clara County Transportation Agency* (1987)	Reaffirmed the use of preferential treatment based on sex to overcome problems in existing affirmative action plans.

Exhibit 3-5

Summary of Selected Supreme Court Cases Affecting EEO

The *Wards Cove* decision had the effect of potentially undermining two decades of gains made in equal employment opportunities. This case could have struck a significant blow to affirmative action. Inasmuch as the potential was there, businesses appeared to be unwilling to significantly deviate from the affirmative action plans that had developed over the years. Accordingly, the perception held by many was, "now that business views affirmative action as a competitive necessity, it (the Supreme Court rulings) just might not matter so much."[73] Of course, it's now a moot point, as the Civil Rights Bill of 1991 nullified many of these Supreme Court rulings.

Cases Concerning Reverse Discrimination

Affirmative action programs are necessary to assure continued employment possibilities for minorities and women. Programs to foster the careers of these two groups have grown immensely. But while this voluntary action may have been needed to correct past abuses, what about the white male?[74] Some white males feel that affirmative action plans work against them. In some situations, this feeling has resulted in less commitment and loyalty to the organization,[75] or to charges of **reverse discrimination.** Although reverse discrimination cases exist, two specific cases of reverse discrimination have been noteworthy: the *Allen Bakke* and the *Brian Weber* cases.

In 1978, the Supreme Court handed down its decision in the case of *Bakke* v. *the Regents of the University of California at Davis Medical School.*[76] Allen Bakke was an applicant to the Davis Medical School for one of the one hundred first-year seats. At that time, U.C. at Davis had a self-imposed quota system to promote its affirmative action plan: That is, of the one hundred first-year seats, sixteen were set aside for minority applicants.

Bakke's charge stemmed from those sixteen reserved seats. His credentials were not as good as those gaining access to the first eighty-four seats, but were better than those minorities targeted for the reserved seats. The issue that finally reached the Supreme Court was, could an institution impose its own quota to correct past imbalances between whites and minorities? The Supreme Court ruled that the school could not set aside those seats, for doing so resulted in "one race being favored over another."[77] Consequently, Bakke was permitted to enter medical school. As a footnote to the case, one often wonders what would have happened if Allen Bakke had waited one more year to apply; a year later, Bakke would have been 40 years old. In an age-protected group, he quite possibly would have been eligible for one of the "reserved" seats.

The Supreme Court's decision in the case of the *United Steelworkers of America* v. *Weber* (1979) appeared to have important implications for organizational training and development practices and for the larger issue of reverse discrimination. In 1974, Kaiser Aluminum and the United Steelworkers Union set up a temporary training program for higher-paying skilled trade jobs, such as electrician and repairer, at a Kaiser plant in Louisiana. Brian Weber, a white employee at the plant who was not selected for the training program, sued on the grounds that he had been illegally discriminated against. He argued that African Americans with less seniority were selected over him to attend the training due solely to their race. The question facing the Court was: Is it fair to discriminate against whites in order to help African Americans who have been long-time victims of discrimination? The Justices said that Kaiser could choose to give special job preference to African Americans without fear of being harassed by reverse discrimination suits brought by other employees. The ruling was an endorsement of voluntary affirmative action efforts—goals and timetables for bringing an organization's minority and female work force up to the percentages they represent in the available labor pool.

English-Only Rules

Can an organization require its employees to speak only English on the job? The answer, for the most part, is yes. At least that is the latest perception, given the Supreme Court's refusal to consider a case involving an employer who has an English-only rule. Accordingly, a Ninth Circuit Court of Appeals decision remains in effect permitting such a policy to exist in organizations located in Alaska, Arizona, California, Hawaii, Idaho, Montana, Nevada, Oregon, and Washington.

At issue here are several items. On the one hand, employers have identified the need to have a common language spoken at the work site. Employers must be able to communicate effectively with all employees, especially when safety or productive efficiency matters are at stake. This, they claim is a business necessity. Consequently, if it is a valid requirement of the job, the practice could be permitted. However, at issue in the precedent case in the Ninth Circuit Court was an employer's desire to have one language because "some workers were using bilingual capabilities to harass and insult other workers in a language they could not understand." And with today's ever-increasing concern with protecting employees, especially women, from hostile environ-

ments, English-only rules serve as one means of reasonable care.

A counterpoint to this English-only rule firmly rests with the work-force diversity issue. Workers in today's organizations come from all nationalities and speak different languages. It's estimated that by the year 2000, about 32 million workers in the United States will speak a language other than English. What about their desire to speak their language, to communicate effectively with their peers, and to maintain their cultural heritage? To them, English-only rules are discriminatory in terms of national origin in that they create an adverse impact for non-English-speaking individuals.

Should employers be permitted to require that only English be spoken in the workplace? Even if it's not necessary for successful performance, or doesn't create a safety or health hazard? Should the Supreme Court view this as a discriminatory practice, or render a decision that would create a single, nationwide standard on English-only? What do you think about this issue?

SOURCE: Jana Howard Carey and Larry R. Seegull, "Beware the Native Tongue: National Origin and English-Only Rules," *HR Legal Report* (Spring 1995), pp. 1–4; and Commerce Clearing House, Human Resources Management, "English–Only Rules Not Necessarily Invalid, Contrary to EEOC Guidelines," *Ideas and Trends* (July 20, 1994), p. 124.

Despite the press coverage that both cases received, as we entered the 1980s many questions remained unanswered. Just how far was a company permitted to go regarding preferential treatment (see "Ethical Decisions in HRM")? In subsequent cases, more information became available. In 1984, the Supreme Court ruled in *Firefighters Local 1784* v. *Stotts*[78] (1984) that when facing a layoff situation, affirmative action may not take precedence over a seniority system: That is, the last in (often minorities) may be the first to go. This decision was further reinforced in *Wyant* v. *Jackson Board of Education*[79] (1986) when the Supreme Court ruled that a collective bargaining agreement giving preferential treatment to preserve minority jobs in the event of a layoff was illegal. And the effects of this case may have been recently felt during the 1993 recession. In a study conducted by both *The Wall Street Journal* and the Government Accounting Office, African Americans and Hispanics were laid off in greater proportions than any other group.[80] On the contrary, in *Johnson* v. *Santa Clara County Transportation* (1987) the Supreme Court did permit affirmative action goals to correct worker imbalances as long as the rights of nonminorities were protected. This ruling had an effect of potentially reducing reverse discrimination claims.

The implications of these cases may be somewhat confusing. What conclusions one needs to draw from these is that any HRM practice may be challenged by anyone. HRM must be able to defend its practices if necessary, and to explain the basis and the parameters on which the decisions were made. Failure to document or to base the decisions on business necessities may lead to serious challenges to the action taken.

ENFORCING EQUAL EMPLOYMENT OPPORTUNITY

Two U.S. government agencies are primarily responsible for enforcing equal employment opportunity laws. They are the Equal Employment Opportunity Commission (EEOC) and the Office of Federal Contract Compliance Programs (OFCCP).

The Role of the EEOC

Any charge leveled against an enterprise regarding discrimination based on race, color, sex, national origin, age, qualified disabilities, or wages due to sex falls under the jurisdiction of the EEOC.[81] The EEOC requires that charges be filed within 180 days of an alleged incident,[82] and that these charges be written and sworn under oath. Once the charges have been filed, the EEOC may progress (if necessary) through a four-step process:[83]

1. The EEOC will notify the organization of the charge within ten days of its filing, and then begin to investigate the charge to determine if the complaint is valid. The company may simply settle the case here, and the process stops.
2. The EEOC will notify the organization in writing of its findings within 120 days. If the charge is unfounded, the EEOC's process stops. However, the individual may still file charges against the company in civil court (called a right-to-sue notice). If there is justification to the charge, the EEOC will attempt to correct the problem through informal meetings with the employer. Again, the company, recognizing that discrimination may have occurred, may settle the case at this point.

3. If the informal process is unsuccessful, the EEOC will begin a formal settlement meeting between the individual and the organization (called a conciliation meeting). The emphasis here is to reach a voluntary agreement between the parties.
4. Should Step 3 fail, the EEOC may file charges in court.

It's important to note that while acting as the enforcement arm of Title VII, the EEOC has the power to investigate claims, but they do not have the power to force organizations to cooperate.

The EEOC is staffed by five presidentially appointed commissioners and staff counsels. It is generally well known that the EEOC is quite understaffed. And as a result, more than 100,000 cases are backlogged.[84] Consequently, the EEOC began prioritizing cases in 1995, attempting to spend more of their time on cases that initially appear to have merit. Furthermore, their enforcement plans are prioritized—with those cases that "raise issues appropriate for widespread or class relief" receiving the highest priority.[85] But even then, the EEOC may decide not to file suit. If conciliation efforts are unsuccessful, the EEOC may simply issue a "right-to-sue" letter to the complainant, and reallocate their resources on other cases. Under these new EEOC directions, it's more important than ever for HRM to investigate the complaints internally, to communicate openly with the EEOC regarding the priority level of the complaint, and even to seek alternative means to resolve the dispute with the individual.[86]

> **The EEOC prioritizes its cases to spend more time on those that have the greatest significance.**

The relief that the EEOC tries to achieve for the individual is regulated by Title VII. If the allegation is substantiated, the EEOC attempts to make the individual whole. That is, under the law, the EEOC attempts to obtain lost wages or back pay, job reinstatement, and other rightfully due employment factors (e.g., seniority or benefits). The individual may also recover attorney fees. However, if the discrimination was intentional, other damages may be awarded. Lastly, under no circumstances may the enterprise retaliate against an individual filing charges—whether or not the person remains employed by the organization.[87] The EEOC monitors that no further adverse action against that individual occurs.

Office of Federal Contract Compliance Program (OFCCP)

In support of Executive Order 11246, the OFCCP enforces the provisions of this order (as amended), as well as Section 503 of the Vocational Rehabilitation Act of 1973 and the Vietnam Veterans Readjustment Act of 1974.[88] Provisions of the OFCCP apply to any organizations, including universities, that have a federal contract or act as a subcontractor on a federal project. The OFCCP operates within the U.S. Department of Labor. Similar to the EEOC, the OFCCP investigates allegations of discriminatory practices and follows a similar process in determining and rectifying wrongful actions. One notable difference is that the OFCCP has the power to cancel an enterprise's contract with the federal government if the organization is not in compliance with EEO laws.

CURRENT ISSUES IN EMPLOYMENT LAW

EEO today continues to address two important issues affecting female employees. These are sexual harassment in the workplace and the glass ceiling initiative. Let's take a closer look at both of these.

Sexual Harassment

Sexual harassment is a serious issue in both public and private sector organizations. More than 25,000 complaints are filed with the EEOC each year.[89] Data indicate that almost all Fortune 500 companies in the United States have had complaints lodged by employees, and about a third of them have been sued.[90] Not only were the settlements in these cases at a substantial cost to the companies in terms of litigation, it is estimated that it costs a "typical Fortune 500 company $6.7 million per year in absenteeism, low productivity, and turnover."[91] That amounts to more than $3 billion annually. Sexual harassment, however, is not just a U.S. phenomenon. It's a global issue.[92] For instance, sexual harassment charges have been filed against employers in such countries as Japan, Australia, Netherlands, Belgium, New Zealand, Sweden, Ireland, and Mexico.[93] While discussions of sexual harassment cases oftentimes focus on the large awards granted by a court, there are other concerns for employers. Sexual harassment creates an unpleasant work environment for organization members and undermines their ability to perform their job. But just what is sexual harassment?

Sexual harassment can be regarded as any unwanted activity of a sexual nature that affects an individual's employment. It can occur between members of the opposite or of the same sex. Although such an activity was generally protected under Title VII (sex discrimination), in recent years this problem has gained more recognition. By most accounts, prior to the mid-1980s this problem was generally viewed as an isolated incident, with the individual committing the act being solely responsible (if at all) for his or her actions.[94] Yet, in the late 1990s, charges of sexual harassment continue to appear in the headlines on an almost regular basis. Do you remember the fury over the sexual harassment allegations made by Paula Jones against President Bill Clinton?[95] Maybe somewhere you read about Sabino Gutierrez's charges against his female supervisor, Maria Martinez, the chief financial officer of California Acrylic Industries,[96] or the $7.1 million award Rena Weeks received in her case against the San Francisco law firm, Baker and McKenzie.[97] And let's not forget the central theme in Michael Crichton's book and subsequent Hollywood movie, *Disclosure*.

Much of the problem associated with sexual harassment is determining what constitutes this illegal behavior. In 1993, the EEOC cited three situations in which sexual harassment can occur. These are instances where verbal or physical conduct toward an individual: (1) creates an intimidating, offensive, or hostile environment; (2) unreasonably interferes with an individual's work; or (3) adversely affects an employee's employment opportunities.

For many organizations, it's the offensive or hostile environment issue that is problematic. Just what constitutes such an environment? Challenging hostile environment situations gained much support from the Supreme Court case of *Meritor Savings Bank* v. *Vinson*.[98] This case stemmed from a situation in which Ms. Vinson initially refused the sexual advances of her boss. However, out of fear of reprisal, she ultimately conceded. But according to court records, it did not stop there. Vinson's boss also "fondled Vinson in front of other employees, followed her into the restroom, and exposed himself to her on various occasions."[99] In addition to supporting hostile environment claims, the *Meritor* case also identified employer liability: That is, in sexual harassment cases, an organization can be held liable for sexual harassment actions by its management team, employees, and even customers![100]

Former Long Beach, California Police Officer Melissa Clerkin was one tough cop. But her toughness couldn't withstand the sexual harassment she encountered at the hands of her former boyfriend and sergeant and fellow officers. After complaining to police officials about the harassment, Clerkin found herself in situations on the street where she needed backup, and no one would arrive. Additionally, she was subjected to being called crude names, as well as getting offensive messages on her patrol car's computer. Although her sexual harassment case was finally settled, and she was awarded about $900,000, Clerkin is saddened that the thing she valued most—being a police officer—was taken from her.

Although the *Meritor* case has implications for organizations, how do organizational members determine if something is offensive? For instance, does sexually explicit language in the office create a hostile environment? How about off-color jokes?[101] Pictures of women totally undressed? The answer is: It could! It depends on the people in the organization and the environment in which they work. Take, for example, pin-up photos and calendars. Lois Robinson, a worker at Jacksonville Shipyards, complained to the company that displays of nude and semi-nude women on calendars and posters were offensive. Additionally, because of these photos, she and the other five females out of a work crew of 846 were subjected to abuse. The company, on the other hand, felt that the pictures, while not in the greatest of taste, were not offensive to the average woman. The Supreme Court ruled for Lois Robinson.[102]

What does this tell us? The point here is that we all must be attuned to what makes fellow employees uncomfortable—and if we don't know, then we should ask! Organizational success entering the new millennium will, in part, reflect how sensitive each employee is toward another in the company.[103] At DuPont, for example, their "A Matter of Respect" program is designed to eliminate sexual harassment through awareness and respect for all individuals.[104] This means understanding one another and, most importantly, respecting others' rights. Similar programs exist at Federal Express, General Mills, and Levi-Strauss.[105]

If sexual harassment carries with it potential costs to the organization, what can a company do to protect itself (see Exhibit 3-6)?[106] The courts want to know two things—did the organization know about, or should it have known about, the alleged behavior; and what did management do to stop it? With the number and dollar amounts of the awards against organizations today, there is even a greater need for management to educate all employees on sexual harassment matters and have mechanisms available to monitor employees [see workplace issues]. Furthermore, "victims" no longer have to prove that their psychological well-being is seriously affected.[107] The Supreme Court ruled in 1993 in the case

1. **Issue a sexual harassment policy describing what constitutes sexual harassment and what is inappropriate behavior.** Just stating that sexual harassment is unacceptable at your organization is not enough. In this policy, specific behaviors that are unacceptable must be identified. The more explicit these unacceptable behaviors, the less chance of misinterpretation later on.

2. **Institute a procedure (or link to an existing one) to investigate sexual harassment charges.** Employees, as well as the courts, need to understand what avenue is available for an employee to levy a complaint. This too, should be clearly stated in the policy and widely disseminated to employees.

3. **Inform all employees of the sexual harassment policy.** Educate these employees (via training) about the policy and how it will be enforced. Don't assume that the policy will convey the information simply because it is a policy. It must be effectively communicated to all employees. Some training may be required to help in this understanding.

4. **Train management personnel how to deal with sexual harassment charges and what responsibility they have to the individual and the organization.** Poor supervisory practices in this area can open the company up to a tremendous liability. Managers must be trained in how to recognize signs of sexual harassment, and where to go to help the "victim." Because of the magnitude of the issue, a manager's performance evaluation should reinforce this "competency."

5. **Investigate all sexual harassment charges immediately.** All means *all*— even those that you suspect are invalid. You must give each charge of sexual harassment your attention, and investigate it by searching for clues, witnesses, and so on. Investigating the charge is also consistent with our societal view of justice. Remember, the alleged harasser also has rights. These, too, must be protected by giving the individual the opportunity to respond. You may also want to have an objective party review the data before implementing your decision.

6. **Take corrective action as necessary.** Discipline those doing the harassing and "make whole" the harassed individual. If you find that the charge can be substantiated, you must take some corrective action, including up to dismissing the individual. If the punishment does not fit the crime, you may be reinforcing or condoning the behavior. The harassed individual should also be given whatever was taken away. For example, if the result of sexual behavior led to an individual's resignation, making whole the person would mean reinstatement, with full back pay and benefits.

7. **Continue to follow up on the matter to ensure that no further harassment occurs or that retaliation does not occur.** One of the concerns that individuals have in coming forward with sexual harassment charges is that there may be some retaliation against them—especially if the harasser has been disciplined. You must continue to observe what is affecting these individuals—including follow-up conversations with them.

8. **Periodically review turnover situations to determine if a potential problem may be arising.** (This may be EEO audits, exit interviews, and the like.) There may be a wealth of information at your disposal that may indicate a problem. For example, if only females are resigning in a particular department, that may indicate that a serious problem exists. Pay attention to your regular reports and search for trends that may be indicated.

9. **Don't forget to privately recognize individuals who bring these matters forward.** Without their courageous effort, the organization might have been faced with tremendous liability. These individuals took a risk in coming forward. You should show your appreciation for that risk. Besides, if others know that such risk is worthwhile, others may feel more comfortable in coming to you when any type of problem exists.

SOURCES: Adapted from Marshall H. Tanick, "No Rhyme for the 'Seinfeld' Firing," *The National Law Journal* (August 18, 1997), p. A-19; Anne B. Fisher, "Sexual Harassment: What to Do," *Fortune* (August 23, 1993), pp. 84–88; Clifford M. Koen, Jr., "Sexual Harassment Claims Stem from a Hostile Work Environment," *Personnel Journal* (August 1990), pp. 97–98; Martha E. Eller, "Sexual Harassment: Prevention, Not Protection," *The Cornell H.R.A. Quarterly* (February 1990), p. 87; Maureen P. Woods and Walter J. Flynn, "Heading Off Sexual Harassment," *Personnel* (November 1989), p. 48; and Jacqueline F. Strayer and Sandra E. Rapoport, "Sexual Harassment: Limiting Corporate Liability," *Personnel* (April 1986), pp. 32–33.

Exhibit 3-6

Protecting the Enterprise from Sexual Harassment Charges

If It's Offensive, It May Be Sexual Harassment

Sexually explicit language. Sexual joking. Sexually suggestive remarks. Inappropriate touching. Displaying your favorite pin-up photo or drawing. Some employees would find some or all behaviors on that list offensive. The fact that some people are offended by some or all of the above can place those actions squarely under the heading of "sexual harassment."

While offering or demanding sexual favors in return for rewards in the workplace clearly qualifies as sexual harassment or sex discrimination, there's a harder-to-recognize kind of harassment defined by the Equal Employment Opportunity Commission; that type of sexual harassment is conduct which "has the purpose or effect of unreasonably interfering with another employee's job performance or creating an intimidating, hostile or offensive work environment."

Title 7 of the 1964 Civil Rights Act prohibits sexual harassment. Any behavior that may be perceived as harassment is prohibited. Suppose someone is told that keeping his/her job, or getting a raise or plum assignment depends on submitting to sexual advances or granting sexual favors; that's sexual harassment, pure and simple.

If it happens to you, report it immediately—to the ethics hot line, to your supervisor or to another supervisor. The reverse situation—offering sexual favors to get a job, an assignment or a raise—can also be sexual harassment. When an employee gains job advantages in exchange for sex, there is discrimination against other employees; that's illegal conduct, as well. Everyone loses.

A hostile work environment is one where sexual conduct between coworkers is offensive to either one of them, or to an observer, and that may include the actions on our list above. Sexual harassment can have a number of negative effects on employees and on the company. It can lead to reduced productivity. An employee trapped in work areas where sexual harassment is tolerated is under stress and becomes less productive. Customers may gain an unfavorable impression of the company's professionalism if they see harassment being tolerated. Supervisors or coworkers can report sexual harassment they observe, resulting in an investigation and discipline of those involved. Knowing what is and what is not acceptable and being sensitive to others' feelings should protect you from harassing anyone.

But what if you feel you are being harassed? A word to the offender might be enough. That person may be unaware of your sensitivity to the behavior. If that doesn't work, report the behavior to your supervisor or another manager, to labor or employee relations or to the ethics hot line. That number is published in every issue of *Profile* and *Missileer*.

Education and training play an important role in cultivating an environment free of harassment. Managers throughout the company have received training in identifying and eliminating sexual harassment problems. Additional training is offered by human resources.

Some people may fear their complaints will be ignored or that reporting an incident will become a negative in their work record. Neither is the case. The company takes all complaints of sexual harassment seriously and investigates each thoroughly and discreetly. Both sides are considered and disciplinary action will be taken against proven violators and false accusers.

DR. CONNIE SITTERLY, CPCM

of *Harris* v. *Forklift Systems, Inc.* "that victims do not have to suffer substantial mental distress in order to be awarded jury awards."[108]

Furthermore, in June 1998, the Supreme Court ruled that sexual harassment may have occurred even if the employee had not experienced any "negative" job repercussions.[109] In this case, Kimberly Ellerth, a marketing assistant at Burlington Industries, filed harassment charges against her boss because he "touched her, suggested she wear shorter skirts, and told her during a business trip that he could make her job 'very hard or very easy'." When Ellerth refused, the harasser never "punished" her; In fact, Kimberly even received a promotion during the time the harassment was ongoing. What the Supreme Court's decision in this case indicates is that "harassment is defined by the ugly behavior of the manager, not by what happened to the worker subsequently."[110]

Before we leave the topic of sexual harassment, we'd be remiss not to mention the case of *Jerold Mackenzie vs. Miller Brewing*, and its implications?[111] In the case, Mackenzie allegedly made inappropriate comments to a female employee based on something that was televised on Seinfeld. In investigating the case, Miller officials determined that Mackenzie acted inappropriately, and his actions constituted sexually harassing a female employee. Consequently, acting in what they believed was good faith, Mackenzie was fired. But Mackenzie challenged his firing, filing suit for wrongful termination. In the end, he was awarded $18 million in punitive damages and $8.2 million in compensatory damages. And $1.5 million of the total award was to be personally paid by the woman who filed the harassment complaint.[112] Needless to say, this case has left some companies wondering just what to do.

What the *Mackenzie* case tells us is that the harasser has rights, too. This means that no action should be taken against someone until a thorough investigation has been conducted. Furthermore, the results of the investigation should be reviewed by an independent and objective individual before any action against the alleged harasser is taken. Even then, the harasser should be given an opportunity to respond to the allegation, and have a disciplinary hearing if desired. Additionally, an avenue for appeal should also exist for the alleged harasser—an appeal heard by someone in a higher level of management who is not associated with the case. There's no doubt the *Mackenzie* case adds new dimensions to sexual harassment issues. But given this precedent setting case, it's well worth the time, effort, and money for HRM to make sure it protects everyone involved in the controversy.

The Glass Ceiling Initiative

In years past, many jobs were formally viewed as being male- or female-oriented. For example, librarians, nurses, and elementary schoolteachers were considered typical jobs for women; by contrast, police officers, truck drivers, and top management positions were regarded as the domain of men. Historically, this attitude resulted in the traditional female-oriented jobs being paid significantly less than the male-oriented positions. This differentiation led to concerns over gender-based pay systems, commonly referred to as the **comparable worth** issue.[113] For instance, a nurse may be judged to have a comparable job to that of a police officer. Both must be trained, both are licensed to practice, both work under stressful conditions, and both must exhibit high levels of effort. But they are not typically paid the same; male-dominated jobs have traditionally been paid more than female jobs. Under comparable worth, estimates of the importance of each job are used in determining and equating pay structures. While the 1963 Equal Pay Act requires that workers doing essentially the same work must initially be paid the same wage (later wage differences may exist due to performance, seniority, merit systems, and the like), the act is not directly applicable to comparable worth. Comparable worth proponents want to take the Equal Pay Act one step further. Under such an arrangement, factors present in each job (e.g., skills, responsibilities, working conditions, effort) are evaluated. A pay structure is based solely on the presence of such factors on the job. The result is that dissimilar jobs equivalent in terms of skills, knowledge, and abilities are paid similarly.

The point of the comparable worth issue revolves around the economic worth of jobs to employers. If jobs are similar, even though they involve different occupations, why shouldn't they be paid the same? The concern here is one of pay disparities: Women still earn less than men. While the disparity is lessening, the fact remains that although significant progress has been made in terms of affirmative action for women, it appears they have reached a plateau in the organization. That is, while laws prohibit organizations from keeping qualified women out of high-paying positions, there appears to be a "glass ceiling" holding them down.

The **glass ceiling** is a term used to reflect why women and minorities aren't more widely represented at the top of today's organizations. The glass ceiling is not, however, synonymous with "classic" discrimination. For example, the Oles Envelope Company, which agreed to pay fifty female employees $220,000 for keeping them in lower paying jobs, was not necessarily indicative of the glass ceiling issue.[114] Rather, the glass ceiling, according to a Department of Labor study, is indicative of "subtle attitudes and prejudices that have blocked [these groups] from climbing the corporate ladder."[115] It appears that while significant gains have been made by minorities and women in gaining entry to organizations, less than 10 percent of senior management positions are held by women and minorities.[116] Although the percentage is low, in Japan it's even worse where only 1 in 2,000 top executives is female.[117] Why are women underrepresented? Although there are cultural issues attributed to the numbers in Japan,[118] in the United States many times females often do not have advocates in the organization, lack appropriate networks, or do not have access to executive search firms.[119] To begin to correct this invisible barrier, the OFCCP is working to expand its audit compliance reviews. In these reviews, the auditors will be looking to see if government contractors do indeed have training and development programs operating to provide career growth to the affected groups. Should these be lacking, the OFCCP plans to take legal action to ensure compliance. It did just that when, in its first settlement ever regarding the glass ceiling, the OFCCP got almost $604,000 in back pay and salary increases for fifty-two women workers at a Virginia hospital.[120]

While the OFCCP's initiative to study this phenomenon is promising, research into this effort is beginning to identify ways to correct the problem.[121] In one study, it was suggested that an organizational practice such as promoting from within and preparing individuals for top-level positions may "eventually shatter the glass ceiling."[122] In organizations like Xerox, Merck, Paine Webber, Pitney Bowes, Mattel, and Hoechst Celanese, this practice has worked well.[123] If society puts more pressure on corporations, in terms of boycotting products they sell or not investing in the companies that are inadequately represented by women in upper management, then more cracks in the "glass" are expected.[124]

SUMMARY

(This summary relates to the Learning Objectives identified on p. 62.)

After reading this chapter, you should know:

1. The Civil Rights Act of 1964, Title VII, gives individuals protection on the basis of race, color, religion, sex, and national origin. In addition to those protected under the 1964 Act, amendments to the act, as well as subsequent legislation, give protection to the disabled, veterans, and individuals over age 40. In addition, state laws may supplement this list and include categories like marital status.

2. The Equal Employment Opportunity Act of 1972 is an important amendment to the Civil Rights Act of 1964, as it granted the EEOC enforcement powers to police the provisions of the Act.

3. Affirmative action plans are good-faith efforts by organizations to actively recruit and hire protected group members, and to show measurable results. Such plans are voluntary actions by an organization.

4. An adverse impact is any consequence of employment that results in a disparate rate of selection, promotion, or termination of protected group members.

Adverse treatment occurs when members of a protected group receive different treatment than other employees. A protected group member is any individual who is afforded protection under discrimination laws.

5. The Americans with Disabilities Act of 1990 provides employment protection for individuals who have qualified disabilities. The Act also requires organizations to make reasonable accommodations to provide qualified individuals access to the job.

6. The Family and Medical Leave Act grants up to twelve weeks of unpaid leave for family or medical matters. Fetal protection laws were overturned because they created an adverse impact for women.

7. A business can protect itself from discrimination charges first by having HRM practices that do not adversely affect protected groups, through supported claims of job relatedness, bona fide occupational qualifications, or through a valid seniority system.

8. *Griggs* v. *Duke Power* was one of the most important Supreme Court rulings as it pertains to EEO. Based on this case, items used to screen applicants had to be related to the job. Additionally, post–*Griggs,* the burden was on the employer to prove discrimination did not occur.

9. Sexual harassment is a serious problem existing in today's enterprises. Sexual harassment is defined as any verbal or physical conduct toward an individual: which (1) creates an intimidating, offensive, or hostile environment; (2) unreasonably interferes with an individual's work; or (3) adversely affects an employee's employment opportunities.

10. The glass ceiling is an invisible barrier existing in today's organizations that is keeping minorities and women from ascending to higher levels in the workplace.

EXPERIENTIAL EXERCISE:
Is it sexual harassment?

Could these situations demonstrate sexual harassment or prohibitive behaviors?

Answer true or false to each question, then compare your responses to the answers provided.

1. A female supervisor frequently praises the work of a highly competent male employee.
2. A male prominently posts a centerfold from a female pornographic magazine.
3. A female employee voluntarily accepts a date with her male supervisor.
4. A male employee is given favored work assignments in exchange for arranging dates for his boss.
5. A female employee is offered a job promotion in exchange for sex.

6. A client pressures a female salesperson for dates and sexual favors in exchange for a large purchase.
7. A female requests that her male assistant stay in her hotel room to save on expenses while out of town at a conference and holds acceptance as a job condition for continued employment.
8. A male has asked two female coworkers to stop embarrassing him by telling jokes of a sexual nature and sharing their sexual fantasies, but they continue, telling him a "real man wouldn't be embarrassed."
9. Although he has shared with his coworker that rubbing his shoulders and arms, calling him "Babe" in front of his coworkers, and pinching him is offensive, she continues to touch him in a way that makes him feel uncomfortable.
10. Al tells Marge an offensive joke, but when Marge says "Al, I don't appreciate your nasty jokes," Al responds, "I'm sorry, Marge, you're right, I shouldn't have told that one at work."

1f 2t 3f 4t 5t 6t 7t 8t 9t 10f

WEB-WISE EXERCISE

Assignment
Search and print findings from the Equal Employment Opportunity Web site www.eeoc.gov

Assignment
Explore and print findings from the Web site for Americans with Disabilities Act Documents Center http://jan-web.icdi.wvu.edu/kinder/, which links to ADA resources and includes sites regarding specific disabilities such as HIV/AIDS, cancer, hearing, visual and mobility impairment, as well as alcohol and drug related.

CASE APPLICATION:
Fair Labor

Two human resource staff members, Jim and Sue, your coworkers, have been arguing throughout lunch whether they should pay overtime to all salaried employees who work over 40 hours a week. Jim believes no one would notice a mistake since the law is so confusing anyway. Sue is afraid of anything that might attract an audit or possible litigation, and believes they should pay all salaried employees who work overtime regardless of the company's cost reduction goals. They ask you what you think and how they can be assured of proceeding fairly and legally.

The Department of Labor (DOL) investigates errors in minimum wage, overtime, immigration, classification of employees regarding their eligibility for overtime pay, and child-labor violations among other compliances.

Are the following statements true or false? Place a **t** for true and **f** for false beside each statement below.

1. If a company pays a salary, they do not have to pay overtime.
2. If you misclassify an employee, DOL may ask you to start paying overtime to the employee and back pay owed.
3. The DOL wins almost all cases of violations that go to litigation, although less than 10 percent goes to litigation.

Answers: **1f   2t   3t**

TESTING YOUR UNDERSTANDING

How well did you fulfill the learning objectives?

1. Why was the outcome of *Griggs* v. *Duke Power* different from the outcome of *Washington* v. *Davis?*
   a. *Washington* v. *Davis* was heard after *Roe* v. *Wade*. *Griggs* v. *Duke Power* was heard before *Roe* v. *Wade*.
   b. Requirements such as aptitude tests and diplomas were shown to be relevant in one case, but not in the other.
   c. The outcomes were not different. Both men were subsequently hired.
   d. The outcomes were not different. Neither man was subsequently hired.
   e. Police officers are exempt from Title VII. Maintenance workers are not exempt from Title VII.
2. Why was additional discrimination legislation passed in 1972?
   a. Times had changed. New rules were needed.
   b. There was such backlash against the 1964 Civil Rights Act that it was repealed.
   c. The original legislation lacked enforcement mechanisms.
   d. Women were not protected under the original legislation.
   e. Age was not protected under the original legislation.
3. Leisure, Inc. is an Equal Employment Opportunity employer, with an active affirmative action program. What does that mean?
   a. Leisure, Inc. actively pursues female and minority candidates and makes good faith efforts to get them into the applicant pool.
   b. Leisure, Inc. hires only females and minorities during a designated five-year period.
   c. Leisure, Inc. systematically retires and fires more white males than any other group of employees.
   d. Leisure, Inc. hires a larger percentage of minorities and females than white males.

e. Leisure, Inc. has historically employed large percentages of females and minorities.
4. Which one of the statements is accurate regarding adverse impact?
   a. Adverse impact may result from a seemingly neutral employment practice.
   b. Adverse impact is a deliberate discriminatory practice.
   c. Adverse impact is reverse discrimination against white males.
   d. Adverse impact is a public attitude toward an organization that refuses to hire female and minority job applicants.
   e. Adverse impact is a public attitude toward an organization that refuses to hire white males.
5. A 35-year-old mother of two has been with her firm for fifteen years. She wants to transfer to the computer room of her organization. She is charging adverse impact for which one of the following conditions found in the posted job description for "Computer Room Assistant"?
   a. Must be able to lift fifty pounds.
   b. High-school diploma or GED required.
   c. Prior military experience preferred.
   d. Must be familiar with organizational communications systems and requirements.
   e. Must be able to file and catalog tape and disk resources.
6. What is the difference between adverse impact and adverse treatment?
   a. There is no difference; the terms are synonymous.
   b. Adverse impact typically refers to organizational hiring practices. Adverse treatment typically refers to organizational promotion and performance evaluation practices.
   c. Adverse impact is physical abuse. Adverse treatment is mental abuse.
   d. Adverse impact is emotional and subjective. Adverse treatment is objective and impersonal.
   e. Adverse impact is legal. Adverse treatment is illegal.
7. It has just come to your attention that one of your accounting department employees has just tested HIV+. What workplace protection to this employee is provided under the law?
   a. Under the 1990 Americans with Disabilities Act, the employee's immediate supervisor and co-workers must be informed within forty-eight hours.
   b. Under the 1990 Americans with Disabilities Act, all job actions must be based on job performance requirements.
   c. Under the 1990 Americans with Disabilities Act, the employee must be assigned a job with other HIV+ workers within six weeks.

d. Under the 1990 Americans with Disabilities Act, the employee will no longer be allowed to meet with other employees outside of her own area.

e. The 1990 Americans with Disabilities Act does not have provision for people with AIDS.

8. Barbara has worked for a major manufacturing firm for five years and is pregnant with her first child. What benefit provision is she allowed under the 1993 Family and Medical Leave Act?

a. No provision. The law is scheduled to be phased in, starting in 1997.

b. No provision. The law covers only vested employees, those who have been employed seven years.

c. She can take up to twelve weeks of paid leave and resume her old job when she returns.

d. She is entitled to her old job or an equivalent position upon returning to work.

e. She is not entitled to pay during her leave, but she can collect unemployment benefits.

9. Mike is a mortgage loan officer for a large financial institution. He has had a roller-coaster year. He took a six-week leave without pay in May to spend time with his newly adopted son. He took a five-week leave without pay in September–October to care for his wife, who had surgery. He is now telling you, the benefits coordinator for his section, that he needs time off (without pay, of course) from Thanksgiving through the first of the year to care for another relative. His father will be out of the hospital around Thanksgiving, but can't be placed in a nursing home until January 1. You need to be sure that he is treated in accordance with the provisions of the 1993 Family and Medical Leave Act. What action will you take?

a. Fire him.

b. Transfer him to a lower paying, less responsible job.

c. Tell him he is entitled to only one additional week this year of unpaid leave, and that other arrangements will have to be worked out with his supervisor and the vice president of benefits.

d. Grant him the leave. Tell him he is not eligible to apply again for additional unpaid leave for twenty-four months.

e. Grant him the leave.

10. You are accused of discriminatory hiring practices by a Hispanic rights group that says the only minorities your organization hires are African-Americans. Which statement is an appropriate application of the 4/5ths rule?

a. In the last year, one hundred African-Americans applied for positions, while only ten Hispanics applied.

b. There are no Spanish-speaking neighborhoods in 4/5ths of the geographical locations of the organization.

c. During the interview process, all applicants who were approved by four of the five interviewers were hired.

d. Forty out of eighty white applicants were hired. Two out of three Hispanic applicants were hired.

e. Eighty percent of all applicants were not hired.

11. An allegation of discrimination could best be supported under which one of the following geographical comparisons test?

a. Company position advertisements state that travel is required, approximately ten to twelve days per month.

b. The Leisure, Inc. company has a policy of promoting from within. They only hire inexperienced, newly graduated applicants, mostly from local universities.

c. A large Miami-based financial institution has no Hispanics on the payroll.

d. Jon, an HIV+ postal worker, was passed over for promotion because of his physical condition. He had successfully completed all training requirements and passed the qualifying examination.

e. Company position available announcements are posted in English, Spanish, and French.

Endnotes

1. Based on Mark Maremont, and Jane A. Sasseen, "Abuse of Power," *Business Week* (May 13, 1996), pp. 86–98.
2. "Settlement Astra," *L.A. Times* (February 6, 1998), p. D-3.
3. Jonathan A. Segal, "The Unprotected Minority," *HRMagazine* (February 1995), pp. 27–33.
4. See, for instance, Frederick R. Lynch and William R. Beer, "You Ain't the Right Color, Pal," *Policy Review* (Winter 1990), p. 64.
5. Cases filed under this act could be heard by a jury. Such opportunity was unavailable under the Civil Rights Act of 1964.
6. Under the Civil Rights Act of 1964, the only remedy is back pay.
7. *Patterson* v. *McLean Credit Union,* 87, U.S. Supreme Court 107 (1989).
8. *1981 Guidebook to Fair Employment Practices* (Chicago: Commerce Clearing House, 1980), p. 16.
9. Ibid.
10. Another stipulation is receiving $50,000 or more of government monies. Thus, a two-person operation that has a government contract for more than $50,000 is bound by Title VII.
11. See, for example, Arthur P. Brief, Robert T. Buttram, Robin M. Reisenstein, S. Douglas Pugh, Jodi D. Callahan, Richard L. McCline, and Joel B. Vaslow, "Beyond Good Intentions: The Next Steps Toward Racial Equality in the American Workplace," *Academy of Management Executive,* Vol. 11, No. 4 (November 1997), pp. 59–71.
12. *Washington Metropolitan Police Department* v. *Davis,* 422 U.S. Supreme Court, 229 (1976).

13. The EEOA of 1972 amended Title VII in several ways, including expanding the definition of employer to include state and local government agencies and educational institutions; reduced the minimum number of employees in private sector organizations from 25 to 15; and gave more power to the EEOC to file suit against alleged violators of Title VII.

14. R. Roosevelt Thomas, Jr., "From Affirmative Action to Affirming Diversity," *Harvard Business Review* (March–April 1990), p. 107.

15. See, for example, Marian N. Ruderman, "Affirmative Action: Does It Really Work," *Academy of Management Executive,* Vol. 10, No. 3 (November 1996), pp 64–66.

16. For an interesting view on this subject, see Alison M. Konrad and Frank Linnehan, "Formalized HRM Structures: Coordinating Equal Employment Opportunity or Concealing Organizational Practices," *Academy of Management Journal,* Vol. 38, No. 3 (Fall 1995), pp. 787–820.

17. See, for instance, Myrtle P. Bell, "Changing Attitudes Toward Affirmative Action: A Current Issue That Calls for Action," Printed in the *Academy of Management Best Paper Proceedings,* Lloyd N. Dosier and J. Bernard Keys, eds. (Boston, MA: August 8–13, 1997), pp. 488–442; John Leo, "Endgame for Affirmative Action," *U.S. News and World Report* (March 13, 1996), p. 18.

18. Thomas Sowell, "The 'Q' Word," *Forbes* (April 10, 1995), p. 61.

19. Steven V. Roberts, "Affirmative Action on the Edge," *U.S. News & World Report* (February 13, 1995), pp. 32–38.

20. Ibid; and Dinesh D'Souza, "Dammed If You Do, Dammed If You Don't," *Forbes* (September 25, 1995), pp. 50–56.

21. Jonathan Kaufam, "White Men Shake Off That Losing Feeling on Affirmative Action," *The Wall Street Journal* (September 5, 1996), p. A-1; and James P. Pinkerton, "Why Affirmative Action Won't Die," *Fortune* (November 13, 1995), p. 191.

22. Adverse impact refers to an employment practice that results in a disparate selection, promotion, or firing of a class of protected group members, whereas adverse treatment affects one or more individuals. See also Commerce Clearing House, *Human Resources Management; Ideas and Trends* (May 12, 1993), p. 64.

23. Jeffrey H. Greenhaus, Saroj Parasuraman, and Wayne M. Wormley, "Effects of Race on Organizational Experiences, Job Performance Evaluations, and Career Outcomes," *Academy of Management Journal,* Vol. 33, No. 1 (1990), pp. 64–86.

24. ADEA is afforded to all individuals age 40 and older who are employed in organizations with twenty or more employees. See, for example, David Israel and Stephen P. Beiser, "Are Age Discrimination Releases Enforceable?" *HRMagazine* (August 1990), p. 80.

25. Executive and high policy-making employees of an organization may still be required to retire. Three conditions must be met, however. These are that they are at least 65 years of age, will receive a pension from the organization of at least $44,000, and have been in this executive or high policy-making position for the previous two years. See, American Association of Retired People, *Age Discrimination in the Job* (Washington, D.C.: AARP, 1992), p. 10.

26. Mollie H. Bowers and David A. DeCenzo, *Essentials of Labor Relations* (Englewood Cliffs, N.J.; Prentice-Hall, 1992), p. 31.

27. Ray Scippa, "Retired Pilots Take to the Skies—Again," *Profiles* (Continental Airlines Magazine) (October 1995), p. 65.

28. The age 60 issue is currently being debated. Questions regarding who medical research was conducted on (e.g., private pilots, not commercial ones) have raised many concerns. However, at this time, mandatory retirement for pilots attaining age 60 still is in force.

29. Katherine Bishop, "Pan Am to Pay Retired Pilots in Age Bias Suit," *The New York Times,* (February 4, 1988), p. A18.

30. See *Price* v. *Maryland Casualty Co.,* 561 F.2d 609, 612 (C.A. 5th Cir., 1977), and Helen Creighton, J.D., R.N., "Age Discrimination," *Nursing Management,* Vol. 20, No. 2 (February 1989), pp. 21–22.

31. Israel and Beiser, p. 81.

32. Adapted from Niki Scott, "Promotion Can't Be Denied Because of Pregnancy," Universal Press Syndicate, reprinted in *The Baltimore Sun* (August 12, 1990), p. M-5.

33. This will obviously vary within companies. Additionally, extended periods can be obtained by the workers using entitled sick and vacation benefits. See David A. DeCenzo and Stephen J. Holoviak, *Employee Benefits* (Englewood Cliffs, N.J.: Prentice-Hall, 1991), p. 30.

34. Lisa J. Raines and Stephen P. Push, "Protecting Pregnant Workers," *Harvard Business Review* (May–June 1986), p. 26.

35. Betty Southard Murphy, Wayne E. Barlow, and D. Diane Hatch, contributing editors, "Supreme Court to Decide Fetal Protection Conflict," *Personnel Journal* (May 1990), p. 12.

36. Stephen Wermeil, "Justices Bar Fetal Protection Policies," *The Wall Street Journal* (March 21, 1991), p. 81.

37. Ibid.

38. This act defines a disability as any condition that curtails one or more major life activities for an individual.

39. Wray Herbert, "Troubled at Work," *U.S. News & World Report* (February 9, 1998), pp. 62–64.

40. Carolyn Hirschman, "Reasonable Accommodations at a Reasonable Cost," *HRMagazine* (September 1997), p. 106; and Francine S. Hall and Elizabeth L. Hall, "The ADA: Going Beyond the Law," *Academy of Management Executive,* Vol. 8, No. 1 (1994), pp. 17–32.

41. Jonathan A. Segal, "Looking for Trouble," *HRMagazine* (July 1997), p. 78.

42. "President Signs Disabilities Act into Law," *Human Resources Management: Ideas and Trends,* No. 227 (Chicago: Commerce Clearing House, August 8, 1990), p. 133.

43. Ibid.

44. Thomas J. Flygare, "Supreme Court Holds That Contagious Diseases Are Handicaps," *Phi Delta Kappa,* Vol. 68 (May 1987), p. 705.

45. Those states were Connecticut, New Jersey, Maine, Minnesota, Oklahoma, Oregon, Rhode Island, Tennessee, Vermont, Washington, West Virginia, and Wisconsin. See "Family Leave," *Human Resources Management: Ideas and Trends,* No. 225 (July 11, 1990), p. 115.

46. The Department of Labor has defined just what counts toward the 50-employee threshold. Specifically, temporary employees and those on permanent layoff do not count toward the 50 minimum [See "Final FMLA Regulations: What Do They Mean for Employers," *HR Legal Report* (Winter 1995), p. 1. Furthermore, under certain circumstances, and in compliance with company policy, the employee or the

122. Gary N. Powell and D. Anthony Butterfield, "Investigating the 'Glass Ceiling' Phenomenon: An Empirical Study of Actual Promotions to Top Management," *Academy of Management Journal,* Vol. 37, No. 1 (1994), pp. 68–86.

123. Linda Himelstein, and Stephanie Anderson Forest, "Breaking Through," *Business Week* (February 17, 1997), pp. 64–70; Linda Himelstein, "Shatterproof Glass Ceiling;" "Xerox Cited for Hiring and Promoting Women," *HR News* (March 1995), p. 14; and Erick Schonfeld, "A Fissure in the Glass Ceiling," *Fortune* (September 5, 1994), p. 15.

124. Elyse Mall, "Why Getting Ahead Is (Still) Tougher for Women," *Working Woman* (July 1994), p. 11.

4. Motivating Employees and Designing Jobs

LEARNING OBJECTIVES

After reading this chapter, you will be able to:

1. Define motivation.
2. Identify the three critical components of motivation in an organizational setting.
3. Discuss the process of motivation.
4. Describe how unsatisfied needs create tension.
5. Explain the difference between functional and dysfunctional tension.
6. Discuss the effort–performance relationship
7. Explain the performance–organizational goal relationship.
8. Describe the organizational goal–individual goal relationships.
9. Identify the five core characteristics of the job characteristics model.
10. Describe the motivational effects of job enrichment and work-at-home.

*I*n 1990, Steven Forth returned to Vancouver, British Columbia, after spending a decade abroad. His time overseas was spent working a variety of odd jobs in the publishing field—specializing in "international rights for Japanese publishing companies." [1] You'd think this experience would have been helpful in starting his career when returning to Vancouver. But what he found was a lot of advice from prospective employers—"with all that experience, become a tour guide." That's some advice that Forth simply ignored.

Instead, in 1992, he started his own company, Fact International, Inc. This organization specializes in providing customized software for companies in East Asia. Its main market niche is in translating software programs developed elsewhere in the world—like the United States—into forms residents in East Asia can use. The company has been growing at 80 to 100 percent a year—a rate

Steven Forth, founder of Fact International, Inc., in Vancouver, British Columbia, recognizes that money is not the only motivator for employees. Although his employees could leave Fact International for better paying jobs, they stay. Why? The primary reason is that Forth gives each employee a part of the business. Thus, as the business grows, so too will their "worth." This has served as a significant motivator for Forth's 25 employees.

that Forth, himself, agrees is too fast. Nonetheless, the $2 million in sales in 1995 were welcomed by all. And this is being done with fewer than 25 employees—individuals from such countries as Poland, Greece, Turkey, China, Japan, and Canada.

The irony behind Fact International's success is that none of the company's employees earn more than $50,000 (Canadian). In fact, most are in the $25–$35,000 range. You'd think that many of these skilled employees would leave Fact. Even Forth, who makes less than $50,000, refuses to accept offers from larger software companies to sell his business—and become an instant millionaire. Why is this so? Forth and his employees believe in what they are doing. They know that one day their efforts will pay off handsomely. That's because Forth gives each employee a stake in the business. Therefore, employees are not just workers, but partners in the organization. And they're hoping their "sweat equity" invested today will someday offer them a major reward. At their current rate of growth and target to take the company to $100 million in sales within a decade, they may just get that reward.

INTRODUCTION

In any organization, success is contingent on how well its employees perform. Up to this point in HRM, we have focused our attention on productive employees through the use of job analysis, proper recruitment and selection techniques, and orientation and training of employees. Although these activities are critical, we cannot assume that they will give us our desired result—

highly energized employees. We can hire individuals with extraordinary competencies, adapt them to the organization and its culture, and further develop their abilities. But this will not assure satisfactory **performance.** We know that an individual's performance is a function of their ability to do the job and their willingness to do it.[2] Recruitment, selection, and training typically focus only on the ability side; thus, a major missing ingredient is one's willingness. Motivation, then, becomes a process of activating this potential in all our employees. For example, even the most mundane topics in a college course can be made exciting by a professor who knows how to "excite" his or her students. By doing those things necessary to keep students involved and their interest piqued, the professor is activating the learning "energies" of these individuals.

In whatever forum—a company, a university, or a one-on-one relationship—the issue at hand is finding ways to motivate people. Let's take a closer look at motivation and how it manifests itself in our organizations.

CHARACTERISTICS OF MOTIVATION

The Motivation Process

Motivation can be defined in terms of some outward behavior. People who are motivated exert a greater effort to perform some task than those who are not motivated.[3] However, saying such is only relative and tells us little. A more descriptive definition of motivation would be the willingness to do something, where this something is conditioned by its ability to satisfy some need for the individual.[4] For instance, consider the amount of effort (willingness) you put into a class you take on a pass/fail basis. Human nature tells us that you exert only enough effort to meet the minimum requirements necessary to pass. That effort is typically less than if you attempted to get an A in the class. So, an individual's level of effort should be considerably higher when the need is to "earn an A," in contrast to merely passing.

Although in a generic sense this definition is correct, it needs to be modified for organizational reasons. That's because the effort put forth by employees can be misguided. Therefore, it must be focused on some **organizational goal.** We often assume that this factor is implied, but it is our contention that it is too important to be left to an assumption. For example, if your goal is to pass the HRM class you are currently enrolled in, you don't put your energies into studying for a chemistry test to prepare for your HRM mid-term examination. Thus, the focus on goals becomes crucial in channeling the effort in the right areas.

There is another reason why this definition needs to be modified. That reason lies in satisfying both organizational and individual needs. As employers, we must ensure that employee needs are met, but in doing so, we must have something tangible on which to base our reward. That something is productive work—effort that assists the organization in meeting its goals and objectives. Consequently, employee motivation can be defined as an individual's willingness to exert effort to achieve the organization's goals, conditioned by this effort's ability to satisfy individual needs. Inherent in this definition, then, are

Process Flow

Exhibit 4-1

Components of motivation.

three components: effort, organizational goals, and individual needs. We have portrayed these three components graphically in Exhibit 4-1. Although we have a general understanding of effort and organizational goals, let's focus for a moment on **individual needs.**

An individual need, in our terminology, reflects some internal state that makes certain outcomes appear attractive. Regarding Exhibit 4-1, note that although individual needs can be satisfied without the achievement of organizational goals (by, for example, winning a $5 million lottery), our purpose here is to focus only on those needs satisfied through work effort in an organization. Needs, and how they relate to our behavior, are depicted in Exhibit 4-2. Our process of motivation begins with an unsatisfied need. Unsatisfied needs are anything that we desire, of which we are deprived. For instance, what if you would just love to purchase a new car? The fact that you don't have one creates an unsatisfied need. Until you do get the automobile, you are deprived of its pleasure.

Whenever we are in a state of **deprivation,** having unsatisfied needs, this results in tension. Tension, as we've come to know it, has a negative connotation. But some tension is absolutely necessary. Rather than group all forms of tension into one term, let's recognize both the positive and negative forms—functional and dysfunctional tension. For motivation to occur, we must have **functional tension.** This "hype" is what gives us the energy to perform. Think about what athletes do before a sporting event: They get themselves "psyched," which is functional tension. As a result of this tension, individuals are able to perform at peak levels. We'll come back to dysfunctional tension shortly.

Given that individuals are experiencing some unsatisfied needs and have the desire to change that, the functional tension they have will cause them to exhibit a particular behavior—in our model, called effort. **Effort** is the outward action of individuals that focuses on a particular goal. These actions are performed so that the required goals can be achieved. If our efforts are successful in achieving our goal, then we expect our needs to be satisfied. Satisfied needs then reduce or eliminate the deprivation we initially experienced. If we worked hard and saved for that car, when we finally make our purchase, we have satisfied that need. Furthermore, when this need is satisfied, our tension is reduced for that particular need, resulting in a temporary calming effect until the next need (like purchasing a house) becomes unsatisfied.

Therefore, we can say that motivated employees are in a state of tension. To relieve this tension, they engage in organizational activities. The greater the tension, the greater the drive to bring about relief. Accordingly, when we see people working hard at some activity, we can conclude that they are driven by a desire to achieve some goal that they perceive as having value to them. The

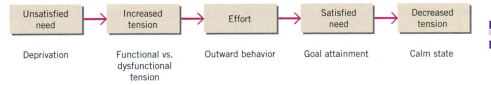

Exhibit 4-2

Process of motivation.

problem, however, is that this is a fragile process, one that requires the blending of many "pieces of the puzzle." If any of these linkages are missing, the willingness to exert energy will decrease.

Barriers to Motivation

Because we are dealing with people—individuals who view things in their own idiosyncratic way—a number of barriers may exist to prevent motivation. These barriers can lie either in the individual or in the organization. Despite the actual reasons for reduced motivation, we can identify some common problems. Let's look again at our diagram of the process of motivation (refer to Exhibit 4-2).

Problems begin to become apparent in the tension phase. During this activity, two major obstacles can exist: **dysfunctional tension** and **apathy.** As we previously mentioned, some tension is crucial to effort. But when that tension becomes dysfunctional, we witness a change in individuals. For instance, suppose that initially an individual was putting forth the effort, but didn't satisfy his or her need. Maybe a second attempt was made, with the same result. At some point, the tension takes a turn for the worse—creating stress and leading to dysfunctional tension. For example, suppose we have two employees working in the public library in a local community. Yearly performance evaluations conducted on employees result in a pay raise. In this library, three evaluation outcomes are possible—outstanding, satisfactory, and needs improvement. The pay increases for each are 8 percent, 4 percent, and 0 percent, respectively. Furthermore, assume the library has a means of quantifying this evaluation based on reference services processed, books loaned out, collections of overdue fines, etc.—and their quality. To be rated "outstanding," one needs a quantitative score of 114 percent with less than a 1 percent error rate; for "satisfactory," 78 percent with less than a 5 percent error rate; and "needs improvement" is anything under 78 percent or an error rate above 5 percent. During the first evaluation, employee A has a score of 109.6 percent with no recorded errors; employee B, 86 percent with a 4 percent error rate. What pay raise do both get? Four percent! For employee A, this is disturbing; an 8 percent pay raise is what she wants (unsatisfied need). So for period two, she tries even harder to get to 114 percent. Employee B, on the other hand, is satisfied with the 4 percent raise. At the end of period two, the evaluations indicate: employee A, 111.1 percent, no errors; employee B, 78.9 percent, 3 percent errors. Their pay raises? Four percent again! By now, employee A is frustrated. She has done all she can to satisfy her needs, but apparently she is unable to do so. So how does dysfunctional tension come into play? This employee knows that she can get an 80 percent rating by working hard until Wednesday afternoon. So she slows down, thus losing her drive. In the end, she gives the company what she believes is fair—effort consistent with a 4 percent pay raise!

Apathy also can play a role in this process. By *apathy* we mean a condition of little or no drive, or just not caring. Although people often encounter problems in an organization—such as being disciplined—when a supervisor's actions result in "making" someone apathetic, the supervisor has broken the employee's spirit. This is one of the greatest motivational problems to overcome—if it can be at all.[5] For instance, consider when a new executive took over a Bay Area hardware chain in San Francisco, bringing in an all new

> **Some tension is absolutely necessary for motivation to occur.**

management team, current management employees were displaced.[6] Although they were productive, this new executive saw them as a remnant of the old regime. As such, many were either let go or demoted to lesser positions in the hardware store. When employees are cast aside, their dignity is often stripped away. And it may only be a short period of time before they leave the organization altogether. But before they do, there is little doubt as to how much productivity the organization will get from them. Because of this phenomenon, employee effort toward goal achievement is often nil.

For motivation to exist, then, it is imperative that certain conditions exist. For HRM, these parameters are the effort–performance relationship; the performance-organizational goal relationship; and the organizational goal–individual goal relationship.[7] However, before we get into these relationships, a few words are in order about our view of motivation. Whenever discussions of motivation occur, there is a tendency to spend considerable time discussing the likes of Abraham Maslow,[8] Douglas McGregor,[9] Frederick Herzberg,[10] David McClelland,[11] J. Stacey Adams,[12] and Victor Vroom.[13] Since you may have reviewed these theorists' contributions in earlier courses, we assume you're already familiar with their theories. Whether or not that assumption holds, we've summarized them briefly in Exhibit 4-3.

Theory	Individual	Summary
Hierarchy of Needs	Abraham Maslow	Five needs rank in an hierarchical order from lowest to highest: physiological, safety, belonging, esteem, and self-actualization. An individual moves up the hierarchy and, when a need is substantially realized, moves up to the next need.
Theory X– Theory Y	Douglas McGregor	Proposes two alternative sets of assumptions that managers hold about human beings: motivations—one, basically negative, labeled Theory X; and the other, basically positive, labeled Theory Y. McGregor argues that Theory Y assumptions are more valid than Theory X and that employee motivation would be maximized by giving workers greater job involvement and autonomy.
Motivation– Hygiene	Frederick Herzberg	Argues that intrinsic job factors motivate, whereas extrinsic factors only placate employees.
Achievement, Affiliation, and Power Motives	David McClelland	Proposes that there are three major needs in workplace situations: achievement, affiliation, and power. A high need to achieve has been positively related to higher work performance when jobs provide responsibility, feedback, and moderate challenge.
Equity Theory	J. Stacey Adams	An individual compares his or her input/outcome ratio to relevant others. If there is a perceived inequity, the individual will augment his or her behavior, or choose another comparison referent.
Expectancy Theory	Victor Vroom	Proposes that motivation is a function of valence (value) of the effort–performance and the performance–reward relationships.

Exhibit 4-3

Recap of classic motivational theories.

A MODEL OF MOTIVATION

The motivation process is complex. Because individuals, and organizations for that matter, are multifaceted, there must exist an appropriate blend of factors that promote needs satisfaction. Furthermore, the factors that must exist may also change frequently—what one has as an unfulfilled need today may not be important tomorrow. Research has shown us that people do change over time; that at various stages in their careers, certain goals are more important than others. For example, consider just two possible "outcomes"—a three-day weekend for the summer months, or a $4,000 annual bonus. That is what Tina Irwin of Friendship Cards[14] posed to her employees. Tina believed that all her employees would value a $4,000 bonus; most of them were under 30 years of age, and she thought that an infusion of that kind of money—almost 10 percent of their salary—would be welcomed. But Tina was mistaken: When she asked her employees what they valued more, the majority asked for the three-day weekend.

Although another group of employees might have responded differently, there's an important message here: That is, to be sure that specific needs are satisfied, you might have to ask employees what those needs are.[15] Even the best motivational device is useless if it misses its intended target. For that direct hit to occur, HRM must ensure that all the potential traps that can sap an individual's motivation are removed. To begin, HRM must ensure that employees clearly see a strong relationship between effort and performance.[16]

The Effort–Performance Relationship

Whenever we hire an employee, there is an implied understanding that we have hired the individual who best fits the job requirements. Accordingly, one of the initial components of the **effort–performance relationship** focuses on one's ability to exert the appropriate effort. We said earlier that effort is an inward reaction that is witnessed as outward behavior. But what should that effort be? For motivation to occur, we must be able to specify what effort is needed. For HRM, this means that jobs must be analyzed properly (and updated frequently) to ensure that the job is defined in terms of the tasks, duties, and responsibilities (Chapter 5). Furthermore, HRM must identify what the job incumbent must possess to be successful. Once these two concepts are in place, HRM must ensure that it has selected the appropriate person for the job (Chapters 6 and 7), adapted them to the organization and trained them in doing the job the company way (Chapter 8). In fact, the effort component is indeed the first two legs of our HRM model—staffing, and training and development. By defining the job properly and selecting the appropriate person, we have those competent, adapted individuals with up-to-date skills, knowledge, and abilities. For job performance purposes, staffing and training and development functions serve to address the "ability" component.

In addition to ability, effort also implies job design. Although we'll look at job design in greater detail later in this chapter, here we want to make sure the organization facilitates productive performance. In doing so, a company must assure that employees have the best equipment available to do the job. Even the best ability on a paper-oriented spreadsheet may not provide the same pro-

Imagine facing this impossible task. What do you think happens to this employee's motivation? Of course, it's hopeless. The real issue here, however, is properly designing jobs. In doing so, work can be made more manageable, more interesting, and ultimately lead to a more productive employee.

ductivity and quality that a computerized version and laser printer would. Consequently, for effort to be exerted, the right tools must be present. Furthermore, the necessary resources must also be readily available. Consider an individual who must spend a considerable part of each day using specific tools. If the tools are located a distance from the job sight, this individual will be less productive than if the tools were readily accessible. Dave Miller, of Lemco Miller Custom Machine Parts, found that just correcting this tool location problem increased worker productivity by almost 20 percent.[17]

Inasmuch as ability and job design are critical to effort, so, too, is the performance dimension. All the effort in the world will be lost if it is not directed toward some end. For HRM, that end is performance. Hence, an individual will make the effort as long as there is a good likelihood that he or she will be a successful performer. But what is successful performance? At this stage of the motivation model, performance must be defined. Supervisors must be trained in establishing work standards and communicating these expectations to their employees. These same supervisors must be able to coach their employees and assist them in achieving their performance levels. And for supervisors to be proficient at this, they must be trained by HRM staff in performance-appraisal processes. Only by showing employees that their effort is required for specified performance, and that if such effort exists they will be successful on the job, will the effort–performance linkage be completed. When that milestone has been achieved, it's time to tie this performance to organizational goals.

The Individual Performance–Organizational Goal Relationship

Whenever employees perform their duties, their effort should be guided toward some end.[18] As we discussed in Chapter 5, that end is meeting organizational goals. If we have determined the strategic nature of our jobs and linked them accordingly to company objectives, then we can best facilitate their attainment by promoting the appropriate performance. Just as we modified the definition of motivation to include organizational goals, so, too, do we need to reveal to employees this critical linkage.

The **individual performance–organizational goal relationship** is designed to provide something of value to the organization. Just as individuals have unsatisfied needs that cause them to behave in a certain manner, so, too, do organizations. But the organization's unsatisfied needs (unfulfilled goals) cannot be satisfied without the effort of its people. If employees' performance is not adequate to meet company objectives, the company will be less able to "reward" its people. For example, consider Lincoln Electric Company. Known for decades as an organization with some of the highest paid blue-collar workers in the world, Lincoln Electric's methodology is one in which employees share in company profits. Each year, management and employees determine what goals are to be met. If those goals are achieved, then employees receive a specified amount. Additionally, if the goals are surpassed, as they have been for years, then the employees receive a bonus. How much will they receive? That amount is directly related to the level of worker performance. Accordingly, through a profit-sharing process, the more the employee performance exceeds organizational goals, the greater their share of the profits. In fact, in situations like this, a performance–organizational goal relationship creates a win-win situation for all involved. Even so, caution is in order. Such a linkage does not occur automatically. Rather, it is a function of many parts of the organization, like an extensive performance-appraisal system—being led in part by HRM.

For the performance–organizational goal relationship to function effectively, the organization must set a clear direction. That is, the organization must set its plans for given time periods and communicate those plans downward in the organization, and employees must have control over the performance measures. At each successive level, then, the plans take on more detail, such that at employee levels, each individual knows why his or her job exists and what role it plays in achieving the organization's objectives. At these levels, then, jobs must be clearly focused. Just as in our first relationship, effort–performance, employees must know what is expected of them. Furthermore, they must know what goal performance is, and how it will be determined.

In most of our organizations, the linkage to successful performance is measured through some performance evaluation instrument. But too often, what we measure, or how we go about the process, may be inappropriate. For example, consider a college professor. Assuming the university has set its objectives, we recognize that one measurement of these objectives is how much students learned. In one simple way, we might assess this information through student evaluations. Are these evaluations an accurate reflection of the performance-organizational goal relationship?

The answer is: it depends. Obviously, student reaction is one piece of information. Yet they are not the only thing. What about student testing and other assignments the faculty members evaluate? Aren't they better predictors of what was learned? If learning is the outcome, measured by a quantifiable student evaluation score, can we be certain that a high score is a valid prediction of high learning? Or that a low score indicates the opposite? Suppose one faculty member is viewed as being easy—a high grader, who entertains the class with a variety of stories. If this individual is rated high, was the university's goal met? Quite possibly, no. Conversely, another professor who is rigid in grading, not overly charismatic in the classroom, and demands quite a bit of work from students may be rated lower, but has helped students learn more.

Whatever the case may be, HRM must ensure that performance evaluations operate properly. Doing so requires significant time and effort by both HRM and the managers who evaluate employees. Because of the intricacies involved, we'll reserve further comments on performance evaluation until the next chapter.

If all is going as planned, we are getting into a better position to motivate our employees. We have defined our jobs, linked them to the strategic nature of the business, communicated to the employees what they must do to be successful, and then measured that effort properly. It is now time to complete the cycle. We have shown employees what they can do for the company; it is now time to show what the organization will do for them. This part is called the **organizational goal–individual goal relationship.**

The Organizational Goal – Individual Goal Relationship

Mediatech, a midwestern videocassette duplicating company, recognized that something was needed to help its employees feel better about work.[19] Mediatech's management apparently noticed that employees tended to be less productive on Friday afternoons—if, in fact, they were on the job at all. To turn around this situation, the company's management decided to institute a lottery. Each week, the company placed $250.00 into a lottery drawing, which would be held at the close of business on selected Fridays. Employee pay stubs would then be placed in a drum, with the winner receiving the cash award. The only stipulation was that the employee had to be present to win. Mediatech's game has resulted in better morale, greater productivity, and much better attendance on Fridays.

The point of the Mediatech example is not the lottery drawing; rather, it is that doing something differently excites employees and reinforces attendance. In the past, however, companies generally did not look for unique and creative ways to "turn on" employees; rather, supervisors became complacent about what people really wanted out of their jobs. For years, companies held that rewarding employees meant giving pay raises and some recognition here and there.[20] If each of us has specific unsatisfied needs that cause us to behave in a particular manner, how can we be expected to meet all those different needs with one reward system? We can't, generally. Rather, we must tailor our rewards to meet those individual needs, if for no other reason than that such a diverse work force exists, one that indicates various needs must be met.[21] That is the thrust of this last linkage. The organization requires specific activities to be met to accomplish its goals; why should employees be any different? Hence, if we truly want to enhance motivation, we must make sure individual goals are met.

If we truly want to enhance motivation, we must make sure individual goals are met.

How can this be done? Through careful assessment of employee needs and a reward system that reflects individual preferences. It's working in companies like Levi—where satisfied employees don't quit, and they remain productive.

If you were to poll every member of your class, you might find that each has a different reason for being there.[22] Some attend because they want to learn more about the subject; some go because it is required, or they fear that missing classes will result in poorer test scores and a lower grade. Some may even be there out of habit—they go to class because that's what they think they're supposed to do. Whatever the reason, each student has a compelling drive that brings him or her to class. Therefore, to satisfy each class member, the instructor must address these diverse needs. But professors will not know what these needs are unless they ask. Ever wonder why some classes start by asking you for your expectations of the course? The instructor is gathering information on your specific needs so that throughout the semester, they can be met. In cases where a student's expectations go outside the intended class syllabus, the instructor knows that additional materials or reading lists may be needed to fulfill that student's expectations. Unfortunately, not all businesses have entirely gotten to this point. There are cases at companies, like TRW and Primerica, where individual rewards are tailored to meet specific individual needs. In such companies, this is done through a process called *flexible compensation*. Let's look at how this works.

In organizations, there's been a tendency to provide uniform benefits. Everyone, for instance, may get medical coverage and reimbursement for night courses taken at the local college. But flexible compensation programs allow people to choose the mix that best fits their needs.[23] Suppose, for example, an individual values more time off from work rather than a bonus or other benefits. Where this freedom to choose does exist, individual choices can be handled. In such companies, employees are presented with a pool of money that reflects increases due to achieving organizational goals through successful performance. Each employee is also presented with a menu of what options are available for the next year and how much each will cost. Employees can choose the benefits they want until they've spent their budgeted amount. Someone wanting more health or life insurance coverage might choose that over more pension contribution, more time off, or extended day care—the employer can purchase those things that are best-suited to his or her individual needs.

Flexible compensation, then, gives choices and allows employees to tailor benefits to their unique needs. Although flexible compensation systems can be expensive to implement and administer, where they exist the benefits have outweighed the costs.[24] We'll revisit this topic in Chapter 13.

In addition to formulating compensation programs, companies also need to review how their reward and recognition programs operate.[25] For example, suppose the local McDonald's hamburger outlet puts the "employee of the month's" name on a sign beside the counter. Not everyone places a high value on such recognition. Doing something that employees see as low in value does not create the desired effect on motivation we want. Consequently, we may want to recognize superior performance by giving employees a choice and letting them select the reward they most value. For example, maybe an employee would like $100.00 in cash, or tickets for two to the local symphony. Maybe an employee would like dinner for herself and her spouse, or a night at a downtown luxury hotel. Or maybe an employee wants to pick out something from a catalog that he has wanted for a long time. Our point is that the same amount of money spent on a plaque might be better spent letting employees select their rewards.[26]

HRM, then, must ensure that processes are in place that result in employees getting something they want. Yet above all, these rewards must be perceived as being directly attributable to their performance. Only by creating and supporting the performance-reward link will both the employee be motivated and rewarded and the organization be more productive and moving toward meeting its goals.

Putting the Pieces Together

The model we have presented has a number of implications. For one, it shows the need for sound inception and development efforts on the part of HRM. It also reveals that pay-for-performance can be beneficial to both employee and company. Until we begin to reinforce that productivity and show that only productivity matters, we will continue to get things other than the productivity that we reward.

Yet there is another point of the model that is interesting: The motivation process can be adapted to reflect corporate values of what is important for both the organization and the employee. We have portrayed this adaptation in Exhibit 4-4.

IMPLICATIONS OF THE MODEL FOR MOTIVATING EMPLOYEES

Organizations today are recognizing the importance of having a highly energized work force. To bring this about, they're using more self-managed work teams, allowing for more worker participation, and empowering their employees.[27] But it is still a long way from being ingrained into the everyday life of most companies.

For example, it has been suggested that supervisors, for whatever reasons, are not providing accurate feedback to individuals about their performance. These supervisors find that identifying group-task goals and linking them to task responsibilities of individual members is a time-consuming operation. Mutual goal setting (the sharing of the goal-setting task with the employee) is avoided by some supervisors because they believe this is an infringement of management prerogatives. In some cases, task goals are identified, performance is evaluated, and the results are conveyed to the employee; yet the employee remains unsure of management's view of his or her accomplishments in terms of preestablished goals. In summary, it appears that many supervisors fail to recognize the importance of establishing goals and performance feedback as would be suggested by the model.

Furthermore, the model suggests that supervisors should ensure that high productivity and good work performance lead to the achievement of personal

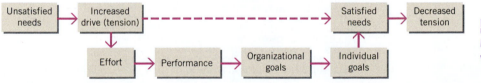

Exhibit 4-4

Motivation process for a work environment.

goals. Again, a review of actual organizational practices reveals many exceptions. Unfortunately, organizations too often fail to allocate rewards in such a way as to optimize motivation. While individual performances tend to be widely divergent—that is, a few outstanding, a few very poor, and the majority surrounding the average-rewards tend to be allocated more uniformly. The result is the over-rewarding of incompetence and the under-rewarding of superior performance. Employees perceive that hard work does not necessarily pay off; they place a low probability on its leading to organizational rewards, and eventually the attainment of personal goals. As such, they do just enough to get by (see Exhibit 4-5).[28]

Internal politics is also a vital determinant of who and what will be rewarded. For example, group acceptance may be a personal goal, and high productivity may hinder rather than support achievement of this goal—that is, if the work group one has joined works at a slower pace, leaves exactly at the end of their shift, and takes their breaks precisely on schedule (irrespective of the work that may need to get done at that moment), one must exhibit those same work behaviors to become "part of the gang." Although, at times, these are the realities of work behavior, our motivational theories tend to overemphasize the decision-making, goal-oriented rationality of human beings. For example, when unemployment is high, there may be a tendency for work groups to work at a pace that helps keep their jobs.

While the preceding discussion presents a rather pessimistic view, we offer some suggestions to help motivate employees, summarized in Exhibit 4-6. These suggestions focus on getting tomorrow's supervisors to understand their employees as individuals, rather than trying to judge them based on their own value system. Again, with a diverse work group, it is unlikely that any supervisor's employees will share all of his or her values.

Exhibit 4-5

Motivation, zeno style.

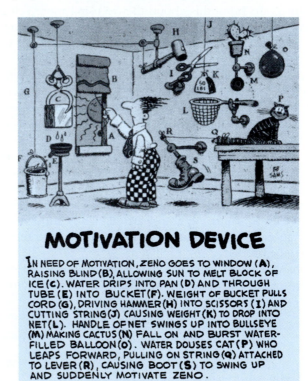

MOTIVATION DEVICE

IN NEED OF MOTIVATION, ZENO GOES TO WINDOW (A), RAISING BLIND (B), ALLOWING SUN TO MELT BLOCK OF ICE (C). WATER DRIPS INTO PAN (D) AND THROUGH TUBE (E) INTO BUCKET (F). WEIGHT OF BUCKET PULLS CORD (G), DRIVING HAMMER (H) INTO SCISSORS (I) AND CUTTING STRING (J) CAUSING WEIGHT (K) TO DROP INTO NET (L). HANDLE OF NET SWINGS UP INTO BULLSEYE (M) MAKING CACTUS (N) FALL ON AND BURST WATER-FILLED BALLOON (O). WATER DOUSES CAT (P) WHO LEAPS FORWARD, PULLING ON STRING (Q) ATTACHED TO LEVER (R), CAUSING BOOT (S) TO SWING UP AND SUDDENLY MOTIVATE ZENO.

1. **Address individual differences.** Recognize that employees are not homogeneous. Rather, each individual possesses a unique set of needs. Accordingly, to effectively motivate any individual, you must understand what those needs are that make them provide the effort.

2. **Properly place employees.** Employees should be properly matched to the job. The best intention will do little for productive behavior if the employee lacks the ability to get the job done. Proper recruiting and selection techniques should assist in creating this match.

3. **Set achievable goals.** Employees often work best when challenging, but achievable goals are mutually set. These hard and specific goals provide the direction employees may need. Continuous feedback on how well employees are performing helps to reinforce their effort.

4. **Individualize rewards.** Realizing that employees have different needs should indicate that rewards, too, may need to be different. What works for one individual may not "motivate" another. As such, one should use their understanding of employee differences and tailor rewards to meet these various needs.

5. **Reward performance.** Rewarding individuals for anything other than performance only reinforces that performance may not matter most. Each reward (individual rewards) must be shown to be the result of achieving organizational goals.

6. **Use an equitable system.** The rewards individuals receive should be viewed as comparable to the effort they have expended. Although perceptions may vary in what is equitable, effort must be made to ensure the reward system used is fair, consistent, and objective.

7. **Don't forget money.** It's easy to get caught up in identifying needs, tailoring rewards, and the like. But don't forget the primary reason most individuals work—money. While it cannot be the sole motivator, failure to use money as a motivator will significantly decrease employee productivity.

Exhibit 4-6

Motivation suggestions.

JOB DESIGNS TO INCREASE MOTIVATION

The Job Characteristics Model

If the type of work a person does is important, can we identify those specific job characteristics that affect productivity, motivation, and satisfaction? A model has been developed by J. Richard Hackman and Greg R. Oldham that identifies five such job factors and their interrelationship. It is called the **job characteristics model.**[29] The research with this model indicates that it can be a useful guide in redesigning the jobs of individuals.[30]

The model specifies five core characteristics or dimensions:

1. *Skill variety*—the degree to which a job requires a variety of different activities so one can use a number of different skills and talents.
2. *Task identity*—the degree to which the job requires completion of a whole and identifiable piece of work.
3. *Task significance*—the degree to which the job has a substantial impact on the lives or work of other people.

4. *Autonomy*—the degree to which the job provides substantial freedom, independence, and discretion to the individual in scheduling the work and in determining the procedures to be used in carrying it out.

5. *Feedback*—the degree to which carrying out the work activities required by the job results in the individual obtaining direct and clear information about the effectiveness of his or her performance.

Exhibit 4-7 presents the model. Notice how the first three dimensions—skill variety, task identity, and task significance—combine to create meaningful work; that is, if these three characteristics exist in a job, we can predict that the incumbents will view their job as being important, valuable, and worthwhile. Notice, too, that jobs that possess autonomy give the job incumbents a feeling of personal responsibility for the results; and that if a job provides feedback, the employees will know how effectively they are performing. From a motivational standpoint, the model says that internal rewards are obtained by individuals when they learn (knowledge of results) that they personally (experienced responsibility) have performed well on a task that they care about (experienced meaningfulness).[31] The more that these three conditions are present, the greater will be the employees' motivation, performance, and satisfaction and the lower will be their absenteeism and likelihood of turnover.[32] As the model shows, the links between the job dimensions and the outcomes are moderated, or adjusted for, by the strength of the individual's growth need; that is, the employee's desire for self-esteem and self-actualization.[33]

This means that individuals with a high growth need are more likely than their low-growth-need counterparts to experience the critical psychological states when their jobs are enriched, and to respond more positively to the psychological states when they are present.

An example of how this model works can be seen at Chaparral Steel, the Midlothian, Texas, steel producer.[34] The industry has had severe problems in the past few decades, but Chaparral Steel has become one of the world's lowest-cost producers. To achieve that distinction, the company began to change the jobs of the employees. Employees were trained to do a variety of jobs that increased task variety, task identity, and task significance. In fact, employees were given the opportunities to redesign production-process machinery to make life easier for them, and to cut costs for the organization. Furthermore,

Exhibit 4-7

The job characteristics model of work motivation.

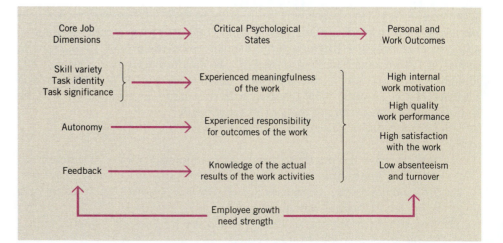

$$\text{Motivating potential score} = \frac{\text{Skill variety} + \text{Task identity} + \text{Task significance}}{3} \times \text{Autonomy} \times \text{Job feedback}$$

Exhibit 4-8
Computing the motivating potential score.

employees are given a lot of freedom to complete their jobs (autonomy) and are recognized by management for a job well done (feedback).

The core job dimensions can be analyzed and combined into a single index called the motivating potential score (MPS) as shown in Exhibit 4-8. Jobs that are high on motivating potential—as derived by answers to specific questions for each dimension—must be high on at least one of the three factors that lead to experiencing meaningfulness, and they must be high on both autonomy and feedback. If jobs score high on motivating potential, the model predicts that motivation, performance, and satisfaction will be positively affected, while the likelihood of absence and turnover is lessened.

Research findings on the job characteristics model have been generally supportive.[35] These studies have shown:

1. People who work on jobs with high-core job dimensions are more motivated, satisfied, and productive than those who do not.
2. People with strong growth needs respond more positively to jobs that are high in motivating potential than do those with weak growth dimensions.
3. Job dimensions operate through the psychological states in influencing personal and work outcome variables, rather than influencing them directly.[36]

These findings support a position that the structure of work is an important influence on an employee's motivation level. Certainly the decision about how a job is to be structured reflects other considerations (such as technology, the environment, plant and equipment, and skill levels) besides its motivational potential. But the design of a job and the way work is scheduled are variables that (1) management can readily influence, and (2) affect an employee's motivation.

Job Enrichment

The most popularly advocated structural technique for increasing an employee's motivational potential is **job enrichment.** To enrich a job, management allows the worker to assume some of the tasks executed by his or her supervisor. Enrichment requires that workers do increased planning and controlling of their work, usually with less supervision and more self-evaluation. From the standpoint of increasing the internal motivation from doing a job, it has been proposed that job enrichment offers great potential.[37] However, job enrichment is successful only when it increases responsibility, increases the employee's freedom and independence, organizes tasks so as to allow individuals to do a complete activity, and provides feedback to allow individuals to correct their own performance.[38] These aspects are precisely what the job characteristics model advocates. In addition, we can say that these factors lead, in part, to a better quality of work life (QWL). Furthermore, job-enrichment efforts will only be successful if the individuals in the enriched jobs find that their needs are met by the "enrichment." If these individuals did not want increased responsibility, for example, then increasing responsibility will not have the desired effect. Successful job enrichment, then, is contingent on worker input.

A successful job enrichment program should ideally increase employee satisfaction and commitment. But since organizations do not exist to create employee satisfaction as an end, there must also be direct benefits to the organization. There is evidence that job enrichment and QWL programs produce lower absenteeism, reduce turnover costs,[39] and increase employee commitment,[40] but on the critical issue of productivity, the evidence is inconclusive, or poorly measured.[41] In some situations, job enrichment has increased productivity; in others, productivity has been decreased. However, when it decreases, there does appear to be a consistently conscientious use of resources and a higher quality of product or service. In other words, in terms of efficiency, for the same input a higher quality of output is obtained; so fewer repairs could increase productivity if the measure included the number of repairs.

Job Rotation

Job rotation offers a potential for dealing with the problem of general worker dissatisfaction caused by over-structuring or career plateauing.[42] It allows employees to diversify their activities and offset the occurrence of boredom.

Horizontal job transfers can break up the monotony inherent in almost any job after the employee's skills have been refined and the newness has worn off. In some cases, this may be after only a few weeks, while in other cases it may be years. Opportunities for diversity, to learn new skills, change supervisors, relocate, or make new job acquaintances can deter or slow the onset of boredom from jobs that have become habitual. Job rotation, therefore, can renew enthusiasm for learning and can motivate workers to better performance.[43]

A more modern version of job rotation can be viewed in terms of project teams. Here, a team of workers combines their varied skills in an attempt to complete some designated project. By working with individuals from other part of the organization—oftentimes those who possess much different skills—employees have the opportunity to expand their "skill portfolio" and learn from one another.

Work at Home

Technology today is providing an unusual opportunity for employees. With the advent of home computers, fax machines, modems, and networked communication lines, certain types of jobs can be completed in the comfort of one's own home. As we mentioned in Chapter 2, many in the work force—especially women—find that work at home affords them the opportunity to combine both their careers and family responsibility.[44] Furthermore, permitting work to be done at a worker's home also gives the organization an opportunity to save money. By having decentralized work sites and supported through telecommunication technology (see Chapter 2), organizations are able to reduce the work space they must either purchase or lease, thus cutting some overhead costs.

Most of the findings about working at home appear promising. Although homework requires different management techniques—like planning and controlling the productive work flow—the flexibility such a practice offers clearly has a positive motivational effect on employees.[45]

Flexible Hours

Another approach toward increasing workers' freedom and their motivation is flextime. **Flextime** is a system whereby employees contract to work a specific number of hours a week but are free to vary the hours of work within certain limits. Each day consists of a common core, usually six hours, with a flexibility band surrounding the core. For example, the core may be 10 A.M. to 4 P.M., with the office actually opening at 7:30 A.M. and closing at 6 P.M. All employees are required to be at their jobs during the common core period, but they are allowed to use their other two hours before and/or after the core time. Some flextime programs allow extra hours to be accumulated and turned into a free day off each month.

Under flextime, employees assume responsibility for completing a specific job, and that increases their feeling of self-worth. It is consistent with the view that people are paid for producing work, not for being at their job stations for a set period of hours; hence, its motivational aspects.

Flextime has been implemented in a number of organizations, such as American Express, IBM, Levi-Strauss, and PepsiCo.[46] In the United States, it is estimated that such scheduling exists in almost 40 percent of all companies.[47] And for many of these organizations, there has been some good news. Flextime appears to contribute to decreased tardiness, reduced absenteeism, less job fatigue, increased organizational loyalty, and improved recruitment. In fact, when you recall the discussion of the composition of our work force, a more positive light is shed on flexible arrangements—for example, flextime enables dual-career couples a better opportunity to balance work and family responsibilities.[48] And with more and more single parents coming into the work force, flexible work arrangements can only better serve both the employer and employee.[49]

How does flexibility in policies in a company like Levi-Strauss help the organization reach its goals? That depends on how you measure it. But at its Knoxville, Tennessee plant by being flexible in dealing with employees, the company has witnessed an increase in employee morale. For this plant, this has resulted in employees staying in their jobs—most more than ten years. That's success!

Although the benefits of flexible scheduling appear plentiful, there is still one major drawback. It produces problems for supervisors in directing employees outside core time periods, or may cause difficulty in evaluating the performance of an employee who may not be seen eight hours a day.[50] But inherent in that statement is part of the problem. Rather than evaluating employees on how much they've been seen—often called "face-time" in organizations—supervisors should concern themselves with "results and productivity."[51] As we described in our motivation model, that should be the only thing that matters. Thus, if a scheduling arrangement permits better performance, there is no logical reason for not implementing one.

UNIQUE MOTIVATION CHALLENGES FOR HRM

Although we've examined a process of motivation understanding current studies of employee motivation are influenced by several significant workplace issues. These include motivating a diversified work force, pay for performance programs, employee stock option programs, and motivating minimum wage employees. Let's take a closer look at each of these issues.

Motivating a Diverse Work Force

To maximize motivation among today's diversified work force, HRM policy makers need to think in terms of *flexibility*.[52] For instance, studies tell us that men place considerably more importance on having autonomy in their jobs than do women. In contrast, the opportunity to learn, convenient work hours, and good interpersonal relations are more important to women than to men.[53] HRM needs to recognize that what motivates a single mother with two dependent children who's working full time to support her family may be very different from the needs of a young, single, part-time worker or the older employee who is working to supplement his or her pension income. Employees have different personal needs and goals that they're hoping to satisfy through their job. Offering various types of rewards to meet these diverse needs can be highly motivating for employees.[54] We've seen some of these before. For instance, family-friendly benefits and flexible work schedules are a response to the varied needs of a diverse work force.[55]

Motivating a diverse work force also means that HRM policies must be flexible by being considerate of *cultural* differences. The theories of motivation we reference were developed largely by U.S. psychologists and validated by studying American workers. Therefore, these theories need to be modified for different cultures.[56]

For instance, the self-interest concept is consistent with capitalism and the extremely high value placed on individualism in countries such as the United States. Because the motivation process presented in this chapter is based on the self-interest motive, it should be applicable to employees in such countries as Great Britain and Australia, where capitalism and individualism are highly valued.[57] In more collectivist nations—such as Venezuela, Singapore, Japan, and Mexico—the link to the organization is the individual's loyalty to the organization, society, or family, rather than his or her self-interest. Employees in collectivist cultures should be more receptive to team-based job design, group goals, and group-performance evaluations. Reliance on the fear of being fired in such

> To maximize motivation among today's diverse work force, HRM policy makers need to think in terms of flexibility.

cultures is likely to be less effective, even if the laws in these countries allow supervisors to fire employees.

Results, however, of several recent studies among employees in countries other than the United States indicate that some aspects of the motivation process are transferable.[58] For instance, the motivation process was presented as a means of changing performance-related behaviors. However, we shouldn't assume that motivation concepts are universally applicable. HRM must adjust its motivational techniques to fit the societal culture.[59] For example, the method of recognizing and embarrassing the worst sales clerks by giving them awards used by a large department store in Xian, China may be effective in China.[60] But doing something that humiliates employees isn't likely to work in North America or Western Europe.

Pay for Performance

What's in it for me? That's a question every person consciously or unconsciously asks before engaging in any form of behavior. Our knowledge of motivation tells us that people do what they do to satisfy some need. Before they do anything, therefore, they look for a payoff or reward. Although there may be many different rewards offered by organizations, most of us are concerned with earning an amount of money that allows us to satisfy our needs and wants. Because pay is an important variable in motivation as one type of reward, we need to look at how we can use pay to motivate high levels of employee performance. And this explains the intent and logic behind pay-for-performance programs (see Exhibit 4-9).

Pay-for-performance programs, like the one used at FormPac, are compensation plans that pay employees on the basis of some performance measure.[61] Piece-rate plans, gainsharing, wage-incentive plans, profit sharing, and lump sum bonuses are examples of pay-for-performance programs.[62] What differentiates these forms of pay from the more traditional compensation plans is that instead of paying an employee for *time* on the job, pay is adjusted to reflect some performance measures. These performance measures might include such things as individual productivity, team or work group productivity, departmental productivity, or the overall organization's profits for a given period.[63]

Performance-based compensation is probably most compatible with the process of motivation we presented. That is, employees should perceive a strong relationship between their performance and the rewards they receive if motivation is to be maximized. If rewards are allocated solely on nonperformance factors—such as seniority, job title, or across the board cost-of-living raises—then employees are likely to reduce their efforts.[64]

Exhibit 4-9

Dilbert's pay-for-performance.

SOURCE: United Features Syndicate, Inc. Used with permission.

Pay-for-performance programs are gaining in popularity in organizations. One survey of 2000 companies found that almost 70 percent of firms surveyed were practicing some form of pay-for-performance for salaried employees.[65] The growing popularity can be explained in terms of a motivation tool. From a motivation perspective, making some or all of a worker's pay conditional on performance measures focuses his or her attention and effort on that measure, then reinforces the continuation of that effort with rewards. However, if the employee, team, or the organization's performance declines, so too does the reward.[66] Thus, there's an incentive to keep efforts and motivation strong. For instance, employees at Hallmark Cards, Inc., in Kansas City have up to 10 percent of their pay at risk. Depending on their productivity on such performance measures as customer satisfaction, retail sales, and profits, employees turn that 10 percent into rewards as high of 25 percent.[67] However, failure to reach the performance measures can result in the forfeiture of the 10 percent of salary placed at risk. Companies like Saturn, Steelcase, TRW, Hewlett-Packard, Du Pont, and AmeriTech use similar formulas where employee compensation is comprised of base and reward pay.[68]

A recent extension of the pay-for-performance concept is called **competency-based compensation.** A competency-based compensation program pays and rewards employees based on the skills, knowledge, or behaviors employees' possess.[69] These competencies may include such behaviors and skills as leadership, problem solving, decision making, or strategic planning. Based on the degree to which these competencies exist, pay levels are established. Pay increases in a competency-based system are awarded for growth in personal competencies, as well as the contributions one makes to the overall organization.[70] Accordingly, an employee's rewards are tied directly to how capable he or she is to contributing to the success of the organization's goals and objectives. We'll look more closely at competency-based pay plans in Chapter 11.

Motivating through Employee Stock Ownership Plans

Many companies are using employee stock ownership plans for improving and motivating employee performance. An **employee stock ownership plan (ESOP)** is a compensation program in which employees become part owners of the organization by receiving stock as a performance incentive. More than 10 million employees in such companies as United Airlines, British Petroleum, Avis, NationsBank, Pfizer, Thrifty Foods, Owens Corning, Weirton Steel, and Starbucks participate in ESOPs.[71] Also, many ESOPs allow employees to purchase additional stocks at attractive, below-market prices. Under an ESOP, employees often are motivated to give more effort because it makes them owners who will share in any gains and losses. The fruits of their labors are no longer just going into the pockets of some unknown owners—the employees are the owners!

Do ESOPs positively affect employee motivation? The answer appears to be yes! The research on ESOPs indicates that they increase employee satisfaction and frequently result in higher performance.[72] For instance, one study compared 45 ESOP companies against 238 companies that did not have ESOPs. The ESOP firms outperformed the non–ESOP organizations in terms of both employment and sales growth.[73] However, other studies showed that productivity in organizations with ESOPs does increase but the impact is greater the longer the ESOP has been in existence.[74] So organizations shouldn't expect immediate increases in employee motivation and productivity if an ESOP is implemented. But over time, employee productivity and satisfaction should go up. Other studies also show that ESOPs work better in smaller, private firms where "worker-input issues are easier to handle." [75]

Although ESOPs have the potential to increase employee satisfaction and work motivation, employees need to psychologically experience ownership in order to realize this potential.[76] What this means is that in addition to merely having a financial stake in the organization, employees need to be regularly informed on the status of the business to have the opportunity to exercise influence over the operation. When these conditions are met, "employees will be more satisfied with their jobs, more satisfied with their organizational identification, motivated to come to work, and motivated to perform well while at work."[77]

Motivating Minimum Wage Employees

Imagine for a moment that your first supervisory job after graduating from college involves overseeing a group comprised of minimum wage employees. Offering more pay to these employees for high levels of performance is out of the question. Your company just can't afford it. What are your motivational options at this point?[78] One of the toughest motivation challenges facing HRM is how to achieve high performance levels among minimum wage workers.

How do you motivate employees who work in jobs that pay at or near minimum wage? In many cases, it won't be money, although that could help. Instead, motivation comes from treating these employees with respect and dignity, sincerely praising them, and recognizing them for a job well done.

One trap many in HRM fall into is thinking that employees are only motivated by money. And although money is important as a motivator, it's not the only "reward" that people seek and that one can use. In motivating minimum wage employees, HRM should look at other types of rewards that serve the function of helping motivate employee performance.

What are some other types of rewards that can be used? Many companies use employee recognition programs such as employee of the month, quarterly employee-performance award ceremonies, or other celebrations of employee accomplishment.[79] Such programs serve the purpose of highlighting employees whose work performance has been of the type and level the organization wants to encourage. HRM must educate supervisors on the power of praise.[80] When used, HRM must ensure that these "pats on the back" are sincere and done for the right reasons; otherwise, employees can see such actions as manipulative.[81]

But we know from the motivation process previously presented that rewards are only part of the motivation equation. We can look to job design, too, for additional insights. In service industries such as travel and hospitality, retail sales, child care, and maintenance, where pay for front-line employees generally doesn't get much above the minimum wage level, successful companies are empowering these front-line employees with more authority to address customers' problems. If we use the JCM to examine this change, we can see that this type of job redesign provides enhanced motivating potential because employees now experience increased skill variety, task identity, task significance, autonomy, and feedback. For instance, at Marriott International, almost every job in its hotel is being redesigned to place more workers in contact with more guests more of the time.[82] These employees are now able to take care of customer complaints and requests that formerly were referred to a supervisor or another department. In addition, employees have at least part of their pay tied to customer satisfaction, so there's a clear link between level of performance and reward. So even though motivating minimum wage employees may be more of a challenge, we can still use what we know about employee motivation to help us come up with some answers.

SUMMARY

This summary relates to the Learning Objectives provided on p. 98.

After having read this chapter you should know:

1. Motivation is the willingness to make every effort to achieve organizational goals conditioned by this effort's ability to satisfy individual needs.

2. The three major components for motivation in an organization setting are effort, organizational goals, and individual needs.

3. The process of motivation begins with an unsatisfied need that creates an increase in tension. This tension causes one to behave in a manner (effort) such that the needs can be satisfied, and tension ultimately reduced.

4. An unsatisfied need is a state of deprivation. Because these needs are something you desire, they cause tension.

5. Tension can be viewed in two forms—functional and dysfunctional. Functional tension is positive and causes an individual to act toward goal attainment. Dysfunctional tension is negative and may lead to problems in performance or attitudes.

6. The effort–performance relationship focuses on the energy exerted by employees and its outcome in terms of performance. The premise of this relationship is that if appropriate effort is exerted, an employee will give a successful performance.

7. The performance–organizational goal relationship focuses on the work achieved and how well it relates to organizational objectives. The premise of this relationship is that if successful performance levels are achieved, then the organization will be meeting its stated goals.

8. The organizational goal–individual goal relationship

focuses on the reward for the employees as it relates to organizational goals. The premise of this relationship is that if organizational goals are met, employees are to be rewarded for their performance. Their rewards will be such that they satisfy individual needs.

9. The job characteristics model consists of skill variety, task identity, task significance, autonomy, and feedback.

10. Job enrichment refers to a situation where workers assume increased responsibility for planning and self-evaluation of their work. This provides an opportunity to fulfill intrinsic and autonomous needs. Working at home enables employees to meet organizational job requirements while simultaneously fulfilling personal needs. Work at home provides the diverse work force with opportunities to combine both work and family.

EXPERIENTIAL EXERCISE:
Motivating Factors

Instructions:

In a class team of three or four members, create a panel of applicants and an interviewer to ask and respond to the following motivation-related questions.

Option: paired sharing—in a team of two, one member assumes the role of interviewer and the other applicant to ask and respond to the following motivation-related questions.

1. When do you feel excited about coming to work and why?
2. When do you feel deflated or demotivated?
3. What does motivation mean to you? Define motivation. Define success. What is the relationship between success and motivation, if any?
4. How do you motivate yourself? Others?
5. What experiences have been the most meaningful on the job? In the classroom?
6. What types of rewards would motivate you in your chosen profession?
7. What person in your life has motivated you and how? What did you learn that you could use to motivate others? Was that person highly motivated? Are you like that person in any way?
8. How do you think human resources functions can help motivate employees? How are motivation and morale related? How could a human resources department contribute to improving morale?
9. If you were the human resources manager, how would you motivate your staff or team?
10. If you were on a project team, how would you motivate your team members?

Team Discussion

Share responses to the following questions with team members and prepare a list of at least three overall findings or conclusions for the class. Assign a timekeeper for the 10 minute discussion and for the one minute oral class conclusions report. Also assign a spokesperson and a recorder to note responses and conclusions.

1. How can you make your work more interesting? Class work?
2. How do you presently demonstrate appreciation for others' work or contributions? When has someone shown their appreciation for your work or contribution? How did you feel?
3. Describe your best and worst experiences of being in on things or feeling apart from things at work and how it affected your motivation.
4. Describe the most motivated persons you know. What do they think or believe or value? What do they do, act or respond? What results have they or do they produce in their lives? Summarize their philosophy in a phrase or sentence.
5. How can you take a more sincere interest in team members or coworkers?
6. Describe what you would like to do and be more than anything.

WEB-WISE EXERCISE

Search and print findings from the following sites:

HR Manager
http://www.auxillium.com/conternts.htm

HRMagazine
http://www.shrm.org/hrmagazine/

HR Headquarters
http://wwwhrhq.com/indexhtml

CASE APPLICATION:
Chorale's Chips and Dips, Inc. — Are You In or Are You Out?

Part 1

Congratulations! You have been asked by the new president of Chorale's Chips N' Dips, Inc. Al Gunner, to lead a new recognition team. Al is concerned that his work force of 586 employees needs to be motivated to achieve higher goals and customer expectations, increased requirements, and more demanding regulations from the (FDA) Food and Drug Administration.

Although he has only been at this plant two months he has observed low morale, unusually high waste and scrap, unclean areas, and as he says "a place that has a lifeless spirit." The plant is dark gray, the lunchroom has one vending machine that requires luck, and the parking lot may even have empty six packs and fast food sacks taking up spaces.

Al overheard employees commenting in the bathroom, "what difference does it make, we get paid the same whether we do or don't. Nobody comes around or notices when you make any extra effort anyway. Makes me want to use their chips and dips for a. . . ." and then they paused when they saw Al.

Al says, "I talked to them, and reassured them and asked them to help me understand what changes they thought needed to be made. They said they couldn't remember the last time they saw a manager in their area.

They said they stay in meetings so much they're clueless to what really goes on and wouldn't know the name of an employee if they were reading their badge.

They said the only information they received was when some supervisor appeared from their cubicle long enough to tell them what they did wrong and threatened them that if it happened again they would be fired. They didn't even get a turkey last year because some guy in human resources was a vegetarian! Most feel they couldn't get another job around here; who would hire them now?

They said they feel beaten, but the overtime is good, and one said, his mission in life was to help make sure his kids didn't have to work in a place like this.

Al continued, "I couldn't sleep last night; I couldn't eat—I want to start turning this place around so these people can have a place they will want to work at and be so proud they will want their families and friends to work here too. It won't be easy, these attitudes and habits were developed over time and it will take time. What I do know is that if we don't change and improve the conditions for employees, if we don't rebuild trust, respect, commitment, recognize reward, and reinvest in them, this business won't be here maybe even two years from now. I can get another job—jump ship—but I won't. I'm committed to either transform this place through employee involvement, or I'll go down with the company; but I won't quit, I WON'T LEAVE—YOU HAVE MY WORD, ON THAT."

Al looks at records, and it seems sick days go fast, and the tendency is for many employees to find any loop hole in law or policy they can to not come to work—and that's costing thousands.

"Also I've noted safety concerns and injuries are higher than a plant this size should be, and in fact in two months, three incidents of violence have occurred, two injuries and a termination."

Al continued, "When I took this job, I knew it would

be a challenge, but I had no idea, I need help and I believe in the work teams and employee involvement. To my knowledge we don't even have a suggestion or a recognition system or offer employee training, but we do have a majority of managers who for too long have gotten by misusing their position power with their autocratic attitudes. I've been walking around and overhearing comments, like 'if I want your opinion I'll give it to you,' 'any Bozzo could figure that out—make me look bad again, and I'll personally walk you to your car.' One man who will remain nameless, came up to me last night, with tears in his eyes, and said, 'you are our last hope—it's so hard to come to work, but after 21 years, where else could I go?' He said it's affecting his relationships with his wife and kids, and he's gotten an ulcer, and he didn't even feel good about himself anymore."

It made me sad, angry, and sick at my stomach. Chips and Dips may be recession proof but it won't really matter in 2000—if there's a lease signed in that year. This company won't make it to 2000 if we do not implement dramatic changes immediately, starting today, this week.

Now, before you tell me yes or no to leading this recognition and reward team, know that you will encounter great resistance even if you're trying to improve conditions in the best interest of the company, employees, and stockholders. You will likely be ridiculed by some unenlightened managers and cynical employees. I don't want to be known as a quitter. That's why I'm asking you, not appointing you. I want a team leader that has heart, a clear sense of purpose, vision, who can lead a team with maybe even a few of the resisters on it. . . .

So, are you in or are you out . . . as recognition team leader?

Question:

1. How would you respond to Al's offer? You're _____ in _____ out. Why or why not? If you responded **out,** share with your class. If you responded **in,** continue.

Part 2

Al adds, "you and your team are going to need some background about the process of motivation, to effectively lead your recognition team.

"They need to understand the basic three components of motivation in an organizational setting such as ours, how their unsatisfied needs creates either functional or dysfunctional tension, and how job enrichment or even work at home could be used to motivate. Also I think the team needs to understand the relationships between individual and organizational goals, and between performance and goals. Let's start with a 15 minute briefing, and each meeting will create some additional teaching moments to build on our knowledge; o.k?"

Al continues, "There's a chapter in this Human Resource Management book, on motivation that you could use to brief me and your team members for 15 minutes in our first recognition team tomorrow. You'll need to call your members, arrange a time, and let me know. I will open the meeting for 15 minutes, then turn it over to you. Questions?"

Assignment:

Instructions:

Be prepared to present a 15 minute summary briefing for your team.

Part 3

Russ Knox was recently named quality assurance team leader and appointed to the new recognition team because of the nature of his position. Chorale's Chips and Dips, Inc.'s.

As the recognition team's leader, when you called Russ to arrange the first meeting, introduce yourself, and share your enthusiasm about the positive contribution that the team can make to the company and employees, Russ interrupted you and stated, "you know, that's the problem around here with quality, coddling these employees. About 80 percent just need to be fired, and go get some new ones. No one recognizes me to do what I get paid to do! Motivation works like this: if you want to keep your job, do it right the first time, every time, and a paycheck should be motivation enough. I didn't get where I am because I got some certificate of appreciation or pen and pencil set. My daddy raised me to have work ethic! Day's pay for a day's work. Anyone who remembers the depression ought to appreciate what they have and not complain. These young people just wanted all handed to them . . . motivate to do their jobs, yeah, right.

"And I think being on some recognition team is a waste of my time, with all the paperwork I have to fill out, but I'm smart enough to know I better not say no to the new president, or he might send me back to shipping for not being 'touchy-feely.'"

"But answer some questions for me first, Team Leader, since I'm on your team. But I don't want to put you on the spot. You think about these questions, and when we meet with Al and the other team members for our 'briefing,' you can tell me then, o.k.?"

Respond to the following questions for the briefing meeting.

Questions:

1. Why should we have to motivate these people to perform their jobs?

2. Why isn't their paycheck sufficient reward?
3. Why should the company have to pay them to do what's expected?
4. How do you think rewards can increase quality or productivity? That's what I care about!
5. How do you think we can get anyone to commit or get them involved now?

Choose one of the following responses:

a. I quit as team member, I thought I could handle the resistance, but it's just not going to be worth it.
b. Good questions! Thanks—other team members may have the same ones and during the briefing will be a good time. Appreciate your input. Wonderful opportunity. Make it a great day!
c. Fine! . . . but call me by my name, not MR./MS Team Leader, all right?
d. say nothing and think, it's only 9:30 in the morning and I still have three more members to go, prepare for this meeting, and get my "real work" done . . . what have I gotten myself into . . . what makes me think I can do this?

(The only "right" answer to Russ's remarks is your answer. . . . b. of course will help to advance the cause and contribution if sincere.)

SOURCE: Compiled from experiences of consultant Dr. Connie Sitterly, names changed. copyright © Dr. Connie Sitterly, Ft. Worth, Texas. Used with permission.

TESTING YOUR UNDERSTANDING

How well did you fulfill the learning objectives?

1. Employee performance is a function of the employee's ability to do a job and
   a. the employee's willingness to do the job.
   b. the supervisor's ability to monitor performance.
   c. effective communication throughout the organization.
   d. the employee's salary.
   e. the organization's culture, plus a good work environment.

2. A vice president of human resources for a large manufacturing firm conducted an employee survey to improve employee benefits and working conditions. The survey showed 97 percent of employees wanted a 30-hour (or less) work week. Why didn't the vice president recommend that change to the benefits manager, according to organizational motivation theory?
   a. The vice president's ability to exert effort was ineffective.
   b. Organizational goals were not defined.
   c. Employees' individual needs changed.

d. Employees' individual needs would not be satisfied.

e. Organizational goals would not be met.

3. Why are beer commercials set in the desert, according to motivation theory?

a. The contrast makes beer look drinkable.

b. An individual's sense of deprivation is heightened by the parched surroundings.

c. It's easier to attain a calm state in the desert.

d. Dysfunctional tension is reduced when distractions are removed.

e. Most human drives are intensified by heat.

4. How can a teacher produce dysfunctional tension in a straight-A student?

a. Give boring lectures.

b. Give difficult tests.

c. Grade term papers on a curve.

d. Require oral presentations as part of the class.

e. Assign grades in a random manner, ranging from A to C, for all written work.

5. Roberta, Ernie's secretary, likes her job and her boss, but she types 40 words per minute and has a 5 percent error rate. Standard performance in the company is 80 words per minute and a 3 percent error rate. Should Ernie send Roberta to secretarial school, according to motivation theory?

a. No. It would embarrass Roberta.

b. Yes. It would strengthen the effort–performance link.

c. No. It would weaken the effort–performance link.

d. Yes. It would strengthen the performance–organization relationship.

e. No. It would weaken the performance–organization relationship.

6. If the goal of an undergraduate business school program is to produce qualified graduates who obtain suitable entry-level positions upon graduation, which question best measures the performance–organizational goal linkage?

a. How many articles do the faculty publish each year, compared to faculty at other similar institutions?

b. How high are the GPAs of graduates, compared to non-business majors in the university?

c. What percentage of the graduates get jobs they want, compared to graduates from other programs during the same year?

d. What positions do graduates hold in organizations seven years after graduation, compared to other graduates from the same year?

e. What percentage of graduates go on for MBA degrees within ten years, compared to graduates of other undergraduate business programs?

7. A vice president of human resources for a large service organization has instituted a program that allows employees to choose up to $1,500 worth of goods or services from a range of annual options, such as more time off, a cash bonus, tuition reimbursement, or new office furniture. What is the vice president doing?

a. Instituting a flexible compensation program to satisfy individual needs.

b. Saving the company money during a downsizing cycle.

c. Simplifying the accounting mechanisms for the entire human resources function.

d. Reducing the number of complaints from workers about their immediate supervisors.

e. Changing the organization to comply with Title VII stipulations.

8. Jobs that score high on the core dimensions are associated with all of these work outcomes in employees with high growth needs except

a. high work satisfaction.

b. experienced responsibility for outcomes.

c. high-quality work performance.

d. high internal work motivation.

e. lower absenteeism.

9. Job enrichment is successful when all of the following are present except

a. responsibility is increased for the employee.

b. pay-for-performance is increased.

c. the employee's freedom and independence is increased.

d. tasks are reorganized so that an individual performs a complete activity.

e. feedback is provided so that the employee may correct his or her own performance.

10. Don pays minimum wage to the 30 workers who help him run the local food bank. How can he motivate them?

a. Make sure he tells them they are appreciated.

b. Make work fun.

c. Let them have as much autonomy as possible.

d. Involve them in day-to-day decisions about the work to be done.

e. All of these.

11. Motivation is all of the following except

a. the process of activating a willingness to work in employees.

b. evident in "energized" students, who want to learn.

c. found in workers who are involved and interested in their work.

d. a necessary component of good job performance.

e. usually measured during the recruitment and selection process.

12. What is the difference between functional tension and dysfunctional tension?

a. There is no difference.

b. Functional tension leads to action that will attain the desired organizational goal. Dysfunctional tension leads to action that thwarts the desired organizational goal.

c. Functional tension leads to action. Dysfunctional tension leads to inaction.

d. Functional tension satisfies needs. Dysfunctional tension does not satisfy needs.

e. Functional tension is more intense than dysfunctional tension.

13. Employers can do all of the following to strengthen the effort-performance link for their employees except

a. coach employees.

b. assist employees in achieving their performance levels.

c. give raises.

d. establish work standards.

e. communicate performance expectations to employees.

14. Marty won a $10 million lottery Saturday. Why, according to motivation theory, did he quit his job on Monday?

a. Marty's ability to exert effort had changed.

b. Organizational goals changed.

c. Marty's individual needs changed.

d. Marty's individual interests changed.

e. Organizational needs were realigned.

15. In the motivation theory presented, how is tension created?

a. Pressure is exerted from outside sources.

b. An individual becomes aware of an unsatisfied need.

c. Pleasure is anticipated.

d. Force for action is triggered.

e. Needs are balanced with equity.

Endnotes

1. Vignette based on "Get 'Em While They're Hot," *Canadian Business* (April 1996), pp. 52–54.

2. See, for instance, Robert McGarvey, "Fire 'Em Up," *Entrepreneur* (March 1996), p. 76.

3. Mark A. Frohman, "Unleash Urgency and Action," *Industry Week* (November 4, 1996), p. 13.

4. See, for example, Victor H. Vroom, *Work and Motivation* (New York: John Wiley, 1964).

5. Carla Joinson, "Re-creating the Indifferent Employee," *HRMagazine* (April 1996), pp. 77–80; and Neil Flanagan and Jarvis Finger, "How to Switch-On Turned-Off Employees," Management (August 1997), p. 19.

6. Raju Narisetti, "Managing Your Career: Shoved Down a Rung? It's Time to Find Another Ladder," *The Wall Street Journal* (September 28, 1994), p. B-1.

7. Our model is based on the expectancy theory of motivation as developed by Victor Vroom. For a complete review of ex-

pectancy theory, see Victor Vroom, *Work and Motivation* (New York: John Wiley, 1964).

8. Abraham Maslow's motivation theory is called "the hierarchy of needs." See Abraham Maslow, *Motivation and Personality* (New York: Harper & Row, 1954).

9. Douglas McGregor's motivation theory is called "Theory X; Theory Y." See Douglas McGregor, *The Human Side of Enterprise* (New York: McGraw-Hill, 1960).

10. Frederick Herzberg's motivation theory is called "the motivation-hygiene theory." See Frederick Herzberg, *Work and the Nature of Man* (New York: World Publishing, 1966).

11. David McClelland's motivation theory is called "the achievement, affiliation and power motives theory." See David C. McClelland, *The Achieving Society* (New York: Van Nostrand Reinhold, 1961).

12. J. Stacey Adams's motivation theory is called "equity theory." See J. Stacey Adams, "Inequity in Social Exchanges," in Leonard Berkowitz (ed.), *Advances in Experimental Social Psychology*, Vol. 2 (New York: Academic Press, 1965), pp. 267–300.

13. Vroom.

14. See, for example, Kenneth A. Kovach, "What Motivates Employees? Workers and Supervisors Give Different Answers," *Business Horizons* (September–October 1987), pp. 58-65.

15. See, "What Do Workers Want?" *Inc.,* (June 1994), p. 12; Commerce Clearing House, "Employers: Employees Want Personal Satisfaction," *Human Resources Management: Ideas and Trends* (November 10, 1993), p. 181; and Nancy K. Austin, "Motivating Employees Without Pay or Promotion," *Working Woman* (November 1994), pp. 17–18.

16. The model of motivation we present for HRM is directly influenced by two of the more contemporary theories of motivation—equity theory and expectancy theory.

17. Phaedra Hise, "The Camera Doesn't Lie," *Inc.* (October 1993), p. 35.

18. Christopher Caggiano, "The Profit Promoting Daily Scorecard," *Inc.* (May 1994), pp. 101–103.

19. Timothy D. Schellhardt, "Eager to Boost Morale: Just Spin the Wheel," *The Wall Street Journal* (September 19, 1990), p. B-1.

20. See, for example, "Motivating Employees," *Personnel Report for the Executive* (New York: Research Institute of America, January 15, 1987), pp. 1–2.

21. Linda Grant, "Happy Workers, High Returns," *Fortune* (January 12, 1998), p. 81; Bob Nelson, Lael Good, and Tom Hill, "Motivate Employees According to Temperament," *HRMagazine* (March 1997), pp. 51–56.

22. See, for example, Jack Stack, "Measuring Morale," *Inc.* (January 1997), p. 29.

23. Richard Wald, "Flexible Benefit Programs Can Be a Key in Linking HR and Business Strategies," *Journal of Compensation and Benefits* (March/April 1997), pp. 23–25.

24. See, for example, David A. DeCenzo and Stephen J. Holoviak, *Employee Benefits* (Englewood Cliffs, N.J.: Prentice-Hall, 1990), Chapter 11.

25. B. Jackson Wixom, Jr., "Recognizing People in a World of Change," *HRMagazine* (June 1995), pp. 65–67.

26. Kerry A. Dolan, "When Money Isn't Enough," *Forbes* (November 18, 1996), pp. 164–170.

27. "Motivating Employees to Excel," *Incentive* (October 1997), pp. 3–8.

28. Kenneth M. Dawson and Sheryl N. Dawson, "How to Motivate Your Employees," *HRMagazine* (April 1990), p. 79.

29. J. Richard Hackman and Greg R. Oldham, "Development of the Job Diagnostic Survey," *Journal of Applied Psychology* (April 1975), pp. 159–70.

30. See, for example, Shaul Fox and Gerald Feldman, "Attention State and Critical Psychological States as Mediators Return Job Dimension and Job Outcomes," *Human Relations,* Vol. 41, No. 3 (March 1988), pp. 229–245; and Dianna L. Stone and Erik R. Eddy, "A Model of Individual and Organizational Factors Affecting Quality-Related Outcomes," *Journal of Quality Management,* Vol. 1, No. 1 (January 1996), pp. 29–31.

31. J. Richard Hackman, "Work Design," in *Improving Life at Work,* J. R. Hackman and J. L. Suttle (Eds.) (Santa Monica, Calif.: Goodyear, 1977), p. 129.

32. "Managers Can Influence Absenteeism," *Manpower Argus* (August 1997), p. 10.

33. J. Barton Cunningham and Ted Eberle, "A Guide to Job Enrichment and Redesign," *Personnel,* Vol. 67, No. 2 (February 1990), p. 57.

34. Adapted from Brian Dumaine, "Unleash Workers and Cut Costs," *Fortune* (May 18, 1992), p. 88.

35. See, for example, "Job Characteristics Theory of Work Redesign," in John B. Miner, *Theories of Organizational Behavior* (Hinsdale, Ill.: Dryden Press, 1980), pp. 231–266; B. T. Loher, R. A. Noe, N. L. Moeller, and M. P. Fitzgerald, "A Meta-analysis of the Relation of Job Characteristics to Job Satisfaction," *Journal of Applied Psychology* (May 1985), pp. 280–289; and M. G. Evans, and D. A. Ondrack, "The Motivational Potential of Jobs: Is a Multiplicative Model Really Necessary?" in S. L. McShane (Ed.), *Organization Behavior, ASAC Conference Proceedings,* Vol. 9, Part 5, Halifax, Nova Scotia (1988), pp. 31–39. It is important to note, however, that while these studies generally support the JCM, there still exists some debate about the dimensions used and the duplicity of some of the dimensions. For an overview of that debate, see Y. Fried and G. R. Ferris, "The Dimensionality of Job Characteristics: Some Neglected Issues," *Journal of Applied Psychology* (August 1986), pp. 419–426.

36. Hackman, pp. 132–133.

37. See, for example, Cunningham and Eberle, p. 57.

38. See, for example, Norm Alster, "What Flexible Workers Can Do," *Fortune* (February 13, 1989), pp. 62–66.

39. See Stephen J. Havolic, "Quality of Work Life and Human Resource Outcomes," *Industrial Relations* (Fall 1991), pp. 469–79.

40. Mitchell W. Fields and James W. Thacker, "Influence on Quality of Work Life on Company and Union Commitment," *Academy of Management Journal* (June 1992), p. 448.

41. For an interesting viewpoint on JCM, see Ronald H. Humphrey, "How Job Charactersitcs Influence Prototypes and the Information Dilution Effect," *Academy of Management Best Paper Proceedings,* Dorothy Perrin Moore, ed. (Vancouver, British Columbia, Canada: August 6–9, 1995), pp. 131–135.

42. Robert A. MacDicken, "Managing the Plateaued Employee," *Association Management,* Vol. 43, No. 7 (July 1991), p. 37.

43. Timothy D. Schellhardt, "Few Employers Give Job Rotation a Whirl," *The Wall Street Journal* (July 21, 1992), p. B-1.

44. Sue Shellenbarger, "Enter the 'New Hero': A Boss Who

45. Knows You Have a Life," *The Wall Street Journal* (May 8, 1996), p. B-1.

45. "The Value of Flexibility," *Inc.* (April 1996), p. 114. Also, for an interesting view on work and home, see Michael P. Cronin, "The Return of Happy Hour," *Inc.* (December 1993), p. 165.

46. See Deutschman, pp. 50–55.

47. Verespej, p. 12.

48. David A. Ralston, "How Flextime Eases Work/Family Tension," *Personnel* (August 1990), pp. 45–48.

49. Helen Paris, "Balancing Work and Family Responsibilities: Canadian Employer and Employee Viewpoints," *Human Resource Planning,* Vol. 13, No. 2 (February 1990), p. 153.

50. Julie Cohen Mason, "Flexing More Than Muscle: Employees Want Time on Their Side," *Management Review* (March 1992), pp. 7–8.

51. Ibid., p. 8.

52. "The Value of Flexibility," *Inc.* (April 1996), p. 114; and B. J. Wixom, Jr., "Recognizing People in a World of Change," *HRMagazine* (June 1995), p. 65.

53. I. Harpaz, "The Importance of Work Goals: An International Perspective," *Journal of International Business Studies* (First Quarter 1990), pp. 75–93.

54. S. Shellenbarger, "Enter the 'New Hero': A Boss Who Knows You Have a Life," *The Wall Street Journal* (May 8, 1996), p. B-1.

55. See also A. Kindelan, "Dependent-Care Accounts Top Family-Friendly Benefits," *HR News* (April 1996), p. 14; and Elizabeth Sheley, "Job Sharing Offers Unique Challenges," *HRMagazine* (January 1996), pp. 46–49.

56. G. Hofstede, "Motivation, Leadership, and Organizations: Do American Theories Apply Abroad?" *Organizational Dynamics* (Summer 1980), p. 55.

57. See, for instance, Nancy H. Leonard, Laura L. Beauvais, and Richard W. School, "A Self Concept-Based Model of Work Motivation," *Academy of Management Best Papers Proceeding,* Dorothy Perrin Moore (Ed.) (Vancouver, British Columbia, Canada: August 6–9, 1995), pp. 322–326.

58. D.H.B. Walsh, F. Luthens, and S. M. Sommer, "Organizational Behavior Modification Goes to Russia: Replicating an Experimental Analysis Across Cultures and Tasks," *Journal of Organizational Behavior Management* (Fall 1993), pp. 15–35; and J. R. Baum et al., "Nationality and Work Role Interactions: A Cultural Contrast of Israel and U.S. Entrepreneurs' Versus Managers' Needs," *Journal of Business Venturing* (November 1993), pp. 499–512.

59. See, for instance, J. K. Giacobbe-Miller and D. J. Miller, "A Comparison of U.S. and Russian Pay Allocation Decisions and Distributive Justice Judgements," in D. P. Moore (Ed.), *Academy of Management: Best Papers Proceedings* (Vancouver, British Columbia, Canada, August 6–9, 1995), pp. 177–181.

60. A. Ignatius, "Now If Ms. Wong Insults a Customer, She Gets an Award," *The Wall Street Journal* (January 24, 1989), p. A-1.

61. R. K. Abbott, "Performance-Based Flex: A Tool for Managing Total Compensation Costs," *Compensation and Benefits Review* (March–April 1993), pp. 18–21; J. R. Schuster and P. K. Zingheim, "The New Variable Pay: Key Design Issues," *Compensation and Benefits Review* (March–April 1993), pp. 27–34; C. R. Williams and L. P. Livingstone, "Another Look at the Relationship Between Performance and Voluntary

Turnover," *Academy of Management Journal* (April 1994), pp. 269–298; A. M. Dickinson, and K. L. Gillette, "A Comparison of the Effects on Productivity: Piece Rate Pay Versus Base Pay Plus Incentives," *Journal of Organizational Behavior Management* (Spring 1994), pp. 3–82; and Shari Caudron, "Spreading Out the Carrots," *Industry Week* (May 19, 1997), pp. 20–24.

62. See, for example, D. Fenn, "Compensation: Bonuses That Make Sense," *Inc.* (March 1996), p. 95; J. H. Sheridan, "Yes to Team Incentives," *Industry Week* (March 4, 1996), p. 64; and H. N. Altmansberger and M. J. Wallace, Jr., "Strategic Use of Goalsharing at Corning," *ACA Journal* (Winter 1995), pp. 64–71.

63. D. A. DeCenzo and S. P. Robbins, *Human Resource Management,* 5th ed. (New York: John Wiley & Sons, 1996), p. 354.

64. G. Grib and S. O'Donnell, "Pay Plans That Reward Employee Achievement," *HRMagazine* (July 1995), pp. 49–50.

65. S. Tully, "Your Paycheck Gets Exciting," *Fortune* (November 1, 1993), p. 83.

66. "Compensation: Sales Managers as Team Players," *Inc.* (August 1994), p. 102.

67. D. Fenn, "Compensation: Goal-Driven Incentives," *Inc.* (August 1996), p. 91; and M. A. Verespej, "More Value for Compensation," *Industry Week* (June 17, 1996), p. 20.

68. S. Overman, "Saturn Teams Working and profiting," *HRMagazine* (March 1995), p. 72.

69. M. E. Lattoni and A. Mercier, "Developing Competency-Based Organizations and Pay Systems," *Focus: A Review of Human Resource Management Issues in Canada* (Calgary, Canada: Towers Perrin, Summer 1994), p. 18.

70. Ibid.

71. Aaron Bernstein, "Should Avis Try Harder–For Its Employees," *Business Week* (August 12, 1996), p. 68; K. Capell, "Options for Everyone," *Business Week* (July 22, 1996), pp. 80–88; A. Bernstein, "United We Own," *Business Week* (March 18, 1996), pp. 96–102; R. McGarvey, "Something Extra," *Entrepreneur* (May 1995), p. 70; and "Reaching for the Top Shelf," *Canadian Business* (January 16, 1997), p. 67.

72. See, for example, T. R. Stenhouse, "The Long and the Short of Gainsharing," *Academy of Management Executive,* Vol. 9, No. 1 (1995), pp. 77–78.

73. C. M. Rosen and M. Quarrey, "How Well Is Employee Ownership Working?" *Harvard Business Review* (September-October 19897), pp. 126-132.

74. S. C. Kumbhakar and A. E. Dunbar, "The Elusive ESOP-Productivity Link: Evidence from U.S. Firm-Level Data," *Journal of Public Economics* (September 1993), pp. 273–283; and S. A. Lee, "ESOP Is a Powerful Tool to Align Employees with Corporate Goals," *Pension World* (April 1994), pp. 40–42.

75. A. Bernstein, "United We Own," *Business Week* (March 18, 1996), p. 102.

76. J. L. Pierce and C. A. Furo, "Employee Ownership: Implications for Management," *Organizational Dynamics* (Winter 1990), pp. 32–43.

77. Ibid., p. 38.

78. S. W. Kelley, "Discretion and the Service Employee," *Journal of Retailing* (Spring 1993), pp. 104–126; S. S. Brooks, "Noncash Ways to Compensate Employees," *HRMagazine* (April 1994), pp. 38–43; and S. Greengard, "Leveraging a Low-Wage Work Force," *Personnel Journal* (January 1995), pp. 90–102.

79. R. McGarvey, "Fire 'Em Up," *Entrepreneur* (March 1996), pp. 76–79.

80. Bob Nelson, "Try Praise: It's the One Employer Incentive Any Small Company Can Afford," *Inc.* (September 1996), p. 115.

81. See, for instance, Christopher Meyer, "What Makes Workers Tick?" *Inc.* (December 1997), pp. 74–81.

82. R. Henkoff, "Finding, Training, and Keeping the Best Service Workers," *Fortune* (October 5, 1994), pp. 110–122.

5. Human Resource Planning and Job Analysis

LEARNING OBJECTIVES

After reading this chapter, you will be able to:

1. Describe the importance of human resource planning.
2. Define the steps involved in the human resource planning process.
3. Explain what Human Resource Management Systems are used for.
4. Define what is meant by the term *job analysis*.
5. Identify the six general techniques for obtaining job analysis information.
6. Describe the steps involved in conducting the job.
7. Explain the difference between job descriptions, job specifications, and job evaluations.
8. Describe the difference between downsizing and rightsizing.
9. Explain what is meant by outplacement services.
10. Discuss what is meant by the term "layoff-survivor" sickness.

*I*magine an organization of about 40 people operating in today's environment without the assistance of an HRM professional. Unusual, problematic? Maybe not, especially when the entrepreneurial owner of the company doesn't want to add bureaucracy to the organization. But what if it is revealed that many of your supervisory employees are spending an inordinate amount of time on HR activities? And having 40 employees means that the organization is covered under such laws as Equal Employment Opportunity and the Americans with Disabilities Acts. Will these individuals perform the related HRM work in a consistent manner? Are policies enforced uniformly? If not, what liabilities are created for the company? Answers to such questions may be unknown. So what does one do given this scenario? You hire a temporary HR gen-

eralist. That's exactly what Bob Freese, CEO of Alphatronix, the software developer in Research Triangle Park, North Carolina, did.[1]

Wanting to create an atmosphere where HR activities were functioning properly, and freeing his supervisory staff from the day-to-day HRM activities that were consuming much of their time, Freese advertised for a three-day-a-week HR manager. Much to his delight, Freese was overwhelmed with applications. It appeared that there were a number of applicants in the area who wanted to work part-time, but still have the opportunity to keep abreast of the HRM field. In essence, the contingent work force struck HR. Many of the applicants wanted to spend more time with their children, and were looking for a position that gave them more flexibility. Alphatronix's position provided that opportunity. More importantly, however, hiring a contingent HRM professional did not have to mean getting one who was a novice in the field or lacking good skills. On the contrary, many of the applicants, like his final selection, Suzanne Jones, had many years of HRM experience.

There is obviously a point in time when a company should retain HRM staff on a full-time basis. But for some organizations, a part-time HRM professional can prove to be beneficial to both parties. At Alphatronix, the company now has its professional HRM member properly handling the myriad of HR activities required in the company—and Suzanne Jones has the opportunity to blend her personal and career goals.

INTRODUCTION

Bob Freese realized that changes do occur in organizations. But adapting to these changes requires all organizational members to understand where the organization is going and to support what the enterprise is about to do. Individuals like Bob and Suzanne Jones understand that before you can depart on a journey, you have to know your destination. Just think about the last time you took a vacation. For example, if you live in Raleigh, North Carolina, and decide to go to a Florida beach for two weeks in the summer, you need to decide specifically what beach—Daytona or Fort Lauderdale—you want to go to and the best route you can take to get you there. In an elementary form, this is what planning is all about—knowing where you are going and how you are going to get there. The same holds true for Human Resource Management.

Whenever an organization is in the process of determining its human resource needs, it is engaged in a process we call **human resource planning.** Human resource planning is one of the most important elements in a successful Human Resource Management program,[2] because it is a process by which an organization ensures that it has the right number and kinds of people, at the right place, at the right time, capable of effectively and efficiently completing those tasks that will help the organization achieve its overall strategic objectives. Human resource planning, then, ultimately translates the organization's overall goals into the number and types of workers needed to meet those goals. Without clear-cut planning, and a direct linkage to the organization's strategic direction, estimation of an organization's human resource needs are reduced to mere guesswork.

This means that human resource planning cannot exist in isolation. It must be linked to the organization's overall strategy.[3] Thirty years ago, few employees in a typical firm, outside of possibly the firm's top executives, really knew about the company's long-range objectives. The strategic efforts also were often no more than an educated guess in determining the organization's direction. But things are different today. Aggressive domestic and global competition, for instance, has made strategic planning virtually mandatory. Although it's not our intention to go into every detail of the strategic planning process in this chapter, senior HRM officials need to understand the process because they're playing a more vital role in the strategic process. It's often HRM's responsibility to lead the entire management team in "showing the best way to take charge of the new workplace." [4] Let's look at a fundamental strategic planning process in an organization.

> **Employment planning cannot exist in isolation. It must be linked to the organization's overall strategy.**

AN ORGANIZATIONAL FRAMEWORK

The strategic planning process in an organization is both long and continuous.[5] At the beginning of the process, the organization's main emphasis is to determine what business it is in. This is commonly referred to as developing the **mission statement.** Why is the mission statement important? Take, for instance, a part of Black and Decker's mission statement—to be the premier manufacturer and marketer of tools. What that statement does is clarify for all organizational members what exactly the company is about. Accordingly, the company specifies clearly why it exists and sets the course for company operations. That is, a sound mission statement facilitates the decision-making process. For example, Black and Decker's decision to sell industrial hand tools and enter that market with its DeWalt line of products is a decision that is within the boundaries set by the mission. However, these same managers would know that any effort to expand the company's product lines to include home appliances is not consistent with the mission. That's why, when Black & Decker in early 1998 reformulated its mission statement to reflect its core business (tools), company officials decided to sell off its home appliance division—like the coffee makers, toaster ovens, mixers, etc.[6] This discussion is not meant to say that mission statements are written in stone; at any time, after careful study and deliberation, they can be changed. For example, the March of Dimes was originally created to facilitate the cure of infantile paralysis (polio). When polio was essentially eradicated in the 1950s, the organization redefined its mission as seeking cures for children's diseases. Nonetheless, the need to specifically define an organization's line of business is critical to its survival.

After reaching agreement on what business the company is in and who its consumers are, senior management then begins to set **strategic goals.**[7] During this phase, these managers define objectives for the company for the next five to twenty years. These objectives are broad statements that establish targets the organization will achieve. For example, Illinois's Continental Banks established broad areas of emphasis. That is, the bank was going to enter three specific banking arenas: corporate and institutional banking, global trading and distribution, and private banking.[8]

After these goals are set, the next step in the strategic planning process begins—the corporate assessment. During this phase, a company begins to analyze its goals, its current strategies, its external environment, its strengths and weaknesses, and its opportunities and threats, in terms of whether or not they can be achieved with the current organizational resources. Commonly referred to as a "gap or SWOT (strengths, weaknesses, opportunities, and threats) analysis," the company begins to look at what skills, knowledge, and abilities are available internally, and where shortages in terms of people skills or equipment may exist. For Continental Bank, this meant looking at what people skills were needed in order to be successful in the new markets. Their analysis resulted in their changing the company's recruiting efforts in an attempt to hire people with the specific international marketing skills they wanted.[9] This phase of the strategic planning process cannot be overstated; it serves as the link between the organization's goals and ensuring that the company can meet its objectives—that is, establishes the direction of the company through strategic planning.

The company must determine what jobs need to be done, and how many and what types of workers will be required. In management terminology, we call this *organizing*. Thus, establishing the structure of the organization assists in determining the skills, knowledge, and abilities required of jobholders.

It is only at this point that we begin to look at people to meet these criteria. And that's where Human Resource Management comes in to play an integral role. To determine what skills are needed, HRM conducts a job analysis. Exhibit 5-1 is a graphic representation of this process. The key message in Exhibit 5-1 is that all jobs in the organization ultimately must be tied to the company's mission and strategic direction. Recall in Chapter 2 our discussion of effectiveness and efficiency in terms of corporate downsizing. Unless jobs can be linked to

Exhibit 5-1

The Strategic Direction–
Human Resource Linkage

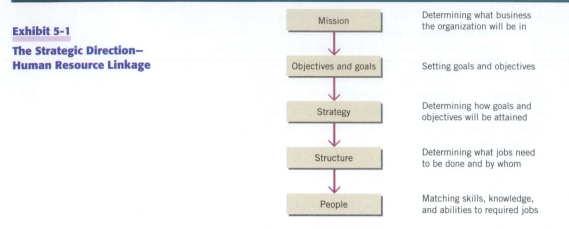

the organization's strategic goals, achieving these goals becomes a moving target. It's no wonder, then, that human resource planning has become more critical in organizations. Let's look at how human resource planning operates within the strategic planning process.

LINKING ORGANIZATIONAL STRATEGY TO HUMAN RESOURCE PLANNING

To ensure that appropriate personnel are available to meet the requirements set during the strategic planning process, human resource managers engage in human resource planning. The purpose of this planning effort is to determine what HRM requirements exist for current and future supplies and demands for workers. For example, if a company has set as one of its goals to expand its production capabilities over the next five years, such action will require that skilled employees be available to handle the jobs. After this assessment, human resource planning matches the supplies and demands for labor, supporting the people component.[10]

Assessing Current Human Resources

Assessing current human resources begins by developing a profile of the organization's current employees. This is an internal analysis that includes information about the workers and the skills they currently possess. In an era of sophisticated computer systems, it is not too difficult for most organizations to generate an effective and detailed human resources inventory report. The input to this report would be derived from forms completed by employees and then checked by supervisors. Such reports would include a complete list of all employees by name, education, training, prior employment, current position, performance ratings, salary level, languages spoken, capabilities, and specialized skills.[11] For example, if internal translators were needed for suppliers, customers, or employee assistance, a contact list could be developed.

From a planning viewpoint, this input is valuable in determining what skills are currently available in the organization. The inventory serves as a guide for supporting new organizational pursuits or in altering the organization's strategic direction. This report also has value in other HRM activities, such as selecting individuals for training and development, promotion, and transfers. The completed profile of the human resources inventory can also provide crucial information for identifying current or future threats to the organization's ability to successfully meets its goals. For example, the organization can use the information from the inventory to identify specific variables that may have a particular relationship to training needs, productivity improvements, and succession planning. A characteristic like technical obsolescence, or workers who are not trained to function with new computer requirements, can, if it begins to permeate the entire organization, adversely affect the organization's performance.

Human Resource Management Systems   To assist in the HR inventory, organizations have implemented a **human resource management system (HRMS).** The HRMS (sometimes referred to as a human resource inventory system [HRIS]) is designed to quickly fulfill the human resource management informational needs of the organization.[12] The HRMS is a database system that keeps important information about employees in a central and accessible location—even information on the global workforce.[13] When such information is required, the data can be retrieved and used to facilitate employment planning decisions. Its technical potential permits the organization to track most information about employees and jobs, and to retrieve that information when needed.[14] An HRMS may also be used to help track EEO data.[15] Exhibit 5-2 is a listing of typical information tracked on an HRMS.

HRMSs have grown significantly in popularity in the past fifteen years. This is essentially due to the recognition that management needs timely information on its people; moreover, new technological breakthroughs have significantly cut the cost of these systems.[16] Additionally, HRMSs are now more "user-friendly"

Group 1   Basic Nonconfidential Information
  Employee name
  Organization name
  Work location
  Work phone number

Group 2   General Nonconfidential Information
  Information in the previous category, plus:
  Social Security number
  Other organization information (code, effective date)
  Position-related information (code, title, effective date)

Group 3   General Information with Salary
  Information in the previous category, plus:
  Current salary, effective date, amount of last change, type of last change and reason
    for last change)

Group 4   Confidential Information with Salary
  Information in the previous category, plus:
  Other position information (EEO code, position ranking and FLSA)
  Education data

Group 5   Extended Confidential Information with Salary
  Information in the previous category, plus:
  Bonus information
  Projected salary increase information
  Performance evaluation information

SOURCE: Joan E. Goodman, "Does Your HRIS Speak English?" *Personnel Journal* (March 1990), p. 81. Used with permission.

Exhibit 5-2

Information Categories of Human Resource Management Systems

and provide quick and responsive reports,[17] especially when linked to the organization's management information system.

At a time when quick analysis of an organization's human resources is critical, the HRMS is filling a void in the human resource planning process. With information readily available, organizations are in a better position to quickly move forward in achieving their organizational goals.[18] Additionally, the HRMS is useful in other aspects of human resource management, providing data support for compensation and benefits programs, as well as providing a necessary link to corporate payroll.[19]

Replacement Charts In addition to the computerized HRMS system, some organizations also generate a separate senior management inventory report. This report, called a **replacement chart,** typically covers individuals in middle-to-upper-level management positions. In an effort to facilitate succession planning[20]—ensuring that another individual is ready to move into a position of higher responsibility—the replacement chart highlights those positions that may become vacant in the near future due to retirements, promotions, transfers, resignations, or death of the incumbent. But not all companies use replacement charts, and this can create confusion, or even worse.[21] For example, at General Electric, no formal charts exist to show who will replace CEO Jack Welch when he leaves. A sudden rush to the hospital in 1995 brought this to light. Even in light of this "scare," a formal replacement chart is still nonexistent.[22] The gravity of having replacement charts was truly witnessed in April 1996 when U.S. Commerce Secretary Ronald Brown's plane crashed while on a trip to the Balkans. On board with Brown were 30 executives from U.S. companies. Those organizations without replacement charts were at a loss for a substantial period of time.[23]

Against this list of positions is placed the individual manager's skills inventory to determine if there is sufficient managerial talent to cover potential future vacancies. This "readiness" chart then gives management an indication of time frames for succession, as well as helping to spot skill shortages that may exist.[24] Should skill shortages exist, human resource management can either recruit new employees or intensify employee development efforts (see Chapter 9).

Exhibit 5-3 A Sample Replacement Chart

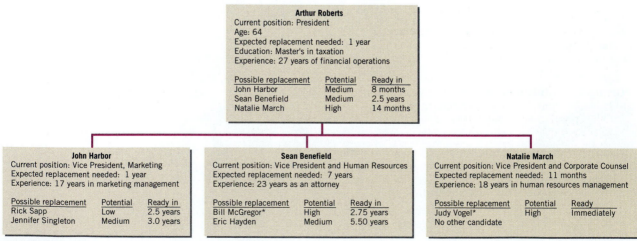

Arthur Roberts
Current position: President
Age: 64
Expected replacement needed: 1 year
Education: Master's in taxation
Experience: 27 years of financial operations

Possible replacement	Potential	Ready in
John Harbor	Medium	8 months
Sean Benefield	Medium	2.5 years
Natalie March	High	14 months

John Harbor
Current position: Vice President, Marketing
Expected replacement needed: 1 year
Experience: 17 years in marketing management

Possible replacement	Potential	Ready in
Rick Sapp	Low	2.5 years
Jennifer Singleton	Medium	3.0 years

Sean Benefield
Current position: Vice President and Human Resources
Expected replacement needed: 7 years
Experience: 23 years as an attorney

Possible replacement	Potential	Ready in
Bill McGregor*	High	2.75 years
Eric Hayden	Medium	5.50 years

Natalie March
Current position: Vice President and Corporate Counsel
Expected replacement needed: 11 months
Experience: 18 years in human resources management

Possible replacement	Potential	Ready
Judy Vogel*	High	Immediately
No other candidate		

* Denotes minority

Replacement charts look very similar to traditional organizational charts. With the incumbents listed in their positions, those individuals targeted for replacement are listed beneath with the expected time in which they will be prepared to take on the needed responsibility. We have provided a sample replacement chart in Exhibit 5-3.

The Demand for Labor

Once an assessment of the organization's current human resources situation has been made and the future direction of the organization has been considered, a projection of future human resource needs can be developed.

It will be necessary to perform a year-by-year analysis for every significant job level and type. In effect, the result is a human resource inventory covering specified years into the future. These pro-forma inventories obviously must be comprehensive, and therefore complex. Organizations usually require a diverse mix of people. That's because employees are not perfectly substitutable for one another within an organization. For example, a shortage of actuaries in an insurance company cannot be offset by transferring employees from the purchasing area where there is an oversupply. If accurate estimates are to be made of future demands in both qualitative and quantitative terms, more information is needed than just to determine that, for example, in the next 24 months, we will have to hire another 85 individuals. Instead, it is necessary to know what types of employees, in terms of skills, knowledge, and abilities, are required. Remember, these skills, knowledge and abilities are determined based on the jobs required to meet the strategic direction of the organization. Accordingly, our forecasting methods must allow for the recognition of specific job needs as well as the total number of vacancies.

CEO extraordinaire, world-renown Jack Welch, of General Electric. Sudden chest pain some years ago and subsequent heart surgery brought to light one important fact. If something were to happen to Jack, who would succeed him? At GE, that answer is unknown. Although there are speculations about who the heir apparent is, no formal plans exist to prepare someone to step into Welch's shoes once he leaves the job.

Estimating the Future Supply of Labor

Estimating changes in internal supply requires the HRM to look at those factors that can either increase or decrease its employee base. As previously noted in the discussion on estimating demand, forecasting of supply must also concern itself with the micro, or unit, level. For example, if one individual in Department X is transferred to a position in Department Y, and an individual in Department Y is transferred to a position in Department X, the net effect on the organization is zero. However, if only one individual is initially involved—say, promoted and sent to another location in the company—it is only through effective human resource planning that a competent replacement will be available to fill the position vacated by the departing employee.

An increase in the supply of any unit's human resources can come from a combination of four sources: new hires, contingent workers, transfers-in, or individuals returning from leaves.[25] The task of predicting these new inputs can range from simple to complex.

Decreases in the internal supply can come about through retirements, dismissals, transfers-out of the unit, layoffs, voluntary quits, sabbaticals, prolonged illnesses, or deaths.[26] Some of these occurrences are obviously easier to predict than others. The easiest to forecast are retirements, assuming that employees typically retire after a certain length of service, and the fact that most organizations require some advance notice of one's retirement intent. Given a history of the organization, HRM can predict with some accuracy how many retirements will occur over a given time period. Remember, however, that retirement, for the most part, is voluntary. Under the Age Discrimination in Employment Act, an organization cannot force most employees to retire.

At the other extreme, voluntary quits, prolonged illnesses, and deaths are difficult to predict—if at all. Deaths of employees are the most difficult to forecast because they are often unexpected. Although Southwest Airlines or Nissan Motors can use probability statistics to estimate the number of deaths that will occur among its employee population, such techniques are useless for forecasting in small organizations or estimating the exact positions that will be affected in large ones. Voluntary quits can also be predicted by utilizing probabilities when the population size is large. In a company like Microsoft, managers can estimate the approximate number of voluntary quits during any given year. In a department consisting of two or three workers, however, probability estimation is essentially meaningless. Weak predictive ability in small units is unfortunate, too, because voluntary quits typically have the greatest impact on such units.

In between the extremes—transfers, layoffs, sabbaticals, and dismissals—forecasts within reasonable limits of accuracy can be made. Since all four of these types of action are controllable by management—that is, they are either initiated by management or are within management's veto prerogative—each type can be reasonably predicted. Of the four, transfers out of a unit, such as lateral moves, demotions, or promotions, are the most difficult to predict because they depend on openings in other units. Layoffs are more controllable and anticipated by management, especially in the short run. Sabbaticals, too, are reasonably easy to forecast, since most organizations' sabbatical policies require a reasonable lead time between request and initiation of the leave. For example, at the McDonald's corporation,[27] employees with ten years of continuous service are eligible for an eight-week sabbatical. The sabbatical can be taken during any eight continuous weeks, but with advanced approval of management. This gives the corporation ample time to find a replacement if needed.

Dismissals, based on inadequate job performance, can usually be forecasted in the same method as voluntary quits, using probabilities where large numbers of employees are involved. Additionally, performance evaluation reports are usually a reliable source for isolating the number of individuals whose employment might have to be terminated at a particular point in time due to unsatisfactory work performance.

Estimated Changes in External Supply

The previous discussion on supply considered internal factors. We will now review those factors outside the organization that influence the supply of available workers. Recent graduates from schools and colleges expand the supply of available human resources. This market is vast and includes everyone from high-school graduates to individuals who have graduated from college; or those who received highly specialized training through an alternative supplier of job skills training. Entrants to the workforce from sources other than schools may also include men and women seeking full or part-time work; students seeking work to pay for their education or support themselves while in school; employees returning from military service; job seekers who have been recently laid off; and so on. Migration into a community may also increase the number of individuals who are seeking employment opportunities and accordingly represent another source for the organization to consider as potential additions to its labor supply.

It should be noted that consideration of only these supply sources just identified tends to understate the potential labor supply because many people can be retrained through formal or on-the-job training. Therefore, the potential supply can differ from what one might conclude by looking only at the obvious sources of supply. For example, with a minimal amount of training, a journalist can become qualified to perform the tasks of a book editor; thus, an organization that is having difficulty securing individuals with skills and experience in book editing should consider those candidates who have had recent journalism or similar experience and are interested in being editors. In similar fashion, the potential supply for many other jobs can be expanded.

Matching the Demand and Supply of Labor

The objective of human resource planning is to bring together the forecasts of future demand for workers and the supply for human resources, both current and future. The result of this effort is to pinpoint shortages both in number and in kind; to highlight areas where overstaffing may exist (now or in the near future); and to keep abreast of the opportunities existing in the labor market to hire qualified employees—either to satisfy current needs or to stockpile "potential candidates" for the future.

Special attention must be paid to determining shortages. Should an organization find that the demand for human resources will be increasing in the future, then it will have to hire or contract with additional staff or transfer people within the organization, or both, to balance the numbers, skills, mix, and quality of its human resources. An often-overlooked action, but one that may be neces-

Exhibit 5-4 Employment Planning and the Strategic Planning Process

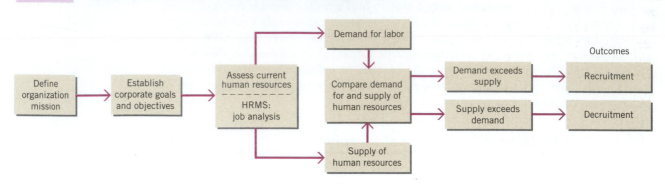

sary because of inadequate availability of human resources, is to change the organization's objectives. Just as inadequate financial resources can restrict the growth and opportunities available to an organization, the unavailability of the right types of employees can also act as such a constraint, even leading to changing the organization's objectives.

As organizations like Sears, Ryder, and Xerox reorganize and reengineer, another outcome is increasingly likely: the existence of an oversupply. When this happens, human resource management must undertake some difficult steps to sever these people from the organization—a process referred to as *decruitment*. We'll return to decruitment under the discussion of corporate downsizing later in the chapter.

Corporate strategic and human resource planning are two critically linked processes; one cannot survive without the other. Accordingly, to perform both properly requires a blending of activities. We have portrayed these linkages in Exhibit 5-4.

DETERMINING ESSENTIAL SKILLS, KNOWLEDGE, AND ABILITIES

Applied Human Resource Systems (AHRS), a corporate training and development firm, has been working with a client that has experienced a 20 percent turnover of engineers over the past eighteen months. An analysis of the resignations indicated that the average length of stay has been only 11 months. Perplexed by this dilemma and the resulting loss to productivity and revenue, consultants from AHRS recommended an investigation to find out why such high turnover levels exist.

A job analysis involves identifying and describing what is happening on a job.

The investigation, while much more complex, involved contacting most of the individuals who resigned to ask them why they quit. The responses were that what they were hired to do and what they were required to do were often two different things. The latter required different skills and aptitudes. Feeling frustrated and bored, and not wanting to jeopardize their career records, they quit. Unfortunately, the company's training costs these past three years had run approximately 300 percent over budget. When one of the senior managers was asked what it was about the job that made it so difficult to properly match the job requirements with people skills, she did not have an answer. It appeared that no one in the organization had taken the time to find out what the jobs were all about. In other words, the job analysis process was lacking.

What Is Job Analysis?

A **job analysis** is a systematic exploration of the activities within a job. It is a technical procedure used to define the duties, responsibilities, and account-abilities of a job. This analysis "involves the identification and description of what is happening on the job . . . accurately and precisely identifying the re-quired tasks, the knowledge, and the skills necessary for performing them, and the conditions under which they must be performed." [28] Let's explore how this can be achieved.

Job Analysis Methods

The basic methods that HRM can use to determine job elements and the es-sential knowledge, skills, and abilities for successful performance include the following:

Observation Method. Using the **observation method,** a job analyst watches employees directly or reviews films of workers on the job. Although the observation method provides firsthand information, workers often do not function most efficiently when they are being watched, and thus distortions in the job analysis can occur. This method also requires that the entire range of ac-tivities be observable. This is possible with some jobs, but impossible for many—for example, most managerial jobs.

Individual Interview Method. Using the **individual interview method,** a team of job incumbents is selected and extensively interviewed. The results of these interviews are combined into a single job analysis. This method is effec-tive for assessing what a job entails, and involving employees in the job analysis is essential.

Group Interview Method. The **group interview method** is similar to the individual interview method except that a number of job incumbents are inter-viewed simultaneously. Accuracy is increased in assessing jobs, but group dy-namics may hinder its effectiveness.

Structured Questionnaire Method. Under the **structured questionnaire method,** workers are sent a specifically designed questionnaire on which they check or rate items they perform on their job from a long list of possible task items. This technique is excellent for gathering information about jobs. How-ever, exceptions to a job may be overlooked, and there is often no opportunity to ask follow-up questions or to clarify the information received.

Technical Conference Method. The **technical conference method** uses supervisors with extensive knowledge of the job. Here, specific job characteris-tics are obtained from the "experts." Although a good data-gathering method, it often overlooks the incumbent workers' perceptions about what they do on their job.

Diary Method. The **diary method** requires job incumbents to record their daily activities. The diary method is the most time consuming of the job analy-sis methods and may have to extend over long periods of time—all adding to its cost.

These six methods are not meant to be viewed as mutually exclusive; no one method is universally superior. Even obtaining job information from the in-cumbents can create a problem, especially if these individuals describe what they think they should be doing rather than what they actually do. The best results, then, are usually achieved with some combination of methods—with information provided by individual employees, their immediate supervisors, a professional analyst, or an unobtrusive source such as filmed observations. In the next section, we'll explore a means of conducting the job analysis.

Conducting the Job Analysis

There are several steps involved in conducting the job analysis. Let's look at how this is done (see Exhibit 5-5).

Understand the Purpose of Conducting the Job Analysis   Before embarking on a job analysis, one must understand the nature and purpose of conducting the investigation. Recognize that job analyses serve a vital purpose in such HRM activities as recruiting, training, setting performance standards, evaluating performance, and compensation. In fact, nearly every activity in HRM revolves around the job analysis.

Understand the Role of Jobs and Values in the Organization   Every job in the organization should have a purpose. Before conducting the job analysis, one must understand the linkage that the job has to the strategic direction of the organization. In essence, one must answer why the job is needed. If an answer cannot be determined, then maybe the job is not needed.

Benchmark Positions   In a large organization, it would be impossible to evaluate every job at one time. Accordingly, by involving employees and seeking their input, selected jobs can be chosen based on how well they represent other, similar jobs in the organization. This information, then, will be used as a starting point in later analysis of the other positions.

Determine How You Want to Collect the Job Analysis Information
Proper planning at this stage permits one to collect the data desired in the most effective and efficient manner. This means developing a process for collecting the data. Several combined methods—like structured questionnaires, group interviews, and technical conferences—should be used. Select the ones, however, that best meet your job analyses goals and timetables.

Seek Clarification, Wherever Necessary   Some of the information collected may not be entirely understood by the job analyst. Accordingly, when this oc-

Exhibit 5-5

Steps in a Job Analysis

curs, one must seek clarification from those who possess the critical information. This may include the employee and the supervisor. Failure to understand and comprehend the information will make the next step in the job analysis process—writing the job description—more difficult.

Develop the First Draft of the Job Description Although there is no specific format that all job descriptions follow, most include certain elements. Specifically, a job description contains the job title, a summary sentence of the job's main activities, the level of authority and accountability of the position, performance requirements, and working conditions. The last paragraph of the job description typically includes the job specifications, or those personal characteristics the job incumbent should possess to be successful on the job.

Review Draft with the Job Supervisor Ultimately, the supervisor of the position being analyzed should approve the job description. Review comments from the supervisor can assist in determining a final job description document. When the description is an accurate reflection, the supervisor should sign off, or approve the document.

Structured Job Analyses Techniques

Now that we realize that job analysis data can be collected in a number of ways, and that there's a process that we can follow to do the work, let us consider other notable job analysis processes. These are the Department of Labor Job Analysis Process and the Position Analysis Questionnaire.

The Department of Labor's Job Analysis Process The **Department of Labor's Job Analysis Process** describes what a worker does by having someone observe and interview the employee. This information is standardized and cataloged into three general functions that exist in all jobs: data, people, and things (see Exhibit 5-6). An employment interviewer, for example, might be found to analyze data, speak to people, and handle things; the job would be coded 2, 6, 7. Exhibit 5-7 shows the listing for the employment interviewer's position. This type of coding of key elements has already been done for thousands of job titles listed in the **Dictionary of Occupational Titles,** which is readily available in most libraries. Use of this publication may significantly re-

Work Functions		
Data	*People*	*Things*
0 Synthesizing	0 Mentoring	0 Setting up
1 Coordinating	1 Negotiating	1 Precision working
2 Analyzing	2 Instructing	2 Operating–controlling
3 Compiling	3 Supervision	3 Driving–operating
4 Computing	4 Diverting	4 Manipulating
5 Copying	5 Persuading	5 Tending
6 Comparing	6 Speaking–signaling	6 Feeding–offbearing
	7 Serving	7 Handling
	8 Taking instructions–helping	

SOURCE: U.S. Department of Labor, *Dictionary of Occupational Titles,* 4th ed. revised (Washington, D.C.: Government Printing Office, 1991), p. xix.

Exhibit 5-6

Department of Labor Job Analysis Process

Exhibit 5-7

Department of Labor Job Narrative

166.267–010   Employment Interviewer
              Alternate title: Placement Interviewer

Interviews job applicants to select persons meeting employer qualifications. Reviews completed application and evaluates applicant's work history, education and training, job skills, salary desired, and physical and personal qualifications. Records additional skills, knowledge, abilities, interests, test results, and other data pertinent to classification, selection, and referral. Searches files of job orders from employers and matches applicant's qualifications with job requirements and employer specifications, utilizing manual search, computer matching services, or employment service facilities. Informs applicant about job duties and responsibilities, pay and benefits, hours and working conditions, company and union policies, promotional opportunities, and other related information. Refers selected applicant to interview with person placing job order according to policy of school, agency, or company. Keeps for future reference records of applicants not immediately selected or hired. May perform reference and background checks. May refer applicants to vocational counseling services. May test or arrange for skills, intelligence, or psychological testing of applicant. May engage in research or follow-up activities to evaluate selection and placement techniques by conferring with management and supervisory personnel. May specialize in interviewing and referring certain types of personnel, such as professional, technical, managerial, clerical, and other types of skilled or unskilled workers. May be known as personnel recruiter and seek out potential applicants and try to interest them in applying for position openings.

SOURCE: Bureau of Labor Statistics, U.S. Department of Labor, *Occupational Outlook Handbook*, 1998–1999 Edition, Bulletin 2500 (Washington, D.C.: Government Printing Office, 1998), pp. 37–9.

duce HRM's burden of gathering information on jobs for its organization. Additionally, the DOL job codes are supplemented with a detailed narrative. So the information regarding the employment interviewer's job would tell us what the jobholder's main functions are, with whom the jobholder speaks, and which things are handled. The DOL technique allows managers to group jobs into job

Exhibit 5-8

Fine's Functional Job Analysis (FJA) Scale

Data	People	Things
1. Comparing	1a. Taking instruction 1b. Serving	1a. Handling 1b. Feeding/off-bearing 1c. Tending
2. Copying	2. Exchanging information	2a. Manipulating 2b. Operating/controlling 2c. Driving/controlling
3a. Computing 3b. Compiling	3a. Coaching 3b. Persuading 3c. Diverting	3a. Precision work 3b. Setting up
4. Analyzing	4a. Consulting 4b. Instructing 4c. Treating	
5a. Innovating 5b. Coordinating	5. Supervising	
6. Synthesizing	6. Negotiating	
	7. Mentoring	

SOURCE: A. S. Fine, *Functional Job Analysis Scales: A Desk Aid* (Kalamazoo, MI: W.E. Upjohn Institute for Employment Research, 1973). Used with permission.

Category	Number of Job Elements
1. *Information input* Where and how does the worker get the information he or she uses on the job?	35
2. *Mental processes* What reasoning, decision making, planning, etc., are involved in the job?	14
3. *Work output* What physical activities does the worker perform and what tools or devices are used?	49
4. *Relationships with other people* What relationships with other people are required in the job?	36
5. *Job context* In what physical and social contexts is the work performed?	19
6. *Other job characteristics* What special attributes exist on this job (e.g., schedule, responsibilities, pay).	41

SOURCE: Reprinted with permission from the Position Analysis Questionnaire, Copyright 1969, Purdue Research Foundation.

Exhibit 5-9

Categories and Their Number of Job Elements of the PAQ

families that require similar kinds of worker behavior. Candidates for these jobs, therefore, should hold similar worker skills.

A variation of the Department of Labor's methodology was developed by a U.S. Employment Service employee, Sidney Fine. Fine developed a process that further described those items listed by the DOL, called the Functional Job Analysis (FJA) (see Exhibit 5-8). In so doing, the FJA provides a more accurate picture of what the jobholder does.[29]

Position Analysis Questionnaire   Developed by researchers at Purdue University, the Position Analysis Questionnaire (PAQ) generates job requirement information that is applicable to all types of jobs. In contrast to the DOL approach, the PAQ presents a more quantitative and finely-tuned description of jobs. The PAQ procedure involves "194 elements that are grouped within six major divisions and 28 sections"[30] (see Exhibit 5-9).

The PAQ allows HRM to scientifically and quantitatively group interrelated job elements into job dimensions. This, in turn, should allow jobs to be compared with each other. However, research on the usefulness of the PAQ is suspect. For the most part, it appears to be more applicable to lower-level, blue-collar jobs.[31]

Purpose of Job Analysis

No matter what method is used to gather data, the information amassed and written down from the job analysis process generates three outcomes: job descriptions, job specifications, and job evaluation. It is important to note that these are the tangible products of the work—not the job analysis, which is the conceptual, analytical process or action from which we develop these outcomes. Let's look at them more closely.

Job Descriptions   A **job description** is a written statement of what the jobholder does, how it is done, under what conditions it is done, and why it is done. It should accurately portray job content, environment, and conditions of employment. A common format for a job description includes the job title, the

Exhibit 5-10

Example of a Job Description

Job Description

Faculty Member, College of Business

Job Title: Faculty Member   **Occupational Code No.** 4554

Reports to: Department Chairperson   **Job No.** 078

Supervises: None   **Date:** 5/14/98

Environmental Conditions: None

Functions: Teach one or more subjects within a prescribed business and economics curriculum.

Duties and Responsibilities:
- Prepare and deliver outside reading assignments.
- Stimulate class discussion.
- Compile, administer, and grade examinations—or assign this work to others.
- Direct research for others working for advanced degree.
- Conduct research in particular field of knowledge and publish findings in professional journals.
- Perform related duties, such as advising students on academic and vocational curricula.
- Serve on faculty committees.
- Provide professional consulting to government and industry.
- Other duties as assigned by department head.

Job Specifications

Job Characteristics: Understanding of instructional methods for traditional and nontraditional students; excellent communication skills; and skilled operation of a personal computer, using word processing, spreadsheet, database management, and statistical packages.

SOURCE: Bureau of Labor Statistics, U. S. Department of Labor, Occupational Outlook Handbook, 1998–1999 Edition, Bulletin 2500 (Washington, D.C.: Government Printing Office, 1998), pp 167–169.

duties to be performed, the distinguishing characteristics of the job, environmental conditions, and the authority and responsibilities of the jobholder. An example of a job description for a faculty member in a College of Business is provided in Exhibit 5-10.

When we discuss employee recruitment, selection, and performance appraisal, we will find that the job description acts as an important resource for: (1) describing the job (either verbally by recruiters and interviewers or in written advertisements) to potential candidates; (2) guiding newly hired employees in what they are specifically expected to do; and (3) providing a point of comparison in appraising whether the actual activities of a job incumbent align with the stated duties. Furthermore, under the Americans with Disabilities Act, job descriptions have taken on an added emphasis in identifying essential job functions.

Job Specifications   The **job specification** states the minimum acceptable qualifications that the incumbent must possess to perform the job successfully. Based on the information acquired through job analysis, the job specification identifies the knowledge, skills, education, experience, certification, and abilities needed to do the job effectively. Individuals possessing the personal characteristics identified in the job specification should perform the job more effectively than those lacking these personal characteristics. The job specification, therefore, is an important tool in the selection process, for it keeps the selector's attention on the list of qualifications necessary for an incumbent to perform the job and assists in determining whether candidates are essentially qualified.

Job Evaluations   In addition to providing data for job descriptions and specifications, job analysis is also valuable in providing the information that makes comparison of jobs possible. If an organization is to have an equitable compensation program, jobs that have similar demands in terms of skills, knowledge, and abilities should be placed in common compensation groups. **Job evaluation** contributes toward that end by specifying the relative value of each job in the organization. Job evaluation, therefore, is an important part of compensation administration, as will be discussed in detail in Chapter 11. In the meantime, you should keep in mind that job evaluation is made possible by the data generated from job analysis.

The Multifaceted Nature of Job Analysis

One of the overriding questions about job analysis is: Are they being conducted properly, if at all? The answer to this question varies, depending on the organization. Generally, most organizations do conduct some type of job analysis. This job analysis extends further, however, than meeting the federal equal employment opportunity requirement. Almost everything that HRM does is directly related to the job analysis process (see Exhibit 5-11). Recruiting, selection, compensation, and performance-appraising activities are most frequently cited as being directly affected by the job analysis. But there are others. Employee training and career development are assisted by the job analysis process by identifying necessary skills, knowledge, and abilities. Where deficiencies exist, training and development efforts can be used. Similar effects can also be witnessed in determining safety and health requirements, and labor relations processes, if a union exists. Accordingly, this often lengthy and complex job analysis process cannot be overlooked.

We cannot overemphasize the importance of job analysis, as it permeates most of the organization's activities. If an organization doesn't do its job analysis well, it probably doesn't perform many of its human resource activities well. If employees in the organization understand human resource activities, they should understand the fundamental importance of job analysis. The job analysis, then, is the starting point of sound human resource management. Without

Exhibit 5-11

The Multifaceted Nature of the Job Analysis

knowing what the job entails, the material covered in the following chapters may be merely an effort in futility.

CURRENT ISSUES IN HUMAN RESOURCE PLANNING

Earlier in this chapter, we identified a situation in human resource planning in which the supply of workers exceeds demand. When that occurs, organizations must begin a process of decruitment. For the most part, that meant downsizing. Recall from Chapter 2 the necessity for such action. The guiding theme was to make the organization more "lean and mean"; in other words, more efficient. But cutting employees for efficiency sake may not be appropriate. Rather, companies today are looking at the need to correctly staff the organization with the needed skills, knowledge, and abilities. We call this rightsizing.[32] Let's look at the downsizing/rightsizing issue facing companies.

Downsizing: Past and Present

Over the past few decades, we have witnessed the continued shrinkage of the once-strong smokestack industries—steel, auto, and rubber.[33] Competition in the high-tech industries has also soared during this time, giving rise to massive layoffs at such companies as Apple and IBM, as well as a host of others in the Silicon Valley. Conglomerates, too, began shedding less profitable business units, or closed down altogether. And the continual increase in foreign competition creates more difficulties for U.S. organizations.

Human resource planning tended to ignore issues in managing declining organizations such as those in the industries described above. Going bankrupt (Wang), divesting holdings (GM), or eliminating unprofitable product lines (Chrysler) are activities that are seldom seen in a growing enterprise. Clearly these activities have a major impact on the employee population. Human resource planning, as we described earlier, had to change to a more strategic focus.[34] As we enter the new millennium, even how we downsize may be changing.

It was believed that in order to cut costs and turn around ailing companies, body counts had to be high. So many companies initiated "quick fix" solutions. And these actions were obvious! By the mid–1990s, nearly every major corporation in the United States had trimmed its work force.[35] It became so commonplace (or we've become so indifferent to the action), that today, massive layoffs don't even make front-page news. But there's more to the story!

Cutting employees didn't always produce the results that companies were looking for.

Cutting employees didn't always produce the results that companies were looking for. Operating costs often didn't decrease. Downsizing was sometimes a short-term fix! What it did do in those cases was to leave fewer people to do the work that was to be done. Consequently, productivity fell. Many companies didn't look at the long-term effects of downsizing.[36] Today, that is changing. In fact, it is estimated that by the year 2000, more than half of the companies that lay off employees will also simultaneously be hiring. How can that be? Isn't such action contradictory? The answer is no! It's actually simple—lying in the concept of human resource planning. That is, companies today are refocusing their efforts on those things that meet their strategic direction. Organizational activities, and jobs that lead to strategic goal attainment and add value to the corporation are getting the necessary resources. And that includes people. For instance, just ten years ago, AT&T employed fewer than 60 people outside the United States. However, with its strategic direction to go global, the company has increased staffing levels to over 70,000 employees.[37]

Don't let the previous paragraph lead you into a false sense of security into believing that the downsizing trend is over. That's not the point of the discussion. Rather, it indicates that companies are more consciously linking their employee needs to the organization's strategy. Those jobs that are not directly linked to strategy are often being eliminated. So instead of downsizing, it's more appropriately called **rightsizing.** That's precisely the point made in Exhibit 5-4!

A Little Help for Our "Friends"

Recall that in our discussion in Chapter 1 of the goals of human resource management, we stated the goal of the maintenance function to be such that commitment and loyalty to the organization are maintained. Under growth circumstances, such a goal is often possible. However, in downsizing or other staff reduction activities, the emphasis of that goal changes. The company must demonstrate its support for the past commitment and loyalty of the severed employee. Outplacement delivers that support. By definition, **outplacement** is a process of assisting "existing employees" with job-help services, psychological counseling, support groups, severance pay, extended health insurance benefits, and detailed communications.[38]

Companies need to recognize that many of these long-term "loyal" employees have no idea how to go about getting a job outside the company. The crucial period for this employee appears to be the first three to six months,[39] in which a number of key factors come into play. First of all is the psychological aspect of looking for a job. Being unsuccessful for more than six months tends to cause an individual to feel that he or she will never get a job; negative self-image can only hurt in interviewing situations. Second is the money issue: After six months, money—even severance pay—may be running out. And this only adds to the psychological problem. That is why the current aspect of outplacement is so crucial—to help these individuals deal with these tough times. Through proper counseling, and offering space and telephone access, outplacement can help.[40] Outplacement does not come cheap—the costs range into the thousands of dollars per individual—but most employers offering outplacement services indicate that it is money well spent.[41]

What about the Survivors?

Many organizations have done a fairly good job of helping layoff victims through a variety of outplacement services. Although some affected individuals react very negatively to such events (the worse case involving returning to the separating organization and committing some form of violence), the assistance offered reveals that the organization does care. Unfortunately, very little has been done for those who have been left behind and have the task of keeping the organization going. Or even revitalizing it!

It may surprise you to learn that the evidence shows both victims and survivors experience similar feelings of frustration, anxiety, and loss.[42] But layoff victims get to start over with a clean slate. This isn't true of survivors. As one

What can you do for the individuals who are working hard in your organization, who are productive, but just need a break. In some organizations, employees get a sabbatical. Kate Newlin, president of the fifteen-person New York public relations firm, The Newlin company, did just that. She took off for two months—getting away from the rat race and spending time on things she really wanted to do. In her case, that was to work on a novel. And not only did she return to work more relaxed, she recognized that the business could run without her controling every aspect. As a result of her "relaxed self," company revenues doubled in a little more than a year's time. Apparently there's something to giving employees a break from the day-to-day grind!

author suggested, "the terms could be reversed: those who leave become survivors, and those who stay become victims."[43] A new syndrome seems to be popping up in more and more organizations: **layoff-survivor sickness.** It's a set of attitudes, perceptions, and behaviors of employees who remain following involuntary employee reductions.[44] Symptoms of this sickness include job insecurity, perceptions of unfairness, depression, stress from increased workloads, fear of change, loss of loyalty and commitment, reduced effort, and an unwillingness to do anything beyond the required minimum job requirements.[45]

To address this survivor syndrome, HRM may want to provide opportunities for employees to talk to counselors about their guilt, anger, and anxiety. Group discussions can also provide an opportunity for the "survivors" to vent their feelings. Some organizations have used downsizing efforts as the spark to implement increased employee participation programs such as empowerment and self-managed work teams. In short, to keep morale and productivity high, every attempt should be made to ensure that those individuals who are still working in the organization know that they are a valuable and much-needed resource.

SUMMARY

This summary relates to the Learning Objectives provided on p. 128.

After having read this chapter, you should know:

1. Human resource planning is the process by which an organization ensures that it has the right number and kinds of people capable of effectively and efficiently completing those tasks that are in direct support of the company's mission and strategic goals.

2. The steps in the human resource planning process include mission formulating, establishing corporate goals and objectives, assessing current human resources, estimating the supplies and demand for labor, and matching demand with current supplies of labor. The two outcomes of this process are recruitment and decruitment.

3. A Human Resource Management System is useful for

quickly fulfilling human resource management information needs by tracking employee information and having that information readily available when needed.

4. Job analysis is a systematic exploration of the activities surrounding and within a job. It defines the job's duties, responsibilities, and accountabilities.

5. The six general techniques for obtaining job information are observation method, individual interview method, group interview method, structured interview method, technical conference method, and diary method.

6. The steps involved in conducting the job analysis include: (a) understanding the purpose of conducting the job analysis; (b) understanding the role of jobs in the organization; (c) benchmarking positions; (d) determining how you want to collect job analysis information; (e) seeking clarification, wherever necessary; (f) developing the first draft of the job description; and (g) reviewing the draft with the job supervisor.

7. Job descriptions are written statements of what the jobholder does (duties and responsibilities); job specifications identify the personal characteristics required to perform successfully on the job; and job evaluation is the process of using job analysis information in establishing a compensation system.

8. Downsizing refers to the process of restructuring the organization that results in the organization reducing its number of employees. Rightsizing may involve downsizing, but more appropriately focuses on having the right people available to work on activities directly related to the strategic direction of the company.

9. The layoff-survivor sickness reflects a set of attitudes, perceptions, and behaviors of employees who have kept their jobs after downsizing has occurred. Symptoms of this sickness include job insecurity, perceptions of unfairness, depression, stress from increased workloads, fear of change, loss of loyalty and commitment, reduced effort, and an unwillingness to do anything beyond the required minimum job requirements.

10. Outplacement services are programs offered by an employer to assist employees being retrained, or those severed from the organization, in obtaining employment. These services include training, resume writing, interviewing techniques, office and clerical assistance, and career counseling.

EXPERIENTIAL EXERCISE:
Job Analysis Information

Describe and compare the technical, people, and conceptual knowledge or skills required to perform tasks of a human resources manager effectively. You may ob-

tain samples directly from a company's manager, with permission, interview a human resources manager, or use any of the related Web sites such as

HR Headquarters

http:www.hrq.com.

Technical

People

Conceptual

Based upon the values indicated in the company's information, what values will be important for the human resources manager to personally possess and how will these be demonstrated in that role?

WEB-WISE EXERCISES

Search and print findings about interviewing, resumes, and job listings from

Jobtrack
http://www.jobtrack.com/

Web Wise
Search and print an occupational title and/or description from the site

U.S. Department of Labor
http://www.dol.gov/ (which links to several department agencies under the Department of Labor supervision)

CASE APPLICATION:
Smelly's Shoes

At 18, Page White began her career with Smelly's Shoes, a shoe retailer, as a stock clerk. Her desire to interact with customers, combined with a knowledge of the shoes and their manufacturers, led her to apply and be promoted to floor salesperson within the first six months. Today, six years later, Page is Regional Manager of a four state area, with combined sales of 2.4 million dollars, from 14 stores, and 143 employees. Sam Smelly believed that anyone, even his relatives, should start the same place he did: at the bottom, then go as far as their energy, talent, desire, and abilities could take them. Promotion from within is embedded in Smelly's culture and heritage, believing that success comes from not only knowing your products, customers, and function, but also the company.

Smelly's management expects employees to assume

responsibility for their own careers and to let management know what position they wish to hold, what they want to learn, and what their long and short term goals are. Such a philosophy isn't for everyone. There is a 22% turnover for new hires within the first year, but it drops to 3% for managers who have adapted to a culture of such high expectations. Page, impressed with your initiative as a part time student and part time employee, challenges you with a special assignment: Page asks you to help her develop a new position titled **"Human Rersource Manager,"** and suggests that if you perform well in the following special assignment, you may be on your way to fast tracking your career at Smelly's too.

Specifically, she asks you to develop a job description, an advertisement for Smelly's Shoes' newsletter, and a job analysis for a **Human Resource Manager** who will report to her at job grade S9. She would like to meet within one week to discuss the descriptions, newsletter advertisement, type of job analysis used and why, and your internal recruiting suggestions.

You are to bring a rough draft for **Human Resource Manager** description and analysis to the meeting. Based upon your drafts an internal search for best candidates will begin.

Assignment

Prepare the following:

1. Job description (to include purpose, duties and responsibilities, work experience requirements, working relationships, educational requirements, skills and competencies, expectations and success factors).
2. Describe the job analysis you will use and why.
3. Internal recruiting suggestions.
4. Create a sample newsletter advertisement.

TESTING YOUR UNDERSTANDING

How well did you fulfill the learning objectives?

1. Diane is vice president of human resources of a large manufacturing firm. When should she become involved in human resource planning for her organization?
   a. She should do all of it as part of her job.
   b. She should never be involved in it. That function belongs in financial management and marketing.
   c. Her real contribution comes after organizational assessment is completed.
   d. She should be included in mission development.
   e. She should be included in the maintenance phase.
2. Supply and demand forecasts, combined, provide all of the following for human resource managers except
   a. highlighting areas where overstaffing might currently exist.
   b. highlighting areas where overstaffing might exist in the future.
   c. pinpointing anticipated shortages in engineering areas.
   d. pinpointing anticipated budget changes in recruiting and maintenance.
   e. keeping abreast of opportunities to stockpile good people for anticipated needs.
3. The vice president of human resources in a large manufacturing firm has just received a gap analysis report. It indicated staffing needs over the next five years for one hundred additional shipping clerks, one hundred fewer shop technicians, one hundred additional sales representatives, and one hundred fewer research specialists. What should the vice president do?
   a. Internal transfers can take care of all these needs.
   b. Corporate outplacement services need to be secured for four hundred employees over the next five years.
   c. Recruiting efforts for research areas need to be increased immediately.
   d. Examine current human resource inventories to determine retirement, internal transfers, and probable dismissals over the next five years.
   e. No additional shipping clerk candidates should be interviewed for five years.
4. Human Resource Management Systems usage has grown significantly in recent years for all of these reasons except
   a. skill demands have become less complex for most of the work force.
   b. technology costs have come down.
   c. managers are often overwhelmed with information.
   d. systems are more user friendly.
   e. staffing decisions need to be made more quickly.
5. During a job analysis, all of these tasks are performed except
   a. duties and responsibilities of a job are defined.
   b. a description of what happens on a job is provided.
   c. skills and abilities necessary to perform a job are precisely identified.
   d. basic pay ranges for a job are set.
   e. conditions under which a job should be performed are described.
6. Job analysis can be performed in all of these ways except
   a. observing hourly workers.
   b. reviewing exit interviews conducted with departing employees.
   c. studying diaries or daily journals that managers kept over a three-month period.
   d. listening to fifteen assembly line workers in a group discussion.
   e. giving workers checklists to indicate which tasks on the list are performed during job execution.

7. Manny, the director of job analysis, must write job descriptions for two hundred new jobs in a new plant for his large manufacturing firm. The new robotics line will make this location different from the other five sites. Ten new supervisors have been recruited from outside the organization because of their experience with robotics production technology. Ten current supervisors have been sent to robotics production training. In addition, 150 workers have been targeted to work on the line, but none of them has any robotics experience. Which job analysis method do you recommend Manny use?
   a. observation
   b. structured questionnaire
   c. technical conference
   d. diary
   e. gap analysis

8. The Purdue University Position Analysis Questionnaire (PAQ) and the Department of Labor Job Analysis Process (JAP) are accurately compared with which statement?
   a. The PAQ is the same as the JAP.
   b. The PAQ is used to develop the JAP.
   c. The PAQ produces a more quantitative and finely tuned job description than the JAP.
   d. The PAQ works more effectively for white-collar, managerial jobs, while the JAP is more effective for blue-collar, unskilled jobs.
   e. The JAP is used only in the public sector. The PAQ is used only in the private sector.

9. Which statement best compares job specifications and job descriptions?
   a. Job description focuses on qualifications for jobholders. Job specification focuses on what the jobholder does.
   b. Job specification focuses on qualifications for jobholders. Job description focuses on what the jobholder does.
   c. Job specification occurs before job analysis. Job description occurs after job analysis.
   d. Job description is the same as job specification.
   e. Job specification occurs after job analysis. Job description occurs before job analysis.

10. Which statement accurately reflects the current state of job analysis in most organizations today?
    a. Job analysis is not done.
    b. Job analysis is performed by senior human resources professionals.
    c. The primary purpose of job analysis is to assist in the recruiting and selection activities.
    d. Job analysis affects most HRM activities.
    e. Job analysis is developed from the human resource skills inventory.

11. Sarah is vice president of human resources in a medium-sized manufacturing firm. She's being sued under the Americans with Disabilities Act for not hiring Mary, who is confined to a wheelchair, to work in the plant. Which document should she use in her company's defense?
    a. Job description
    b. Job analysis
    c. Job evaluation
    d. Affirmative action report
    e. Job specification

12. If outplacement costs can range into thousands of dollars per employee, why do downsizing organizations have outplacement centers?
    a. They do not. Downsizing organizations use outplacement firms.
    b. They do not. Outplacement is only performed by organizations in growth mode.
    c. The costs are overstated. Outplacement is usually around $100 per employee.
    d. Outplacement is a refocused goal in the downsizing organization to reward loyalty and commitment in employees.
    e. Outplacement centers are required under Title VII.

Endnotes

1. Michael P. Cronin, "The Affordable HR Pro," *Inc.* (October 1994), p. 121.
2. See, for example, Max Messmer, "Strategic Staffing for the 90s," *Personnel Journal* (October 1990), p. 92.
3. Patrick M. Wright, Dennis L. Smart, and Gary C. McMahan, "Matches Between Human Resources and Strategy Among NCAA Basketball Teams," *Academy of Management Journal,* Vol. 38, No. 4 (Winter 1995), pp. 1052–1074; Martin J. Plevel, Sandy Nells, Fred Lane, and Randall S. Schuler, "AT&T Global Business Communications Systems: Linking HR with Business Strategy," *Organizational Dynamics* (1994), pp. 59–71. See also, Randall S. Schuler, "Strategic Human Resources Management: Linking the People with the Strategic Needs of the Business," *Organizational Dynamics* (1992), pp. 18–32.
4. Messmer, p. 96.
5. As previous users have concurred, while strategic planning cannot be oversimplified in a two-page discussion, a quick overview is in order. With respect to the strategic nature of business, we recommend for a comprehensive review of strategic planning: James Brian Quinn, Henry Mintzberg, and Robert M. James, *The Strategic Process* (Englewood Cliffs, N.J.: Prentice-Hall, 1988).
6. Amy Barrett and Gail DeGeorge, "Home Improvement at Black & Decker," *Business Week* (May 11, 1998), pp. 54–56.
7. Goals that are established are a function of a number of factors. Such issues as the economy, government influences, market maturity, technological advances, company image, and location will factor into the analysis. See, for example, Henry J. Sredl and William J. Rothwell, *Professional Training Roles and Competencies,* Vol. 1 (Maine: HRD Press, 1987), p. 154.
8. Todd S. Nelson, "Continental Banks on New Hiring Plan," *Personnel Journal* (November 1990), p. 95.

9. Ibid., p. 95.

10. See, for instance, John E. Delery, and D. Harold Doty, "Modes of Theorizing in Strategic Human Resource Management: Tests of Universalistic Contingency and Configurational Performance Predictions," *Academy of Management Journal,* Vol. 38, No. 4 (August 1996), pp. 802–835.

11. Joan E. Goodman, "Does Your HRS Speak English?" *Personnel Journal* (March 1990), p. 81.

12. William A. Minneman, "Strategic Justification for an HRIS that Adds Value," *HRMagazine* (December 1996), pp. 35–38.

13. Sandra E. O'Connell, "Systems Issues of International Business," *HRMagazine* (March 1997), pp. 36–41.

14. Jeffrey B. Arthur, "Effects of Human Resource Systems on Manufacturing Performance and Turnover," *Academy of Management Journal,* Vol. 37, No. 3 (Summer 1994), pp. 670–687.

15. See, for example, John Spirig, "HRIS," *Employment Relations Today,* Vol. 16, No. 54 (Winter 1989/1990), pp. 347–50.

16. Stephen G. Perry, "The PC-Based HRIS," *Personnel Administrator* (February 1988),

17. Even with new generation software, some difficulties still exist. For example, generating reports still requires knowledge of computer "lingo."

18. Jeffrey Knapp, "Trends in HR Management Systems," *Personnel* (April 1990), pp. 56–57. See also John P. Polard, "HRIS: Time Is of the Essence," *Personnel Journal* (November 1990), pp. 42–43.

19. Ibid., pp. 60–61.

20. David Greising, "What Other CEOs Can Learn from Goizueta," *Business Week* (November 3, 1997), p. 38; and Jennifer Wing, "Succession Planning Smooths Return to Business-as-Usual," *HR News* (May 1996), p. 11.

21. John A. Byrne, Jennifer Reingold, and Richard A. Melcher, "Wanted: A Few Good CEOs," *Business Week* (August 11, 1997), pp. 64–70.

22. Linda Grant, "GE: The Envelope Please," *Fortune* (June 26, 1995), p. 89; Tim Smart, "Who Could Replace Jack Welch," *Business Week* (May 29, 1995), p. 32; and William M. Carley, CEO's Heart Surgery Is Giving GE a Case of Succession Jitters," *The Wall Street Journal* (May 24, 1995), pp. A-1; A-5.

23. Jennifer Wing, "Co-Workers Absorb Loss of Leaders in Plane Crash," *HR News* (May 1996), pp. 1; 10.

24. "Succession: Are You Prepared?" *HRMagazine* (November 1996), p. 19.

25. See, for example, Courtney von Hippel, Stephen L. Mangum, David B. Greenberger, Robert L. Heneman, and Jeffrey D. Skoglind, "Temporary Employment: Can Organizations and Employees Both Win," *Academy of Management Executive* (February 1997), pp. 93–103; Thomas C. Greble, "A Leading Role for HR in Alternative Staffing," *HRMagazine* (February 1997), pp. 99–103; Michael A. Verespej, "Skills on Call," *Industry Week* (June 3, 1996), pp. 46–51; Richard A. Melcher, "Manpower Upgrades Its Resume," *Business Week* (June 10, 1996), pp. 81–82; Glenn Burkins, "Temporary Employment Is Growing in Popularity, Some Schools Report," *The Wall Street Journal* (June 4, 1996), p. A-1; Lucy A. Newton, "Stiff Competition for Talented Temps," *HRMagazine* (May 1996), pp. 91–94; "Rent-a-Worker," *Profiles* (October 1995), p. 15; and Paul Klebnikov, "Focus, Focus, Focus," *Forbes* (September 11, 1995), pp. 42–44.

26. Mark Henricks, "Time Out," *Entrepreneur* (October 1995), pp. 70–74.

27. Commerce Clearing House, "Sabbaticals: a Good Investment for McDonald's," *Human Resources Management: Ideas and Trends* (May 11, 1994), pp. 77, 84.

28. Richard Henderson, *Compensation Management: Rewarding Performance,* 6th ed. (Englewood Cliffs, N.J.: Prentice Hall, 1994), p. 137.

29. Sidney A. Fine, *Functional Job Analysis Scales: A Desk Aid,* No. 7 (Kalamazoo, Mich.: WE UpJohn Institute for Employment Research, 1973).

30. Henderson, p. 168.

31. See Wayne Casio, *Applied Psychology in Personnel Management,* 4th ed. (Englewood Cliffs, N.J.: Prentice Hall, 1991), p. 207; see also Stephanie K. Butler and Robert J. Harvey, "A Comparison of Holistic Versus Decomposed Rating of Position Analysis Questionnaire Work Dimensions" *Personnel Psychology,* Vol. 41, No. 4 (Winter 1988), pp. 761–71.

32. Tomasz Mroczkowski and Masao Hannaoka, "Effective Rightsizing Strategies in Japan and America: Is There a convergence of Employment Practices," *Academy of Management Executive,* Vol. 11, No. 2 (May 1997), pp. 57–66.

33. See, for example, Louis S. Richman, "America's Tough New Job Market," *Fortune* (February 24, 1992), pp. 52–61.

34. See for example, John A. Byrne, "Why Downsizing Looks Different These Days," *Business Week* (October 19, 1994), p. 43.

35. Data taken from: "Taking an Ax to Allied," *Business Week* (November 4, 1991), p. 70; Donna Milbank, "Goodyear Plans to Further Cut Its Work Force," *The Wall Street Journal* (March 14, 1991), p. A-4; Neil Templin, "Ford to End Some Benefits to Executives, Cut Payroll," *The Wall Street Journal* (March 1, 1991), p. A-1; Laurie M. Grossman, "Pepsi to Take $62.3 Million in Change While Cutting 1,800 Jobs at Frito-Lay," *The Wall Street Journal* (September 17, 1991), p. A-4; and Paul B. Carroll, "IBM Plans $3 Billion Charge and About 20,000 Jobs Cut," *The Wall Street Journal* (November 27, 1991), p. A-3.

36. John E. Gutknecht and J. Bernard Keys, "Mergers, Acquisitions, and Takeovers: Maintaining Morale of Survivors and Protecting Employees," *Academy of Management Executive,* Vol. 7, No. 3 (1993), p. 26.

37. John A. Byrne, p. 43.

38. See, for example, Richard L. Bunning, "The Dynamics of Downsizing," *Personnel Journal* (September 1990), p. 73.

39. Ibid.; see also Elaine M. Duffy, Richard M. O'Brien, William P. Brittian, and Stephen Cuthrell, "Behavioral Outplacement: A Shorter, Sweeter Approach," *Personnel* (March 1988), pp. 28–33.

40. Bunning, p. 73; see also Robert Volino, "Beyond Outplacement," *Information Week* (February 18, 1991), p. 24.

41. "Most Employers Laud `Outplacement' Firms, but Few Demur," *The Wall Street Journal* (October 1, 1991), p. A-1.

42. See, for instance, D. M. Noer, *Healing the Wounds* (San Francisco, CA: Jossey-Bass, 1993).

43. Ibid., p. 11.

44. Ibid., p. 13; see also "Survivors of Layoffs Often Feel Guilty," *Manpower Argus* (November 1996), p. 10; see also Elizabeth Wolfe Morrison and Sandra Robinson, "When Employees Feel Betrayed: A Model of How Psychological Contract Violation Develops," *Academy of Management Journal,* Vol. 22, No. 1 (January 1997), pp. 226–256.

45. Tom Brown "Sweatshops of the 1990s," *Management Review* (August 1996), pp. 13–18.

6. Recruiting and the Foundations of Selection

LEARNING OBJECTIVES

After reading this chapter, you will be able to:

1. Define what is meant by the term *recruiting*.
2. Identify the dual goals of recruiting.
3. Explain what constrains human resource managers in determining recruiting sources.
4. Identify the principal sources involved in recruiting employees.
5. Discuss the benefits derived from a proper selection process.
6. Identify the primary purpose of selection activities.
7. Describe the selection process.
8. List three types of validity.
9. Explain how validity is determined.
10. Define validity generalization.

After organizations have established their strategic direction and developed a corresponding employment plan, the organization must turn its attention to getting the right people. The jobs that have been identified, and their associated skills point to very specific types of employees that are required. But these employees don't just magically appear—nor do they frequently come knocking on the organization's door. Instead, the company must embark on an employment process of finding and hiring qualified people.

That process starts when the organization notifies the "public" that openings exist. The organization wants to get its information out such that a large number of potentially qualified applicants respond. Then, after several interactions with the most promising of these candidates, employees are hired. These candidates will best demonstrate the skills, knowledge, and abilities to successfully perform the job.

Years ago, this entire process was dominated by paper and face-to-face interactions. Technology, today, is changing that. For individuals like Henry Liang, the job search has gone to the "Net."[1] Many jobs in organizations today are

Henry Liang found a unique way to demonstrate to prospective employers that he was "technology" oriented. Instead of mass mailing resumés, Henry developed a web page, and let recruiters review his actual skills and abilities. While paper methods still are dominant, the use of the Internet in the years ahead appears to be helping to better match employees with the jobs employers have.

heavily influenced by technology. In fact, technology-related jobs in the United States grew by 320 percent in the late 1990s, and that growth is predicted to continue through the early years of the new millennium.[2] Accordingly, candidates must be able to demonstrate that they have the requisite skills to meet and offer something to organizations. But explaining them in a letter to an employer often doesn't have the same effect as showing potential employers what you can do. When Henry, a University of Pennsylvania senior, wanted to let employers know he understood technology, he opted for an electronic resumé. By developing a "home page" on the Internet, Liang was able to refer potential employers to his Web page that he had designed. The electronic resumé, however, was only the beginning. Through the creation of links to other Web pages, applicants—like Henry—are able to refer recruiters to a variety of Web sites that provide substantial data about them. For example, Liang provided the details about his college, as well as his major course of study, showed some of his completed works, and even graphically highlighted other pertinent data about his "fit" with the organization.

The use of the Internet for job hunting will continue to gain momentum. (We'll look at this phenomenon more in Appendix A.) It's also safe to say that a competitive advantage can be gained for highly technical jobs by using the Internet as a means of displaying one's skills. And in the end, as Henry Liang found, that's what employers really wanted.

INTRODUCTION

Successful human resource planning is designed to identify an organization's human resource needs. Once these needs are known, an organization will want to do something about meeting them. The next step, then, in the staffing function—assuming, of course, that demand for certain skills, knowledge, and abilities is greater than the current supply—is recruiting. This activity makes it possible for a company to acquire the people necessary to ensure the continued operation of the organization. *Recruiting* is the process of discovering potential candidates for actual or anticipated organizational vacancies. Or, from another perspective, it is a linking activity—bringing together those with jobs to fill and those seeking jobs.

In this chapter, we'll explore the activities surrounding "getting" employees into the organization. We'll do this by looking at the fundamental activities surrounding recruiting and selection.

RECRUITING GOALS

For the recruiting process to work effectively, there must be a significant pool of candidates to choose from—and the more diversity within that group the better. Achieving a satisfactory pool of candidates, however, may not be that easy, especially in a tight labor market. For example, CDI, the largest engineering services firm in the United States, was having difficulty filling such jobs as product designer and computer modelers. As an incentive to boost the number of applicants, the company offered a drawing for a multipurpose vehicle, or a Caribbean cruise for two, to those qualified individuals who sent resumes.[3] The first goal of recruiting, then, is to communicate the position in such a way that job seekers respond. Why? The more applications received, the better the recruiter's chances for finding an individual who is best suited to the job requirements.

Simultaneously, however, the recruiter must provide enough information about the job that unqualified applicants can self-select themselves out of job candidacy. For instance, when Ben & Jerry's was searching for a new CEO a few years ago, someone with a conservative political view, with a classical, bureaucratic perspective of management, would not want to apply because that individual wouldn't fit the renowned countercultural ways of the company. Why is having potential applicants remove themselves from the applicant pool important to human resource management? Typically, when applications are received, the company acknowledges their receipt. That acknowledgment costs time and money. Then there are the application reviews and a second letter sent, this time rejecting the applications. Again, this incurs some costs. Accordingly, whenever possible, applications from those who are unqualified must be discouraged. A good recruiting program should attract the qualified, and not the unqualified. Meeting this dual objective will minimize the cost of processing unqualified candidates.

Factors That Affect Recruiting Efforts

Although all organizations will, at one time or another, engage in recruiting activities, some do so to a much larger extent than others. Obviously, size is one factor; an organization with 100,000 employees will find itself recruiting continually. So, too, will fast-food firms, smaller-service organizations, as well as firms that pay lower wages. Certain other variables will also influence the extent of recruiting. Employment conditions in the community where the organization is located will influence how much recruiting takes place. The effectiveness of past recruiting efforts will show itself in the organization's historical ability to locate and keep people who perform well. Working conditions and salary and benefit packages offered by the organization will influence turnover and, therefore, the need for future recruiting. Organizations that are not growing, or those that are actually declining, may find little need to recruit. On the other hand, organizations that are growing rapidly, like Home Depot, Nucor, and U.S. Healthcare will find recruitment a major human resource activity.[4]

Recruitment efforts, even in these growing companies, are no easy task. Recall in Chapter 2 the discussion of skill deficiencies. Quality workers are becoming harder to locate. Therefore, HRM will have to develop new strategies to locate and hire those individuals possessing the skills the company needs.[5] United Parcel Service (UPS), for example, found a creative way to locate talented people.[6] Having problems finding workers in its three New Jersey facilities, UPS met with a local public employment agency that offered, among other services, employment counseling. By UPS describing the type of employee it was seeking, this agency sought to match its clients with UPS needs. This cooperation effort resulted in about 1,500 new employees for the company.

Constraints on Recruiting Efforts

While the ideal recruitment effort will bring in a satisfactory number of qualified applicants who will take the job if it is offered, the realities cannot be ignored. For example, the pool of qualified applicants may not include the "best" candidates; or the "best" candidate may not want to be employed by the organization. These and other **constraints on recruiting efforts** limit human resource recruiters' freedom to recruit and select a candidate of their choice. However, we can narrow our focus by suggesting five specific constraints.

Image of the Organization   We noted that the prospective candidate may not be interested in pursuing job opportunities in the particular organization. The image of the organization, therefore, should be considered a potential constraint. If that image is perceived to be low, the likelihood of attracting a large number of applicants is reduced.[7] Many college graduates know, for example, that the individuals who occupy the top spots at Disney earn excellent salaries, are given excellent benefits, and are greatly respected in their communities. Among most college graduates, Disney has a positive image. The hope of having a shot at one of its top jobs, being in the spotlight, and having a position of power results in Disney having little trouble in attracting college graduates into entry-level positions. Microsoft, too, enjoys a positive image—to the point where the company receives more than 12,000 resumés a month![8] But not all graduates hold a positive image of some large organizations. More specifically, their image of some organizations is pessimistic. In a number of communities, local firms have a reputation for being in a declining industry; engaging in practices that result in polluting the environment, poor-quality products, and unsafe working conditions; or being indifferent to employees' needs. Such reputations can and do reduce these organizations' abilities to attract the best personnel available.[9]

> **Microsoft Corporation receives more than 12,000 resumes a month.**

Attractiveness of the Job   If the position to be filled is an unattractive job, recruiting a large and qualified pool of applicants will be difficult. In recent years, for instance, many employers have been complaining about the difficulty of finding suitably qualified individuals for "manual labor" positions. In a job market where unemployment rates are low, and where a wide range of opportunities exists creating competition for these workers, a shortage results. Moreover, any job that is viewed as boring, hazardous, anxiety-creating, low-paying, or lacking in promotion potential seldom will attract a qualified pool of applicants. Even during economic slumps, people have refused to take many of these jobs.[10]

Internal Organizational Policies   Internal organizational policies, such as "promote from within wherever possible," may give priority to individuals inside the organization. Such policies, when followed, typically ensure that all positions, other than the lowest-level entry positions, will be filled from within the ranks. Although this is promising once one is hired, it may reduce the number of applications.[11]

Government Influence   The government's influence in the recruiting process should not be overlooked. An employer can no longer seek out preferred individuals based on non-job-related factors such as physical appearance, sex, or religious background. An airline wishing to staff all its flight attendant positions with attractive females will find itself breaking the law if comparably qualified male candidates are rejected on the basis of sex—or female candidates are rejected on the basis of age.

Recruiting Costs   The last constraint, but certainly not lowest in priority, is one that centers on recruiting costs. Recruiting efforts by an organization are expensive. Sometimes continuing a search for long periods of time is not possible because of budget restrictions. Accordingly, when an organization considers various recruiting sources, it does so with some sense of effectiveness in mind—like maximizing its recruiting travel budget by first interviewing employees over the phone or through videoconferencing.

RECRUITING FROM AN INTERNATIONAL PERSPECTIVE

When beginning to recruit for overseas positions, the first step, as always, is to define the relevant labor market.[12] For international positions, however, that market is the whole world.[13] As mentioned in Chapter 2, we first must decide if we want to send an American overseas, recruit in the host country where the position is, or ignore nationality and do a global search for the best person available.[14] Thus, our possibilities are to select someone from the United States, the host country, or a third country. It's important to make a proper choice, if for no other reason than it's estimated that the cost of failure in an international assignment approximates $250,000.[15]

To some extent, this basic decision depends on the type of occupation and its requirements, as well as the stage of national and cultural development of the overseas operations. Although production, office, and clerical occupations are rarely filled beyond a local labor market, executive and sometimes scientific, engineering, or professional managerial candidates may be sought in national or international markets. If the organization is searching for someone with extensive company experience to launch a very technical product in a country where it has never sold before, it will probably want a home-country national. This approach is often used when a new foreign subsidiary is being established and headquarters wants to control all strategic decisions, but technical expertise and experience are needed. It is also appropriate where there is a lack of qualified host-country nationals in the work force.

In other situations it might be more advantageous to hire a **host-country national (HCN),** assuming there is a choice. For an uncomplicated consumer product it may be a wise corporate strategic decision to have each foreign subsidiary acquire its own distinct national identity.[16] Clothing has different styles of merchandising, and an HCN may have a better feel for the best way to market the sweaters or jeans of an international manufacturer.

Sometimes the choice may not be entirely left to the corporation. In some countries, most African nations for example, local laws control how many **expatriates** a corporation can send. There may be established ratios, such as twenty host-country nationals must be employed for every American granted working papers. Using HCNs eliminates language problems and avoids problems of expatriate adjustment and the high cost of training and relocating an expatriate with a family. It also minimizes one of the chief reasons international assignments fail—the family's inability to adjust to their new surroundings.[17] Even when premiums are paid to lure the best local applicants away from other companies, the costs of maintaining the employee are significantly lower than with sending an American overseas. In some countries, where there are tense political environments, an HCN is less visible and can somewhat insulate the U.S. corporation from hostilities and possible terrorism.

The third option, recruiting regardless of nationality, develops an international executive cadre with a truly global perspective. On a large scale this type of recruiting may reduce national identification of managers with particular organizational units. For example, automobile manufacturers may develop a Taiwanese parts plant, a Mexican assembly operations, and a U.S. marketing team, creating internal status difficulties through its different treatment of each country's employees.

RECRUITING SOURCES

Recruiting is more likely to achieve its objectives if recruiting sources reflect the type of position to be filled. For example, an ad in the business employment section of *The Wall Street Journal* is more likely to be read by a manager seeking an executive position in the $150,000-to-$225,000-a-year bracket than by an automobile assembly-line worker seeking to find employment. Similarly, an interviewer who is seeking to fill a management training position and visits a two-year vocational school in search of a college graduate with undergraduate courses in engineering and a master's degree in business administration is looking for "the right person in the wrong place."

Certain recruiting sources are more effective than others for filling certain types of jobs. As we review each source in the following sections,[18] the strengths and weaknesses in attempting to attract lower-level and managerial-level personnel will be emphasized.

The Internal Search

Many large organizations will attempt to develop their own employees for positions beyond the lowest level. These can occur through an **internal search** of current employees, who have either bid for the job, been identified through the organization's human resource management system, or even been referred by a fellow employee. The advantages of such searches—a "promote from within wherever possible" policy—are:[19]

▶ It is good public relations.

▶ It builds morale.

▶ It encourages good individuals who are ambitious.

▶ It improves the probability of a good selection, since information on the individual's performance is readily available.

▶ It is less costly than going outside to recruit.

▶ Those chosen internally already know the organization.

▶ When carefully planned, promoting from within can also act as a training device for developing middle- and top-level managers.

There can be distinct disadvantages, however, to using internal sources. It can be dysfunctional to the organization to utilize inferior internal sources only because they are there, when excellent candidates are available on the outside. However, an individual from the outside, in contrast with someone already employed in the organization, may appear more attractive because the recruiter is unaware of the outsider's faults. Internal searches may also generate infighting among the rival candidates for promotion, as well as decreasing morale levels of those not selected.

The organization should also avoid excessive inbreeding. Occasionally it may be necessary to bring in some "new blood" to broaden the current ideas, knowledge, and enthusiasm, and to question the "we've-always-done-it-that-way" mentality. As noted in the discussion of human resource inventories in Chapter 5, the organization's HRM files should provide information as to which employees might be considered for positions opening up within the organization. Most organizations can utilize their computer information system to generate an output of those individuals who have the desirable characteristics to potentially fill the vacant position.

In many organizations, it is standard procedure to post any new job openings and to allow any current employee to "apply" for the position. This action, too, receives favorable marks from the EEOC. The posting notification can be communicated on a central "positions open" bulletin board in the plants or offices, in the weekly or monthly organization newsletter, or, in some cases, in a specially prepared posting sheet from human resources outlining those positions currently available. Even if current employees are not interested in the position, they can use these notices to individuals for employment within the organization—the employee referral.

Employee Referrals/Recommendations

One of the best sources for individuals who will perform effectively on the job is a recommendation from a current employee.[20] Why? Because employees rarely recommend someone unless they believe that the individual can perform adequately. Such a recommendation reflects on the recommender, and when someone's reputation is at stake, we can expect the recommendation to be based on considered judgment. **Employee referrals** also may have acquired more accurate information about their potential jobs. The recommender often gives the applicant more realistic information about the job than could be conveyed through employment agencies or newspaper advertisements. This information reduces unrealistic expectations and increases job survival. As a result of these pre-selection factors, employee referrals tend to be more acceptable applicants, to be more likely to accept an offer if one is made, and, once employed, to have a higher job survival rate. Additionally, employee referrals are an excellent means of locating potential employees in those hard-to-fill positions. For example, because of the difficulty in finding computer programmers, engineers, or nurses with specific skills required by the organization, some organizations have turned to their employees for assistance. In many of these organizations, these specifically identified hard-to-fill positions include a reward if an employee referral candidate is hired. In doing so, both the organization and the employee benefit; the employee receives a monetary reward and the organization receives a qualified candidate without the major expense of an extensive recruiting search.

There are, of course, some potentially negative features of employee referral. For one thing, recommenders may confuse friendship with job performance competence. Individuals often like to have their friends join them at their place of employment for social and even economic reasons; for example, they may be able to share rides to and from work. As a result, a current employee may recommend a friend for a position without giving an unbiased consideration to the friend's job-related competence. Employee referrals may also lead to nepotism, that is, hiring individuals who are related to persons already employed by the organization. Although such actions may not necessarily align with the objective of hiring the most qualified applicant, interest in the organization and loyalty to it may be long-term advantages. Finally, employee referrals may also minimize an organization's desire to add diversity to the work place.[21]

Employee referrals do, however, appear to have universal application. Lower-level and managerial-level positions can, and often are, filled by the recommendation of a current employee. In higher-level positions, however, it is more likely that the referral will be a professional acquaintance rather than a friend with whom the recommender has close social contact. In jobs where specialized expertise is important, and where employees participate in professional organizations that foster the development of this expertise, it can be expected that current employees will be acquainted with, or know about, individuals they think would make an excellent contribution to the organization.

The External Searches

In addition to looking internally for candidates, it is customary for organizations to open up recruiting efforts to the external community. These efforts include advertisements, employment agencies, schools, colleges and universities, professional organizations, and unsolicited applicants.

Advertisements　　The sign outside the construction location reads: "Now Hiring—Carpenters." The newspaper advertisement reads:

> *Telemarketing Sales. We are looking for someone who wants to assume responsibility and wishes to become part of the fast-growing cellular telephone business. No previous sales experience required. Salary to $35,000. For appointment, call Mr. Reynolds at 1-888-555-0075.*

Most of us have seen both types of advertisements. When an organization wishes to communicate to the public that it has a vacancy, advertisement is one of the most popular methods used. However, where the advertisement is placed is often determined by the type of job. Although it is not uncommon to see blue-collar jobs listed on placards outside the plant gates, we would be surprised to find a vice presidency listed similarly. The higher the position in the organization, the more specialized the skills, or the shorter the supply of that resource in the labor force, the more widely dispersed the advertisement is likely to be. The search for a top executive might include advertisements in a national publication, like *The Los Angeles Times,* for example. On the other hand, the advertisement of lower-level jobs is usually confined to the local daily newspaper or regional trade journal.

A number of factors influence the response rate to advertisements. There are three important variables: identification of the organization, labor market conditions, and the degree to which specific requirements are included in the advertisement. Some organizations place what is referred to as a **blind-box ad,** one in which there is no specific identification of the organization. Respondents are asked to reply to a post office box number or to an employment firm that is acting as an agent between the applicant and the organization. Large organizations with a national reputation seldom use blind advertisements to fill lower-level positions; however, when the organization does not wish to publicize the fact that it is seeking to fill an internal position, or when it seeks to recruit for a position where there is a soon-to-be-removed incumbent, a blind-box advertisement may be appropriate.

Although blind ads can assist HRM in finding qualified applicants, many individuals are reluctant to answer them. Obviously, there is the fear, sometimes unjustified, that the advertisement has been placed by the organization in which the individual is currently employed. Also, the organization itself is frequently a key determinant of whether the individual is interested; therefore, potential candidates may be reluctant to reply. Further deterrents are the bad reputation that advertisements have received because of organizations that place ads when no position exists in order to test the supply of workers in the community, to build a backlog of applicants, or to identify those current employees who are interested in finding a new position; or to satisfy affirmative action requirements when the final decision, for the greater part, has already been made.

The job analysis process is the basic source for the information placed in the ad. A decision must be made as to whether the ad will focus on descriptive elements of the job (job description) or on the applicant (job specification). The choice made will often affect the number of replies received. If, for example, you are willing to sift through 1,000 or more responses, you might place a national ad in *The New York Times* or the *Chicago Tribune,* or a regional newspaper's employment section similar to the one in Exhibit 6-1. However, an advertisement in these papers that looks like Exhibit 6-2 might attract less than a dozen replies.

The difference between Exhibits 6-1 and 6-2 is obvious. Exhibit 6-1 uses more applicant-centered criteria to describe the successful candidate. Most individuals perceive themselves as having confidence and seeking high "income." More important, how can an employer measure these qualities? The response rate should therefore be high. In contrast, Exhibit 6-2 describes a job requiring precise abilities and experience. The requirements of at least "seven years of progressive experience in nursing leadership," a master's in Nursing Administration, and a doctorate in a related field are certain to limit the respondent pool.

SALES: ADVANCE YOUR CAREER

$95,000/YEAR
SALES/MANAGEMENT
$170,000 + YEARLY

We are a dynamic national marketing organization in MD, D.C., & VA, offering individual and corporate benefit packages.

WE OFFER YOU

- $1,000-$4,000 weekly comm.
- Rapid advancement/management opportunities
- 20 Qualified leads every week
- 5 day work week
- Trips for 2, twice yearly
- Incentives & bonuses

WE WANT

Enthusiastic, positive, goal oriented people who want to be in control of their lives and income. Truly a ground floor opportunity for those who have what it takes to succeed. If you are one of these people and are looking for an unlimited opportunity and $100,000 your first year, call Monday.

SOURCE: Anonymous, printed in *The Sunday Sun: Employment* (October 30, 1994).

Exhibit 6-1

Job advertisement with a high response rate likely.

Employment Agencies   We will describe three forms of employment agencies: public or state agencies, private employment agencies, and management consulting firms. The major difference between these three sources is the type of clientele served. All states provide a public employment service. The main function of these agencies is closely tied to unemployment benefits, since benefits in some states are given only to individuals who are registered with their state employment agency. Accordingly, most public agencies tend to attract and list individuals who are unskilled or have had minimum training. This, of course, does not reflect on the agency's competence, but rather, on the image of public agencies. State agencies are perceived by prospective applicants as having few high-skilled jobs, and employers tend to see such agencies as having few high-skilled applicants. Therefore public agencies tend to attract and place predominantly low-skilled workers. The agencies' image as perceived by both applicants and employers thus tends to result in a self-fulfilling prophecy; that is, few high-skilled individuals place their names with public agencies, and, similarly, few employers seeking individuals with high skills list their vacancies or inquire about applicants at state agencies.

Vice President, Nursing. Merryvale Medical Center, a 665-bed community teaching medical center located in Cleveland, Ohio, is seeking a top-level, highly creative nursing executive who will be a key member of the leadership team within the Merryvale Health System. The successful candidate will work closely with corporate officers, physicians, and staff in continuing the growth of the Medical Center. The position will be responsible for all aspects of nursing operations, including administration, education, research and practice; will be fiscally accountable for the nursing department; and will be responsible for the delivery of innovative models for interdisciplinary care. This person will possess a progressive vision of professional nursing practice and a proven track record as a leader in the nursing field. A Master's in Nursing Administration, plus the possession of a doctorate (Ph.D., Sc.D., Ed.D.) in a related field; 7–10 years' progressive experience in nursing leadership; and licensure as a registered nurse are required.

SOURCE: Adapted from Christina Murray Younger, Manager, Employment Services, *The Baltimore Sun*, (July 31, 1994).

Exhibit 6-2

Job advertisement with a low response rate likely.

Charging upwards of 35 percent of a manager's first-year's salary means that excellent services must be provided to an organization. Executive search firms, like Tampa, Florida-based Sterling-Sharpe, do just that. In essence, they perform most of the "recruiting" activities for an organization for a specific position, and present a slate of qualified candidates for final selection by client members.

Yet this image may not always be the case. For example, a nationwide computer network at the Employment Security Commission acts as a clearinghouse for professional-level jobs. In this case, a public agency may be a good source for such applicants.

How does a private employment agency, which has to charge for its services, compete with state agencies that give their service away? They must do something differently from what the public agencies do, or at least give that impression.[22]

The major difference between public and private employment agencies is their image; that is, private agencies are believed to offer positions and applicants of a higher caliber. Private agencies may also provide a more complete line of services. They may advertise the position, screen applicants against the criteria specified by the employer, and provide a guarantee covering six months or a year as protection to the employer should the applicant not perform satisfactorily. The private employment agency's fee can be totally absorbed by either the employer or the employee, or it can be split. The alternative chosen usually depends on the demand–supply situation in the community involved.

The third agency source consists of the management consulting, **executive search,** or "headhunter" firms. Agencies of this type—such as Korn/Ferry and Heidrick & Struggles—are actually specialized private employment agencies. They specialize in middle-level and top-level executive placement,[23] as well as hard-to-fill positions such as actuaries or computer programmers. In addition to the level at which they recruit, the features that distinguish executive search agencies from most private employment agencies are their fees, their nationwide contacts, and the thoroughness of their investigations. In searching for an individual of vice-president caliber, whose compensation package may be far in excess of $200,000 a year, the potential employer may be willing to pay a very high fee to locate exactly the right individual to fill the vacancy. A fee up to 35 percent of the executive's first-year salary is not unusual as a charge for finding and recruiting the individual.[24]

Executive search firms canvass their contacts and do preliminary screening. They seek out highly effective executives who have the skills to do the job, can effectively adjust to the organization, and most important, are willing to consider new challenges and opportunities. Possibly such individuals are frustrated by their inability to move up in their current organization at the pace at which they are capable, or they recently may have been bypassed for a major promotion. The executive search firm can act as a buffer for screening candidates and, at the same time, keep the prospective employer anonymous.[25] In the final stages, senior executives in the prospective firm can move into the negotiations and determine the degree of mutual interest.

Schools, Colleges, and Universities

Educational institutions at all levels offer opportunities for recruiting recent graduates. Most educational institutions operate placement services where prospective employers can review credentials and interview graduates. Most also provide employers an opportunity to witness a "prospective employee's" performance through cooperative arrangements and internships.[26]

Whether the educational level required for the job involves a high-school diploma, specific vocational training, or a college background with a bachelor's, master's, or doctoral degree, educational institutions are an excellent source of potential employees.[27]

High schools or vocational–technical schools can provide lower-level applicants; business or secretarial schools can provide administrative staff personnel; and two- and four-year colleges and graduate schools can often provide professional and managerial-level personnel. While educational institutions are usually viewed as sources for inexperienced entrants to the work force, it is not uncommon to find individuals with considerable work experience using an educational institution's placement service. They may be workers who have recently returned to school to upgrade their skills, or former graduates interested in pursuing other opportunities.

Professional Organizations

Many **professional organizations,** including labor unions, operate placement services for the benefit of their members. The professional organizations include such varied occupations as industrial engineering, psychology, accounting, legal, and academics. These organizations publish rosters of job vacancies and distribute these lists to members. It is also common practice to provide placement facilities at regional and national meetings where individuals looking for employment and companies looking for employees can find each other—building a network of employment opportunities.

Professional organizations, however, can also apply sanctions to control the labor supply in their discipline. For example, although the law stipulates that unions cannot require employers to hire only union members, the mechanisms for ensuring that unions do not break this law are poorly enforced. As a result, it is not unusual for labor unions to control supply through their apprenticeship programs and through their labor agreements with employers. Of course, this tactic is not limited merely to blue-collar trade unions. In those professional organizations where the organization placement service is the focal point for locating prospective employers, and where certain qualifications are necessary to become a member (such as special educational attainment or professional certification or license), the professional organization can significantly influence and control the supply of prospective applicants.

Cyberspace Recruiting   One of the newer arenas for locating resumes of qualified employees is looking on the Internet.[28] Companies like Eli Lilly, Grolier Electronic Publishing, Wells Fargo Bank, Fidelity Investments, General Electric, Levi Strauss, Bristol Technology, and Cisco Systems have found the use of the World-Wide-Web advantageous in filling their positions.[29] In fact, nearly half of all major U.S. companies use the Internet to recruit for positions from the "$15,000 entry level jobs to senior executive posts paying deep into six figures." [30] Individuals like Henry Liang, too, have found that using his own web page has given him greater exposure to potential employers, and in doing so, demonstrates certain skills that he possesses. As we move forward in the years ahead, we can expect Web searches—for both employers and employees—to become a more abundant element in the recruiting process.[31]

Unsolicited Applicants   Unsolicited applications, whether they reach the employer by letter, telephone, or in person, constitute a source of prospective applicants. Although the number of unsolicited applicants depends on economic conditions, the organization's image, and the job seeker's perception of the types of jobs that might be available, this source does provide an excellent supply of stockpiled applicants. Even if there are no particular openings when the applicant contacts the organization, the application can be kept on file for later needs.

Unsolicited applications made by unemployed individuals, however, generally have a short life. Those individuals who have adequate skills and who would be prime candidates for a position in the organization if a position were currently available usually find employment with some other organization that does have an opening. However, in times of economic stagnation, excellent prospects are often unable to locate the type of job they desire and may stay actively looking in the job market for many months.

Applications from individuals who are already employed can be referred to many months later and can provide applicants who (1) are interested in considering other employment opportunities, and (2) regard the organization as a possible employer.

Recruitment Alternatives

Much of the previous discussion on recruiting sources implies that these efforts are designed to bring into the organization full-time, permanent employees. However, economic realities, coupled with management trends such as rightsizing, have resulted in a slightly different focus. Companies today are looking at hiring temporary help (including retirees), leasing employees, and using the services of independent contractors.[32]

Temporary Help Services   Organizations like the Kelly Temporary Services, Accountemps, and Temp-Force Inc. can be a source of employees when individuals are needed on a temporary basis. Temporary employees are particularly valuable in meeting short-term fluctuations in HRM needs.[33] While traditionally developed in the office administration area, the temporary staffing service has expanded its coverage to include a broad range of skills. It is now possible, for example, to hire temporary nurses, computer programmers, accountants, librarians, drafting technicians, secretaries, even CEOs.[34]

Software development companies have to be especially creative in finding qualified applicants. Using the technologies that are available, companies like CLAM Associates, a Cambridge, Massachusetts software developer, are going into cyberspace to search for applicants. Kathy Santos, CLAM's Webmaster, has designed a homepage that informs applicants about job openings, as well as educates these applicants about the company. Kathy's work is paying off, as she receives about five applications each day from the Web site.

In addition to specific temporary help services, another quality source of temporary workers is older workers, those who have already retired or have been displaced by rightsizing in many companies.[35] An aging work force and an individual's desire to retire earlier, have created skill deficiencies in some disciplines. Older workers bring those skills back to the job. In fact, at Monsanto, the company has capitalized on this rich skill base by establishing its own temporary, in-house employment agency, the Retiree Resource Corps (RRC).[36] Then, when there is a need for temporary help somewhere in the organization, the RRC provides the needed talent pool. For Monsanto, such a temporary work force is saving the company almost $2 million a year.

While the reasons many of these older workers wish to continue to work vary,[37] they bring with them several advantages. These include "flexibility in scheduling, low absenteeism, high motivation, and mentoring abilities for younger workers."[38] It was these very attributes that the first ten sales representatives of Everyday Learning Company, the Evanston, Illinois, publishing organization specializing in elementary school math curriculum books, brought to the job.[39] By their fifth year, they had helped the founder, Jo Anne Schiller, build a business that generates more than $2 million annually and has its books in over 2,000 schools.

Employee Leasing   Whereas temporary employees come into an organization for a specific short-term project, leased employees typically remain with an organization for longer periods of time. Under a leasing arrangement, individuals work for the leasing firm.[40] When an organization has a need for specific employee skills, it contracts with the leasing firm to provide a certain number of trained employees. For example, consider Robert Half International. As a leasing firm, Robert Half has on its staff fully trained accountants ready to meet an organization's accounting needs. If tax season requires additional tax accountants, Robert Half can supply them; the same holds true for other accounting areas. One reason for leasing's popularity is cost.[41] The acquiring organization pays a flat fee for the employees. The company is not responsible for benefits

Hiring Contingent Workers

Hiring temporary or contingent workers provides an organization with great flexibility. It enables the organization to deal with peak performance times without having to add permanent staff to its payroll. For many workers, especially older workers and individuals who wish to spend more time on personal matters, like child rearing, this part-time work serves a fundamental need. It permits them to explore those things they prefer to explore, without being hampered by the requirements of a full-time position. But not every contingent worker sees part-time work in the same light. It is suggested that almost several million workers would prefer to work full-time, but can't find anything but part-time employment. As such, the organizational emphasis on a contingent work force is adversely affecting today's workers.

Part-time workers often don't receive the benefits that full-time employees get. They often receive no health insurance benefits, nor enjoy an opportunity to participate in a company-sponsored retirement plan. They have little opportunity, if any, of career advancement, and their tenure with an organization is as long as the project they are working on.

Organizations, however, appear to gain in this scenario. Hiring contingent workers is a cost-effective means of staffing the organization. And, oftentimes, by employing part-time employees, they may be exempt from certain federal EEO regulations. But that may not make it right. Are these organizations exploiting contingent workers? Are they acting responsibly toward a society that keeps them in business? Or are we headed down that proverbial historical path where one day, more federal legislation will be passed to protect the contingent worker? The Clinton administration's desire for 100 percent health coverage of all Americans was brought to the forefront because so many workers, like the contingent work force, did not have health insurance. Are organizations exploiting contingent workers? What do you think?

or other costs, like social security payments, it would incur for a full-time employee. This is because leased employees are, in fact, employees of the leased firm. Furthermore, when the project is over, employees are returned to the leasing company, thus eliminating any cost associated with layoffs or discharge.

Leased employees are also well-trained individuals. They are screened by the leasing firm, trained appropriately, and often go to organizations with an unconditional guarantee. Thus, if one of these individuals doesn't work out, the company can get a new employee, or make arrangements to have its fee returned. There are also benefits from the employee's point of view. Some of today's workers prefer more flexibility in their lives. Working with a leasing company and being sent out at various times allows these workers to work when they want, for the length of time they desire. But a word of caution exists with respect to **employee leasing.** The IRS has very stringent requirements that must be met for an organization to legitimately hire employees under a leasing arrangement.

Independent Contractors   Another means of recruiting is the use of independent contractors. Often referred to as consultants, independent contractors are taking on a new meaning. Companies may hire independent contractors to do very specific work at a location on or off the company's premises. For instance, claims-processing, or medical and legal transcription activities can easily be done at one's home and forwarded to the employer on a routine basis. With the growing use of personal computers, fax machines, and voice mail, employers can ensure that home work is being done in a timely fashion.

Independent contractor arrangements benefit both the organization and the individual. Because the company does not have to regard this individual as an employee, it saves costs associated with full-or part-time personnel, like social security taxes and workers' compensation premiums. Additionally, such opportunity is also a means of keeping good individuals associated with your company. Suppose an employee wants to work, but also be at home when the kids are home. This cannot be done through typical work arrangements, but allowing the individual to work at home, on his or her time, can generate a win–win solution to the problem.

Last Call

We have identified a number of sources of potential candidates. If we've achieved our goal and located a number of qualified applicants, it's time to begin to filter through the stack. This filtering process is called selection.

GOALS OF THE SELECTION PROCESS

A recent HRM graduate went on her first interview.[42] Not knowing what to expect, she prepared as best she could. She was dressed exquisitely in a new navy pinstriped suit and was carrying her new black leather Tumi briefcase. As she entered the human resource management office, she encountered two doors. On the first door was, "Human Resource Management Majors." On the second was, "All Other Majors." She entered door 1, which opened up to two more doors. On door 1 was, "3.45 or better GPA"; door 2, "All Other GPAs." Having a 3.73 GPA, she once again entered door 1, and found herself facing yet two more choices. Door 1 stated, "Took Compensation and Benefits Course," and door 2, "Didn't Take Compensation and Benefits." Because this course was not required for her major, she went through door 2. Upon opening the door, she found a box with preprinted letters saying, "Your qualifications did not meet the expectations of the job. Thanks for considering our organization. Please exit to the right."

Although fictional, this story illustrates the fundamental issues involved in the selection process. All selection activities exist for the purpose of making effective selection decisions. Each activity is a step in the process that results in a prediction—managerial decision makers seeking to predict which job applicants will be successful if hired. Successful, in this case, means performing well on the criteria the organization uses to evaluate its employees. For a sales position, for example, the criteria should be able to indicate to the assessors which applicants will generate a high volume of sales; for a teaching position, such as a college professor, they should predict which applicants will get high student evaluations or generate many high-quality publications or both.

The Selection Process

Selection activities typically follow a standard pattern, beginning with an initial screening interview and concluding with the final employment decision. The **selection process** typically consists of eight steps: (1) initial screening interview, (2) completing the application form, (3) employment tests, (4) comprehensive interview, (5) background investigation, (6) a conditional job offer; (7) medical or physical examination, and (8) the permanent job offer. Each step represents a decision point requiring some affirmative feedback for the process to continue. Each step in the process seeks to expand the organization's knowl-

Exhibit 6-3 The selection process

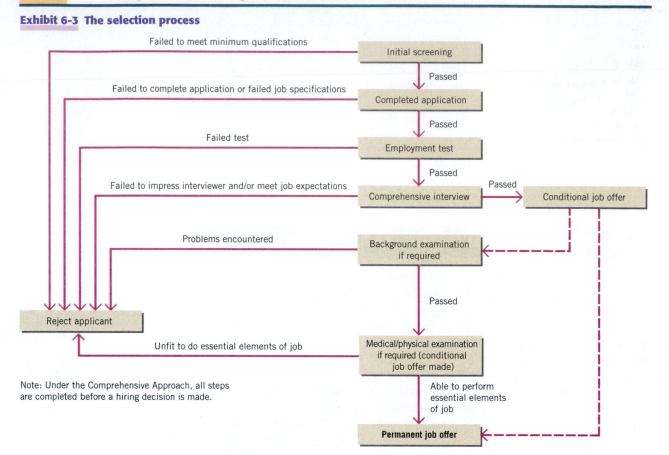

Note: Under the Comprehensive Approach, all steps
are completed before a hiring decision is made.

edge about the applicant's background, abilities, and motivation, and it increases the information from which decision makers will make their predictions and final choice. However, some steps may be omitted if they do not yield data that will aid in predicting success, or if the cost of the step is not warranted. Applicants should also be advised what specific screening will be done, such as credit checks, reference checking, and drug tests. The flow of these activities is depicted in Exhibit 6-3. Let us take a closer look at each.

Initial Screening   As a culmination of our recruiting efforts, we should be prepared to initiate a preliminary review of potentially acceptable candidates. This **initial screening** is, in effect, a two-step procedure: (1) the screening of inquiries and (2) the provision of screening interviews.

If our recruiting effort has been successful, we will be faced with a number of potential applicants. Based on the job description and job specification, some of these respondents can be eliminated. Factors that might lead to a negative decision at this point include inadequate or inappropriate experience, or inadequate or inappropriate education. There might also be other "red flags" identified, such as gaps in the applicant's job history, many brief jobs, or numerous courses and seminars instead of appropriate education.

The screening interview is also an excellent opportunity for HRM to describe the job in enough detail so the candidates can consider whether they are really serious about applying. Sharing job description information with the individual frequently encourages the unqualified or marginally qualified to voluntarily withdraw from candidacy, with a minimum of cost to the applicant or the organization. Costs, too, can be minimized with the screening interview by using videoconferencing.[43]

Another important point during the initial screening phase is to identify a salary range. Most workers are concerned about their salaries, and while a job opening may sound exciting, a low salary may preclude an organization from obtaining excellent talent. During this phase, if proper HRM activities have been conducted, there should be no need to mask salary data.

Completion of the Application Form   Once the initial screening has been completed, applicants are asked to complete the organization's **application form.** The amount of information required may be only the applicant's name, address, and telephone number. Some organizations, on the other hand, may request the completion of a more comprehensive employment profile. In general terms, the application form gives a job-performance-related synopsis of what applicants have been doing during their adult life, their skills, and their accomplishments.

Applications are also useful in that they obtain information the company wants. Additionally, completing the application serves as another hurdle; that is, if the job requires one to follow directions and the individual fails to do so on the application, that is a job-related reason for rejection. Lastly, applications require a signature attesting to the truthfulness of the information given, and to give permission to check references. If at a later point the company finds out the information is false, it can result in the immediate dismissal of the individual.

Employment Tests   Organizations historically relied to a considerable extent on intelligence, aptitude, ability, and interest tests to provide major input to the selection process. Even handwriting analysis (graphology) and honesty tests have been used in the attempt to learn more about the candidate—information that supposedly leads to more effective selection.

Technology is assisting recruiters in cost-saving ways. Whereas face-to-face interviews previously involved paying for someone to travel to the company's location (or the recruiter going to the applicant), technology is eliminating much of that expense. Through the use of videoconferencing, recruiters can replicate the "visual" aspects of face-to-face interviews, at a fraction of the cost.

In the 1970s and early 1980s, reliance on traditional written tests for selection purposes decreased significantly. This was attributed directly to legal rulings requiring employers to justify as job-related any test that is used.[44] Given the historical difficulty and costs in substantiating this relationship, some organizations merely eliminated employment testing as a selection device.

Since the mid–1980s, however, that trend has reversed. It is estimated that more than 60 percent of all organizations use some type of employment test today.[45] For these organizations, there is recognition that scrapping employment tests was equivalent to "throwing out the baby with the bath water." They have come to recognize that some tests are quite helpful in predicting who will be successful on the job. The key in employment testing, then, is to use a test that accurately predicts job performance. We will discuss the issue of predicting job success later in the chapter.

The Comprehensive Interview   Those applicants who pass the initial screening, application form, and required tests are typically given a **comprehensive interview.** The applicant may be interviewed by HRM interviewers, senior managers within the organization, a potential supervisor, potential colleagues, or some or all of these. In fact, in a company like Disney, applicants are interviewed by some forty people.[46]

The comprehensive interview is designed to probe areas that cannot be addressed easily by the application form or tests, such as assessing one's motivation, ability to work under pressure, and ability to "fit in" with the organization.[47] However, this information must be job related. The questions asked and the topics covered should reflect the job description and job specification information obtained in the job analysis. This means that not only the "obvious" illegal questions should be avoided, so too should inappropriate questions.[48] We'll take a much more in-depth look at interviews in the next chapter.

> **The interview is designed to assess one's motivation and ability to fit into the organization.**

Background Investigation   The next step in the process is to undertake a **background investigation** of those applicants who appear to offer potential as employees. This can include contacting former employers to confirm the candidate's work record and to obtain their appraisal of his or her performance, contacting other job-related and personal references, verifying the educational accomplishments shown on the application,[49] verifying an individual's legal status to work in the United States (via the Employment Eligibility Verification, I-9 Form; see Exhibit 6-4), checking credit references and criminal records; and even using third-party investigators, like Pinkerton Investigative Services, to do the background check.[50]

Common sense dictates that HRM find out as much as possible about its applicants before the final hiring decision is made. Failure to do so can have a detrimental effect on the organization, both in terms of cost and morale. But getting the needed information may be difficult, especially when there may be a question about invading one's privacy. In the past, many organizational policies stated that any request for information about a past employee be sent to HRM. Then, HRM typically only verified employment dates and positions held. Why? Companies wanted to stay away from being sued by a previous employee and simply verified "the facts."[51] But that has changed.

Based on a concept of **qualified privilege,** some courts have ruled that employers must be able to talk to one another about employees. Additionally, about half of the states have laws which protect employers from "good-faith ref-

EMPLOYMENT ELIGIBILITY VERIFICATION (Form I-9)

Exhibit 6-4

Immigration Reform and Control Act of 1986

1	**EMPLOYEE INFORMATION AND VERIFICATION:** (To be completed and signed by employee.)

Name: (Print or Type) Last	First	Middle	Birth Name

Address: Street Name and Number	City	State	ZIP Code

Date of Birth (Month/Day/Year)		Social Security Number	

I attest, under penalty of perjury, that I am (check a box):

☐ 1. A citizen or national of the United States.

☐ 2. An alien lawfully admitted for permanent residence (Alien Number A _____).

☐ 3. An alien authorized by the Immigration and Naturalization Service to work in the United States (Alien Number A _____ ,

or Admission Number _____ , expiration of employment authorization, if any _____).

I attest, under penalty of perjury, the documents that I have presented as evidence of identity and employment eligibility are genuine and relate to me. I am aware that federal law provides for imprisonment and/or fine for any false statements or use of false documents in connection with this certificate.

Signature	Date (Month/Day/Year)

PREPARER/TRANSLATOR CERTIFICATION (To be completed if prepared by person other than the employee). I attest, under penalty of perjury, that the above was prepared by me at the request of the named individual and is based on all information of which I have any knowledge.

Signature	Name (Print or Type)	
Address (Street Name and Number)	City	State	Zip Code

2	**EMPLOYER REVIEW AND VERIFICATION:** (To be completed and signed by employer.)

Instructions:

Examine one document from List A and check the appropriate box, _OR_ examine one document from List B _and_ one from List C and check the appropriate boxes. Provide the *Document Identification Number* and *Expiration Date* for the document checked.

List A	List B	List C
Documents that Establish Identity and Employment Eligibility	Documents that Establish Identity **and**	Documents that Establish Employment Eligibility
☐ 1. United States Passport	☐ 1. A State-issued driver's license or a State-issued I.D. card with a photograph, or information, including name, sex, date of birth, height, weight, and color of eyes. (Specify State)_____)	☐ 1. Original Social Security Number Card (other than a card stating it is not valid for employment)
☐ 2. Certificate of United States Citizenship		☐ 2. A birth certificate issued by State, county, or municipal authority bearing a seal or other certification
☐ 3. Certificate of Naturalization	☐ 2. U.S. Military Card	
☐ 4. Unexpired foreign passport with attached Employment Authorization	☐ 3. Other (Specify document and issuing authority)	☐ 3. Unexpired INS Employment Authorization Specify form
☐ 5. Alien Registration Card with photograph		# _____
Document Identification	*Document Identification*	*Document Identification*
# _____	# _____	# _____
Expiration Date (if any)	*Expiration Date (if any)*	*Expiration Date (if any)*
_____	_____	_____

CERTIFICATION: I attest, under penalty of perjury, that I have examined the documents presented by the above individual, that they appear to be genuine and to relate to the individual named, and that the individual, to the best of my knowledge, is eligible to work in the United States.

Signature	Name (Print or Type)	Title
Employer Name	Address	Date

Form I-9 (05/07/87)
OMB No. 1115-0136

U.S. Department of Justice
Immigration and Naturalization Service

erences."[52] Accordingly, these discussions may be legal and may not invade one's right to privacy so long as the discussion is a legitimate concern for the business—and in some cases if the applicant has given permission for the background investigation to take place. For example, had a Midwest hospital learned that one of its anesthesiologist applicants had lost his license in three states for substance abuse, it clearly would not have hired him.[53]

Moreover, some courts have also endorsed a company defense called the "After-Acquired Evidence Doctrine," which has been used to significantly reduce the organization's liability to discrimination claims. The essence of this controversial doctrine involves evidence that a company acquires after some action has been taken against an employee—like a termination. In cases where this defense has been used, the courts have ruled that even if discrimination did occur, the company may not be responsible because some sort of "resumé fraud" existed. Of course, the company had to have made its hiring decision without this information, and the employee's action involved some sort of misconduct that company policy indicates could be grounds for dismissal.[54]

Conditional Job Offer If a job applicant has "passed" each step of the selection process so far, it is typically customary for a **conditional job offer** to be made. Conditional job offers usually are made by an HRM representative (we'll revisit this momentarily). In essence, what the conditional job offer implies is that if everything checks out "okay—passing a certain medical, physical, or substance abuse test—" the conditional nature of the job offer will be removed and the offer will be permanent.

Physical/Medical Examination The next to last step in the selection process may consist of having the applicant take a **medical/physical examination.** Remember, however, that in doing so a company must show that the reasoning behind this requirement is job related. Physical exams can only be used as a selection device to screen out those individuals who are unable to physically comply with the requirements of a job. For example, firefighters are required to perform a variety of activities that require a certain physical condition. Whether it is climbing a ladder, lugging a four-inch water-filled hose, or carrying an injured victim, these individuals must demonstrate that they are fit for the job.

Aside from its use as a screening tool, there is another purpose for the physical exam: to show that minimum standards of health exist to enroll in company health and life insurance programs. Additionally, a company may use this exam to provide base data in case of an employee's future claim of injury on the job. This occurs, however, after one has been hired. In both cases, the exam is paid for by the employer.

One last event fits appropriately under medical examination: the drug test. As we'll mention in Chapter 13, increasingly more companies require applicants to submit to a drug test. Where in this process that test occurs is somewhat immaterial; the fact remains that failing an employment drug test may result in the rejection of an applicant.

Job Offer Those individuals who perform successfully in the preceding steps are now considered to be eligible to receive the employment offer. Who makes the final employment offer? The answer is, it depends. For administrative purposes (processing salary forms, maintaining EEO statistics, ensuring a statement exists which states that employment is not guaranteed, etc.), the offer typically is made by an HRM representative. But that individual's role should be only administrative. The actual hiring decision should be made by the manager in the department where the vacancy exists. While this might not be the situation in all organizations, the manager of the department should have this authority. First, the applicant will eventually work for this manager and therefore a good "fit" between boss and employee is necessary. Second, if the decision made is not correct, the hiring manager has no one else to blame. It's also important to remember—as we previously mentioned in recruiting—that those finalists who don't get hired deserve the courtesy of being notified that they didn't get the job.

It's Now Up to the Candidate

If the organization selection process has been effective in differentiating between those individuals who will make successful employees and those who will not, the selection decision is now in the hands of the applicant. Is there anything management can do at this stage to increase the probability that the individual to whom an offer is made will accept? Assuming that the organization has not lost sight of the process of selection's dual objective—evaluation and a good fit—we can expect that the potential employee has a solid understanding of the job being offered and what it would be like to work for the organization. Yet it might be of interest at this point to review what we know about how people choose a job. This subject—job choice—represents selection from the perspective of the potential employee rather than the organization.

Research indicates that people gravitate toward jobs that are compatible with their personal orientation.[55] Individuals appear to move toward matching their work with their personality. Social individuals lean toward jobs in clinical psychology, foreign service, social work, and the like. Investigative individuals are compatible with jobs in biology, mathematics, and oceanography. Careers in management, law, and public relations appeal to enterprising individuals. This approach to the matching of people and jobs suggests that management can expect a greater proportion of acceptances if it has properly matched the candidate's personality to the job and to the organization, making the good fit.[56]

Not surprisingly, most job choice studies indicate that an individual's perception of the attractiveness of a company is important.[57] People want to work where their expectations are positive and where they believe their goals can be achieved. This, coupled with conclusions from previous research, should encourage management to ensure that those to whom offers are made can see that the job is compatible with their personality and goals.[58]

Before we leave this last step in the selection process, we should ask, What about those applicants to whom we did not make an offer?[59] We believe that those involved in the selection process should carefully consider how rejected candidates are treated. What is communicated and how it is communicated will have a central bearing on the image that the rejected candidates will have of the organization. And that image may be carried for a lifetime. The young college graduate rejected for a position by a major computer manufacturer may a decade later be the influential decision maker for his or her current employer's computer purchases. The image formed many years earlier may play a key part in the decision. In this same vein, it was said that Richard Nixon never forgave FBI Director J. Edgar Hoover for the Bureau's rejection of Nixon's application following his graduation from law school.

The Comprehensive Approach

We have presented the general selection process as being comprised of multiple hurdles—beginning with a screening interview and culminating with a final selection decision. This discrete selection process is designed so that tripping over any hurdle puts one out of the race. This approach, however, may not be the most effective selection procedure for every job. If, for example, the application form shows that the candidate has only two years of relevant experience, but the job specification requires five, the candidate is rejected without going any further in the process. Yet, in many jobs, negative factors can be counterbalanced by positive factors.[60] Poor performance on a written test, for example, may be offset by several years of relevant job experience. This suggests that sometimes it may be advantageous to do comprehensive rather than discrete selection. In **comprehensive selection,** all applicants are put through every step of the selection process, and the final decision is based on a comprehensive evaluation of the results from all stages.

The comprehensive approach overcomes the major disadvantage of the discrete method (eliminating potentially good employees simply because they receive an acceptable, but low evaluation at one selection step). The comprehensive method is more realistic. It recognizes that most applicants have weaknesses as well as strengths. But it is also more costly, since all applicants must go through all the screening hurdles. Additionally, the method consumes more of management's time and can demoralize many applicants by building up hope. Yet in those instances where many qualities are needed for success in the job, and where finding candidates who are strong on all qualities is unlikely, the comprehensive approach is probably preferable to the typical discrete method.

No matter which approach is used or which steps are involved, one critical aspect must be present: the devices used must measure job-related factors; that is, these devices must be able to indicate how one would perform on the job. That's critical for business success; and it's necessary to defend and respond to an allegation that the hiring practices are discriminatory.

KEY ELEMENTS FOR SUCCESSFUL PREDICTORS

We are concerned with selection activities that can help us predict which applicants will perform satisfactorily on the job. In this section, we want to explore the concepts of reliability, validity, and cut scores. For illustration purposes, we will emphasize these elements as they relate to employment tests, but they are relevant to any selection device.

Reliability

For any predictor to be useful, the scores it generates must possess an acceptable level of **reliability** or consistency of measurement. This means that the applicant's performance on any given selection device should produce consistent scores each time the device is used.[61] For example, if your height were measured every day with a wooden yardstick, you would get highly reliable results, but if you were measured daily by an elastic tape measure, there would probably be considerable disparity between your height measurements from one day to the next. Your height does not change from day to day—the variability is due to the unreliability of the measuring device.

Similarly, if an organization uses tests to provide input to the selection decision, the tests must give consistent results. If the test is reliable, any single individual's scores should remain fairly stable over time, assuming that the characteristic it is measuring is also stable. An individual's intelligence, for example, is generally a stable characteristic, and if we give applicants an IQ test, we should expect that someone who scores 110 in March would score close to 110 if tested again in July. If, in July, the same applicant scored 85, the reliability of the test would be highly questionable. On the other hand, if we were measuring something like an attitude or a mood, we would expect different scores on the measure, because attitudes and moods change.

Validity

High reliability may mean little if the selection device has low *validity,* that is, if the measures obtained are not related to some relevant criterion, such as job performance. For example, just because a test score is consistent is no indication that it is measuring important characteristics related to job behavior. It must also differentiate between satisfactory and unsatisfactory performance on the job. We should be aware of three specific types of validity: content, construct, and criterion related.

Content Validity   **Content validity** is the degree to which the content of the test or questions about job tasks, as a sample, represents the situations on the job. All candidates for that job are given the same test or questions so applicants can be properly compared. A simple example of a content-valid test is a typing test for a word-processing position. Such a test can approximate the work to be done on the job; the applicant can be given a typical sample of typing, and his or her performance can be evaluated based on that sample. Assuming that the tasks on the test, or the questions about tasks, constitute an accurate sample of the tasks on the job (ordinarily a dubious assumption at best), the test is content valid.[62]

Construct Validity   **Construct validity** is the degree to which a test measures a particular trait related to successful performance on the job.[63] These traits are usually abstract in nature, such as the measure of intelligence,[64] and are called constructs. Construct validity is complex and difficult. In fact, it is the most difficult type of validity to prove because you are dealing with constructs, or abstract measures.

Criterion-related Validity   **Criterion-related validity** is the degree to which a particular selection device accurately predicts the level of performance or important elements of work behavior. This validation strategy shows the relationship between some predictor (test score, for example) and a criterion, job performance (e.g., production output or managerial effectiveness). To establish criterion-related validity, either of two approaches can be used: **predictive validity** or **concurrent validity.**

To validate a test predictively, an organization would give the test (with an unknown validity) to all prospective applicants. The test scores would not be used at this time; rather, applicants would be hired as a result of successfully completing the entire selection process. At some prescribed date, usually at least a year after being hired, the applicants' job performance would be evaluated by their supervisors. The ratings of the evaluations would then be compared with the initial test scores, which have been stored in a file over the period. At that time, an analysis would be conducted to see if there was any relationship between test scores (the predictors) and performance evaluation (the measure of success on the job, or the criterion). If no clear relationship exists, the test may have to be revised. However, if the organization can statistically show that the employees who scored below some predetermined score, called a **cut score** (determined in the analysis), were unsuccessful performers, then management could appropriately state that any future applicants scoring below the cut score would be ineligible for employment. What happens to those unsuccessful performers? They are handled like any other employee who has experienced poor evaluations: training, transfer, discipline, or discharge.

The **concurrent validity** method validates tests using current employees as the subjects. These employees are asked to take a proposed selection test experimentally. Their scores are immediately analyzed, revealing a relationship

Exhibit 6-5

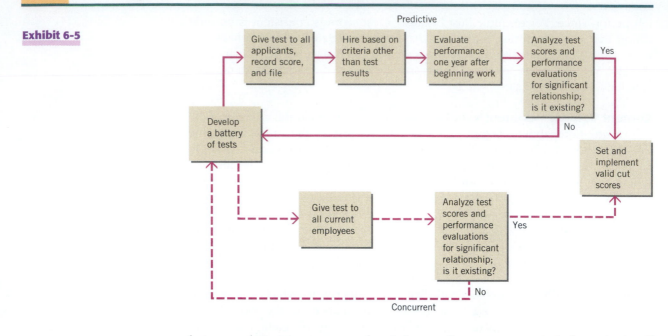

between their test scores and existing performance appraisal data. Again, if there is a relationship between test scores and performance, then a valid test has been found.

Predictive validity is the preferred choice. Its advantage over concurrent validity is that it is demonstrated by using actual job applicants, whereas concurrent validity focuses on current employees. Both validation strategies are similar, with the exception of the people who are tested and the time that elapses between gathering of predictor and criterion information (see Exhibit 6-5).

While the costs associated with each method are drastically different, predictive validation strategies should be used if possible. Concurrent validity, although better than no validity at all, leaves many questions to be answered.[65] Its usefulness has been challenged on the premise that current employees know the jobs already and that a learning process takes place. Thus, there may be little similarity between the current employee and the applicant.

The Validity Analysis

Correlation coefficients used to demonstrate the statistical relationships existing between an individual's test score and his or her job performance are called validity coefficients. The correlation analysis procedure can result in a coefficient ranging from $+1$ to -1 in magnitude. The closer the validity coefficient is to the extreme (1), the more accurate the test;[66] that is, the test is a good predictor of job performance. For example, Exhibit 6-6 contains two diagrams. In each diagram, we are trying to determine if a positive relationship exists between test scores and successful job performance.

In diagram A, there is no relationship. Statistically speaking, the score on the test bears no relationship between test score and performance. In this case, our test is not valid. It does not help us distinguish between the successful and unsuccessful job performers. Diagram B reveals that there is a positive relationship between test scores and job performance. Those individuals scoring higher

Exhibit 6-6 Validity correlation analysis.

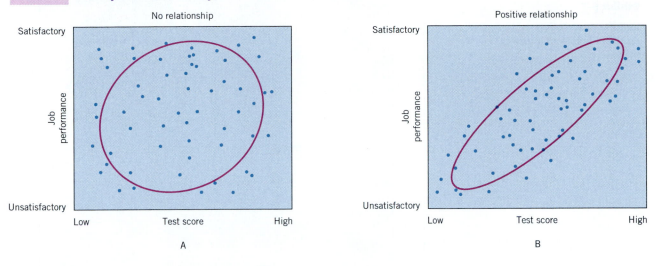

A

B

on the test have a greater probability of being successful in their jobs than those scoring lower. Based on this relationship, this test appears to be valid. When we have a valid test as determined by our correlation analysis, we are then able to identify the test score that distinguishes between successful and unsuccessful performers (the cut score).

Cut Scores and Their Impact on Hiring

In this discussion, we have been referring to test scores and their ability to predict successful job performance. By using our statistical analyses, we are able to generate a point at which applicants scoring below that point are rejected. We refer to this as a cut score.[67] However, existing conditions (e.g., availability of applicants) may cause an organization to change the cut score. If cut scores do change, what impact will this have on hiring applicants who will be successful on the job? Let us review again the positive relationship we found in our validity correlation analysis. We have reproduced the main elements in the graph in Exhibit 6-7. Let us assume that after our analysis, we determined that our cut score should be 70. At this cut score, we have shown that the majority of the applicants who scored above 70 have a greater probability of being successful performers on the job; the majority scoring below 70, unsuccessful performers. If we change our cut score, however, we alter the number of applicants in these categories. For example, suppose the organization faces a "buyer's market" for particular positions. Because of the many potential applicants, the organization can afford to be very selective. In a situation such as this, the organization may choose to hire only those applicants who meet the most extreme criteria. To achieve this goal, the organization increases its cut score to 98. By increasing the cut score from 70 to 98, the organization has rejected all but two candidates (areas A and B in Exhibit 6-7). However, many potentially successful job performers also would be rejected (individuals shown in area C). What has happened here is that the organization has become more selective and has put more faith in the test than is reasonable. If there were one hundred applicants and only two were hired, we could say that the selection ratio (the ratio of number hired to the number of applicants) is 2 percent. A 2

Exhibit 6-7

Validity correlation analysis after cut score is raised.

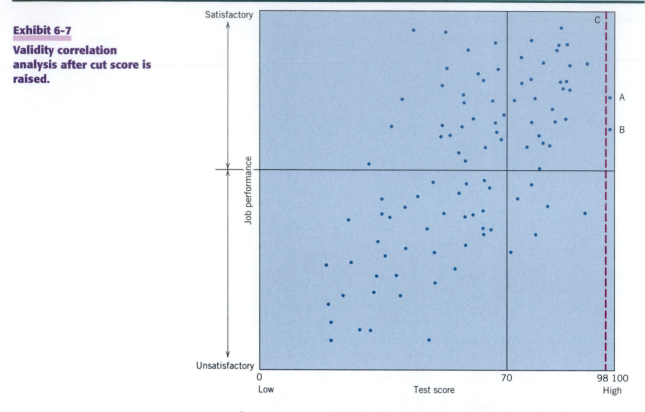

percent selection ratio means that the organization is very particular about who is hired.

Lowering the cut score also has an effect. Using the same diagram, let us lower our cut score to 50 and see what results. We have graphically portrayed this in Exhibit 6-8. By lowering the cut score from 70 to 50, we have increased our number of eligible hires who have a greater probability of being successful on the job (area D). At the same time, however, we have also made eligible more applicants who could be unsuccessful on the job (area E). Although using a hiring process where we know that more unsuccessful applicants may be hired seems not to make sense, conditions may necessitate the action. Labor market conditions may be such that there is a low supply of potential applicants who possess particular skills. For example, in some cities, finding a good computer modeler may be difficult. Because the supply is low, coupled with many openings, companies may hire individuals on the spot (more commonly referred to as an open-house recruiting effort). In this approach, the organization hires almost all the applicants who appear to have the skills needed (as reflected in a score of 50), putting them on the job, and filtering out the unsuccessful employees at a later date. While this may not appear to be effective, the organization is banking on the addition of individuals in area D of Exhibit 6-8.

Validity Generalization

In the late 1970s, two researchers published a model that was able to support a phenomenon called **validity generalization.**[68] Validity generalization refers to a situation where a test may be valid for screening applicants for a variety of jobs and performance factors across many occupations.[69] For example,

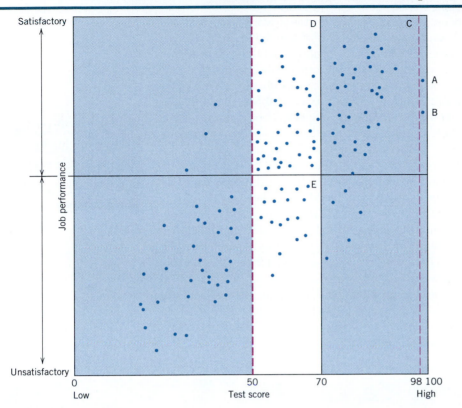

Exhibit 6-8

Validity correlation analysis after cut score is lowered.

the Department of Labor's General Aptitude Test (GATB) was shown to be valid for five hundred jobs studied in terms of the test's ability to predict job performance and training success irrespective of race.[70] What distinguishes validity generalization is its use of a statistical technique called *meta-analysis*. Through meta-analysis, researchers can determine correlations that may exist among numerous variables, and correct or adjust for any variances that may exist in predictor–criterion relationships.

SELECTION FROM AN INTERNATIONAL PERSPECTIVE

The selection criteria for international assignments are broader in scope than those for domestic selection. To illustrate the point, in addition to such factors as technical expertise and leadership ability, an international assignment requires greater attention to personality and especially to flexibility in the design. The individual must have an interest in working overseas and a talent for relating well to all types of people. The ability to relate to different cultures and environments, a sensitivity to different management styles, and a supportive family are often selection requirements.

Not surprisingly, many corporations consider personal factors of maturity and age, as well as the "family situation factor," far more important in their international assignments than in domestic placements. Although not all expatriates are married, many human resource managers believe that marital stability reduces a person's likelihood of returning home early and in many countries enhances the individual's social acceptability.[71]

American women have been successful in the business world, and it is unacceptable in our culture to discriminate on the basis of gender in employment, but organizations know that some Middle Eastern countries will not grant working papers to American women executives. On the other hand, in Asia, where common wisdom has held that women executives are less effective, the opposite has proven true! Although few Asian women are at or above middle-management levels, American women are often highly respected because they have risen to be experts in their fields. Thus, past reluctance to assign women to overseas positions where culture rather than law once made them rare is vanishing, and American women in Asia and Latin America are more common.[72] Not only may the candidate's gender be considered, but also the social acceptability of single parents, unmarried partners, and blended families.

> **Women executives from America are highly respected in Asia because they have risen to be experts in their fields.**

In addition, personal factors such as health, background, and education may be considered in international placements. In fact, the ideal candidate for many corporations is an older couple in good health, with no young children at home and a long and stable marital history. These are all factors that would play no role in domestic assignments.

When younger candidates are appropriate, many American corporations seek foreign students on U.S. university campuses who want to return to their home countries. These students provide a well-educated labor pool with experience in both their home and American cultures.

SUMMARY

This summary relates to the Learning Objectives provided on p. 154.

After having read this chapter, you should know:

1. Recruitment is the discovering of potential applicants for actual or anticipated organizational vacancies.
2. The two goals of recruiting are to generate a large pool of applicants from which to choose while simultaneously providing enough information for individuals to self-select out of the process.
3. Influences that constrain HRM in determining recruiting sources include image of the organization, attractiveness and nature of the job, internal policies, government requirements, and the recruiting budget.
4. The principal sources of recruiting employees include internal search, advertisements, employee referral/recommendations, employment agencies, temporary rental services, schools, colleges, universities, professional organizations, the Internet, and casual or unsolicited applicants. Employee leasing, temporary employees, and independent contractors continue to also be a good source of employees.
5. Proper selection can minimize the costs of replacement and training, reduce legal challenges, and result in a more productive work force.
6. The primary purpose of selection activities is to predict which job applicant will be successful if hired. During the selection process, candidates are also informed about the job and organization.

7. The discrete selection process would include the following: initial screening interview, completion of the application form, employment tests, comprehensive interview, background investigation, conditional job offer, physical or medical examination, and the permanent job offer.
8. There are three validation strategies. These are content, construct, and criterion-related validity.
9. Validity is determined either by discovering the extent to which a test represents actual job content, or through statistical analyses that show the test used relates to an important job-related trait, or to performance on the job.
10. Validity generalization refers to a process whereby tests are validated for numerous occupations through the use of meta-analysis.

EXPERIENTIAL EXERCISE:
Role-Play, The Interview Part 1

Alan Berstein is an impatient, results-oriented, innovative, hard-working focused entrepreneur, who likes to be surrounded with aggressive, highly creative skilled, focused team players that are flexible, change driven, informed, cutting edge skilled professionals much like himself in work ethic, but like diverse groups.

He believes that professionals with different backgrounds, culture, race, national origin, sex, and any other factors contribute to better solutions and creativity. He wants only those who are as committed as he is to growing a company that produces the industry standard which will become the benchmark in intranet and software technology. That means willing to work 60 or 90 hours a week if the project requires and dedication and passion to customers, HI-5-TECH, and the project team.

Mr. Berstein may start people out with slightly below industry average salaries, but you know he rewards performance and tenure. He's reputed to double a salary when a developer exceeds expectations. He also contributes his company's stock to employees' benefit package, subject to their length of employment, and at the current rate, a person might retire a millionaire if he or she can last the pace.

Still interested?

Discuss, why or why not, comparing responses with your paired team member.

Role play

Next, role play in pairs, one member choosing the role of Alan Berstein, the other as the applicant for the job of People Manager upon graduation. Switch roles. Reach a consensus which would progress to a second and final interview and why.

EXPERIENTIAL EXERCISE:
Role-Play, The Interview Part 2

Alan Berstein was impressed with your responses and calls you back for the second interview. He says for you to prepare responses to the questions below:

1. What Web sites would you use to recruit from an international perspective, because he wants not only a diverse talent in the United States but he wants to sell products overseas and wants employees who can better understand those customers.
   What Web sites would you use to define relevant labor markets, and give him an example of the Asian market.
2. Would you consider being an expatriate, why or why not?
3. Where and how will you recruit minorities because he wants his company to "look like America and think like the world"?
4. Why should he hire you instead of promoting his administrative assistant who is good with people?
5. What ideas do you have on developing an employee referral system that provides some type of incentives

or rewards for those hired that remain six months or more because "likes attract".
6. The last time he ran an ad in the *Wall Street Journal* and *USA Today* he got 1000 responses! Is that good or bad? What thoughts do you have on that?
7. He read about some computer company that employed children to test and use the software. Why do you think they would use children, and how could HI-5-TECH adapt a concept like that?

EXPERIENTIAL EXERCISE:
Role-Play, Final Interview Part 3

Next, role play in pairs, one member choosing the role of Alan Berstein, the other applicant for the job of People Manager upon graduation. Reach a consensus which would be hired and why.

WEB-WISE EXERCISES

Search and print findings from the following Web sites:

(AJB) American's Job Bank, sponsored by the Department of Labor (DOL) in cooperation with various state employment services through AJB. Any U.S. employer or any foreign company legally authorized to operate a business in the United States may list its job openings with this public employment service. No charge or fees are involved with using this service.

Additional Web sites regarding career topics include:

E-SPAN's Interactive Employment Network: espan.com

On-line Career Center.occ.com

(SHRM) the Society for Human Resource Management: http://www.shrm.org

Career Web: cweb.com

Job Web: jobweb.com

Career Mosaic: http://www.careermosaic.com/ for job information as well as data on current job opportunities

Boston Consulting Group: http://www.bcg.com/
One of the best strategy consulting firms in the nation. This site has some information on recruiting and careers.

CareerPath.com & The Monster Board: www.careerpath.com-www.monsterboard.com
CareerPath.com posts classified ads from newspapers. The Monster Board lets companies post openings and job seekers post resumes.

Web Wise   National Business Employment Weekly:
http://www.nbew.com/
Job search and career guidance information

CASE APPLICATION:
You're the Expert

A friend of the family, Alan Berstein, learns that you are completing a human resource management course, that you are graduating next year, and asks you for your recommendations about hiring some new people.

The founder and president, Alan Berstein, of a small computer training and software development company, HI-5-Tech, currently employs 23 employees, but needs to hire five highly skilled superstars within two months to fulfill a new contract to create a customized intranet for Ameriglobal Healthcare, Inc.

Alan usually handles personnel issues, but with the expansion, he has little time to search, interview, check references, train new hires, and keep up with changing regulations. He shares that he does not wish to spend any more money on people than necessary since he also needs to purchase faster computers and printers immediately. He isn't currently active in any associations because he says "he's too busy running a company to go eat some rubber chicken for two hours."

He feels that working for his company is an opportunity to get cutting-edge experience, and that is his company's number one benefit. He asks you how he can get the right superstars with the least money, in the shortest possible time. Based on Hi-5-Tech's track record, his company should continue its fast growth. Alan says that he might like to hire you when you graduate next year to handle the "people stuff," if he likes what he hears. He's also going to talk with a few other upcoming graduates from his alma mater—others in your human resource management class.

Alan closes with "I only have ten minutes, so jot down your five best ideas and be specific, and I'll be back in five minutes to discuss them."

List five specific recommendations for how Mr. Berstein might search, recruit, select, interview, and hire the highly skilled individuals. You think you would like to go to work for him upon graduation, because although he seems demanding, his company's fast growth could mean rapid advancement and opportunities for you, and you suspect that you would never be bored.

Team Discussion:

Share and discuss your recommendations with your class team. Based on each member's recommendations, if Mr. Berstein benchmarked each member's recommendations, which would he hire as the "people stuff" person and why? What criteria do you think Mr. Berstein would use to compare each of you if you were candidates for the position. Use input from your team to develop a candidate evaluation chart.

TESTING YOUR UNDERSTANDING

How well did you fulfill the learning objectives?

1. Recruiting efforts are usually lighter in organizations
   a. that are large, rather than small.
   b. that are growing, rather than declining.
   c. that have poor, rather than good, compensation packages.
   d. that have good, rather than poor, working conditions.
   e. that are service, rather than public sector.

2. Which of the following indicates effective recruiting efforts for a director of recruiting for a large corporation?
   a. Recruiting costs have increased 8 percent during the last two years.
   b. The applicant pool is increasing in size.
   c. The Director of Recruiting's secretary spends three times as much time acknowledging ad responses from under-qualified applicants as she did a year ago.
   d. The director of recruiting's secretary spends less than one-third of the time acknowledging ad responses from under-qualified applicants as she did a year ago.
   e. The applicant pool is becoming global.

3. The director of recruiting at a medium-sized East Coast manufacturer, is unable to hire the best people for her company because of a new restriction that no longer pays airfare for college recruiters. Therefore, her staff is limited to going to college job fairs within a 150-mile radius of the company. What one of the following recruiting constraints is most affecting her organization?
   a. Organizational image.
   b. Job unattractiveness.
   c. Internal organizational politics.
   d. Government's influence.
   e. Costs.

4. Bob needs to hire two managers for a Pittsburgh paint manufacturing plant by the end of the year. His organization is under pressure to have females and minorities better represented at top levels of the organization. Currently, all executives are white and male. What recruiting technique should he use?
   a. Employee referrals.
   b. Public employment agencies.
   c. Headhunters.
   d. College placement centers.
   e. Walk-in.

5. A manager of human resources of a small accounting firm needs 2,000 extra person hours of work during the first two weeks of every April for data entry and word processing. What is the manager's best recruiting alternative?
   a. Independent contractors.
   b. Professional organizations.
   c. Employee leasing.
   d. College placement centers.
   e. Temporary help.

6. Which of the following is the most successful selection outcome for the XYZ organization?
   a. Ann was hired by XYZ, but she was unable to perform the job.
   b. Amy was hired by XYZ, but she was bored and left after three weeks.
   c. Andrea was hired by XYZ, and she quit the firm two months later for a better offer.
   d. Angela was not hired by XYZ, but she got an equivalent job with another firm (where she has done very well).
   e. Arnie was not hired by XYZ and could not get an equivalent job anywhere else in town.

7. A director of recruiting for a large U.S.-based global corporation is looking for a country manager for a newly acquired South American affiliate. Her best choice, to minimize language, culture, and family problems, is a
   a. home-country national.
   b. host-country national.
   c. local expatriate.
   d. third-country national.
   e. new foreign subsidiary.

8. Don, director of international staffing for a large U.S.-based manufacturing firm, needs to hire a production manager for an Asian country. He should make all of the following considerations except
   a. an Asian female would not be a likely candidate, being regarded as less effective.
   b. a married employee will be less acceptable than a single one.
   c. health requirements for this assignment are more important than for a domestic assignment.
   d. prior experience in Hong Kong and other Pacific Rim countries would be a plus.
   e. an American female would be highly respected and regarded as an expert in her field.

9. Julie, vice president of human resources for a large manufacturing firm, is concerned that 40 percent of the clerical workers hired last year lacked basic reading, writing, and filing skills. She thinks these workers should have been eliminated from the applicant pool, as early as the _____ step of the selection process.
   a. application forms
   b. physical examination

   c. comprehensive interview
   d. employment tests
   e. background investigation

10. Jan runs an employment agency that provides experienced secretarial help. She gives typing tests to job candidates to make sure they can type as part of the selection process. This test is an example of
    a. content validity.
    b. reliability.
    c. construct validity.
    d. differential validity.
    e. predictive validity.

11. Ruth runs an employment agency that provides experienced secretarial help. She gives typing tests to applicants during the selection process, but she does not hire based on these scores. She compares these test scores to their performance evaluations six months after employment. What is Ruth doing?
    a. Establishing reliability.
    b. Establishing content validity.
    c. Using cut scores.
    d. Establishing predictive validity.
    e. Decontextualizing construct validity.

12. Marion is the selection manager for a large manufacturing organization. The machinists test has a validity coefficient of .75. Scores typically run evenly from 0 to 100 with 50 as the average. Marion expects 1,000 employees in this year's applicant pool to fill 75 openings. What cut score is appropriate?
    a. 750
    b. 90
    c. 100
    d. 50
    e. She should interview all the applicants.

13. In the recruiting process, positive self-removal happens when
    a. human resources gets out of the hiring loop. Working divisions advertise for and interview their own job candidates.
    b. there is a streamlined human resources office arrangement. Candidates can escort themselves out, thus reducing the need for receptionists and security personnel.
    c. all applicants are encouraged to apply for jobs.
    d. unqualified applicants do not apply for jobs.
    e. women and minority applicants are discouraged and do not apply for jobs.

14. How does the selection process differ when hiring for international versus domestic positions?
    a. There is no difference.
    b. Married employees are preferred for domestic employment. Single employees are preferred for international assignments.
    c. Personality is more important for international assignments. Technical expertise is more important for domestic employment.

d. Gender discrimination is not allowed in domestic or international situations.

e. Age discrimination is not allowed in domestic or international situations.

15. Standard selection activities follow which pattern?

a. Screen, physical exam, comprehensive interview, tests, decision.

b. Physical exam, screen, tests, conditional job offer, interview, decision.

c. Background investigation, screen, physical examination, decision.

d. Physical examination, conditional job offer, background investigation, forms completion, decision.

e. Forms completion, comprehensive interview, background investigation, decision.

16. Predictive validity is preferred to concurrent validity because

a. it is easier to establish.

b. it is quicker to establish.

c. it is cheaper to establish.

d. it focuses on current employees.

e. it focuses on current job applicants.

17. Criterion-related validity may be established by

a. predictive or concurrent validity.

b. cut scores or construct validity.

c. content or construct validity.

d. reliability or cut scores.

e. concurrent or contaminant validity.

Endnotes

1. Margaret Mannix, "A Paper Resume? It's Passe," *U.S. News & World Report* (October 30, 1995), p. 90.

2. "Hottest Corporate Jobs Are Unheard Of," *The Sun: Business* (February 11, 1996), p. E8. See also, Patrick Scheetz, "Best, Worst Majors for Job-Hunting Grads," *Employment Research Institute* (East Lansing, MI: Michigan State University), in *USA Today* (May 29, 1996), p. B11.

3. Justin Martin, "One Company's Hiring Binge," *Fortune* (February 7, 1994), p. 14.

4. See, for example, Wendy Zellner, Robert D. Hof, Richard Brandt, Stephen Baker, and David Greising, "Go-Go Goliaths," *Business Week* (February 13, 1995), pp. 80–81.

5. Andrew S. Bargerstock and Gerald Swanson, "Four Ways to Build Cooperative Recruitment Alliances," *HRMagazine* (March 1991), p. 49.

6. Ibid., pp. 50-51.

7. "Code Words," *The Wall Street Journal* (September 12, 1995), p. A-1; and Linda B. Robin, "Recruitment: Troubleshooting Recruitment Problems," *Personnel Journal* (September 1988), p. 94.

8. "Wired for Hiring: Microsoft's Slick Recruiting Machine," *Fortune* (February 5, 1996), p. 123.

9. See, for instance, Daniel B. Turban and Daniel W. Greening, "Corporate Social Performance and Organizational Attractiveness to Prospective Employers," *Academy of Management Journal*, Vol. 40, No. 3 (June 1997), pp. 658–672.

10. See, for example, Stephen J. Holoviak and David A. DeCenzo, contributing eds., "Service Industry Seeks Summer Help," *Audio Human Resource Report*, Vol. 1, No. 9 (October 1990), p. 5.

11. Ken Jordan, "Play Fair and Square When Hiring from Within," *HRMagazine* (January 1997), pp. 49–51.

12. Linda Micco, "Global Recruiting Called Essential for Many Firms," *HR News* (May 1998), p. 15.

13. Donna Fenn, "International: Opening Up and Overseas Operation," *Inc.* (June 1995), p. 89; and Pamela Sebastian, "Expatriate Employees," *The Wall Street Journal* (March 9, 1995), p. A-1.

14. See, for instance, Clair Poole, "The New Nationalization," *Latin Trade* (June 1998), pp. 71–72; and "Hire Power," *Canadian Business* (December 1996), p. 56.

15. C. Grove, "An Ounce of Prevention: Supporting International Job Transitions," *Employment Relations Journal*, Vol. 17, No. 2 (Spring 1990), p. 111.

16. Robert J. Grossman, "HR in Asia," *HRMagazine* (July 1997), p. 106.

17. See, for example, Barbara Fitzgerald-Turner, "Myths of Expatriate Life," *HRMagazine* (June 1997), p. 65.

18. See, for example, Michelle Neely Martinez, "Looking for Young Talent? Inroads Helps Diversify Efforts," *HRMagazine* (March 1996), pp. 73–75.

19. Jack Stack, "The Next in Line," *Inc.* (April 1998), p. 43.

20. Thomas A. Stewart, "In Search of Elusive Tech Workers," *Fortune* (February 16, 1998), p. 171; Andy Bargerstock and Hank Engle, "Six Ways to Boost Employee Referral Programs," *HRMagazine* (December 1994), pp. 72–79.

21. Kathryn Tyler, "Employees Can Help Recruit New Talent," *HRMagazine* (September 1996), p. 60.

22. See, for example, Clyde J. Scott, "Recruitment: Employing a Private Employment Firm," *Personnel Journal* (September 1989), pp. 78–83.

23. See, for example, Jennifer Reingold and Nicole Harris, "Casting for a Different Set of Characters," *Business Week* (December 8, 1997), pp. 38–39.

24. Ibid.; and Perri Capbell, "When a Recruiter Comes Knocking, Be Ready to Respond," *The Wall Street Journal* (August 6, 1996), p. B-1.

25. Gayle Sato Stodder, "Getting Personnel," *Entrepreneur* (October 1995), p. 94.

26. Christopher Caggiano, "Beyond Campus Recruiting," *Inc.* (April 1998), p. 115.

27. Linda Thornburg, "Employers and Graduates Size Each Other Up," *HRMagazine* (May 1997), pp. 76–79; and Robert W. Thompson. "Job-Hunting Students Seek Balance," *HR News* (May 1997), p. 2.

28. Gary Meyer, "Recruiting Systems Linked to the Internet," *HRMagazine* (April 1997), pp. 42–47; Samantha Drake, "HR Departments Are Exploring the Internet," *HRMagazine* (December 1996), pp. 53–56; Sandra E. O'Connell, "Technology in the Employment Office," *HRMagazine* (August 1996), pp. 31–38; and Stephenie Overman, "Cruising Cyberspace for the Best Recruits," *HRMagazine* (February 1995), pp. 52–55.

29. Donna Fenn, "The Right Fit," *Inc. 500* (1997), p. 106, Patricia Nakache, "Best Practices: Cisco's Recruiting Edge," *Fortune* (September 29, 1997), p. 275; "The Home-Page Help Wanteds," *U.S. News & World Report* (October 30, 1995), p. 88.

30. Justin Martin, "Changing Jobs? Try the Net," *Fortune* (March 2, 1998), p. 205.

31. Justin Martin, "Changing Jobs? Try the Net," *Fortune* (March 2, 1998), pp. 205–208; Donna Fenn "Hiring: Recruiting in Cyberspace," *Inc.* (November 1995), p. 93; and Jacqueline M. Graves, "IBM Alums Find Real Jobs the Virtual Way," *Fortune* (May 1, 1995), p. 32.

32. Patricia W. Hamilton, "Staffing on a Shoestring," *Executive Female* (July/August 1995), pp. 32–34; and John Ross, "Effective Ways to Hire Contingent Personnel," *HRMagazine* (February 1991), pp. 52–53.

33. Ibid., p. 53. See also Steve Bergsman, "Setting Up a Temporary Shop," *HRMagazine* (February 1990), pp. 46–49.

34. "The Temporary Help Business," *The Wall Street Journal* (February 25, 1992), p. A-1.

35. See, for example, American Association of Retired Persons, *How to Recruit Older Workers* (Washington, D.C.: American Association of Retired Persons, 1993).

36. Lee Phillion and John R. Brugger, "Encore! Retirees Give Top Performance as Temporaries," *HRMagazine* (October 1994), pp. 74–77.

37. Reasons cited by the American Association of Retired Persons include the need to make money, to get health insurance coverage, to develop skills, to use their time more productively, to feel useful, to make new friends, to provide some structure to their daily lives, or to have a sense of achievement. See "How to Recruit Older Workers," p. 27.

38. American Association of Retired Persons and the Society for Human Resource Management, *The Older Workforce: Recruitment and Retention* (Washington, D.C.: American Association of Retired Persons, 1993), p. 1.

39. Susan Greco, "Recruiting the Newly Retired," *Inc.* (August 1993), p. 23.

40. Caution is warranted regarding for whom an individual works. Generally, the employee is the responsibility of the leasing company. But under certain circumstances, like long-term duration of the lease, the acquiring organization may be the employer of record, with the leasing company handling a variety of HRM associated paperwork. See Jane Easter Bahls, "Employees for Rent," *Nation's Business* (June 1991), p. 36.

41. Bargerstock and Swanson, p. 50.

42. This story was influenced by an example in Arthur Sloan, *Personnel: Managing Human Resources* (Englewood Cliffs, N.J.: Prentice-Hall, 1983), p. 127.

43. Karl O. Magnusen and K. Galen Kroeck, "Videoconferencing Maximizes Recruiting," *HRMagazine* (August 1995), pp. 70–71.

44. See the Albemarle Paper Company reference in Chapter 3.

45. See, for example, E. James Randall and Cindy H. Randall, "Review of Salesperson Selection Techniques and Criteria: A Managerial Approach," *International Journal of Research in Marketing*, Vol. 7, No. 2 (December 1990), pp. 81–95.

46. Ronald Henkoff, "Finding, Training, and Keeping the Best Service Workers," *Fortune* (October 3, 1994), p. 118.

47. Clifford E. Montgomery, "Organizational Fit Is Key to Job Success," *HRMagazine* (January 1996), pp. 94–96; and Donna Fenn, "Promoting' Getting the Right Fit," *Inc.* (February 1995), p. 111.

48. Stephenie Overman, "Bizarre Questions Aren't the Answer," *HRMagazine* (April 1995), p. 56.

49. See, for example, "What Personnel Offices Really Stress in Hiring," *The Wall Street Journal* (March 6, 1991), p. A-1.

50. "Responsible Background," ad in *HRMagazine* (February 1991), p. 50.

51. Paul W. Barada, "Reference Checking Is More Important Than Ever," *HRMagazine* (November 1996), p. 49.

52. Frances A. McMorris, "Ex-Bosses Face Less Peril Giving Honest Job References," *The Wall Street Journal* (July 8, 1996), p. B-1; Elizabeth Bahnsen and Adrienne Loftin, "Handle Reference Requests Consistently; Stick to Facts, " *HR News* (December 1995), p. 16; and Bill Leonard, "Reference-Checking Laws: Now What?" *HRMagazine* (December 1995), p. 57.

53. Paul W. Barada, "Reference Checking Is More Important Than Ever," p. 49.

54. See, for example, Theresa Donahue Egler, "White Lies Limit Employee Recovery in Discrimination Lawsuits," *HRMagazine* (November 1994), pp. 30–32.

55. See, for example, Joyce Lain Kennedy and Dr. Darryl Laramore, *Career Book* (Lincolnwood, Ill.: National Textbook Company, 1988), Section 6; John L. Holland, *Making Vocational Choices: A Theory of Vocational Personalities and Work Environments,* 2nd ed. (Englewood Cliffs, N.J.: Prentice-Hall, 1985); and John L. Holland, Gary D. Gottfredson, and Deborah Kimili Ogwawa, *RIASEC Codes with 12 Dictionary of Holland Occupational Codes: A Comprehensive Cross-Index of Holland's DOT Occupations* (Palo Alto, Calif.: Consulting Psychologists Press, Inc., 1982).

56. See David E. Bowen, Gerald E. Ledford, Jr., and Barry R. Nathan, "Hiring for the Organization, Not the Job," *Academy of Management Executive,* Vol. 5, No. 4 (November 1991), pp. 35–51.

57. See, for example, Sara L. Rynes, Robert D. Bretz, and Barry Gerhart, "The Importance of Recruitment in Job Choice: A Different Way of Looking," *Personnel Psychology,* Vol. 44, No. 3 (Autumn 1991), pp. 487–521.

58. See, for example, Charles A. O'Reilly III, David I. Caldwell, and Richard Mirable, "A Profile Comparison Approach to Person v. Job Fit: More Than a Mirage," in Jerry L. Wall and Lawrence R. Jauch, Eds., *Academy of Management Best Papers Proceedings,* Las Vegas (August 9–12, 1992), pp. 237–42.

59. See, for example, Thomas F. Casey, "Making the Most of a Selection Interview," *Personnel* (September 1990), pp. 41–43.

60. See, for instance, "Hiring: Measure of Success," *Industry Week* (February 1996), p. 11.

61. As one reviewer correctly pointed out, there are several methods of determining reliability. These include equivalent form, test–retest method, and internal consistency forms of reliability. Their discussion, however, goes well beyond the scope of this text.

62. See, for example, Wayne Casio, *Applied Psychology in Personnel Management* (Englewood Cliffs, N.J.: Prentice-Hall, 1991), pp. 151–54.

63. For an interesting perspective on the use of construct validity, see Linn Van Dyne and Jeffrey A. LePine, "Helping and Voice Extra-Role Behaviors: Evidence of Construct and Predictive Validity," *Academy of Management Journal* (February 1998), pp. 108–119.

64. See, for example, Richard Kern, "IQ Tests for Salesmen Make a Comeback," *Sales and Marketing* (April 1988), pp. 42–46.

65. A limitation of concurrent validity is the possibility of restricting the range of scores in testing current employees. This occurs because current employees may have been in the upper range of applicants. Those not hired were unde-

sirable for some reason. Therefore, these scores theoretically should represent only the top portion of previous applicant scores.

66. A specific correlation coefficient for validation purposes is nearly impossible to pinpoint. There are many variables that will enter into the picture, such as the sample size, the power of the test, and what is measured. However, for EEO purposes, correlation coefficients must be indicative of a situation where the results are predictive of performance that is greater than one where chance alone dictated the outcomes.

67. Cut scores are determined through a set of mathematical formulas—namely, a regression analysis and the equation of a line. We refer you to any good introductory statistics text for a reminder of how these formulas operate.

68. Frank L. Schmidt and John E. Hunter, "Developing a General Solution to the Problem of Validity Generalization," *Journal of Applied Psychology,* Vol. 62, No. 5 (October 1977), pp. 529–539.

69. Lauress L. Wise, Jeffrey McHenry, and John P. Campbell, "Identifying Optimal Predictor Composites and Testing for Generalizability Across Jobs and Performance Factors," *Personnel Psychology,* Vol. 43, No. 2 (Summer 1990), pp. 355-366.

70. Frank L. Schmidt, Kenneth Pearlman, John E. Hunter, and Hannah Rothstein Hirsh, "Forty Questions About Validity Generalization and Meta-Analysis," *Personnel Psychology,* Vol. 38, No. 4 (Winter 1985), pp. 697–822.

71. See, for example, Kathy B. Strawn and Steven P. Nurney, "Outsource Expatriate Support for High quality, Low Costs," *HRMagazine* (December 1995), pp. 65–69.

72. Michelle Neely Martinez, "Myths About Women Expatriates Bad for Business," *HR News* (February 1996), p. B-3.

7. Selection Devices

LEARNING OBJECTIVES

After reading this chapter, you will be able to:

1. Identify the purpose of selection devices.
2. Discuss why organizations use application forms.
3. Describe the usefulness of weighted application forms.
4. Explain the primary purposes of performance simulation tests.
5. Describe assessment centers and how they are conducted.
6. Explain graphology tests and their use in the selection process.
7. Discuss the problems associated with job interviews, and means of correcting them.
8. Identify the steps involved in properly interviewing candidates.
9. Specify the organizational benefits derived from realistic job previews.
10. Explain the purpose of background investigations.

*T*ruth, it's often said to be stranger than fiction. While this adage could be debated, when it comes to employment selection, it appears to hold true. That's because anyone who's ever worked in the screening process—especially reviewing cover letters, resumés, or interviewing—typically has some fascinating story to tell. Like what? Well, consider the following items that have been taken from events in organizations like Snelling and Snelling, and Robert Half.[1] For your convenience, we've italicized the blunder.

▶ When asked to fill out the reason for leaving his last job, this applicant stated it was because he was *laid out*.

▶ In a cover letter to a major corporation, this applicant noted that he was experienced in *private relations*.

▶ Imagine the embarrassment this applicant must have felt when he proofread his cover letter and noticed that he had written "*As indicted,* I have five years of analyzing investments.

▶ Or, would you hire this applicant with *WordPurpose* and *Locust* skills?

▶ Of course, this applicant was correct when she noted that this was just a "*ruff draft* of her resumé."

▶ How about the applicant who was dressed to the "9s" for an interview at a well-known *"conservative" organization*—tailored dark-blue pin-striped Armani suit, white spread-collar Egyptian-broadcloth shirt, a red power tie, black polished cap-toe shoes; and *multiple facial-piercings, including four in each ear, his tongue, one in his left nostril.*

▶ After several minutes in an interview, the job applicant interrupted the recruiter and asked *what the IBM in the company name stood for.*

▶ Another applicant, when asked why he wanted to work for the major regional bank for which he was applying, responded he didn't know because he *would really prefer to work for the bank's competitor, which is much closer to his home.*

▶ This applicant, in response to a question why he was applying for the job, stated he wanted the position *to pay his bills.*

Wouldn't it be nice if the selection process were this clear cut? Sure would make things easier!. Of course, these are the exaggerations. And HR practition-

Here's one to test your limits. Everything about this candidate's resumé looks great. But when he shows up for the interview, he appears with multiple body piercings, which you know go against the grain of the conservative culture of the organization. Do you believe this individual "fits?" How would you react to him in an interview setting?

ers usually are not this lucky to have their decisions handed to them on silver platters. Instead, a lot of careful planning and careful thought is required. That's what we want to look at in this chapter.

INTRODUCTION

As we noted in the last chapter, the selection process is composed of a number of steps. Each of these steps provides decision makers with information that will help them predict whether an applicant will prove to be a successful job performer.[2] One way to conceptualize this is to think of each step as a higher hurdle in a race. The applicant able to clear all the hurdles wins the race—victory being the receipt of a job offer. And how long this takes varies. The process may take weeks, or as in the case of Toyota U.S., the selection process could take almost two years (see Exhibit 7-1)![3]

The selection steps presented in Chapter 6 attempt to make predictions based on either evaluating the past or sampling the present. The application form, background investigation, and comprehensive interview attempt to find out what the applicant has done in the past and then to project these past experiences and accomplishments into the future. You should be aware that this method of prediction implies certain assumptions concerning the relationship of the past to the future. Specifically, it assumes that a candidate's past behavior can be a guide for predicting future behavior, and that the candidate will remain the same person in the future that he or she was in the past.[4] While these

Exhibit 7-1

Selection excellence at Toyota.

Want a Job at Toyota Motor Manufacturing plant in Georgetown, Kentucky? Here's what you can expect in their hiring process over the coming months:

What's Assessed?	And How?	
Technical skills	Phase I:	Applicants complete applications, and watch a
Technical Performance		Interpersonal Skills one-hour video about the work
Leadership		environment.
Problem-solving Skills	Phase II:	Applicants complete Kentucky's Department of
Health Assessment		Employment Services' Situation Judgement
		Inventory—measuring one's ability to work in a team, and other interpersonal skills.
	Phase III:	Applicants participate in a four-hour program designed to assess individual and group problem-solving skills. Applicants are observed by Toyota screening experts.
		Assembly-line applicants also participate in a five-hour assembly simulation.
	Phase IV:	One-hour interview with a group of Toyota interviewers.
	Phase V:	Conditional Toyota employee. Applicants undergo two-and one-half hours of physical and substance testing at an area hospital.
	Phase VI:	Employee is closely monitored by seasoned employees who assess job performance for the next six months.

SOURCE: Based on information contained in Micheline Maynard, "Toyota Devises Grueling Work-out for Job Seekers," *USA Today* (August 11, 1997), p. 3B; Gary Dessler, "Value-Based Hiring Builds Commitment," *Personnel Journal* (November 1993), pp. 98–102; and "Choosing the Right People," *HRMagazine* (March 1990), pp. 66–70.

assumptions may be accurate and this approach satisfactory, it appears that devices like job-related tests, where relevant, may also be good predictors because they sample present behavior in order to predict future behavior.

It is logical that selection devices that simulate actual work behavior and are as current as possible should stand the best chance for being good predictors.[5] But is this true in practice? In the following pages, we will review the devices discussed in Chapter 6. Since each of these devices is a potential "device" in the selector's "tool kit," and using several in combination often is best, we want to look carefully at each in the context of how good a tool it is, and under what conditions it should be used.

It's logical that selection devices that simulate actual work behavior have the best chances for being good predictors.

THE APPLICATION FORM

The Civil Rights Acts of 1964 and 1991 and subsequent amendments, executive orders, court rulings, and other legislation have made it illegal to discriminate on the basis of sex, race, color, religion, national origin, disability, and age. The only major exceptions to these guidelines involving age, sex, and religion are cases where it can be shown that these criteria are bona fide occupational qualifications (BFOQ).

Many of the items that traditionally appeared on the **application form**—religion, age, marital status, occupation of spouse, number and ages of children,

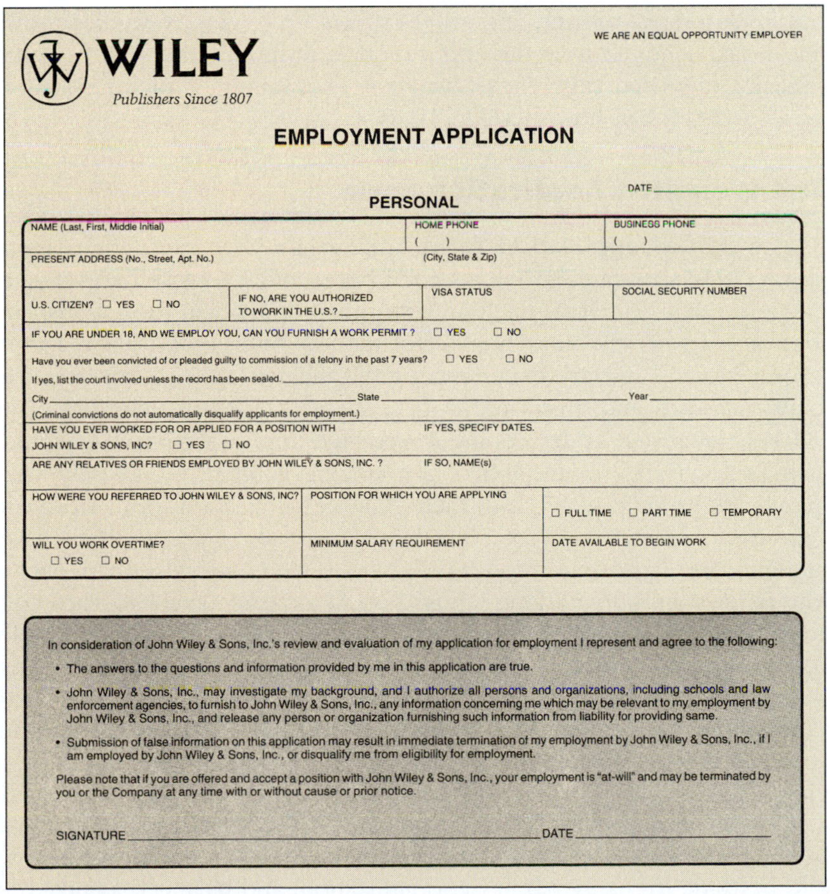
WILEY
Publishers Since 1807

WE ARE AN EQUAL OPPORTUNITY EMPLOYER

EMPLOYMENT APPLICATION

DATE ______

PERSONAL

NAME (Last, First, Middle Initial) | HOME PHONE ( ) | BUSINESS PHONE ( )

PRESENT ADDRESS (No., Street, Apt. No.) | (City, State & Zip)

U.S. CITIZEN? ☐ YES ☐ NO | IF NO, ARE YOU AUTHORIZED TO WORK IN THE U.S.? ______ | VISA STATUS | SOCIAL SECURITY NUMBER

IF YOU ARE UNDER 18, AND WE EMPLOY YOU, CAN YOU FURNISH A WORK PERMIT? ☐ YES ☐ NO

Have you ever been convicted of or pleaded guilty to commission of a felony in the past 7 years? ☐ YES ☐ NO

If yes, list the court involved unless the record has been sealed. ______

City ______ State ______ Year ______

(Criminal convictions do not automatically disqualify applicants for employment.)

HAVE YOU EVER WORKED FOR OR APPLIED FOR A POSITION WITH JOHN WILEY & SONS, INC? ☐ YES ☐ NO | IF YES, SPECIFY DATES.

ARE ANY RELATIVES OR FRIENDS EMPLOYED BY JOHN WILEY & SONS, INC. ? | IF SO, NAME(s)

HOW WERE YOU REFERRED TO JOHN WILEY & SONS, INC? | POSITION FOR WHICH YOU ARE APPLYING | ☐ FULL TIME ☐ PART TIME ☐ TEMPORARY

WILL YOU WORK OVERTIME? ☐ YES ☐ NO | MINIMUM SALARY REQUIREMENT | DATE AVAILABLE TO BEGIN WORK

In consideration of John Wiley & Sons, Inc.'s review and evaluation of my application for employment I represent and agree to the following:

- The answers to the questions and information provided by me in this application are true.
- John Wiley & Sons, Inc., may investigate my background, and I authorize all persons and organizations, including schools and law enforcement agencies, to furnish to John Wiley & Sons, Inc., any information concerning me which may be relevant to my employment by John Wiley & Sons, Inc., and release any person or organization furnishing such information from liability for providing same.
- Submission of false information on this application may result in immediate termination of my employment by John Wiley & Sons, Inc., if I am employed by John Wiley & Sons, Inc., or disqualify me from eligibility for employment.

Please note that if you are offered and accept a position with John Wiley & Sons, Inc., your employment is "at-will" and may be terminated by you or the Company at any time with or without cause or prior notice.

SIGNATURE ______ DATE ______

Exhibit 7-2
Sample application form.

hobbies could not be proved to be job-related.[6] Given this reality, it should not be surprising to find different application forms now. Since the onus is on management to demonstrate that information supplied by applicants is job-related, items that cannot be demonstrated to be job related should be omitted.

In addition to these changes being made, one important aspect has been added. Applications typically include a statement giving the employer the right to dismiss an employee for falsifying information (see Exhibit 7-2).[7] They also typically indicate that employment is at the "will" of either party (the employer or the employee can end the work relationship), and that the employee understands that employment is not guaranteed. Furthermore, the applicant is giving the company permission to obtain previous work history. Of course, an applicant has the right not to sign the application. In that event, however, one's application is removed from consideration.

The fact that application forms have had to be revised should not be interpreted as an indictment of the application form as an effective predictor. Such is not the case; in fact, evidence indicates that hard and relevant biographical data on the application that can be verified—for example, rank in high-school graduating class—may be a more valid measure of potential job performance than many of the intelligence, aptitude, interest, and personality items that traditionally have been used in the selection decision.[8] Additionally, when application form items have been appropriately weighted to reflect job relatedness, we find that the application can successfully predict performance criteria for such diverse groups as salesclerks, engineers, factory workers, district managers, clerical employees, draftspersons, and army officers.[9] A review of studies using biographical data acquired from the application form found a number of items that successfully predicted differences between short-tenure and long-tenure employees.[10] Let's look at how these are used.

The Weighted Application Form

The **weighted application form** appears to offer excellent potential in helping recruiters to differentiate between potentially successful and unsuccessful job performers. To create such an instrument, individual form items, such as number of years of schooling, number of months on last job, salary data for all previous jobs, and military experience, are validated against performance and turnover measures and given appropriate weights. Let's assume, for example, that HRM is interested in developing a weighted applicant form that would predict which applicants for the job of accountant, if hired, would stay with the company. They would select from their files the application forms from each of two groups of previously hired accountants—one, a group that had short tenure with the organization (adjusters who stayed, say, less than one year), and the other, a group with long tenure (say, five years or more). These old application forms would be screened item by item to determine how employees in each group responded. In this way, management would discover items that differentiate the groups. These items would then be weighted relative to how well they differentiate applicants. If, for example, 80 percent of the long-tenure group had a college degree, the possession of a college degree might be given a weight of 4. But if 30 percent of the long-tenure group had prior experience in a Big 6 accounting firm, while 20 percent of the short-tenure did, this item might be given a weight of only 1. Note, of course, that this procedure would have to be done for every job in the organization, and balanced against the factors of those that do not fall into the majority category; that is, while 80 percent of the long-tenure individuals had a college degree, we would need to factor into our weighing scheme those who had a college degree and were successful on the job, but only had short tenure with the company.

Items that predict long tenure for an accountant might be totally different from items that predict long tenure for an engineer or even an financial analyst. However, with the continued improvement in sophisticated computer software, the task of developing the application for each job may be more manageable.[11]

A Successful Application

The application form, as noted earlier, has had wide success in selection for a number of diverse jobs. For instance, in various positions in the hotel industry, analysis of the application form has been valuable. In one study, it was found that seven items on the application were highly predictive of successful performance as measured by job tenure.[12]

Evidence that the application form provides relevant information for predicting job success is well supported across a broad range of jobs. Care must be taken to ensure that application items are validated for each job. Also, since the predictive ability of items may change over time, the items must be continuously reviewed and updated. Finally, management should be aware of the possibility that the application information given is erroneous. A background investigation can verify most of the data.

EMPLOYMENT TESTS

In this section, we want to look at **employment tests**—the better-known written tests that attempt to assess intelligence, abilities, and personality traits, as well as the lesser-known performance simulation tests, including work sampling and the tests administered at assessment centers. In addition, we will look at and evaluate the validity of polygraph tests and handwriting analysis as selection devices, and will see how the use of tests may be different in a global environment.

Written Tests

We noted in the last chapter that **written tests** historically have served as significant input into the selection decision. And although there was a hiatus after the *Griggs v. Duke Power* decision in the mid-1970s, a number of companies recognized that testing served a vital purpose.[13] There has been renewed interest in written tests, since those that have been validated can aid significantly in the acquisition of efficient and effective workers.[14] However, let us remind you that the company has the sole responsibility for demonstrating that tests used for hiring or promotion are related to job performance.

There are literally hundreds of tests that can be used by organizations as selection tools.[15] One can use tests that measure intellect, spatial ability, perception skills, mechanical comprehension, motor ability, personality traits, as well as "reading, math, and mechanical dexterity skills." [16] It is not the purpose of this text to review each of these test categories; that is generally the province of books in applied industrial psychology.[17]

Performance Simulation Tests

To avoid criticism and potential liability that may result from the use of psychological, aptitude,[18] and other types of written tests, there has been increasing interest in the use of **performance simulation tests.** The single identifying characteristic of these tests is that they require the applicant to engage in specific behaviors necessary for doing the job successfully. In contrast to the types of tests discussed above, performance simulation tests should more easily meet the requirement of job-relatedness because they are made up of actual job behaviors rather than surrogates.[19]

Work Sampling   **Work sampling** is an effort to create a miniature replica of a job. Applicants demonstrate that they possess the necessary talents by actually doing the tasks. By carefully devising work samples based on job analysis data, the knowledge, skills, and abilities needed for each job are determined. Then each work sample element is matched with a corresponding job performance element. For example, a work sample for a bank teller at First USA Bank involving computation on a calculator would require the applicant to make similar computations. At Home Depot, a potential check-out clerk is screened for a job to scan the prices of your purchases quickly and accurately. Most go through a similar work-sampling session where supervisors demonstrate how to scan accurately, ensuring that the product did indeed ring up. Then the candidate is given an opportunity to show that he or she can handle the job. Work sampling, then, reflects actual "hands-on" experience.

The advantages of work sampling over traditional pencil-and-paper tests are obvious. Because content is essentially identical to job content, work sampling should be a better predictor of short-term performance and should minimize discrimination.[20] Additionally, because of the nature of their content and the methods used to determine content, well-constructed work sample tests should

How are applicants for cashiers jobs at Home Depot screened to determine if they can properly scan customer purchases? They are put through a work sampling test to determine if they can accurately and effectively do the job.

easily meet EEOC content validity requirements.[21] The main disadvantage is the difficulty in developing good work samples for each job. Furthermore, work sampling is not applicable to all levels of the organization. It is often difficult to use for managerial jobs because it is hard to create a work sample test that can address the full range of managerial activities. In the following section, we will look at a type of performance simulation test that is more directly related to midlevel managerial positions.

Assessment Centers A more elaborate set of performance simulation tests, specifically designed to evaluate a candidate's managerial potential, is administered in **assessment centers.** Assessment centers use procedures that incorporate group and individual exercises. Applicants go through a series of these exercises and are appraised by line executives, practicing supervisors, and/or trained psychologists as to how well they perform. As with work sampling, because these exercises are designed to simulate the work that managers actually do, they tend to be accurate predictors of later job performance. In some cases, however, the assessment center also includes traditional personality and aptitude tests.

How does an assessment center work? Essentially, the procedure goes something like this:[22]

1. A small group of applicants come to the assessment center.
2. The assessment center has approximately six to eight assessors, some of whom are trained psychologists, while others are managers at least two levels above the individual being assessed, who have been trained as assessors.
3. For about two to four days, the assessees are asked to participate in exercises such as:
   a. Interviews
   b. "In-basket" exercises, where applicants solve day-to-day problems that managers might find in their in-baskets
   c. Case exercises
   d. Leaderless group discussions
   e. Business games
   f. Personality tests
   g. General ability tests
4. Assessors, usually in pairs, observe and record the behavior of applicants in group and individual situational problems. A clinical psychologist summarizes the personality tests.
5. Each assessee is rated on twenty to twenty-five characteristics (such as organization and planning, decision making, creativity, resistance to stress, and oral communication skills).
6. A judgment is made about the assessee's potential for meeting the job requirements.

Assessment centers typically operate as described in Exhibit 7-3. Evidence supporting the effectiveness of assessment centers is impressive. They have consistently demonstrated results that predict later job performance in professional positions like sales, as well as lower- to midlevel management positions.[23] Even when the costs of conducting assessment center evaluations are taken into account—training of assessors, consultant fees, time away from the

Day 1 Orientation Meeting

Management Game: "Conglomerate" Forming different types of conglomerates is the goal, with four-person teams bartering companies to achieve their planned result. Teams set their own acquisition objectives and must plan and organize to meet them.

Background Interview A 90-minute interview conducted by an assessor.

Group Discussion: "Management Problems" Short cases calling for various forms of management judgment are presented to groups of four. In one hour the group, acting as consultants, must resolve the cases and submit its recommendation in writing.

Individual Fact-finding and Decision-making Exercises: "The Research Budget" The participants are told that they have just taken over as division manager. They are given a brief description of an incident in which their predecessor has recently turned down a request for funds to continue a research project. The research director is appealing for a reversal of the decision. The participants are given fifteen minutes to ask questions to dig out the facts in the case. Following this fact-binding period, they must present their decisions orally with supporting reasoning and defend it under challenge.

Day 2

In-basket Exercise: "Section Manager's In-basket" The contents of a section manager's in-basket are simulated. The participants are instructed to go through the contents, solving problems, answering questions, delegating, organizing, scheduling, and planning, just as they might do if they were promoted suddenly to the position. An assessor reviews the contents of the completed in-basket and conducts a one-hour interview with each participant to gain further information.

Assigned Role Leaderless Group Discussion: "Compensation Committee" The Compensation Committee is meeting to allocate $8,000 in discretionary salary increases among six supervisory and managerial employees. Each member of the committee (participant) represents a department of the company and is instructed to "do the best they can" for the employee from their department.

Analysis, Presentation, and Group Discussion: "The Pretzel Factory" This financial analysis problem has the participant role-play a consultant called in to advise Carl Flowers of the C.F. Pretzel Company on two problems: what to do about a division of the company that has continually lost money, and whether the corporation should expand. Participants are given data on the company and are asked to recommend appropriate courses of action. They make their recommendation in a seven-minute presentation after which they are formed into a group to come up with a single set of recommendations.

Days 3 and 4

Assessors meet to share their observations on each participant and to arrive at summary evaluations relative to each dimension sought and overall potential.

job, purchase of tests and exercises, and so on—the payoffs in terms of more effective selection are usually more than justified.[24] For instance, AT&T has assessed thousands of employees in its management development center and has found the center to be very effective in indicating which individuals would be successful on jobs that provide greater responsibility and accountability.[25]

One note of caution has been offered concerning the impressive and consistent results from assessment center selection. It has been proposed that the measures of job performance may be contaminated.[26] Assessment center results may not be valid because they generally use the success measures of promotions and salary increases as determinants of "job performance." Given that promotions and salary increases may not be based solely on performance, assessment evaluators will come up with effective results if they know what factors senior management actually uses to make advancement and salary increment decisions. Accordingly, assessors may not be evaluating true performance, but such nonperformance-related factors as the candidate's social skills, likeability, "proper" background, appearance, or attitude. For instance, assessors who correctly realize that upper-level managers like and tend to promote "yes types" and conformists may unintentionally assess candidates for these traits. Whenever assessment center ratings and success measures contain a common component unrelated to job performance, the results will be contaminated and the validity of the procedure questionable.

Other Tests

Two other tests—**graphology** (handwriting analysis) and polygraph (lie detector) and honesty tests—receive a fair amount of media attention. Because of this attention, and the controversy surrounding their validity, we will conclude our discussion of tests with a brief review of these devices, and look at testing issues in a global arena.

Graphology   It has been said that an individual's handwriting can suggest the degree of energy, inhibitions, and spontaneity to be found in the writer, disclosing idiosyncrasies and elements of balance and control from which many personality characteristics can be inferred.[27] Although most scientists doubt the validity of handwriting analysis, it is estimated that more than 3,000 U.S. organizations, including Ford, General Electric, and the CIA, consult graphologists to supplement their usual HRM procedures.[28] When used, graphology can be considered as an employment test. The argument is made that a large percentage of occupational failures are due to personality defects, not lack of education or ability. Given the inadequacies of many standardized methods for assessing personality characteristics, handwriting analysis, if it really does tell us something about applicants' personality, might have validity, but only if the job analysis had identified these personalities (see Exhibit 7-4).

In spite of the relatively large number of organizations that admit to using graphology, there is little substantial evidence to support this method as a valid selection device.[29]

Polygraph and Honesty Tests   The use of lie detectors for verifying information on the application form can only be used for specific jobs, such as police

The reason I am applying for this job is twofold. First, I believe I can offer the organization several special skills ... *In conclusion, I believe there is a good match between the organization and ...*	In graphology, an analyst would evaluate the writing sample provided by the applicant. That evaluation would present a psychological profile.

Exhibit 7-4
Using graphology.

Have you ever cheated on a test? Be careful, that may not be a correct answer.

officer or federal agents such as those from the National Security Agency, that typically require security clearance. While the polygraph may be a reasonably valid instrument when used by competent examiners, it could be abused in certain situations. Because of this potential for abuse, the Employee Polygraph Protection Act of 1988 (followed by many other state laws) prohibits the use of polygraph testing as a uniform prerequisite of employment. However, a second-generation polygraph technique, honesty tests, is thriving.[30]

Honesty tests are designed to assess an individual's integrity, to predict those who are more likely to steal from an employer[31] or otherwise act in a manner unacceptable to the organization. Although the questions asked may appear to be relatively innocent, those taking the test do not know how they will be interpreted. For example, the response to "Have you ever cheated on a test in your life?" may not have a correct response on its face value. If you say yes, you admit that you've cheated; a no response might indicate that you are lying. Nonetheless, the question patterns are such that even those who try to "outsmart" the test often fail. These tests often contain questions that repeat themselves in some fashion, and the examiner then looks for consistency in responses.

Since polygraphs are all but unusable for the typical firm, honesty testing has become more widespread. By the late 1990s, nearly one-fourth of all American Management Association affiliated firms used honesty tests.[32] In fact, their use has become so extensive that it has grown into a $50-million-a-year business for these honesty-psychological testing firms.[33]

Testing in a Global Arena   Many of the standard selection techniques described in this text are not easily transferable to international situations. Where the decision has been made to recruit and employ host-country nationals, typical American testing will be acceptable in some countries, but not in others. For example, although handwriting or graphology tests are sometimes used in the United States, they are frequently used in France. In Great Britain, most psychological tests like graphology, polygraph, and honesty tests are rarely used in employment. Accordingly, whenever American corporations prepare to do business abroad, their practices must be adapted to the cultures, and regulations, of the country in which they will operate.[34]

INTERVIEWS

Whether we're discussing initial screening interviews or comprehensive interviews, a common question arises: Are interviews effective for gathering accurate information from which selection decisions can be made? The **interview** has proven to be an almost universal selection tool—one that can take a number of forms. They can revolve around a one-on-one encounter between the interviewer and the applicant (the traditional interview) or involve several individuals who interview an applicant at once (the panel interview). Interviews can follow some predetermined pattern wherein both the questions and the expected responses are identified (a **situational interview**[35]). Interviews can also be designed to create a difficult environment in which the applicant is "put to the test" to assess his or her confidence levels. These are frequently referred to as the **stress interview** (see HRM Ethics).

Irrespective of how the interview is conducted, it is understood that few people get jobs without one or more interviews. This is extremely interesting,

ETHICAL DECISIONS IN HRM

Your interview day has finally arrived. You are all dressed up to make that lasting first impression. You finally meet Ms. Langley, as she shakes your hand firmly and invites you to get comfortable. Your interview has started! This is the moment you've waited for.

The first few moments appear mundane enough. The questions to this point, in fact, seem easy. Your confidence is growing. That little voice in your head keeps telling you that you are doing fine—just keep on going. Suddenly, the questions get tougher. Ms. Langley leans back, and asks about why you want to leave your current job—the one you've been in for only eighteen months. As you begin to explain that you wish to leave for personal reasons, she begins to probe more. Her smile is gone. Her body language is different. All right, you think, be honest. So you tell Ms. Langley you want to leave because you think your boss is unethical and you don't want your reputation tarnished being associated with this individual. This has led to a number of public disagreements with your boss, and you're tired of dealing with the situation any longer. Ms. Langley looks at you and replies: "If you ask me, that's not a valid reason for wanting to leave. Appears to me that you should be more assertive about the situation. Are you sure you're confident enough and have what it takes to make it in this company?"

How dare she talk to you that way! Who does she think is? So you respond with an angry tone in your voice. And guess what, you've just fallen victim to one of the tricks of the interviewing business—the stress interview.

Stress interviews are becoming more commonplace in today's business. Every job produces stress, and at some point in time every worker has a horrendous day. So these types of interviews become predictors of how you may react at work under less than favorable conditions. How so? Interviewers want to observe how you'll react when you are put under pressure. Those who demonstrate the resolve and strength to handle the stress indicate a level of professionalism and confidence. It's those characteristics that are being assessed. Individuals who react to the pressure interview in a more positive manner indicate that they should be more able to handle the day-to-day irritations that exist at work. Those who don't, well. . . .

On the other hand, they are staged events. Interviewers deliberately lead applicants into a false sense of security—the comfortable interaction. Then suddenly and drastically, they change. They go on the attack. And it's usually a personal affront that picks on a weakness they've uncovered about the applicant. It's possibly humiliating; at the very least it's demeaning.

So, should stress interviews be used? Should interviewers be permitted to assess professionalism and confidence, and how one reacts to the everyday nuisances of work by putting applicants into a confrontational scenario? Does getting angry in an interview when pressured indicate one's propensity toward violence should things not always go smoothly at work? Should HRM advocate the use of an activity that could possibly get out of control? What's your opinion?

SOURCE: Vignette based on Stephen M. Pollan and Mark Levine, "How to Ace a Tough Interview," *Working Woman* (July 1994), p. 49.

given that the validity of the interview as a selection tool has been the subject of considerable debate. Let's look at the research findings regarding interviews.

The Effectiveness of Interviews

Unfortunately for recruiters, interview situations aren't always this cut and dried. Rather, many factors enter into the deliberation in determining if a candidate is a "good fit" for the organization.[36] Although interviews are typically part of every job search process, summaries of research on interviewing have concluded that the reliability and validity of interviews are generally low.[37] Despite its popularity, the interview is expensive, inefficient, and often not job related.[38]

More specifically, a review of the research has generated the following conclusions:[39]

1. Prior knowledge about the applicant can bias the interviewer's evaluation.
2. The interviewer often holds a stereotype of what represents a "good" applicant.

3. The interviewer often tends to favor applicants who share his or her own attitudes.
4. The order in which applicants are interviewed often influences evaluations.
5. The order in which information is elicited influences evaluations.
6. Negative information is given unduly high weight.
7. The interviewer may make a decision as to the applicant's suitability in the first few minutes of the interview.
8. The interviewer may forget much of the interview's content within minutes after its conclusion.
9. Structured and well-organized interviews are more reliable.
10. The interview is most valid in determining an applicant's organizational fit, level of motivation, and interpersonal skills.

These conclusions, generated over the past few decades, still hold today. Let's elaborate on a few of them.

When an interviewer has already seen the candidate's resumé, application form, possible test scores, or appraisals of other interviewers, bias may be introduced. In such cases, the interviewer no longer relies on the data gained in the interview alone. Based on the data received prior to the interview, an image of the applicant is created. Much of the early part of the interview, then, becomes an exercise wherein the interviewer compares the actual applicant with the image formed earlier.

For example, a classic study of interviewer stereotyping focused on the Canadian Army.[40] In this study, it was concluded that Army interviewers developed a stereotype of what was a good job applicant. But this stereotype was not an individual bias; rather, it was one that was typically shared by all interviewers who had a reasonable amount of experience and who operated in a similar environment. This stereotype changed very little during the interview; in fact, most interviewer decisions changed very little during the interview. Based on this research, which appears to be still valid today, a "good applicant" is probably characterized more by the absence of unfavorable characteristics than by the presence of favorable ones.[41] Thus, negative information in an interview has a greater impact on assessment of evaluations than does positive information.

In addition to interviewer bias is something that is directly related to the applicant's actions. This is referred to as **impression management.** Impression management refers to one's attempt to project an image that will result in receiving a favorable outcome.[42] Thus, if an applicant can say or do something that is viewed favorably by the interviewer, then that person may be viewed more favorably for the position. For example, suppose you find out that the interviewer values workers who can work seven days a week, twelve-plus hours a day, if needed. Understandably, few if any jobs can sustain this work schedule over a long period of time. But that's the interviewer's view nonetheless. Accordingly, making statements of being a workaholic, which conforms to this interviewer's values, may result in creating a positive impression.

Interviewers often have a remarkably short and inaccurate memory. For example, in one study of an interview simulation, a twenty-minute videotape of a selection interview was played for a group of forty interviewers. Following the playing of the tape, the interviewers were given a twenty-question test. Although all the questions were straightforward and factual, the average number

Impression management research tells us that if this applicant is able to project an appropriate image in the interview, a favorable outcome can be achieved. So far he appears to be doing fine as he's apparently made good eye contact and has the interviewer focusing intently on what he's saying. Maybe her smile does indicate that he is making a favorable impression!

of wrong answers was ten. The researchers' conclusion? Even in a short interview, the average interviewer remembers only half of the information.[43] However, taking notes during an interview has been shown to reduce memory loss.[44] Note-taking is also useful—albeit possibly disconcerting for the interviewee—for getting more accurate information and for developing a clearer understanding of the applicant's fit by allowing follow-up questions to be asked. Companies like MPR, a personnel consultant service in Chicago, go even one step further.[45] They tape record interviews. Recruiters that do tape interviews have found that more thorough responses are elicited—and like videoconferencing, are cost effective.[46] Furthermore, taping the interview serves as one means of showing that all candidates were given equal treatment. Of course, a recruiter cannot record the interview without the permission of the applicant.

Evidence lends strong support to the view that structured interviews are more reliable and valid than unstructured interviews.[47] When two interviewers are allowed to use their own idiosyncratic pattern for questions and evaluation, they will frequently arrive at two different decisions. This happens, in part, because a different set of questions will elicit different information from the same applicant. Unstructured interviews thus make for very low reliability among the various interviewers' outcomes.

Another research finding points out that the interview offers the greatest value as a selection device in determining an applicant's organizational fit, level of motivation, and interpersonal skills.[48] This is particularly true of senior management positions. Accordingly, it is not unlikely for candidates for these positions to go through many extensive interviews with executive recruiters, company executives, and even board members before a final decision is made. Similarly, where teams have the responsibility to hire their own members, it is commonplace for each team member to interview the applicant.

One final issue about interviews revolves around when the interviewer actually makes the decision. Early studies, like the Canadian Army example, indi-

"There Are Ways To Avoid Mistakes in Hiring"

As an owner or manager, it may seem like your rights to hire, interview, retain and terminate employees are diminishing.

Learning too little too late is a continuing frustration and challenge as managers and entrepreneurs seek to work within legal limitations to obtain information about possible candidates.

For example, a manager recently hired a seemingly outstanding applicant only to see the newly hired department head resign one week later—realizing his inability to fulfill the job's expectations. Upon closer investigation, it seemed the candidate had projected the right experience and credentials on paper—not falsifying, but embellishing in the name of a competitive job market.

In fact, the resume and cover letter were the best the manager had seen, thanks to the candidate's outside professional assistance. Resume writers may help to project images on paper to secure employment, but it takes more than illusions to keep a job. Implying or exaggerating accomplishments is not only poor judgment; it's bad business.

As managers and entrepreneurs, we are going to make hiring mistakes. We may not detect some situations, such as an exaggerated resume, but others can be prevented more easily by knowing our rights as employers—not only what we cannot do, but what we can do. So what can we do?

1. Prior to interviewing applicants, update and prepare a list of job requirements, duties and responsibilities so that you and the applicant will understand the expectations of the position. After all, the longer a position is open and the more desperate you are to fill it, the more likely you are to make the position fit the candidate—any candidate.

2. Don't panic. Hire a temporary, contract or subcontract out some of the workload, or ask others to assist during the transition rather than hiring the wrong person.

3. Ask such questions as: What are your long- and short-range goals? Why are you interested in this position? What do you consider to be your greatest strengths and weaknesses? Why should I hire you? In what specific ways do you think you can make a contribution to the company? Do you have plans for continuing education?

4. Before you extend an offer, check references, including several supervisors or managers, even with an exemplary interview and seemingly perfect matched background. Even though many companies forbid anyone but the personnel department to provide information about former employees and it may seem like little information can be gained, I repeat: Check references, including education references.

The answer to the question, "Would you rehire this individual?" may not provide all you need to know, but it's a start.

5. Get applicants' permission to check references by obtaining a signed release form saying that they agree to your calling their references to ask about their background and work performance. Ask for former supervisors or managers, and if the applicant cannot provide them as references, ask why not.

6. Don't depend on letters that only provide partial information. Call and talk with someone, asking open-ended questions and listening for content as well as hesitation and inflections. If you do not feel adept, ask your personnel or human resources manager to check references or hire a consultant or reference checking service.

7. Sample questions to ask those you wish to check references with include one or more of the following: Why didn't you persuade him/her to stay? How well did he/she take criticism or suggestions given in his/her last performance appraisal process? Go over the part of the resume that relates to the reference and ask for comments.

8. Avoid questions that indirectly or directly identify age; physical characteristics, such as height, weight, hair or eye color; religious affiliation; marital and family status; medical history, work absenteeism due to illness or physical limitations; or child- or adult-care obligations.

It may take time, effort and patience to match the right person to the right job, but regardless of the process, consider the alternatives: the dismissal process.

DR. CONNIE SITTERLY, CPCM

cated that interviewers made their choice to hire or not hire a candidate within the first few minutes of the interview. While that belief was widely held, subsequent research does not support these findings.[49] In fact, this research showed that initial impressions may have little effect, unless that is the only information available for an interviewer to use.

So what sense can we make of these issues raised about interviews? And where might interviews be most appropriate? If interviews will continue to have a place in the selection decision, they appear to be more appropriate for the high-turnover jobs, and the less routine ones like middle- and upper-level managerial positions. In jobs where these characteristics are important in determining success, the interview can be a valuable selection input. In nonroutine activities, especially senior managerial positions, failure (as measured by voluntary terminations) is more frequently caused by a poor fit between the individual and the organization than by lack of competence on the part of the individual.[50] Interviewing can be useful, therefore, when it emphasizes the candidate's ability to fit into the organization rather than specific technical skills.

Becoming a More Effective Interviewer

The differences we have described may seem to cast a dark cloud over the interview. But the interview is far from worthless. It can help us to better assess the candidate, as well as be a valuable vehicle for relaying information to prospective employees.

For anyone who interviews prospective job candidates, whether as a recruiter in HRM or in any other capacity, there are several suggestions we can offer for improving the effectiveness of interviews.

Obtain Detailed Information About the Job for Which Applicants Are Being Interviewed When such information is unavailable, you may tend to rely more on factors less relevant to the job, allowing bias to enter into the assessment. You should therefore, at a minimum, have a copy of the recent position description as an information source. You are now ready to structure the interview.

Structure the Interview So That the Interview Follows a Set Procedure Reliability is increased when the interview is designed around a constant structure. A fixed set of questions should be presented to every applicant. In the trade-off between structure and consistency versus nonstructure and flexibility, structure and consistency have proved to be of greater value for selection purposes. The structured interview also aids you in comparing all candidates' answers to a like question.

Review the Candidate's Application Form and/or Resumé This step helps you to create a more complete picture of the applicant in terms of what is represented on the resume/application, and what the job requires (from step 1). This will help you to identify specific areas that need to be explored in the interview. For example, areas not clearly defined on the resume but essential for job success become a focal point for interview discussion.

Put the Applicant at Ease Assume the applicant will be nervous. For you to obtain the kind of information you will need, the applicant will have to be put at ease. Introduce yourself, and open with some small talk like the weather, the traffic coming to the interview, etc.[51] But be careful: don't venture into illegal areas with small talk about the applicant's family. Keep it impersonal!

Ask Your Questions The questions you are asking should be behaviorally based. Such questions are designed to require applicants to provide detailed descriptions of their actual job behaviors.[52] You want to elicit concrete examples of how the applicant demonstrates certain behaviors, the same behaviors that are necessary for successful performance on the job for which the interview is being held. If you are unsatisfied with the applicant's response, probe deeper to seek elaboration. The key here is to let the applicant talk. A big mistake is to do most of the talking yourself.[53] During this part of the interview, take notes. Given the propensity to forget what was actually said during the interview, notes should be taken. This will lead to increased accuracy in evaluation.

Conclude the Interview   Let the applicant know that all of your questioning is finished. Summarize what you have heard from the applicant, and give the applicant an opportunity to correct something that is unclear; or discuss anything that you may have not addressed in the interview. Inform the applicant what will happen next in the process, and when he or she can expect to hear from you.

Complete a Post-Interview Evaluation Form   Along with a structured format should go a standardized evaluation form. You should complete this item-by-item form shortly after the interviewee has departed—while the information and your notes are still fresh in your mind. The information on this evaluation can then be summarized into an overall rating, or impression, for the candidate. This approach increases the likelihood that the same frame of reference is applied to each applicant.

BACKGROUND INVESTIGATION

Background investigations are intended to verify that what was stated on the application form is correct and accurate information. And while a chief means of verifying that data comes from reference checks, HRM has witnessed significant changes in this area. For instance, by the late 1980s, organizations began questioning how much information should be given to another employer. These questions arose over the fear of being sued for giving information that had a negative effect on an individual's employment prospects elsewhere. The result is that as employee privacy rights issues began to hit the courts,[54] employers all but abandoned giving references—except for verifying employment! For instance, consider the following.[55] Larry Buck, an insurance broker with Frank B. Hall and Company, was having trouble getting employment in the field after being fired from Hall. Believing that his previous employer was sabotaging his job search efforts, Buck hired a private investigator to contact Hall and Company, posing as a prospective employer. What the investigator got was an earful. Buck, it appeared, was referred to as a "Jekyll and Hyde person, a classic sociopath." Those comments by his previous employer cost Frank B. Hall and Company about $2 million in a legal settlement. Why? The Supreme Court held that the comments were malicious and libelous.[56]

As we mentioned in the last chapter, the past few years have witnessed a changing of the Court's opinion toward background investigations and employee privacy issues.[57] This is a result of companies being held liable for the actions of their employees—especially those who later commit some sort of violence at the work place.[58] It is safe to assume that companies today need to

off the mark by Mark Parisi

EMPLOYMENT HISTORY
• SINGLE-HANDEDLY CLIMBED HUGE MOUNTAIN IN A DEATH-DEFYING MANNER TO FETCH PAIL OF LIFE-GIVING LIQUID, ALL WHILE RISKING SERIOUS HEAD INJU

JACK PADS HIS RESUME

www.offthemark.com
ATLANTIC FEATURE © 1997 MARK PARISI

Poor Jack, he just can't get the break he wants! That's because a good selection process ensures that the information obtained from an applicant is true, and actually reflects the candidate's work behaviors. In this case, it appears that Jack may have slightly exaggerated his work history.

expend some effort in investigating an applicant's background. There is documentation that supports the premise that a good predictor of an individual's future behavior is his or her past behavior,[59] as well as data that suggest that one-third of all applicants exaggerate their backgrounds or experiences.[60] Accordingly, companies must assess the liability that potential employees may create, and delve into their backgrounds in as much depth as necessary to limit the risk.[61] For example, local school systems must go to great extremes to ensure that potential teachers do not pose a risk to children. Similarly, hospitals need to feel confident that the doctors, nurses, and staff they hire are drug free. Should an unfortunate event occur, the courts may find fault in how HRM handled the background investigation.

In conducting a background investigation, two methods can be used: the internal or the external investigation. In the *internal* investigation, HRM undertakes the task of questioning former employers, personal references, and possibly credit sources.[62] Although this is a viable option, and one avidly used, unless the investigation process is handled thoroughly, little useful information may be found. On the other hand, the *external* means involves using a reference-checking firm.[63] Although there is a greater cost associated with this investigation, such firms have a better track record of gathering pertinent information, as well as being better informed on privacy rights issues.[64] However it is done, documentation is the important element.[65] Should an employer be called upon to justify what has or has not been found, supporting documentation is invaluable.

MEDICAL/PHYSICAL EXAMINATIONS

For jobs that require certain physical characteristics, the physical examination has some validity. However, this includes a very small proportion of jobs today. Should a medical clearance be required to indicate that the applicant is physically fit for the essential job elements, a company must be able to show that it is a job-related requirement. Failure to do so may result in the physical examination creating an adverse impact. Also, the company must keep in mind the Americans with Disabilities Act. Thus, even a valid physical examination may only be required after a conditional job offer. Having a physical disability may not be enough to exclude an individual from the job. Companies, as we mentioned in Chapter 3, may be required to make reasonable accommodations for these individuals.

THE REALISTIC JOB PREVIEW: CLOSING THE DEAL

Rich Falts was a recent graduate of Duke University's MBA program. During the recruiting process with one company, the aspiring marketing manager was guaranteed that he would be closely involved in the company's annual sales meeting—working with several key decision makers in the marketing division. Impressed by the thought of having an active part in the meeting, Rich found the job offer very appealing. He accepted the job and within weeks was actively involved in the sales meetings. He saw to it that power-point presentation software was loaded on the computer for each presenter. He also made sure that "token" gifts for attendees were placed at their assigned seats. Additionally, he worked closely with the hotel staff to ensure that beverages and "goodies" for breaks were readily available. This, Rich later found out, was the "involvement" he was promised. In frustration, Rich Falts quit.

The primary purpose of selection devices is to identify individuals who will be effective performers. But it is not in an interviewer's best interest to find good prospects, hire them, and then have them leave the organization. Therefore, part of selection should be concerned with reducing voluntary turnover and its associated costs.[66] One device to achieve that goal is the **realistic job preview** (RJP). What is a realistic job preview? It may include brochures, films, plant tours, work sampling, or merely a short script made up of realistic statements that accurately portray the job. The key element in RJP is that unfavorable as well as favorable information about the job is shared. While the RJP is not normally treated as a selection device, it should take place during the interview and it has demonstrated effectiveness as a method for increasing job survival among new employees, so we've included it here.

The key element in RJP is that both favorable and unfavorable information about the job is shared with the candidate.

Every applicant acquires during the selection process a set of expectations about the organization and about the specific job the applicant is hoping to be offered. It is not unusual for these expectations to be excessively inflated as a result of receiving almost uniformly positive information about the organization and job during recruitment and selection activities.[67] Evidence suggests, however, that interviewers may be erring by giving applicants only favorable information. More specifically, research leads us to conclude that applicants who have been given a realistic job preview (as well as a realistic preview of the organization) hold lower and more realistic expectations about the job they will be doing and are better prepared for coping with the job and its frustrating elements. Realistic job previews also appear to work best for those jobs that are more attractive to the individual,[68] resulting in lower turnover rates.[69] Most studies demonstrate that giving candidates a realistic job preview before offering them the job reduces turnover without lowering acceptance rates.[70] Of course, it is not unreasonable to suggest that exposing an applicant to RJP may also result in the hiring of a more committed individual.

SELECTION FOR SELF-MANAGED TEAMS

Much of the discussion about selection devices throughout the past two chapters has assumed one fact. That is, somewhere in HRM lies the responsibility for the selection process. Today, however, that may not always be the case. Companies like Perdue Farms (the chicken company of Frank Perdue), General Mills, Corning, Motherwear, Toyota, and Federal Express,[71] are more team oriented, and they empower their employees to take responsibility for the day-to-day functions in their areas. Accordingly, these employees may now work without direct supervision and take on the "administrative" responsibilities that were once performed by their supervisor.[72] One aspect of this change has been a more active role in hiring their coworkers.[73]

Consider a time when you took a course that required a group project. How was your team formed? Did the professor assign you to a group, or were you permitted to form the group yourself? Assuming your professor permitted you to select your own group, what did you look for in a potential group member? Other students who shared your values in getting the work done, on time, and of a high quality? Those who you knew would pull their own weight, and

Jody Wright, president of Motherwear—a Northampton, Massachusettts catalog company—has found it beneficial to have her employees play a major role in hiring team members. As she sees it, it's the employees who will have to work with the new employee and will have to be comfortable in the work relationships they build.

not let one or two in the group do all of the work? Well, that's the same premise behind self-managed work-team selection. In any organization, a critical link to success is how well employees perform their jobs. It is also understood that when those jobs require the interaction of several individuals, or a team, coming together as a unified unit takes time.[74] The length of that time, however, is a function of how the team views its goals and priorities, and how open and trusting group members are. What better way to begin this team-building than to have the "personalities" involved actually making the hiring decision.

When workers are empowered to hire their coworkers, they bring to the selection process varied experiences and backgrounds. This enables them to "better assess applicants' skills in their field of expertise."[75] They, too, like your class project, want to hire someone they can count on, who will perform his or her duties, and not let the others down. This means that they focus their attention on the job duties required, and those special skills and qualifications needed to be successful. From our previous discussion of validation (Chapter 6), that's precisely the focus of the selection process. In this case, a more objective evaluation may be obtained. But that's not to say that self-managed work teams are not without problems. If these workers are unfamiliar with proper interviewing techniques, or the legal ramifications of their hiring decisions, they too, could experience many of the difficulties often associated with interviews.

SUMMARY

This summary relates to the Learning Objectives provided on p. 190.

After reading this chapter, you should know:

1. Selection devices provide managers with information that will help them predict whether an applicant will prove to be a successful job performer.
2. The application form is effective for acquiring hard biographical data—data that can ultimately be verified.
3. Weighted applications are useful in that through statistical techniques, linkage can be determined between certain relevant information and the prediction of job success.
4. Performance simulation tests require the applicant to engage in specific behaviors that have been demonstrated to be job related. Work sampling and the assessment center, which are performance simulations, receive high marks for their predictive capability.
5. Assessment centers are a type of performance simulation test. They are concluded over a few days, with a number of observers studying how the individuals handle or react to various business situations.
6. Graphology is the analysis of handwriting. Its validity is questionable.
7. Interviews consistently achieve low marks for reliability and validity. These, however, are more the result of interviewer problems as opposed to the interview itself. Interviewing validity can be enhanced by using a structured process.

8. Steps involved in properly interviewing involve: (1) obtain detailed information about the job for which applicants are being interviewed; (2) structure the interview so that the interview follows a set procedure; (3) review the candidate's application form and/or resumé; (4) put the applicant at ease; (5) ask your questions; (6) conclude the interview; and (7) complete a post-interview evaluation form.
9. Realistic job previews reduce turnover by giving the applicant both favorable and unfavorable information about the job.
10. Background investigations are valuable when they verify hard data from the application; they tend, however, to offer little practical value as a predictive selection device.

EXPERIENTIAL EXERCISE: Benchmark "Show and Tell"

Instructions

Ask (with permission) a human resource representative or personnel manager from your university, college, a current employer, church, or other organization for samples of a blank application form, appraisal form, reference inquiry, orientation package, exit interview form, or sample blank personnel file, annual report or company brochure, needs assessments, attitude survey forms, or any related human resource or personnel sample forms that might be provided.

Benchmarking Discussion

Share, compare, and discuss similarities and differences with your class team and other teams for benchmarking purposes.

Individual Decision

If you were a human resource manager, selecting from the choices, which would you choose and why?

Class Consensus Decision

Discuss, share, and develop a class comparison chart to determine which sample forms are the most preferred overall by class participants as a whole.

WEB-WISE EXERCISES

Search and print findings about current job opportunities in human resources from the Web site.

Career Mosaic
http://www.careermosaic.com
For job information as well as data on current job opportunities.

Online Career Center
http://www.occ.com
Offers over 250 companies that post listings of employment opportunities. Listing is especially strong in hi-tech area.

Search and Find
Compliance assistance information available from Department of Labor (DOL) which provides reference guides, fact sheets on a variety of topics, under Fair Labor Standards Act (FLSA). Prints recordkeeping requirements and fact sheets on related topics of interest.
       http://www.dol.gov/)

CASE APPLICATION:
Frank's Catering

After twenty-one years as a field technologist with Nation's Co. Frank Crepes chose to quit, believing that he would not be given a suitable severance package if lay-offs continued and that the company's future seemed questionable.

Moreover, Frank perceived many of the recent management decisions and changes as little more than desperate survival measures that unfairly regarded its employees. Frank quit, and he was right; there was no severance package. Using what little retirement he had earned, Frank with his wife, Juanita, started a mobile catering business. They would travel to outdoor events, preparing inexpensive, quality food for fair prices and friendly service. They have an opportunity to expand to three other locations on the property of their primary client, if they are willing to increase staff. Although it would complicate their operations, they would have an opportunity to earn back the retirement fund which they spent starting the business. Frank is afraid of the process of hiring people. Juanita thinks it would be helpful to have someone who could speak Spanish because they have so many customers who speak Spanish.

One of his customers, Tomisina Wolfe, says he has a cousin who needs a job, is a great cook, but can't find a job because of a disability. Frank would like to interview the cousin, but doesn't know how to properly ask questions. He has never managed, interviewed, selected, or had any experience with the selection process. He doesn't know what questions are illegal, he is not familiar with pertinent laws, he does not know how to properly interview, screen, or test an applicant, or conduct a reference or background check.

He does know he needs your advice because if he doesn't hire three people within two weeks who can ensure their level of quality, service, cleanliness and service, and who they can trust in a predominantly cash business, their primary customers will select another supplier to meet their need. Although they can't afford to pay you, they will serve you a free dinner for two each month for a year, or cater a dinner party for twelve, while you coach them on how to proceed, and ask questions.

Based on what you have learned from human resource management, what advice will you give Frank and Juanita?

Option

You may wish to form a class team of three and role play, two serving as Frank and Juanita to ask questions, and the other to share expertise to expand their knowledge and abilities legally and effectively interview, screen, hire, recruit, test, and evaluate potential applicants.

TESTING YOUR UNDERSTANDING

How well did you fulfill the learning objectives?
1. A director of selection at a large toy store is reviewing the selection techniques used by three sales specialist interviewers. One relies solely on the inter-

view, but does not thoroughly read the application form and never does a background check. A second does not trust the interview outcomes, and conducts extensive background checks on each applicant. A third looks for related work experiences on the application form and asks each applicant to handle a specific sales situation in the interview. The director concludes that

a. Interviewers one and two are better than interviewer three because they rely on one selection device.

b. Interviewer three does not assess past or current work-related behaviors.

c. The three interviewers all perform roughly equivalent processes.

d. Each interviewee should be seen by all three interviewers to improve the quality of the interview process.

e. A selection test should be written and added to the devices used.

2. A director of selection for a large manufacturing organization wants to weight application forms for employees in the new robotics plant. That plant, scheduled to open in eleven months, will utilize new technology that will create substantially different job requirements than any existing organizational jobs. How should the director proceed?

a. Delay the opening of the plant until a weighted application is developed for current jobs in the robotics plant.

b. Wait until the plant has been open a year, then examine the application forms for good and poor workers to identify patterns of differences.

c. Hire a consultant to conduct the analysis and submit a valid report on the reliability of weighted application forms.

d. Examine work records from good and poor performers over the last five years. Identify differences in application form items.

e. A weighted application form is inappropriate for a robotics plant. They work only in the sales and financial areas of a company where hard biographical data are more readily available.

3. College professors interviewing for jobs at a small private New England area university are asked to prepare and deliver a "class" for selected students. Given this information, which one of the following statements is most correct?

a. This is an example of an in-basket simulation. It is unique to hiring faculty in universities.

b. The class session is a type of work sampling, at least for the teaching part of the job.

c. The "class" represents an assessment center for new faculty to determine the new faculty member's rank.

d. The "class" is part of the interviewing process used to determine attainment of a specialized degree.

e. The "class" is an atypical feedback test.

4. As part of the selection process, a day-care center in Boston has each applicant come to work for a day before final hiring decisions are made. Why?

a. The decision makers have a chance to evaluate the hands-on capabilities of each applicant.

b. The organization is understaffed. This is a system to get free help.

c. Title VII requires this for all child-care providers.

d. This process takes less time than a real interview.

e. Workdays have replaced background checking in most child-care organizations.

5. How do employment tests differ from performance simulation tests?

a. Employment tests are conducted before hiring decisions are made. Performance simulation tests are conducted after hiring decisions are made.

b. Employment tests are conducted after hiring decisions are made. Performance simulation tests are conducted before hiring decisions are made.

c. Performance simulation tests are paper-and-pencil exercises. Employment tests are measured by manager observation.

d. Performance simulation tests have high content validity. Employment tests may also have construct validity.

e. Employment tests are more expensive than performance simulation tests.

6. What is the difference between work sampling and assessment centers?

a. Work sampling is another term used to describe the assessment center.

b. Work sampling is a type of employment test. Assessment centers are a performance evaluation technique.

c. Work sampling procedures usually have fewer evaluators than assessment centers.

d. Assessment centers usually take less time to conduct than work sampling procedures.

e. Assessment centers are usually done for blue-collar work. Work sampling procedures are conducted for managerial job candidates.

7. Gina interviews candidates for technical consultant positions in a large aerospace firm. She was trained to do this last year, because of her extensive technical background and job knowledge. At the end of a typical day, she has interviewed eight to ten people. She asks them all the same questions, in the same order. At 5 P.M. she fills out standard forms for each person, and forwards her recommendations to corporate. She complains that she makes mistakes, and can't really remember facts and details about his candidates while completing the evaluation forms. What

should be done to make Gina's interviews more effective?

a. Nothing can be done. Interviews are not effective predictors of successful job performance.

b. Gina should ask a different set of questions with each applicant.

c. Gina should conduct no more than four interviews per day.

d. Gina should learn some memory-enhancing techniques.

e. Gina should take notes.

8. What could have been done differently in the case of Rich Falts, the Duke University graduate who quit his job because he had to perform what he considered menial tasks during his first annual sales meeting?

a. The interviewer should have offered Rich coffee during the interview process, to model appropriate behavior.

b. The company should have offered Rich more money to help ease the burden of performing routine tasks.

c. The interviewer should have told Rich that the early part of his assignment would include menial tasks.

d. The interviewer should have been honest with Rich and told him that the firm did not have a job suitable for someone with his credentials.

e. The company should review all of its job descriptions.

9. Realistic job previews are fine, but what do you do when you have a job that no one wants to take? Bill had been interviewing for more than two months for the position of manager in his southeastern chemical-processing plant. The hours would be long. The workers were often unwilling to work. The plant was old, with inefficient equipment. Bill spoke frankly to the 35 prospective candidates he interviewed. Not one of these individuals decided to continue to pursue the job.

a. Bill should consider job redesign or plant relocation. The problem in this case is not with interviewing techniques.

b. Bill should hire a consultant to teach him how to present a realistic job preview in more favorable terms.

c. Bill should keep interviewing. The right person, dedicated and challenge-seeking, will turn up.

d. Bill should raise the salary for the "hard-to-fill" position.

e. Bill should let someone else do the interviewing.

10. A vice president of human resources for a large service organization wants to start a background investigation process on all new employees in her company who have access to financial information or funding, such as accountants. How should she proceed?

a. Begin a policy of credit checking for new employees.

b. Call former employers of potential employees.

c. Be suspicious of any employee who has held more than two jobs in any five-year period. Hire a professional to follow such an individual for a period of time before hiring.

d. Give candidates polygraph tests.

e. Hire an external investigator for a more thorough job than could be done internally.

11. Don is interviewing Candy, who is confined to a wheelchair, for a computer programming position in his company. She has passed the usual selection criteria—the employment test, the background check, and all interviews. What should Don do?

a. Have Candy take a physical examination before hiring her.

b. Recommend that Candy be hired if she can supply a desk/chair arrangement that would be suitable.

c. Recommend that Candy be hired.

d. Conduct more interviews with Candy.

e. Interview employees who would have to work with Candy.

12. A vice president of human resources wants to exclude physical examinations from the selection process. In the past year, his firm has been sued twice because of the physical. However, most jobs in the machine shop require moving heavy, sensitive machines. What else can the organization do to protect its equipment investment?

a. Perform a thorough background check.

b. Add weighted items to the application form about health club memberships.

c. Close the production facility.

d. Initiate a work sampling procedure for the jobs in question.

e. Ask applicants about their physical abilities during the intensive interview.

13. Biographical data on job application forms

a. are illegal under civil rights legislation.

b. are often good predictors of future job success.

c. are seldom good predictors of future job success.

d. are useful only to identify mental lapses indicated by large time periods between jobs.

e. are standardized across all U.S. organizations.

14. How do organizations use application forms, since civil rights legislation changed the contents?

a. They have no real use. In fact, most companies are eliminating application forms.

b. They are used to avoid adverse impact.

c. Validated information, such as class standing, can be a good predictor of job success.

d. They are used to document ADA compliance.

e. They are used to validate Title VII compliance.

15. All of these statements are true about assessment centers except
    a. personality tests may be included in the assessment.
    b. groups of applicants are evaluated together.
    c. applicants may be asked to solve day-to-day problems that managers find in their in-baskets.
    d. the most important element is the leaderless group discussion.
    e. evaluation is done by groups of assessors.

16. In your text, graphology is
    a. not recommended for use. There is little evidence to support its use as a selection technique.
    b. recommended for checking educational level.
    c. recommended for validating job skills.
    d. recommended for identifying personality defects.
    e. recommended for job analysis.

17. Bernie runs a chain of florists shops on the east coast. She could have used all of the following to try to find honest employees for her cashier's jobs except
    a. reference checking.
    b. intelligence testing.
    c. honesty tests.
    d. graphology.
    e. background investigation.

18. Why do realistic job previews result in lower turnover rates?
    a. When unfavorable information is disclosed, most candidates are no longer interested, so fewer job offers are made.
    b. They do not result in lower turnover rates.
    c. Providing unfavorable information instead of favorable information about a job helps people brace for the realities of work. When a new employee finds out the job is not all bad, they are less inclined to voluntarily resign.
    d. Training that provides new employees coping skills helps to reduce turnover.
    e. More committed employees are hired.

Endnotes

1. Employment situations are based on vignettes cited in Vivian Pospisil, "Resume' Gaffes," *Industry Week* (March 1996), p. 10; Rochelle Sharpe, "Checkoffs," *The Wall Street Journal* (August 8, 1995), p. A-1; and Tom Washington, "Selling Yourself in Job Interviews," *National Business Employment Weekly* (Spring/Summer 1993), p. 30.

2. For an interesting view on selection, see Orlando Behling, "Employee Selection: Will Intelligence and Conscientiousness Do the Job?" *Academy of Management Executive,* Vol. 12, No. 1 (January 1998), pp. 77–86.

3. Micheline Maynard, "Toyota Devises Grueling Workout for Job Seekers," *USA Today* (August 11, 1997), p. 3B.

4. Pierre Mornell, "Zero Defect Hiring," *Inc.* (March 1998), p. 77.

5. Richard Sisley, "The Recruitment Gamble–Improving the Odds," *Management* (May 1997), pp. 22–24.

6. See also Elizabeth Bahnsen, "Questions to Ask, and Not to Ask, Job Applicants," *HR News* (November 1996), pp. 10–11.

7. Saundra Jackson and Nan McGrane, "Get Application Form Before Offering Job," *HR News* (June 1996), p. 13.

8. Wayne F. Casio, *Applied Psychology in Personnel Management* (Englewood Cliffs, N.J.: Prentice-Hall, 1991), p. 265. See also Edson G. Hammer and Lawrence S. Kleinman, "Getting to Know You," *Personnel Administration,* Vol. 33 (May 1988), pp. 86–92.

9. Wayne Casio, p. 265. See also Edson G. Hammer and Lawrence S. Kleinman, pp. 86–92.

10. See, for example, Brooks Mitchell, "Bio Data: Using Employment Applications to Screen New Hires," *Cornell Hotel and Restaurant Administration Quarterly,* Vol. 29, No. 4 (February 1989), pp. 56–61.

11. See, for example, M. C. Smith, J. M. Smith, and D. I. George, "Improving Access through a Software Design for the Weighted Application Form," *Journal of Occupational Psychology,* Vol. 61, No. 3 (September 1988), pp. 257–64.

12. Mitchell, p. 58. The seven items were not specifically identified so that the competitive edge the hotel had in hiring practices would not be weakened.

13. Carla Joinson, "Is After-Hire Testing the Best Solution," *HRMagazine* (July 1997), p. 120; and Adrienne Loftin and Rebecca Hastings, "Research Helps to Avoid Testing-Related Problems," *HR News* (February 1997), p. 11.

14. See, for instance, Lorie Parch, "Workshop: Testing . . . 1, 2, 3," *Working Woman* (October 1997), pp. 74–78; and Leonard A. White, Mark C. Young, and Robert N. Kilcullen, "Selecting the Best Employees for Your Organization," *B&E Review* (October-December 1995), p. 9.

15. Jack J. Kramer and Jane Close Conoley, supplement to *The Tenth Mental Measurements Yearbook* (Lincoln, Neb.: Buros Institute of Mental Measurements, 1990).

16. John A. Parnel, "Improving the Fit Between Organizations and Employees," *SAM Advanced Management Journal* (Winter 1998), pp. 35–42; and Jerry Flint, "Can You Tell Applesauce from Pickles?" *Forbes* (October 9, 1995), p. 108.

17. John B. Miner, *Industrial Psychology* (New York: McGraw-Hill, 1992).

18. See, for instance, Rudy M. Yandrick, "Employers Turn to Psychological Tests to Predict Applicants' Work Behavior," *HR News* (November 1995), pp. 2, 13; and Wade Lambert, "Flunking Grade: Psychological Tests Designed to Weed Out Rogue Cops Get a 'D'," *The Wall Street Journal* (September 11, 1995), p. A-1.

19. Jonathan A. Segal, "Take Applicants for a Test Drive," *HRMagazine* (December 1996), pp. 120–122.

20. See, for example, Walter C. Borman and Glenn L. Hallman, "Observation Accuracy for Assessors of Work Sample Performance: Consistency Across Task and Individual Differences Correlates," *Journal of Applied Psychology,* Vol. 76, No. 4 (February 1991), p. 11. See also Ivan T. Robertson and Sylvia Downs, "Work Sample Tests of Trainability: A Meta Analysis," *Journal of Applied Psychology,* Vol. 74, No. 3 (June 1989), pp. 402–10.

21. See, for example, Cynthia D. Fisher, Lyle F. Schoenfeldt, and

James B. Shaw, *Human Resource Management* (Boston: Houghton Mifflin, 1990), p. 264.

22. See, for example, Lisa McDaniel, "Group Assessments Produce Better Hires," *HRMagazine* (May 1995), pp. 72–76; and Jeffrey R. Schneider and Neil Schmitt, "An Executive Approach to Understanding Assessment Center Dimension and Exercise Constructs," *Journal of Applied Psychology,* Vol. 77, No. 1 (February 1992), pp. 32–35.

23. Craig Russell, "Selecting Top Corporate Leaders: An Example of Biographical Information," *Journal of Management,* Vol. 16, No. 1 (March 1990), p. 74.

24. George Munchos III and Barbara McArthur, "Revisiting the Historical Use of Assessment Centers in Management Selection and Development," *Journal of Management Development,* Vol. 10, No. 1 (1991), p. 5.

25. Interview with George Shaffer, AT&T Assessment Director, March 12, 1992. Cost figures are not released according to company policy regarding proprietary information.

26. See, for example, Victor Dulewicz, "Improving Assessment Centers," *Personnel Management,* Vol. 23, No. 6 (June 1991), pp. 50–55.

27. See Alessandra Bianchi, "The Character-Revealing Handwriting Analysis," *Inc.* (February 1996), pp. 77–79; and David L. Kurtz, C. Patrick Flecnor, Louis E. Boon, and Virginia M. Rider, "CEOs: A Handwriting Analysis," *Business Horizons,* Vol. 32, No. 1 (January–February 1989), pp. 41–43.

28. Ibid., p. 41.

29. Alan Fowler, "An Even-Handed Approach to Graphology," *Personnel Management,* Vol. 23, No. 3 (March 1991), pp. 40–43. See also "Graphology: The Power of the Written Word," *Economist,* Vol. 2315, No. 7659 (June 11, 1990), p. 97.

30. David Nye, "Son of the Polygraph," *Across the Board,* Vol. 26, No. 6 (June 1989), p. 20.

31. See Rom Zemke, "Do Honesty Tests Tell the Truth?" *Training,* Vol. 27, No. 10 (October 1990), pp. 75–81. Also see Robin Inwald, "Those Little White Lies of Honesty Vendors," *Personnel,* Vol. 67, No. 6 (June 1990), p. 52.

32. Jerry Beilinson, "Applicant Screening Methods: Under Surveillance," *Personnel,* Vol. 67, No. 12 (December 1990), p. 3.

33. See Zemke, p. 75.

34. Jonathan A. Segal, "Mirror, Mirror On the Wall," *HRMagazine* (March 1996), pp. 29–34.

35. Steven D. Maurer and Thomas W. Lee, "Situational Interview Accuracy in a Multiple Rating Context," *Academy of Management Best Papers Proceedings,* Lloyd N. Dosier and J. Bernard Keys, eds. (August 8–13, 1997), pp. 149–153; and Steven D. Maurer and Thomas W. Lee, "Toward a Resolution of Contrast Error in the Employment Interview: A Test of the Situational Interview," *Academy of Management Best Papers Proceedings,* Dorothy P. Moore, ed. (August 14–17, 1994), pp. 132–36.

36. For a discussion on fit and its appropriateness to the interviewing process, see "The Right Fit," *Small Business Reports* (April 1993), p. 28.

37. See, for example, A. I. Huffcutt and W. Arthur, Jr., "Hunter and Hunter (1984) Revisited: Interview Validity for Entry-Level Jobs," *Journal of Applied Psychology* (April 1994), pp. 184–90; M. A. McDaniel, D. L. Whetzel, F. L. Schmidt, and S. D. Maurer, "The Validity of Employment Interviews: A Comprehensive Review and Meta-Analysis," *Journal of Applied Psychology* (August 1994), pp. 599–616; and Herbert

George Baker and Morris S. Spier, "The Employment Interview: Guaranteed Improvement in Reliability," *Public Personnel Management* (Spring 1990), pp. 85–87.

38. Gary N. Powell, and Laurel R. Goulet, "Recruiters' and Applicants' Reactions to Campus Interviews and Employment Decisions," *Academy of Management Journal,* Vol. 39, No. 6 (December 1996), pp. 1619–1640; and Robert C. Dipboye, *Selection Interviews: Process Perspectives* (Cincinnati: Southwestern Publishing Co., 1992), pp. 6–9.

39. See Charles Foster and Lynn Godkin, "Employment Selection in Health Care: The Case for Structured Interviewing," *Health Care Management Review* (Winter 1998), p. 46; Cynthia Kay Stevens, "Effects of Preinterview Beliefs on Applicants' Reactions to Campus Interviews," *Academy of Management Journal,* Vol. 40, No. 4 (August 1997), pp. 947–966; and Baker and Spier, p. 87; and Dipboye, Chapter 1.

40. Edward C. Webster, *Decision Making in the Employment Interview* (Montreal: Industrial Relations Center, McGill University, 1964).

41. Dipboye, p. 8; and Baker and Spier, p. 87.

42. For a more detailed discussion of impression management, see Amy L. Kristof and Cynthia Kay Stevens, "Applicant Impression Management Tactics: Effects on Interviewer Evaluations and Interview Outcomes," *Academy of Management Best Papers Proceedings,* Dorothy P. Moore, ed. (August 14–17, 1994), pp. 127–131.

43. Reported in Robert E. Carlson, Paul W. Thayer, Eugene C. Mayfield, and Donald A. Peterson, "Improvements in the Selection Interview," *Personnel Journal* (April 1971), p. 272.

44. Dipboye, p. 201.

45. Michael P. Cronin, "Try Taping Those Interviews," *Inc.* (September 1994), p. 120.

46. Robin Rimmer Hurst, "Video Interviewing: Take One!" *HRMagazine* (November 1996), pp. 100–104

47. See, for example, Wayne F. Casio, *Applied Psychology in Personnel Management,* 4th ed. (Englewood Cliffs, N.J.: Prentice-Hall, 1991), p. 271.

48. Ibid.

49. See, for example, Casio, p. 273; A. Phillips and R. L. Dipboye, "Correlation Tests of Predictions from a Process Model of the Interview," *Journal of Applied Psychology,* Vol. 74 (1989), pp. 41–52; M. Ronald Buckley and Robert W. Edner, "B. M. Springbett and the Notion of the 'Snap Decision' in the Interview," *Journal of Management,* Vol. 14, No. 1 (March 1988), pp. 59–67.

50. See, for example, Dipboye, pp. 39–45.

51. For an interviewee's perspective on small talk, see Jack Wolfe, "The Power of Babble," *Men's Health* (November 1996), pp. 74–76.

52. "Interviewing: It's How You Play the Game," *Inc.* (December 1995), p. 120.

53. Robert McGarvey, "Good Questions," *Entrepreneur* (January 1996), p. 87.

54. Steven C. Bahls and Jane Easter Bahls, "Point of Reference," *Entrepreneur* (June 1997), pp. 84–85.

55. Stories adapted from "Revenge of the Fired," *Newsweek* (February 11, 1987), pp. 46–47.

56. Ibid.

57. Jennifer Click, "SHRM Survey Highlights Dilemmas of Reference Checks," *HR News* (July 1995), p. 13.

58. See, for example, Society of Human Resource Management,

Reference-Checking Survey (Alexandria, VA: SHRM, 1995); and Gregory Service, "Keeping Out of Court," *Security Management Supplement* (July 1990), p. 11A.

59. Paul Falcone, "Getting Employers to Open Up on a Reference Check," *HRMagazine* (July 1995), pp. 58–63; Michael A. McDaniel, "Biographical Constructs for Predicting Employee Suitability," *Journal of Applied Psychology,* Vol. 74, No. 6 (December 1989), pp. 964–970; and Michael Tadman, "The Past Predicts the Future," *Security Management,* Vol. 33, No. 7 (July 1989), pp. 57–61.

60. Commerce Clearing House, *Human Resources Management: Ideas and Trends* (May 17, 1992), p. 85.

61. Ellen Alderman and Caroline Kennedy, "Privacy," *Across the Board* (March 1996), pp. 32–35; and Norman D. Bates, "Understanding the Liability of Negligent Hiring," *Security Management Supplement* (July 1990), p. 7A.

62. Edward A. Robinson, "Beware–Job Seekers Have No Secrets," *Fortune* (December 29, 1997), p. 285.

63. William T. Hill, "Getting Help from the Outside," *Security Management Supplement* (July 1990), p. 15A.

64. Ibid.

65. Commerce Clearing House, pp. 439–440.

66. Michael W. Mercer, "Turnover: Reducing the Costs," *Personnel,* Vol. 65, No. 12 (December 1988), p. 36.

67. See, for example, Bruce M. Meglino, Angelo S. DeNisi, Stuart A. Youngblood, and Kevin J. Williams, "Effects of Realistic Job Previews," *Journal of Applied Psychology,* Vol. 79, No. 2 (May 1988), pp. 259–266.

68. Bruce M. Meglino and Angelo S. DeNisi, "Realistic Job Previews: Some Thoughts on Their More Effective Use in Managing the Flow of Human Resources," *Human Resources Planning,* Vol. 10, No. 3 (Fall 1987), p. 157.

69. Ibid.

70. See, for example, Robert J. Vanderberg and Vida Scarpello, "The Matching Model: An Examination of the Processes Underlying Realistic Previews," *Journal of Applied Psychology,* Vol. 75, No. 1 (February 1990), pp. 60–67.

71. Donna Fenn, "Hiring: Employees Take Charge," *Inc.* (October 1995), p. 111; William R. Coradetti, "Teamwork Takes Time and a Lot of Energy," *HRMagazine* (June 1994), p. 74; and Brian Dumaine, "Who Needs a Boss?" *Fortune* (May 7, 1990), pp. 52–62.

72. Dale E. Yeatts, Martha Hipskind, and Debra Barnes, "Lessons Learned from Self-Managed Work Teams," *Business Horizons* (July/August 1994), pp. 11–18.

73. "How to Form Hiring Teams," *Personnel Journal* (August 1994), pp. 14–17.

74. See for example, Alexander Mikalachki, "Creating a Winning Team," *Business Quarterly* (Summer 1994), pp. 14–22.

75. "How to Form Hiring Teams," p. 14.

8. Socializing, Orienting and Developing Employees

LEARNING OBJECTIVES

After reading this chapter, you will be able to:

1. Define socialization
2. Identify the three stages of employee socialization.
3. Identify the key personnel involved in orientation.
4. Explain why employee training is important.
5. Define training.
6. Describe how training needs evolve.
7. Indicate what is meant by the term *organizational development* and the role of the change agent.
8. Describe the methods and criteria involved in evaluating training programs.
9. Explain issues critical to international training and development.

It should come to no one's surprise that the United States has become a predominantly service economy. In fact, the Bureau of Labor Statistics indicates that almost 80 percent of all employment in the United States is in providing services and that percentage will grow during the next decade. Success in this industry is a function of many factors. Unquestionably, however, is one primary factor—the individuals providing the service. Given this service trend and the importance of people, an appropriate question for service organizations is: What are you doing to attract and keep the best service workers?[1] When the management of Marriott Hotels posed that question to themselves, they responded, "much, much more!"

Marriott Hotels used to hire doormen, bellmen, front desk clerks, and concierges in droves. These front-line people were the first point of contact with customers. As such, you'd expect that the hotel would want to have these people represent the "best" the hotel had to offer. Yet, when these employees were hired, they were often brought together for an hour and told of the benefits they'd receive. After that, they were put to work—often with little idea of what to do, or how Marriott expected them to do their jobs. The re-

Several years ago, these "front-line" employees at Marriott would have received a one-day orientation and then been "thrown" into their jobs. Frustrated, many quit. Of those remaining, they struggled with doing their jobs properly. All that has changed today thanks to a ninety-day orientation program at Marriott designed to truly acclimate employees to their jobs—and to customer service.

sults? You guessed it! Customers often weren't happy about the service they were getting. Moreover, neither were these same employees happy about what they were doing. More than 40 percent of the new employees quit within the first three months on the job. But all this began to change in the early 1990s.

It started when Marriott launched its new employee orientation and training program. Instead of the one-hour, here's-your-benefits speech, new employees go through an intensive ninety-day orientation and training program. It begins with new employees attending an initial eight-hour session. During the session, new employees are bombarded with information about what quality service means. Much of that focus promotes how to please customers, and what role each employee plays in making the hotel a success. Yes, they still get their benefits information. It just doesn't dominate orientation. And that speech is a bit easier to swallow, especially considering the extravagant lunch that is served as a welcome-aboard gesture.

During the remaining "89 days," new employees are assigned to a buddy who will continue the orientation and provide job-specific training. Employees and their buddies also attend refresher courses, which reinforce the hotel's commitment to both its employees and customers. And at the end of the ninety-day orientation, new employees, their buddies, and guests are invited to a gala banquet—a reward for "learning the ropes."

How successful is Marriott's new employee orientation and training program? If success at the hotels can be measured by customer response times, then they are highly successful. Prior to this new program, it took an average of fifteen minutes from the time customers stepped onto the curb in front of the hotel until they were in their rooms. Today, that time has been cut to under three minutes!

INTRODUCTION

When we talk about socializing, orienting, and developing employees, we are referring to a process of helping new employees adapt to their new organizations and work responsibilities. These programs are designed to assist employees to fully understand what working is about in the organization, and to get them to become fully productive as soon as possible. In essence, it's about learning the ropes! This means that employees understand and accept the behaviors that the organization views as desirable, and that when exhibited, will result in each employee attaining his or her goals.[2]

In this chapter, we'll explore the arena of socializing, orientating, and developing employees. We'll first look at the socialization process, and what organizations should do when employees first join an organization. We'll then proceed to explore their training and later development efforts designed to ensure a supply of highly skilled employees.

THE OUTSIDER–INSIDER PASSAGE

When we talk about **socialization,** we are talking about a process of adaptation. In the context of organizations, the term refers to all passages undergone by employees. For instance, when you begin a new job, accept a lateral transfer, or get a promotion, you are required to make adjustments. You must adapt to a new environment—different work activities, a new boss, a different and most likely a diverse group of coworkers, and probably a different set of standards for what constitutes good performance.[3] Although we recognize that this socialization will go on throughout our careers—within an organization as well as between organizations—the most profound adjustment occurs when we make the first move into an organization: the move from being an outsider to being an insider. The following discussion, therefore, is limited to the outsider–insider passage, or what is more appropriately labeled organization-entry socialization.

Socialization

Do you remember your first day in college? What feelings did you experience? Anxiety over new expectations? Uncertainty over what was to come? Excitement at being on your own and experiencing new things? Fear based on all those things friends said about how tough college courses were? Stress over what classes to take, and what professors to get? Well, you probably experienced many of these things. And entry into a job is no different. For organizations to assist in the adjustment process, a few matters must be understood. We'll call these the assumptions of employee socialization.[4]

The Assumptions of Employee Socialization

Several assumptions underlie the process of socialization. The first is that socialization strongly influences employee performance and organizational stability. Also, new members suffer from anxiety; socialization does not occur in a vacuum; and the way in which individuals adjust to new situations is remarkably similar. Let's look a little closer at each of these assumptions.

Socialization Strongly Influences Employee Performance and Organizational Stability   Your work performance depends to a considerable degree on knowing what you should or should not do. Understanding the right way to do a job indicates proper socialization. Furthermore, the appraisal of your performance includes how well you fit into the organization. Can you get along with your co-workers? Do you have acceptable work habits? Do you demonstrate the right attitude? These qualities differ among jobs and organizations. For instance, on some jobs you will be evaluated higher if you are aggressive and outwardly indicate that you are ambitious. On another job, or on the same job in another organization, such an approach might be evaluated negatively. As a result, proper socialization becomes a significant factor in influencing both your actual job performance and how it is perceived by others.[5]

Organizational Stability Is Also Increased through Socialization[6]   When, over many years, jobs are filled and vacated with a minimum of disruption, the organization will be more stable. Its objectives will be more smoothly transferred between generations. Loyalty and commitment to the organization should be easier to maintain because the organization's philosophy and objectives will appear consistent over time. Given that most managers value high employee performance and organizational stability, the proper socialization of employees should be important.

New Members Suffer from Anxiety   The outsider—insider passage is an anxiety-producing situation. Stress is high because the new member feels a lack of identification—if not with the work itself, certainly with a new superior, new co-workers, a new work location, and a new set of rules and regulations. Loneliness and a feeling of isolation are not unusual. This anxiety state has at least two implications. First, new employees need special attention to put them at ease. This usually means providing an adequate amount of information to reduce uncertainty and ambiguity. Second, the existence of tension can be positive in that it often acts to motivate individuals to learn the values and **norms** of their newly assumed role as quickly as possible.[7] We can conclude, therefore, that the new member is anxious about the new role but is motivated to learn the ropes and rapidly become an accepted member of the organization.

Socialization Does Not Occur in a Vacuum   The learning associated with socialization goes beyond the formal job description and the expectations that may be made by people in human resources or by the new member's manager. Socialization is influenced by subtle and less subtle statements and behaviors offered up by colleagues, management, employees, clients, and other people with whom new members come in contact.

The Way In Which Individuals Adjust to New Situations Is Remarkably Similar   This holds true even though the content and type of adjustments may vary. For instance, as pointed out previously, anxiety is high at entry and the new member usually wants to reduce that anxiety quickly. The information obtained during the recruitment and selection stages is always incomplete and usually distorted. New employees, therefore, must alter their understanding of their role to fit more complete information they get once they are on the job. The point is that there is no instant adjustment—every new member goes through a settling-in period that tends to follow a relatively standard pattern.

The Socialization Process

Socialization can be conceptualized as a process made up of three stages: prearrival, encounter, and metamorphosis.[8] The first stage encompasses the learning the new employee has gained before joining the organization. In the second stage, the new employee gets an understanding of what the organization is really like, and deals with the realization that the expectations and reality may differ. In the third stage, lasting change occurs. Here, new employees become fully trained in their jobs, perform successfully, and "fit" in with the values and norms of coworkers.[9] These three stages ultimately affect new employees' productivity on the job, their commitment to the organization's goals, and their decision to remain with the organization.[10] Exhibit 8-1 is a graphic representation of the socialization process.

The **prearrival stage** explicitly recognizes that each individual arrives with a set of organizational values, attitudes, and expectations. These may cover both the work to be done and the organization. For instance, in many jobs, particularly high-skilled and managerial jobs, new members will have undergone a considerable degree of prior socialization in training and in school.[11] Part of teaching business students is to socialize them to what business is like, what to expect in a business career, and what kind of attitudes professors believe will lead to successful assimilation in an organization. Prearrival socialization, however, goes beyond the specific job. The selection process is used in most organizations to inform prospective employees about the organization as a whole. In addition, of course, interviews in the selection process also act to ensure the inclusion of the "right type"—determining those who will fit in![12] "Indeed, the ability of individuals to present the appropriate face during the selection process determines their ability to move into the organization in the first place. Thus, success depends on the degree to which aspiring members have correctly anticipated the expectations and desires of those in the organization in charge of selection." [13]

Upon entry into the organization, new members enter the **encounter stage.** Here the individuals confront the possible dichotomy between their expectations—about their jobs, their coworkers, their supervisors, and the organization in general—and reality. If expectations prove to have been more or less accurate, the encounter state merely provides a reaffirmation of the perceptions generated earlier. However, this is often not the case. Where expectations and

Exhibit 8-1

A socialization process.

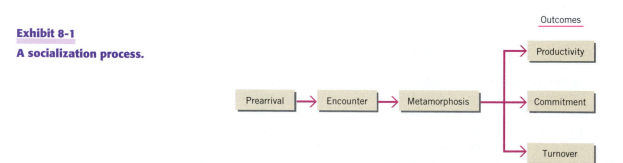

reality differ, new employees must undergo socialization that will detach them from their previous assumptions and replace these with the organization's pivotal standards.[14] For example, at Micron Technology Inc., of Boise, Idaho, new employees are indoctrinated into the company's use of work teams.[15] Because many new employees were unsure of how to quickly assimilate into work groups, and what that meant to them as an employee of Micron, the organization created its fifteen-hour "Reaching High Performance" (RHP) program. During this process, employees gain a better understanding of team participation, taking responsibility, employee involvement, and organizational change.

Socialization, however, cannot solve all the expectation differences. At the extreme, some new members may become totally disillusioned with the actualities of their jobs and resign. It's hoped that proper selection, including the realistic job preview, would significantly reduce this latter occurrence.

Finally, the new member must work out any problems discovered during the encounter stage. This may mean going through changes—hence, we call this the **metamorphosis stage.** But what is a desirable metamorphosis? Metamorphosis is complete—as is the socialization process—when new members have become comfortable with the organization and their work teams. In this situation, they will have internalized the norms of the organization and their coworkers; and they understand and accept these norms.[16] New members will feel accepted by their peers as trusted and valued individuals. They will become confident that they have the competence to complete their jobs successfully. They will have gained an understanding of the organizational system— not only their own tasks but the rules, procedures, and informally accepted practices as well. Finally, they will know how they are going to be evaluated. That is, they've gained an understanding of what criteria will be used to measure and appraise their work. They'll know what is expected of them and what constitutes a "good" job. Consequently, as Exhibit 8-1 shows, successful metamorphosis should have a positive effect on new employees' productivity and the employee's commitment to the organization, and should reduce the likelihood that the employee will leave the organization anytime soon.[17]

If HRM recognizes that certain assumptions hold for new employees entering an organization and that they typically follow a three-staged socialization process, they can develop a program to begin helping these employees adapt to the organization. Let's turn our attention, then, to this aspect of organizational life—socializing our new employees through the new-employee orientation process.

THE PURPOSE OF NEW-EMPLOYEE ORIENTATION

New-employee **orientation** covers the activities involved in introducing a new employee to the organization and to his or her work unit. It expands on the information received during the recruitment and selection stages, and helps to reduce the initial anxiety we all feel when beginning a new job. For example, an orientation program should familiarize the new member with the organization's objectives, history, philosophy, procedures, and rules; communicate relevant HRM policies such as work hours, pay procedures, overtime requirements, and company benefits; review the specific duties and responsibilities of the new member's job; provide a tour of the organization's physical facilities; and introduce the employee to his or her manager and coworkers.

Exhibit 8-2

Sample Orientation Agenda

NEW EMPLOYEE: Karen Bradley	
B.S. in Finance	
University of Delaware, 1999.	
JOB TITLE:	Financial Analyst
DEPARTMENT:	Accounting and Finance
8:15 a.m.	Report to Human Resources: Receive new-employee package, including brochures describing the organization's history, products, and philosophy.
8:15–8:30	Welcome by company president.
8:30–9:00	Mr. Reynolds, Employment: Review Employment policies and practices.
9:00–10:00	Ms. Bateman, Training and Development: Review Training, Development, and Career Development Program offerings.
10:00–10:20	Break
10:20–10:50	Mr. Caldwell, Compensation: Overview and philosophy of company pay practices.
10:50–12:00	Ms. Reed, Benefits: Overview and enrollment for eligible benefits.
12:00–12:30	Mr. Wright, Employee Relations: Overview of safety, health, and communications programs.
12:30–1:30	Lunch with Mr. Haight (new employee's supervisor).
1:30–3:00	Supervisory Orientation. Provides a detailed tour of the Finance Department. Reviews the Department's overall structure. Discusses daily job routine and department policies and rules. Explains job expectations. Introduces new employee to her coworkers.
3:00–4:00	Tour of physical plant.
4:00–5:00	New employee is on her own to familiarize herself with and set up her office.

Exhibit 8-2 illustrates a generic new-employee orientation agenda used in one organization.

Who is responsible for orienting the new employee? This can be done by either the new employee's supervisor, the people in HRM, or some combination thereof. In many medium-sized and most large organizations, HRM takes charge of explaining such matters as overall organizational policies and employee benefits. In other medium-sized and most small firms, new employees will receive their entire orientation from their supervisor. Exhibit 8-2 demonstrates a situation where the process is shared between the HRM staff and the new employee's supervisor.

Of course, the new employee's orientation may not be formal at all. For instance, in many small organizations, orientation may mean the new member reports to her supervisor, who then assigns the new member to another employee who will introduce her to those persons with whom she will be working closely. This may then be followed by a quick tour to show her where the lavatory is, how to make her way to the cafeteria, and how to find the coffee machine. Then the new employee is shown to her desk and left to fend for herself.

Although these programs may function differently, it is our contention that new-employee orientation requires much more. For instance, in today's dynamic organizations, it is imperative that new employees understand what the organization is about.[18] More specifically, these individuals need to understand the organization's culture.

Learning the Organization's Culture

Every organization has its own unique **culture.** This culture includes long-standing, and often unwritten, rules and regulations; a special language that facilitates communication among members; shared standards of relevance as to the critical aspects of the work that is to be done; matter-of-fact prejudices; standards for social etiquette and demeanor; established customs for how members should relate to peers, employees, bosses, and outsiders; and other traditions that clarify what is appropriate and "smart" behavior within the organization and what is not.[19] An employee who has been properly socialized to the organization's culture, then, has learned how things are done, what matters, and which work-related behaviors and perspectives are acceptable and desirable and which ones are not. In most cases, this involves input from many individuals.

> **Every organization has its own unique culture.**

The CEO's Role in Orientation

Prior to the mid-1980s, new-employee orientation operated, if at all, without any input from the company's executive management (see Meet Bo Pilgrim). But that began to change, due in part to consultants and authors such as Tom Peters strongly advocating that senior management "manage by walking around."[20] What Peters and others advocated was that senior managers become highly visible in the organization, meeting and greeting employees, and listening to employee concerns. At the same time, these individuals were given the opportunity to talk about the company—where it is going and how it is going to get there. In management terminology, this was called *visioning*. As more and more successful companies began to be cited in business literature for their leaders' ability to be involved in the work force, one question arose. If it appeared to work well for existing employees, what would it do for new employees joining the organization? The answer appears to be a lot.[21]

One of the more stressful aspects of starting a new job is the thought of entering the unknown. Although a previous organization may have done something that made you leave—like having no upward mobility—at least you knew what you had. But starting a new job is frightening. Did you do the right thing, make the right choice? Having the CEO present from day one addressing new employees helps to allay some of those fears. The CEO's first responsibility is to welcome new employees aboard and talk to them about what a good job choice they made.[22] In fact, this segment of new-employee orientation can be likened to a cheerleading pep rally. The CEO is in a position to "turn on" these new employees by talking about what it is like to work for the organization. In addition, the CEO is in a position to begin to discuss what really matters in the company—an indoctrination to the organization's culture.[23]

When a CEO is present, the company is sending the message that it truly cares for its employees. Employee satisfaction concepts are sometimes thrown around an organization to such an extent that they are nothing more than ruses to pay lip service to the idea. But this senior company official's presence validates that the company really is concerned—the CEO's commitment to making the first day special is evidenced by his or her presence. And even when scheduling conflicts may arise, companies can be prepared: Levi Strauss uses videotaped messages that carry the same message.[24]

Meet

BO PILGRIM
CEO of Pilgrim's Pride Corporation

Bo Pilgrim, co-founder and CEO of Pilgrim's Pride Corporation, knows that the success story of Pilgrim's Pride is a success story of people. Whether it is a line worker in one of Pilgrim's sixteen U.S. or six Mexico locations, or the director of accounting in corporate headquarters, all have been part of a team that has turned Pilgrim's Pride into one of the most successful chicken companies in the world.

Realizing this, Mr. Pilgrim embarked on a mission to change the corporate culture in 1989. After reading and hearing much about Total Quality Management and Continuous Improvement, Bo, as he is known to all, made a major change in the decision-making process at Pilgrim's Pride. Since the company's birth in October 1946, most decisions were made at the top and passed down through the organization, a process not uncommon in many large companies. But Bo was excited about a new management style and enthusiastically started training his management team in the Continuous Improvement philosophy. After considering many options, he chose a customized approach based primarily on the teachings of Dr. Edward Deming.

The training was intense. All of top management was trained first and finally all of the over 13,000 Partners, as the employees of Pilgrim's Pride are called, were schooled. Bo's program is based on the fourteen points of Continuous Improvement.

1. Constancy of Purpose
2. Adopt a New Style of Management
3. Cease Dependence on Inspection
4. Avoid Doing Business on Price Tag Alone
5. Continuous Improvement of Processes
6. Training and Re-training
7. Improvement of Leadership
8. Drive out Fear
9. Departments Must Work Together
10. Continuous Improvement Provides Its Own Motivation
11. Work Standards and Quotas Shall not Limit Our Performance
12. Remove Barriers that Rob Partners of Their Right to Pride of Workmanship
13. Institute Education and Self-Improvement
14. Do It!

Each new Partner receives training as a part of their orientation into Pilgrim's Pride. They are told that they are empowered, and expected, to make suggestions to improve their job process. A formal system is in place to make that happen; it's called the Action Request Memo (ARM). Any Partner can submit an ARM to their location's Continuous Improvement Council. The Council forwards the ARM to the person they determine can best respond. A response is given to the Partner within 7 days. To date there have been well over 1000 ARMS submitted. If an ARM requires it, a Process Improvement Team (PIT) is formed and assigned to study the issue addressed by the ARM. There are PITs working every day at Pilgrim's Pride. Over 100 have been utilized so far. The savings as a result of process improvements have been in the millions of dollars.

The success of Continuous Improvement at Pilgrim's Pride is not surprising. With Continuous Improvement, the person closest to the job is given credit as being the one most likely to understand the challenges associated with that job and is the best one to evaluate their work processes. Continuous Improvement and the ARM form give them an avenue to improve their own job. Instead of a few people at the top making decisions, Pilgrim's Pride has over 10,000 decision makers with the power to make a real difference in their work life.

Continuous Improvement has evolved into more than just another management style; it is a way of life. And it is alive and well at Pilgrim's Pride.

HRM's Role in Orientation

In our introductory comments we stated that the orientation function can be performed by HRM, line management, or a combination of the two. Inasmuch as Exhibit 8-2 indicates a preference for a combination strategy, it is our contention that HRM plays a major role in new-employee orientation—the role of coordination, which ensures that the appropriate components are in place. In addition, HRM also serves as a participant in the program. Consequently, it is important to recognize what HRM must do. For example, in our discussion of making the job offer (Chapter 6), we emphasized that the offer should come from human resources. This was necessary to coordinate the administrative activities surrounding a new hire. The same holds true for new-employee orientation. Depending on the recruiting that takes place, there should be a systematic schedule of when new employees join a company.

As job offers are made and accepted, HRM should instruct the new employee when to report to work. However, before the employee formally arrives, HRM must be prepared to handle some of the more routine needs of these individuals; for example, new employees typically have a long list of questions about benefits. More proactive organizations like Xerox and AT&T prepare a package for new employees. This package generally focuses on the important decisions that a new employee must make—decisions like the choice of health insurance, institutions for direct deposit of paychecks, and tax withholding information. By providing this information a few weeks before an individual starts work, the HRM unit in these companies gives new hires ample time to make a proper choice—quite possibly, a choice that must be made in conjunction with a working spouse's options. Furthermore, forms often require information that most employees do not readily keep with them—for example, social security numbers of family members and medical histories. Accordingly, having that information before the new-employee orientation session saves time.[25] HRM's second concern revolves around its role as a participant in the process. Most new employees' exposure to the organization thus far has been with HRM, but after the hiring process is over, HRM quickly drops out of the picture unless there is a problem. Therefore, HRM must spend some time in orientation addressing what assistance it can offer to employees in the future. This point cannot be minimized. HRM provides an array of services, like career guidance and training, to other areas of the company. Although these areas generally are unable to go outside the organization for their HRM needs, HRM cannot become complacent. They must continue to provide their services to the employees, and departments, of the organization. And one means of affecting this service is to let these new employees know what else HRM can do for them.

WHAT IS EMPLOYEE TRAINING?

Every organization, like Marriott Corporation, needs to have well adjusted, trained and experienced people to perform the activities that must be done. As jobs in today's dynamic organizations have become more complex, the importance of employee education has increased. When jobs were simple, easy to learn, and influenced to only a small degree by technological changes, there was little need for employees to upgrade or alter their skills. But that situation rarely exists today. Instead, rapid job changes are occurring, requiring employee skills to be transformed and frequently updated.[26] In organizations, this takes place through what we call employee training.

Training is a learning experience in that it seeks a relatively permanent change in an individual that will improve the ability to perform on the job. We typically say training can involve the changing of skills, knowledge, attitudes, or behavior.[27] It may mean changing what employees know, how they work, their attitudes toward their work, or their interaction with their coworkers or supervisor.

For our purposes, we will differentiate between **employee training** and **employee development** for one particular reason. Although both are similar in the methods used to affect learning, their time frames differ. Training is more present-day oriented; its focus is on individuals' current jobs, enhancing those specific skills and abilities to immediately perform their jobs.[28] For example, suppose you enter the job market during your senior year of college, pursuing a job as a marketing representative. Although you have a degree in Marketing, when you are hired, some training is in order. Specifically, you'll need to learn the company's policies and practices, product information, and other pertinent selling practices. This, by definition, is job-specific training, or training that is designed to make you more effective in your current job.

Employee development, on the other hand, generally focuses on future jobs in the organization.[29] As your job and career progress, new skills and abilities will be required. For example, if you become a sales territory manager, the skills needed to perform that job are quite different from those required for selling the products. Now you will be required to supervise a number of sales representatives; requiring a broad-based knowledge of marketing and very specific management competencies like communication skills, evaluating employee performance, and disciplining problem individuals. As you are groomed for positions of greater responsibility, employee development efforts will help prepare you for that day.[30]

Irrespective of whether we are involved in employee training or employee development, the same outcome is required. That is, we are attempting to help individuals learn! Learning is critical to everyone's success, and it's something that will be with us throughout our working lives. But learning for learning's sake does not happen in a vacuum. Rather, it is a function of several events that occur, with the responsibility for learning being a shared experience between the "teacher" and the "learner" (see Exhibit 8-3).

Exhibit 8-3
Principles of learning.

Learning Is Enhanced When the Learner Is Motivated.	An individual must want to learn. When that desire exists, the learner will exert a high level of effort. There appears to be valid evidence to support the adage, "You can lead a horse to water, but you can't make him drink."
Learning Requires Feedback.	Feedback, or knowledge of results, is necessary so that learners can correct their mistakes. Feedback is best when it is immediate rather than delayed; the sooner individuals have some knowledge of how well they are performing, the easier it is for them to compare performance to goals and correct their erroneous actions.
Reinforcement Increases the Likelihood That a Learned Behavior Will Be Repeated.	The principle of reinforcement tells us that behaviors that are positively reinforced (rewarded) are encouraged and sustained. When the behavior is punished, it is temporarily suppressed but is unlikely to be extinguished. What is desired is to convey feedback to the learners when they are doing what is right to encourage them to keep doing it.
Practice Increases a Learner's Performance.	When learners actually practice what they have read or seen, they gain confidence and are less likely to make errors or to forget what they have learned.
Learning Begins Rapidly, Then Plateaus.	Learning rates can be expressed as a curve that usually begins with a sharp rise, then increases at a decreasing rate until a plateau is reached. Learning is very fast at the beginning, but then plateaus as opportunities for improvement are reduced.
Learning Must Be Transferable to the Job.	It doesn't make much sense to perfect a skill in the classroom and then find that you can't successfully transfer it to the job. Therefore, training should be designed for transferability.

Training and EEO

Much of our previous discussions of EEO have centered on the selection process. Undoubtedly, it is most prevalent in the hiring process, but its application to training cannot be overlooked. Remember under the definition of adverse impact, we referenced any HRM activity that adversely affects protected group members in hiring, firing, and promoting. So how does training fall into the EEO realms? Let's briefly take a look.

Training programs may be required for promotions, job bidding (especially in unionized jobs), or for salary increases. Under any of these scenarios, it is the responsibility of the organization to ensure that training selection criteria are related to the job. Furthermore, equal training opportunities must exist for all employees.

Organizations should also pay close attention to training completion rates. If protected group members fail to pass training programs more frequently than the "majority group," this might indicate dissimilarities in the training that is offered. Once again, organizations should monitor these activities, and perform periodic audits to ensure full compliance with EEO regulations.

Determining Training Needs

Now that we have a better understanding of what training is, we can look at a more fundamental question for organizations. That is, how does an organization assess whether there is a need for training? We propose that HRM can determine this following a process depicted in Exhibit 8-4.[31]

Recall from Chapter 5 that these questions demonstrate the close link between employment planning and the determination of training needs. Based on our determination of the organization's needs, the type of work to be done, and the type of skills necessary to complete this work, our training programs should follow naturally.[32] Once we can identify where deficiencies lie, we have a grasp of the extent and nature of our training needs.

What kinds of signals can warn employee supervisors that employee training may be necessary? The more obvious ones relate directly to productivity—especially inadequate job performance or a drop in productivity. The former is likely to occur in the early months on a new job. When a supervisor sees evidence of inadequate job performance, assuming the individual is making a satisfactory effort, attention should be given to raising the worker's skill level.[33] When a supervisor is confronted with a drop in productivity, it may suggest that skills need to be fine-tuned. Of course it could be related to other factors, too—

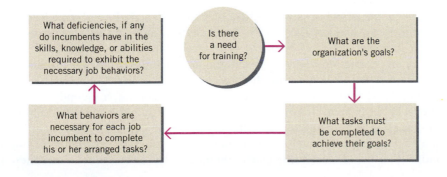

Exhibit 8-4

Determining training needs.

like a lack of resources or equipment malfunctions. That's why it's imperative to pinpoint the problem precisely.

In addition to productivity measures, a high reject rate or larger than usual scrappage may indicate a need for employee training. A rise in the number of accidents reported can also suggest some type of retraining is necessary.[34] Furthermore, the changes that are being imposed on workers as a result of a job redesign or a technological breakthrough demand training.

A word of caution on training, however, is in order. If deficiencies in performance are uncovered, it doesn't necessarily follow that the manager should take corrective action. It is important to put training into perspective. It has costs, which may be high, ranging from $350 to $1,400 per employee trained;[35] and training should not be viewed as a cure-all for what "ails" the organization. Rather, training should be judged by its contribution to performance, where performance is a function of skills, abilities, motivation, and the opportunity to perform. Managers must also compare the value received from the increase in performance that can be attributed to training with the costs incurred in that training.

Once it has been determined that training is necessary, training goals must be established. Management should explicitly state what results are sought for each employee. It is not adequate merely to say the change in employee knowledge, skills, attitudes, or behavior is desirable; we must clarify what is to change, and by how much. These goals should be tangible, verifiable, timely, and measurable. They should be clear to both the supervisor and the employee. For instance, a firefighter might be expected to jump from a moving fire truck traveling at fifteen miles per hour, successfully hook up a four-inch hose to a hydrant, and turn on the hydrant, all in less than forty seconds. Such explicit goals ensure that both the supervisor and the employee know what is expected from the training effort.

Training Approaches

The most popular training and development methods used by organizations can be classified as either on-the-job or off-the-job training.[36] In the following pages, we will briefly introduce the better-known techniques of each category.

On-the-Job Training   The most widely used training methods take place on the job. The popularity of these methods can be attributed to their simplicity and the impression that they are less costly to operate. On-the job training places the employees in actual work situations and makes them appear to be immediately productive. It is learning by doing. For jobs that either are difficult to simulate or can be learned quickly by watching and doing, on-the-job training makes sense.

One of the drawbacks of on-the-job training can be low productivity while the employees develop their skills. Another drawback can be the errors made by the trainees while they learn. However, when the potential problems trainees can create are minimal, where training facilities and staffs are limited or costly,[37] or where it is desirable for the workers to learn the job under normal working conditions, the benefits of on-the-job training frequently offset the drawbacks. Let's look at two types of on-the-job training: apprenticeship programs and job instruction training (JIT).

People seeking to enter skilled trades—to become, for example, heating/air conditioning/ventilation technicians, plumbers, or electricians—are often required to undergo **apprenticeship training** before they are elevated to master-mechanic status. Apprenticeship programs put the trainee under the guidance of a master worker. The argument for apprenticeship programs is that the required job knowledge and skills are so complex as to rule out anything less than a period of time where the trainee understudies a skilled master.[38]

During World War II, a systematic approach to on-the-job training was developed to prepare supervisors to train employees. This approach was called **job instruction training (JIT).** JIT proved highly effective and became extremely popular. JIT consists of four basic steps:

1. preparing the trainees by telling them about the job and overcoming their uncertainties
2. presenting the instruction, giving essential information in a clear manner
3. having the trainees try out the job to demonstrate their understanding
4. placing the workers in the job, on their own, with a designated resource person to call upon should they need assistance.[39]

Job instruction training application can achieve impressive results.[40] By following these steps, studies indicate that employee turnover can be reduced.[41] Higher levels of employee morale have been witnessed, as well as decreases in employee accidents.[42]

Off-the-Job Training   Off-the-job training covers a number of techniques—classroom lectures, films, demonstrations, case studies and other simulation exercises, and programmed instruction. The facilities needed for each technique vary from a small, makeshift classroom to an elaborate development center with large lecture halls, supplemented by small conference rooms with sophisticated instructional technology equipment. We have summarized the majority of these methods in Exhibit 8-5. Because of its growing popularity in today's technology-oriented organizations, however, programmed instruction warrants a closer look.

The **programmed instruction** technique can be in the form of programmed tests and manuals, or video displays, while in some organizations sophisticated teaching machines are utilized. All programmed instruction approaches have a common characteristic. They condense the material to be

Classroom Lectures	Lectures designed to communicate specific interpersonal, technical, or problem-solving skills.
Videos and Films	Using various media productions to demonstrate specialized skills that are not easily presented by other training methods.
Simulation Exercises	Training that occurs by actually performing the work. This may include case analysis, experiential exercises, role playing, or group decision making.
Computer-Based Training	Simulating the work environment by programming a computer to imitate some of the realities of the job.
Vestibule Training	Training on actual equipment used on the job, but conducted away from the actual work setting—a simulated work station.
Programmed Instruction	Condensing training materials into highly organized, logical sequences. May include computer tutorials, interactive video disks, or virtual reality simulations.

Exhibit 8-5

Off-the-job training methods.

learned into highly organized, logical sequences that require the trainee to respond. The ideal format provides for nearly instantaneous feedback that informs the trainee if his or her response is correct.

For example, popular today with the purchase of computer software is an accompanying tutorial program. This tutorial walks the user through the software application, giving the individual opportunities to experiment with the program. These tutorials, then, form one basis of programmed instruction.

As technology continues to evolve, we can expect programmed instruction to become more dominant. Two noticeable versions, **interactive video disks** (IVDs) and **virtual reality,** are gaining momentum in corporate training. Interactive video disks (IVDs) (sometimes referred to as multimedia technology) allow users to interact with a personal computer while simultaneously being exposed to multimedia elements.[43] This "motion picture" enables the trainee to experience the effect of his or her decision in real-time mode.[44] In the past few years, the Internet, along with the advances in multimedia presentations, has taken this concept to an even higher plateau. A number of companies, such as Pitney Bowes, Applied Learning, and IBM, have begun using IVDs.[45] In fact, it is estimated that approximately 16 percent of all companies that train use them.[46] In many of these organizations, employees experience greater learning in such areas as mathematics, interpersonal skills, and marketing skills.[47]

Virtual reality is a newer concept in corporate training.[48] Virtual-reality systems simulate actual work activities by sending various messages to the brain. For example, one type of virtual reality requires an individual to place a helmet over his or her head. Inside this helmet are sensors that display both visual and audio simulations of an event. For instance, skiers can be taught to ski through virtual reality. Under the system, an individual standing on dry land can be made to feel like he or she is actually skiing downhill, with the speed, obstacles, and weather being simulated. This sophisticated simulation allows for individuals to interact with their environment as if they were really there. Although such systems are promising, their expense at this time precludes their use except for extremely large organizations and very complex jobs.

EMPLOYEE DEVELOPMENT

Employee development, by design, is more future oriented and more concerned with education than employee job-specific training. By education we mean that employee development activities attempt to instill sound reasoning processes—to enhance one's ability to understand and interpret knowledge—rather than imparting a body of facts or teaching a specific set of motor skills. Development, therefore, focuses more on the employee's personal growth. Successful employees prepared for positions of greater responsibility have analytical, human, conceptual, and specialized skills. They are able to think and understand. Training, per se, cannot overcome an individual's inability to understand cause-and-effect relationships, to synthesize from experience, to visualize relationships, or to think logically. As a result, we suggest that employee development be predominantly an education process rather than a training process.[49]

It is important to consider one critical component of employee development: All employees, regardless of level, can be developed. Historically, devel-

Playing Coach Is Part of the Job, So Learn to Read Signals

Increasingly, managers must assume the role of "coach." In fact, some organizations officially have changed titles from managers to coaches. Changing titles doesn't change abilities, but with training and practice, managers—by whatever name—can learn to coach and counsel their employees more effectively.

With the change toward teamwork, empowerment and managing by influence, acquiring such skills is imperative for the success of both corporations and their employees. Coaching and counseling improves efficiency and productivity and prevents situations from escalating, while enhancing job satisfaction and confidence when attitude or performance problems occur.

Some managers suffer from the Ostrich Syndrome—hiding their heads in the sand in the hope that the problem or employee will go away. Too pressed for time, afraid that they may give the wrong advice and be blamed for it or just not having any solutions for a particular situation, managers may avoid counseling/coaching.

But as managers, we must accept coaching and counseling as a part of our jobs, however uncomfortable it may be. It means regularly providing employees with feedback about their performance—not just at appraisal time—providing appropriate on-going training, support and encouragement, viewing them as partners in the process, giving credit when deserved and providing information about the company and its goals, as well as their role, responsibilities and expectations in meeting them.

If you have employees blocked from career opportunities, dissatisfied with their jobs, needing help setting priorities or feeling stressed, burned out and insecure, your counseling skills are going to be tested. Employees may not tell you initially that they have a problem, but they will give you an assortment of clues, such as missed deadline, absenteeism and decreased quality and productivity. They may show less initiative or interest, or become irritable or withdrawn. Your job is to find out why their attitude or performance is waning; could it be that they were not recognized for some work or they are frustrated because of a lack of time, training or feedback? After all, most employees believe that their managers either can or should read minds.

Maybe it's time to reassess what's happening. For example, have you as a manager taken time to explain expectations, directions and priorities, and have you removed obstacles and reinforced performance? When it's time to practice your new coaching/counseling insights, carefully plan what you are going to say in advance, then allow enough time without distractions or interruptions to discuss how the situation is affecting performance, to listen without becoming defensive and to obtain enough information to develop an action plan of improvement. Invite the employee to propose solutions or alternatives. Be prepared to have a follow-up session to review progress and to reinforce improvements.

Sometimes even the best coaches/counselors have to cut their losses if and when performance continues to decline, which may call for more severe measures such as probation, demotion, transfer, termination or disciplinary action if other alternatives such as transfer, retraining or restructuring a job are impossible. But on the optimistic side, if the coaching or counseling session is effective, everybody wins—the company, employee and manager. Attitude or performance improves, communication lines up and both managers and employees can build on the situation.

Think about the alternatives—not saying anything, not taking action. But don't wait too long. The problem may persist, even if the opportunity to fill the job doesn't.

DR. CONNIE SITTERLY, CPCM

---

opment was reserved for potential management personnel. Although it is critical for individuals to be trained in specific skills related to managing—like planning, organizing, leading, controlling, and decision making—time has taught us that these skills are needed by nonmanagerial employees as well. The use of work teams, reductions in supervisory roles, allowing workers to participate in setting the goals of their jobs, and a greater emphasis on quality and customers have changed the way developing employees is viewed (see Workplace Issues). Accordingly, organizations now require new employee skills, knowledge, and abilities. Thus, as we go through the next few pages, note that those methods used to develop employees in general are the same as those used to develop future management talent.

All employees, no matter what level, can be developed.

Employee Development Methods

Some development of an individual's abilities can take place on the job. We will review several methods, three popular on-the-job techniques (job rotation, assistant-to positions, and committee assignments) and three off-the-job methods (lecture courses and seminars, simulation exercises, and outdoor training).

Job Rotation   **Job rotation** involves moving employees to various positions in the organization in an effort to expand their skills, knowledge, and abilities. Job rotation can be either horizontal or vertical. Vertical rotation is nothing more than promoting a worker into a new position. In this chapter, we will emphasize the horizontal dimension of job rotation, or what may be better understood as a short-term lateral transfer.

Job rotation represents an excellent method for broadening an individual's exposure to company operations and for turning a specialist into a generalist. In addition to increasing the individual's experience and allowing him or her to absorb new information, it can reduce boredom and stimulate the development of new ideas. It can also provide opportunities for a more comprehensive and reliable evaluation of the employee by his or her supervisors.

Assistant-To Positions   Employees with demonstrated potential are sometimes given the opportunity to work under a seasoned and successful manager, often in different areas of the organization. Working as staff assistants or, in some cases, serving on "special boards," these individuals perform many duties under the watchful eye of a supportive coach. In doing so, these employees get exposure to a wide variety of management activities and are groomed for assuming the duties of the next higher level.

Committee Assignment   Committee assignments can provide an opportunity for the employee to share in decision making, to learn by watching others, and to investigate specific organizational problems. When committees are of a temporary nature, they often take on task-force activities designed to delve into a particular problem, ascertain alternative solutions, and make a recommendation for implementing a solution. These temporary assignments can be both interesting and rewarding to the employee's growth.

Appointment to permanent committees increases the employee's exposure to other members of the organization, broadens his or her understanding, and provides an opportunity to grow and make recommendations under the scrutiny of other committee members. In addition to the on-the-job techniques described above, we will briefly discuss three of the more popular ones: lecture courses and seminars, simulations, and outdoor training.

Lecture Courses and Seminars   Traditional forms of instruction revolved around formal lecture courses and seminars. These offered an opportunity for individuals to acquire knowledge and develop their conceptual and analytical abilities. For many organizations, they were offered in-house by the organization itself, through outside vendors, or both.

Today, however, technology is allowing for significant improvements in the training field. A growing trend at companies such as Pacific Bell, British Columbia Telecom, and the City of Los Angeles[50] is to provide lecture courses and

C. Richard Truex, an executive with Sanofi Winthrop, Inc., a pharmaceutical company in New York, finds off-the-job training can be very beneficial. As part of his development in becoming more decisive and forceful, he has attended programs like this leadership course at the Center for Creative Leadership in Greensboro, NC.

seminars revolving around what we call distance learning.[51] Through the use of digitized computer technology, a facilitator can be in one location giving a lecture, while simultaneously being transmitted over fiber-optic cables, in real time, to several other locations. For example, British Airways uses distance learning to train its employees for supervisory positions.[52] Workers, located in ten different countries, are afforded the opportunity to receive training from five different organizations that otherwise would not be possible without incurring travel costs.[53]

Over the past few years, we've witnessed an expansion of lecture courses and seminars for organizational members. This has been in the form of returning to college classes,[54] either for credit toward a degree or by way of "continuing education" courses. Either way, the outcome is the same. Employees are taking the responsibility to advance their skills, knowledge, and abilities in an effort to enhance their value-addedness to their current, or "future" employer.

Simulations   **Simulations** were previously cited in Exhibit 8-5 as a training technique. While critical in training employees on actual work experiences, simulations are probably even more popular for employee development. The more widely used simulation exercises include case studies, decision games, and role plays.

The *case-study-analysis* approach to employee development was popularized at the Harvard Graduate School of Business. Taken from the actual experiences of organizations, these cases represent attempts to describe, as accurately as possible, real problems that managers have faced. Trainees study the cases to determine problems, analyze causes, develop alternative solutions, select what they believe to be the best solution, and implement it. Case studies can provide stimulating discussions among participants, as well as excellent opportunities for individuals to defend their analytical and judgmental abilities. It appears to be a rather effective method for improving decision-making abilities within the constraints of limited information.

Simulated decision games and role-playing exercises put individuals in the role of acting out supervisory problems. *Simulations,* frequently played on a computer programmed, provide opportunities for individuals to make decisions and to witness the implications of their decisions on other segments of the organization. Airlines, for instance, find that simulations are a much more cost-effective means of training pilots—especially in potentially dangerous situations. And, should the trainee's decision be a poor one, there typically would be no adverse effects on the learner—other than an explanation of why his or her choice was not a good one. *Role playing* allows the participants to act out problems and to deal with real people. Participants are assigned roles and are asked to react to one another as they would have to do in their managerial jobs.

The advantages of simulation exercises are the opportunities to attempt to "create an environment" similar to real situations managers face, without the high costs involved should the actions prove to be undesirable. Of course, the disadvantages are the reverse of this: it is difficult to duplicate the pressures and realities of actual decision making on the job, and individuals often act differently in real-life situations than they do in a simulated exercise.

Outdoor Training   A 1990s trend in employee development has been the use of outdoor (sometimes referred to as wilderness or survival) training. The primary focus of such training is to teach trainees the importance of working together; gelling as a team.[55] Outdoor training typically involves some major emotional and physical challenge. This could be white-water rafting, mountain climbing, paint-ball games, or surviving a week in the "jungle." The purpose of such training is to see how employees react to the difficulties that nature presents to them. Do they face these dangers alone? Do they "freak"? Or are they controlled and successful in achieving their goal? The reality is that today's business environment does not permit employees to "stand alone." This has reinforced the importance of working closely with one another, building trusting relationships, and succeeding as a member of a group.[56]

ORGANIZATIONAL DEVELOPMENT

Although our discussion so far has been related to the people side of business, it is important to recognize that organizations change from time to time. With the changes experienced with respect to downsizing, rightsizing, continuous improvements, diversity, and reengineering, it is necessary to move the organization forward through a process we call **organizational development (OD).** OD has taken on a renewed importance today. Brought about by continuous-improvement goals, many organizations have drastically changed the way they do business. For example, companies such as Ryder Trucks, GTE, Motorola, and Union Carbide are making "radical changes in business processes to achieve breakthrough results."[57] Attainment of these goals, however, directly affects the operations and the people of the organization.

Whenever change occurs, four areas are usually affected: the organization's systems, its technology, its processes, and its people. No matter what the change is, or how minor it may appear, understanding the effect of the change is paramount for it to be supported and lasting. That is where OD comes in to play. OD efforts are designed to support the strategic direction of the business. For instance, if work processes change, people will need to learn new production methods, procedures, and maybe obtain new skills. OD becomes instrumental in bringing about the change. How so? Whenever change occurs, the effect of that change becomes an organizational culture issue. Accordingly, OD efforts must be expended to ensure that all organizational members support the new culture and provide whatever assistance is needed to bring the new culture to fruition.

The basis of organizational development, then, is to help people adapt to change. Although there are different perspectives on how that change should occur, one of the best descriptions of the change process was illustrated by Kurt Lewin.[58] According to Lewin, change occurs over three stages. These include the unfreezing of the status quo, the change to the new state, and refreezing to ensure that the change becomes permanent. We have graphically portrayed this process in Exhibit 8-6.

What Lewin identified was the movement in the organization away from the status quo. Portraying the status quo in Exhibit 8-6 as circles, the change effort helps the organization move in the direction of the squares. Through OD efforts, the intervention can take place, with the change effort supported by continual reinforcement to make it permanent.

Of course change doesn't always happen in a nicely predicted way. Moreover, in today's dynamic environments, change has taken on unprecedented proportions—likened to rafting in "white waters." The **"white water" metaphor** takes into consideration that environments are both uncertain and dynamic. To get a feeling for what managing change might be like when you have to continually maneuver in uninterrupted rapids, consider attending a college that had the following curriculum: courses vary in length. Unfortunately, when you sign up, you don't know how long a course will last. It might go for two weeks or thirty weeks. Furthermore, the instructor can end a course any time he or she wants, with no prior warning. If that isn't bad enough, the length of the class changes each time it meets—sometimes it lasts twenty minutes, while other times it runs for three hours—and determination of the time of the next class meeting is set by the instructor during the previous class. Oh yes, there's one more thing. The exams are all unannounced, so you have to be ready for a test at any time. To succeed positively and proactively in this college, you would have to be incredibly flexible and be able to respond quickly to every changing condition. Students who are too structured or unable to adjust may not survive.

A growing number of employees and managers are coming to accept that their jobs are much like what these students would face in such a college. The stability and predictability of Lewin's model don't frequently exist. Disruptions

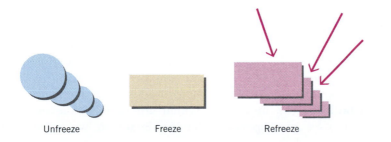

Exhibit 8-6
Lewin's change process.

Unfreeze   Freeze   Refreeze

in the status quo are not occasional and temporary, followed by a return to equilibrium. Most of today's professionals never get out of the rapids. They face constant change, bordering on chaos. These managers are being forced to play a game they've never played before, which is governed by rules that are created as the game progresses.[59] Is the "white water" metaphor merely an overstatement? No! Take the case of Harry Quadracci, founder and president of Quad/Graphics, Inc., a commercial printing firm based in Pewaukee, Wisconsin.[60] Founded in 1971, the company is one of the largest and fastest-growing printers in the United States. It prints such magazines as *Time, People,* and *Architectural Digest.* The company now employs more than 3,000 people and has sales in excess of $800 million a year. Quadracci attributes his company's success to its ability to act fast when opportunities arise. Change and growth are among the few constants at Quad/Graphics. He encourages his people to "act now, think later." The company has no budgets because it is moving too fast—its annual growth rate during the past decade has been an astounding 40 percent! As Quadracci points out, when every department looks 30 percent different every six months, budgets aren't much use. Instead of budgets, each of the company's ten divisions is measured against its own previous performance.

OD Methods

Development efforts in human resource management go beyond the individual. There are instances, like changing an organization's culture, where system-wide change and development are required. Organizational development techniques have been created to change the values and attitudes of people and the structure of organizations in order to make them more adaptive.

Included among the more popular OD techniques are three approaches that rely heavily on group interactions, participation, and collaboration. These are climate surveys, team building, and third-party intervention.[61]

Climate Surveys   One tool for assessing attitudes held by organizational members, identifying discrepancies among member perceptions, and solving these differences is the **climate survey.** Organization members may be asked to respond to a set of specific questions or may be interviewed to determine what issues are relevant. A questionnaire (see Exhibit 8-7) typically asks members for their perceptions and attitudes on a broad range of topics, such as decision-making practices; leadership; communication effectiveness; coordination between units; and satisfaction with the organization, job, co-workers, and their immediate supervisor.

The data from this questionnaire are tabulated. These data then become the springboard for identifying problems and clarifying issues that may be creating difficulties for people.

Addressing these difficulties hopefully will result in the group agreeing on commitments to various actions that will remedy the problems that have been identified.

Team Building   Organizations are composed of people working together to achieve a common end. Since people are frequently required to work in groups, considerable attention has been focused on OD for team building.

Team building can be applied within groups or at the intergroup level where activities are interdependent. For our discussion, we will emphasize the

Rate each of the following statements using the following scale:

1 = strongly agree
2 = agree
3 = undecided
4 = disagree
5 = strongly disagree

1. The environment in this organization is conducive to productive work.	5	4	3	2	1
2. Getting ahead in this organization is strictly a function of one's performance.	5	4	3	2	1
3. My salary is fair and competitive.	5	4	3	2	1
4. Employee benefits are appropriate and meet my personal needs.	5	4	3	2	1
5. I have the opportunity to make decisions about my job for those things that affect it.	5	4	3	2	1
6. I have an open and trusting relationship with my boss.	5	4	3	2	1
7. Clear work expectations exist for my job.	5	4	3	2	1
8. My job challenges me to use my skills, knowledge, and abilities.	5	4	3	2	1
9. The organization encourages a team environment.	5	4	3	2	1
10. Managers of this organization have a clear direction for the next ten years.	5	4	3	2	1

Exhibit 8-7

A sample climate survey.

intragroup level. The activities included in team building typically include goal setting, development of interpersonal relations among team members, role analysis to clarify each member's role and responsibilities, and team process analysis. Of course, team building may emphasize or exclude certain activities depending on the purpose of the development effort and the specific problems with which the team is confronted. Basically, however, team building attempts to use high interaction among group members to increase trust and openness.

Third-party Intervention   Third-party intervention seeks to change the attitudes, stereotypes, and perceptions that groups have of each other. For example, in one company, the marketing representatives saw HRM as having a bunch of "smiley-types who sit around and plan company picnics." Such stereotypes have an obvious negative impact on the coordinating efforts between the departments that leads to conflict.

Although there are a number of approaches for third-party intervention, conflict resolution strategies are often dominant.[62] In **conflict resolution,** the OD practitioner attempts to get both parties to see the similarities and differences existing between them, and focus on how the differences can be overcome. Achieving some movement toward reducing these differences is often gained through consensus building—or finding a solution that is acceptable to both parties.

The Role of Change Agents

No matter what role OD takes in an organization, it requires facilitation by an individual well versed in organization dynamics. In HRM terms, we call this person a **change agent.**[63] Change agents are responsible for fostering the environment in which change can be made, working with the affected employees to

Being a fully functioning team member requires a lot of trust. At wilderness training camps, individuals like this executive learn to trust one another, and they learn that their success is dependent on the help of others. Together, there's no mountain a team can't climb!

help them adapt to the change that is taking place. To achieve this goal, change agents must possess two critical skills—the ability to take risk, and outstanding communication skills.[64] Change agents may be either internal employees, often associated with the training and development function of HRM, or external consultants.

Successful applications of the change agent role have been witnessed in many organizations, among them W. T. Grant, Sears, Inland Steel, and the New York City Police Department.[65] In all cases, change was brought about through the concerted efforts of one individual who championed the process—the change agent.

A Special OD Case: The Learning Organization

Imagine you've just entered the grand ballroom of the Loews Anatole in Dallas, and your senses are picking up some strange occurrences. There are several hundred people gathered, milling around with the constant drone of a beating drum in the background. Bird and other animal sounds permeate the air every so often, as your eyes glance at the seaside sunset on the giant projection screen in front of the room. Have you just walked into a religious experience, or a seminar on the latest diet fad? No! You've just been exposed to a seminar on the learning organization.

Based on research by MIT Professor Peter Senge, the **learning organization** attempts to promote change—change that will result in the organization radically transforming itself. Senge describes the learning organization as one that "values, and thinks competitive advantages derive from, continued learning." The learning organization attacks the premise that the status quo is good enough. It then fosters an environment where open, trusting work relationships abound—resulting in the revitalization of the organization.[66]

Learning organizations possess five characteristics. These are systems thinking, personal mastery, mental models, shared vision, and team learning. As *Fortune* magazine writer Brian Dumaine summarizes, to fully develop the learning organization, "people need to put aside their old ways of doing thinking (mental models), learn to be open with others (personal mastery), understand how their company really works (systems thinking), for a plan everyone can agree on (shared vision), and then work together to achieve that vision (team learning)." [67] How widespread is the belief in the learning organization as a means of creating an OD transformation? Organizations subscribing to the "learning organization" concept read like a who's who in corporate America—including Ford, Federal Express, Intel, AT&T, and Motorola.

> **The learning organization fosters an environment of open, trusting work relationships.**

EVALUATING TRAINING AND DEVELOPMENT EFFECTIVENESS

Any training or development implemented in an organization effort must be cost effective. That is, the benefits gained by such programs must outweigh the costs associated with providing the learning experience. Only by analyzing such programs can effectiveness be determined. It is not enough to merely assume that any training an organization offers is effective; we must develop substantive data to determine whether our training effort is achieving its goals—that is, if it's correcting the deficiencies in skills, knowledge, or attitudes that were assessed as needing attention.[68] Note, too, that training and development programs are expensive—exceeding $56 billion annually for American workers.[69] The costs incurred alone justify evaluating the effectiveness.

How Do We Evaluate Training Programs?

It is easy to generate a new training program, but if the training effort is not evaluated, it becomes possible to rationalize any employee-training efforts. It would be nice if all companies could boast returns on investments in training as do Motorola executives, who claim they receive $30 in increased productivity for every dollar spent on training,[70] as well as a 139 percent increase in sales productivity.[71] But such a claim cannot be made without properly evaluating training.

Can we generalize how training programs are typically evaluated? The following is probably generalizable across organizations: Several managers, representatives from HRM, and a group of workers who have recently completed a training program are asked for their opinions. If the comments are generally positive, the program may get a favorable evaluation and the organization will continue it until someone decides, for whatever reason, it should be eliminated or replaced.

The reactions of participants or managers, while easy to acquire, are the least valid; their opinions are heavily influenced by factors that may have little to do with the training's effectiveness—things like difficulty, entertainment value, or personality characteristics of the instructor. However, trainees' reactions to the training may in fact provide feedback on how worthwhile the participants viewed the training. Beyond general reactions, training must also be evaluated in terms of how much the participants learned, how well they are using their new skills on the job (did their behavior change) and whether the training program achieved its desired results (reduced turnover, increased customer service, etc.).[72]

Performance-Based Evaluation Measures

We'll explore three popular methods of evaluating training programs. These are the post-training performance method, the pre-post-training performance method, and the pre-post-training performance with control group method.

Post-Training Performance Method   The first approach is referred to as the **post-training performance method.** Participants' performance is measured after attending a training program to determine if behavioral changes have been made. For example, assume we provide a week-long seminar for HRM recruiters on structured interviewing techniques. We follow up one month later with each participant to see if, in fact, the techniques addressed in the program were used, and how. If changes did occur, we may attribute them to the training. But caution must be in order, for we cannot emphatically state that the change in behavior was directly related to the training. Other factors, like reading a current HRM journal or attending a presentation at a local Society of Human Resource Management, may have also influenced the change. Accordingly, the post-training performance method may overstate the benefits of training.

Pre-Post-Training Performance Method   In the **pre-post training performance method,** each participant is evaluated prior to training and rated on actual job performance. After instruction—of which the evaluator has been kept unaware—is completed, the employee is reevaluated. As with the post-training performance method, the increase is assumed to be attributed to the instruction. However, in contrast to the post-training performance method, the pre-post-performance method deals directly with job behavior.

Pre-Post-Training Performance with Control Group Method   The most sophisticated evaluative approach is the **pre-post-performance with control group method.** Under this evaluation method, two groups are established and evaluated on actual job performance. Members of the control group work on the job but do not undergo instruction. On the other hand, the experimental group is given the instruction. At the conclusion of training, the two groups are reevaluated. If the training is really effective, the experimental group's performance will have improved, and its performance will be substantially better than that of the control group. This approach attempts to correct for factors, other than the instruction program, that influence job performance.

Although a number of methods for evaluating training and development programs may exist, these three appear to be the most widely recognized. Furthermore, the latter two methods are preferred, because they provide a stronger measure of behavioral change directly attributable to the training effort.

INTERNATIONAL TRAINING AND DEVELOPMENT ISSUES

Important components of international human resource management include both cross-cultural training and a clear understanding of the overseas assignment as part of a manager's development.

Training

Cross-cultural training is necessary for expatriate managers and their families before, during, and after foreign assignments. It is crucial to remember that when the expatriates arrive, they are the foreigners, not the host population. Before the employee and family are relocated to the overseas post, it is necessary to provide much cultural and practical background.[73] Language training is essential for everyone in the family.

Although English is the dominant business language worldwide, relying on English puts the expatriate at a disadvantage. The expatriate will be unable to read trade journals and newspapers, which contain useful business information, and will be reliant on translators, which at best only slow down discussions and at worst "lose things" in the process. Even if an expatriate manager is not fluent, a willingness to try communicating in the local language makes a good impression on the business community—unlike the insistence that all conversation be in English. Foreign-language proficiency is also vital for family members to establish a social network and accomplish the everyday tasks of maintaining a household. Americans may be able to go to the produce market and point at what they recognize on display, but if the shop has unfamiliar meats or vegetables, it helps to be able to ask what each item is and even better to understand the answers!

But cross-cultural training is much more than just language training. It should provide an appreciation of the new culture including details of its history and folklore, economy, politics (both internal and its relations with the United States), religion, social climate, and business practices. It is easy to recognize that religion is highly important in daily life in the Middle East, but knowledge of the region's history and an understanding of the specific practices and beliefs is important to avoid inadvertently insulting business associates or social contacts.

All this training can be carried out through a variety of techniques. Language skills are often provided through classes and tapes, while cultural training utilizes many different tools. Lectures, reading materials, videotapes, and movies are useful for background information, while cultural sensitivity is more often taught through role playing, simulations, and meetings with former international assignees,[74] as well as natives of the countries now living in the United States.

While all this training in advance of the overseas relocation is important, cultural learning takes place during the assignment as well. One American corporation provides some of the following suggestions for adapting to a foreign environment: Forget the word foreign. Learn how things get done: at work, at home, at schools, at social gatherings. Watch television, even if you don't understand it yet. Read newspapers, as many as possible. Visit parks, museums, and zoos. Make friends with local people and learn from them. Plan vacations and day trips in the new country.[75]

After the overseas assignment has ended and the employee has returned, more training is required for the entire family. All family members must re-acclimate to life in the United States. The family must face changes in the extended family, friends, and local events that have occurred in their absence. Teenagers find reentry particularly difficult, as they are ignorant of the most recent jargon and the latest trends, but often are more sophisticated and mature than their local friends. The employee also must adjust to organizational changes, including the inevitable promotions, transfers, and resignations that have taken place during his or her absence. Returnees are anxious to know where they fit in, or if they have been gone for so long that they no longer are on a career path.

Development

In the current global business environment, the overseas assignment should be a vital component in the development of top-level executives. However, so far this is truer in Europe and Japan than it is in the United States. Many American managers return with broader experiences than what appears on paper, having been relatively independent of headquarters. Particularly, midlevel managers have experienced greater responsibilities than others at their level, having frequently acquired greater sensitivity and flexibility to alternative ways of doing things. Unfortunately they are often ignored and untapped after their return.

One survey showed that although 70 percent of international assignments were presented as career opportunities, only 30 percent of the sample's respondents were told anything about their career after returning. Only 23 percent reported being promoted upon their return, while 18 percent reported being demoted. Only 54 percent reported there was a specific job waiting for them.[76] It is vital for the organization to make the overseas assignment part of a career de-

Imagine that you've just been transferred to work for your company's Tehran, Iran subsidiary. Somewhat excited at the opportunity, you encounter a glitch on your first day. You're handed a copy of a manual (pictured) that you're expected to follow. But you can't read it. It's printed in Farsi, and you speak just enough to get by, but don't read it at all. As a result, your success on the job just might be affected. Language training undoubtedly would have helped!

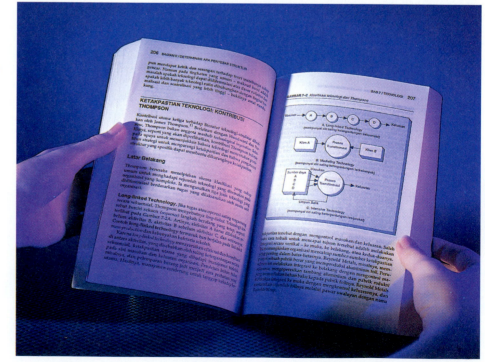

velopment program. In the absence of such a developmental program, two negative consequences often occur. First, the recently returned manager who is largely ignored or underutilized becomes frustrated and leaves the organization. This is extremely costly, because the investment in developing this individual is lost and the talent the individual has will likely be recruited by a competitor, either at home or overseas.

Second, when overseas returnees are regularly underutilized or leave out of frustration, other potential expatriates become reluctant to accept overseas posts, inhibiting the organization's staffing ability. When the overseas assignment is completed, the organization has four basic options. First, the expatriate may be assigned to a domestic position, beginning the repatriation process. Hopefully, this new assignment will build on some of the newly acquired skills and perspectives. Second, the return may be temporary, with the goal of preparing for another overseas assignment. This might be the case where a manager has successfully opened a new sales territory and is being asked to repeat that success in another region. Third, the expatriate may seek retirement, either in the United States or in the country in which she or he spent the last few years. Finally, employment may be terminated, either because the organization has no suitable openings or because the individual has found opportunities elsewhere.

All of these options involve substantial expenses or a loss in human investment. A well-thought-out and organized program of employee development is necessary to make overseas assignments a part of the comprehensive international human resource management program.[77]

SUMMARY

This summary relates to the Learning Objectives provided on p. 218.
After having read this chapter, you should know:

1. Socialization is a process of adaptation. Organization-entry socialization refers to the adaptation that takes place when an individual passes from outside the organization to the role of an inside member.

2. The three stages of employee socialization are the pre-arrival, the encounter, and the metamorphosis states.

3. The key people in orientation are the CEO and the representatives from HRM. The CEO's role is to welcome the new employees, reaffirm their choice of joining the company, and discuss the organization's goals and objectives while conveying information about the organization's culture. Each function in HRM has a specific role in orientation to discuss what employee services they can offer in the future.

4. Employee training has become increasingly important as jobs have become more sophisticated and influenced by technological and corporate changes.

5. Training is a learning experience that seeks a relatively permanent change in individuals that will improve their ability to perform on the job.

6. An organization's training needs will evolve from seeking answers to these questions: (a) What are the organization's goals? (b) What tasks must be completed to achieve these goals? (c) What behaviors are necessary for each job incumbent to complete his or her assigned tasks? and (d) What deficiencies, if any, do incumbents have in the skills, knowledge, or attitudes required to perform the necessary behaviors?

7. Organization development is the process of affecting change in the organization. This change is facilitated through the efforts of a change agent.

8. Training programs can be evaluated by post-training performance, the pre-post-training performance, or the pre-post-training performance with control group methods. In the evaluation, focus is placed on trainee reaction, what learning took place, and how appropriate the training was to the job.

9. International issues in training and development include cross-cultural training, language training, and economic issues training.

EXPERIENTIAL EXERCISES
Orienting Employees

Identify, call, and ask the human resource manager if you may observe part or all of an upcoming orientation or training program of your college or university, employer, nonprofit organization, or a company, as a part of class assignment.

Benchmarking Activity

Summarize your orientation experience in a one- to two-page report, then share your experience with your class or team. What guidelines, policies, or standards did your organization practice regarding orientation? Discuss and compare.

EXPERIENTIAL EXERCISE:
Interview with an Internal Trainer

Instructions

Interview the human resource manager, organization development specialist, or employee involvement or training coordinator about the training programs that are provided for employees and managers.

Sample interview questions may include, but are not limited to:

1. How do you determine a training budget? by a percent of sales or profits or operating dollars, of is left open?
2. What courses do you offer? how have topics or methods changed?
3. Which courses are mandatory and which are voluntary?
4. Do you monitor individual training plans?
5. Do you have a recommended or required number of training hours per employee?
6. Do you have a training plan or catalogue?
7. Do you have a formal mentor program?
8. How do you determine the topics or participants? Do you use samples needs analysis or surveys?
9. What forms of training do you use such as seminars, computer-based, satellite teleconferences, etc.?
10. Who trains and how do they qualify or certify to train in the company? Summarize your interview in a one- to two-page report and share your conclusions with your class or team.
11. How do they measure results of training outcomes?
12. How do they evaluate training, materials, and presenters? Can they provide a sample evaluation?
13. How do they respond to individual requests for specific training needs not available through preset courses?
14. Are there any incentives for completing courses?
15. Are courses provided on company time or personal time?
16. How does the training offered reflect the culture, philosophy, goals, or strategic issues of the company?

WEB-WISE EXERCISES

From the sites listed below, search and print findings on three or more topics from the following list:

▶ training
▶ distance learning
▶ simulation
▶ satellite
▶ seminars
▶ organizational development
▶ computer-based learning
▶ corporate universities
▶ knowledge organization
▶ orientation
▶ competency-based learning
▶ pay for learning
▶ coaching and counseling
▶ mentoring
▶ job instruction training

Society for Human Resource Management
http://www.shrm.org/
HR Magazine
http://www.shrm.org/docs/Hrmagazine.html

CASE APPLICATION:
Common Sense Isn't Always Common Practice

Imagine that you are the employee involvement coordinator and wish to propose a company-wide training in quality improvement to help address the 2 to 3 million dollars lost each month in scrap, waste, and overtime. Although the training has been developed and four employee trainers have been certified to present the program, you anticipate a lack of support based on past experience and comments noted below from management.

Currently, the fifty-year-old parts manufacturing company, QuikParts, Inc. is generating less than a 3 percent return for stockholders due to scrap, waste, overtime, late shipments, and overall poor quality. Both stockholders and customers are unhappy, and morale and productivity are low. You know you must try to persuade management to support the EI and training efforts in the best interest of the company. You perceive the present management team/Executive Committee overall to be unenlightened about training, coaching, organizational development, and that persuading them to provide quality improvement training won't be easy.

A new plant manager is hired with the mandate to "shape up the place, and solve its quality problems."

You propose offering a half-day program, customized for the company entitled "Quality Improvement," to create awareness and involve employees in applying quality concepts to their areas. You recommend to the Executive Committee that the program be completed by both employees and supervisors and managers on all three shifts within the six months, starting in two weeks.

The plant manager, Nick, considers such training "soft," and he does not want to give employees time away from their machines. He says employees "need to pay more attention, and get the parts out the door to meet schedules."

The engineering manager, Joe, adds that when it comes to quality, "meeting customer requirements should be enough; anything else is a waste of time."

The general manager, Tom, adds, "I don't read books, and I never did like school—now is not the time when we're so far behind schedule. Three hours of training is too much when they—including the certified employee trainers—are needed on the shop floor, instead of trying to sound like some expert on the topic. Other companies may train, but I don't think we can afford the luxury right now."

Mary Alice is the front office manager, and she thinks that "training might give employees and managers an opportunity to work out some problems together and understand each other's viewpoint. There is no better time than now to make the time—waiting will just make things worse, and if things get much worse, none of us will be here."

Discussion

Discuss possible responses by role-playing the situation with four team members. Each member will play a role: either Nick, Joe, Tom, or Mary Alice.

Before role-playing, however, discuss what each management team member must think, value, or believe about employees and quality, and how each might act, or react, to related situations and decisions, and the consequences or impact to the company, employees, and themselves.

Respond to the management team's/Executive Committee's comments, and persuade them to allow you to coordinate quality improvement training.

TESTING YOUR UNDERSTANDING

How well did you fulfill the learning objectives?

1. The vice president of human resources wants to include the CEO in the orientation process. What would be the best way to do this?
   a. Have the CEO explain the company benefits packages.
   b. Have the CEO dress up like a clown and sing or do a stunt. That will help employees realize she is just one of the team members.
   c. Have the CEO moderate the film about the first hundred years of company history.
   d. Have the CEO share the vision of the organization, what she hopes to accomplish, and to welcome the new employees to that vision.
   e. Have the CEO go to lunch with each new employee.

2. Some companies send a packet of benefits information to the employee's home a week or so before the new employee starts work. All of these reasons were given for this arrangement except
   a. time is not used during formal orientations to have an employee fill out forms.
   b. decisions about insurance coverage often have to be made in conjunction with coverage already provided by a working spouse.
   c. often, employees change their mind about working for a firm when they see the benefits options in writing. Sending the information home reduces embarrassing scenes in the human resources office.
   d. some of the forms require information that a person would not routinely carry to work.
   e. this process expedites handling routine needs.

3. Your text describes CEO involvement in orientation programs in all of these ways, except
   a. they welcomed new employees aboard and told them they made a good job choice, like leading a pep rally.
   b. they indoctrinated new employees into the organization's culture by sharing the philosophy and mission of the organization.
   c. they advocated company goals.
   d. they conducted company tours.
   e. they emphasized the importance of communications by having an open question-and-answer period.

4. In which of these organizations is employee training least important?
   a. An organization that is switching to a robotics manufacturing facility.
   b. An organization that can easily recruit employees with the skills and experience necessary to perform jobs.
   c. An organization that has been in existence more than a hundred years.
   d. An organization that is developing major new products.
   e. An organization that is entering the global arena for marketing.

5. Dana, with a recent B.S. in Human Resource Management, was hired as a compensation analyst by a

major organization. What training is she likely to get before she starts work?

a. No training. She should be able to function from day one.

b. Formal training in compensation plans, and alternative financial systems. She could be sent to a local university for some course work.

c. The company will send her for an MBA before they will let her go to work.

d. She may need job-specific training, such as a new computer package, or how to interpret internally developed pay graphs and charts.

e. She should spend several weeks designing her career plans and alternatives for the next ten to fifteen years.

6. A director of training for a medium-sized computer software manufacturer has just been asked by a systems software development manager to develop a training program to help fifty programmers "remember" to log off of the system when they have completed online debugging procedures. The system automatically logs off after twenty seconds of keyboard idle-time. The training director estimates $10,000 to develop and deliver such a training exercise. The computer time is valued at $.01 for each ten seconds logged on time. He checks around and finds that none of the other five software development managers has a similar log-off problem. What should he do?

a. Develop the program. The cost of the $10,000 training program is clearly justified by an estimated savings of at least $1.00 each day.

b. Develop the program. Training exists to meet the needs of users. Challenging the systems software development manager, or questioning him, would only alienate him.

c. Do not develop the program. There is no real performance problem identified.

d. Do not develop the program. The problem is not a training problem.

e. Develop the program. It could be marketed later to other computer software firms.

7. Jean just qualified for flight school in a military organization. She is learning to fly wearing a helmet that has sensors to project a horizon and the control panel of her plane. She wears a special glove that interfaces with the helmet projection. What kind of training did Jean receive?

a. Simulation.

b. Vestibule training.

c. Virtual reality.

d. Experiential exercise.

e. Programmed instruction.

8. Last week, Barbara spent the morning watching Liz work. Then, she took Liz to lunch to talk to her about how to improve her job performance. They have been friends for years, and Barbara is the office manager of a local real estate company. Liz, on the other hand, is a new real estate agent. What is going on in this scenario?

a. Barbara and Liz are part of a job rotation program.

b. Barbara is coaching Liz.

c. Liz is an assistant to Barbara.

d. Liz and Barbara are part of a short-term lateral transfer.

e. None of the above

9. How does mentoring compare to orientation?

a. Mentoring is done when an employee is being prepared for jobs of greater responsibility. Orientation is done when an employee first joins an organization.

b. Mentoring is done by the supervisor. Orientation is conducted by peers.

c. Mentoring is a required process. Orientation is optional.

d. Mentoring is generally regarded as a negative experience by the employee. Orientation is generally regarded as a positive experience by the employee.

e. Mentoring and orientation are the same thing.

10. When is employee counseling an appropriate approach for dealing with performance problems?

a. When training is too costly.

b. When the performance problem is ability related.

c. When the manager cannot identify the problem.

d. When the performance problem is related to employee willingness to perform the job.

e. When the performance problem occurs often.

11. Cara, director of training for a large manufacturing organization, has developed a program on sexual harassment in the workplace. All employees are given a questionnaire describing various workplace behaviors and asked to determine whether or not sexual harassment is occurring. They will complete a similar questionnaire at the end of the training program. What training evaluation method will Cara use with these questionnaires?

a. Supervisor and incumbent opinion.

b. Test–retest method.

c. Pre-post performance method.

d. Experimental-control group method.

e. Employee inventory.

12. Don, an MBA from a prestigious school who speaks fluent German, Japanese, and English, was hired by a U.S.-based global organization for international marketing. He was sent to Japan as director of marketing for a year. He returned to the United States for six months and then was sent to Germany for a year as director of marketing. He was expecting a

promotion to vice president of international marketing when he returned to corporate. Instead, he was assigned as west coast regional manager. Why do you think he received this assignment?

a. People with prestigious MBAs often have higher opinions of their abilities than do the organizations who employ them.

b. Don must have made some really big mistakes in his overseas assignments to be demoted like that.

c. Most foreign assignments result in demotions. The experience is viewed as a vacation and not to be rewarded.

d. This assignment is not surprising. A recent survey showed that 18 percent of all returning expatriates were demoted upon return.

e. This assignment only seems like a demotion. The position of regional manager will give him a lot more autonomy than he had as a country-level manager.

13. Training needs may be assessed by answering the questions that are listed here except:

a. What, historically, has worked well in this organization?

b. What are the organization's goals?

c. What behaviors are necessary to complete assigned tasks?

d. What tasks are needed to achieve the organization's goals?

e. What skill deficiencies do job incumbents have, related to tasks needed to achieve organizational goals?

14. Why are training programs evaluated in industry?

a. They cannot be evaluated.

b. With downsizing, everything in industry is being evaluated.

c. Evaluation is a necessary component of establishing training effectiveness.

d. Evaluation is required for Title VII compliance.

e. Employees have the right to comment on the training they receive.

Endnotes

1. Case based on information contained in Ronald Henkoff, "Finding, Training, and Keeping the Best Service Workers," *Fortune* (October 3, 1994), pp. 110–16.

2. See, for instance, Blake E. Ashforth and Alan M. Saks, "Socialization Tactics: Longitudinal Effects on Newcomer Adjustment," *Academy of Management Journal,* Vol. 39, No. 1 (February 1996), pp. 149–178; and Cheryl L. Adkins, "Previous Work Experience and Organizational Socialization: A Longitudinal Examination," *Academy of Management Journal,* Vol. 38, No. 3 (October 1995), pp. 839–862.

3. See, for example, Jitendra M. Mishra and Pam Strait, "Em-ployee Orientation: The Key to Lasting and Productive Results,' *Health Care Supervisor* (March 1993), pp. 19–29; Henry L. Tosi, *Organizational Behavior and Management: A Contingency Approach* (Boston, Mass.: PWS Kent Publishing, 1990), pp. 233–235; also John Van Maanen, "People Processing: Strategies of Organizational Socialization," in Henry L. Tosi's *Organizational Behavior and Management: A Contingency Approach,* pp. 65–66.

4. See, for instance, R. L. Falcione and C. E. Wilson, "Socialization Process in Organizations," in G. M. Goldhar and G. A. Barnett (eds.), *Handbook of Organizational Communication* (Norwood, N.J.: Ablex Publishing, 1988), pp. 151–170; N. J. Allen and J.P. Meyer, "Organizational Socialization Tactics: A Longitudinal Analysis of Links to Newcomers' Commitment and Role Orientation," *Academy of Management Journal* (December 1990), pp. 847–858; V. D. Miller and F. M. Jablin, "Information Seeking During Organizational Entry: Influences, Tactics, and a Model of Process," *Academy of Management Review* (January 1991), pp. 92–120; and J. A. Chatam, "Matching People and Organizations: Selection and Socialization in Public Accounting Firms," *Administrative Science Quarterly* (September 1991), pp. 459–84.

5. Shirley A. Hopkins and Willie E. Hopkins, "Organizational Productivity 2000: A Work Force Perspective," *SAM Advanced Management Journal* (Autumn 1991), pp. 44–48.

6. See, for example, Timothy J. Fogarty, "Organizational Socialization in Accounting Firms: A Theoretical Framework and Agenda for Future Research," *Accounting, Organizations, and Society* (February 1992), pp. 129–150.

7. Coy A. Jones and William R. Crandall, "Determining the Source of Voluntary Employee Turnover," *SAM Advanced Management Journal* (March 22, 1991), p. 16.

8. John Van Maanen, and Edgar H. Schein, "Career Development," in J. Richard Hackman and J. Lloyd Suttle (eds.), *Improving Life at Work* (Santa Monica, Cal.: Goodyear, 1977), pp. 58–62. See also J. P. Wanous, A. E. Reichers, and S. D. Malik, "Organizational Socialization and Group Development," *Academy of Management Review,* Vol. 9 (1992), pp. 670–683.

9. D. C. Feldman, "The Multiple Socialization of Organization Members," *Academy of Management Review* (April 1981), p. 310.

10. For a thorough discussion of these issues, see Jennifer A. Chatman, "Matching People and Organizations: Selection and Socialization in Public Accounting Firms," *Administrative Science Quarterly* (September 1991), pp. 459–85.

11. For example, see Lisa K. Gundry, "Fitting into Technical Organizations: The Socialization of Newcomer Engineers," *IEEE Transactions of Engineering Management* (November 1993), p. 335.

12. For an interesting viewpoint on selection fit and socialization, see Isaiah O. Ugboro, "Loyalty, Value Congruency, and Affective Organizational Commitment: An Empirical Study," *Mid-American Journal of Business* (Fall 1993), pp. 29–37.

13. Ibid., p. 59.

14. Rabindra N. Kanungo and Jay A. Conger, "Promoting Altruism as a Corporate Goal," *Executive* (August 1993), pp. 37–48; Elizabeth Wolfe Morrison, "Longitudinal Study of the Effects of Information Seeking on Newcomer Socialization," *Journal of Applied Psychology* (April 1993), pp. 173–183;

and Laurie K. Lewis and David R. Seinbold, "Innovation Modification During Intraorganizational Adoption," *Academy of Management Review* (April 1993), pp. 322–54.

15. Karen Bridges, Gail Hawkins, and Keli Elledge, "From New Recruit to Team Members," *Training and Development* (August 1993), pp. 55–59.

16. Cheri Ostroff and Steve W. J. Kozlowski, "Organizational Socialization as a Learning Process: The Role of Information Acquisition," *Personnel Psychology* (Winter 1992), pp. 849–874.

17. Tayla N. Bauer and Stephen G. Green, "Effect of Newcomer Involvement in Work-Related Activities: A Longitudinal Study of Socialization," *Journal of Applied Psychology* (April 1994), pp. 211–223.

18. See, for example, Alice M. Starcke, "Building a Better Orientation Program," *HRMagazine* (November 1996), pp. 107–113; and H. Eugene Baker III and Daniel C. Feldman, "Linking Organizational Socialization Tactics with Corporate Human Resource Management Strategies," *Human Resource Management Review,* Vol. 1, No. 3 (Fall 1991), pp. 193–202.

19. John Van Maanen and Edgar H. Schein, "Toward a Theory of Organizational Socialization," in *Research in Organizational Behavior,* Barry M. Staw (ed.) (Greenwich, Conn.: JAI Press, 1979), p. 210. See also, "New Employee Orientation: Ensuring a Smooth Transition," *Small Business Report,* Vol. 13, No. 7 (July 1988), pp. 40–43.

20. See Thomas J. Peters and Robert H. Waterman, *In Search of Excellence: Lessons from America's Best Run Companies* (New York: Harper & Row, 1982).

21. Adapted from Richard F. Federico, "Six Ways to Solve the Orientation Blues," *HRMagazine,* Vol. 36, No. 5 (May 1991), p. 69.

22. See, for example, Nancy K Austin, "Giving New Employees a Better Beginning," *Working Woman* (July 1995), pp. 20–22; 74.

23. Martha I. Finney, "Employee Orientation Programs Can Help Introduce Success," *HR News* (October 1995), p. 2; and Andre Nelson, "New Employee Orientation: Are They Really Worthwhile?" *Supervision,* Vol. 51, No. 11 (November 1990), p. 6.

24. Allan Halcrow, "A Day in the Life of Levi Strauss," *Personnel Journal,* Vol. 67, No. 11 (November 1988), p. 14.

25. See, for example, Joseph F. McKenna, "Training: Welcome Aboard," *Industry Week,* Vol. 238, No. 21 (November 6, 1989), pp. 31–38.

26. Ronald Henkoff, "Companies That Train Best," *Fortune* (March 22, 1993), p. 62; and Commerce Clearing House, "Quality Challenge for HR: Linking Training to Quality Program Goals," 1994 *SHRM/CCH Survey* (June 22, 1994), p. 1.

27. See, for example, Richard G. Zalman, "The Basics of In-House Skills Training," *HRMagazine* (February 1991), pp. 74–78.

28. David E. Bartz, David R. Schwandt, and Larry W. Hillman, "Difference Between 'T and D,'" *Personnel Administrator* (June 1989), p. 164.

29. Ibid. A case can also be built that development can also occur for a current job, where, for example, a new skill is required because one will have greater responsibility. Nonetheless, we will differentiate these two primarily by time frames.

30. Martin M. Broadwell, "The Case for Pre-Supervisory Training," *Training* (October 1996), pp. 103–107.

31. Commerce Clearing House, "Interview with George Odiorne," *Human Resource Management: Ideas and Trends,* No. 165 (March 22, 1988), p. 45.

32. Carla Joinson, "A Return to Good Manners," *HRMagazine* (February 1997), p. 88; Candice Harp, "Link Training to Corporate Mission," *HRMagazine* (August 1995), p. 65; Teresa L. Smith, "Job-Related Materials Reinforce Basic Skills," *HRMagazine* (July 1995), p. 84; Michael Dulworth and Robert Shea, "Six Ways Technology Improves Training," *HRMagazine* (May 1995), p. 33; and Gale Cohen Ruby, "Basic Training," *Entrepreneur* (December 1994), p. 129.

33. Frederick Kuri, "Basic-Skills Training boosts Productivity," *HRMagazine* (September 1996), p. 73.

34. Neville C. Tompkins, "Lessons in Many Languages," *HRMagazine* (March 1996), pp. 94–96.

35. Commerce Clearing House, "Training and Retention Programs," *Topical Law Reports: Human Resources Management Personnel Practices/Communication* (January 1990), p. 555.

36. See, for example, Lakewood Research and Training Magazine, "Instructional Methods: Charting the Top 10," in Carla Joinson, "Make Your Training Stick," *HRMagazine* (May 1995), p. 55.

37. "Our Employees Need Specialized Training: What Can We Offer?" *Inc.* (January 1997), p. 82.

38. Beth Rogers, "The Making of a Highly Skilled Worker," *HRMagazine* (July 1994), p. 62.

39. Leslie A. Bryan, Jr., "An Ounce of Prevention for Workplace Accidents," *Training and Development Journal,* Vol. 44, No. 7 (July 1990), p. 101.

40. William J. Rothwell and H. C. Kazanas, "Planned OJT Is Productive OJT," *Training and Development Journal,* Vol. 44, No. 10 (October 1990), pp. 53–56.

41. Kathryn Tyler, "Tips for Structuring Workplace Literacy Programs," *HRMagazine* (October 1996), p. 112.

42. Ibid., p. 55, and Bryan, Jr., p. 102.

43. Sandra E. O'Connell, "CD-ROMs Offer Practical Advantages for HR," *HRMagazine* (November 1996), p. 35–38.

44. Richard P. Lookatch, "How to Talk to a Talking Head," *Training and Development Journal,* Vol. 44, No. 9 (September 1990), pp. 63–65.

45. See Jo McHale and David Flegg, "Training Extra: Screentest," *Personnel Management,* Vol. 23, No. 6 (June 1991), p. 69; Patricia A. Galagan, "IBM Faces the Future Again," *Training and Development Journal,* Vol. 44, No. 3 (March 1990), p. 36; and Bob Filipczak, "Leaders of the Pack," *Training,* Vol. 26, No. 12 (December 1989), p. 49.

46. Chris Lee, "Who Gets Trained in What," *Training,* Vol. 28, No. 10 (October 1991), p. 57.

47. William W. Lee, "Bridging the Gap with IVD," *Training and Development Journal,* Vol. 44, No. 3 (March 1990), p. 64.

48. See, for example, Samuel Greengard, "'Virtual' Training Becomes Reality," *Industry Week* (January 19, 1998), p. 72; Tom Simmons, "Virtual Reality," *Inc.* (October 1995), p. 23; and Gene Bylinsky, "The Marvels of Virtual Reality," *Fortune* (June 3, 1991), p. 138.

49. Debra Eller, "Motorola Trains VPs to Become Growth Leaders," *HRMagazine* (June 1995), pp. 82–87.

50. "Training for Telecommuting," *Manpower Argus* (November 1996), p. 8; Bob Filipczak, "Distance Teamwork," *Training* (April 1994), p. 71; and Randall Johnson, "Alternative Methods: Technology, Good Client Relations Help Training to Thrive," *Training* (July 1992), p. B-05.

51. Ibid.

52. Jane Pickard, "Training on Another Plane," *Personnel Management* (August 1992), pp. 45–47.

53. See for example, Michael Emery, and Margaret Schubert, "A Trainer's Guide to Videoconferencing," *Training* (June 1993), pp. 59–64; and Bob Filipczak, "Distance Teamwork," *Training* (April 1994), p. 71.

54. James Bredin, "Broadening Horizons," *Industry Week* (October 1997), p. 68.

55. Mark Henricks, "Excellent Adventures," *Entrepreneur* (July 1995), p. 58; and Keith Green, "Leadership Program a Life-Altering Experience," *HR News* (March 1995), p. 4.

56. See, for example, "Survival Training for Employees," *ABC World News Tonight/American Agenda* (July 21, 1993).

57. Thomas A. Stewart, "Reengineering: The Hot New Managing Tool," *Fortune* (August 23, 1994), pp. 41–48.

58. Kurt Lewin, *Field Theory in Social Science* (New York: Harper & Row, 1951).

59. See, for instance, Tom Peters, *Thriving on Chaos* (New York: Alfred A. Knopf, 1987).

60. Phyllis Berman, "Harry's a Great Story Teller," *Forbes* (February 27, 1995), pp. 112–116; Janet Bamford, "Changing Business as Usual," *Working Woman* (November 1993), p. 62; "Interview with Harry V. Quadracci," *Business Ethics* (May–June 1993), pp. 19–21; and Daniel M. Kehrer, "The Miracle of Theory Q," *Business Month* (September 1989), pp. 45–49.

61. R. Wayne Pace, Phillip C. Smith, and Gordon E. Mills, *Human Resource Development* (Englewood Cliffs, N.J.: Prentice-Hall, 1991), p. 131.

62. Ibid.

63. See Scott Kerr, "Managing Change Successfully," *Leadership and Organization Development Journal*, Vol. 12, No. 1 (January 1991), p. 2.

64. E. J. Muller, "How to Be an Agent of Change," *Distribution*, Vol. 90, No. 13 (1991), p. 24.

65. See William Weitzel and Ellen Johnson, "Reversing the Downward Spiral: Lesson from W. T. Grant and Sears Roebuck," *Academy of Management Review*, Vol. 5, No. 3 (August 1991), pp. 7–22; Alan L. Wilgus, "Forging Change in Spite of Adversity," *Personnel Journal*, Vol. 70, No. 9 (September 1991), pp. 60–67; and Kevin Doyle, "The Many Behind the Men in Blue," *Incentive*, Vol. 165, No. 11 (November 1991), pp. 39–45.

66. Dominic Bencivenga, "Learning Organizations Evolve in New Directions," *HRMagazine* (October 1995), pp. 69–73.

67. Brian Dumaine, "Mr. Learning Organization," *Fortune* (October 17, 1994), pp. 147–157.

68. Maureen Minehan, "Skills Shortage in Asia," *HRMagazine* (March 1996), p. 152.

69. Michael A. Verespej, "Formal Training: Secondary Education?" *Industry Week* (January 5, 1998, p. 42; Bill Leonard, "Cover Story," *HRMagazine* (July 1996), p. 75; Jacquelyn S. DeMatteo, Gregory H. Dobbins, and Kyle M. Lundby, "The Effects of Accountability on Training Effectiveness," *Academy of Management Best Papers Proceedings,* Dorothy P. Moore, ed. (August 4–17, 1994), p. 122; and Ronald Henkoff, "Companies that Train Best," p. 62.

70. Ronald Henkoff, "Companies That Train Best," p. 62.

71. Linda Grant, "A School for Success," *U.S. News & World Report* (May 22, 1995), p. 53.

72. See, for example, R. E. Catalano and D. L. Kirkpatrick, "Evaluating Training Programs–The State of the Art," *Training and Development Journal* (May 1968), pp. 2–9.

73. See, for example, Joseph W. Weiss and Stanley Bloom, "Managing in China: Expatriate Experiences in Training," *Business Horizons,* Vol. 33, No. 3 (May-June 1990), pp. 23–29.

74. S. Ronen, "Training the International Assignee," in I. L. Goldstein & Associates (eds.), *Training and Development in Organizations* (San Francisco: Jossey-Bass, 1989), pp. 417–453.

75. From an undated Bristol-Myers handout.

76. G. Oddou, teaching note in "The Overseas Assignment: A Practical Look," *International Human Resource Management,* M. Mendenhall and G. Oddou (eds.) (Boston: PWS-Kent Publishing, 1991), pp. 259–269.

77. See, for instance, Ellen Van Velsor and Jean Brittain Leslie, "Why Executives Derail: Perspectives Across Time and Cultures," *Academy of Management Executive*, Vol 9, No. 4 (May 1995), pp. 62–72.

9. Managing Careers

LEARNING OBJECTIVES

After reading this chapter, you will be able to:

1. Explain who is responsible for managing careers.
2. Describe what is meant by the term *career*.
3. Discuss the focus of careers for both the organization and individuals.
4. Describe how career development and employee development are different.
5. Explain why career development is valuable to organizations.
6. Identify the five stages involved in a career.
7. List the Holland Vocational Preferences.
8. Describe the implications of Personality Typologies and jobs.
9. Identify several suggestions that you can use to manage your career more effectively.

What do you do if after spending several years getting your college education, you can't find a job that suits your needs? Although statistics reveal that about 80 percent of all college graduates do find a job within six months after graduation, with three-fourths of these in career starting positions, for some individuals, that's not enough. They want to make their mark on the world, get rich, and simultaneously help enhance the quality of living for all people. For many, such opportunities are limited, especially in the United States. So enterprising individuals, like Michael Giles, find their opportunities by going abroad.[1]

Michael Giles is the kind of person people both wonder about and admire. He was a graduate of the prestigious Columbia Law School and was in high demand when he entered the market. He accepted a position as a marketer for IBM, which paid him an annual salary of $160,000. Working outside of Washington, D.C., Michael appeared to have it all—a challenging and well-paying career, and an endless future for such a bright individual. But Michael wanted

252

An individual's career often-times takes one in different directions. That's precisely the case with Michael Giles. After graduating from a prestigious law school and working for a major company in the United States, he had a "wonderful" future ahead of him. But Giles decided to chuck it all—to do something that was more meaningful to him. Moving to South Africa, he started a Laundromat business—an action that gave "something back to the community." Michael's happier today than he has ever been, and his entrepreneurial initiative is rewarding him well.

more. He wanted the lifestyle great wealth could provide, but he wanted to give something back—especially to the black residents in deplorable living conditions in South Africa. At age 35, he quit his job with IBM and moved to Soweto, a small South-African township just outside of Johannesburg. Leaving behind the luxury of living in a nice section of the D.C. suburbs, Michael moved into an area where there was no running water or even primitive sewer systems. No doubt many thought he was crazy!

In adversity, however, Michael saw prosperity. He applied for, and received, a $9.3 million loan from the U.S. government's Overseas Private Investment Corporation. With this money, he founded the Quick-Wash-Dry Clean USA Corporation. Today, Michael's firm is completing the building of 108 coin-operated laundromats that will provide laundry services to most of South Africa's black communities. Michael's career dream to give back to the community, while simultaneously making a decent living, appears to be happening. He's making life better for a group of individuals, which fulfills his need to do the right thing! And his entrepreneurial spirit is being richly rewarded.

INTRODUCTION

Career development is important to us all. We know that people sometimes have difficulties achieving their career goals. This reflects the new and unexpected complexities that managers must now confront in their efforts to mobilize and manage their employees. The historical beliefs that every employee

253

would jump at the chance for a promotion, that competent people will somehow emerge within the organization to fill arising vacancies, and that a valuable employee will always be a valuable employee are no longer true. Lifestyles, too, are changing. We are becoming increasingly aware of the different needs and aspirations of employees. If HRM representatives are to be assured that they will have competent and motivated people to fill the organization's future needs, they should be increasingly concerned with matching the career needs of employees with the requirements of the organization.

It's important to note that while career development has been an important topic in HRM-related courses for several decades, we have witnessed some drastic changes over the past ten years. Years ago, career development programs were designed to assist employees in advancing their work lives. HRM's focus was to provide information and assessments needed to help employees realize their career goals. Career development was also a way for an organization to attract and retain highly talented personnel. But those days are all but disappearing in today's dynamic work environment—and so too are jobs as we have known them for the past several decades. Downsizing, restructuring, contingent workers, etc. have drawn us to one significant conclusion about managing careers. That is, you, the individual, are responsible for your career.[2] It's not the organization's obligation! Sadly, some 3 million employees have learned this the hard way the past few years.[3] Therefore, you must be prepared to do whatever is necessary to advance your career.

> **You, the individual, are solely responsible for managing your career.**

That's not to say the organization doesn't have a vested interest in you. It does! In fact, the more marketable you are because of your skills, the more value you add to the organization. How willing the organization is to invest in you—recognizing that you may leave the organization when another opportunity arises—however, rests within the corporate culture. If you're fortunate enough to be part of this type of organization, then you should take advantage of the shared responsibility toward your career development.[4] But don't get the false sense of security that all organizations view developing you that way. It simply isn't the industry norm.

It's within this realm that this chapter is presented. We'll review some of the basics of career development for you, and what role HRM plays today in offering its assistance. But throughout the chapter, remember, it's up to you to manage your career. If you don't, no one else will!

WHAT IS A CAREER?

The term **career** has a number of meanings. In popular usage it can mean advancement ("He's moving up in his career"), a profession ("She has chosen a career in medicine"), or stability over time (career military).[5] For our purposes, we will define career as "the pattern of work-related experiences that span the course of a person's life."[6] Using this definition, it is apparent that we all have or will have careers. The concept is as relevant to transient, unskilled laborers as it is to engineers and physicians. For our purposes, therefore, any work, paid or unpaid, pursued over an extended period of time, can constitute a career. In addition to formal job work, careers can include schoolwork, homemaking, or volunteer work. Furthermore, career success is defined not only objectively in terms of promotion, but also subjectively, in terms of satisfaction.

Individual versus Organizational Perspective

The study of careers takes on a very different orientation, depending on whether it is viewed from the perspective of the organization or of the individual. A key question in career development, then, is, "With whose interests are we concerned?" From an organizational or HRM viewpoint, career development involves tracking career paths and developing career ladders. HRM seeks information to direct and to monitor the progress of special groups of employees, and to ensure that capable professional, managerial, and technical talent will be available to meet the organization's needs. Career development from the organization's perspective is also called *organizational career planning*.

In contrast, individual career development, or career planning, focuses on assisting individuals to identify their major goals and to determine what they need to do to achieve these goals. Note that in the latter case the focus is entirely on the individual and includes his or her life outside the organization, as well as inside. So while organizational career development looks at individuals filling the needs of the organization, individual career development addresses each individual's personal work career and other lifestyle issues.[7] For instance, an excellent employee, when assisted in better understanding his or her needs and aspirations through interest inventories, life-planning analysis, and counseling, may even decide to leave the organization if it becomes apparent that career aspirations can be best achieved outside the employing organization. Employee expectations today are different from employee expectations a generation ago. Sex-role stereotypes are crumbling as people are less restricted by gender-specific occupations. Additionally, our lifestyles are more varied, with, for example, more dual-career couples today than ever before. Both career approaches (individual and organizational) have value. This chapter blends the interests of both the individual within the organization and the organization itself. However, since the primary focus of human resource management is the interest of careers to the organization, we will primarily emphasize this area. We will, however at the end of the chapter, take a special look at how you can better manage your career.

Career Development versus Employee Development

Given our discussions in Chapter 8 on employee development, you may be wondering what, if any, differences there are between **career development** and employee development. These topics have a common element,[8] but there is one distinct difference—the time frame.

Career development looks at the long-term career effectiveness and success of organizational personnel. By contrast, the kinds of development discussed in the last chapter focused on work effectiveness or performance in the immediate or intermediate time frames. These two concepts are closely linked; employee training and development should be compatible with an individual's career development in the organization. But a successful career program, in attempting to match individual abilities and aspirations with the needs of the organization, should develop people for the long-term needs of the organization and address the dynamic changes that will take place over time.

Career Development: Value for the Organization

Assuming that an organization already provides extensive employee development programs, why should it need to consider a career development program as well? A long-term career focus should increase the organization's effectiveness in managing its human resources. More specifically, we can identify several positive results that can accrue from a well-designed career development program.

Ensures Needed Talent Will Be Available   Career development efforts are consistent with, and are a natural extension of, strategic and employment planning. Changing staff requirements over the intermediate and long term should be identified when the company sets long-term goals and objectives. Working with individual employees to help them align their needs and aspirations with those of the organization will increase the probability that the right people will be available to meet the organization's changing staffing requirements.[9]

Improves the Organization's Ability to Attract and Retain High-talent Employees   Outstanding employees will always be scarce, and there is usually considerable competition to secure their services. Such individuals may give preference to employers who demonstrate a concern for their employees' future. If already employed by an organization that offers career advice, these people may exhibit greater loyalty and commitment to their employer. Importantly, career development appears to be a natural response to the rising concern by employees for the quality of work life and personal life planning. As more individuals seek jobs that offer challenge, responsibility, and opportunities for advancement, realistic career planning becomes increasingly necessary. Additionally, social values have changed so that more members of the work force no longer look at their work in isolation. Their work must be compatible with their personal and family interests and commitments. Again, career development should result in a better individual–organization match for employees and thus lead to less turnover.

Ensures that Minorities and Women Get Opportunities for Growth and Development   As discussed in previous chapters, equal employment opportunity legislation and affirmative-action programs have demanded that minority groups and women receive opportunities for growth and development that will prepare them for greater responsibilities within the organization. The fair employment movement has served as a catalyst to career development programs targeted for these special groups. Recent legislation, such as the Americans with Disabilities Act, offers an even greater organizational career challenge. Furthermore, courts frequently look at an organization's career development efforts with these groups when ruling on discrimination suits.

Reduces Employee Frustration   Although the educational level of the work force has risen, so too, have their occupational aspirations. However, periods of economic stagnation and increased concern by organizations to reduce costs have also reduced opportunities. This has increased frustration in employees who often see a significant disparity between their aspirations and actual opportunities. When organizations cut costs by downsizing, career paths, career tracks, and career ladders often collapse.[10] Career counseling can result in more realistic, rather than raised, employee expectations.

Enhances Cultural Diversity   The work force in the next decade will witness a more varied combination of race, nationality, sex, and values in the organization.[11] Effective organizational career development provides access to all levels of the organization for more varied types of employees. Extended career opportunities make cultural diversity, and the appreciation of it, an organizational reality.[12]

Promotes Organizational Goodwill   If employees think their employing organizations are concerned about their long-term well-being, they respond in kind by projecting positive images of the organization into other areas of their lives (e.g., volunteer work in the community).[13] For instance, Walt works for a long-distance phone carrier. He also coaches Little League baseball with other parents in the community. When he expresses his trust of the phone company, because of their expressed career interest, his friends might consider proposed rate hikes in a tolerant light.

Career Development: Value for the Individual

Effective career development is also important for the individual. In fact, as we've previously mentioned, it is more important today than ever. Because the definitions of careers and what constitutes success have changed, the value of

Marion Manigo-Truell is quite typical of individuals in today's dynamic market. That is, she has followed what once would be considered an unusual career path. She's worked in a bank, a hotel, and in the investment field. Each step of the way, she learned new skills—all of which have helped her earn bigger job titles and more money.

individual career development programs has expanded. Career success may no longer be measured merely by an employee's income or hierarchical level in an organization. Career success may now include using one's skills and abilities to face expanded challenges, or having greater responsibilities and increased autonomy in one's chosen profession.[14] Intrinsic career development, or "psychic income," is desired by contemporary workers who are seeking more than salary and security from their jobs.[15] Contemporary workers seek interesting and meaningful work; such interest and meaning are often derived from a sense of being the architect of one's own career.[16]

Careers are both **external** and **internal.** The external career involves properties or qualities of an occupation or an organization.[17] For example, a career in business might be thought of as a sequence of jobs or positions held during the life of the individual: undergraduate degree in business; sales representative for a construction supply house; graduate training in business; district manager in a "Do-It-Yourself" hardware chain; president of a small housing inspection and appraisal firm; retirement. External careers may also be characterized by such things as career ladders within a particular organization (employment recruiter, employment manager, HRM director, vice president HRM).

The individual career encompasses a variety of individual aspects or themes: accumulation of external symbols of success or advancement (bigger office with each promotion);[18] threshold definition of occupational types (i.e., physicians have careers, dog catchers have jobs);[19] long-term commitment to a particular occupational field (i.e., career soldier);[20] a series of work-related positions;[21] and, work-related attitudes and behaviors.[22]

With careers being the pattern of work-related experiences that span the course of a person's life, we must understand that both personal relationships and family concerns are also intrinsically valued by employees. Subjective and objective elements, then, are necessary components of a theoretical perspective, which captures the complexity of career.[23] Success can then be defined in external terms. For example, if after five years at the same company you get a promotion, and Ryan, a colleague who was hired the same day you were for the same type of job, has not yet been promoted, then you are more successful than Ryan. The external definition also states that a certified public accountant is more successful than a dog catcher. However, if you consider the subjective, internal valuation of success, the story may be different. A dog catcher who defines his job as protecting children and others in the community from danger, who goes home proud at night because he has successfully and compassionately captured dogs that day, is successful in his career. Compare that to a CPA who works only to buy a new sports car so she can escape from the drudgery of her day-to-day office life of dealing with clients, accounting forms, and automated systems. Is she more or less successful than the dog catcher?

This differentiation of internal from external is important to the manager who wants to motivate employees (Exhibit 9-1). Different employees may respond to different motivational tools. For instance, Darin is working as a consultant for you, looking to earn enough money to purchase a time-share in a condo in Florida. Diane, your newest software developer, joined the company with the expectation that within four years she will have obtained her Master's degree and in a supervisory position in the company. Would they respond equally to the opportunity to be trained in interpersonal skills? Would both of them be as likely to accept (or reject) a transfer to another city? Probably not, because both have different drives. Thus, we can say that internal and external

Exhibit 9-1 Internal and External Events and Career Stages

Stage	External Event	Internal Event
Exploration	Advice and examples of relatives, teachers, friends, and coaches	Development of self-image of what one "might" be, what sort of work would be fun
	Actual successes and failures in school, sports and hobbies	Self-assessment of own talents and limitations
	Actual choice of educational path—vocational school, college, major, professional school	Development of ambitions, goals, motives, dreams
		Tentative choices and commitments, changes
Establishment	Explicit search for a job	Shock of entering the "real world"
	Acceptance of a job	Insecurity around new tasks of interviewing, applying, being tested, facing being turned down
	Induction and orientation	
	Assignment to further training or first job	Making a "real" choice; to take a job or not; which job; first commitment
	Acquiring visible job and organizational membership trappings (ID card, parking sticker, uniform, organizational manual)	Fear of being tested for the first time under *real* conditions, and found out to be a fraud
	First job assignment, meeting the boss and co-workers	Reality shock—what the work is really like, doing the "dirty work"
	Learning period, indoctrination	Forming a career strategy, how "to make it"— working hard, finding mentors, conforming to an organization, making a contribution
	Period of full performance—"doing the job"	
		This is "real," what I'm doing matters
		Feeling of success or failure—going uphill, either challenging or exhausting
		Decision to leave organization if things do not look positive
		Feeling of being accepted fully by the organization, "having made it"—satisfaction of seeing "my project"
Mid-Career	Leveling off, transfer, and/or promotion	Period of settling in or new ambitions based on self-assessment
	Entering a period of maximum productivity	More feeling of security, relaxation, but danger of leveling off and stagnation
	Becoming more of a teacher/mentor than a learner	Threat from younger, better trained, more energetic, and ambitious persons—"Am I too old for my job?"
	Explicit signs from boss and co-workers that one's progress has plateaued	Possible thoughts of "new pastures" and new challenges—"What do I really want to do?"
		Working through mid-life crisis toward greater acceptance of oneself and others
		"Is it time to give up on my dreams? Should I settle for what I have?"
Late Career	Job assignments drawing primarily on maturity of judgment	Psychological preparation for retirement
		Deceleration in momentum
	More jobs involving teaching others	Finding new sources of self-improvement off the job, new sources of job satisfaction through teaching others
Decline	Formal preparation for retirement	Learning to accept a reduced role and less responsibility
	Retirement rituals	Learning to live a less structured life
		New accommodations to family and community

SOURCE: Adapted from John Van Maanen and Edgar H. Schein, "Career Development," in *Improving Life at Work* (ed.), J. Richard Hackman and J. Lloyd Suttle (Santa Monica, CA: Goodyear, 1977), pp. 55–57; and D. Levinson, *The Seasons of a Man's Life.*

career events may be parallel, but result in different outcomes. We have displayed these events in Exhibit 9-1. They are discussed in the context of career stages, the topic discussed in the next section.

Mentoring and Coaching

It has become increasingly clear over the years that employees who aspire to higher management levels in organizations often need the assistance and advocacy of someone higher up in the organization.[24] These career progressions often require having the favor of the dominant "in-group," which sets corporate goals, priorities, and standards.[25]

When a senior employee takes an active role in guiding another individual, we refer to this activity as **mentoring** or **coaching.** Just as baseball coaches observe, analyze, and attempt to improve the performance of their athletes, "coaches" on the job can do the same. The effective coach, whether on the diamond or in the corporate hierarchy, gives guidance through direction, advice, criticism, and suggestion in an attempt to aid the employee's growth.[26] These individuals offer to assist certain junior employees in terms of providing a support system. This system, in part, is likened to the passing of the proverbial baton—that is, the senior employee shares his or her experiences with the protégé, providing guidance on how to make it in the organization.[27] Accordingly, in organizations such as Motorola, Tenneco, and Prudential,[28] that promote from within, those who aspire to succeed must have the "corporate support system"[29] in their favor. This support system, guided by a mentor, vouches for the candidate, answers for the candidate in the highest circles within the organization, makes appropriate introductions, and advises and guides the candidate on how to effectively move through the system [see Carolyn Bufton Elman]. In one study, this effort generated significant outcomes.[30] For example, these researchers found that where a significant mentoring relationship existed, those protégés had more favorable and frequent promotions, were paid significantly more than those who were not mentored,[31] had a greater level of commitment to the organization, and had greater career success.[32] But there was a caution in this study; that is, those benefits that accrued because of mentoring generally often went to white male employees. Why this outcome? In the past, women and minorities have found it difficult to get a mentor,[33] and therefore their upward mobility was often limited.

The technique of senior employees coaching individuals has the advantages that go with learning by doing, particularly the opportunities for high interaction and rapid feedback on performance. Unfortunately, its two strongest disadvantages are: (1) its tendencies to perpetuate the current styles and practices in the organization; and (2) its heavy reliance on the coach's ability to be a good teacher. In the same way that we recognize that all excellent Hall-of-Fame baseball players don't make outstanding baseball coaches, we cannot expect all excellent employees to be effective coaches. An individual can become an excellent performer without necessarily possessing the knack of creating a proper learning environment for others to do the same; thus, the effectiveness of this technique relies on the ability of the coach. Coaching of employees can occur at any level and can be most effective when the two individuals do not have any type of reporting relationship.

Recall from Chapter 3 the discussion of the glass ceiling.[34] One of the main reasons for its existence is that women previously didn't have many role models

CAROLYN BUFTON ELMAN

Executive Director, American Business Women's Association

Few leaders have direct career experience beginning with childhood, but Carolyn Bufton Elman was destined for the role of leader ever since her father, Hilary Bufton Jr., founded the American Business Women's Association in 1949. Recognizing the enormous contribution working women could make in our country, Mr. Bufton created the Association to support women reaching their educational and career goals. Nearly fifty years after the founding of ABWA, Ms. Elman is carrying out her father's work and expanding the foundation he laid to help and empower the 80,000 members of ABWA and all working women across the country.

At a young age Ms. Elman learned by her father's example about the value of relationships. While traveling across the country on family vacations, Mr. Bufton couldn't resist making a phone call while stopping for gas or paying a quick visit to the many ABWA members who lived in the cities and towns the Bufton family traveled through. As a young woman in high school and college, Ms. Elman spent her summers working part-time at ABWA, filling in for staff members who were on vacation. Learning every aspect of ABWA from various perspectives gave Ms. Elman valuable insight into the workings of the Association as well as important knowledge about ABWA members and their needs.

Ms. Elman graduated with honors from Beloit College in Wisconsin and taught in secondary schools near Milwaukee and later in St. Louis. She did postgraduate work at the University of Wisconsin, the University of Utah School of Business, and she graduated from the Smith Management Program at Smith College in Northampton, Mass.

In 1985, following the death of her father, Ms. Elman was appointed ABWA's assistant executive director to work closely with her mother, Ruth Bufton, who was serving as the Association's executive director. Ms. Elman's vast knowledge of ABWA, proven business skills and her education in management made her the logical choice to lead the Association when Mrs. Bufton relinquished her formal duties with ABWA. In January 1986, Carolyn Bufton Elman was endorsed by ABWA's National Board to serve as executive director of the Association.

Under Ms. Elman's direction, ABWA has produced comprehensive educational business programs for thousands of working women across the United States; most notable are: the Express Network® and the Business Skills Grants and Loans program. Her goal is to offer something to every businesswoman, from those who are established in their jobs or own their own businesses to those re-entering the workforce or just beginning their careers.

One of the accomplishments Ms. Elman is most proud of is the growth of the ABWA scholarship program, the Stephen Bufton Memorial Education Fund, which has awarded more than $10 million in scholarships to women enabling them to become business entrepreneurs, executives and professionals.

Ms. Elman is a recognized leader in American business and an authority on workplace issues that affect women. She offers her insight and experience in solving economic and social dilemmas of American society through Leadership America, the Women's Bureau of the U.S. Department of Labor, and Glass Ceiling Commission Testimony. Additionally Ms. Elman has served on the International Federation for Business Education; the Center for International Business Advisory Committee at the University of Missouri, Kansas City; American Express Financial Advisors' Distinguished Women's Advisory Board; and the Women's World Banking Innovation Council.

While remaining focused on the goals set by her father, providing education and training to working women, Ms. Elman has her eye on the future and is launching a national program to mentor women who are currently on welfare and entering the workforce. By providing support and encouragement to these women, their transition into the workforce will be more successful. Making connections has been an important benefit of ABWA membership. Through mentoring, these women will be introduced to a network of working women who will be positive role models and sources of support. Ms. Elman hopes ABWA will help move 200 women from welfare to work by the year 2000.

Ms. Elman has set some very high goals for the Association and businesswomen everywhere. Her varied interests and activities support the participative style of leadership she uses to help herself and others reach those goals. She is a true advocate for working women and will continue to crumble barriers, reach for new heights, and create awareness and opportunity for all women in business.

sitting at top levels in the organization who could help them through the system.[35] Although there was no excuse for this situation, there may be some explanation. Mentors sometimes select their protégés on the basis of seeing themselves, in their younger years, in the employee. Since men rarely can identify with younger women, many are unwilling to play the part of their mentor.[36] Of course, as women have battled their way into the inner circle of organizational power, some success is being witnessed.[37]

Additionally, organizations are beginning to explore ways of advocating cross-gender mentoring. This revolves around identifying the problems associated with such an arrangement,[38] deciding how they can be handled effectively, and providing organizational support.[39] Unfortunately, the effects of corporate downsizing in the 1990s—and to some extent, concerns about appearances of sexual harassment—significantly curtailed this effect.[40]

CAREER STAGES

One traditional way to analyze and discuss careers is to consider them in stages or steps.[41] Progression, from a beginning point through growth and decline phases to a termination point, is typically a natural occurrence in one's work life. Most of us begin to form our careers during our early school years. Our careers begin to wind down as we reach retirement age. We can identify five career stages that are typical for most adults, regardless of occupation: exploration, establishment, mid-career, late career, and decline. These stages are portrayed in Exhibit 9-2.

The age ranges for each stage in Exhibit 9-2 are intended to show general guidelines. For some individuals pursuing certain careers, this model may be too simplistic. The key is, however, to give your primary attention to the stages rather than the age categories. For instance, someone who makes a dramatic change in career to undertake a completely different line of work at age 45 will have many of the same establishment-stage concerns as someone starting at age 25. On the other hand, if the 45-year-old started working at 25, he or she now has 20 years of experience, as well as interests and expectations that differ from those of a peer who is just starting a career at middle age. Of course, if the 45-year-old individual is a newly admitted college student who starts college once her children have grown, she will have more in common—career stage wise—with the 23-year-old sitting next to her than she will with the 45-year-old full

Exhibit 9-2

Career Stages

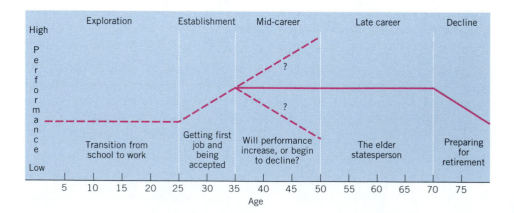

professor who is teaching the class. So don't get hung-up on the age generalizations in Exhibit 9-2. They're presented simply for points of reference.

Exploration

Many of the critical choices individuals make about their careers are made prior to entering the work force on a paid basis. What we hear from our relatives, teachers, and friends, what we see on television, in the movies, or on the Internet, helps us to narrow our career choice alternatives, leading us in certain directions. Certainly, the careers, interests, and aspirations of family members and financial resources will be heavy factors in determining our perception of what careers are available or what schools, colleges, or universities we might consider.

The **exploration period** ends for most of us as we make the transition from formal education programs to work. From an organizational standpoint, this stage has the least relevance, since it occurs prior to employment. It is, of course, not irrelevant. The exploration period is a time when a number of expectations about one's career are developed, many of which are unrealistic. Such expectations may lie dormant for years and then pop up later to frustrate both employee and employer.

Successful career exploration strategies involve trying a lot of potential fields to see what you like or don't like. The college internships and cooperative education programs are excellent exploration tools. You are given the opportunity to see your future co-workers firsthand and to do, day in and day out, a "real" job. Some successful internships lead to job offers. From a career-stage perspective, an internship that helps you realize that you're bored to death with the work is also a successful one. In the exploration stage we form our attitudes toward work (doing homework, meeting deadlines, taking or avoiding short-cuts, attendance), and our dominant social relationship patterns (easygoing, domineering, indifferent, likable, obnoxious). Therefore, exploration is preparation for work.

> **When you establish your career, you are trying to find your niche and make your mark.**

Establishment

The **establishment period** begins with the search for work and includes getting your first job, being accepted by your peers, learning the job, and gaining the first tangible evidence of success or failure in the "real world."[42] It begins with uncertainties and anxieties, and is, indeed, dominated by two problems: finding a "niche" and "making your mark."

Finding the right job takes time for many of us. In fact, you may know a 38-year-old who has held a series of seemingly unrelated jobs (for instance, after high school, clerk in a sporting goods store, three years; Navy, six years; police dispatcher, four years; small business owner, three years; over-the-road truck driver, now). This person has looked for a niche—or attempted to establish one—for nearly 20 years! A more typical pattern is to recognize that we may not change as frequently as the individual above. On the other hand, your first "real" job probably won't be with the company from which you retire. Thorough career exploration helps make this part of establishment an easier step.

The second problem of the establishment stage, "making your mark," is characterized by making mistakes, learning from those mistakes, and assuming increased responsibilities.[43] However, individuals in this stage have yet to reach their peak productivity, and rarely are they given work assignments that carry great power or high status. As shown in Exhibit 9-2, this stage is experienced as "going uphill." The career takes a lot of time and energy. There is often a sense of growth, of expectation, or anticipation, such as a hiker feels when approaching a crest, waiting to see what lies on the other side. And, just as a hiker "takes" a hill when she stands at the crest, the establishment stage has ended when you have "arrived" (made your mark). Of course, at this time you're considered a seasoned veteran. Consequently, you're now responsible for your own mistakes.

Mid-Career

Many people do not face their first severe career dilemmas until they reach the **mid-career stage.**[44] This is a time when individuals may continue their prior improvements in performance, level off, or begin to deteriorate. Therefore, although the challenge of remaining productive at work after you're "seasoned" is a major challenge of this career stage, the pattern ceases to be as clear as it was for exploration and establishment. Some employees reach their early goals and go on to even greater heights. For instance, a worker who wants to be the vice president of HRM by the time he's 35 to 40 years old might want to be CEO by the time he's 55 to 60 if he has achieved the prior goal. Continued growth and high performance are not the only successful outcomes at this stage. Maintenance, or holding onto what you have, is another possible outcome of the mid-career stage. These employees are plateaued, not failed. **Plateaued** mid-career employees can be very productive.[45] They are technically competent—even though some may not be as ambitious and aggressive as the climbers. They may be satisfied to contribute a sufficient amount of time and energy to the organization to meet production commitments; they also may be easier to manage than someone who wants more. These employees are not deadwood, but good, reliable employees and "solid citizens." An example

Many individuals are rarely prepared for that first major set-back in their careers. For Bernie Marcus and Arthur Blank, they didn't have any reason to think that their careers weren't moving forward. Both were successful managers at Handy Dan's (a retailer of hardware goods headquartered in Los Angeles). Then, unsuspectingly, they were fired. Unsure of what to do, and being unwilling to feel sorry for themselves, they decided to start the business they always feared—the hanger-sized warehouse home improvement center. Today, we know the business they started as Home Depot.

would be the same HRM vice president who decides at 40 to not go for the next promotion, but to enjoy other aspects of his life more—pursuing his hobbies, while still performing well on the job.

The third option for mid-career deals with the employee whose performance begins to deteriorate. This stage for this kind of employee is characterized by loss of both interest and productivity at work.[46] Organizations are often limited to relegating such individuals to less conspicuous jobs, reprimanding them, demoting them, or severing them from the organization altogether. The same HRM vice president could become less productive if, by 42, he realizes that he will never be CEO and tries to "wait it out" for 13 years until he can take early retirement. Fortunately, some affected individuals can be reenergized by moving them to another position in the organization. This can work to boost their morale and their productivity.[47]

Late Career

For those who continue to grow through the mid-career stage, the **late career** is usually a pleasant time when one is allowed the luxury to relax a bit and enjoy playing the part of the elder statesperson. It is a time when one can rest on one's laurels and bask in the respect given by less experienced employees. Frequently during the late career, individuals are no longer expected to outdo their levels of performance from previous years. Their value to the organization typically lies heavily in their judgment, built up over many years and through varied experiences. They can teach others based on the knowledge they have gained.[48]

For those who have stagnated or deteriorated during the previous stage, on the other hand, the late career brings the reality that they will not have an everlasting impact or change the world as they once thought. Employees who decline in mid-career may fear for their jobs. It is a time when individuals recognize that they have decreased work mobility and may be locked into their current job. One begins to look forward to retirement and the opportunities of doing something different. Mere plateauing is no more negative than it was during mid-career. In fact, it is expected at late career. The marketing vice president who didn't make it to executive vice president might begin delegating more to her next in line. Life off the job is likely to carry far greater importance than it did in earlier years, as time and energy, once directed to work, are now being redirected to family, friends, and hobbies.

Decline (Late Stage)

The **decline** or **late stage** in one's career is difficult for just about everyone, but, ironically, is probably hardest on those who have had continued successes in the earlier stages. After decades of continued achievements and high levels of performance, the time has come for retirement. These individuals step out of the limelight and relinquish a major component of their identity. For those who have seen their performance deteriorate over the years, it may be a pleasant time; the frustrations that have been associated with work are left behind. For the plateaued, it is probably an easier transition to other life activities.

Adjustments, of course, will have to be made regardless of whether one is leaving a sparkling career or a hopeless job. The structure and regimentation that work provided will no longer be there. Work responsibilities are generally fewer, and life is often less structured due to the absence of work. As a result, it is a challenging stage for anyone to confront.

However, as we live longer, healthier lives, coupled with laws removing age-related retirement requirements, 62 or 65 ceases to be a meaningful retirement demand. Some individuals shift their emphasis from one type of work to another—either paid or volunteer work. Oftentimes, the key element in this decision is the financial security one has. Those who have adequate funds to "maintain their lifestyles in retirement" are more likely to engage in activities that they desire. For instance, former CEO of Kodak, Kay Whitmore, moved on to do something he had always wanted—leading the Mormon Mission of Southern England—after retiring from the film-producing company.[49] Unfortunately, those less financially secure may not be able to retire when they want, or find that they have to seek gainful employment in some capacity to supplement their retirement income.

CAREER CHOICES AND PREFERENCES

The best career choice is the choice that offers the best match between what you want and what you need. Good career choice outcomes for any of us should result in a series of positions that give us an opportunity for good performance, make us want to maintain our commitment to the field, and give us high work satisfaction. A good career match, then, is one in which we are able to develop a positive self-concept and to do work that we think is important.[50] Let's look at some of the existing research that can help us formulate in which careers we may best "fit."

Holland Vocational Preferences

One of the most widely used approaches to guide career choices is the **Holland vocational preferences model.**[51] This theory consists of three major components. First, Holland found that people have varying occupational preferences; we do not all like to do the same things. Second, his research demonstrates that if you have a job where you can do what you think is important, you will be a more productive employee. Personality of workers may be matched to typical work environments where that can occur. Third, you will have more in common with people who have similar interest patterns and less in common with those who don't. For instance, assume Karen hates her job; she thinks it is boring to waste her time packing and unpacking trucks on the shipping dock of a manufacturing firm, and would rather be working with people in the recruiting area. Pat, on the other hand, enjoys the routine of her work; she likes the daily rhythm and the serenity of loading and unloading the warehouse. Do Karen and Pat get the same satisfaction from their jobs? There's a good chance that they don't. Why? Their interests, expressed as occupational interests, are not compatible.

The Holland vocational preferences model identifies six vocational themes (realistic, investigative, artistic, social, enterprising, conventional) presented in Exhibit 9-3. An individual's occupational personality is expressed as some combination of high and low scores on these six themes. High scores indicate that you enjoy those kinds of activities. Although it is possible to score high or low on all six scales, most people are identified by three dominant scales. The six

Exhibit 9-3 Holland's General Occupational Themes.

Realistic Rugged, robust, practical, prefer to deal with things rather than people mechanical interests. Best matches with jobs that are Agriculture, Nature, Adventure, Military, Mechanical.

Investigative Scientific, task-oriented, prefer abstract problems, prefer to think through problems rather than to act on them, not highly person-oriented, enjoy ambiguity. Corresponding jobs are Science, Mathematics, Medical Science, Medical Service.

Artistic Enjoy creative self-expression, dislike highly-structured situations, sensitive, emotional, independent, original. Corresponding jobs are Music/Dramatics, Art, Writing.

Social Concerned with the welfare of others, enjoy developing and teaching others, good in group settings, extroverted, cheerful, popular. Corresponding jobs are Teaching, Social Service, Athletics, Domestic Arts, Religious Activities.

Enterprising Good facility with words, prefer selling or leading, energetic, extroverted, adventurous, enjoy persuasion. Corresponding jobs are Public Speaking, Law/Politics, Merchandising, Sales, Business Management.

Conventional Prefer ordered, numerical work, enjoy large organizations, stable, dependable. Corresponding job is Office Practices.

themes are arranged in the hexagonal structure shown in Exhibit 9-4. This scale model represents the fact that some of the themes are opposing, while others have mutually reinforcing characteristics.

For instance, Realistic and Social are opposite each other in the diagram. A person with a realistic preference wants to work with things, not people. A person with a social preference wants to work with people, no matter what else they do. Therefore, they have opposing preferences about working alone or with others. Investigative and Enterprising are opposing themes as are Artistic and Conventional preferences.

An example of mutually reinforcing themes is the Social-Enterprising-Conventional (SEC) vocational preference structure. Sally, for example, likes working with people, being successful, and following ordered rules. That combination is perfect for someone willing to climb the ladder in a large bureaucracy.

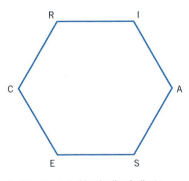

Letters connected by the line indicate reinforcing themes; letters not connected represent opposing themes

Exhibit 9-4

Structure of Holland's Themes

What about Bob? He's Realistic-Investigative-Artistic, preferring solitary work to large groups, asking questions to answering them, and making his own rules instead of following someone else's. How does Bob fit into a large bureaucracy? Some may see his preferred actions labeling him as a troublemaker. Where would he fit better? Possibly in a research lab! Both the preference of the scientist and the environment of the research lab are characterized by a lack of human interruptions and a concentration on factual material. That's consistent with the Realistic-Investigative-Artistic profile.

The Schein Anchors

Edgar Schein has identified *anchors,* or personal value clusters, that may be satisfied or frustrated by work. When a particular combination of these personal value clusters (technical–functional competence, managerial competence, security—stability, creativity, and autonomy—independence) is held by the worker and characteristically offered by the organization, that person is "anchored" in that job, organization, or industry.[52] Most people have two or three value clusters that are important to them. If an organization satisfies two out of three, that is considered a stable match. For instance, Donny is a recent college graduate. He wants to use his human resources degree. His father was laid off when his organization downsized last year, and he never wants to have to deal with that type of uncertainty. Schein would describe Donny's anchors as technical competence and security-stability. His current job choices are marketing on a commission basis for a new credit card company, or recruiting for an established and growth-oriented computer firm. Which job should he take? Based on his combination of value clusters, at this time the recruiting job appears to better match Donny's preferences.

Jung and the Myers-Briggs Typologies

One of the more widely used methods of identifying personalities is the **Myers-Briggs Type Indicator (MBTI)**®*.[53] Building on the works of the early psychologist, Carl Jung, the MBTI uses four dimensions of personality to identify 16 different personality types—for example, ISTJ, ENFP, and so on—based on one's responses to an approximately 100 item questionnaire (see Exhibit 9-5). More than 2 million individuals each year in the United States alone take the MBTI. It's used in such companies as Apple computer, AT&T, Exxon, 3M, as well as many hospitals, educational institutions, and the U.S. armed forces.[54] These personality dimensions can be matched to work environments, much as Holland vocational preferences are used. People with different personality attributes express different job skills and are compatible with other workers with similar personality structures.

The EI dimension measures an individual's orientation toward the inner world of ideas (I) or the external world of the environment (E). The sensing-intuitive dimension indicates an individual's reliance on information gathered from the external world (S) or from the world of ideas (I). Thinking–feeling reflects one's preference to evaluate information in either an analytical manner (T) or based on values and beliefs (F). Lastly, the judging–perceiving index reflects one's attitude toward the external world, which is either task completion oriented (J) or information-seeking (P). Using this information, then, let's de-

---

* The Myers-Briggs Type Indicator and MBTI are registered trademarks of Consulting Psychologists Press, Inc.

Exhibit 9-5 Characteristics Frequently Associated with Myers-Briggs Types

		Sensing Types S		Intuitive Types N	
		Thinking T	Feeling F	Feeling F	Thinking T
Introverts I	Judging J	**ISTJ** Quiet, serious dependable, practical matter-of-fact. Value traditions and loyalty.	**ISFJ** Quiet, friendly, responsible, thorough, considerate. Strive to create order and harmony.	**INFJ** Seek meaning and connection in ideas. Committed to firm values. Organized and decisive in implementing vision.	**INTJ** Have original minds and great drive for their ideas. Skeptical and independent, have high standards of competence for self and others.
Introverts I	Perceiving P	**ISTP** Tolerant and flexible. Interested in cause and effect. Values efficiency.	**ISFP** Quiet, friendly, sensitive. Likes own space. Dislikes disagreements and conflicts.	**INFP** Idealistic, loyal to their values. Seek to understand people and help them fulfill their potential.	**INTP** Seeks logical explanations. Theoretical and abstract over social interactions. Skeptical, sometimes critical. Analytical.
Extroverts E	Perceiving P	**ESTP** Flexible and tolerant. Focus on here and now. Enjoy material comforts. Learn best by doing.	**ESFP** Outgoing, friendly. Enjoy working with others. Spontaneous. Learn best by trying a new skill with other people.	**ENFP** Enthusiastic, imaginative. Wants a lot of affirmation. Rely on verbal fluency and ability to improvise	**ENTP** Quick, ingenious, stimulating. Adept at generating conceptual possibilities, and analyzing them strategically. Bored by routine.
Extroverts E	Judging J	**ESTJ** Practical, realistic, matter-of-fact, decisive. Focus on getting efficient results. Forceful in implementing plans.	**ESFJ** Warmhearted, cooperative. Want to be appreciated for who they are and for what they contribute.	**ENFJ** Warm, responsive, responsible. Attuned to needs of others. Sociable, facilitate others, provide inspirational leadership.	**ENTJ** Frank, decisive, assumes leadership. Enjoys long-term planning and goal setting. Forceful in presenting ideas.

scribe someone who is identified as an INFP (introvert–intuitive–feeling–perceptive). Under Myers-Briggs, the INFP individual would be someone who is quiet and reserved and generally in deep thought, sees the "big picture," is flexible and adaptable, likes a challenge, looks for complete information before making a decision, and cares for others.[55]

Just as each individual has a psychological typology, so too do jobs. As such, this body of work would indicate that employees will be better performers if they are appropriately matched to the job. For example, consider the job of a computer programmer. This job requires an individual to work with details, to work autonomously much of the time, and to complete complex programs according to a set schedule. Using the Myers-Briggs profiles, this job would be viewed as having characteristics of introversion, sensing, thinking, judging (ISTJ). Would the description of the INFP person above be a good match for this job? Probably not—it may not provide what the INFP is looking for. Accordingly, to be better matched to the job, research would suggest that the employee share the same personality type.

MANAGING YOUR CAREER

The career is dead—long live the career. A play on words or an insight into today's careers? Maybe it's a little bit of both. Nonetheless, it's the title of Douglas T. Hall's new book.[56] For several decades, Douglas Hall has been highly regarded for his research about people's careers. And similar to what we've previously discussed, careers are changing. The greatest difference is that you, the individual, are responsible for developing and managing your career.[57] We'll look at suggestions to help you in developing your career—whichever your field of interest.

Making Your Career Decision

The best career choice is the choice that offers the best match between what you want out of life and what you need. Good career choice outcomes should result in a series of positions that give you an opportunity to be a good performer, make you want to maintain your commitment to your career, lead to highly satisfying work, and be able to give you the proper balance between work and personal life. A good career match, then, is one in which you are able to develop a positive self-concept, to do work that you think is important, and to lead the kind of life you desire.[58] Identifying this is referred to as *career planning*.

Career planning is designed to assist you in becoming more knowledgeable of your needs, values, and personal goals. This can be achieved through the following three-step, self-assessment process.[59]

Identify and Organize Your Skills, Interests, Work-Related Needs, and Values   The best place to begin is by drawing up a profile of your educational record. List each school attended from high school on. What courses do you remember as liking most and least? In what courses did you score highest and lowest? In what extracurricular activities did you participate? Are there any specific skills that you acquired? Are there other skills in which you have gained proficiency?

Next, begin to assess your occupational experience. List each job you have held, the organization you worked for, your overall level of satisfaction, what you liked most and least about the job, and why you left. It's important to be honest in covering each of these points.

Convert This Information into General Career Fields and Specific Job Goals   By completing step 1, you should now have some insights into your interests and abilities. What you need to do now is look at how these can be converted into the kind of organizational setting or field of endeavor with which you will be a good match. Then you can become specific and identify distinct job goals.

Careers

WORKPLACE ISSUES

Susan has worked in the same position as an executive assistant for 12 years, and has reached the top grade level for her career path in her company. Becoming bored and disenchanted with the lack of challenge and opportunities, she fears "burnout" as well as boredom. Nevertheless, she does not want to leave the company regardless of the lack of openings in the company due to recent downsizing. Lately, she has realized her feelings of powerlessness and frustration are affecting her attitude and consequently her performance.

Susan is experiencing feelings and a work-state common to those who experience rapid company downsizing, specialized careers or employment in smaller companies with shorter career ladders. Regardless of the situation, Susan and others experiencing symptoms of career burnout, boredom or blockage do have a number of options. To overcome burnout, boredom or blockage recharge your career by taking responsibility and accountability for enriching your own position and maximizing your career potential. For example, before quitting, talk with your manager. Although Susan has been with the company for 12 years, she has not had a raise in three years and does not believe she will be given another raise or opportunity without going into management. She does not want to go into management and sees no other alternative than to stay and be miserable,

and since misery loves company, make what coworkers are left miserable too.

Susan, like so many others, needs to have a chat with her manager rather than assuming or reading minds. What is the worst thing that could happen if the situation was discussed and the manager had an opportunity to respond, possibly support a plan of action? What could be gained? Frequently situations continue unresolved until a termination or resignation is the only option. However, taking charge of your own career destiny can prevent many terminations and resignations, as well as bring renewed fulfillment by choosing from the following strategies:

1. Take books home and read the operations manuals, annual reports, training materials, trade journals, product information, newsletters—anything and everything to learn new information and gain a new perspective.
2. Volunteer to start or join teams or committees to meet fresh faces and potential career contacts.
3. Review your current job description, highlighting the tasks or responsibilities you prefer to perform the best. Write your dream job description—how do they compare? Is it possible to incorporate more of the dream job into your current job? If not, what would it take to get that dream job?
4. Enroll in seminars and courses. It's back to school time—why not you? Countless opportunities for internal, public, computer—on line and tutorials courses as well as vocational, non-traditional and academic offerings abound. Stagnation and obsolescence is a personal choice. Consider unique course opportunities

such as the Fast-Track Management Program at Texas Woman's University which offers a series of five, three-weekend credit courses in courses such as leadership, management, communication, and relations, and supervision.
5. Soul search. What would you really like to be or do when you grow up, considering that you still want to grow? What skills, contacts, credentials, and abilities will you need, and are you willing to pay the price?
6. Network—join clubs, organizations, church groups, to gain the contacts, role models, support and learning opportunities and to do the same for someone else.
7. Tap your internal and external resources as well as human resources or personnel department. They may be delighted to assist someone positively, a refreshing change from personnel problems and paperwork. After all, people can't help you if they do not know what you need.
8. Reassess your needs, values and set some goals—share them with your boss or tell someone who cares. If no one seems to, then start a new list. Look into your own crystal ball, your heart, mind or your consciousness—among the confusion is that inner guiding voice, and so far betting on yourself may be your best bet.

And Susan . . . finally got the courage to talk with her manager who encouraged her to delegate and reassign tasks to free her to develop computer and customer service skills in order to qualify for the upcoming promotion and raise. True story. . . . Really.

DR. CONNIE SITTERLY, CPCM

What fields are available? In business? In government? In nonprofit organizations? Your answer can be broken down further into areas such as education, financial, manufacturing, social services, or health services. Identifying areas of interest is usually far easier than pinpointing specific occupations. When you are able to identify a limited set of occupations that interest you, you can start to align these with your abilities and skills. Will certain jobs require you to move? If so, would this be compatible with your geographic preferences? Do you have the educational requirements necessary for the job? If not, what additional schooling will be needed? Does the job offer the status and earning potential that you aspire to? What is the long-term outlook for jobs in this field? Does the career suffer from cyclical employment? Since no job is without its drawbacks, have you seriously considered all the negative aspects? When you have fully answered questions such as these, you should have a relatively short list of specific job goals.

Test Your Career Possibilities Against the Realities of the Organization or the Job Market   The final step in this self-assessment process is testing your selection against the realities of the marketplace. This can be done by going out and talking with knowledgeable people in the fields, organizations, or jobs you desire. These informational interviews should provide reliable feedback as to the accuracy of your self-assessment and the opportunities in the fields and jobs that interest you (see Workplace Issues on page 271).

Achieving Your Career Goals

We, as many authors, wish we had a foolproof process to give you. Nothing would make our jobs easier than if we could say emphatically, follow these steps and you'll be guaranteed career success. Of course, we all know that such a guarantee could never be given. But that's not to imply that achieving your career goals are left simply to chance. Instead, there are suggestions on how to "survive" in most organizations, as well as ways that you might use to make inroads toward building a successful career (see Exhibit 9-6).

The following discussion provides a dozen suggestions based on proven tactics that many individuals have used to advance their careers.[60]

Exhibit 9-6

Steps in managing your career.

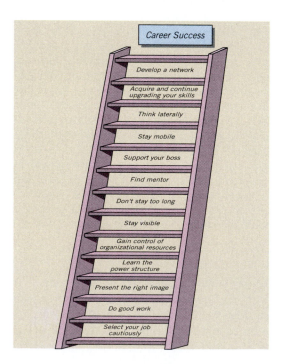

Select Your First Job Judiciously　All first jobs are not alike. Where you begin in the organization has an important effect on your subsequent career progress. Specifically, evidence suggests that if you have a choice, you should select a powerful department as the place to start your career.[61] A power department is one where crucial and important organizational decisions are made. If you start out in departments that are high in power within the organizations, you're more likely to advance in the organization—and ultimately throughout your career.

Do Good Work　Good work performance is a necessary (but not sufficient) condition for career success. The marginal performer may be rewarded in the short term, but his or her weaknesses are bound to surface eventually and cut off career advancement. Your good work performance is no guarantee of success, but without it, the probability of a successful career is low.

Present the Right Image　Assuming that your work performance is in line with other successful employees, the ability to align your image with that sought by the organization is certain to be interpreted positively. You should assess the organization's culture so that you can determine what the organization wants and values. Then you need to project that image in terms of style of dress; organizational relationships that you should and shouldn't cultivate; whether you should project a risk-taking or risk-averse stance; whether you should avoid, tolerate, or encourage conflict; the importance of getting along well with others; and so forth.

Learn the Power Structure　The authority relationships defined by the organization's formal structure, as shown by an organizational chart, explain only part of the influence patterns within an organization. It's of equal or greater importance to know and understand the organization's power structure. You need to learn "who's really in charge, who has the goods on whom, what are the major debts and dependencies"—all things that won't be reflected in neat boxes on the organization chart. Once you have this knowledge, you can work within the power structure with more skill and ease.[62]

Gain Control of Organizational Resources　The control of scarce and important organizational resources is a source of power. Knowledge and expertise are particularly effective resources to control. They make you more valuable to the organization and therefore more likely to gain job security and advancement.

Stay Visible　Because the evaluation of performance effectiveness can be very subjective, it's important that your boss and those in power in the organization be made aware of your contributions. If you're fortunate enough to have a job that brings your accomplishments to the attention of others (or have a mentor who's ensuring that this information is made known), taking direct measures to increase your visibility might not be needed. But your job may require you to handle activities that are low in visibility, or your specific contribution may be indistinguishable because you're part of a group endeavor. In such cases, without creating the image of a braggart, you'll want to call attention to yourself by giving progress reports to your boss and others. Other tactics include being seen at social functions, being active in your professional associations, and developing powerful allies who speak positively of you.

Marguerite Piret had a dream. She wanted to run an organization that gave her opportunities to work closely with people, and one that richly rewarded her. But she knew that she couldn't do this right out of college. Instead, she started small, learning her "trade" from the bottom up. She left her employer every few years, moving into a new job that afforded her more exposure and greater experience. In the end, she achieved her goal—Marguerite is now president of a small investment banking firm in Boston.

Don't Stay Too Long in Your First Job   The evidence indicates that, given a choice between staying in your first job until you've "really made a difference," or accepting going onto another job (either in your current organization or for another one), you should opt for making the change.[63] By moving quickly through different jobs, you signal to others that you're on the fast track. This, then, often becomes a self-fulling prophecy. The message for you is to start fast by seeking early transfers or promotions from your first job.

Find a Mentor   This item is so important it needs to be singled out. Remember a mentor is someone from whom you can learn and who can encourage and help you (see Ethical Decisions in HRM). The evidence indicates that finding a sponsor who is part of the organization's power core is essential for you to make it to grow in your career.[64]

Support Your Boss   Your immediate future is in the hands of your current boss. He or she evaluates your performance, and you're unlikely to have enough power to successfully challenge this supervisor. Therefore, you should make the effort to help your boss succeed, be supportive if your boss is under siege from other organizational members, and find out what he or she will be using to assess your work effectiveness.[65] Don't undermine your boss. Don't speak negatively of your boss to others. If your boss is competent, visible, and possesses a power base, he or she is likely to be on the way up in the organization. Being perceived as supportive, you might find yourself pulled along too. If

Special Mentoring Programs for Women and Minorities

We have been witnessing many discussions lately regarding how more women and minorities can break through the glass ceiling. There is no doubt that these groups are underrepresented at the top echelons of organizations. Several reasons have been well documented detailing why this occurred. One of those reasons centers around the issue of mentoring.

Finding, or getting, a mentor to support you is rarely easy. In fact, more often than not, a mentor approaches you to begin the relationship. In the past, many of these individuals happened to be white males; and historically, women and minorities found it difficult to gain the favor of these mentors simply because mentors preferred someone more like them.

With the changing work force composition, employment legislation, and changing societal views of women and minorities in the workplace, mentoring relationships for this group are occurring more frequently. But it is not, as yet, fully ingrained in the minds and hearts of some managers. Consequently, a number of organizations have developed special mentoring programs for women and minorities—formalizing a practice that typically naturally evolved. In some respects, this may be the best way at this time to help further advance these two groups. Leaving it up to nature just doesn't work well. The prevalence of the glass ceiling dilemma attests to that. On the other hand, can a mentoring relationship be forced, and regulated? The crux of these relationships is for an individual to become very close to his or her protégé in an effort to further one's career. Won't forcing these people together—two individuals who have not come together naturally—lead to a constrained relationship? Given the degree of conflict that may arise between the two, it's possible more harm than good for the protégé's career may result.

Should women and minorities be given special treatment in the mentoring relationship by having organizational policies dictating who will mentor and how it will be handled? Should there be special guidelines to ensure that mentoring for women and minorities occurs? And what about the white male? Is he being left out? What do you think?

---

your boss's performance is poor and his or her power is low, you need to move to another job. A mentor may be able to help you arrange this. It's hard to have your competence recognized or your positive performance evaluation taken seriously if your boss is perceived as incompetent.

Stay Mobile   You're likely to move upward more rapidly if you indicate your willingness to move to different geographical locations and across functional lines within the organization. Career advancement may also be facilitated by your willingness to change organizations.[66] Working in a slow-growth, stagnant, or declining organization should make mobility even more important to you.

Think Laterally   The suggestion to think laterally acknowledges the changing world of work. Because of organizational restructuring and downsizing, there are fewer rungs on the promotion ladder in many large organizations. To survive in this environment, it's a good idea to think in terms of lateral career moves.[67] It's important to recognize that lateral movers in the 1960s and 1970s were presumed to be mediocre performers—the plateaued worker. That presumption doesn't hold in many cases today. Lateral shifts are now a viable career consideration. They give you a wider range of experiences, which enhances your long-term mobility. In addition, these moves can help energize you by making your work more interesting and satisfying. So if you're not moving ahead in your organization, consider a lateral move internally or a lateral shift to another organization.

Think of Your Career in Terms of Skills You're Acquiring and Continue Upgrading Those Skills   Organizations need employees who can readily adapt to the demands of the rapidly changing marketplace. By focusing on skills that you currently have and continuing to learn new skills you can establish your value to the organization. It's employees who don't add value to an organization are the ones whose jobs (and career advancement) are in jeopardy.

Work Harder Than Ever at Developing a Network   Our final suggestion is based on the recognition that having a network of friends, colleagues, neighbors, customers, suppliers, etc. can be a useful tool for career development.[68] If you spend some time cultivating relationships and contacts throughout your industry and community, you'll be prepared if "worse comes to worse" and your current job is eliminated. Even if your job is in no danger of being cut, having a network can prove beneficial in getting things done.

Some Final Words of Wisdom

Have you ever pondered the freight train career ride of the baby-boom generation that occurred from the 1960s through the 1980s? Did you ever wonder what existed that promoted some of these meteoric career heights in such a quick period? Were the baby boomers smarter than the generation Xers; or were they just luckier? A precise answer is difficult to pinpoint, but clearly luck played a major role. How so? Consider that during the 1960s, organizations in the United States experienced unprecedented growth. This meant new markets opened up, bringing along with it many new jobs. Organizations during this period became overly hierarchical, which translated into the creation of managerial positions for almost any task that existed.

Undoubtedly, many of the baby boomers were in the right place, at the right time. But don't chalk it up solely to luck. The baby boomers were better educated than the generation preceding them, and they brought an aggressive trait to the work force that was rarely witnessed before. Furthermore, accepting most any challenging assignment, being willing to relocate, and having the support of mentors all fostered a career boom. Unfortunately, this prosperity didn't last forever. In fact, many of these baby boomers who skyrocketed to the top in their first 10 to 15 years on the job were the ones hardest hit by the downsizing that began in the late 1980s. For them, and those that have followed, fast-tracked career progression may be a thing of the past. Our organizations just cannot afford to promote workers in droves as they once did. And, many of the jobs that served as stepping-stones to careers may be lost forever.

What, then, can you do to keep your career alive in today's dynamic organizations? The answer may lie in the acronym DATA.[69]

The D stands for desire. Although experience was once perceived as the best preparation for the future, past experience may actually be a hindrance. The past may promote a status quo mentality—one that is ill-fitted to a dynamic environment. Instead, your desire will be a key factor in your career growth. If you desire to be the best in your field, continually strive to excel, and perform under a variety of difficult situations, you'll have an advantage over those who don't possess this trait.

Secondly, you must have the *Ability* to perform the required work. This means that you can never sit back on your laurels and bask in that glory. Rather, you must continually upgrade your skills, knowledge, and abilities to assist you in becoming the best at your job. This also means looking closely inside and identifying your strengths and weaknesses, capitalizing on the strengths and working to develop the weaknesses.

Your desire to be the best you can be is a key element in your career growth.

You must also have an appropriate *Temperament*. The security of yesterday's jobs is gone.[70] You are on your own in many circumstances. And when the job is done, so too, might be your association with the organization. Being such, you must have a disposition that easily adjusts to an everchanging work situation. Rigidity and the desire for security may be the ultimate killers of your career.

Finally, you must possess a variety of *Assets*. This means that whatever resources the job requires, you must be able to provide them. This may be networking contacts, equipment, or even time commitments—all resources that contribute to a successful performer.

Succeeding in tomorrow's organizations needn't be a hopeless cause. You must recognize that yesterday's career paths don't exist everywhere. But with proper preparation and a positive mind-set, you can open the doors to career growth.[71] This time, however, it will be solely your responsibility.

SUMMARY

This summary relates to the Learning Objectives provided on p. 252.

After having read this chapter you should know:

1. The responsibility for managing a career belongs to the individual. The organization's role is to provide assistance and information to the employee, but is not responsible for growing an employee's career.
2. A career is a sequence of positions occupied by a person during a course of a lifetime.
3. Career development from an organizational standpoint involves tracking career paths and developing career ladders. From an individual perspective, career development focuses on assisting individuals in identifying their major career goals and to determining what they need to do to achieve these goals.
4. The main distinction between career development and employee development lies in their time frames. Career development focuses on the long-range career effectiveness and success of organizational personnel. Employee development focuses on more of the immediate and intermediate time frames.
5. Career development is valuable to an organization because it (1) ensures needed talent will be available; (2) improves the organization's ability to attract and retain high-talent employees; (3) ensures that minorities and women get opportunities for growth and development; (4) reduces employee frustration; (5) enhances cultural diversity; (6) assists in implementing quality; and (7) promotes organizational goodwill.
6. The five stages in a career are exploration, establishment, mid-career, late-career, and decline.
7. The Holland Vocational Preferences are realistic, investigative, artistic, social, enterprising, and conventional.
8. Typology focuses on personality dimensions including extroversion–introversion; sensing–intuition; thinking–feeling; and judging–perceiving. These four "pairs" can be combined into 16 different combination profiles. With this information, personality of jobs can be matched to personality of individuals.
9. Some suggestions for managing your career include: (1) Select your first job judiciously; (2) do good work; (3) present the right image; (4) learn the power structure; (5) gain control of organizational resources; (6) stay visible; (7) don't stay too long in your first job; (8) find a mentor; (9) support your boss; (10) stay mobile; (11) think laterally; (12) think of your career in terms of skills you're acquiring and continue upgrading those skills; and (13) work harder than ever at developing a network.

EXPERIENTIAL EXERCISE:
Career Insights

Imagine that you enter the elevator on your way to an interview for an entry-level job at the company for which you would most like to work. However, the elevator stalls, and the one other individual pulls out her mobile phone and calls security. After he hangs up, he says, "Well, it will be 15 or 20 minutes, let me introduce myself, I'm Hans Schultz, president, of ProSearch Solutions."

Introduce yourself and maximize your opportunity by answering his questions that follow:

1. Who do you think is responsible for your career?
2. What are your plans to continue your education?
3. Why did you pick your chosen career?
4. In a meeting with our human resources manager yesterday, he said there's a difference between ca-

reer and employment development. Do you know the difference?

5. What phase of your career development are you in?

6. What style are you according to Myers-Briggs Typologies?

7. How would you match what you want out of life and your career? Career goals? Job goals?

8. What are your skills, interests, work-related needs and values?

9. What courses do you like best and least? Most challenging and most difficult?

10. Have you ever had a mentor? Share that experience.

11. How would you demonstrate loyalty to your company? Support for your manager?

12. Describe your desire? Abilities? Temperament? Assets? What in the past and present would demonstrate that by examples?

WEB-WISE EXERCISES

Search and print findings about jobs in human resource consulting from the following Web sites:

Career Magazine
http://www.careermag.com/careermag/

Career Advice from the Princeton Review
http://www.review.com/careers/index.cfm

Jobs in Consulting

http://www.cob.ohio-state-fin/jobs/consult.htm
Offers information for those interested in a career in management consulting. You may choose areas of generalist, benefits, employee relations, compensation, or other areas of interest. This site contains information on skill requirements in consulting, key job areas, print resources, and links to other Internet resources.

Assignment
Search and print findings about job listings in human resource from the following Web site:

Jobtrack http://www.jobtrack.com/
Offers information on job listings, employers, tips on interviewing and resumés, and links to other helpful sites. Also gives read and print tips on interviewing and resumés and notes other future sites for future reference.

Assignment
Search and print findings about employment opportunities of interest from the following Web site: **Outline Career Center http://www.occ.com**
More than 250 companies post listings of employ-

ment opportunities here. Listing is especially strong in the hi-tech area.

Boston Consulting Group http://www.bcg.com/
This is one of the best strategy consulting firms in the nation. This site has some information on recruiting and careers.

Career Mosaic http://www.careermosaic.com/
Gives job information as well as data on current job opportunities.

Career Path.com & The Monster Board www.careerpath.com-www.monsterboard.com
CareerPath.com posts classified ads from newspapers. The Monster board lets companies post openings and job seekers post resumes.

National Business Employment Weekly http://www.nbew.com/
Gives you job search and career guidance information.

(AJB) America's Job Bank, sponsored by the Department of Labor (DOL) in cooperation with various state employment services through AJB, any U.S. employer or any foreign company legally authorized to operate a business in the United States, may list its job openings with this public employment service. No charge or fees are involved with using this service.

Additional Web sites regarding career topics include:

E-SPAN's Interactive Employment Network:
    espan.com
On-line Career Center.occ.com
(SHRM) the Society for Human Resource Management http://www.shrm.org
Career Path careerpath.com
Career Web cweb.com
Job Web jobweb.com

CASE APPLICATION:
Happiness Is . . .

Michelle, Carlos, and Becky have invited you to join them for coffee and discuss careers. Michelle believes that if she could find a career that could make her happy, everything else in her life would improve and she could gain an opportunity for the recognition, approval, money, influence, confidence, and satisfaction that she desires.

Becky, a friend who is majoring in education to become a career counselor, suggests that it's not that simple; it takes balancing and meshing personal values, interests, skills, knowledge, feelings, beliefs, and preferences with those of an organization to gain the right match for optimal success. She adds that she read recently that only about 3 percent of college students take advantage of career programs or counseling offered in their colleges and universities, and she intends to take advantage of more career courses, any assessments, counseling, seminars, career days, computer programs . . . anything available to help her understand better who she is and what she might want.

Carlos says he depends on his intuition, and has been lucky in the past. Things have always come to him when he has needed help, like when he didn't know where to get money for college. A man who worked with his father told him about scholarships available for employees' children.

He watched his father come home every night from a job he hated for 23 years, complaining about his work, his boss, and co-workers, but says it won't happen to him. He will quit, he will not waste his life going to a place he hates.

Becky suggests that you visit the college career center, answer the following questions, and meet later to discuss responses. Carlos says it will be important to be totally honest about preferences. Michelle offers that everyone should also consider what each would be willing to do to achieve success, because she knows she'll do whatever it takes to succeed. Becky suggests that the team use a comparison chart like the one used in the human resource management class. Becky adds that the team needs to agree on roles, and she volunteers to be the team leader. She suggests that Michelle be the recorder, Carlos be the timekeeper, and you be the discussion facilitator next time to help keep them on track.

The team accepts their roles, agrees to complete the four steps, and meet later in the week for coffee and discussion.

Instructions:

1. Visit the career center. (Perhaps it would be more interesting and fun for your team to visit the center together.)
2. Discuss resources available with a career counselor.
3. Do steps 1 and 2 and summarize the information obtained.
4. Complete a comparison chart to evaluate criteria against career options.

TESTING YOUR UNDERSTANDING

How well did you fulfill the learning objectives?

1. Carol is a wife and mother. She has raised four children, and now wants to do something else. She spends most of her time in volunteer activities—save the whales, quilting, great books clubs, church work. What could she change to have a successful career?
   a. Get paid for the work she does.
   b. Stick to only one volunteer activity for a period of more than fifteen years.
   c. Carol does have a successful career.
   d. Carol could have more children.
   e. If Carol felt satisfied as wife, mother, and volunteer worker, her career could be regarded as successful.

2. A vice president of human resources for a large, high-technology firm fights to attract and retain highly skilled workers. She is hiring a new manager of training and development. She wants a progressive person who is in tune with the needs of the workers and is aware of emerging trends in career management. What comment would be a danger signal in an interview with a prospective candidate?
   a. A major focus of the job is developing career ladders and tracking career paths.
   b. Monitoring the progress of special groups, such as minorities and managers, is an important part of the job.
   c. The needs of dual-career couples should be handled in the same ways as single employees to avoid favoritism.
   d. Lifestyle issues and individual analysis should be part of the career planning services offered to employees.
   e. Employee needs and goals should be assessed. Today's worker has different expectations than those of a generation ago.

3. Robin has worked for the same manufacturing firm for twenty years. Last week, after a training session, she decided to quit, return to school, and open a florist shop. What kind of session did Robin attend?
   a. Individual career development.
   b. Organizational career management.
   c. Employee development.
   d. Employee training.
   e. Employee inventory.

4. John, vice president of human resources, has just cut the career development program from his budget in response to a 35 percent budget cut directive. What is likely to happen?
   a. Good employees will not be affected.
   b. All employee training functions will become more effective and efficient because of this action.
   c. In the short term, employees will work harder.
   d. In the long term, employees will be less committed and satisfied with the organization.
   e. The other training functions can easily replace these programs.

5. A large federal agency conducts career management workshops for its employees. More than 30 percent of workshop attendees leave for employment elsewhere within a year. The program is considered to be a great success in career management because it

a. keeps those employees out of other training sessions.

b. increases cultural diversity.

c. reduces employee frustration.

d. reduces organizational goodwill.

e. promotes organizational globalization.

6. Sean is a 27-year-old college senior. He will graduate in the spring with an MBA in Accounting and return to full-time work as a senior accountant for the firm that paid his way through school. Identify Mike's career stage.

a. Decline.

b. Maintenance.

c. Exploration.

d. Establishment.

e. Mid-career.

7. Jane is an accounting major and refinishes furniture in her spare time. She is well organized and uses a very impressive time-management calendar. She seems friendly enough, and belongs to several campus groups, but is not an officer in any of them. What is Jane's Holland type?

a. Realistic-Investigative-Artistic.

b. Social-Enterprising-Conventional.

c. Social-Conventional-Realistic.

d. Investigative-Enterprising-Artistic.

e. Realistic-Conventional-Artistic.

8. Gloria works for a large bank as a teller manager. She likes the steady hours, the predictable schedule, the pleasant co-workers, the good working relationships with her employees, and the status of the bank. What Schein anchors are important to Gloria?

a. Security, managerial competence.

b. Security, creativity.

c. Technical competence, security.

d. Creativity, autonomy, technical competence.

e. Creativity, autonomy, security.

9. Based on a comparison of Holland's vocational preferences and the Jungian/Myers-Briggs Typology, which statement is accurate?

a. A realistic person is likely to be intuitive.

b. A social person is likely to be an extrovert.

c. An investigative person is likely to be thinking.

d. An artistic person is likely to be judging.

e. An enterprising person is likely to be an introvert.

10. Joanne is an Extrovert-Sensing-Thinking-Judging Jungian type. What job would be best for her?

a. A shoe clerk. She could meet lots of people, measure feet, sell the shoes, and move on to the next customer.

b. A waitress. She could meet lots of people, anticipate their dining needs, make sure everyone in the dining party was happy, and look forward to repeat business.

c. A rocket scientist. She could work in her lab,

away from people, and make whatever experiments she wanted, whenever she wanted.

d. A veterinarian. She could work with animals, not people, extend the limits of physical diagnosis in her treatments, and move on to the next dog.

e. A grade-school teacher. She could work with children, help them be creative, help socialize them, and know that, for years to come, she influenced their lives.

11. Matt quit school when he was 16 to work full-time at the local fast-food emporium to pay for his car and his video games. Now, at 36, he wants to try something else. What should Matt do?

a. Finish high school.

b. Get into the management training program at the fast-food emporium.

c. Spend some time sorting and identifying his skills, interests, needs, and values.

d. Just say, "No."

e. Check the want ads and interview for other jobs.

12. Individual career management is different today than it was a generation ago for all of these reasons except

a. sex-role stereotypes are crumbling.

b. employee expectations are different.

c. the impact of other life roles and responsibilities on work life has been recognized.

d. choices are more important. There is little opportunity today to change a career, once it has been launched.

e. lifestyles are more varied.

Endnotes

1. Lee Smith, "Landing That First Real Job," *Fortune* (May 16, 1994), p. 94; and William Echikson, "Young Americans Go Abroad and Strike It Rich," *Fortune* (October 17, 1994), p. 186.

2. Patricia Buhler, "Managing Your Career: No Longer Your Company's Responsibility," *Supervision* (November 1997), pp. 23–26.

3. "Three Million U.S. Jobs Cut in Seven Years, *Manpower Argus* (March 1996), p. 3; Manuel London, "Redeployment and Continuous Learning in the 21st Century: Hard Lessons and Positive Examples from the Downsizing Era," *Academy of Management Executive,* Vol. 10, No. 4 (November 1996), pp. 67–78; "New paths to Success," *Fortune* (June 12, 1995), p. 90; and Bill Leonard, "Downsized & Out: Career Survival in the '90s" *HRMagazine* (June 1995), pp. 89–92.

4. Carolyn Griffith, "Building a Resilient Work Force," *Training* (Winter 1998), pp. 54–60.

5. Douglas T. Hall, *Careers in Organizations* (Santa Monica, Calif.: Goodyear Publishing, 1976); and J. Van Maanen and E. H. Schein, "Career Development," in J. R. Hackman and J. L. Suttle (eds.), *Improving Life at Work: Behavioral Sci-*

ences Approaches to Organizational Change (Santa Monica, Calif.: Goodyear Publishing, 1977), pp. 341–355.

6. Jeffrey H. Greenhaus, *Career Management* (New York: Dryden Press, 1987), p. 6.

7. See, for instance, E. P. Cook, "1991 Annual Review: Practice and Research in Career Counseling and Development, 1990," *Career Development Quarterly* (February 1991), pp. 99–131.

8. For an interesting overview of the similarities, see Thomas A. Stewart, "Planning a Career in a World Without Managers," *Fortune* (March 20, 1995), pp. 72–80.

9. Donna Fenn, "Homegrown Employees," *Inc.* (July 1995), p. 93.

10. Justin Martin, "Employees Are Fighting Back," *Fortune* (August 8, 1994), p. 12.

11. See M. Koden and J. B. Rousener, *Workforce America: Managing Employee Diversity as a Vital Resource* (Homewood, Ill.: Irwin Publishing, 1991).

12. "Promoting a Development Culture in Your Organization: Using Career Development as a Change Agent," *HRMagazine* (February 1998), pp. 132–133; Kenneth Labich, "Making Diversity Pay," *Fortune* (September 9, 1996), p. 177; Rose Mary Wentling, "Breaking Down Barriers to Women's Success," *HRMagazine* (May 1995), pp. 79, 81.

13. R. S. Bangar, "Human Resource Development–Career and Skill," *Employment News* (January 17/23, 1998), p. 1.

14. Hal Lancaster, "Professionals Try Novel Way to Assess and Develop Skills," *The Wall Street Journal* (August 2, 1995), p. B-1.

15. D. Yankelovich and J. Immerwahl, "The Emergence of Expressivism Will Revolutionize the Contract Between Workers and Employers," *Personnel Administrator* (December 1983), pp. 34–39, 114.

16. See B. B. Grossman and R. J. Blitzer, "Choreographing Careers," *Training and Development* (November 1991), pp. 68–89; R. Chanick, "Career Growth for Baby Boomers," *Personnel Journal* (January 1992), pp. 40–44.

17. Van Maanen and Schein.

18. Ibid.

19. Douglas T. Hall, *Careers in Organizations* (Santa Monica, Calif.: Goodyear Publishing, 1976).

20. Van Maanen and Schein.

21. See M. London and S. A. Stumpf, *Managing Careers* (Reading, Mass.: Addison Wesley, 1982); and A. S. Miner, "Organizational Evolution and the Social Ecology of Jobs," *American Sociological Review* (Fall 1991), pp. 772–785.

22. Cook, p. 99.

23. Greenhaus, p. 6.

24. Bennett J. Tepper, "Upward Maintenance Tactics in Supervisory Mentoring and Nonmentoring Relationships," *Academy of Management Journal*, Vol. 38, No. 4 (May 1995), p. 1191; Patricia Schiff Estess, "A Few Good Mentors," *Entrepreneur* (September 1995), p. 83; and Commerce Clearing House, "Should Your Company Encourage Mentoring?" *Human Resources Management: Ideas and Trends* (July 20, 1994), p. 122.

25. Sue Shellenbarger, "Corporate America Grooms Women Execs," *Working Woman* (October 1993), pp. 13–14.

26. See, for example, James A. Wilson and Nancy S. Elman, "Organizational Benefits of Mentoring," *Academy of Management Executive*, Vol. 4, No. 4 (November 1990), pp. 88–94.

27. Ibid.

28. Sue Shellenbarger, p. 13.

29. Michelle Neely Martinez, *HRMagazine*, Vol. 36, No. 6 (June 1991), p. 46.

30. George F. Dreher and Ronald A. Ash, "A Comparative Study of Mentoring Among Men and Women in Managerial Professional, and Technical Positions," *Journal of Applied Psychology*, Vol. 75, No. 5 (October 1990), pp. 539–546.

31. For an excellent discussion of these issues, see William Whitely, Thomas W. Dougherty, and George F. Dreher, "Relationship of Career Mentoring and Socioeconomic Origin to Managers' and Professionals' Early Career Progress," *Academy of Management Journal*, Vol. 34, No. 5 (June 1991), pp. 331–351.

32. Daniel B. Turban and Thomas W. Dougherty, "Protégé Personality, Mentoring, and Career Success," in Jerry L. Wall and Lawrence R. Jauch (eds.), *Academy of Management Best Papers Proceedings 1992*, Las Vegas, Nevada (August 9–12, 1992), p. 419.

33. For a discussion of mentoring and minorities, see David A. Thomas, "The Impact of Race on Managers' Experiences of Developmental Relationships: An Intra-Organizational Study," *Journal of Organizational Behavior*, Vol. 11, No. 6 (November 1990), pp. 479–492. For an opposing view of mentoring and women/race issues, see Belle Rose Ragins and Terri A. Scandura, "Gender and the Termination of Mentoring Relationships," *Academy of Management Best Papers Proceedings*, Dorothy P. Moore (ed.), (August 14–17, 1994), pp. 361–365.

34. Michael D. Esposito, "Affirmative Action and the Staffing Demands of the 1990s," *Journal of Compensation and Benefits*, Vol. 6, No. 4 (January–February 1991), p. 41.

35. Cheryl McCortie, "Mentoring Young Achievers," *Black Enterprise*, Vol. 21, No. 11 (June 1991), p. 336.

36. See, for example, Stephen C. Bushardt, Cherie Elaine Fretwell, and B. J. Holdnak, "The Mentor/Protege Relationship: A Biological Perspective," *Human Relations*, Vol. 44, No. 6 (June 1991), pp. 619–639.

37. See, for example, Belle Rose Ragins and Terri A. Scandura, "Gender Differences in Expected Outcomes of Mentoring Relationships," *Academy of Management Journal* (1994), pp. 957–971.

38. John Lorinc, "The Mentor Gap—Older Men Guiding Younger Women: The Perils and Payoffs," *Canadian Business*, Vol. 63, No. 9 (September 1990), p. 93.

39. See Ronald J. Burke and Carol A. McKeen, "Mentoring in Organizations: Implications for Women," *Journal of Business Ethics*, Vol. 9, No. 4 (April–May 1990), pp. 317–332.

40. "Mentoring Programs Face Hard Times in the `90s," *The Wall Street Journal* (March 24, 1992), p. A-1.

41. See, for example, Donald E. Super, *The Psychology of Careers* (New York: Harper & Row, 1957); Edgar Schein, *Career Dynamics: Matching Individual and Organizational Needs* (Reading, Mass.: Addison Wesley, 1978); and Daniel J. Levinson, C. N. Darrow, E. B. Klein, M. H. Levinson, and B. McKee, *A Man's Life* (New York: Knopf, 1978).

42. For an interesting account of career failures and the success that can follow, see Patricia Sellers, "So You Fail, Now Bounce Back," *Fortune* (May 1, 1995), pp. 48–66.

43. See Anne Fisher, "Six Ways to Supercharge Your Career," *Fortune* (January 13, 1997), pp. 46–48.

44. Betsy Morrie, "Executive Women Confront Mid-Life Crisis," *Fortune* (September 18, 1995), pp. 60–86; and Jaclyn Fier-

man, "Beating the Mid-Life Career Crisis," *Fortune* (September 6, 1993), p. 51.

45. See Mary Beth Regan, "Your Next Job," *Business Week* (October 13, 1997), pp. 64–72 Frederic M. Hudson, "When Careers Turn Stale," *Next* (Lakewood, Calif.: American Association of Retired Persons, 1994), p. 3; and Julie Connelly, "Have You Gone as Far as You Can Go?" *Fortune* (December 26, 1994), p. 231.

46. Harvey Schachter, "Careers," *Canadian Business* (April 1997), p. 70; Shari Caudron, "Downshifting Yourself," *Industry Week* (May 20, 1996), p. 126; Ronald Henkoff, "So You Want to Change Your Job," *Fortune* (January 15, 1996), p. 52; and Shari Caudron, "Pursue Your Passion," *Industry Week* (September 2, 1996), p. 27.

47. Adele Scheele, "Moving Over Instead of Up," *Working Woman* (November 1993), pp. 75–76.

48. See, for instance, Belle Rose Ragins, "Diversified Mentoring Relationships in Organizations: A Power Perspective," *Academy of Management Review,* Vol. 22, No. 2 (April 1997), pp. 482–521.

49. "Kay Whitmore's New Sense of Mission," *Business Week* (September 26, 1994), p. 8.

50. D. E. Super, "A Life-span Life Space Approach to Career Development," *Journal of Vocational Behavior,* Vol. 16 (Spring 1980), pp. 282–298. See also E. P. Cook, pp. 99–131, and M. Arthur, *Career Theory Handbook* (Englewood Cliffs, N.J.: Prentice-Hall, 1991). See also Louis S. Richman, "The New Worker Elite," *Fortune* (August 22, 1994), pp. 56–66.

51. John Holland, *Making Vocational Choices,* 2nd. ed. (Englewood Cliffs, N.J.: Prentice-Hall, 1985).

52. For an interesting discussion of Schein anchors, see Edgar H. Schein, "Career Anchors Revisited: Implications for Career Development in the 21st Century," *Academy of Management Journal,* Vol. 10, No. 1 (January 1996), pp. 80–88.

53. Isabel Briggs-Myers, *Introduction to Type* (Palo Alto, CA: Consulting Psychologists Press, 1980).

54. Stephen P. Robbins, *Organizational Behavior: Concepts, Controversies, Applications* (Englewood Cliffs, NJ: Prentice-Hall, Inc., 1996), p. 93.

55. Ibid., pp. 7–8.

56. D. T. Hall and Associates, *The Career Is Dead—Long Live the Career: A Relational Approach to Careers* (San Francisco, CA: Jossey-Bass, 1996). See also Douglas T. Hall, Protean Careers of the 21st Century," *Academy of Management Journal,* Vol. 10, No. 4 (November 1996), pp. 8–16; and Hal Lancaster, "A New Social Contract to Benefit Employer and Employee," *The Wall Street Journal* (November 29, 1994), p. B-1.

57. Hal Lancaster, "Managing Your Career: You, and Only You, Must Stay in Charge of Your Employability," *The Wall Street Journal* (November 15, 1994), p. B-1.

58. D. E. Super, "A Life-span Life Space Approach to Career Development," *Journal of Vocational Behavior,* Vol. 16 (Spring 1980), pp. 282–298; E. P. Cook, pp. 99–131, M. Arthur, *Career Theory Handbook* (Englewood Cliffs, NJ: Prentice Hall, 1991); L. S. Richman, "The New Worker Elite," *Fortune* (August 22, 1994), pp. 56–66; Lynne Cusack, "Is It Time for a

Career Change?" *Working Mother* (April 1998), p. 31; T. S. Price, "Surviving Job Change," *Industry Week* (February 19, 1996), p. 57; and Julie Connelly, "How to Choose Your Next Career," *Fortune* (February 6, 1995), p. 145.

59. I. R. Schwartz, "Self-Assessment and Career Planning: Matching Individuals and Organizational Goals," *Personnel* (January–February 1979), p. 48.

60. A. N. Schoonmaker, *Executive Career Strategy* (New York: American Management Association, 1971); A. J. DuBrin, *Fundamentals of Organizational Behavior: An Applied Perspective,* 2nd ed. (Elmsford, NY: Pergamon Press, 1978), Chapter 5; E. E. Jennings, "Success Chess," *Management of Personnel Quarterly* (Fall 1980), pp. 2–8; and R. Henkoff, "Winning the New Career Game," *Fortune* (July 12, 1993), pp. 46–49.

61. J. E. Sheridan, J. W. Slocum, Jr., R. Buda, and R. C. Thompson, "Effects of Corporate Sponsorship and Departmental Power on Career Tournaments," *Academy of Management Journal* (September 1990), pp. 578–602.

62. C. Perrow, *Complex Organizations: A Critical Essay* (Glenwood, IL: Scott, Foresman, 1972), p. 43.

63. J. E. Sheridan, J. W. Slocum, Jr., R. Buda, and R. C. Thompson, "Effects of Corporate Sponsorship and Departmental Power on Career Tournaments."

64. G. F. Dreher and R. A. Ash, "A Comparative Study of Mentoring Among Men and Women in Managerial, Professional, and Technical Positions," *Journal of Applied Psychology* (October 1990), pp. 539–546.

65. Hal Lancaster, "How to Learn Your Job's Potential, Skills You'll Need," *The Wall Street Journal* (February 6, 1996), p. B-1; Hal Lancaster, "When Your Boss Doesn't Like You, It's Detente or Departure," *The Wall Street Journal* (August 15, 1995), p. B-1; and Eugene Allen, "Should You Be Friends with Your Boss?" *Working Woman* (November 1995), p. 72.

66. Justin Martin, "Job Surfing: Move On to Move Up," *Fortune* (January 13, 1997), pp. 50–54.

67. See, for example, D. Kirkpatrick, "Is Your Career on Track," *Fortune* (June 2, 1990), pp. 38–48; A. Saltzman, "Sidestepping Your Way to the Top," *U.S. News & World Report* (October 17, 1990), pp. 60–61; and B. Nussbaum, "I'm Worried About My Job," *Business Week* (October 7, 1991), pp. 94–97.

68. Hal Lancaster, "Many Are Still Looking to Leave Small Ponds for Deeper Waters," *The Wall Street Journal* (September 5, 1995), p. B-1; and Khush Pittenger, "Networking Strategies for Minority Managers," *Academy of Management Executive* (November 1996), p. 62.

69. William Bridges, "The End of the Job," *Fortune* (September 19, 1994), p. 72; and Patricia Sellers, "Don't Call Me Slacker!" *Fortune* (December 12, 1994), pp. 181–182.

70. See also Louis S. Richman, "Getting Past Economic Insecurity," *Fortune* (April 17, 1995), pp. 161–168.

71. See, for instance, John H. Sheridan, "Selling Skills, Not Experience," *Industry Week* (January 8, 1996), pp. 15–18; Hall Lancaster, "Managers Beware: You're Not Ready for Tomorrow's Jobs," *The Wall Street Journal* (January 24, 1995), p. B-1.

10. Evaluating Employee Performance

LEARNING OBJECTIVES

After reading this chapter, you will be able to:

1. Describe the link between performance management systems and motivation.
2. Identify the three purposes of performance management systems and who is served by them.
3. Explain the six steps in the appraisal process.
4. Discuss what is meant by absolute standards in performance management systems.
5. Describe what is meant by relative standards in performance management systems.
6. Discuss how MBO can be used as an appraisal method.
7. Explain why performance appraisals might be distorted.
8. Identify ways to make performance management systems more effective.
9. Describe what is meant by the term 360-degree appraisal.
10. Discuss how performance appraisals may differ in foreign countries.

*E*very year, most employees experience an evaluation of their past performance. This may take the form of a five-minute, informal discussion between employees and their supervisors, or a more elaborate, several-week process involving many specific steps. Irrespective of their formality, however, employees generally see these evaluations as having some direct effect on their work lives. They may result in increased pay, a promotion, or assistance in personal development areas for which the employee needs some training. As a result, any evaluation of employees' work can create an emotionally charged event. That's the reaction Joe Malik of AT&T had.[1]

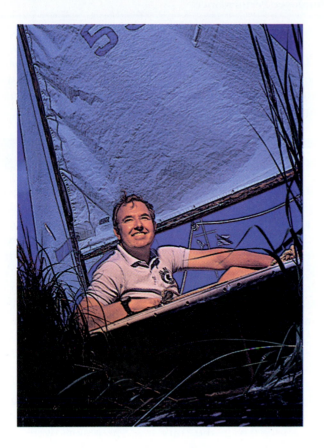

Joe Malik thought he was doing his job exceptionally well. Although he had some areas that he knew he should continue developing, it wasn't until he was exposed to a 360-degree feedback process that he learned the "truth" about his work behaviors. Armed now with this constructive feedback, Joe is working on making things better for his employees.

Joe Malik is the manager of a team of engineers at AT&T in New Jersey. He is an individual who prides himself on recognizing his strengths and weaknesses. He makes every attempt to capitalize on those strengths and works fervently on developing efforts to overcome the weaknesses. His biggest problem, he thought, was his temper. In the past, Joe just blew his stack—and it was no surprise to anyone when Joe flew off the handle at work. He understood that this interfered with his work and with relationships he had on the job. Understandably, Joe had been working very hard to overcome this problem. No performance appraisal was needed to confirm that this was a problem.

Although an active believer in getting and receiving feedback, Joe was startled to learn that his employees viewed him as having a bigger problem. A function of his temperament, Joe wondered? No! His employees thought Joe had no vision for where the group was heading! Team members reported to Joe that whenever any of them asked about the future plans for their work group, Joe would just "scrunch up in his chair." Everyone perceived this as Joe's way of evading the question—a tough one at that. Moreover, his body language indicated to these employees that he might know some unsettling news and just didn't want to share it. Fear became rampant! Sadly, though, their perceptions were the furthest from the truth. Interestingly enough, Joe prided himself as being a visionary. How else could he manage a group of professionals developing prototypes for the phone system's networking system? Unfortunately, Joe kept his visions to himself. Through AT&T's performance feedback process, Joe was able to appreciate and understand the results of his behavior. Joe now knows that his employees have a strong desire to understand where they are going, and what his future plans are for the unit. He now communicates such information to team members regularly. As a result, team members are less frustrated, and Joe has overcome one of his shortcomings— all because the performance management system at AT&T worked effectively.

Even though Joe still scrunches up in his chair, it's not because he's unsure how to respond to employee questions. That's just Joe!

INTRODUCTION

Because the performance evaluation is not the simple process it once was, it is now more critical to perform one while simultaneously focusing on key activities of the job. For example, should Joe Malik's body language have become part of his performance evaluation? How about how well he serves as a mentor to his employees? Moreover, should Joe's employees have had input into his effectiveness at work? But let's not focus these questions solely on Joe Malik. What about employees in an organization. Should their ability to perform tasks in a timely and accurate manner matter in an evaluation of their work? How about how employees interacts with customers? Questions like the ones posed for Joe, as well as employees in general, cannot be overlooked. And that's exactly how senior management at Ameritech Corporation viewed a similar situation.[2]

To answer what employees did, management established a task force to identify the key performance measures of a specific job. During the course of one review, a task force developed eight specific measurable skills, in this case for a position of secretary in the company. These skills were business awareness, communication skills, decision making, flexibility, adaptability, initiative, interpersonal skills, and organizational skills[3]—all requisites for success on the job. Taking information from a job analysis, the task force then developed the standards from which performance would be measured.

If we want to know how well our employees are doing, we've got to measure their performance—not necessarily an easy task. Many factors go into the performance evaluation process, such as why do we do them, who should benefit from the evaluation, what type of evaluation should be used, and what problems we might encounter. This chapter seeks answers to these and several other important factors in the **performance-appraisal process.** By developing a valid performance management system, we can maximize the relationship in our motivational model that focuses on the effort–performance linkage. Let's review that linkage.

THE LINKAGE TO MOTIVATION

As we discovered in Chapter 4, just because employees have the ability to do the job does not ensure that they will perform satisfactorily. A critical dimension of their effectiveness is their willingness to exert high energy levels—their motivation. Theoretically, as supervisors we should be interested in ends, not means. In other words, we need to ensure that the job gets done![4] As one basketball coach remarked in appraising his point guard's game winning but unorthodox three-point jumper: "It ain't pictures that matter, it's points. However you cut it, that shot's the difference between an NCAA tournament bid and go-

Exhibit 10-1

Performance evaluations and the motivation process.

ing home for the off-season." Similarly, we need to be concerned with quality results.[5] It really is performance that counts! Although it may be difficult for some individuals in supervisory positions to accept, they shouldn't be appraising employees on how to do things, but rather on whether they can "score." We propose, accordingly, that organizations exist to "score," rather than to provide an environment for individuals to "look like players." Just like the basketball coach, supervisors must be concerned with evaluating their employees on the "points" and not on the "pictures."

Performance is a vital component of the motivation model.[6] Specifically, we must be concerned with the link between effort and performance, and between performance and rewards (see Exhibit 10-1). Employees have to know what is expected of them, and they need to know how their performance will be measured. Furthermore, employees must feel confident that if they exert an effort within their capabilities, it will result in a better performance as defined by the criteria by which they are being measured. Finally, they must feel confident that if they perform as they are being asked, they will achieve the rewards they value.[7] Do people see effort leading to performance, and performance to the rewards that they value? If not, the motivational aspects of evaluating performance deteriorate.

In summary, performance appraisals and their outcomes play a vital part in the model of motivation. If the objectives that individual employees are seeking are unclear, if the criteria for measuring that objective attainment are vague, if employees lack confidence that their efforts will lead to a satisfactory appraisal of their performance, or if they feel that there will be an unsatisfactory payoff by the organization when their performance objectives are achieved, we can expect individuals to work considerably below their potential. If we have done our job to acquire capable people and develop their basic abilities to do the job, we must also make sure that they know what behaviors are required of them; understand how they are going to be appraised; and believe that the appraisal will be conducted in a fair and equitable manner. Lastly, employees must anticipate that their performance will be recognized by proper rewards.[8] That's the premise for what you'll be reading in the remaining pages of this chapter.

PERFORMANCE MANAGEMENT SYSTEMS

Performance management systems involve a number of activities. They are more than simply reviewing what an employee has done. These systems must fulfill several purposes.[9] Moreover, they are oftentimes constrained by difficulties in how they operate. Let's look at these two major areas.

The Purposes

Two decades ago performance evaluations were designed primarily to tell employees how they had done over a period of time, and to let them know

Performance evaluations should address feedback, development, and documentation concerns.

what pay raise they would be getting. This was the *"feedback"* mechanism in place. Although this may have served its purpose then, today there are additional factors that must be addressed. Specifically, performance evaluations should also address *development* and *documentation* concerns.[10]

Performance appraisals must convey to employees how well they have performed on established goals. It's also desired to have had these goals and performance measures mutually set between the employee and the supervisor. As our motivation model suggested (Chapter 4), without proper two-way feedback about one's effort and its effect on performance, we run the risk of decreasing an employee's "drive." However, equally as important to feedback is the issue of development.[11] By development, we are referring to those areas in which an employee has a deficiency or weakness, or an area that simply could be better if some effort was expended to enhance performance. For example, suppose a college professor demonstrates extensive knowledge in his or her field and conveys this knowledge to students in an adequate way. Although this individual's performance may be regarded as satisfactory, his or her peers may indicate that some improvements could be made. In this case, then, development may include exposure to different methods of teaching, such as bringing into the classroom more experiential exercises, real-world applications, case analyses, etc.[12]

Finally comes the issue of **documentation.** A performance evaluation system would be remiss if it did not concern itself with the legal aspects of employee performance. Recall in Chapter 3 the discussion about EEO and the need for job-related measures. Those job-related measures must be performance-supported when an HRM decision affects current employees. For instance, suppose a supervisor has decided to terminate an employee. Although the supervisor cites performance matters as the reason for the discharge, a review of recent performance appraisals of this employee indicates that performance was evaluated as satisfactory for the last two review periods. Accordingly, unless this employee's performance significantly decreased (and assuming that proper methods to correct the performance deficiency were performed), personnel records do not support the supervisor's decision. This critique by HRM is absolutely critical—to ensure that employees are fairly treated and that the organization is "protected." Additionally, in our discussion of sexual harassment in Chapter 3, we addressed the need for employees to keep copies of past performance appraisals. If retaliation (such as termination or poor job assignments) for refusing a supervisor's advances occurs, existing documentation can show that the personnel action was inappropriate (see Ethical Decisions in HRM). That's because it may not be consistent with past performance—but attributable to something else, like the harassment!

Because documentation issues are prevalent in today's organizations, HRM must make the effort to ensure that the evaluation systems used support the legal needs of the organization. However, even though the performance appraisal process is geared to serve the organization, we should also recognize two other important players in the process: employees and their appraisers. Through timely and accurate feedback and development we can better serve employees' needs. In doing so, we may also be in a better position to show the effort—performance linkage.

Next, we should keep in mind the needs of the appraiser. If feedback, development, and documentation are to function effectively, appraisers must have a performance system that is appropriate for their needs—a system that facilitates giving feedback and development information to their employees, and one

The Inaccurate Performance Appraisal

Most individuals recognize the importance of effective performance management systems in an organization. Not only are they necessary for providing feedback to employees and for identifying personal development plans, they serve a vital legal purpose. Furthermore, organizations that fail to accurately manage employee performance often find themselves facing difficult times in meeting their organizational goals.

Most individuals would also agree that performance appraisals must meet Equal Employment Opportunity requirements. That is, they must be administered in such a way that they result in a fair and equitable treatment for the diversity that exists in the workplace. Undeniably, this is an absolute necessity. But what about those gray areas—instances where an evaluation meets legal requirements, but verges on a questionable practice. For example, what if a manager delib-

erately evaluates a favored employee higher than one he likes less, even though the latter is a better promotional candidate? Likewise, what if the supervisor avoids identifying areas for employee development for individuals, knowing that the likelihood of career advancement for these employees is stalemated without the better skills?

Supporters of properly functioning performance appraisals point to two vital criteria that managers must bring to the process—sincerity and honesty. Yet, there are no legislative regulations, like EEO laws, that enforce such ethical standards. Thus, they may be, and frequently are, missing from the evaluation process.

Can an organization have an effective performance-appraisal process without sincerity and honesty dominating the system? Can organizations develop an evaluation process that is ethical? Should we expect companies to spend training dollars to achieve this goal? What do you think?

SOURCE: Larry L. Axline, "Ethical Considerations of Performance Appraisals," *Management Review* (March 1994), p. 62.

that allows for employee input. For example, if appraisers are required to evaluate their employees using inappropriate performance measures, or answer questions about employees who have little bearing on the job, then the system may not provide the same benefits as one where such negatives are removed. In contrast to evaluations used decades ago, it's acceptable, and absolutely necessary, for the evaluation criteria used to be different for some jobs. Tailoring the evaluation process to the job analysis and the organization's and employee's goals, is the difference between an evaluation system that is satisfactory, to one that is an integral part of the HRM process.

To create the performance management system we desire, however, we must recognize that difficulties in the process may exist. We must look for ways to either overcome these difficulties or find ways to deal with them more effectively. Let's turn our attention to these challenges.

Difficulties in Performance Management Systems

When you consider that three constituencies coexist in this process—employees, appraisers, and organizations—coordinating the needs of each may cause problems. By focusing on the difficulties, we can begin to address them in such a way that we can reduce their overall consequence in the process. In terms of difficulties, two primary categories can be addressed—(1) the focus on the individual, and (2) the focus on the process.

Focus on the Individual Do you remember the last time you received a graded test from a professor and felt that something was marked incorrect that wasn't wrong, or that your answer was too harshly penalized? How did you feel about that? Did you accept the score and leave it at that, or did you question the instructor? Whenever performance evaluations are administered (and tests are one form of performance evaluations), we run into the issue of having people seeing "eye-to-eye" on the evaluation. Appraising individuals is probably one of the more difficult aspects of a supervisor's job. Why? Because emotions are involved, and sometimes supervisors just don't like to do appraisals.[13] We all think we are performing in an outstanding fashion, but that just may very well be our perception. And although our work is good, and a boss recognizes it, it may not be seen as outstanding. Accordingly, in evaluating performance, emotions may arise. And if these emotions are not dealt with properly (we'll look at ways to enhance performance evaluations later in this chapter), they can lead to greater conflict. In fact, consider the aforementioned test example, assuming you confronted the professor. Depending on the encounter, especially if it is aggressive, both of you may become defensive. And because of the conflict, nothing but ill feelings may arise. For appraisers, the same thing applies. You both differ on the performance outcomes.[14]

When that occurs, it may lead to a situation in which emotions overcome both parties. This is not the way for evaluations to be handled. Accordingly, our first concern in the process is to remove the emotion difficulty from the process. When emotions do not run high in these meetings, employee satisfaction of the process increases,[15] and additionally, this satisfaction carries over into future job activities, where both the employee and supervisor have opportunities to have ongoing feedback in an effort to fulfill job expectations.[16]

Focus on the Process   Wherever performance evaluations are conducted, there is a particular structure that must be followed. This structure exists to facilitate the documentation process that often allows for some sort of a quantifiable evaluation. Additionally, HRM policies often exist that dictate performance outcomes. For example, if a company ties performance evaluations to pay increases, consider the following potential difficulty. Sometime during spring, managers develop budgets for their units—budgets that are dictated and approved by upper management. Now in this budget for the next fiscal year, each manager's salary budget increases by 4 percent. As we enter the new fiscal year, we evaluate our employees. One in particular has done an outstanding job and is awarded a 6 percent raise. What does this do to our budget? To average 4 percent, some employees will get less than the 4 percent salary increase. Consequently, company policies and procedures may present barriers to a properly functioning appraisal process.

Furthermore, to get these numbers to balance means that rather than accentuating the positive work behaviors of some employees, an appraiser focuses on the negative.[17] This can lead to a tendency to search for problems, which can ultimately lead to an emotional encounter. We may also find from the appraiser's perspective some uncertainty about how and what to measure, or how to deal with the employee in the evaluation process.[18] Frequently, appraisers are poorly trained in how to evaluate an employee's performance. Because of this lack of training, appraisers may make errors in their judgment, or permit biases to enter into the process. We'll talk more about these problems later.

Because difficulties may arise, we should begin to develop our performance appraisal process so that we can achieve maximum benefit from it. This maximum benefit can be translated into employee satisfaction with the process. Such satisfaction is achieved by creating an understanding of the evaluation criteria used, permitting employee participation in the process, and allowing for development needs to be addressed.[19] To begin doing so requires us to initially understand the appraisal process.

One of the best reasons for having effective performance management systems is that they can help reduce situations like this. Everyone needs to understand that emotions may run high in an evaluation. However, with a proper design and effective implementation (like training) such barriers can be significantly avoided.

Effectively Evaluating Employees

How does one properly conduct the performance appraisal process? We offer the following steps that can assist in this endeavor.

Prepare for, and Schedule, the Appraisal in Advance Before meeting with employees, some preliminary activities should be performed. You should at a minimum review employee job descriptions, period goals that may have been set, and performance data on employees you may have. Furthermore, you should schedule the appraisal well in advance to give employees the opportunity to prepare their data, too, for the meeting.

Create a Supportive Environment to Put Employees at Ease Performance appraisals conjure up several emotions. As such, every effort should be made to make employees comfortable during the meeting, such that they are receptive to constructive feedback.

Describe the Purpose of the Appraisal to Employees Make sure employees know precisely what the appraisal is to be used for. Will it have implications for pay increases, or other personnel decisions? If so, make sure employees understand exactly how the appraisal process works, and its consequences.

Involve the Employee in the Appraisal Discussion, Including a Self-Evaluation Performance appraisals should not be a one-way communication event. Although as supervisor, you may believe that you have to talk more in the meeting, that needn't be the case. Instead, employees should have ample opportunity to discuss their performance, raise questions about the facts you raise, and add their own data/perceptions about their work. One means of ensuring that two-way communications occurs is to have employees conduct a self-evaluation. You should actively listen to their assessment. This involvement helps to create an environment of participation.[20]

Focus Discussion on Work Behaviors, Not on the Employees   One way of creating emotional difficulties is to attack the employee. Being such, you should keep your discussion on the behaviors you've observed. Telling an employee, for instance that his report stinks doesn't do a thing. That's not focusing on behaviors. Instead, indicating that you believe that not enough time was devoted to proofreading the report describes the behavior you may be having a problem with.

Support Your Evaluation with Specific Examples   Specific performance behaviors help clarify to employees the issues you raise. Rather than saying something wasn't good (subjective evaluation) you should be as specific as possible in your explanations. So, for the employee who failed to proof the work, describing that the report had five grammatical mistakes in the first two pages alone would be a specific example.

Positive as well as negative feedback helps employees to gain a better understanding of their performance.

Give Both Positive and Negative Feedback   Performance appraisals needn't be all negative. Although there is a perception that this process focuses on the negative, it should also be used to compliment and recognize good work. Positive, as well as negative, feedback helps employees to gain a better understanding of their performance. For example, although the report was not up to the quality you expected, the employee did do the work and completed the report in a timely fashion. That's behavior that deserves some positive reinforcement.

Ensure Employees Understand What Was Discussed in the Appraisal
At the end of the appraisal, especially where some improvement is warranted, you should ask employees to summarize what was discussed in the meeting. This will help you to ensure that you have gotten your information through to the employee.

Generate a Development Plan   Most of the performance appraisal revolves around feedback and documentation. But, another component is needed. Where development efforts are encouraged, a plan should be developed to describe what is to be done, by when, and what you, the supervisor, will commit to aid in the improvement/enhancement effort.

PERFORMANCE APPRAISALS AND EEO

Performance evaluations are an integral part of most organizations. Properly developed and implemented, the performance appraisal process can help an organization achieve its goals by developing productive employees. Although there are many types of performance evaluation systems, each with its own advantages and disadvantages, we must be aware of the legal implications that arise.

EEO laws require organizations to have HRM practices that are bias free. For HRM, this means that performance evaluations must be objective and job related. That is, they must be reliable and valid! Furthermore, under the Americans with Disabilities Act, performance appraisals must also be able to measure "reasonable" performance success. To assist in these matters, two factors arise: (1) The performance appraisal must be conducted according to some established intervals; and (2) appraisers must be trained in the process.[21] The reasons for this become crystal clear when you consider that any employee action, like a promotion or termination, must be based on valid data—data prescribed from the performance evaluation document.[22] These objective data often support the "legitimacy" of employee actions.[23]

The Appraisal Process

The appraisal process (Exhibit 10-2) begins with the establishment of performance standards in accordance with the organization's strategic goals. These should have evolved out of the company's strategic direction—and, more specifically, the job analysis and the job description discussed in Chapter 5. These performance standards should also be clear and objective enough to be understood and measured. Too often, these standards are articulated in ambiguous phrases that tell us little, such as "a full day's work" or "a good job." What is a "full day's work" or a "good job"? The expectations a supervisor has in terms of work performance by her employees must be clear enough in her mind so that she will be able to, at some later date, communicate these expectations to her employees, mutually agree to specific job performance measures, and appraise their performance against these established standards.

Once performance standards are established, it is necessary to communicate these expectations; it should not be part of the employees' job to guess what is expected of them. Too many jobs have vague performance standards, and the problem is compounded when these standards are set in isolation and do not involve the employee.[24] It is important to note that communication is a two-way street; mere transference of information from the supervisor to the employee regarding expectations is not communication! The third step in the appraisal process is the measurement of performance. To determine what actual performance is, it is necessary to acquire information about it. We should be concerned with how we measure and what we measure.

Four common sources of information are frequently used by managers regarding how to measure actual performance: personal observation, statistical re-

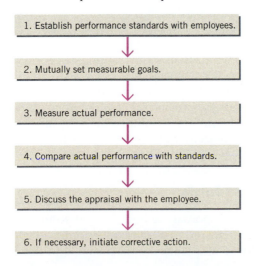

1. Establish performance standards with employees.

2. Mutually set measurable goals.

3. Measure actual performance.

4. Compare actual performance with standards.

5. Discuss the appraisal with the employee.

6. If necessary, initiate corrective action.

Exhibit 10-2

The Appraisal Process.

ports, oral reports, and written reports. Each has its strengths and weaknesses; however, a combination of them increases both the number of input sources and the probability of receiving reliable information. What we measure is probably more critical to the evaluation process than how we measure, since the selection of the wrong criteria can result in serious, dysfunctional consequences. And what we measure determines, to a great extent, what people in the organization will attempt to excel at. The criteria we measure must represent performance as it was mutually set in the first two steps of the appraisal process.

The fourth step in the appraisal process is the comparison of actual performance with standards. The point of this step is to note deviations between standard performance and actual performance so that we can proceed to the fifth step in the process—the discussion of the appraisal with the employee. As we mentioned previously, one of the most challenging tasks facing appraisers is to present an accurate assessment to the employee. Appraising performance may touch on one of the most emotionally charged activities—the evaluation of another individual's contribution and ability.[25] The impression that employees receive about their assessment has a strong impact on their self-esteem and, very importantly, on their subsequent performance. Of course, conveying good news is considerably less difficult for both the appraiser and the employee than conveying the bad news that performance has been below expectations. In this context, the discussion of the appraisal can have negative as well as positive motivational consequences.

The final step in the appraisal is the identification of corrective action where necessary. Corrective action can be of two types: one is immediate and deals predominantly with symptoms, and the other is basic and delves into causes. Immediate corrective action is often described as "putting out fires," whereas basic corrective action gets to the source of deviation and seeks to adjust the difference permanently. Immediate action corrects something right now and gets things back on track. Basic corrective action asks how and why performance deviated. In some instances, appraisers may rationalize that they do not have the time to take basic corrective action and therefore must be content to "perpetually put out fires." Good supervisors recognize that taking a little time to analyze the problem today may save more time tomorrow when the problem may get bigger.

APPRAISAL METHODS

The previous section described the appraisal process in general terms. In this section we will look at specific ways in which HRM can actually establish performance standards and devise instruments that can be used to measure and appraise an employee's performance. Three different approaches exist for doing appraisals: Employees can be appraised against (1) absolute standards, (2) relative standards, or (3) objectives. No one approach is always best; each has its strengths and weaknesses.

Absolute Standards

Our first group of appraisal methods uses **absolute standards.** This means that employees are compared to a standard; and their evaluation is independent of any other employee in a work group. Included in this group are the follow-

"Performance Appraisals Needn't Be a Dreaded Task"

It's almost Monday, so you begin your week by thinking of one of your most dreaded occurrences at work. Is it being laid off? Finding out your division will be permanently eliminated at 4:30 today? Being informed that several departments will merge and everyone is included but you? Conducting or completing a performance evaluation?

Of these dreaded occurrences, we have some control over only one: performance appraisals.

Your career progression, or lack of it, is not just the result of luck and timing, but also your recognized achievements, recorded as part of the performance appraisal process. And learning more about the performance appraisal process—whether it's formal or informal—will help ensure your next review will bring the positive results you want.

Performance appraisals for the most part are dreaded and perceived negatively. Most people are pretty sure about two things: they don't want to give one, and they don't want to get one. But if more managers understood how to properly administer a performance appraisal, and if more employees understood clearly how to prepare for one, the dread could be minimized, and the appraisal could be utilized as it was intended: as a tool to recognize achievements, correct substandard performance, and identify new skills and responsibilities on which to focus.

Problems arise in conducting performance appraisals because few managers possess adequate skills, training or experience to administer effective reviews.

A performance appraisal is a management aid which shows how an employee has performed against a set of predetermined criteria. The manager usually discusses the review with an employee in a one-to-one meeting shortly before the annual salary review date. Some managers provide a sample form to employees beforehand to compare perceptions and to better mutually prepare an action plan during the meeting. Other managers provide no opportunity for employees to provide feedback or to prepare for the review. These managers normally allow little employee feedback during the review.

Appraisals should benefit both the supervisor and the employee. They help the manager identify capable replacements for higher-level jobs, improve morale and give the manager input for the employee's development.

Employees want feedback and want to know how well they're doing. Appraisals let the employee know how the supervisor feels about his/her performance, provide an opportunity to change behavior and allow the employee an opportunity to present suggestions for improvement.

DR. CONNIE SITTERLY, CPCM

ing methods: the essay appraisal, the critical incident appraisal, the checklist, the adjective rating scale, forced choice, and behaviorally anchored rating scales. Let's look at each of these, focusing on their strengths and weaknesses.

The Essay Appraisal   Probably the simplest method of appraisal is to have the appraiser write a narrative describing an employee's strengths, weaknesses, past performance, potential, and suggestions for improvement. The strength of the **essay appraisal** lies in its simplicity. It requires no complex forms or extensive training to complete. The essay appraisal is also valuable in providing specific information, much of which can be easily fed back and understood by the employee.

However, inherent in this method are several weaknesses. Because the essays are unstructured, they are likely to vary widely in terms of length and content. This makes it difficult to compare individuals across the organization. And, of course, some raters are better writers than others. So a "good" or "bad" evaluation may be determined as much by the rater's writing skill as by the employee's actual level of performance. This method also provides only qualitative data. HRM decisions generally improve when useful quantitative data is obtained because it enables employees to be compared and ranked more objectively.

In spite of its inherent weaknesses, the essay appraisal is a good start. It's also very beneficial if used in conjunction with other appraisal methods.

The Critical Incident Appraisal **Critical incident appraisal** focuses the rater's attention on those critical or key behaviors that make the difference between doing a job effectively and doing it ineffectively. The appraiser writes down anecdotes describing what the employee did that was especially effective or ineffective. For example, a police sergeant might write the following critical incident about one of her officers: "Brought order to a volatile situation by calmly discussing options with an armed suspect during a hostage situation which resulted in all hostages being released, and the suspect being apprehended without injury to any individual. Note that with this approach to appraisal, specific behaviors are cited, not vaguely defined individual traits. A behavior-based appraisal such as this should be more valid than trait-based appraisals because it is clearly more job related. It is one thing to say that an employee is "aggressive," "imaginative," or "relaxed," but that does not tell us anything about how well the job is being done. Critical incidents, with their focus on behaviors, judge performance rather than personalities.

The strength of the critical incident method is that it looks at behaviors. Additionally, a list of critical incidents on a given employee provides a rich set of examples from which employees can be shown which of their behaviors are desirable and which ones call for improvement. Its drawbacks are basically that: (1) appraisers are required to regularly write these incidents down, and doing this on a daily or weekly basis for all employees is time-consuming and burdensome for supervisors; and (2) critical incidents suffer from the same comparison problem found in essays—mainly, they do not lend themselves easily to quantification. Therefore the comparison and ranking of employees may be difficult.

The Checklist Appraisal In the **checklist appraisal,** the evaluator uses a list of behavioral descriptions and checks off those behaviors that apply to the employee. As Exhibit 10-3 illustrates, the evaluator merely goes down the list and checks off "yes" or "no" to each question.

Once the checklist is complete, it is usually evaluated by the HRM staff, not the appraiser completing the checklist. Therefore the rater does not actually evaluate the employee's performance; he or she merely records it. An analyst in HRM then scores the checklist, often weighing the factors in relationship to their importance to that specific job. The final evaluation can then be returned to the appraiser for discussion with the employee, or someone from HRM can provide the feedback to the employee.

The checklist appraisal reduces some bias in the evaluation process since the rater and the scorer are different. However, the rater usually can pick up the positive and negative connections in each item—so bias can still be introduced. From a cost standpoint, too, this appraisal method may be inefficient if there are a number of job categories for which an individualized checklist of items must be prepared.

Exhibit 10-3

Sample checklist items for appraising customer service representative.

	Yes	No
1. Are supervisor's orders usually followed?	_____	_____
2. Does the individual approach customers promptly?	_____	_____
3. Does the individual suggest additional merchandise to customers?	_____	_____
4. Does the individual keep busy when not servicing a customer?	_____	_____
5. Does the individual lose his or her temper in public?	_____	_____
6. Does the individual volunteer to help other employees?	_____	_____

Exhibit 10-4 Sample of adjective rating scale items and format.

Performance Factor	Performance Rating				
Quality of work is the accuracy, skill, and completeness of work.	☐ Consistently unsatisfactory	☐ Occasionally unsatisfactory	☐ Consistently satisfactory	☐ Sometimes superior	☐ Consistently superior
Quality of work is the volume of work done in a normal workday.	☐ Consistently unsatisfactory	☐ Occasionally unsatisfactory	☐ Consistently satisfactory	☐ Sometimes superior	☐ Consistently superior
Job knowledge is information pertinent to the job that an individual should have for satisfactory job performance.	☐ Poorly informed about work duties	☐ Occasionally unsatisfactory	☐ Can answer most questions about the job	☐ Understands all phases of the job	☐ Has complete mastery of all phases of the job
Dependability is following directions and company policies without supervision.	☐ Requires constant supervision	☐ Requires occasional follow-up	☐ Usually can be counted on	☐ Requires very little supervision	☐ Requires absolute minimum of supervision

The Adjective Rating Scale Appraisal   One of the oldest and most popular methods of appraisal is the **adjective rating scale.**[26] An example of some rating scale items is shown in Exhibit 10-4. Rating scales can be used to assess factors such as quantity and quality of work, job knowledge, cooperation, loyalty, dependability, attendance, honesty, integrity, attitudes, and initiative. However, this method is most valid when abstract traits like loyalty or integrity are avoided, unless they can be defined in more specific behavioral terms.[27]

To use the adjective rating scale, the assessor goes down the list of factors and notes the point along the scale or continuum that best describes the employee. There are typically five to ten points on the continuum. In the design of the rating scale, the challenge is to ensure that *both* the factors evaluated *and* the scale points are clearly understood and are unambiguous to the rater. Should ambiguity occur, bias is introduced.

Why are rating scales popular? Although they do not provide the depth of information that essays or critical incidents do,[28] they are less time-consuming to develop and administer. They also provide a quantitative analysis that is useful for comparison purposes. Furthermore, in contrast to the checklist, there is more generalization of items so that comparability with other individuals in diverse job categories is possible.[29]

The Forced-Choice Appraisal   Have you ever completed one of those tests that presumably gives you insights into what kind of career you should pursue? (Questions might be, for example, "Would you rather go to a party with a group of friends or attend a lecture by a well-known political figure?") If so, then you are familiar with the forced-choice format. The **forced-choice appraisal** is a special type of checklist where the rater must choose between two or more statements. Each statement may be favorable or unfavorable. The appraiser's job is to identify which statement is most (or in some cases least) descriptive of the individual being evaluated. For instance, students evaluating their college instructor might have to choose between: "(a) keeps up with the schedule identified in the syllabus; (b) lectures with confidence; (c) keeps interest and attention of class; (d) demonstrates how concepts are practically applied in today's organizations; or (e) allows students the opportunity to learn concepts on their own." All the preceding statements could be favorable, but we really don't know. As with the checklist method, to reduce bias, the right answers are not known to the rater; someone in HRM scores the answers based on the "answer" key for the job being evaluated. This key should be validated so HRM is in a position to say that individuals with higher scores are better-performing employees.

The major advantage of the forced-choice method is that, because the appraiser does not know the "right" answers, it reduces bias and distortion.[30] For example, the appraiser may like a certain employee and intentionally want to give him a favorable evaluation, but this becomes difficult if one is not sure which response is most preferred. On the negative side, appraisers tend to dislike this method; many dislike being forced to make distinctions between similar-sounding statements. Raters also may become frustrated with a system in which they do not know what represents a "good" or "poor" answer. Consequently, they may try to second-guess the scoring key in order to get the formal appraisal to align with their intuitive appraisal.

The Behaviorally Anchored Rating Scales

An approach that has received considerable attention by academics in past years involves **behaviorally anchored rating scales (BARS).** These scales combine major elements from the critical incident and adjective rating scale approaches. The appraiser rates the employees based on items along a continuum, but the points are examples of actual behavior on the given job rather than general descriptions or traits. The enthusiasm surrounding BARS grew from the belief that the use of specific behaviors, derived for each job, should produce relatively error-free and reliable ratings. Although this promise has not been fulfilled,[31] it has been argued that this may be due partly to departures from careful methodology in the development of the specific scales themselves rather than to inadequacies in the concept.[32] BARS, too, have also been found to be very time-consuming.

Behaviorally anchored rating scales specify definite, observable, and measurable job behavior. Examples of job-related behavior and performance dimensions are generated by asking participants to give specific illustrations of effective and ineffective behavior regarding each performance dimension; these behavioral examples are then translated into appropriate performance dimensions. Those that are sorted into the dimension for which they were generated are retained. The final group of behavior incidents are then numerically scaled to a level of performance that each is perceived to represent. The identified incidents which have high rater agreement on performance effectiveness are retained for use as anchors on the performance dimension. The results of these processes are behavioral descriptions, such as anticipates, plans, executes, solves immediate problems, carries out orders, or handles emergency situations. Exhibit 10-5 is an example of a BARS for an employee relations specialist's scale.

The research on BARS indicates that while it is far from perfect, it does tend to reduce rating errors. Possibly its major advantage stems from the dimensions generated, rather than from any particular superiority of behavior over trait anchors.[33] The process of developing the behavioral scales is valuable for clarify-

Performance dimension scale development under BARS for the dimension "Ability to Absorb and Interpret Policies for an Employee Relations Specialist."

Exhibit 10-5

Sample BARS for an employee relations specialist.

This employee relations specialist

	9	Could be expected to serve as an information source concerning new and changed policies for others in the organization
Could be expected to be aware quickly of program changes and explain these to employees	8	
	7	Could be expected to reconcile conflicting policies and procedures correctly to meet HRM goals
Could be expected to recognize the need for additional information to gain a better understanding of policy changes	6	
	5	Could be expected to complete various HRM forms correctly after receiving instruction on them
Could be expected to require some help and practice in mastering new policies and procedures	4	
	3	Could be expected to know that there is always a problem, but go down many blind alleys before realizing they are wrong
Could be expected to incorrectly interpret guidelines, creating problems for line managers	2	
	1	Could be expected to be unable to learn new procedures even after repeated explanations

Source: Reprinted from *Business Horizons* (August 1976), Copyright 1976 by the Foundation for the School of Business at Indiana University. Used with permission.

ing to both the employee and the rater which behaviors represent good performance and which don't. Unfortunately, it, too, suffers from the distortions inherent in most rating methods.[34] These distortions will be discussed later in this chapter.

Relative Standards

In the second general category of appraisal methods, individuals are compared against other individuals. These methods are **relative standards** rather than absolute measuring devices. The most popular of the relative methods are group order ranking, individual ranking, and paired comparison.

Group Order Ranking   **Group order ranking** requires the evaluator to place employees into a particular classification, such as "top 20 percent." This method, for instance, is often used in recommending students to graduate schools. Evaluators are asked to rank the student in the top 5 percent, the next 5 percent, the next 15 percent, and so forth. But when used by appraisers to evaluate employees, raters deal with all their employees in their area. So, for example, if a rater has twenty employees, only four can be in the top fifth; and, of course, four also must be relegated to the bottom fifth.

The advantage of this group ordering is that it prevents raters from inflating their evaluations so everyone looks good or from forcing the evaluations so everyone is rated near the average—outcomes that are not unusual with the adjective rating scale. The main disadvantages surface, however, when the number of employees being compared is small. At the extreme, if the evaluator is looking at only four employees, it is quite possible that all may be excellent, yet the evaluator may be forced to rank them into top quarter, second quarter, third quarter, and low quarter! Theoretically, as the sample size increases, the validity of relative scores as an accurate measure increases; but occasionally the technique is implemented with a small group, utilizing assumptions that apply to large groups.

Another disadvantage, which plagues all relative measures, is the "zero-sum game" consideration. This means that any change must add up to zero. For example, if there are twelve employees in a department performing at different levels of effectiveness, by definition, three are in the top quarter, three are in the second quarter, and so forth. The sixth-best employee, for instance, would be in the second quartile. Ironically, if two of the workers in the third or fourth quartiles leave the department and are not replaced, then our sixth-best employee now falls into the third quarter. Because comparisons are relative, an employee who is mediocre may score high only because he or she is the "best of the worst"; in contrast, an excellent performer who is matched against "stiff" competition may be evaluated poorly, when in absolute terms his or her performance is outstanding.

Individual Ranking The **individual ranking** method requires the evaluator merely to list the employees in order from highest to lowest. In this process, only one employee can be rated "best." If the evaluator is required to appraise thirty individuals, this method assumes that the difference between the first and second employee is the same as that between the twenty-first and the twenty-second. Even though some of these employees may be closely grouped, this method typically allows for no ties. In terms of advantages and disadvantages, the individual ranking method carries the same pluses and minuses as group order ranking. For example, individual ranking may be more manageable in a department of six employees than in one where a supervisor must evaluate the 19 employees that report to her.

Paired Comparison The **paired comparison** method is calculated by taking the total of $[N(N-1)]/2$ comparisons. A score is obtained for each employee by simply counting the number of pairs in which the individual is the preferred member. It ranks each individual in relationship to all others on a one-on-one basis. If ten employees are being evaluated, the first person is compared, one by one, with each of the other nine, and the number of times this person is preferred in any of the nine pairs is tabulated. Each of the remaining nine persons, in turn, is compared in the same way, and a ranking is formed by the greatest number of preferred "victories." This method ensures that each employee is compared against every other, but the method can become unwieldy when large numbers of employees are being compared.

Objectives

The third approach to appraisal makes use of objectives. Employees are evaluated on how well they accomplished a specific set of objectives that have been determined to be critical in the successful completion of their job. This approach is frequently referred to as **management by objectives (MBO).**[35] Management by objectives is a process that converts organizational objectives into individual objectives. It consists of four steps: (1) goal setting, (2) action planning, (3) self-control, and (4) periodic reviews.

In goal setting, the organization's overall objectives are used as guidelines from which departmental and individual objectives are set. At the individual level, the supervisor and employee jointly identify those goals that are critical to fulfilling the requirements of the job as determined by job analysis. These goals are agreed on and then become the standards by which the employee's results will be evaluated.

In action planning, the means are determined for achieving the ends established in goal setting; that is, realistic plans are developed to attain the objectives. This step includes identifying the activities necessary to accomplish the objective, establishing the critical relationships between these activities, estimating the time requirements for each activity, and determining the resources required to complete each activity.

Self-control refers to the systematic monitoring and measuring of performance—ideally, by having the employee review his or her own performance. Inherent in allowing employees to control their own performance is a positive image of human nature. The MBO philosophy is built on the assumption that employees can be responsible, can exercise self-direction, and do not require external controls and threats of punishment to motivate them to work toward their objectives. This, from a motivational point of view, would be representative of Douglas McGregor's Theory Y (see Exhibit 4-3, p. 103 in Chapter 4).

Finally, with periodic progress reviews, corrective action is initiated when behavior deviates from the standards established in the goal-setting phase. Again, consistent with the MBO philosophy, these supervisor-employee reviews are conducted in a constructive rather than punitive manner. Reviews are not meant to degrade the employee but to aid in future performance. These reviews should take place at least two or three times a year. What will these objectives look like? It is important that they be tangible, verifiable, and measurable. This means that, wherever possible, we should avoid qualitative objectives and substitute quantifiable statements. For example, a quantitative objective might be "to cut, each day, 3,500 yards of cable to standard five-foot lengths, with a maximum scrap of 50 yards," or "to prepare, process, and transfer to the treasurer's office, all accounts payable vouchers within three working days from the receipt of the invoice."

MBO's advantages lie in its results-oriented emphasis. It assists the planning and control functions and provides motivation, as well as being an approach to performance appraisal. That's because employees know exactly what is expected of them and how they will be evaluated. Moreover, employees understand that their evaluation will be based on the success in achieving mutually agreed on objectives. Finally, it's expected that employees should have a greater commitment to the objectives they have participated in developing than to those unilaterally set by their boss.

> **MBO's advantages lie in its results-oriented emphasis.**

The major disadvantage of MBO is that it is unlikely to be effective in an environment where management has little trust in its employees. This type of environment could be one where management makes decisions autocratically and relies heavily on external controls to direct employee behavior. The amount of time needed to implement and maintain an MBO process may also cause problems. Many activities must occur to set it up, such as meetings between supervisors and employees to set and monitor objectives. These meetings can be very time-consuming. Additionally, it may be difficult to measure whether the MBO activities are being carried out properly. The difficulty involved in properly appraising the supervisor's efforts and performance as they carry out their MBO activities may cause it to fail.

FACTORS THAT CAN DISTORT APPRAISALS

The performance appraisal process and techniques that we have suggested present systems in which the evaluator is free from personal biases, prejudices, and idiosyncrasies.[36] This is defended on the basis that objectivity minimizes the potential arbitrary and dysfunctional behavior of the evaluator, which may be detrimental to the achievement of the organizational goals. Thus, our goal should be to use direct performance criteria where possible.

It would be naive to assume, however, that all evaluators impartially interpret and standardize the criteria upon which their employees will be appraised. This is particularly true of those jobs that are not easily programmable and for which developing hard performance standards is most difficult—if not impossible. These would include, but are certainly not limited to, such jobs as researcher, teacher, engineer, and consultant. In the place of such standards, we can expect appraisers to use nonperformance or subjective criteria against which to evaluate individuals.

A completely error-free performance appraisal is only an ideal we can aim for.[37] In reality, most appraisals fall short of this ideal. This is often due to one or more actions that can significantly impede objective evaluation.[38] We've briefly described them below.

Leniency Error

Every evaluator has his or her own value system that acts as a standard against which appraisals are made. Relative to the true or actual performance an individual exhibits, some evaluators mark high, while others mark low. The former is referred to as positive **leniency error,** and the latter as negative leniency error. When evaluators are positively lenient in their appraisal, an individual's performance becomes overstated. In doing so, the performance is rated higher than it actually should be. Similarly, a negative leniency error understates performance, giving the individual a lower appraisal.

If all individuals in an organization were appraised by the same person, there would be no problem. Although there would be an error factor, it would be applied equally to everyone.[39]

The difficulty arises when we have different raters with different leniency errors making judgments. For example, assume a situation where both Jones and Smith are performing the same job for a different supervisor, with absolutely identical job performance. If Jones's supervisor tends to err toward positive leniency while Smith's supervisor errs toward negative leniency, we might be confronted with two dramatically different evaluations.

Halo Error

The **halo error** or effect is a "tendency to rate high or low on all factors due to the impression of a high or low rating on some specific factor." [40] For example, if an employee tends to be conscientious and dependable, we might become biased toward that individual to the extent that we will rate him or her positively on many desirable attributes.

People who design teaching appraisal forms for college students to fill out in evaluating the effectiveness of their instructor each semester must confront the halo effect. Students tend to rate a faculty member as outstanding on all criteria when they are particularly appreciative of a few things he or she does in the classroom. Similarly, a few bad habits—like showing up late for lectures, being slow in returning papers, or assigning an extremely demanding reading requirement—might result in students evaluating the instructor as "lousy" across the board.

One method frequently used to deal with the halo error is "reverse wording" the evaluation questions so that a favorable answer for, say, question 17 might be 5 on a scale of 1 through 5, while a favorable answer for question number 18 might be 1 on a scale of 1 through 5. Structuring the questions in this manner seeks to reduce the halo error by requiring the evaluator to consider each question independently. Another method, which can be used where there is more than one person to be evaluated, is to have the evaluator appraise all ratees on each dimension before going on to the next dimension.

Similarity Error

When evaluators rate other people in the same way that the evaluators perceive themselves, they are making a **similarity error.** Based on the perception that evaluators have of themselves, they project those perceptions onto others. For example, the evaluator who perceives himself or herself as aggressive may evaluate others by looking for aggressiveness. Those who demonstrate this characteristic tend to benefit, while others who lack it may be penalized.

Low Appraiser Motivation

What are the consequences of the appraisal? If the evaluator knows that a poor appraisal could significantly hurt the employee's future—particularly opportunities for promotion or a salary increase—the evaluator may be reluctant to give a realistic appraisal. There is evidence that it is more difficult to obtain accurate appraisals when important rewards depend on the results. [41]

Central Tendency

It is possible that regardless of who the appraiser evaluates and what traits are used, the pattern of evaluation remains the same. It is also possible that the evaluator's ability to appraise objectively and accurately has been impeded by a failure to use the extremes of the scale. When this happens, we call the action **central tendency.** Central tendency is "the reluctance to make extreme ratings (in either direction); the inability to distinguish between and among ratees; a form of range restriction." [42] Raters who are prone to the central tendency error

Imagine you're teaching these students in this sales management class. Are there some assumptions that you can make about the grades that may be given? If you assume that everyone will do average work, and proceed to give everyone a "C," then you have encountered a rating error referred to as *central tendency*.

are those who continually rate all employees as average. For example, if a supervisor rates all employees as 3, on a scale of 1 to 5, then no differentiation among the employees exists. Failure to rate employees as 5, for those who deserve that rating, and as 1, if the case warrants it, will only create problems, especially if this information is used for pay increases.

Inflationary Pressures

A middle manager in a large Utah-based company could not understand why he had been passed over for promotion. He had seen his file and knew that his average rating by his supervisor was 88. Given his knowledge that the appraisal system defined "outstanding performance" at 90 or above, "good" as 80 or above, "average" as 70 or above, and "inadequate performance" as anything below 70, he was at a loss to understand why he had not been promoted—considering his near-outstanding performance appraisal. The manager's confusion was somewhat resolved when he found out that the "average" rating of middle managers in his organization was 92. This example addresses a major potential problem in appraisals—inflationary pressures. This, in effect, is a specific case of low differentiation within the upper range of the rating choices.

Inflationary pressures have always existed but appear to have increased as a problem over the past three decades. As "equality" values have grown in importance in our society, as well as fear of retribution from disgruntled employees who fail to achieve excellent appraisals, there has been a tendency for evaluation to be less rigorous and negative repercussions from the evaluation reduced by generally inflating or upgrading appraisals. However, by inflating these evaluations, many organizations have found themselves in a difficult position when having to defend their personnel action in the case of discharging an employee.[43]

Inappropriate Substitutes for Performance

It is the unusual job where the definition of performance is absolutely clear and direct measures are available for appraising the incumbent. In many jobs it is difficult to get consensus on what is "a good job," and it is even more difficult to get agreement on what criteria will determine performance. For a salesperson the criteria are affected by factors such as economic conditions and actions of competitors—factors outside the salesperson's control. As a result, the appraisal is frequently made by using substitutes for performance—criteria that, it is believed, closely approximate performance and act in its place. Many of these substitutes are well chosen and give a good approximation of actual performance. However, the substitutes chosen are not always appropriate. It is not unusual, for example, to find organizations using criteria such as effort, enthusiasm, neatness, positive attitudes, conscientiousness, promptness, and congeniality as substitutes for performance. In some jobs, one or more of these criteria are part of performance. Obviously, enthusiasm does enhance the effectiveness of a teacher: You are more likely to listen to and be motivated by a teacher who is enthusiastic than by one who is not; and increased attentiveness and motivation typically lead to increased learning. But enthusiasm may in no way be relevant to effective performance for many accountants, watch repairers, or copy editors. So what may be an appropriate substitute for performance in one job may be totally inappropriate in another.

Attribution Theory

There is a concept in management literature called **attribution theory.** According to this theory, employee evaluations are directly affected by a "supervisor's perceptions of who is believed to be in control of the employee's performance—the employer or the manager."[44] Attribution theory attempts to differentiate between those things that the employee controls (internal) versus those that the employee cannot control (external). For example, if an employee fails to finish a project that he has had six months to complete, a supervisor may view this negatively if he or she believes that the employee did not manage either the project or his time well (internal control). Conversely, if the project is delayed because top management requested that something else be given a higher priority, a supervisor may see the incomplete project in more positive terms (external control).

One research study found support for two key generalizations regarding attribution:[45]

1. When appraisers attribute an employee's poor performance to internal control, the judgment is harsher than when the same poor performance is attributed to external factors.
2. When an employee is performing satisfactorily, appraisers will evaluate the employee favorably if the performance is attributed to the employee's own efforts than if the performance is attributed to outside forces.

While attribution theory is interesting and sheds new light on rater effects on performance evaluations, continued study of the topic is needed. Yet it does provide much insight on why unbiased performance evaluations are important. An extension of attribution theory relates to what is called **impression management.** Impression management takes into account how the employee influences the relationship with his or her supervisor. In one study, impression management was viewed as having an effect on performance ratings. In such a case, when the employee "positively impressed his or her supervisor," the outcome was seen as a higher performance rating.[46]

CREATING MORE EFFECTIVE PERFORMANCE MANAGEMENT SYSTEMS

The fact that evaluators frequently encounter problems with performance appraisals should not lead us to throw up our hands and give up on the concept. There are things that can be done to make performance appraisals more effective. In this section, we offer some suggestions that can be considered individually or in combination.

Use Behavior-based Measures

As we have pointed out, the evidence favors behavior-based measures over those developed around traits. Many traits often considered to be related to good performance may, in fact, have little or no performance relationship. Traits like loyalty, initiative, courage, reliability, and self-expression are intuitively appealing as desirable characteristics in employees. But the relevant question is: Are individuals who rate high on those traits higher performers than those who rate low? Of course we can't definitively answer this question. We know that there are employees who rate high on these characteristics and are poor performers. Yet, we can find others who are excellent performers but do not score well on traits such as these. Our conclusion is that traits like loyalty and initiative may be prized by appraisers, but there is no evidence to support the notion that certain traits will be adequate synonyms for performance in a large cross section of jobs.

A second weakness in traits is the judgment itself. What is "loyalty"? When is an employee "reliable"? What you consider "loyalty," we may not. So traits suffer from weak inter-rater agreement. Behavior-derived measures can deal with both of these objections. Because they deal with specific examples of performance—both good and bad—we avoid the problem of using inappropriate substitutes. Additionally, because we are evaluating specific behaviors, we increase the likelihood that two or more evaluators will see the same thing. You might consider a given employee as "friendly" while we might perceive her as "standoffish." But when asked to rate her in terms of specific behaviors, we might both agree that in terms of specific behaviors, she "frequently says "'good morning' to customers," "willingly gives advice or assistance to coworkers," and "always consolidates her cash drawer at the end of her work day."

Combine Absolute and Relative Standards

A major drawback to individual or absolute standards is that they tend to be biased by positive leniency; that is, evaluators lean toward packing their subjects into the high part of the rankings. On the other hand, relative standards suffer when there is little actual variability among the subjects. The obvious solution is to consider using appraisal methods that combine both absolute and relative standards. For example, you might want to use the adjective rating scale and the individual ranking method. This dual method of appraisal, incidentally, has been instituted at some universities to deal with the problem of grade inflation. Students get an absolute grade—A, B, C, D, or F—and next to it is a relative mark showing how this student ranked in the class. A prospective employer or graduate school admissions committee can look at two students who each got a B in their international finance course and draw considerably different conclusions about each when, next to one grade it says "ranked 4th out of 33," while the other says "ranked 17th out of 21." Clearly, the latter instructor gave a lot more high grades!

Provide Ongoing Feedback

A few years back, a nationwide motel chain advertised, "The best surprise is no surprise." This phrase clearly applies to performance appraisals. Employees like to know how they are doing. The "annual review," where the appraiser shares the employees' evaluations with them, can become a problem. In some cases, it is a problem merely because appraisers put off such reviews. This is particularly likely if the appraisal is negative. But the annual review is additionally troublesome if the supervisor "saves up" performance-related information and unloads it during the appraisal review. This creates an extremely trying experience for both the evaluator and employee. In such instances it is not surprising that the supervisor may attempt to avoid confronting uncomfortable issues that, even if confronted, may only be denied or rationalized by the employee.[47]

The solution lies in having the appraiser share with the employee both expectations and disappointments on a frequent basis. By providing the employee with repeated opportunities to discuss performance before any reward or punishment consequences occur, there will be no surprises at the time of the formal annual review. In fact, where ongoing feedback has been provided, the formal sitting-down step shouldn't be particularly traumatic for either party. Additionally, in an MBO system that actually works, ongoing feedback is the critical element.

Have Multiple Raters

As the number of raters increases, the probability of attaining more accurate information increases.[48] If rater error tends to follow a normal curve, an increase in the number of raters will tend to find the majority clustering about the middle. If a person has had ten supervisors, nine of whom rated him or her excellent and one poor, then we must investigate what went into that one. Maybe this rater was the one who identified an area of weakness where training is needed, or an area to be avoided in future job assignments. Therefore, by moving employees about within the organization to gain a number of evaluations, we increase the probability of achieving more valid and reliable evaluations.[49] Of course, we are making the assumption that the process functions properly, and bias free![50]

Use Peer Evaluations Have you ever wondered why a professor asks you to evaluate the contributions of each other's work when a group or team project is used in the class? The reasoning behind this action is that the professor cannot tell what every member did on the project, but only what the overall product quality was. And at times, that may not be fair to everyone—especially if a member or two in the group left most of the work up to the remaining group members.

Similarly, supervisors find it difficult to evaluate their employees' performance because they are not observing them every moment of the work day. Unfortunately, unless they have this information, they may not be making an accurate assessment. And if their goal of the performance evaluation is to identify deficient areas and provide constructive feedback to their employees, they have been providing a disservice to these workers by not having all the information. Yet how do they get this information? One of the better means is through **peer evaluations.** Peer evaluations are conducted by the employees' co-workers—people explicitly familiar with the behaviors involved in their jobs.[51] For example, at Digital Equipment Corporation, all team members evaluate one another.[52] This is done because co-workers are the ones most aware of each others' day-to-day work behavior and should be given the opportunity to provide the supervisor with some feedback.[53]

The main advantage to peer evaluation is that (1) there is a tendency for co-workers to offer more constructive insight to each other so that, as a unit, each will improve; and (2) their recommendations tend to be more specific regarding job behaviors. Unless specificity exists, constructive measures may be hard to obtain.[54] But caution is in order because these systems, if not handled properly, could lead to increases in halo effects and leniency errors,[55] and fear among employees.[56] Thus, along with training our supervisors to properly appraise employee performance, so too must we train peers to evaluate one another.

A slight deviation from peer assessments is a process called the **upward appraisal,** or the reverse review.[57] Used in such companies as Pratt and Whitney, Dow Chemical, Citicorp, and AT&T, upward appraisals permit employees to offer frank and constructive feedback to their supervisors on such areas as leadership and communication skills.[58]

360-Degree Appraisals

An appraisal device that seeks performance feedback from such sources as oneself, bosses, peers, team members, customers, and suppliers has become very popular in contemporary organizations.[59] It's called the **360-degree appraisal.**[60] It's being used in approximately 90 percent of the Fortune 1000 firms, which includes such companies as DuPont, Nabisco, Warner-Lambert, Mobil Oil, Cook Children Health Care System, and General Electric, and UPS (see Meet David Blackwell).[61]

In today's dynamic organizations, traditional performance evaluations systems may be archaic. Delayering has resulted in supervisors having greater work responsibility and more employees reporting directly to them. Accordingly, in some instances, it is almost impossible for supervisors to have extensive job knowledge of each of their employees. Furthermore, the growth of project teams and employee involvement in today's companies places the responsibility of evaluation where people are better able to make an accurate assessment.[62]

The 360-degree feedback process also has some positive benefits for development concerns. Many managers simply do not know how their employees truly view them and the work they have done. For example, Jerry Wallace,

Meet

DAVID BLACKWELL

Assistant Vice-President HR Cook Children's Health Care System

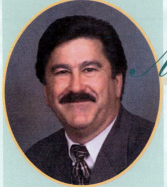

David Blackwell is assistant vice president of human resources for Cook Children's Health Care System in Fort Worth, Texas. In his twenty years in human resources, Blackwell has encountered many new issues with trying to meet the diverse human resource needs of the health care industry.

With many mergers and consolidations in the industry, Blackwell learned that joining organizations that do complimentary but different work (vertical integration) requires the employee cultures to mesh but not necessarily merge. Because the health care divisions are in different stages of their organizational development and growth, HR services, programs, policies, and practices must reflect those differences.

Blackwell began at Fort Worth Children's Hospital in 1978 as an intern while attending graduate school. Before graduation, he was hired as the director of personnel for Fort Worth Children's Hospital and as a result of a merger, assumed the same responsibilities for the W. I. Cook Children's Hospital. He was a key member of the management team responsible for merging the employee cultures of the two hospitals even though many staff initially resisted this change. Blackwell successfully integrated the two compensation and benefit programs, as well as the personnel policies and practices of the two hospitals.

Today, Cook Children's Health Care System is a regional referral center, including the 183-bed flagship hospital, Cook Children's Medical Center, a primary and sub-specialty care physician group with over thirty offices in fifteen Texas cities and a home health agency. The System serves children over a ninety-county area of North and West Texas.

As assistant vice president of human resources, Blackwell is a member of the administrative councils of the medical center and the physician network and reports directly to the System's Chief Executive Officer.

One human resource program in which an improvement was sought was performance management. Blackwell implemented a 360 Performance Assessment and Customer Evaluation (PACE) tool designed to provide feedback to employees from multiple sources. Employees receive feedback on their performance and their department or unit's performance from patient and physician surveys; and peer, internal customer, and supervisory evaluations. PACE has been well received by employees and supervisors except for the distribution and collection of forms. The next version of PACE will be an automated, Intranet-based system that reduces paper transitions and allows information to be distributed, completed, and collected on-line.

In the competitive managed care environment of health care today, resources are tight and imagination is required to meet the human resource needs of the organization. Blackwell believes programs such as PACE are a step in the right direction.

Blackwell is certified as a senior professional in human resources (SPHR). He is a member of the Society for Human Resource Management, American Society of Healthcare Human Resource Administration, and Dallas-Fort Worth Healthcare Human Resource Association. He is a past president and board member of the Dallas-Fort Worth Healthcare Human Resource Association. He received his Bachelor of Science in Education from the University of North Texas in 1972. He attended graduate school at the University of Texas at Arlington, School of Social Work.

GM's Saturn plant's head of personnel viewed himself as being up-to-date on all the latest management techniques.[63] While Jerry viewed himself open to change and flexible to new ideas, feedback from his employees indicated that Jerry was a "control" freak. After some soul-searching, plus an assessment from an external leadership group, Jerry realized his employees were right. He finally understood why nobody wanted to be on a team with him and why he had to do everything himself.[64] In this case, the 360-degree feedback instrument eliminated a strong barrier to Jerry's career progression.

Research studies into the effectiveness of 360-degree performance appraisals are reporting positive results. These stem from having more accurate feedback, empowering employees, reducing the subjective factors in the evaluation process, and developing leadership in an organization (see Meet David Blackwell).[65]

Rate Selectively

It has been suggested that appraisers should only rate in those areas in which they have significant job knowledge. If raters make evaluations on only those dimensions for which they are in a good position to rate, we can increase the inter-rater agreement and make the evaluation a more valid process. This approach also recognizes that different organizational levels often have different orientations toward ratees and observe them in different settings. In general, therefore, we recommend that, in terms of organizational level, appraisers should be as close as possible to the individual being evaluated. Conversely, the more levels separating the evaluator and employee, the less opportunity the evaluator has to observe the individual's work behavior and, not surprisingly, the greater the possibility for inaccuracies.

The specific application of these concepts results in having immediate supervisors or co-workers as the major input into the appraisal and having them evaluate those factors that they are best qualified to judge. For example, it has been suggested that when professors are evaluating secretaries within a university, they use such criteria as judgment, technical competence, and conscientiousness, whereas peers (other secretaries) use such criteria as job knowledge, organization, cooperation with co-workers, and responsibility.[66] Such an approach appears both logical and more reliable, since people are appraising only those dimensions of which they are in a good position to make judgments.

In addition to taking into account where the rater is in the organization or what he or she is allowed to evaluate, selective rating should also consider the characteristics of the rater. If appraisers differ in traits, and if certain of these traits are correlated with accurate appraisals while others are correlated with inaccurate appraisals, then it seems logical to attempt to identify effective raters. Those identified as especially effective could be given sole responsibility for doing appraisals, or greater weight could be given to their observations.

Train Appraisers

If you cannot find good raters, the alternative is to make good raters. Evidence indicates that the training of appraisers can make them more accurate raters.[67] Common errors such as halo and leniency can be minimized or eliminated in workshops where supervisors can practice observing and rating behaviors. Why should we bother to train these individuals? Because a poor appraisal is worse than no appraisal at all.[68] These negative effects can manifest themselves as demoralizing employees, decreasing productivity, and making the company "liable for wrongful termination damages."[69]

INTERNATIONAL PERFORMANCE APPRAISAL

In evaluating employee performance in international environments, other factors come into play. For instance, the cultural differences between the parent country and the host country must be considered. The cultural differences between the United States and England are not as great as those between the United States and China, for example. Thus, hostility or friendliness of the cultural environment in which one manages should be considered when appraising employee performance.

Who Performs the Evaluation?

There are also issues to consider regarding who will be responsible for the evaluations: the host-country management or the parent-country management? Although local management would generally be considered a more accurate gauge, it typically evaluates expatriates from its own cultural perspectives and expectations, which may not reflect those of the parent country. For example, in some countries, a participatory style of management is acceptable, while in other countries, hierarchical values make it a disgrace to ask employees for ideas. This could vastly alter a supervisor's performance appraisal.[70]

Confusion may arise from the use of parent-country evaluation forms if they are misunderstood, either because the form has been improperly translated, not translated at all, or because the evaluator is uncertain what a particular question means. The home-office management, on the other hand, is often so remote that it may not be fully informed on what is going on in an overseas office. Because they lack access and because one organization may have numerous foreign operations to evaluate, home-office managements often measure performance by quantitative indices, such as profits, market shares, or gross sales.[71] However, "simple" numbers are often quite complex in their calculations and data are not always comparable. For example, if a company has many operations in South America, it must be aware of the accounting practices in each country. Peru, for instance, counts sales on consignment as firm sales, while Brazil does not. Local import tariffs can also distort pricing schedules, which alter gross sales figures, another often-compared statistic. Even when the measurements are comparable, the comparison country will have an effect. For example, factory productivity levels in Mexico may be below those of similar plants in the United States, but American-owned plant productivity in Mexico may be above that of similar Mexican-owned plants. Depending on where the supervisor's results are compared, different outcomes may occur. Accordingly, such issues complicate parent-country management performance evaluations by numerical criteria, or indices.

Which Evaluation Format Will Be Used?

Other issues surround the question of selecting the best format to use in performance appraisals. If we have an overseas operation that includes both parent-country nationals (PCNs) and host-country nationals (HCNs), we must determine if we will use the same forms for all employees. While most Western countries accept the concept of performance evaluation, some cultures interpret it as a sign of distrust or even an insult to an employee. This complicates a decision to use one instrument like an adjective rating scale for all employees. On the other hand, using different formats for PCNs and HCNs may create a dual track in the subsidiary, in turn creating other problems.

The evaluation form presents other problems. If there is a universal form for the entire corporation, an organization must determine how it will be translated accurately into the native language of each country. English forms may not be readily understood by local supervisors. For example, clerical and office jobs do not always have identical requirements in all cultures. As a result, some U.S. multinationals may be hesitant about evaluating HCNs and TCNs (third-country nationals). In some countries, notably those who support the Communist ideology, all workers are rewarded only when the group performs—with

Should a manager at this Wal-Mart in Mexico be required to use the corporate evaluation developed and used extensively in the United States? If so, will the evaluation need to be translated into Spanish? Questions such as these need to be addressed when evaluating employees in the global village.

punishment or discipline being highly limited. You'll find this, for example, in the hotel industry in the People's Republic of China. Without the ability to reward good individual performance or to punish poor performance, there is little motivation to have any evaluation at all.[72]

Although the subject of international performance appraisal continues to receive research attention, two general recommendations have been suggested as follows.

▶ Modify the normal performance criteria of the evaluation sheet for a particular position to fit the overseas position and site characteristics. Expatriates who have returned from a particular site or the same country can provide useful input into revising criteria to reflect the possibilities and constraints of a given location.[73]

▶ Include a current expatriate's insights as part of the evaluation. This means that nonstandardized criteria, which are difficult to measure, will be included, perhaps on a different basis for each country. This creates some administrative difficulties at headquarters, but in the long run will be a more equitable system.[74]

SUMMARY

This summary relates to the Learning Objectives provided on p. 284.

After having read this chapter, you should know:

1. Performance management systems serve in the process of linking effort and performance. Only through effective means of making this linkage apparent can an organization develop its rewards based on performance.

2. The three purposes of performance management systems are feedback, development, and documentation. They are designed to support the employees, the appraisers, and the organization.

3. The six-step appraisal process is to: (1) establish performance standards with employees; (2) set measurable goals (manager and employee); (3) measure actual performance; (4) compare actual performance

with standards; (5) discuss the appraisal with the employee; and (6) if necessary, initiate corrective action.

4. Absolute standards refer to a method in performance management systems whereby employees are measured against company-set performance requirements. Absolute standard evaluation methods involve the essay appraisal, the critical incident approach, the checklist rating, the adjective rating scale, the forced-choice inventory, and the behaviorally anchored rating scale (BARS).

5. Relative standards refer to a method in performance management systems whereby employees' performance is compared to other employees. Relative standard evaluation methods include group order ranking, individual ranking, and paired comparisons.

6. MBO is used as an appraisal method by establishing a specific set of objectives for an employee to achieve and reviewing performance based on how well those objectives have been met.

7. Performance appraisal might be distorted for a number of reasons, including: leniency error, halo error, similarity error, central tendency, low appraiser motivation, inflationary pressures, and inappropriate substitutes for performance.

8. More effective appraisals can be achieved with behavior-based measures, combined absolute and relative ratings, ongoing feedback, multiple raters, selective rating, trained appraisers, peer assessment, and rewards to accurate appraisers.

9. In 360-degree performance appraisals evaluations are made by oneself, supervisors, employees, team members, customers, suppliers, and the like. In doing so, a complete picture of one's performance can be assessed.

10. Performance management systems may differ in the international spectrum in terms of who performs the evaluation and the format used. Cultural differences may dictate that changes in the U.S. performance management system are needed.

EXPERIENTIAL EXERCISE:
The 360° Performance

As human resource management students, you and your class team have been asked to conduct a thirty-minute presentation for ten to fifteen supervisors (including Shelia) at the next supervisors meeting, since supervisors have not adapted as well as desired by management to a change in appraisal system.

Develop a thirty-minute presentation about the purposes of the performance management systems, who benefits, the basic six steps, clarify the difference between relative and absolute standards, possible distortions, and introduce the 360-degree feedback system.

WEB-WISE EXERCISE

Search and print findings of interest from the following sites.

National Performance Review
http://www.npr.gov

CASE APPLICATION:
A Stunning Performance Review

"Juan," said team leader, Shelia Thompson, "that dreaded time of year is here, and I've got to do your evaluation this week. So let's meet after lunch and get it done. For a Hispanic male I think you've handled working for a woman better than I would have thought, so I think you'll pass. I really don't know much about your job, but you can fill me in at 1:00 P.M. Just think about how you intend to improve your attitude and performance, so I can get to my 1:30 P.M. meeting with the VP on time. The new form I'll read at lunch—1:00 P.M. in my office?"

Juan gazes in disbelief but is reluctant to say anything, at least until after the appraisal. At lunch he shares her comments with his co-worker, Chuck McFarley, and asks, What do you think she meant, would you say anything? Do you think my appraisal could possibly be fair? She talks down to me and criticizes me when I make a mistake, but doesn't tell me how to improve. I don't think I have a problem with her because she is a woman boss, I just don't like the way she treats me. Chuck, what would you do?"

Chuck responds, "I don't know what being a Hispanic male has to do with anything, but I think I'd mention it to someone in human resources. I don't know if I'd do it now before you meet with her or wait till after the appraisal, but I wouldn't let it go. Maybe she thinks that's humor; it's not. Maybe she's not aware and needs to become aware or maybe she is aware, and just doesn't care; either way, I think it needs to be discussed so feelings and perceptions won't affect your future relationship or performance.

"That's what I would do; but you have to do what you feel is right. I haven't had a problem with her, but then she invites me to happy hour, and I go because I don't want to offend her; and I don't even drink. Whatever you do, document."

If you were Juan, how would you respond?

a. Call or go by HR before the interview.
b. Call or go by HR after the interview.
c. Open the interview by asking her to clarify her remarks.

d. If it's a good evaluation, say nothing.

e. If it's a poor evaluation, go to HR and file a written complaint.

f. Call an agency or get an attorney; skip HR and skip Shelia.

g. Interrupt her lunch to clarify comments before the interview.

h. Say nothing and hope the feelings of demotivation, hurt, resentment, and anger fade with time.

i. Other

Juan decides to say nothing until after the appraisal is over, then he will ask her what she meant by the comments, how he perceived it, felt, and what he would like in the future.

When he shows up for the interview, she says, "come in."

"Hey, I checked everything average, because I don't think anyone is perfect, and if I gave you an excellent 5 rating, you wouldn't understand when I would ask you to improve or do more, better, or faster. Almost everyone is getting average. I'd like a better than average team, but some of us would have to try harder, and take instruction better, wouldn't we? OK, sign at the bottom and I'll give it to the vice president when I see him in a minute. We'll talk more tomorrow. Don't be discouraged; the vice president is a Hispanic male."

Stunned again, Juan does not want to sign the form but is on his way to human resources to file a formal complaint against Shelia.

Assignment

If you were the HR representative assigned to coach Shelia on the appraisal process, what are at least ten suggestions you would share with her?

TESTING YOUR UNDERSTANDING

How well did you fulfill the learning objectives?

1. Performance management systems lead to employee motivation in all of these ways except
   a. work objectives are clarified.
   b. criteria for measuring work objectives are specified.
   c. employees have confidence that their efforts will lead to satisfactory job performance.
   d. employees have confidence that satisfactory job performance will lead to an acceptable reward.
   e. individual value systems are identified.

2. A director of direct purchase accounts always has trouble with his people after performance appraisals. They quit, call in sick for a week, or sabotage operations. During a conversation with Rhonda, the vice president of human resources, the director complained about the performance evaluation process, "I have a bunch of babies working for me. They all expect me to tell them what good performance is. Part of their job is figuring out what they are supposed to do." What would be the best response from Rhonda?
   a. Sympathize. Agree that the director's employees are babies.
   b. Help the director develop corrective action steps for his employees.
   c. Tell the director that performance standards should be set with employees, and objectives should be clearly agreed to.
   d. Tell the director to set clear performance expectations for his employees. It is his job, not theirs.
   e. Show the director the performance objectives Rhoda uses for her employees. Suggest that the director use those objectives.

3. Marc is a marketing analyst. His boss periodically observes his work on specific parts of his job (client calls, conducting meetings, attending seminars, etc.) and writes down, using specific behavioral descriptions, what she sees him doing. What appraisal technique is she using?
   a. graphic rating scale
   b. critical incident
   c. BARS
   d. checklist appraisal
   e. forced-choice comparison

4. Compare the group order ranking and the individual ranking techniques for performance evaluation.
   a. The techniques are the same.
   b. Individual ranking is disadvantaged because you may be forced to identify the "best of the best" in one set of employees and the "best of the worst" in another set. Group order ranking does not have this problem.
   c. Group order ranking is disadvantaged because you may be forced to identify the "best of the best" in one set of employees and the "best of the worst" in another set. Individual ranking does not have this problem.
   d. Individual ranking forces the evaluator to compare all employees to each other. Group order ranking does not.
   e. Individual ranking allows no ties. Group order ranking allows ties.

5. If you had an MBO agreement with your professor about what to do to get an A in this class, which would be the best (in terms of MBO standards) objective?
   a. Get an A for doing the best you can.
   b. Get an A for excellent work on tests, quizzes, and projects.

c. Get an A for a score of 96 or better on this test.

d. Get an A for interesting contributions to class.

e. Get an A if you are in the better part of the class.

6. Tommy rates Adam, an average worker, "excellent" on all of his performance evaluations. The rest of the staff suspects that Adam gets high ratings because he graduated from the same prestigious university and was a member of the same fraternity as Tommy. If this were accurate, what rating error has the staff identified?

   a. Similarity error

   b. Halo error

   c. Leniency error

   d. Central tendency

   e. Inflationary pressures

7. According to attribution theory, if in a supervisor's judgment an employee's poor performance is attributable to external factors,

   a. the employee will be more harshly rated.

   b. the employee will be favorably rated.

   c. the supervisor's perception will be jaded by impression management influence.

   d. there exists an internal focus of control.

   e. the poor performance will be viewed in more positive terms.

8. Which of the following is an example of an upward appraisal?

   a. A manager refers to earlier performance appraisals of subordinates before evaluating them.

   b. Peer evaluation is employed.

   c. Several managers form teams to evaluate all their employees collectively.

   d. Employees evaluate their managers.

   e. Managers evaluate employees' traits, rather than their behaviors.

9. The 360-degree appraisal process

   a. provides feedback from a variety of individuals who have knowledge of an employee's performance.

   b. works best in large organizations.

   c. aids in developing competitive intelligence about competing organizations.

   d. diminishes the effect of development in the performance appraisal process.

   e. all the above

10. Samantha, vice president of a large transnational firm, explains that because of cultural and language differences between the parent and most subsidiary countries, her organization has chosen to evaluate performance only "by the numbers." Gross sales figures and factory productivity levels are used. What is wrong with this approach?

    a. Nothing. Most firms are using this technique for international performance evaluation.

    b. Each country's accounting practices must be considered when recording sales. (For example, some countries record consignments as sales.)

    c. Language differences affect factory productivity levels.

    d. Sales figures cannot be easily converted to a common currency designation.

    e. The effort is redundant. Either gross sales or factory productivity levels should be sufficient.

11. Good performance management systems are designed to provide

    a. performance information and salary updates.

    b. disciplinary action and salary updates.

    c. feedback, development, and documentation.

    d. training, documentation, and salary updates.

    e. communication and documentation.

12. Performance management systems must satisfy the needs of

    a. employees, appraisers, organizations.

    b. employees, customers, supervisors.

    c. customers, managers, human resources professionals.

    d. employees, organizations, customers.

    e. human resources professionals, supervisors, managers.

13. The three approaches for performance appraisal are

    a. absolute standards, tangential standards, nominal standards.

    b. absolute standards, relative standards, objectives.

    c. absolute standards, objectionable standards, peer review.

    d. absolute standards, relative standards, peer review.

    e. relative standards, peer review, objectives.

14. MBOs are likely to be ineffective in

    a. global organizations.

    b. hierarchical organizations that are implementing TQM.

    c. service-sector organizations.

    d. manufacturing plants with more than three production facilities.

    e. hierarchical organizations in which managers traditionally do not trust subordinates and do not delegate.

15. Advantages of MBO include all of the following except

    a. employees have greater commitment to objectives they set.

    b. employees know what is expected of them.

    c. MBO provides a basis for performance evaluation.

    d. MBO is a time-saving way to set goals.

    e. employees know that performance is defined in terms of successfully meeting stated objectives.

16. Under which condition should an expatriate be evaluated by the host-country management instead of by parent-country management?

    a. When the evaluation forms are not properly translated.

b. When a hostile cultural environment exists.

c. When the home office is so remote that it cannot be fully informed about overseas operations.

d. When the economic base of the parent country differs drastically from the host company.

e. When the expatriate is from the parent country.

Endnotes

1. Brian O'Reilly, "360-Feedback Can Change Your Life," *Fortune* (October 17, 1994), pp. 64–65.

2. Danielle R. McDonald, "Performance Review Designed by Secretaries for Secretaries," *Journal of Compensation and Benefits,* Vol. 7, No. 7 (November/December 1991), pp. 36–38.

3. Ibid.

4. See, for example, Joseph P. McCarthy, "A New Focus On Achievement," *Personnel Journal,* Vol. 70, No. 2 (February 1991), pp. 74–76.

5. Philip Ricciardi, "Simplify Your Approach to Performance Measurement," *HRMagazine* (March 1996), p. 99; and Mike Deblieux, "Performance Reviews Support Quest for Quality," *H.R. Focus,* Vol. 68, No. 11 (November 1991), pp. 3–4.

6. See, for example, Jeffrey A. Bradt, "Pay for Impact," *Personnel Journal,* Vol. 70, No. 5 (May 1991), pp. 76–79; and Kathleen A. Guinn and Roberta J. Corona, "Putting a Price on Performance," *Personnel Journal,* Vol. 70, No. 5 (May 1991), pp. 72–77.

7. Brian Murray and Barry Gerhart, "An Empirical Analysis of a Skill-Based Pay Program and Plant Performance Outcomes," *Academy of Management Journal,* Vol. 41, No. 1 (January 1998), p. 68; and James M. Jenks, "Do Your Performance Appraisals Boost Productivity?" *Management Review,* Vol. 80, No. 6 (June 1991), p. 45.

8. See Sandra O'Neal and Madonna Palladino, "Revamp Ineffective Performance Management," *Personnel Journal* (February 1992), pp. 93–102.

9. Suzanne S. Masterson and M. Susan Taylor, "Total Quality Management and Performance Appraisal: An Integrative Perspective, *Journal of Quality Management* (January 1996), p. 73.

10. We would like to recognize Dr. Peter F. Norlin, an organizational consultant specializing in performance management systems, for providing the framework terminology for the purposes, who is served, and inherent difficulties.

11. Robert J. Sahl, Ph.D., "Design Effective Performance Appraisals," *Personnel Journal* (October 1990), pp. 56–57.

12. See Stuart Feldman, "Amoco Keeps Its Employees in the Big Picture," *Personnel* (June 1991), p. 24.

13. Mary Mavis, "Painless Performance Evaluations," *Training and Development* (October 1994), p. 40; and Herbert H. Meyer, "A Solution to the Performance Appraisal Feedback Enigma," *Academy of Management Executive* (February 1991), p. 68.

14. For a discussion on perception differences, see Kenneth P. Carron, Robert L. Cardy, and Gregory H. Dobbins, "Performance Appraisals as Effective Management or Deadly Management Disease: Two Initial Empirical Investigations,"

Group and Organizational Studies (June 1991), pp. 143–59.

15. See, for example, Maria Castanda and Afsaneh Nahavandi, "Link of Manager Behavior to Supervisory Performance Rating and Subordinate Satisfaction," *Group and Organizational Studies* (December 1991), pp. 357–66.

16. Ibid.; and Robert B. Campbell and Lynne Moses Garfinkel, "Strategies for Success," *HRMagazine* (June 1996), p. 104.

17. See Gary English, "Tuning Up for Performance Management," *Training and Development Journal* (April 1991), pp. 56–60.

18. Donald W. Myers, Wallace R. Johnston, and C. Glenn Pearce, "The Role of Human Interaction Theory in Developing Models of Performance Appraisal Feedback," *SAM Advanced Management Journal* (Summer 1991), p. 28.

19. See Barry R. Nathan, Allan M. Mohrman, Jr., and John Milliman, "Interpersonal Relations as a Context for the Effects of Appraisal Interviews on Performance and Satisfaction: A Longitudinal Study," *Academy of Management Journal* (June 1991), pp. 352–363.

20. Stephen M. Pollan and Mark Levine, "Maximizing Your Performance Review, "*Working Woman* (December 1993), p. 74; and Elaine McShulskis, "Involve Employees in Performance Appraisals," *HRMagazine* (April 1997), p. 24.

21. Robert J. Nobile, "The Law of Performance Appraisals," *Personnel* (January 1991), p. 7.

22. Larry L. Axline, "Ethical Considerations of Performance Appraisals," *Management Review* (March 1994), p. 62.

23. See David C. Martin and Kathy M. Bartol, "The Legal Ramifications of Performance Appraisal: An Update," *Employee Relations Law Review* (Autumn 1991), pp. 257–286.

24. Kathyrn Tyler, "Careful Criticism Brings Better Performance," *HRMagazine* (April 1997), p. 57.

25. Jack Stack, "The Curse of the Annual Performance Review," *Inc.* (May 1997), pp. 39–40; and Dick Grote, "Handling Employee Reviews," *Incentive* (October 1997), p. 32.

26. Richard Henderson, *Compensation Management: Rewarding Performance,* 6th ed. (Englewood Cliffs, N.J.: Prentice-Hall, 1994), p. 433.

27. Ahron Tziner and Richard Kopelman, "Effects of Rating Format on Goal-Setting: A Field Experiment," *Journal of Applied Psychology* (May 1988), p. 323.

28. See, for example, Dennis M. Daley, "Great Expectations, or a Tale of Two Systems: Employee Attitudes Toward Graphic Rating Scales and MBO-Based Performance Appraisal," *Public Administration Quarterly* (Summer 1991), pp. 188–201.

29. Richard Henderson, *Compensation Management: Rewarding Performance,* 6th ed. (Englewood Cliffs, N.J.: Prentice-Hall, 1994), p. 433.

30. Mary L. Tenopyr, "Artificial Reliability of Forced-Choice Scales," *Journal of Applied Psychology* (November 1988), pp. 749–751.

31. See Kevin R. Murphy, "Criterion Issues in Performance Appraisal Research: Behavioral Accuracy Versus Classification Accuracy," *Organizational Behavior and Human Decision Processes* (October 1991), pp. 45–50.

32. H. John Bernardin and Richard W. Beatty, *Performance Appraisal: Assessing Human Behavior at Work* (Boston: Kent Publishing, 1984), p. 86.

33. See, for example, Kevin R. Murphy and Virginia A. Pardaffy, "Bias in Behaviorally Anchored Rating Scales: Global or Scale Specific," *Journal of Applied Psychology* (April 1989),

pp. 343–346. See also Michael J. Piotrowski, Janet L. Barnes-Farrell, and Francine H. Esris, "Behaviorally Anchored Bias: A Replication and Extension of Murphy and Constans," *Journal of Applied Psychology* (October 1988), pp. 827–828.

34. Ibid.

35. For an overview of MBO, see Peter F. Drucker, *The Practice of Management* (New York: Harper & Row, 1954).

36. See, for instance, Nancy E. Day, "Can Performance Raters Be More Accurate? Investigating the Benefits of Prior Knowledge of Performance Dimensions," *Journal of Managerial Issues* (Fall 1995), pp. 323–343.

37. Henderson, pp. 428–429.

38. See, for example, William H. Bommer, Jonathan L. Johnson, and Gregory A. Rich, "An Extension of Heneman's Meta-Analysis of Objective and Subjective Measures of Performance," *Academy of Management Best Papers Proceedings,* Dorothy P. Moore (ed.), (August 14–17, 1994), pp. 112–116.

39. For an interesting discussion of leniency errors, see Jeffrey S. Kane, H. John Bernardin, Peter Villanova, and Joseph Peyrefitte, "Stability of Rater Leniency: Three Studies," *Academy of Management Journal,* Vol. 38, No. 4 (November 1995), pp. 1036–1051.

40. Bernardin and Beatty, p. 140.

41. Ibid., p. 270.

42. Ibid., p. 139.

43. Jonathan A. Segal, "Are Your Performance Appraisals Just and Act?" *HRMagazine* (October 1995), pp. 45–50.

44. David Kipnis, Karl Price, Stuart Schmidt, and Christopher Stitt, "Why Do I Like Thee: Is It Your Performance or My Orders?" *Journal of Applied Psychology* (June 1981), pp. 324–328.

45. Ibid.

46. See, for example, Sandy J. Wayne, Isabel K. Graf, and Gerald R. Ferris, "The Role of Employee Influence Tactics in Human Resource Decisions," *Academy of Management Best Papers Proceedings,* Dorothy Perrin Moore (ed.), (Vancouver, British Columbia, Canada, August 6–9, 1995), pp. 156–160; Sandy J. Wayne and Robert C. Liden, "Effects of Impression Management on Performance Ratings: A Longitudinal Study," *Academy of Management Journal,* Vol. 38, No. 1 (February 1995), pp. 232–260; and Sandy J. Wayne and K. Michele Kacmar, "The Effects of Impressive Management on the Performance Appraisal Process," *Organization Behavior and Human Decision Processes* (February 1991), pp. 70–88.

47. See, for example, Bernardin and Beatty, pp. 271–276.

48. An assumption has been made here. That is, these raters have specific performance knowledge of the employee. Otherwise, more information may not be more accurate information. For example, if the raters are from various levels in the organization's hierarchy, these individuals may not have an accurate picture of the employee's performance; thus, quality of information may decrease.

49. See, for example, Hannah R. Rothstein, "Interrater Reliability of Job Performance Ratings: Growth to Asymptote Level with Increasing Opportunity to Observe," *Journal of Applied Psychology* (June 1990), pp. 322–327. See also Mary D. Zalesny, "Rater Confidence and Social Influence in Performance Appraisals," *Journal of Applied Psychology* (June 1990), pp. 274–289.

50. For an interesting perspective on aspects to avoid when using multiple raters, see Susan Haworth, "The Dark Side of Multi-Rater Assessments," *HRMagazine* (May 1998), pp. 106–114.

51. Kathleen A. Guinn, "Performance Management for Evolving Self-Directed Work Teams," *ACA Journal* (Winter 1995), pp. 74–79; Stephanie Gruner, "The Team-Building Peer Review," *Inc.* (July 1995), pp. 63–65; and Ted H. Shore, Lynn McFarlane, and George C. Thornton III, "Construct Validity of Self- and Peer Evaluations of Performance Dimensions in an Assessment Center," *Journal of Applied Psychology* (February 1992), pp. 42–54.

52. Carol A. Norman and Robert A. Zamacki, 'Team Appraisals—Team Approach," *Personnel Journal* (September 1991), p. 101.

53. Catherine M. Petrini, "Upside-Down Performance Appraisals," *Training and Development Journal* (July 1991), pp. 15–22.

54. See, for example, Martin L. Ramsey and Howard Lehto, "The Power of Peer Review," *Training and Development* (July 1994), pp. 38–41.

55. See Jiing-Lib Farh, Albert A. Cannella, and Arthur G. Bedian, "Peer Ratings: The Impact of Purpose on Rating Quality Acceptance," *Group and Organization Studies* (December 1991), pp. 367–386.

56. Marilyn Moats Kennedy, "Where Teams Drop the Ball," *Across the Board* (September 1993), p. 9.

57. Irene H. Buhalo, "You Sign My Report Card—I'll Sign Yours," *Personnel* (May 1991), p. 23.

58. Stephanie Gruner, "Turning the Tables," *Inc.* (May 1996), p. 87; Joann S. Lublin, "Turning the Tables: Underlings Evaluate Bosses," *The Wall Street Journal* (October 4, 1994), pp. B1, B11; and Jerry Baumgartner, "Give It to Me Straight," *Training and Development* (July 1994), pp. 49–51.

59. Richard Lepsinger and Anntoinette D. Lucia, "360 Degree Feedback and Performance Appraisal," *Training* (September 1997), pp. 62–70; Mark R. Edwards and Ann J. Ewen, "Moving Multisource Assessment Beyond Development," *ACA Journal* (Winter 1995), pp. 82–93; and John F. Milliman, Robert A. Zawacki, Carol Norman, Lynda Powell, and Jay Kirksey, "Companies Evaluate Employees from All Perspectives," *Personnel Journal* (November 1994), p. 99.

60. Ibid., pp. 99–104.

61. Leanne Atwater and David Waldman, "Accountability in 360 Degree Feedback," *HRMagazine* (May 1998), p. 96; Robert Hoffman, "Ten Reasons You Should Be Using 360-Degree Feedback," *HRMagazine* (April 1995), p. 82; and "Companies Where Employees Rate Executives," *Fortune* (December 27, 1993), p. 128.

62. Phaedra Brotherton, "Candid Feedback Spurs Changes in Culture," *HRMagazine* (May 1996), pp. 47–52.

63. Brian O'Reilly, "360 Feedback Can Change Your Life," *Fortune* (October 17, 1994), p. 96.

64. Ibid.

65. See, for example, Dianne Nilsen, "Self-Observer Rating Discrepancies: Once an Over-rater, Always an Overrater," *Human Resource Management* (Fall 1993), pp. 265–282; Walter W. Turnow, "Perceptions or Reality: Is Multi-Perspective Measurement a Means or an End?" *Human Resource Management* (Fall 1993), pp. 221–230; Manuel London and Richard W. Beatty, "360-Degree Feedback as a Competitive Advantage," *Human Resource Management* (Fall 1993), pp. 353–373; Robert E. Kaplan, "360-Degree Feedback PLUS:

Boosting the Power of Co-Worker Rating for Executives," *Human Resource Management* (Fall 1993), pp. 299–315; and Hal Lancaster, "Performance Reviews Are More Valuable When More Join In," *The Wall Street Journal* (July 9, 1996), p. B1.

66. W. C. Borman, "The Rating of Individuals in Organizations: An Alternative Approach," *Organizational Behavior and Human Performance* (August 1974), pp. 105–124.

67. Christopher P. Neck, Greg L. Stewart, Charles C. Manz, "Thought Self-leadership as a Framework for Enhancing the Performance of Performance Appraisers," *Journal of Applied Behavior Science* (September 1995), pp. 279–280; Beverly Dugan, "Effects of Assessor Training on Information Use," *Journal of Applied Psychology* (November 1988), pp. 743–748; and Clinton O. Longenecker, Dennis A. Gioia, and Henry P. Sims, Jr., "Behind the Mask: The Politics of Employee Appraisal," *Academy of Management Executive* (August 1987), p. 191.

68. Charles Lee, "Poor Performance Appraisals Do More Harm than Good," *Personnel Journal* (September 1989), p. 91.

69. Ibid.

70. See Peter J. Dowling, Randall S. Schuler, and Denice E. Welch, *International Dimensions of Human Resource Management,* 2d ed. (Belmont, Calif.: Wadsworth, 1994), pp. 103–120; and G. Oddou and M. Mendenhall, "Expatriate Performance Appraisal: Problems and Solutions," in M. Mendenhall and G. Oddou (eds.), *International Human Resource Management* (Boston: PWS Kent Publishing, 1991), pp. 364–374.

71. G. Oddou and M. Mendenhall, "Expatriate Performance Appraisal: Problems and Solutions," in M. Mendenhall and G. Oddou (eds.), *International Human Resource Management* (Boston: PWS Kent Publishing, 1991), p. 366.

72. J. S. Solomon, "Employee Relations Soviet Style," *Personnel Administrator,* Vol. 30, No. 10 (October 1985), pp. 79–86. See also "Rewarding Individuals Hinders Team Performance," *HRMagazine* (November 1996), p. 16.

73. Dowling, Schuler, and Welch, pp. 113–115; and Oddou and Mendenhall, pp. 372–374.

74. Ibid.

11. Establishing Rewards and Pay Plans

LEARNING OBJECTIVES

After reading this chapter, you will be able to:

1. Describe the link between rewards and motivation.
2. Explain the various classifications of rewards.
3. Discuss why some rewards are considered membership-based.
4. Define the goal of compensation administration.
5. Discuss job evaluation and its four basic approaches.
6. Explain the evolution of the final wage structure.
7. Describe competency-based compensation programs.
8. Discuss why executives are paid significantly higher salaries than other employees in an organization.
9. Identify what is meant by the balance sheet approach to international compensation.

$\mathcal{T}$om Warner owns a plumbing, heating, and air-conditioning business in Montgomery County, Maryland. In the early 1990s, he faced a major dilemma. His company's main customers—commercial property–management firms—were looking for ways to cut costs. In doing so, many of these property-management firms simply decided to hire their own "handymen" and eliminate the contract work with Warner. Consequently, Warner had some major decisions to make about his 250-person work force.[1]

Not wanting to lay off his workers who had been so dedicated over the years, Warner decided to restructure his operation into territories, which comprised approximately 10,000 households each. Each of his workers was assigned to a territory, and all were told that they could operate in each territory as if they were running their own business. Of course to make all of this work, there had to be something of value that these area directors desired. He pro-

Tom Warner has found that giving his employees the opportunity to act as if they are running their own business has been highly successful. Not only have these employees witnessed significant pay increases, in doing so Warner's revenues have grown substantially.

vided training for each "area technical director" in sales techniques, budgeting, negotiating, cost estimating, and how to handle customer complaints. Warner believed that if he had a strong core of technically superb, friendly, and ambitious employees, they could operate like small-town "handymen" despite the realization that they were part of a large organization.

Has Warner's program been successful? From all indications, it has been an unqualified success. The area directors developed a strong sense of pride and ownership in their territories. They not only were able to "fix pipes and repair heaters," they were able to generate referrals. All technicians were also able to schedule their own work, handle their own equipment, develop their own estimates and advertising campaigns, and collect their own receivables. While these were important rewards that the technicians desired, there was also the question of money! Would Warner's program increase the technician's "bottom-line?" If you consider the case of Ron Inscoe as an indicator, it appears on this dimension, too, workers are satisfied. For example, as a 34-year-old technician, Ron never made more than $60,000 a year in the heating, air-conditioning, and ventilation field. Yet, in his first year after joining Warner, Ron made $103,000. He exceeded that salary the following year when his gross income was $126,000. From a reward and compensation point of view, Warner Plumbing employees are extremely happy—and Tom Warner has seen his business grow by more than 200 percent in just under 24 months!

INTRODUCTION

"What's in it for me?" That is a question nearly every individual consciously or unconsciously asks before engaging in any form of behavior. Our knowledge of motivation tells us that people do what they do to satisfy some need. Before they do anything, therefore, they look for a payoff or reward.

The most obvious reward employees get from work is pay, and we will spend the major part of this chapter addressing pay as a reward as well as how

Effort → Performance → Organizational goals → Individual goals

Rewards

compensation programs are established. However, rewards also include promotions, desirable work assignments, and a host of other less obvious payoffs—a smile, peer acceptance, or a kind word of recognition.

THE LINKAGE TO MOTIVATION

The place of rewards in our motivation model was made clear in Chapter 4. Since people behave in ways that they believe are in their best interests, they constantly look for payoffs for their efforts. They expect good job performance to lead to organizational goal attainment, which in turn leads to satisfying their individual goals or needs (see Exhibit 11-1). Organizations, then, use rewards to motivate people. They rely on rewards to motivate job candidates to join the organization. They rely on rewards to get employees to come to work and perform effectively once they are hired.[2]

In the following section, we will review the various types of rewards over which supervisors have discretion, and look at the properties of effective rewards, with particular emphasis on using rewards in ways that are consistent with the motivation model.

TYPES OF EMPLOYEE REWARDS

There are several ways to classify rewards. We have selected three of the most typical dichotomies: intrinsic versus extrinsic rewards, financial versus nonfinancial rewards, and performance-based versus membership-based rewards. As you will see, these categories are far from being mutually exclusive, yet all share one common thread—they assist in maintaining employee commitment.[3]

Intrinsic versus Extrinsic Rewards

Intrinsic rewards are the personal satisfactions one gets from the job itself. These are self-initiated rewards, such as having pride in one's work, having a feeling of accomplishment, or being part of a work team. Job enrichment, for instance, discussed in Chapter 10, can offer intrinsic rewards to employees by making work seem more meaningful.[4] **Extrinsic rewards,** on the other hand, include money, promotions, and benefits. Their common thread is that they are external to the job and come from an outside source, mainly management. For example, Apple Computer gives a PC to each of its employees. After one year on the job, the PC becomes the employee's personal property.[5] Consequently, if an employee experiences feelings of achievement or personal growth from a job, we would label such rewards as intrinsic. If the employee receives a salary increase or a write-up in the company magazine, we would label these rewards as extrinsic. The general structure of rewards has been summarized in Exhibit 11-2.

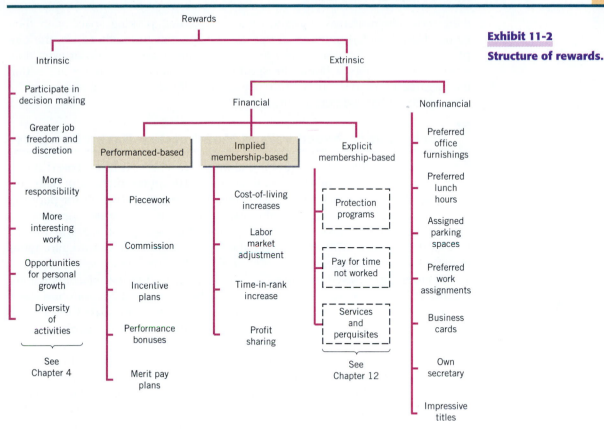

Exhibit 11-2
Structure of rewards.

Financial versus Nonfinancial Rewards

Rewards may or may not enhance the employee's financial well-being. If they do, they can do this directly—through for instance, wages, bonuses, or profit sharing—or indirectly—through employer-subsidized benefits such as pension plans, paid vacations, paid sick leaves, and purchase discounts.

Nonfinancial rewards cover a smorgasbord of desirable "extras" that are potentially at the disposal of the organization. Their common link is that they do not increase the employee's financial position. Instead of enhancing the employee's finances, nonfinancial rewards emphasize making life on the job more attractive. The nonfinancial rewards that we will identify represent a few of the more obvious; however, the creation of these rewards is limited only by HRM's ingenuity and ability to "use them to motivate" desirable behavior.

The saying, "One person's food is another person's poison," applies to the entire subject of rewards, but specifically to the area of nonfinancial rewards. What one employee views as "something I've always wanted," another might find relatively useless. Therefore, HRM must take great care in providing the "right" nonfinancial reward for each person. Yet where selection has been done properly, the benefits by way of increased performance to the organization should be significant.

Some workers, for example, are very status conscious. A plush office, a carpeted floor, a large cherry desk, or signed artwork may be just the office furnishing that stimulates an employee toward top performance. Similarly, status-oriented employees may value an impressive job title, their own business cards, their own administrative assistant, or a well-located parking space with their name clearly painted underneath the "Reserved" sign. In another case, the employee may value the opportunity to dress casually while at work, or even do a portion of one's job at home. Irrespective of the "incentive," these are within the organization's discretion. And when carefully used, they may provide a stimulus for enhanced performance.

Performance-based versus Membership-Based Rewards

The rewards that the organization allocates can be said to be based on either performance or membership criteria. While HR representatives in many organizations will vigorously argue that their reward system pays off for performance, you should recognize that this isn't always the case. Few organizations actually reward employees based on performance—a point we will discuss later in this chapter. Without question, the dominant basis for reward allocations in organizations is membership.

Performance-based rewards are exemplified by the use of commissions, piecework pay plans, incentive systems, group bonuses, merit pay, or other forms of pay-for-performance plans. On the other hand, membership-based rewards include cost-of-living increases, benefits, and salary increases attributable to labor–market conditions, seniority or time in rank, credentials (such as a college degree or a graduate diploma), or future potential (e.g., the recent MBA out of a prestigious university). The key point here is that membership-based rewards are generally extended regardless of an individual's, group's, or organization's performance. The difference between the two is not always obvious. In practice, performance may be only a minor determinant of rewards, despite academic theories holding that high motivation depends on performance-based rewards.

WHAT IS COMPENSATION ADMINISTRATION?

Why do sales directors at G&K Services in Minnetonka, Minnesota, earn more than the route delivery drivers? Intuitively, you might say that the sales directors are more skilled and have greater job responsibility, so they should earn more. But how about sales managers who specialize in the unique field of fire retardant clothing used in such organizations that specialize in petroleum and chemical products? Should they make more or less than the sales director who supervises sales of "traditional" work clothing products? The answers to questions such as these lie in job evaluation.

Job evaluation is the process whereby an organization systematically establishes its compensation program. In this process, jobs are compared in order to arrive at each job's appropriate worth within the organization. In this section we will discuss the broader topic of compensation, narrow our discussion to job evaluation methods, and conclude with a review of an increasingly controversial topic—executive compensation.

Employees exchange work for rewards. Probably the most important reward, and indeed the most obvious, is money. But all employees don't earn the same amount of money. Why? The search for this answer moves us directly into the topic of compensation administration.

The goals of **compensation administration** are to design a cost-effective pay structure that will attract, motivate, and retain competent employees. It should also be one that will be perceived as fair by employees. *Fairness* is a term that frequently arises in the administration of an organization's compensation program. Organizations generally seek to pay the least that they have to in order to minimize costs, so fairness means a wage or salary that is adequate for the demands and requirements of the job. Of course, fairness is a two-way street. Employees, too, want fair compensation. As we pointed out in our earlier discussion of motivation, if employees perceive an imbalance in the relation of their efforts–rewards ratio to some comparative standard, they will act to correct the inequity. So the search for fairness is pursued by both employers and employees.

> **The goals of compensation administration are to design a cost-effective pay structure that will attract, motivate, and retain competent employees.**

Government Influence on Compensation Administration

In Chapter 3, we described how government policies shape and influence HRM. This influence, however, is not equally felt in all areas. For example, collective bargaining and the employee selection process are heavily constrained by government rules and regulations. In contrast, this influence is less in the areas of employment planning and orientation. Compensation administration falls into the former category. Government policies set minimum wages and benefits that employers must meet, and these policies provide protection for certain groups (see Exhibit 11-3). The laws and regulations we will discuss are not meant to comprehensively cover government's influence on compensation administration. Rather, they are presented as highlights. The point of these highlights should be to make you aware that government constraints reduce HRM's discretion on compensation decisions. An abundance of laws and regulations define the general parameters within which managers decide what is fair compensation. Let's look at some of these.

Fair Labor Standards Act   The **Fair Labor Standards Act (FLSA),** passed in 1938, contained several provisions that affected organizations and their compensation systems. These included issues surrounding minimum wages, overtime pay, record-keeping and child labor restrictions. Nearly all organizations, except the smallest businesses, are covered by the FLSA.

The Act also identified two primary categories of employees—*exempt* and *nonexempt*. **Exempt employees** would include, for instance, employees in professional and managerial jobs. Under the Act, jobs categorized as exempt are not required to meet FLSA standards, especially in the area of overtime pay. On the other hand, **nonexempt employees** receive certain protections under the FLSA. Specifically, employees in these jobs are eligible for premium pay—typically time and one-half—when they work more than 40 hours in a week. Moreover, these jobs must be paid at least the minimum wage, which in September 1997 was raised to $5.15 an hour.

Both federal and state governments have also enacted laws requiring employees who contract with the government to pay what are called *prevailing wage rates*. In the federal sector, the secretary of labor is required to review industry rates in the specific locality to set a prevailing rate which becomes the minimum under the contract prescribed under the Walsh–Healy Act. Under this act government contractors must also pay time-and-a-half for all work in excess of eight hours a day or forty hours a week.

The Civil Rights and the Equal Pay Acts   The Civil Rights and the Equal Pay Acts, among other laws, protect employees from discrimination. Just as it is ille-

Exhibit 11-3

Federal Minimum Wage.

YOUR RIGHTS

Under the Fair Labor Standards Act

Federal Minimum Wage

$5.15

Minimum Wage of at least $5.15 per hour beginning September 1, 1997.
Certain full-time student learners, apprentices, and workers with disabilities may be paid less than the minimum wage under special certificates issued by the Department of Labor.

Tip credit—The tip credit which an employer may claim with respect to "Tipped Employees" is 50 percent of the applicable minimum wage.

Overtime Pay
At least 1½ times your regular rate of pay for all hours worked over 40 in a workweek.

Child Labor
An employee must be at least sixteen years old to work in most non-farm jobs and at least eighteen to work in non-farm jobs declared hazardous by the Secretary of Labor. Youths fourteen and fifteen years old may work outside school hours in various non-manufacturing, non-mining, non-hazardous jobs under the following conditions:

No more than—
3 hours on a school day or eighteen hours in a school week;
8 hours on a non-school day or forty hours in a non-school week.

Also, work may not begin before 7 a.m. or end after 7 p.m., except from June 1 through Labor Day, when evening hours are extended to 9 p.m. Different rules apply in agricultural employment.

Enforcement
The Department of Labor may recover back wages either administratively or through court action, for the employees that have been underpaid in violation of the law. Violations may result in civil or criminal action.

Fines of up to $10,000 per minor may be assessed against employers who violate the child labor provisions of the law and up to $1,000 per violation against employers who willfully or repeatedly violate the minimum wage or overtime provisions. This law *prohibits* discriminating against or discharging workers who file a complaint or participate in any proceedings under the Act.

Note:
Certain occupations and establishments are exempt from the minimum wage and/or overtime pay provisions.
Special provisions apply to workers in Puerto Rico and American Samoa.
Where state law requires a higher minimum wage, the higher standard applies.
FOR ADDITIONAL INFORMATION, CONTACT the Wage and Hour Division office nearest you—listed in your telephone directory under United States Government, Labor Department.
The law requires employees to display this poster where employees can readily see it.

Source: U.S. Department of Labor, Employment Standards Administration, Wage and Hour Division, Washington, D.C. 20210. WH Publication 1088. Revised October 1996, U.S. Government Printing Office: 1996—300-812.

gal to discriminate in hiring, organizations cannot discriminate in pay on the basis of race, color, creed, age, or sex.

The **Equal Pay Act** of 1963 mandates that organizations compensate men and women doing the same job in the organization the same rate pay. The Equal Pay Act was designed to lessen the pay gap between male and female pay rates. Although progress is being made, women in general still earn roughly

Meet

CONNIE SITTERLY, EDD
Management Training Specialists

Connie Sitterly is a trainer with passion in her purpose. As her philosophy states; "People are the most important assets to any organization and we are dedicated to enhance the performance of each individual." Often referred to as *The Workplace Doctor*, Sitterly's enthusiasm is contagious as she works diligently with employees, management, and teams toward resolutions and a common vision.

Connie Sitterly specializes in training and consulting on the hard-core workplace issues such as *"Conflict Resolution," "Sexual Harassment," "Diversity,"* confronting every company or organization today as well as *"Interpersonal Skills," "Negativity," "Problem Solving," "Teambuilding," "Quality Improvement," "Marginal Performers," "Discipline & Praise."*

To enable clients to gain an ongoing return on their training investments, Management Training Specialists offers a Train-Your-Trainer Certification Process program on twenty-plus topics. Each designated trainer, with the client's company, is personally trained and coached by Sitterly to present and facilitate with confidence, producing consistently excellent results.

Connie Sitterly has written over three hundred newspaper articles on workplace issues and is published by Prentice-Hall, Harper and Row, Harper-Collins, and Crisp Publishing Companies, among others. She is author of *The Female Entrepreneur, The Woman Manager,* and is a recurrent radio and television guest. Besides her fifteen years as an entrepreneur with Management Training Specialists, Fort Worth, Texas, Dr. Sitterly is also an adjunct professor in the Department of Business and Economics at Texas Woman's University in Denton, where she teaches fast-track courses in management, supervision, human relations, communication, and leadership.

Since its formation in 1983, Management Training Specialists has developed and presented programs for over 350 clients in four countries and contin-ues to build a broad client base by providing sustainable results and support. MTS is unique in four critical areas: customization from intensive preparation through presentations by credentialed, experienced professionals; twenty-plus Train-Your-Trainer certification process programs; integration of training-consulting which enables the development of supplemental systems and tools into the programs and manuals; and support and follow-up by a dedicated staff who demonstrates what MTS trains, publishes and counsels.

A full-service consulting and training-development provider, Management Training Specialists consults on a variety of workplace issues including culture transformation, change, teaming, quality-service improvement, employee involvement, interpersonal skills—enabling both organizations and professionals to achieve a competitive edge as they position themselves for the year 2000 and beyond. MTS designs each program to specifically meet your needs, issues and requirements. While developing and presenting training programs is a significant component, Management Training Specialists can also design related processes, procedures, and policies to ensure implementation, reinforcement, and application of strategies and plans.

---

75 percent of what their male counterparts earn.[6] Some of this difference is attributable to perceived male-versus-female dominated occupations, but the Equal Pay Act requires employers to eliminate pay differences for the same job. That is, all salaries must be established on the basis of skill, responsibility, effort, and working conditions.[7] For example, if an organization is hiring customer service representatives, new employees, irrespective of their sex, must be paid the same initial salary because the attributes for the job are the same. It is important to note that the Equal Pay Act typically affects only initial job salaries. If two workers, one male and one female, perform at different levels during the course of the year, it is conceivable that if performance is rewarded, in the next period their pay may be different. This is permitted under the act!

Recall also from Chapter 3 our discussion on comparable worth. Although job evaluation techniques, described later, can reduce this concern, comparable worth is not an Equal Pay Act concern. Rather it is a societal issue designed to further reduce the male–female pay disparity. Yet it is interesting to note that while comparable worth continues to be debated, especially in this era of work-force diversity, other countries have moved forward to correct the situation. For instance, in Canada, the 1988 Ontario Pay Equity Act went into effect.[8] Under this law, Canadian employers must equate salaries in the female-dominated jobs in their organizations with those in the male-dominated ones. For example, in reviewing this law, Canadian lawmakers found that the skills, knowledge, and abilities of nursing assistants in hospitals were comparable to plumbers working in the same location. Accordingly, under the law, these nursing assistants were given a 17 percent pay increase.[9]

JOB EVALUATION AND THE PAY STRUCTURE

The essence of compensation administration is job evaluation and the establishment of a pay structure. Let's now turn our attention to the topic job evaluation and a discussion of how it is done.

What Is Job Evaluation?

In Chapter 5, we introduced job analysis as the process of describing the duties of a job, authority relationships, skills required, conditions of work, and additional relevant information. We stated that the data generated from job analysis could be used to develop job descriptions and specifications, as well as to do job evaluations. By *job evaluation,* we mean using the information in job analysis to systematically determine the value of each job in relation to all jobs within the organization. In short, job evaluation seeks to rank all the jobs in the organization and place them in a hierarchy that will reflect the relative worth of each. It's important to note that this is a ranking of jobs, not people. Job evaluation assumes normal performance of the job by a typical worker. So, in effect, the process ignores individual abilities or the performance of the jobholder.

The ranking that results from job evaluation is the means to an end, not an end in itself. It should be used to determine the organization's pay structure. Note that we say "should"; in practice, we'll find that this is not always the case. External labor market conditions, collective bargaining, and individual skill differences may require a compromise between the job evaluation ranking and the actual pay structure. Yet even when such compromises are necessary, job evaluation can provide an objective standard from which modifications can be made.

Isolating Job Evaluation Criteria

The heart of job evaluation is the determination of what criteria will be used to arrive at the ranking. It is easy to say that jobs are valued and ranked by their relative job worth, but there is far more ambiguity when we attempt to state what it is that makes one job higher than another in the job structure hierarchy. Most job-evaluation plans use responsibility, skill, effort, and working conditions as major criteria,[10] but each of these, in turn, can be broken down into more specific terms. Skill, for example, is often measured "through the intelligence or mental requirements of the job, the knowledge required, motor or manual skills needed, and the learning that occurs."[11] But other criteria can and have been used: supervisory controls, complexity, personal contacts, and the physical demands needed.[12]

You should not expect the criteria to be constant across jobs. Since jobs differ, it is traditional to separate jobs into common groups. This usually means that, for example, production, clerical, sales, professional, and managerial jobs are evaluated separately. Treating like groups similarly allows for more valid rankings within categories, but still leaves unsettled the importance of criteria between categories. Separation by groups may permit us to say the position of software developer in the Development group requires more mental effort than that of a shipping supervisor, and subsequently receives a higher ranking; but it does not readily resolve whether greater mental effort is necessary for software designers than for customer service managers.

Methods of Job Evaluation

There are four basic methods of job evaluation currently in use: ordering, classification, factor comparison, and point method.[13] Let's review each of these.

Ordering Method   The **ordering method** requires a committee—typically composed of both management and employee representatives—to arrange jobs in a simple rank order, from highest to lowest. No attempt is made to break down the jobs by specific weighted criteria. The committee members merely compare two jobs and judge which one is more important, or more difficult to perform. Then they compare another job with the first two, and so on until all the jobs have been evaluated and ranked.

The most obvious limitation to the ordering method is its sheer inability to be managed when there are a large number of jobs. Imagine the difficulty of trying to rank hundreds or thousands of jobs in the organization! It could be impossible to do the rankings correctly. Other drawbacks to be considered are the subjectivity of the method—there are no definite or consistent standards by which to justify the rankings—and because jobs are only ranked in terms of order, we have no knowledge of the distance between the ranks.

Classification Method   The **classification method** was made popular by the U.S. Civil Service Commission, now the Office of Personnel Management (OPM). The OPM requires that classification grades be established. These classifications are created by identifying some common denominator—skills, knowledge, responsibilities—with the desired goal being the creation of a number of distinct classes or grades of jobs. Examples might include shop jobs, clerical jobs, sales jobs, etc., depending, of course, on the type of jobs the organization requires.

Once the classifications are established, they are ranked in an overall order of importance according to the criteria chosen, and each job is placed in its appropriate classification. This latter action is generally done by comparing each position's job description against the classification description. At the OPM, for example, evaluators have classified both Budget and Finance Clerk I and Typist III positions as GS-5 grades, while Contracts and Procurement officers, and IRS Audit Supervisory jobs have both been graded as GS-13.

The classification method shares most of the disadvantages of the ordering approach, plus the difficulty of writing classification descriptions, judging which jobs go where, and dealing with jobs that appear to fall into more than one classification. On the plus side, the classification method has proven itself successful and viable in classifying millions of kinds and levels of jobs in the civil service.

Exhibit 11-4 Factor Comparison Method (Selected Jobs)

Jobs	Hourly Pay	Mental Requirements	Skill Requirements	Physical Requirements	Responsibility	Working Conditions
Maintenance Electrician	$17.80	$4.35	$5.25	$2.60	$3.60	$2.00
Inventory Control Specialists	14.95	4.05	4.65	2.00	3.25	1.00
Warehouse Stocker	12.60	2.75	3.50	1.80	2.30	2.25
Administrative Assistant	11.15	3.25	3.00	1.00	2.65	1.25
Maintenance Electrician Helper	10.85	2.85	2.20	2.40	1.80	2.00

Factor Comparison Method The **factor comparison method** is a sophisticated and quantitative ordering method. The evaluators select key jobs in the organization as standards. Those jobs chosen should be well known, with established pay rates in the community, and they should consist of a representative cross section of all jobs that are being evaluated. Jobs fitting these requirements are called benchmark jobs. Typically, fifteen to fifty key jobs are selected by the committee.[14]

What factors in the benchmark positions will the other jobs be compared against? These criteria are usually mental requirements, skill requirements, physical requirements, responsibility, and working conditions. Once the key jobs are identified and the criteria chosen, committee members rank the key jobs on the criteria. The next step is the most interesting dimension in the factor comparison method. The committee agrees on the base rate (usually expressed on an hourly basis) for each of the key jobs and then allocates this base rate among the five criteria (see Exhibit 11-4). For example, in one organization the job of maintenance electrician was chosen as a key job with an hourly rate of $17.80. The committee allocated $4.35 to mental effort, $5.25 to skill, $2.60 to physical effort, $3.60 to responsibility, and $2.00 to working conditions. These amounts then became standards by which other jobs in the organization could be evaluated.

The final step in factor comparison requires the committee to compare its overall judgments and resolve any discrepancies. The system is in place when the allocations to the key jobs are clear and understood, and high agreement has been achieved in committee members' judgments about how much of each criteria every job has. Then, the committee must slot the remaining jobs not used in the initial analysis.

Drawbacks to factor comparison include its complexity; its use of the same five criteria to assess all jobs, when, in fact, jobs differ across and within organizations; and its dependence on key jobs as anchor points. "To the extent that one or more key jobs change over time either without detection or without correction of the scale, users of the job comparison scale are basing decisions on what might be described figuratively as a badly warped ruler."[15] On the positive side, factor comparison requires a unique set of standard jobs for each organization, so it is a tailor-made approach. As such, it is automatically designed to meet the specific needs of each organization. Another advantage is that jobs are compared with other jobs to determine a relative value, and since relative job values are what job evaluation seeks, the method is logical.

Point Method The last method we will present breaks down jobs based on various identifiable criteria (such as skill, effort, and responsibility) and then allocates points to each of these criteria. Depending on the importance of each criterion to performing the job, appropriate weights are given, points are summed, and jobs with similar point totals are placed in similar pay grades.

An excerpt from a **point method** chart for administrative assistant II positions is shown in Exhibit 11-5. Each job would be evaluated by deciding, for example, the degree of education required to perform the job satisfactorily. The first degree might require the equivalent of skill competencies associated with ten years of elementary and secondary education; the second degree might require competencies associated with four years of high school; and so forth.

The point method offers the greatest stability of the four approaches we have presented. Jobs may change over time, but the rating scales established under the point method stay intact. Additionally, the methodology underlying the approach contributes to a minimum of rating error. On the other hand, the point method is complex, making it costly and time-consuming to develop. The key criteria must be carefully and clearly identified, degrees of factors have to be agreed upon in terms that mean the same to all raters, the weight of each criterion has to be established, and point values must be assigned to degrees. While it is expensive and time-consuming to both implement and maintain, the point method appears to be the most widely used method. Furthermore, this method can be effective for addressing the comparable worth issue [see Chapter 3].[16]

Job Class: Clerk

Factor	1st Degree	2nd Degree	3rd Degree	4th Degree	5th Degree
Skill					
1. Education	22	44	66	88	110
2. Problem solving	14	28	42	56	70
Responsibility					
1. Safety of others	5	10	15	20	25
2. Work of others	7	14	21	28	35

Exhibit 11-5

Excerpts from a Point Method

2. Problem solving:

This factor examines the types of problems dealt with in your job. Indicate the one level that is most representative of the majority of your job responsibilities.

Degree 1: Actions are performed in a set order per written or verbal instruction. Problems are referred to supervisor.

Degree 2: Solves routine problems and makes various choices regarding the order in which the work is performed within standard practices. May obtain information from varied sources.

Degree 3: Solves varied problems that require general knowledge of company policies and procedures applicable within area of responsibility. Decisions made based on a choice from established alternatives. Expected to act within standards and established procedures.

Degree 4: Requires analytical judgment, initiative, or innovation in dealing with complex problems or situations. Evaluation not easy because there is little precedent or information may be incomplete.

Degree 5: Plans, delegates, coordinates, and/or implements complex tasks involving new or constantly changing problems or situations. Involves the origination of new technologies or policies for programs or projects. Actions limited only by company policies and budgets.

SOURCE: Material reprinted with permission of The Dartnell Corporation, Chicago, IL 60640.

Establishing the Pay Structure

Once the job evaluation is complete, its data generated become the nucleus for the development of the organization's pay structure.[17] This means pay rates or ranges will be established that are compatible with the ranks, classifications, or points arrived at through job evaluation.

Any of the four job evaluation methods can provide the necessary input for developing the organization's overall pay structure. Each has its strengths and weaknesses, but because of its wide use, we will use the point method to show how point totals are combined with wage survey data to form wage curves.

Wage Surveys   Many organizations use surveys to gather factual information on pay practices within specific communities and among firms in their industry.[18] This information is used for comparison purposes. It can tell compensation committees if the organization's wages are in line with those of other employers and, in cases where there is a short supply of individuals to fill certain positions, may be used to actually set wage levels.[19] Where does an organization get wage salary data? The U.S. Department of Labor, through its Bureau of Labor Statistics, regularly publishes a vast amount of wage data broken down by geographic area, industry, and occupation. Many industry and employee associations also conduct **wage surveys** and make their results available. But organizations can conduct their own surveys, and many large ones do!

It would not be unusual, for instance, for the HRM director at Moen in Chicago to regularly share wage data on key positions. Jobs such as maintenance engineer, electrical engineer, computer programmer, or administrative assistant would be identified, and comprehensive descriptions of these jobs would be shared with firms in the industry—like Motorola, Control Data, or Rockwell Technologies.[20] In addition to the average wage level for a specific job, other information frequently reviewed includes entry-level and maximum wage rates, shift differentials, overtime pay practices, vacation and holiday allowances, the number of pay periods, and the length of the normal work day and work week.

Exhibit 11-6

A wage curve.

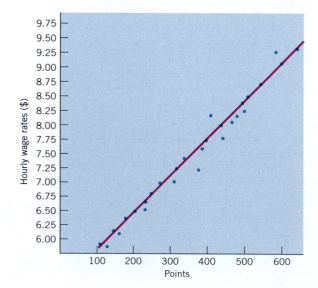

Wage Curves After the compensation committee arrives at point totals from job evaluation and obtains survey data on what comparable organizations are paying for similar jobs, a wage curve can be fitted to the data. An example of a wage curve is shown in Exhibit 11-6. This example assumes use of the point method and plots point totals and wage data. A separate wage curve can be constructed based on survey data and compared for discrepancies.

A completed wage curve tells the compensation committee the average relationship between points of established pay grades and wage base rates. Furthermore, it can identify jobs whose pay is out of the trend line. When a job's pay rate is too high, it may be identified as a "red circle" rate. This means that the pay level is frozen or below-average increases are granted until the structure is adjusted upward to put the circled rate within the normal range. Of course, there will be times when a wage rate is out of line but not red circled. The need to attract or keep individuals with specific skills may require a wage rate outside the normal range. To continue attracting these individuals, however, may ultimately upset the internal consistencies supposedly inherent in the wage structure. It also should be pointed out that a wage rate may be too low. Such undervalued jobs carry a "green circle" rate, and attempts may be made to grant these jobs above-average pay increases—or salary adjustments.

The Wage Structure It is only a short step from plotting a wage curve to developing the organization's **wage structure.** Jobs that are similar—in terms of classes, grades, or points—are grouped together. For instance, pay grade 1 may cover the range from 0 to 150 points, pay grade 2 from 151 to 300 points, and so on. As shown in Exhibit 11-7, the result is a logical hierarchy of wages.[21] The more important jobs are paid more; and as individuals assume jobs of greater importance, they rise within the wage hierarchy. Jobs may also be paid in accordance to what is commonly referred to as *knowledge or competency-based pay*.[22] We'll return to this topic shortly.

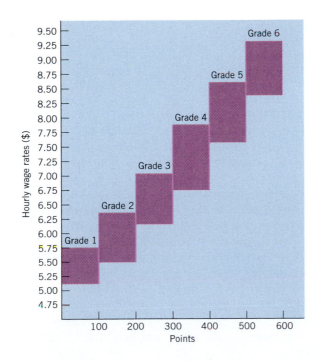

Exhibit 11-7

A sample wage structure.

Irrespective of the determinants, notice that each pay grade has a range and that the ranges overlap. Typically, organizations design their wage structures with ranges in each grade to reflect different tenure in positions, as well as levels of performance. Additionally, while most organizations create a degree of overlap between grades, employees who reach the top of their grade can only increase their pay by moving to a higher grade. However, wage structures are adjusted every several years [if not every year] so employees who've topped-out in their pay grade aren't "maxed-out" forever.

SOME SPECIAL CASES OF COMPENSATION

As organizations are rapidly changing in the dynamic world in which they exist, so, too, are compensation programs. Most notably, organizations are finding that they can no longer continue to increase wage rates by a certain percentage each year (a cost-of-living raise), without some comparable increase in performance. Subsequently, more organizations are moving to varied themes of the pay-for-performance systems. These may include incentive compensation plans, and competency and team-based compensation. Let's take a closer look at each of these.

Incentive Compensation Plans

In addition to the basic wage structure, organizations that are sincerely committed to developing a compensation system that is designed around performance will want to consider the use of incentive pay. Typically given in addition to—rather than in place of—the basic wage, incentive plans should be viewed as an additional dimension to the wage structure we have previously described. Incentives can be paid based on individual, group, or organization-wide performance—a pay-for-performance concept.

Individual Incentives   Individual incentive plans pay off for individual performances.[23] During the 1990s, these plans had been the biggest trend in compensation administration in the United States.[24] Popular approaches included merit pay, piecework plans, time-savings bonuses, and commissions.

One popular and almost universally used incentive system is merit pay.[25] Under a **merit pay plan,** employees who receive merit increases have a sum of money added to their base salary. Somewhat likened to a cost-of-living raise, merit pay differs in that the percentage of increase to the base wage rate is attributable solely to performance. Those who perform better generally receive more merit pay.

While the merit pay plan is the most widely used, the best-known incentive is undoubtedly piecework. Under a straight **piecework plan,** the employee is typically guaranteed a minimal hourly rate for meeting some preestablished standard output. For output over this standard, the employee earns so much for each piece produced. Differential piece-rate plans establish two rates—one up to standard, and another when the employee exceeds the standard. The latter rate, of course, is higher to encourage the employee to beat the standard. Individual incentives can be based on time saved as well as output generated. At Jacobs Engineering Group in Pasadena, California, engineers are not given annual pay raises. Rather, based on their performance, these individuals are given an

Providing incentives can be a worthwhile reward for employees. At Philip Morris, for example, employees have chosen to accept company stocks in lieu of salary increases. This concept links employee compensation directly to their performance. The better they perform, the more their stock will rise!

incentive bonus. For the past few years, this bonus has averaged more than 5 percent of their annual salary—greater than the cost-of-living adjustments if tied to inflation.[26] As with piecework, the employee can expect a minimal guaranteed hourly rate, but in this case, the bonus is achieved for doing a standard hour's work in less than sixty minutes. Employees who can do an hour's work in fifty minutes obtain a bonus that is some percentage (say 50 percent) of the labor saved.

Salespeople frequently work on a commission basis. Added to a lower base wage, they get an amount that represents a percentage of the sales price. On toys, for instance, it may be a hefty 25 or 30 percent. On sales of multi-million-dollar aircraft or city sewer systems, commissions are frequently 1 percent or less.

Individual incentives work best where clear performance objectives can be set and where tasks are independent.[27] If these conditions are not met, individual incentives can create dysfunctional competition or encourage workers to "cut corners." Co-workers can become the enemy, individuals can create inflated perceptions of their own work while deflating the work of others, and the work environment may become characterized by reduced interaction and communications between employees. And if corners are cut, quality and safety may also be compromised. For example, when Monsanto tied workers' bonuses to plant safety, covering up accidents was encouraged.[28]

A potentially negative effect with incentive for performance is that you may "get what you pay for." Since the incentives are tied to specific goals (which are only part of the total outcomes expected from a job), people may not perform the unmeasured, and thus not rewarded, activities in favor of the measured, rewarded ones. For example, if your school held a colloquium and brought in a guest speaker, and your instructor decided to take your class, would you go? Your response might be contingent on whether the colloquium was a requirement, the content of which could be included on an exam, and where attendance was taken. But if it was just for your information, attending might not be as high a priority. Despite the potential negative repercussions that individual incentives can cause in inappropriate situations, they are undoubtedly widespread in practice.

Sometimes, merit pay, too, has been used as a substitute for cost-of-living raises.[29] And similar to the cost-of-living raise, merit monies accrue permanently to the base salary, and become the new base from which future percentage increases can be calculated. The problem with merit pay or a cost-of-living system, then, is that pay increases may be always expected. But what if the company has a bad year, or employees don't produce what is expected of them? Under these traditional systems, wage increases still are expected. Theoretically, they should give some of their salary back!

Organizations today are looking at this latter idea. Specifically, they are requiring employees to place a percentage of their salary at risk. For example, employees at Hallmark Cards, Inc., in Kansas City, have up to 10 percent of their pay placed at risk. Depending on their productivity on such performance measures as customer satisfaction, retail sales, and profits, employees can turn the 10 percent "at-risk" pay into rewards as high as 25 percent.[30] However, failure to reach the performance measures can result in the forfeiture of the 10 percent salary placed at risk. Companies like Saturn, Steelcase, TRW, Hewlett-Packard, DuPont, Eastman Chemical, and Ameri-Tech use similar formulas where employee compensation is comprised of a base rate and reward pay.[31]

> **Employees at Hallmark Cards have up to 10 percent of their pay placed at risk.**

Group Incentives   Each individual incentive option we described also can be used on a group basis; that is, two or more employees can be paid for their combined performance. When are group incentives desirable? They make the most sense where employees' tasks are interdependent and thus require cooperation.[32]

Plant-wide Incentives   The goal of **plant-wide incentives** is to direct the efforts of all employees toward achieving overall organizational effectiveness. This type of incentive, like that of DuPont, produces rewards for all employees based on organization-wide cost reduction or profit sharing.[33] Kaiser Steel, for example, developed in one of its plants a cost-reduction plan that provides monthly bonuses to employees.[34] The amount of the bonus is determined by computing one-third of all increases in productivity attributable to cost savings as a result of technological change or increased effort. Additionally, Lincoln Electric has had a year-end bonus system for decades, which in some years has provided an annual bonus "ranging from a low of 55 percent to a high of 115 percent of annual earnings."[35] The Lincoln Electric plan pays off handsomely when employees beat previous years' performance standards. Since this bonus is added to the employee's salary, it has made the Lincoln Electric workers some of the highest-paid electrical workers in the United States.[36]

One of the best-known organization-wide incentive systems is the **Scanlon Plan.**[37] It seeks to bring about cooperation between management and employees through the sharing of problems, goals, and ideas. (It is interesting to note that many of the quality circle programs instituted in the 1980s were a direct outgrowth of the Scanlon Plan.[38]) Under Scanlon, each department in the organization has a committee composed of supervisor and employee representatives. Suggestions for labor-saving improvements are funneled to the committee and, if accepted, cost savings and productivity gains are shared by all employees, not just the individual who made the suggestion. Typically, about 80 percent of the suggestions prove practical and are adopted.

Another incentive plan that started in the early 1990s is called IM-PROSHARE.[39] **IMPROSHARE,** which is an acronym for Improving Productivity through Sharing, uses a mathematical formula for determining employees' bonuses.[40] For example, if workers can save labor costs in producing a product, a predetermined portion of the labor savings will go to the employee. Where IMPROSHARE exists, productivity gains up to 18 percent have been identified, with most of the gains coming from reduced defects and less production downtime.[41]

Profit-sharing plans, or gainsharing plans, are also plant-wide incentives.[42] They allow employees to share in the success of a firm by distributing part of the company's profits back to the workers. In essence, employees become owners of the company. The logic behind profit-sharing plans is that they increase commitment and loyalty to the organization. For instance, at Science Applications International Corporation, a high-tech research and engineering company in San Diego,[43] workers own almost half of the business. Each employee is entitled to a number of shares of company stock based on how profitable the company is over the year. As such, when employees encounter problems with customers, or the work process, it is in their best interest to take corrective action; you are more likely to be cost conscious if you share in the benefits. On the negative side, employees often find it difficult to relate their efforts to the profit-sharing bonus. Their individual impact on the organization's profitability may be minuscule. Additionally, factors such as economic conditions and actions of competitors—which are outside the control of the employees—may have a far greater impact on the company's profitability than any actions of the employees themselves.[44]

All the plant-wide incentives suffer from what is known as a *dilution effect*. It is hard for employees to see how their efforts result in the organization's overall performance. These plans also tend to distribute their payoffs at wide intervals; a bonus paid in March 1999 for your efforts in 1998 loses a lot of its reinforcement capabilities. Finally, we should not overlook what happens when organization-wide incentives become both large and recurrent. When this happens, it is not unusual for the employee to begin to anticipate and expect the bonus. Employees may adjust their spending patterns as if the bonus were a certainty. The bonus may lose some of its motivating properties. When that happens, it can be perceived as a membership-based reward.[45]

Competency-Based Compensation

So far in our discussion of establishing pay plans, we've implied one specific aspect of the process. That is, we pay jobs. People who hold those jobs just happen to get the salary assigned to that position. That assumption, however, has started to change in several organizations—like Consolidated Diesel, Famous Footwear, and Eli Lily and Company[46]—which are advocating something radically different.[47] Rather than thinking of the job as the most critical aspect to the organization, organizations are viewing the employees as one of their competitive advantages. When that conviction dominates organizational philosophy, compensation programs become one of rewarding competencies, or the "skills, knowledge, and behaviors"[48] employees possess. This is commonly referred to as **competency-based compensation.**

Exhibit 11-8

A Sample Banding.

Band		Salary Range
Band	VIII:	$150,000–175,000
Band	VII:	85,000–125,000
Band	VI:	70,000–90,000
Band	V:	55,000–80,000
Band	IV:	40,000–60,000
Band	III:	25,000–45,000
Band	II:	20,000–40,000
Band	I:	15,000–25,000

SOURCE: Based on the banding compensation program at Coregis Group, Inc., *ACA Journal* (Winter 1995), p. 53.

What in essence has occurred is a pay scheme based on the specific competencies an employee possesses. These may include knowledge of the business and its core competencies, skills to fulfill these core requirements, and demonstrated employee behaviors such as leadership, problem solving, decision making, and planning.[49] Based on the degree to which these competencies exist, pay levels are established. In competency-based pay plans, these pre-set levels are called **broad-banding.** A variety of banding programs have been witnessed—some with as few as four bands with no salary ranges, to others with as "many as 13 bands and multiple salary ranges per band."[50] For example, Exhibit 11-8 shows an eight-band compensation program that exists at Coregis Group, Inc. Broad-Banding, too, can be used in developing wage structures on factors other than skills.

Those who possess a level of competencies within a certain range will be grouped together in a pay category. Pay increases then, are awarded for growth in personal competencies, as well as the contribution one makes to the organization. Accordingly, career and pay advancement may not be tied to a promotion, per se, but rather to how much more one is capable of contributing to the organization's goals and objectives.

If you are making the connection to a few pages ago when we discussed the point method of job evaluation, you are reading attentively. However, the point method looked specifically at the job, and its worth to the company. Competency-based pay plans assesses these "points" based on the value added by the employee in assisting the organization in achieving its goals. As more organizations move toward competency-based pay plans, HRM will play a critical role. Just as we discussed in Chapter 5 with respect to human resource planning, once the direction of the organization is established, attracting, developing, motivating, and retaining competent individuals become essential. This will continue to have implications for recruiting, training and development, career development, performance appraisals, as well as pay and reward systems.[51] Not only will HRM ensure that it has the right people at the right place, but it will have assembled a competent team of employees who add significant value to the organization.

Team-Based Compensation

You've just been handed a copy of the course syllabus for a business policy course you're taking this semester, and quickly your eyes glance at how the final grade will be calculated: two tests—a midterm and a final—and a class project. Intrigued, you read further about the class project. You and four other classmates will be responsible for thoroughly analyzing the company's operations. You are to make recommendations about the company's financial picture, human resources, product lines, competitive advantage, and strategic direction. The group is to turn in a report of no less than fifty pages, double-spaced, and make a thirty-minute presentation to the class about your suggested turnaround. The report and presentation account for 75 percent of the course grade, and each member will receive the grade given by the instructor for the project. Not fair? Too much riding on the efforts of others? Welcome to the world of **team-based compensation.**

In today's changing organizations, much more emphasis has been placed on involving employees in most aspects of the job that affect them. When organizations group employees into teams and empower them to meet their goals, teams reap the benefits of their productive effort. That is, team-based compensation plans are tied to team-based performance. For example, at MacAllister Machinery, distributors of Caterpillar tractors in Indianapolis, bonus goals were established for its managers. If goals were achieved, they all shared in the "glory." If any of the managers failed, the entire team would not receive a dime of bonus money. How did the managers react? They pulled together and helped one another, resulting in sales increasing almost 25 percent and profits rising nearly 30 percent. Consequently, each manager received a bonus amounting to 50 percent of his or her salary.[52] The concept is now being driven down to the employee population! Similar programs also exist at DuPont, Monsanto, American Express,[53] DEC, and General Motors.[54]

Under a team-based compensation plan, team members who have worked on achieving—and in many cases, exceeding—established goals often share equally in the rewards (although, in the truest sense, teams allocate their own rewards). By providing for fair treatment of each team member, group cohesiveness

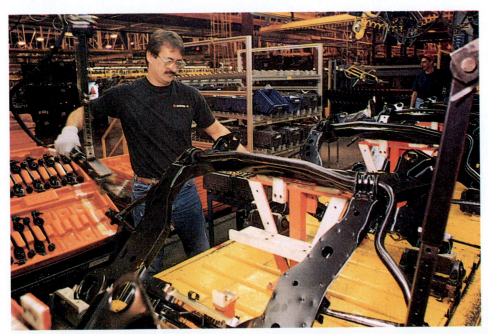

Teams at Saturn find that they can increase their rewards for meeting, and exceeding, their production and quality goals. Moreover, by putting some of their pay at risk, they can earn up to 10 percent extra—based on how well their entire team performs.

Motivating Your Employees

The last thing we would like to do is give one more minute of our workday or what is left of our patience to the 10 to 20 percent of our "challenging employees," that seem to increasingly preoccupy our thoughts and conversations, when our best efforts and coaching sessions seem to fall on deaf ears. Managers/teamleaders simply want employees/team members to fulfill responsibilities in the most time, cost efficient, pleasant manner possible, except sometimes it doesn't seem quite so simple.

Take Ms. U. Owe Me for instance. She possesses basic technical skills to do the job, but basic it is and basic it will be without taking personal responsibility for learning new skills such as an additional computer software program on her own time.

Ms. U. Owe Me may not be motivated—after all, there should be time at work to learn new programs and there should be a personal instructor available as needed—or should there? How do you motivate an employee who expects "the company" to provide all training and development on company time and at company expense?

And Abby Attitude. Abby has a disease—the bad attitude disease—and unfortunately it's beginning to affect the team. It started with complaints about too much to do, grew to include criticisms of the company and manage-

ment, until Abby starts her day the same way she ends it—resenting, defending, denying ownership for her share of affairs.

Take Dave Defensive too, please somebody take Dave. Ask Mr. Defensive and he'll tell you in 30 seconds or less, it's not his fault—it's his boss, it's the company, it's too much to do, not enough time, he can't be responsible. As a manager, on your list of things to do today, be sure you motivate Dave—the tough part will be figuring out how.

Today even productivity is no longer enough—being busy isn't enough. In order to provide our customers with superior—no excuse—on-time, pleasurable service, we must have committed, motivated employees who display a consistent spirit of energy, joy, trust and cooperation.

Regardless of the type of company or position, we all want to work with employees who will occasionally volunteer to come in on their own time, perhaps a Saturday to get caught up, attend a course on their own time and expense, check out business books and videos and return them in a timely manner without being asked or forced, master software programs on their own time, and of course view their positions as a privilege, not a right, an opportunity to grow and contribute.

Perhaps if we all—managers and employees alike—gave ourselves a daily attitude check, adjusted it on the way to work, consciously tried to strengthen relationships throughout the day, and checked sporadically to see if any humor could be extracted, we could avoid the pending fate of Ms. U. Owe Me, Abby Attitude or Dave Defen-

sive. Perhaps if we took ownership not only for the results we produce but the process in which they are achieved. Why not compare how we believe our manager or team leader would rate our attitude with how we rate our own, and if there is a gap, make conscious choices on how to improve it?

Since attitude is a do-it-yourself project and can make or break jobs and careers, we—or Ms. U. Owe Me, Ms. Attitude and Mr. Defensive—might also ask these ten questions:

1. Does this attitude seem to follow me from job to job?
2. How would my co-workers rate my attitude?
3. Do I allow minor issues to become major ones?
4. How open am I to feedback or do I hear it as personal criticism?
5. How long would I pay someone who demonstrated a similar spirit?
6. Is my attitude affecting my working relationships or performance?
7. Is it possible to repair damaged relationships?
8. When a change or suggestion is introduced, do I support it or for every reason given, state at least why it won't work?
9. And speaking of suggestions, do I propose solutions when I voice a complaint, defense, or concern?

After all, this is a new week, new day, why not a new attitude? If not, well, that's another article, another speech, yet another seminar.

DR. CONNIE SITTERLY, CPCM

---

is encouraged.[55] Yet, this does not occur overnight. Rather, it is a function of several key components being in place.[56] For instance, for teams to be effective, they must have a clear purpose and goals. They must understand what is expected of them and that their effort is worthwhile. Teams must also be provided the necessary resources to complete their tasks.[57] Because their livelihood may rest on accomplishing their goals, a lack of requisite resources may doom a team effort before it begins. And finally, there must be mutual trust among the team members. They must respect one another, effectively communicate with one another, and treat each member fairly and equitably. Without these, serious obstacles to teams may exist, which might defeat the purpose that group cohesiveness can foster.

EXECUTIVE COMPENSATION PROGRAMS

Executive pay is merely a special case within the topic of compensation, but it does have several twists that deserve special attention. First, the base salaries of executives are higher than those of low-level managers or operative personnel, and we want to explain why this is so. Second, executives frequently operate under bonus and stock option plans that can dramatically increase their total compensation.[58] A senior executive at American Express, General Electric, or MBNA can, in a good year, earn $10 million, $15 million, or more on top of the base salary.[59] We want to briefly look at how such compensations come about and why. Finally, executives receive perquisites (called perks) or special benefits that others do not. What are these, and how do they impact on executive motivation? These are the topics in this section on compensation.

Salaries of Top Managers

Sanford Weill, Chairman and CEO of the Travelers Group, was recently awarded a salary that made people stop to check if the numbers were correct. In 1997, Coss collected more than $230 million in salary, bonuses, and stock-based incentives.[60] Weill is not alone in this "high salary" category. The 20 top paid CEOs of U.S. companies like Coca-Cola, Intel, Morgan Stanley, Dean Witter, and Occidental Petroleum, averaged more than $60 million in total compensation in 1997. That's more than a 35 percent increase over their 1996 salaries. Incidentally, during this same time frame, the average worker's pay raise was in the 3 percent range (see "Ethical Dilemmas in HRM").[61] Interesting, too, is that not one woman is included in the category of the highest paid CEO in Corporate America. The highest paid woman in Corporate America is Linda Wachner, Chair, CEO, and President of Warnaco Group and Authentic Fitness, who made just nearly $11.5 million in 1997.[62] Moreover, U.S. Chief Executive Officers, on average, make anywhere from 2 to 5 times the compensation of their counterparts in the global village.[63]

It is well known that executives in the private sector receive considerably higher compensation than their counterparts in the public sector. Midlevel executives regularly earn base salaries of $150,000 to $225,000; the CEO of a billion-dollar corporation can expect a minimum total compensation package in excess of $9 million, while base salaries of $1 million or more are not unusual among senior management of Fortune 100 firms. In fact, 480 of the top two executives in the nation's largest 366 companies had salaries exceeding $1 million.[65] How do organizations justify such extraordinary salaries for their executives? The answer is quite simple: economics and motivation.[66] In economic terms, we know that top managers are expected to demonstrate good decision-making abilities. This attribute may not be widely held by all workers. As a result, the supply of qualified senior executives is scarce, and organizations have bid up the price for this talent. They must keep their salaries in line with the competition or potentially lose an executive to another organization. That's exactly what the Board at

Are We Paying U.S. Executives Too Much?

Are we paying U.S. executives too much? Is an average salary in excess of $60 million justifiable? In any debate, there are two sides to the issue. Support for paying this amount is the fact that these executives have tremendous organizational responsibilities. They not only have to manage the organization in today's environment, they must keep it moving into the future. Their jobs are not 9-to-5 jobs, but rather six to seven days a week, often ten to fourteen hours a day. If jobs are evaluated on the basis of skills, knowledge, abilities, and responsibilities, executives should be highly paid.[64] Furthermore, there is the issue of motivation and retention. If you want these individuals to succeed and stay with the company, you must provide a compensation package that motivates them to stay. Incentives based on various measures also provide the impetus for them to excel.

On the other hand, most of the research done on executive salaries questions the linkage to performance. Even when profits are down, many executives are paid handsomely. In fact, American company executives are regarded as some of the highest paid people in the world. On average, their salaries have increased by more than 40 percent per year, while the average worker's salary has increased only about 3 percent during the same time frame. Furthermore, U.S. executives make two to five times the salaries of their foreign counterparts. That's an interesting comparison, especially when you consider that some executives in Japan-based organizations perform better.

Do you believe that U.S. executives are overpaid? What's your opinion?

Source: Wany Grossman and Robert E. Hoskisson, "CEO Pay at the Crossroads of Wall Street and Main: Toward the Strategic Design of Executive Compensation," *The Academy of Management Executive* (February 1998), pp. 43–57; Rana Dogar, "Nineteenth Annual Salary Report," *Working Woman* (February 1998), pp. 24–25; and John Mariotti, "How Much Is Too Much?" *Industry Week* (March 2, 1998), p. 68.

ConAgra learned when its CEO Charles Harper left his $1.27 million job to lead RJR Nabisco—for a $1.18 million raise![67] High salaries also act to attract both top executives and lower level managers. For instance, when Susan Angelo, vice president of Brunswick Savings Bank, wanted to attract excellent executive candidates, she put together a unique compensation package.[68] Under her program, executives are able to go beyond salary deferrals to include deferring their bonuses also. What this has achieved is a flexible compensation system that can be tailored to each executive's needs. High pay not only encourages top-level managers to perform well in order to keep their jobs, but also acts to stimulate lower level managers to work hard so that they can someday move up the ladder to "the big money."[69]

Supplemental Financial Compensation

In 1996, the average compensation for executives in the Fortune 500 companies in the United States was $7.8 million.[70] This figure, as previously mentioned, includes their total compensation—base salary plus bonuses and stock options.[71] Bonuses and stock options dramatically increase the total compensation that executives receive. Much of this additional compensation is obtained through a deferred bonus—that is, the executive's bonus is computed on the basis of some formula, usually taking into account increases in sales and profits. This bonus, although earned in the current period, may be distributed over several future periods. Therefore, it is not unusual for an executive to earn a $1 million bonus but have it paid out at $50,000 a year for twenty years. The major purpose of such deferred compensation is to increase the cost to the executive of leaving the organization. In almost all cases, executives who voluntarily terminate their employment must forfeit their deferred bonuses. One of the main reasons why there are so few voluntary resignations among the ranks of senior management at General Motors is that these executives would lose hundreds of thousands of dollars in deferred income.

Who's the highest paid female executive in the United States? That honor belongs to Linda Wachner, president and CEO of Warnaco and Authentic Fitness Corporations. Her 1996 compensation topped the $10 million mark. Outstanding pay, but clearly well below the highest paid male executive!

Interestingly, another form of bonus, the "hiring bonus," has arisen in the last decade, purposely designed to help senior executives defray the loss of deferred income. It is now becoming increasingly popular to pay senior executives a hiring bonus to sweeten the incentive for them to leave their current employer and forfeit their deferred bonuses and pension rights. These bonuses often do provide deferred income to compensate for loss of pension rights. For example, Kodak paid George Fisher a $5 million signing bonus, and IBM paid Louis Gerstner $4.9 million to join the company to compensate them for giving up deferred compensation and pension and retirement rights.[72]

Stock options also have been a common incentive offered to executives. They generally allow executives to purchase, at some time in the future, a specific amount of the company's stock at a fixed price. Under the assumption that good management will increase the company's profitability and, therefore, the price of the stock, stock options are viewed as performance-based incentives.[73] It should be pointed out, however, that the use of stock options is heavily influenced by the current status of the tax laws. In recent years, tax reform legislation has taken away some of the tax benefits that could accrue through the issuance of stock options.[74] The success, however, of these IRS changes to curb CEO compensation is limited at best. Deferred pay[75] and supplemental retirement plans appear to be vehicles that skirt around the legalities of tax regulations.

Supplemental Nonfinancial Compensation: Perquisites

Executives are frequently offered a smorgasbord of **perquisites** not offered to other employees. The logic of offering these perks, from the organization's perspective, is to attract and keep good managers and to motivate them to work hard in the organization's interest. In addition to the standard benefits offered to all employees (see Chapter 13), some benefits are reserved for privileged executives. They range from an annual physical examination (worth several hundred dollars) to interest-free loans of millions of dollars,[76] which can be worth $100,000 a year or more. Popular perks include the payment of life insurance premiums,[77] club memberships, company automobiles, liberal expense accounts, supplemental disability insurance, supplemental retirement accounts, post-retirement consulting contracts, and personal financial, tax, and legal counseling.[78] Some also may be given mortgage assistance;[79] for example, in organizations like Kaiser Permanente, mortgage loans up to $380,000 are given. At Church and Dwight of Piscataway, New Jersey, not only are individuals able to get up to 15 percent of their mortgage from the employer, if they remain on the job for five years and are active in the community as a volunteer, their debt is considered paid in full.[80]

A popular benefit for top executives that gained popularity in the 1980s and continues today is the golden parachute. The **golden parachute** was designed by top executives as a means of protecting themselves if a merger or hostile takeover occurred.[81] These "parachutes" typically provide either a severance salary to the departing executive or a guaranteed position in the newly created (merged) operation. And at Chrysler, a merger or hostile takeover itself may not be necessary. If in the event of a takeover, for instance, the "acquirer moves to get top executives fired even before a takeover is completed," the golden parachute automatically kicks in.[82] The concept here is to provide an incentive for the executive to stay with the company and "fight" the hostile takeover—rather than leave the organization.

INTERNATIONAL COMPENSATION

Probably the most complex function of international human resource management is the design and implementation of an equitable compensation program.[83] The first step in designing an international compensation package is to determine if there will be one policy applying to all employees or whether parent-country nationals (PCNs), host-country nationals (HCNs), and third-country nationals (TCNs) will be treated differently. Currently American PCNs and HCNs are commonly treated separately, often also differentiating among types of expatriate assignments (temporary or permanent transfer) or employee status (executive, professional, or technical). It is also necessary to thoroughly understand the statutory requirements of each country to ensure compliance with local laws.[84] International compensation packages in the United States generally utilize the "balance-sheet approach," which considers four factors: base pay, differentials, incentives, and assistance programs.[85]

> International compensation packages generally utilize base pay, differentials, incentives, and assistance programs.

Base Pay

Ideally this is equal to the pay of employees in comparable jobs at home, but the range of pay scales in most countries is far narrower than in the United States. Thus, where a middle manager in a U.S. factory might earn $75,000 a year, the same manager in Germany might earn $110,000. However, the U.S. higher level executive might earn $500,000 and her counterpart in Germany only $150,000.00. How can human resource managers satisfy the middle manager who earns a third less than the counterpart where he works, while also satisfying the German executive who earns less than her U.S. counterpart?

In addition to considerations of fairness among overseas employees, foreign currencies and laws must be considered. Should expatriates be paid in U.S. dollars, or the local currency—or a combination of the two? How will the organization deal with changes in currency values? Are there restrictions on either bringing in or taking out dollars or the local currency? If so, how will savings be handled? Should salary increases be made according to the same standards as those established for domestic employees, or according to local standards? Will the expatriate pay U.S. or foreign income taxes?

Taxation is a major factor in calculating equitable base pay rates. If there are substantial differences in tax rates, as for instance in Sweden, where income taxes are about 50 percent, will the base pay be adjusted for the actual loss of net income? While the U.S. Department of State has negotiated agreements with every country to determine where income will be taxed, the protection of income from a tax rate other than the domestic one creates new administrative requirements for the organization. Almost all multinational corporations have some tax protection plan so that the expatriate doesn't pay more in taxes than if she were in her home country.

Differentials

The cost of living is not the same around the world, although the value of the dollar to foreign currencies will affect price; a six-pack of Coca-Cola may cost $2.39 in New York, $3.55 in Paris, and $5.51 in Tokyo; a gallon of premium gasoline $1.26 in New York, $3.69 in Paris, and $4.19 in Tokyo.[86] Differentials are intended to offset the higher costs of overseas goods, services, and housing. The Department of State, which has employees in almost every country in the world, publishes a regularly updated comparison of global costs of living that is used by most multinational corporations for providing differentials to maintain the standards of living the expatriate would enjoy if he or she were home.[87]

Incentives

Not all employees are willing to be separated for long periods of time from family, friends, and the comfort of home support systems. Thus, mobility inducements to go on foreign assignments are regularly offered. These may include monetary payments or services, such as housing, car, chauffeur, and other incentives. But how should a hardship premium be paid? As a percent of salary? In a lump sum payment? In the home or the foreign currency? If foreign housing is provided, what happens to the vacant home back in the States or to the family housing situation when they eventually return? Incentives require careful planning before, during, and after the overseas assignment.

Assistance Programs

As with any relocation, the overseas transfer requires a lot of expenditures for the employee's family. Some of the assistance programs commonly offered by multinational corporations include: household goods shipping and storage; major appliances; legal clearance for pets and their shipment; home sale/rental protection; automobile protection; temporary living expenses; travel, including pre-relocation visits and annual home leaves; special/emergency return leaves; education allowances for children; club memberships (for corporate entertaining); and security (including electronic systems and bodyguards).

Clearly the design of a compensation system for employees serving overseas is complex and requires enormous administrative expertise, particularly when an organization has expatriates posted in forty or fifty different countries.

SUMMARY

This summary relates to the Learning Objectives provided on p. 320.
After having read this chapter, you should know:

1. Rewards are the final link in the motivation model. After the effort has been expended, successful performance happens, and organizational goals are achieved, individuals are now ready to have their particular goals met. These goals, or rewards, can come in a variety of types.

2. Rewards can be classified as (1) intrinsic or extrinsic, (2) financial or nonfinancial, or (3) performance-based or membership-based.

3. Some rewards are membership-based because one receives them for simply belonging to the organization. Employee benefits are an example of membership-based rewards, in that every employee gets them irrespective of performance levels.

4. Compensation administration seeks to design a cost-effective pay structure that will not only attract, motivate, and retain competent employees, but also be perceived as fair by these employees.

5. Job evaluation systematically determines the value of each job in relation to all jobs within the organization. The four basic approaches to job evaluation are: (1) the ordering method, (2) the classification method, (3) the factor comparison method, and (4) the point method.

6. The final wage structure evolves from job evaluation input, wage survey data, and the creation of wage grades.

7. Competency-based compensation views employees as a competitive advantage in the organization. Compensation systems are established in terms of the knowledge and skills employees possess, and the behaviors that they demonstrate. Possession of these three factors is evaluated and compensated according to a broad-banded salary range established by the organization.

8. Executive compensation is higher than that of rank-and-file personnel and also includes other financial and nonfinancial benefits not otherwise available to operative employees. This is done to attract, retain, and motivate executives to higher performance levels.

9. The balance sheet approach to international compensation takes into account base pay, differentials, incentives, and assistance programs.

EXPERIENTIAL EXERCISE:
Wage Structures

Interview a **compensation specialist** in the human resources department of your employer, college, university, hospital, or other organization by asking the following questions within 15 minutes. Summarize your results in a one- to two-paged typed report for your class team discussion or class 5 minute presentation. You may also want to develop a comparison chart based on your team's results, depending on your findings.

Questions

1. Could you share a job description of a compensation specialist?
2. Do you participate in wage surveys? Could you provide results of a recent survey or samples of types of questions asked?
4. What factors are considered in developing wage surveys?
5. What type of plans are used here—piecework, merit, team based, competency based, or other? How are they implemented?
6. Do you use the Scanlon Plan, IMPROSHARE or another system?
7. Do you have any samples or printouts of forms used?

WEB-WISE EXERCISES

Search and print findings of interest from the following sites:
Web Wise
Benefitslink http://www.benefitslink.com/
Search, record the Web address for future reference and for your team, and print findings for the following organizations:

American Benefits Association

Families and Work Institute

National Council on Aging

Bureau of National Affairs

Pension Benefit Guaranty Corporation
http://www.pbgc.gov
Visit the Web site of Benefit Software, Inc. for information about benefit statements and to receive a sample benefit statement:

http://www.bsiweb.com

Search and print findings from the following sites:

American Compensation Association
http:/www.acaonline.org/

Search and print findings about compensation, design, implementation, and management of employee compensation programs from Web site **American Compensation Association http://www/ahrm.org/aca.htm.** This organization is composed of academics, consultants, and professionals active in design, implementation, and management of employment compensation programs.

CASE APPLICATION:
Pay for Performance

A Pittsburgh-based company, Black Box Corporation which markets computer network and other communication devices, developed an innovative solution providing compensation and productivity. After it flattened its organization, management was unable to offer promotions like those offered prior to the flattening. In response, the company offered employees the ability to advance themselves in skills and compensation. For example, an order-entry clerk who starts at the $17,000 to $20,000 level can make as much as $35,000 by increasing their value to the company, as measured by a number of objective tests.

Pay for performance has worked so well for Black Box Corporation that it has integrated incentives into nearly every aspect of its culture. Black Box uses a system of objective criteria by which management can measure both employee and company performance. Employees are divided into three classes—developmental, competent, and premium—according to their impact on the company and are then paid according to a range within those categories as determined by objective evaluations. For example, order-entry clerks increase their value as they improve their ability to speak to their inter-

national customers in their native languages. Black Box monitors and tests clerks on the number of calls they can field and how well they handle them, the number of errors, etc.

Each measure comes with pay consequences because each contributes to productivity and customer satisfaction. The company also reimburses 100 percent of tuition for job-related course work if the employee can demonstrate competency when the course is completed. Many employees can leap over several pay grades even when they just joined the company. Black Box believes that if someone can perform consistently to the next level of expectation, then they have earned the right to be at the next level and to be compensated accordingly. If employees don't perform up to the level of their compensation, they can be downgraded, but the company gives them a set period of time to raise their performance. The results are impressive; Black Box has continued to expand the company without increasing its head count.
permission pending

Adapted from Alan Reder, "Pay, "75 Best Business Practices for Socially Responsible Companies," Chap. 12, G. P. Putnam's Sons, 1995.

Questions

1. Would you prefer a compensation system as described or a more traditional system, and why?
2. What advantages do you think such a pay for performance system provides?
3. What challenges would such a system face with employees?

TESTING YOUR UNDERSTANDING

How well did you fulfill the learning objectives?
1. Employees respond to organizational rewards for all of these reasons except
   a. people behave in ways that they believe are in their best interests.
   b. people constantly look for payoffs for their efforts.
   c. people expect that good job performance will lead to organizational goal attainment that will lead to satisfying individual needs or goals.
   d. organizations use rewards to motivate employees.
   e. employees often respond to peer pressure.
2. What is the difference between financial and nonfinancial rewards?
   a. Financial rewards (such as salary) are taxable. Nonfinancial rewards (such as daycare spending accounts) provide tax shelters.
   b. Financial rewards are a matter of public record. Nonfinancial rewards are not a matter of public record.

c. Financial rewards make life better off the job. Nonfinancial rewards make life better on the job.

d. Financial rewards are fixed according to a compensation schedule. Nonfinancial rewards are variable in nature.

e. Financial rewards provide the same motivation levels for all employees. Nonfinancial rewards provide differing levels of motivation.

3. Good organizational reward systems have all of the following qualities except

a. they are individualized to reflected differences in what employees consider important to them.

b. they are perceived as equitable.

c. they are visible and flexible.

d. they are based on seniority.

e. they are allocated at a relatively low cost.

4. Fairness, in the context of a compensation system, means all of the following except

a. a wage adequate for the demands of the job, from the organization's perspective.

b. employees' perception of an appropriate balance in terms of their efforts–rewards ratio compared to a relevant standard.

c. employees' perception that they are treated better than similar workers in competing organizations.

d. pay rates are established according to a job's comparative worth.

e. reasonable cost-minimization by organizations.

5. A compensation analyst for a large firm is completing a job evaluation for her organization. Identifiable criteria for jobs (skill, effort, responsibility) were determined and points were assigned, based on weighting factors. Several degrees of competency were identified for each of the job criteria. All jobs were then categorized according to these rating scales. What job evaluation method was used?

a. ordering

b. classification

c. factor comparison

d. point method

e. core specification

6. Rachel works for a textile manufacturer as a seamstress. She is paid $0.05 for each sleeve she sews an hour, up to 100 sleeves. She is paid $0.09 for each sleeve she produces over the first 100. What kind of compensation system is used?

a. piecework

b. time-saving bonus

c. commission

d. Scanlon Plan

e. IMPROSHARE

7. Last year, an aerospace engineer made $110,000. His annual base pay was $100,000. The remainder was calculated based on his ability to work faster than the standard hour's work. What kind of compensation system was used?

a. piecework

b. time-saving bonus

c. commission

d. Scanlon Plan

e. IMPROSHARE

8. Competency-based compensation systems can best be described as

a. paying employees according to their knowledge, skills, and demonstrated behaviors.

b. paying employees according to how educated they are and the number of advanced degrees they possess.

c. pay systems that promote team-based incentives.

d. incentive systems whereby strategic goals of the organization are replaced by the value-added nature of employee skills.

e. paying employees according to a piecework system whereby a sophisticated formula is used to determine the dollar value of the employee's bonus.

9. Team-based compensation programs reward employees for achieving unit and organizational goals. Under which situation would a team-based compensation most likely function well?

a. A situation in which a team of workers perform mutually exclusive, independent tasks.

b. A situation in which a team of workers have mutual distrust for one another.

c. A situation where work tasks are woven together such that the work of any one individual is difficult to assess.

d. A situation in which competition among employees is encouraged and fostered.

e. A situation in which group values conform to limiting production.

10. United States organizations justify high salaries for their executives in all of these ways except

a. good decision-making ability is not widely represented in the work force.

b. global competition requires that the United States matches the salaries given to executives in other countries.

c. organizations must pay high prices for scarce executives.

d. high salaries are necessary to keep executives from going over to the competition.

e. high executive salaries attract good workers throughout managerial levels of an organization.

11. Bill, a U.S. computer programmer, reluctantly moved his family to Saudi Arabia for a three-year assignment with his firm. A hardship premium, equal to his annual U.S. salary, was deposited in a U.S. account for each six months of his assignment. What kind of pay factor was used?

a. base pay

b. differentials

c. bonuses

d. incentives

e. assistance programs

12. All of the following questions should be addressed when considering base pay for expatriates except
   a. is the cost of living the same in the host country as in the United States?
   b. will the expatriate pay U.S. or foreign income tax?
   c. should expatriates be paid in U.S. dollars or local currency?
   d. are there restrictions on taking money into or out of the host country?
   e. should salary increases be made according to local standards or U.S. standards?

13. Membership-based rewards include all of the following except
   a. cost-of-living allowances.
   b. benefit provisions.
   c. pay increases for seniority.
   d. pay increases for completion of a college degree.
   e. commissions.

14. Compensation administration is
   a. more heavily influenced by government policies than is strategic human resource planning.
   b. less influenced by government policies than is strategic human resource planning.
   c. less influenced by government policies than is orientation.
   d. influenced at the state, but not the national, level.
   e. influenced at the national, but not the state, level.

15. Specific provisions of the Fair Labor Standards Act include all of the following except
   a. child labor laws.
   b. overtime pay of at least $1\frac{1}{2}$ times regular pay for all hours worked over forty per week.
   c. some categories of workers, such as apprentices or full-time students, may be paid less than the minimum wage under special certificates issued by the Department of Labor.
   d. where federal law differs from state law, federal law prevails.
   e. minimum wage and other relevant information must be posted publicly where employees can readily see it.

16. Pay adjustments designed to maintain the standard of living for an expatriate that she would enjoy at home are called
   a. base pay.
   b. differentials.
   c. bonuses.
   d. incentives.
   e. assistance programs.

Endnotes

1. Vignette is based on J. Finegan, "Pipe Dreams," *Inc.* (August 1994), pp. 64–70.

2. Stephenie Overman, "How Hot Is Your Reward System?" *HRMagazine* (November 1994), p. 51.

3. Clifford J. Mottaz, "Determinants of Organizational Commitment," *Human Relations* (June 1988), pp. 467–482.

4. Philip A. Rudolph and Brian H. Kleiner, "The Art of Motivating Employees," *Journal of Managerial Psychology* (May 1989), pp. i–iv.

5. Jim Braham, "A Rewarding Place to Work," *Industry Week* (September 18, 1989), p. 15.

6. "The Pay Gap Narrows, But," *Fortune* (September 19, 1994), p. 32.

7. Judith M. Collins and Paul M. Muchinsky, "An Assessment of the Construct Validity of Three Job Evaluation Methods: A Field Experiment," *Academy of Management Journal,* Vol. 36, No. 4 (1993), p. 895.

8. "Pay Equity," *Executive Female* (March–April 1991), p. 9.

9. Ibid.

10. Richard Henderson, *Compensation Management: Rewarding Performance,* 6th ed. (Englewood Cliffs, N.J.: Prentice-Hall, 1994), p. 223.

11. Ibid.

12. Ibid.

13. John D. McMullen and Cynthia G. Brondi, "Job Evaluation Generate the Numbers," *Personnel Journal* (November 1986), p. 62.

14. See, for example, Henderson, p. 266.

15. David W. Bedler, *Compensation Administration* (Englewood Cliffs, N.J.: Prentice-Hall, 1974), p. 157.

16. Richard D. Arvey, "Sex Bias in Job Evaluation Procedures," *Personnel Psychology* (Summer 1986), pp. 316–318.

17. For a thorough mathematical discussion of various methods of determining the pay structure, see Henderson, Chap. 11, "Design a Base Pay Structure."

18. Henderson, pp. 315–316.

19. Jack C. O'Brien and Robert A. Zawacki, "Salary Surveys: Are They Worth the Effort?" *Personnel* (October 1985), pp. 70–73.

20. Margaret Dyekman, "Take the Mystery Out of Salary Surveys," *Personnel Journal* (June 1990), p. 105.

21. See, for example, Rosabeth Moss Kanter, "The Attack on Pay," *Harvard Business Review* (March–April 1987), pp. 60–67.

22. Earl Ingram II, "Compensation: The Advantage of Knowledge-Based Pay," *Personnel Journal* (April 1990), p. 138.

23. Stephen H. Applebaum and Barbara T. Shapiro, "Pay for Performance: Implementation of Individual and Group Plans," *Journal of Management Development* (July 1991) pp. 30–40.

24. Joseph Spiers, "Wages Are Starting to Inch Up," *Fortune* (June 1, 1992), p. 17.

25. Luis R. Gomez-Mejia and David B. Balkin, "Effectiveness of Individual and Aggregate Compensation Strategies," *Industrial Relations* (1989), pp. 431–445.

26. Ibid., p. 20.

27. Hoyt Doyel and Thomas Riley, "Incentive Plans," *Management Review* (March 1987), pp. 36–37; and K. Dow Scott, Steven E. Markham, and Richard W. Robers, "Compensation," *Personnel Journal* (September 1987), pp. 114–115.

28. Howard Gleckman, Sandra Atchison, Tim Smart, and John A. Byrne, "Bonus Pay: Buzzword or Bonanza?" *Business Week* (November 14, 1994), p. 62.

29. L. Kate Beatty, "Pay and Benefits Break Away from Tradition," *HRMagazine* (November 1994), p. 64.

30. Donna Fenn, "Compensation: Goal-Driven Incentives," *Inc.* (August 1996), p. 91; and Michael A. Verespej, "More Value for Compensation," *Industry Week* (June 17, 1996), p. 20.

31. Michael A. Verespej, "Top-to-Bottom Incentives," *Industry Week* (February 3, 1997), p. 30; and Stephanie Overman, "Saturn Teams Working and Profiting," *HRMagazine* (March 1995), p. 72.

32. Thomas B. Wilson, "Group Incentives: Are You Ready?" *Journal of Compensation and Benefits* (November 1990), pp. 25–29.

33. Commerce Clearing House, *Human Resource Management: Ideas and Trends* (May 17, 1990), p. 84.

34. Harold Stieglitz, "The Kaiser Steel Union Sharing Plan," *National Industrial Conference Board Studies in Personnel Policy Number 187* (New York, 1963).

35. Henderson, p. 461. For an interesting overview of the Lincoln Electric program, see Richard M. Hodgetts, "Discussing Incentive Compensation with Donald Hastings of Lincoln Electric," *Compensation and Benefits Review* (September/October 1997), pp. 60–66; and Richard M. Hodgetts, "A Conversation with Donald F. Hastings of the Lincoln Electric Company," *Organizational Dynamics* (Winter 1997), pp 68–72.

36. Ibid., p. 462

37. Ibid., pp. 455–458.

38. Ibid., p. 457; and Charles R. Gowen III, "Gainsharing Programs: An Overview of History and Research," *Journal of Organizational Behavior Management* (1990), pp. 77–99.

39. Roget T. Kaufman, "The Effects of IMPROSHARE on Productivity," *Industrial and Labor Relations Review* (January 1992), p. 311.

40. Ibid.

41. Ibid., pp. 319–322.

42. Ronald Recardo and Diane Pricone, "How to Determine Whether Gainsharing Is for You," *Industrial Management* (January/February 1996), pp. 12; and Robert McGarvey "Share the Wealth," *Entrepreneur* (April 1997), pp. 78–79.

43. Based on Nancy J. Perry, "Talk About Pay for Performance," *Fortune* (May 4, 1992), p. 77.

44. See John Greenwald, "Workers: Rules and Rewards," *Time* (April 15, 1991), pp. 42–43.

45. Spragins, p. 79.

46. Peter V. LeBlanc, and Christian M. Ellis, "The Many Faces of Banding," *ACA Journal* (Winter 1995), p. 53.

47. Towers Perrin, "Competency-Based Pay: Paying People, Not Jobs," presented at *The National Conference on Using Competency-Based Tools and Applications to Drive Organizational Performance* (Boston, Mass.: November 2–4, 1994), p. 8.

48. Bill Merrick, "Skill-and Competency-Based Compensation," *Credit Union Magazine* (June 1996), p. 11; and Marc E. Lattoni, and Andree Mercier, "Developing Competency-Based Organizations and Pay Systems," *Focus: A Review of Human Resource Management Issues in Canada* (Calgary, Canada: Towers Perrin, Summer 1994), p. 18.

49. Gary I. Bergel, "Choosing the Right Pay Delivery System to Fit Banding," *Compensation and Benefits Review* (July–August 1994), pp. 34–39; and Sandra O'Neal, "Competencies: The DNA of the Corporation," *ACA Journal* (Winter 1993/94), pp. 6–12.

50. Peter V. LeBlanc and Christian M. Ellis, "The Many Faces of Banding," p. 54; and Larry Reissman, "Nine Common Myths About Broadbands," *HRMagazine* (August 1995), pp. 79–85.

51. Lattoni and Mercier, p. 7.

52. "Compensation: Sales Managers as Team Players," *Inc.* (August 1994), p. 102.

53. Howard Gleckman, Sandra Atchison, Tim Smart, and John A. Byrne, "Bonus Pay: Buzzword or Bonanza?" *Business Week* (November 14, 1994), pp. 62–64.

54. T. M. Wellborne and L. R. Gomez-Mejia, "Team Incentives in the Work Place," in L. Berger (ed.), *Handbook of Wage and Salary Administration* (New York: McGraw-Hill, 1991), pp. 236–247.

55. Henderson, p. 407.

56. See Stephen P. Robbins and David A. DeCenzo, *Fundamentals of Management* (Englewood Cliffs, N.J.: Prentice-Hall, 1995), p. 262.

57. See, for instance, C. James Novak, "Proceed with Caution When Paying Teams," *HRMagazine* (April 1997), pp. 73–75.

58. Wany Grossman, and Robert E. Hoskisson, "CEO Pay at the Crossroads of Wall Street and Main: Toward the Strategic Design of Executive Compensation," *The Academy of Management Executive* (February 1998), pp. 43–57.

59. Jennifer Reingold, Richard A. Melcher, and Gary McWilliams, "Executive Pay," *Business Week* (April 20, 1998), pp. 64–70.

60. Ibid., p. 64.

61. See, for instance, John Mariotti, "How Much Is Too Much?" *Industry Week* (March 2, 1998), p. 68.

62. "Is Warnaco Chairman an Overpaid Woman?" *Baltimore Sun* (April 11, 1998), p. C-12; and Rana Dogar, "Nineteenth Annual Salary Report," *Working Woman* (February 1998), pp. 24–25.

63. "Chief Executive Pay in 12 Countries," *Manpower Argus* (February 1997), p. 4; and "Executive Pay in Europe," *Manpower Argus* (November 1996), p. 4.

64. Sal F. Marino, "Chief Executives Are Underpaid," *Industry Week* (April 20, 1998), p. 22.

65. Based on data presented in Jennifer Reingold, "Executive Pay," pp. 71–111.

66. Dawn Harris and Constance Helfat, "Specificity of CEO Human Capital and Compensation," *Strategic Management Journal* (December 1997), pp. 895–920; and Rob Norton, "Making Sense of the Boss's Pay," *Fortune* (October 3, 1994), p. 36.

67. "If the Pay's the Thing, Jump Ship," *Business Week* (Febraury 12, 1996), p. 8.

68. Jill Andresky Frazer, "Beyond the 401(K)," Inc. (July 1991), pp. 103–104.

69. David Berman, "Do They Deserve It?" *Canadian Business* (September 26, 1997), p. 31.

70. Jennifer Reingold, "Executive Pay," p. 65.

71. For a good review of stock options and their use in organizations, see Edward O. Welles, "Stock Options," *Inc.* (February 1998), pp. 85–97; and Roger Brossy and John E. Balkcom, "Case Studies: Executive Compensation: Finding a Balance in the Quest for Value," *Compensation and Benefits Review* (January–February 1998), pp. 29–34.

72. Ibid.

73. For another perspective on stock options and their effect on profits, see Edward O. Welles, "Stock Options," *Inc.* (February 1998), p. 97; and Jack Stack, "The Problem with Profit Sharing," *Inc.* (November 1996), pp. 67–69.

74. Mark D. Fefer, "Your CEO Will Get Paid," *Fortune* (October 3, 1994), p. 18.

75. Ibid. Under IRS regulations, beginning in 1994, annual salaries paid to a company's five top officers in a publicly held firm are not tax deductible if the salaries are over $1 million. Most companies have simply ignored this new ruling, while others are deferring the excess income for these executives until retirement.

76. "In a Cost-Cutting Era, Many CEOs Enjoy Imperial Perks," *The Wall Street Journal* (March 7, 1995), p. B1; B16.

77. Current tax laws require tax to be paid on that amount of premium paid on life insurance over $50,000. Furthermore, Section 89 of the IRS Tax Code requires that those perks offered to the higher paid employees, that are not given to the average employee, be considered taxable income to the recipient.

78. See, for example, Felix Kessler, "Executive Perks Under Fire," *Fortune* (July 22, 1985), pp. 29–30.

79. "Housing Assistance Gain as an Employee Benefit," *The Wall Street Journal* (September 24, 1991), p. A-1.

80. Ibid.

81. Jennifer Reingold, "Where Parting Is Such a Sweet Deal," *Business Week* (March 31, 1997), pp. 42–43.

82. Gabriella Stern and Joann S. Lublin, "Chrysler Has Bold New Idea–In Parachutes," *The Wall Street Journal* (July 12, 1995), pp. B1; B11.

83. For further reading on international compensation, see J. Blade Corwin, "Compensation Survey: What It Costs to Hire an Offshore Sourcing Manager," *Bobbin* (February 1998), pp. 58–59; and Peter J. Dowling, Randall S. Schuler, and Denice E. Welch, *International Dimensions of Human Resource Management,* 2nd ed. (Belmont, Calif.: Wadsworth, 1994), Chapter 6.

84. Anne V. Corey, "Ensuring Strength in Each Country: A Challenge for Corporate HQ Global HR Executives," *Human Resource Planning,* Vol. 14, No. 1 (1991), pp. 1–8.

85. Edward M. Mervosh, "Managing Expatriate Compensation," *Industry Week* (July 21, 1997), pp. 13–18; and Calvin Reynolds, "Compensation of Overseas Personnel," in *Handbook of Human Resources Administration,* 2d ed., Joseph J. Famularo (ed.) (New York: McGraw-Hill, 1986), pp. 56-2, 56-3.

86. "I'll Take Manhattan," *Fortune* (May 1991), p. 120.

87. "How Far the Paycheck Stretches," *Global Finance* (February 1998), pp. 8–9; and U.S. Department of State, *Indexes of Living Costs Abroad, Quarters, Allowances, and Hardship Differentials* (Washington, D.C.: Bureau of Labor Statistics, published quarterly).

12. Employee Benefits

LEARNING OBJECTIVES

After reading this chapter you will be able to:

1. Explain the linkage of benefits to motivation.
2. Discuss why employers offer benefits to their employees.
3. Contrast Social Security, unemployment compensation, and workers' compensation benefits.
4. Identify and describe three major types of health insurance options.
5. Discuss the important implications of the Employee Retirement Income Security Act.
6. Outline and describe major types of pension programs offered by organizations.
7. Explain the reason companies offer vacation benefits to their employees.
8. Describe the purpose of disability insurance programs.
9. Discuss what is meant by the term family-friendly benefits.
10. List the various types of flexible benefit option programs.

*W*alk toward the office of Fran Sussner Rogers, at Work/Family Directions, and posted on the outside of her Boston, Massachusetts, office door is a sign: "President Fran's Office—Otherwise Known as Mom." This nameplate on her door was made by her son and done in magic marker.[1]

Fran Rogers has always believed that meeting the needs of employees required more than simply paying them and offering a slate of employee benefits. That's because she recognized that balancing the realities of one's work and personal life is difficult. More importantly, she knew that problems employees face in their personal lives will ultimately show up on their performance at work. One of the more critical problems is associated with finding quality child

Fran Sussner Rodgers recognized that productivity and commitment suffer when employees must choose between ambition and caring for personal needs and family. She saw many workplace adaptations that could solve this dilemma in a way that is good for the organization and the individual. Fran started Work/Family Directions, an organization that helps companies with employee issues—like finding adequate child care and elder care providers and creating flexible workplaces and management practices.

care. She believed that companies had to help their employees in this endeavor. Otherwise, productivity would be adversely affected. Helping employees, after all, was the humane thing to do. It was also a way for an organization to provide an employee benefit that employees desire.

Work/Family Directions began in 1983. Working with a client organization, IBM, Rogers attempted to help the organization's employees find quality child care in the Boca Raton, Florida, area. Rogers succeeded in helping these IBM employees—and Work/Family Directions was off and running. Today, the company has grown to 247 employees and has revenues of $50 million. Its client list now boasts corporations such as Xerox, American Express, and NationsBank.

Fran Sussner Rogers may have found a secret to one aspect of employee benefits: by helping companies recognize that giving something of value to its employees can reap many benefits for all involved. She continues her crusade for organizations to make significant investments in work- and family-related issues. She wants organizations to do more—like helping individuals with problems they face not only with day care or elder care, but with anything that employees deal with over their life cycle.

INTRODUCTION

When an organization is designing its overall compensation program, one of the critical areas of concern is what benefits should be provided. Today's workers expect more than just an hourly wage or a salary from their employer;

they want additional considerations that will enrich their lives. These considerations in an employment setting are called **employee benefits.**[2] Employee benefits have grown in importance and variety over the past several decades. Once perceived as an added feature for an organization to provide its employees, employee benefit administration has transformed itself into a well-thought-out, well-organized package. Employers realize that the benefits provided to employees have an effect on whether applicants accept their employment offers or, once employed, whether workers will continue to stay with the organization. Benefits, therefore, are necessary components of an effectively functioning compensation program.[3]

The irony, however, is that while benefits must be offered to attract and retain good workers, benefits as a whole do not directly affect a worker's performance. Benefits are generally membership-based, offered to employees regardless of their performance levels. While this does not appear to be a logical business practice, there is evidence that the absence of adequate benefits and services for employees contributes to employee dissatisfaction and increased absenteeism and turnover.[4] Accordingly, because the negative effect of failing to provide adequate benefits is so great, organizations spend tens of billions of dollars annually to ensure that valuable benefits are available for each worker.

Over the decades, the nature of benefits has changed drastically. The benefits offered in the early 1900s clearly were different from those offered today. In the early 1900s, much emphasis was placed on time off from work. As the first personnel departments arrived on the scene, their main emphasis was to ensure that workers were "happy and healthy." This meant that their responsibility was to administer such benefits as scheduled vacations, company picnics, and other social activities for workers. Later, around the late 1930s, the practice of having employees complete a sign-up card for some type of health insurance came about. Those days of simplicity for the organization, unfortunately, are long gone. Federal legislation, labor unions, and the changing work force have all led to growth in benefit offerings. Today's organizational benefits are more widespread, more creative, and clearly more abundant. As indicated in Exhibit 12-1, the benefits offered to employees as we enter the new millennium are designed to ensure something of value for each worker.

The Costs of Providing Employee Benefits

Most of us are aware of inflation and the effect it has had on the wages and salaries of virtually every job in the United States. It seems incredible that only sixty-five years ago, a worker earning $100.00 a week was ranked among the top 10 percent of wage earners in the United States. Although we are aware that hourly wages and monthly salaries have increased slightly in recent years, we often overlook the more rapid growth in benefits offered to employees. Since the cost of employing workers includes both direct compensation and the corresponding benefits and services, the growth in both benefits and services has resulted in dramatic increases in labor costs to organizations. What do these dramatic cost increases mean for employers? From 1980 to 1996, the cost of providing something of value to each employee increased from $5,560 to $10,213 per year,[5] with the greatest cost being incurred in retiree benefits.[6] Furthermore,

HEALTH INSURANCE		OTHER BENEFITS:	
Medical Care	82	Employee Parking	88
Extended Care	67	Educational Assistance	85
Dental	62	Employee Assistance Programs	62
Vision	26	Travel Insurance	44
Substance Abuse Treatment	80	Severance Pay	42
		Flexible Spending Accounts	12
RETIREMENT PLANS:		Wellness Programs	37
Defined Benefit	56	Relocation Allowance	31
Defined Contribution	49	Elder Care	31
401 (k)s	29	Child Care	7
Profit Sharing	13		
Stock Plans	8	PAID TIME OFF:	
		Vacations	97
LIFE/DISABILITY:		Holidays	91
Life	91	Funeral Leave	90
Accident	44	Funeral Leave	83
Long-term Disability	41	Sick Leave	65
		Military Leave	54
		Personal Leave	21

SOURCE: U.S. Bureau of the Census, *Statistical Abstracts of the United States, 1997* (Washington, D.C.: Government Printing Office, 1997), p. 435.

Exhibit 12-1

Major employee benefit offered (percent of employers participating).

in the early 1980s, the cost of employee benefits was just over 9 percent of corporate revenues generated.[7] Today, benefit and service offerings add about 40 percent to an organization's payroll cost.[8] And that's comparable to benefit costs in other countries—like Russia where the additional benefit payroll cost is 39 percent.[9]

Employers have also found that benefits present attractive areas of negotiation when large wage and salary increases are not feasible. For example, if employees were to purchase life insurance on their own, they would have to pay for it with net dollars, that is, with what they have left after paying taxes. If the organization pays for it, the benefit is nontaxable (the premiums paid on insurance up to $50,000) for each employee.[10]

Benefits for the New Millennium

There has been a dramatic increase in the number and types of benefits offered and an equally sensational increase in their costs. What has triggered the sweeping changes in benefits offerings that will carry us into the next millennium? The answer to that question lies, in part, in the demographic composition of the work force.

Benefits offered to employees reflect many of the trends existing in our labor force. As the decades have witnessed drastic changes in educational levels, family status, and employee expectations, benefits have had to be adjusted to meet the needs of the workers.[11] What specifically have we seen over the past

Benefits offered to employees reflect many of the trends existing in our labor force.

few decades with respect to demographic changes? Let's explore a few factors to show why the benefits offered today are different from those offered thirty years ago.

Recall from Chapter 2 our discussion of the changing work force. Let's review this matter with an eye on benefits. As recently as the early 1960s, the work force was composed of a relatively homogeneous group—predominately males. This typical male had a wife who stayed home and cared for their children—necessitating a relatively standard benefit need. That is, most of these workers required a retirement plan, sick leave, vacation time, and health insurance. Providing these to workers was customary, and for the most part, uncomplicated. However, the typical worker of the early 1960s is rare in today's work force. Dual-career couples, singles, singles with children, and individuals caring for their parents (elder care) are now widely prevalent in the work force.[12] Equally important is the topic of benefit coverage for a worker's significant other—called **domestic partner benefits.** Domestic partner benefits typically include medical, dental, or vision coverage for an employee's live-in partner—whether or not that live-in partner is the opposite sex. Approximately 10 percent of all major corporations—like Apple Computer and Disney—offer such benefits.[13]

Today's organizations must be able to satisfy diverse benefit needs of its employees. Consequently, organizational benefit programs are being adjusted to reflect a different focus. This is required in order to achieve the goal of "something of value" for each worker.

The Linkage to Motivation

Wait a minute! The linkage to motivation? In the previous chapter, and even a few paragraphs ago, we stated that benefits are membership-based, and are provided to employees regardless of performance. How, then, can they be linked to the motivation process? If you're seeing this potential contradiction, you're paying close attention.

Let's review the motivation process we laid out several chapters ago (see Exhibit 12-2). Benefits may become a critical link to this process if organizations tailor them to meet the specific needs of employees. For instance, if each employee is given the same benefits package, regardless of their situation or needs (the traditional approach), then, yes, benefits may have little effect on one's motivation. But if employees have the opportunity to pick and choose the benefits most useful to them, then behavior can be influenced. Let's explain this using a classroom analogy.

Your professor has laid out a syllabus that attempts to meet your specific needs. In the syllabus, you were informed of the professor's policy permitting each student to drop one test score—their lowest grade of the four exams scheduled in the course. While that consideration (benefit) may be available to everyone, it may not be appealing enough. After all, you still have to take all four exams, and generally, you have done well in classes like this. Getting four "A's" on the exams, and getting to drop one for final grade determination, may not meet your individual goal. Hence, its effect on your performance may be minimal. However, your professor is well known and respected in the business community. You know that a letter of recommendation from the professor to a specific company representative could provide you that edge you need to land that "great" job you want after graduation. But the professor doesn't write letters

Exhibit 12-2

Benefits and the link to motivation.

of recommendation freely. Instead, you notice on the syllabus that letters of recommendations will be written only for students who achieve a class standing in the top 5 percent. You value this benefit, so you have to perform so as to be one of the "chosen," in order to fulfill your individual goal.

So while it's generally true that organizations may not get the most out of their benefits packages, there are avenues available that can change that outcome. Before we discuss some of those mechanisms, however, it's important to frame what we mean by the term *benefit administration*.

In putting together a benefits package, two issues must be considered: (1) what benefits must be offered by law, and (2) what benefits and services should be offered to make the organization attractive to applicants and current workers. First, we'll explore the **legally required benefits.**

LEGALLY REQUIRED BENEFITS

United States organizations must provide certain benefits to their employees regardless of whether they want to or not, and they must be provided in a nondiscriminatory manner. With a few exceptions, the hiring of any employee requires the organization to pay Social Security premiums,[14] unemployment compensation, and workers' compensation. Additionally, any organization with 50 or more employees must provide Family and Medical Leave. The premium payments associated with many of these legally required benefits are either shared with employees (as in the case of Social Security), or borne solely by the organization, in an effort to provide each employee with some basic level of financial protection at retirement, termination, or as a result of injury. These benefits also provide a death benefit for dependents in case of a worker's death. Finally, employers must permit employees to take time off from work for certain personal reasons.

The United States, however, is not the only industrialized nation to have legally required benefits. Many others, like Norway, Canada, and China, have them, too. In China, for example, starting in 1995, employees in Chinese firms are provided unemployment insurance, medical insurance, and a retirement plan.[15] While it is not possible to discuss benefit offerings in the industrialized nations, it's important to understand the legally required benefits offered in the United States. Let's look at each of these.

Social Security

A source of income for American retirees, disabled workers, and for surviving dependents of workers who have died, has been the benefits provided by **Social Security** insurance. Social Security also provides some health insurance coverage through the federal government-sponsored Medicare program. In 1997, Social Security benefits exceeded $100 billion a year,[16] covering more than 170 million workers in the United States.[17]

Social Security insurance is financed by contributions made by the employee and matched by the employer, computed as a percentage of the employee's earnings. In 1998, for instance, the rate was 12.4 percent (6.2 percent levied on both the employee and the employer) of the worker's earnings up to $68,400, or a maximum levy of $4,240.80. Additionally, 2.9 percent is assessed for medicare on all earned income. Similar to Social Security, both the employer and employee split this assessment, paying 1.45 percent each in payroll taxes.[18]

To be eligible for Social Security, employees must be employed for a minimum of forty quarters, or ten years of work. During this work period, employees must have also earned a minimum of $630 per quarter. Prior to 1983, employees became eligible for full benefits at age 65. With revisions to Social Security laws, those born after 1938 will have to wait an additional two years before receiving full retirement benefits.

Keep in mind, however, that Social Security is not intended to be employees' sole source of retirement income—although in 1997 nearly 40 percent of all retirees relied on this benefit as their primary source of income.[19] Social Security benefits vary, based on the previous year's inflation, one's additional earnings, and the age of the recipient. For 1997, the maximum monthly Social Security retirement check was $1,125—with the average monthly check being $746.[20] Given longer life expectancies, and a desire to maintain one's current standard of living, workers today are expected to supplement Social Security with their own retirement plans.[21] (We'll look at these shortly.) This is true whether or not Social Security will still be around in the year 2030!

Unemployment Compensation

Unemployment compensation laws provide benefits to employees who meet the following conditions: are without a job, have worked a minimum number of weeks, submit an application for unemployment compensation to their State Employment Agency, register for available work, and are willing and able to accept any suitable employment offered them through their State Unemployment Compensation Commission. The premise behind unemployment compensation is to provide an income to individuals who have lost a job through no fault of their own (e.g., layoffs, plant closing).

The funds for paying unemployment compensation are derived from a combined federal and state tax imposed on the taxable wage base of the employer. At the federal level, the unemployment tax (called FUTA) is 6.2 percent on the first $7,000 of earnings of employees.[22] States that meet federal guidelines are given a 5.4 percent credit, thus reducing the federal unemployment tax to .08 percent, or $56 per employee.[23]

State unemployment compensation tax is often a function of a company's unemployment experience; that is, the more an organization lays off employees, the higher its rate. Rates for employers range from 0.0 to 3.0 percent of state-established wage bases.[24] Eligible unemployed workers receive an amount that varies from state to state but is determined by the worker's previous wage rate and the length of previous employment. Compensation is provided for only a limited period—typically, the base is twenty-six weeks[25] but may be extended by the state another twenty-six weeks during times when unemployment runs excessively high.

Unemployment compensation and parallel programs for railroad, federal government, and military employees cover more than 75 percent of all members in the work force. Major groups that are excluded include self-employed workers, employees who work for organizations employing fewer than four individuals, household domestics, farm employees, and state and local government employees. As recent recessions have demonstrated, unemployment compensation provides stable spending power throughout the nation. In contrast to the early 1930s, when millions of workers lost their jobs and had no compensatory income, unemployment compensation provides a floor that allows individuals to continue looking for work while receiving assistance through the transitory period from one job to the next.[26]

Workers' Compensation

Every state currently has some type of **workers' compensation** to compensate employees (or their families) for death or permanent or total disability resulting from job-related endeavors, irrespective of fault for the accident. Federal employees and others working outside the U.S. border are covered by separate legislation. The rationale for workers' compensation is to protect employees' salaries and to attribute the cost for occupational accidents and rehabilitation to the employing organization. This accountability factor considers workers' compensation costs as part of the labor expenses incurred in meeting the organization's objectives.

Workers' compensation benefits are based on fixed schedules of minimum and maximum payments. For example, the loss of an index finger may be calculated at $500, or the loss of an entire foot at $5,000. When comprehensive disability payments are required, the amount of compensation is computed by considering the employee's current earnings, future earnings, and financial responsibilities.

The entire cost of workers' compensation is borne by the organization. Its rates are set based on the likelihood of an accident, the actual history of company accidents, the type of industry and business operation, and the likelihood of accidents occurring. The organization, then, protects itself by covering its risks through insurance. Some states provide an insurance system, voluntary or required, for the handling of workers' compensation. Some organizations may also cover their workers' compensation risks by purchasing insurance from private insurance companies. Finally, some states allow employers to be self-insurers. Self-insuring—while usually limited to large organizations—requires the employer to maintain a fund from which benefits can be paid.

Most workers' compensation laws stipulate that the injured employee will be compensated by either a monetary allocation or the payment of medical expenses, or a combination of both. Almost all workers' compensation insurance programs, whether publicly or privately controlled, provide incentives for employers to maintain good safety records. Insurance rates are computed based on the organization's accident experience; hence employers are motivated to keep accident rates low.[27]

Family and Medical Leave Act

The last legally required benefit facing organizations who have fifty or more employees is the Family and Medical Leave Act of 1993. Recall from our discussion in Chapter 3 (see pp. 71-72), that the FMLA was passed to provide employees the opportunity to take up to twelve weeks of unpaid leave each year for family or medical reasons. Interestingly, while this is a major improvement for parents in the United States, employees in Norway have been given much superior family leave. Fathers are granted four weeks of paid leave upon the birth of a child. Mothers, on the other hand, receive either fifty-two weeks of leave paid at 80 percent of their salary or forty-two weeks off at 100 percent of their salary.[28]

VOLUNTARY BENEFITS

The voluntary benefits offered by an organization are limited only by management's creativity and budget. As Exhibit 12-1 illustrated, many different benefits are offered—almost all of which carry significant costs to the employer. Some of the most common and critical ones are health insurance, retirement plans, time off from work, and disability and life insurance benefits. We will delay the discussion of benefits that deals with health issues, like employee assistance programs, until the next chapter.

Health Insurance

All individuals have health-care needs that must be met, and most organizations today offer some type of **health insurance** coverage to their employees. This coverage has become one of the most important benefits for employees because of the tremendous increases in the cost of health care.[29] In fact, health care costs U.S. businesses more than $174 billion annually, and although the

How does an organization like the Seattle-based Starbucks Coffee Company attract and retain star employees? Very simply. Based on the philosophy of CEO Howard Schultz, all employees are provided very competitive benefits. For example, all employees are provided excellent health insurance. But there's more to this story. Part-time employees—those working at least 20 hours a week—are provided an excellent benefits package, too. They not only receive health insurance, but they get paid vacations and stock options. And what does Starbucks get for this? In a fast-food industry where turnover reaches upward of 400 percent per year, Starbucks' turnover is 80 percent less. As Starbucks' director of compensation and benefits stated, "People come here for the benefits, and they stay for them."

costs in the late 1990s are leveling off, they're still a major concern for organizations.[30] Without health insurance, almost any family's finances could be depleted at any time if they had to pay for a major illness. The purpose of health insurance is to protect the employee and his or her immediate family from the catastrophes of a major illness and to minimize their out-of-pocket expenses for medical care.

Any type of health insurance offered to employees generally contains provisions for coverage that can be extended beyond the employee. Specifically, the employee, the employee's spouse and children may be covered. Health-care coverage generally focuses on hospital and physician care. It also typically covers major medical expenses. The specific types of coverage offered to employees will vary based on the organization's health insurance policy. Generally, three types appear more frequently than others: traditional health-care coverage, Health Maintenance Organizations (HMOs), and Preferred Provider Organizations (PPOs) (sometimes referred to as point-of-service (POS) or network plans).[31] All three are designed to provide protection for employees, but each does so in a different way. There is also increasing interest in employer-operated options such as self-funded insurance. Let's look at each of these various types.

Traditional Health Insurance When health insurance benefits began decades ago, generally one type of health insurance was offered: the traditional membership program. The cost of this insurance to the employee, if any, was minimal. This traditional insurance generally was provided (and is to some extent today) through a Blue Cross and Blue Shield Organization.[32] However, it's not uncommon to see traditional health insurance programs being offered by such companies as Cigna, Connecticut General, or Prudential.

Since its inception in 1929, Blue Cross and Blue Shield (BC/BS) insurance has served as the dominant health-care insurer in the United States. Blue Cross and Blue Shield plans offer special arrangements to their members in return for a guarantee that medical services will be provided. Blue Cross organizations are concerned with the hospital end of the business. These hospitals contract with **Blue Cross** to provide hospital services to members, and agree to receive reimbursement from the health insurer for their fees incurred. The reimbursement is often paid on a per diem basis for days stayed in the hospital or by paying a percentage of the total bill.[33]

The other component of the health insurer is the **Blue Shield** organization. Whereas Blue Cross has special arrangements with the hospitals, Blue Shield tries to achieve the same by signing up doctors to participate in Blue Shield coverage. This participation feature means that a doctor is willing to accept the payment from Blue Shield as payment in full for services rendered. These payments are generally based on what are called "Usual, Customary, and Reasonable" (UCR) fees. The UCR fees are reflective of physician fees charged in an area.[34]

For many organizations, the costs associated with the "cadillac" of the health insurance plan have become prohibitive. Even passing these costs on to the employee has not met with much success. As such, traditional health-care coverage is rapidly being replaced by the other two plan types. Traditional insurers like Blue Cross and Blue Shield, too, have begun to offer other types of health insurance coverage options to employers in order to help contain rising health-care benefit costs.

Health Maintenance Organizations   **Health Maintenance Organizations (HMOs)** are designed to provide quality health care at a fixed expense for its members. People's needs have changed, and with these changing needs comes the expectation that they can obtain good health care at a reasonable cost. Under traditional coverage, preventive care is generally not covered. For instance, visiting a physician for routine baby immunizations or gynecological exams would not be paid for under the terms of traditional health insurance coverage. Accordingly, the costs of such care are borne solely by the employee.

To meet this growing concern and provide the desired services to employees, HMOs were created. This creation stemmed from the passage of the **Health Maintenance Act of 1973,** which required employers who extended traditional health insurance to their employees to also offer alternative health-care coverage options. HMOs seek efficiencies by keeping health-care costs down; one means of achieving that goal is by providing preventive care.

An HMO like Kaiser Permanente is "an organization that generally delivers broad, comprehensive health care to a specific, voluntary enrolled population . . . on a fixed, periodic payment basis."[35] Since their inception, they have grown rapidly in the United States. It is estimated that there are more than 300 HMOs operating in the United States, providing services to more than 24 million members, and growing "at a 25 percent annual pace."[36] Exhibit 12-3 is a sample of HMO coverage. The major disadvantage, however, is that under an HMO, to get "full" coverage, one must receive services from the service center location that is selected. Furthermore, to be seen outside of the HMO, or for other services, individuals must either receive permission from their HMO physician or incur a greater out-of-pocket expense. Accordingly, under an HMO arrange-

Exhibit 12-3

Sample health maintenance organization coverage.

Coverage Conditions	Coverage (HMO Facility Only)
Physician	
Primary Care	100% after $5 Co-pay
Specialists	100% after $10 Co-pay
In-Patient Care	100% (When preauthorized by Plan)
Out-Patient Care	100% (When preauthorized by Plan)
Hospital	100% (When preauthorized by Plan)
Surgery	100% (When preauthorized by Plan)
Maternity Benefits	100% (When preauthorized by Plan)
Well-Baby Care	100% after $5 Co-pay
Immunizations	100% (When preauthorized by Plan)
Dental Coverage	100%
Diagnostic	100%
Preventive	100% after $10 Co-pay
Deductibles	
Individual	None
Family	None
Out-of-Pocket Maximums	
Individual	None
Family	None

SOURCE: State of Maryland, *Summary of Maryland State Employees Health Benefits,* 1998 (November 1997), pp. 11–19.

ment, freedom of health-care choice is significantly limited. This limiting feature has been one of the greatest concerns some individuals have regarding using an HMO. However, for many, the cost savings far outweigh the imposed restrictions.

Preferred Provider Organizations   Preferred Provider Organizations (PPOs) are health-care arrangements where an employer or insurance company has agreements with doctors, hospitals, and other related medical service facilities to provide services for a fixed fee. In return for accepting this fixed fee, the employer or the insurer promises to encourage employees to use their services. The encouragement often results in additional services being covered. PPOs often have lower premiums than traditional health insurance programs.[37] Moreover, insurance companies offering the PPO also provide valuable information to employers. Through utilization review procedures, the PPO can provide data to help the employer determine unnecessary plan use. For example, elective surgery often requires pre-authorization—which stipulates the approved procedures and hospital stay, if any. These "checks" can act as "gatekeepers" designed to contain health-care costs (see Exhibit 12-4).

How can a PPO benefit the employee? Through the agreement reached between the employer and the insurance company, a PPO can provide much the same service that an HMO provides. The difference is that an individual is not required to use a specific facility—like a designated hospital. So long as a physician or the medical facility is participating in the health network, the services are covered. The individual, in the case of a participating physician, typically incurs a fixed out of pocket expense (defined by the agreement). In those

Coverage Conditions	In Network	Out of Network
Physician		
Primary Care	100% after $15 Co-pay	80% after Deductible
Specialists	100% after $20 Co-pay	80% after Deductible
In-Patient Care	100%	80% after Deductible
Out-Patient Care	100%	80% after Deductible
Hospital	100% for 365 Days	80% after Deductible
Surgery	100%	80% after Deductible
Maternity Benefits	100%	80% after Decuctible
Well-Baby Care	100% after $15 Co-pay	80% after Deductible
Immunizations	100%	80% after Deductible
Dental Coverage		
Diagnostic	Not Covered	
Preventive	Not Covered	
Deductibles		
Individual	None	$250
Family	None	$500
Out-of-Pocket Maximums		
Individual	None	$3,000
Family	None	$6,000

SOURCE: State of Maryland, *Summary of Maryland State Employees Health Benefits,* 1998 (November 1997), pp. 11–19.

Exhibit 12-4

Sample Preferred Provider Organization (Point of Service) coverage.

cases, the PPO takes the form of traditional health insurance. However, if an employee decides to go elsewhere for services, then the service fee is reimbursed according to specific guidelines.

PPOs attempt to combine the best of both worlds—the HMO and traditional insurance. These networks may well be the fastest growing form of health plans in the United States.

Employer-Operated Coverage   Although the types of insurance programs mentioned above are the most popular means of health insurance today, many companies are looking for other options that will assist them in containing the rising health-care costs they incur. To this end, some companies have begun reviewing the concept of being self-insured, and in many of these instances, using the assistance of a third-party administrator (TPA).[38] A movement in health-insurance coverage witnessed in the 1980s was the formation of self-funded programs. Some organizations, such as the State of Maryland and General Binding Corporation, have ventured into the insurance business to reduce health insurance costs. Under a self-funding arrangement, an "employer provides a formal plan to employees under which the employer directly pays and is liable for some or all of the benefits promised under the plan."[39] This insurance plan is customarily established and operated under an arrangement called a **voluntary employees beneficiary association** (VEBA). In this case, the employer typically establishes a trust fund to pay for the health benefits used.[40] For the most part, this employer trust fund has received favorable treatment from the IRS.

Health Insurance Continuation   What happens to an employee's health insurance coverage if that employee leaves the organization, or maybe is laid off? The answer to that question lies in the **Consolidated Omnibus Budget Reconciliation Act (COBRA).** One of the main features established by the COBRA was the continuation of employee benefits for a period up to three years after the employee leaves the company.[41] Because of high unemployment rates in the early 1980s, supplemented by the downsizing of corporate America, large numbers of individuals were out of work, and more importantly, no longer had medical insurance. To combat this problem, COBRA was enacted in 1985. When employees resign or are laid off through no fault of their own—like the expansive downsizing that occurred in the early 1990s—they're eligible for a continuation of their health insurance benefits for a period of 18 months, although under certain conditions, the time may be extended to 29 months.[42] The cost of this coverage is paid by the employee. The employer may also charge the employee a small administrative fee for this service. However, COBRA requires employers to offer this benefit through the company's current group health insurance plan, which is a rate that is typically lower than if the individual had to purchase the insurance himself or herself.

RETIREMENT PROGRAMS

Retiring from work today does not guarantee a continuation of one's standard of living. Social Security cannot sustain the lifestyle most of us grow accustomed to in our working years. Therefore, we cannot rely on the government as the sole source of our retirement income. Instead, Social Security payments must be just one component of a properly designed retirement system.[43] The other components are retirement monies we may receive from our organization and savings we have amassed over the years. Irrespective of the retirement vehicles used, it is important to recognize that retirement plans are highly regulated by the **Employee Retirement Income Security Act (ERISA)** of 1974. Let's take a brief look at ERISA before we discuss the different retirement programs.

ERISA was passed to deal with one of the largest problems of the day imposed by private pension plans—employees were not getting their benefits. That was due chiefly to the design of the pension plans, which almost always required a minimum tenure with the organization before the individual had a guaranteed right to pension benefits, regardless of whether or not they remained with the company. These permanent benefits—or the guarantee to a pension when one retires or leaves the organization—are called **vesting rights.** In years past, employees had to have extensive tenures in an organization before they were entitled to their retirement benefits—if they were entitled at all. This meant, for instance, that a 60-year-old employee with twenty-three years of service who left the company—for whatever reason—would have no right to a pension benefit. ERISA was enacted to prevent such abuses.

> **Vesting rights guarantee an employee's right to a pension benefit.**

ERISA requires employers who decide to provide a pension or profit sharing plan to design their retirement program under specific rules. Typically, each plan must convey to employees "new eligibility requirements for coverage, breaks in service, restoration of service following a break, plan payment methods, and new vesting requirements." [44] Currently, vesting rights in organizations typically come after six years of service, and pension programs must be available to all employees over age 21. [45] Employees, too, with fewer than six years of service may receive a pro-rated portion of their "retirement" benefit. This shorter vesting period, which came into effect with the 1986 Tax Reform Act, is crucial for employees, especially when one considers that the length of service in companies today is shorter. With this shorter vesting period, employees who leave companies after six years generally can carry their retirement rights with them. That is, ERISA enables pension rights to be portable. [46]

ERISA also created guidelines for the termination of a pension program. Should an employer voluntarily terminate a pension program, the **Pension Benefit Guaranty Corporation (PBGC)** must be notified. Similarly, the act permits the PBGC, under certain conditions (such as inadequate pension funding), to lay claim on corporate assets—up to 30 percent of net worth to pay benefits that had been promised to employees. Additionally, when a pension plan is terminated, the PBGC requires the employer to notify workers and retirees of any financial institution that will be handling future retirement programs for the organization. [47]

Another key aspect of ERISA is its requirement for a company to include what is commonly called a **Summary Plan Description (SPD).** Summary Plan Descriptions are designed to serve as a vehicle to inform employees about the benefits offered in the company in terms the "average" employee can understand. [48] This means that employers are required to inform employees on the details of their retirement plans, including such items as "the retirement plan requirements (including eligibility, forfeiture, complaint procedures); their rights under ERISA; information on how the plan is funded; and their accumulated benefits." [49]

Finally, it's important to note that another law has had a significant effect on ERISA. This is the 1984 Retirement Equity Act. While the Retirement Equity

Act decreased plan participation from age 25 to 21, its main effect was that it "made it easier for women to earn and maintain pension and retirement benefits."[50] The Retirement Equity Act also requires plan participants to receive spouse approval before a participant is able to waive survivor benefits.

Defined Benefit Plans

In years past, the most popular pension was a **defined benefit plan.** This plan specifies the dollar benefit workers will receive at retirement. The amount typically revolves around some fixed monthly income for life or a variation of a lump sum cash distribution. The amount and type of the benefit is set, and the company contributes the set amount each year into a trust fund. The amount contributed each year is calculated on an actuarial basis—considering variables such as length of service, how long plan participants are expected to live, their lifetime earnings, and how much return the trust portfolio will receive (e.g., 5 percent or 10 percent annually). The pension payout formulas used to determine retirement benefits vary widely.

Over the past fifteen years, defined benefit plans have received some criticism. Employees have identified a need to receive more retirement benefits and to be permitted to make their own contributions to retirement plans. At the New York Mercantile Exchange, for example, employees requested that management consider making changes to the retirement plan in effect. Recognizing that another retirement vehicle met employees needs better, the company discontinued its defined benefit plan and implemented a money purchase plan and 401(k) combination.[51]

Defined Contribution Plans

Defined contribution plans are different from defined benefit plans in at least one very important area—no specific dollar benefits are fixed. That is, under a defined contribution plan, each employee has an individual account, to which both the employee and the employer may make contributions.[52] The plan establishes rules for contributions. For example, the Humana, Inc. defined contribution pension plan allows employees to select both a money purchase plan (described next) and a profit-sharing plan with the company matching up to 6 percent of salary. In a defined contribution plan, the money is invested and projections are offered as to probable retirement income levels. However, the company is not bound by these projections, and accordingly, unfunded pension liability problems do not occur. For this reason, defined contribution plans have become a popular trend in new qualified retirement planning.

Additionally, variations in plan administration frequently allow the employee some selection in the investment choices. For instance, an employee may select bonds for security, common stocks for appreciation and an inflation hedge, or some type of money market fund.

Money Purchase Pension Plan   Money purchase pension plans are one type of defined contribution plans. Under this arrangement, the organization commits to deposit a fixed amount of money or a percentage of the employee's pay annually into a fund.[53] Under IRS regulations, however, the maximum permitted is 25 percent of worker pay. Under money purchase plans, no specific retirement dollar benefits are fixed as they are under a defined benefit plan.

However, companies do make projections of probable retirement income based on various interest rates, but the company is not bound to the projection.

Profit-Sharing Plans   Profit-sharing pension plans are yet another variation of defined contribution plans. Under these plans, companies, like Fisher-Price, contribute to a trust fund account an optional percentage of each worker's pay (maximum allowed by law is 15 percent). This, of course, is guided by the profit level in the organization. The operative word in profit-sharing plans here is "optional." The company is not bound by law to make contributions every year. It should be noted, however, that although employers are not bound by law, the majority of employers feel a moral obligation to make a contribution. Often they will keep to a schedule, even in times when profits are slim or nonexistent.[54]

Individual Retirement Accounts   From 1982 to 1986, the Individual Retirement Account (IRA) was the darling of retirement planning. The law permitted each worker to defer paying taxes on up to $2,000 of earned income per year ($2,225 for employee and spouse where spouse did not work) with interest on these accounts also accumulating on a tax-deferred basis. This was a tax shelter for the average person, a good way to build a nest egg. Anyone who had earned income could invest in an IRA. The purpose of an IRA was to make the individual partly responsible for his or her retirement income.

IRAs were very popular for the few years they received favorable tax status. However, with the Tax Reform of 1986, IRAs became significantly limited for many workers. To be eligible for deferring income to an IRA, workers now must meet specific conditions, such as not participating in a recognized retirement program at work and falling under limits on the adjusted annual income. For instance, a single individual making $35,000 a year ($50,000 for married taxpayers) with a company-paid pension would no longer qualify for a tax deduction from their IRA contribution. The purpose of the tax reform was to focus IRAs on lower income workers who might not have a retirement program at their place of work, or for those who deserve to augment the one they have.

Roth IRAs   Effective in 1998, a new version of the IRA was signed into law. This was called the Roth IRA. In a Roth IRA, an employee can contribute up to $2,000 annually to an account. However, the money is not deposited on a pre-tax basis. Instead, the money grows tax-free, and after reaching a certain age, the money can be withdrawn tax-free. As with the regular IRA, there are conditions for being eligible to contribute to a Roth IRA based on compensation.

401(k)s   Under the Tax Equity and Fiscal Responsible Act (TEFRA), capital accumulation programs, more commonly known as **401(k)s** or thrift-savings plans, were established. A 401(k) program is named after the IRS tax code section that created its existence. These programs permit workers to set aside a certain amount of their income on a tax-deferred basis through their employer. In 1998, the maximum amount of deferral was $10,100.

In many cases, what differentiated the employer-sponsored 401(k) from an IRA was the amount permitted to be set aside, and the realization that many companies contributed an amount to the 401(k) on the employee's behalf.[55] Because of this matching feature, many companies call their 401(k) a matching-contribu-

Exhibit 12-5

Other retirement plans.

Plan	About the Plan
403(B)	Designed to be the 401(k) counterpart for educational and nonprofit organizations.
Simplified Employee Retirement Plans	Designed for an employer or the self-employed individual. Permits contributions up to 15 percent of net profit, or $30,000 (whichever is less).
Keogh Plans	Available to the self-employed, permits contributions of 15 percent of net profit, or $30,000 (whichever is less). The main distinction between a Keogh and an SEP lies in the annual report filing requirement of the IRS.
Stock Option Plans	Under these plans, an individual can purchase company stock through payroll deductions. The stock is generally sold at a discount to the employee, or at straight market value without the use of, or commissions for, a broker.

tion plan, meaning that both the employer and the employee are working jointly to create a retirement program. For instance, at Coram Health Care, for every dollar of gross income employees defer to the plan, the company makes a matching contribution of 25 cents, up to a maximum match of 6 percent of salary. It's important to note that employee contributions are immediately vested. The employee has a vested right in the employer's contribution vested after 5 years.

401(k) programs have been popular with employees since their inception. Both employers and employees have found that there are advantages to offering capital accumulation plans. The cost of providing retirement income for employees is lower, and employees can supplement their retirement program and often participate in investments. Employees are offered the ease of contributing to their 401(k) through payroll deductions. In some instances, the matching-contribution program may be offered to supplement the employer's non-contributory (defined benefit) retirement plan. Additionally, regardless of the mechanics of the program, employers are heavily regulated on offering employees investment advice.[56]

Other Retirement Vehicles   While we've described the major retirement plans, we would be remiss not to mention the following that are appropriate retirement vehicles for selected groups of workers. These are 403(b)s, Simplified Employee Pension Plans (SEPs), Keogh Plans, and Stock Option Plans (ESOPS—Employee Stock Ownership Plans), PAYSOPS (Payroll-Based Stock Ownership Plans), and TRASOPS (Tax-Benefit Based Stock Ownership Plans). Exhibit 12-5 provides a summary of these retirement alternatives for certain groups of workers.

Paid Time Off

There are a number of benefits that provide pay for time off from work. The most popular of these are vacation and holiday leave and disability insurance, which includes sick leave and short- and long-term disability programs. Although we'll present these as separate items, some organizations today are lumping all paid time off into a single "bank." As the time is used, it is charged to one's account—regardless of whether it's used for vacation, or sick leave.[57]

Vacation and Holiday Leave   After employees have been with an organization for a specified period of time, they usually become eligible for a paid vaca-

David Mason, founder of a St. Louis-based architecture and engineering firm, learned something valuable from a job candidate. Trying to "land" a highly sought-after candidate, everything appeared to be going well. That is, until the candidate stated he wanted every other Friday off. Mason thought it just might be interesting to do. Consequently, he implemented a work-schedule benefit where employees work 7:30–5:30 each day, working 81 hours over nine days—and get every other Friday off. As a result, productivity in the firm has increased, and there has been a significant increase in unsolicited job applicants. Customers, too, have found the schedule workable. As for Mason, he enjoys spending every other Friday with his family.

tion. Common practice is to relate the length of vacation to the length of tenure and job classification in the organization. For example, after six months' service with an organization, an employee may be eligible for one week's vacation; after a year, two weeks; after five years, three weeks; and after ten or more years, four weeks. It is interesting to note that U.S. workers have one of the shortest vacation periods of many industrialized nations. For example, while U.S. workers enjoy fifteen to twenty days off each year, on average, employees in France, England, Germany, and Hong Kong are offered up to thirty days a year.[58]

The rationale behind the paid vacation is to provide a break in which employees can refresh themselves. This rationale is important, but is sometimes overlooked. For example, in a situation where employees accrue a certain amount of vacation time and can sell back to the company any unused vacation days, the regenerative "battery charging" intent is lost. While the cost may be the same to the employer (depending on how long vacation time can be accrued), employees who do not take a break ultimately may be adversely affecting themselves.

Holiday pay is paid time off while observing some special event—federally mandated holidays (like New Year's Day, President's Day, Martin Luther King's Birthday, Memorial Day, Labor Day, Thanksgiving, and Christmas), company-provided holidays (like Christmas Eve and New Year's Eve), or personal days (days employees can take off for any reason). In the United States, employees average ten paid holidays per year.[59] Most other countries are similar, with averages of nine paid holidays in the United Kingdom, eleven in Brazil, seventeen in Japan, and a maximum of nineteen in Mexico.[60]

Disability Insurance Programs   Employees today recognize that salary continuation for injuries and major illnesses is almost more important than life insurance. For most employees, there is a greater probability that they will have a disabling injury requiring an extended absence from work of more than ninety days than that they will die before their retirement.[61] Programs to address this area of need can be broken down into two broad categories—*short-term disability* and *long-term disability* programs.

Almost all employers offer some type of short-term disability plan. Categories under this heading include the company sick-leave policy, short-term disability programs,[62] state disability laws, and workers' compensation. The focus of each is to provide replacement income in the event of an injury or a short-term illness.[63] For many, this short-term period is defined as being six months or less in duration.

One of the most popular types of short-term disability programs is a company's sick-leave plan. Most organizations, such as General Motors and Federal Express, provide their employees with pay for days not worked because of illness. Sick leave is allocated on the basis of a specific number of days a year,[64] often accrued on a cumulative basis. In some organizations, too, the number of days may be expanded relative to years of service with the organization. Each year of employment may entitle the worker to two additional days' sick leave. Regardless of whether sick leave is used, it would continue to accumulate (usually up to some maximum number of days); those individuals who have been with the company the longest would have accumulated the most sick-leave credit.

Sick-leave abuse has often been a problem for organizations. Some research into the area indicates that "only 45 percent of sick leave days are used for personal illnesses."[65] The belief, too, that one should amass sick leave for use later in life is quickly diminishing. That belief may have been popular when a person joined an organization early in life and retired from that company, but with today's mobility, long-term focus has little meaning. This is especially alarming when we consider that sick days are not usually transferable to another organization. Thus, the "use them or lose them" concept may only hinder productivity. Attempts have been made recently to combat this potential for sick-leave abuse. This has come in the form of financial incentives to individuals who do not fully use their sick leave for the year. In a number of organizations, for example, in an effort to reward attendance, companies have what is called "well pay." Well pay focuses on providing a monetary inducement for workers not to use all of their sick leave. This incentive can be in the form of buying back the unused sick leave, lumping sick-leave days into the years of service in calculating retirement benefits, or even having special drawings for those who qualify. For instance, at Northwest Airlines, to combat absenteeism during peak production times, the airlines place names of employees who don't miss work into a drawing. Winners receive Corvettes, Ford Explorers, or cash equivalents.[66] These incentives intend to serve as a bonus and encourage judicious use of sick time.[67] It's interesting to note that in some cases, employees come to work ill when they really shouldn't so as not to "lose" the incentive pay. However, rather than resting and taking care of themselves, they spread their "germs" to others. In early 1998, for instance, a virulent strain of flu ravaged many organizations. Employees exposing other employees to the "flu bug" resulted, at times, in nearly entire departments having to close down.

If health insurance coverage is unable to prevent a major illness from occurring, and an extended period of time off work does not provide for ample recuperation, then employees may need the benefits provided under a long-term disability program. Similar to their short-term disability counterparts, long-term disability programs are designed to provide replacement income for an employee who is no longer able to return to work and where short-term coverage has expired. The period of time before long-term disability becomes effective is usually six months. Some type of long-term disability coverage is in effect in almost 99 percent of all companies and is provided on a temporary or permanent basis.[68] By definition, a temporary disability is one in which an individual cannot perform his or her job duties for the first twenty-four months after injury or illness. Permanent, long-term disability is when an individual is unable to perform in any occupation.[69]

The benefits paid to employees is customarily set between 50 and 67 percent, with 60 percent salary replacement the most common. In most plans, there is a maximum monthly payment of replacement income that lies between 70 and 80 percent of gross pay.[70] This may be as little as $2,000, or greater than $10,000.[71] In most cases, long-term disability payments continue until the individual reaches age 65.[72]

Survivor Benefits

To provide protection to the families of employees, many companies offer life insurance as a benefit. Life insurance programs, one of the more popular employee benefit,[73] typically come in two varieties—*noncontributory* and *contributory* policies. Our major focus in this context is on the noncontributory variety, for that is the one generally completely employer funded.

Group Term Life Insurance   When a company offers group term life insurance to its employees,[74] the standard policy provides for a death benefit of one to five times their annual rate of pay, with most including a double indemnity provision—that is, should an employee's death result from an accident, the benefit is twice the policy value. More than 90 percent of all companies provide this coverage.[75]

Death benefits offered are generally linked to one's position in the organization. Generally speaking, the more "valuable" an employee is defined in terms of his or her level in the organization, the greater the death benefit offered. Those at lower levels of the organization typically receive one to one and one-half their annual wage as a benefit, whereas top-level employees may receive as much as three times their salary.[76]

Travel Insurance   Another insurance plan offered to many employees is travel insurance. Under this policy, employees' lives are covered in the event of death while traveling on company time. This insurance typically provides a lump-sum payment, from $50,000 to $1 million. Depending on any unique provisions of a policy, as long as an employee is conducting business-related activities when the death occurs, the insurance typically will be paid. For example, if a salesperson's day typically begins by traveling to a client's place of business from his or her residence, coverage begins as soon as this person gets into the car. If he or she is killed going to that location, then this insurance is activated. The key element is when death occurred. An employee who normally commutes to work would not be covered under an employer-paid travel insurance benefit if an accident happened on the way.

Family-Friendly Benefits

Family-friendly benefits are so named because they represent benefits that are supportive of caring for one's family.

In a few instances in previous chapters, we referred to something called the family-friendly organization. What makes the organization family-friendly? That answer lies in the benefits it offers. **Family-friendly benefits** are so named because they represent flexible benefits that are supportive of caring for one's family. See Meet Jeanne Baker and Robin Birdsong. These would include such benefits as flextime, child and elder care, dependent-care flexible spending accounts, part-time employment, relocation programs, telecommuting, summer day camp, adoption benefits,[77] and parental leave.[78] Some of the more notable companies that offer such benefits are American Express, Corning, Dow, Hoechst Celanese, Johnson & Johnson, and NationsBank.[79] At the heart of such programs, however, is a means for increasing child- and elder-care benefits.[80] While flexible spending accounts mentioned previously have assisted in "affording" this care, more employees are seeking ways of having quality child care and elder care in close proximity to them; this is especially true of organizations that operate staggered shifts or around the clock.[81]

A number of societal issues are at stake here. Dual-career couples with children and/or elderly live-in parents need to have some assurance that child- or elder-care programs are available to them without major disruptions to their lives. No longer is it acceptable to assume that other family members or friends will provide this care, although in many cases that is what occurs. Nonetheless, many HRM representatives recognize that when their employees face a choice between their jobs and their families, the vast majority of employees clearly place their job second. For example, although sick leave is supposed to be used for the employee's illness only, when a child of that employee is sick and no child care is available, it is likely the employee will call in sick in order to care for their dependent. One company, Nyloncraft, Inc., recognized that it was experiencing tremendous turnover because of child-care conflicts. Accordingly, company officials established what is now regarded as the nation's first employer-owned child-care facility.[82] The purpose was to promote increased productivity, improve attendance, lessen turnover, and the like.[83] And at Johnson & Johnson, absenteeism among employees who took advantage of family-friendly benefit offerings—like flexible work hours and family leaves—was 50 percent less than their work force as a whole.[84] While there are legal and insurance ramifications to be addressed, in locations where these programs operate, employee morale has increased. In addition, companies have also developed cooperative efforts to address this issue; for example, American Express, IBM, Work Family Directions, and Allstate Insurance have joined forces to offer quality child care at a facility that is in close proximity to all of their employees.[85] Similar to the need for child care is the need for elder care. Elder care refers to a situation in which children become more responsible for the care of an aged parent. It's estimated that approximately 12 percent of the work force have some elder-care responsibilities,[86] resulting in significant productivity losses for their organizations.[87] The same issues arise regarding facilities, quality providers, and so forth.

The Service Side of Benefits

In addition to the benefits described above, organizations offer a wealth of services employees may find desirable. These services can be provided to the

Meet

JEANNE BAKER AND ROBIN BIRDSONG

CEO and President of Employer Resource Network, Inc., respectively

Imagine the perfect partnership between two people who have learned that developing a good working relationship is a matter of trust, compromise, and a passion for their business. Baker and Birdsong have created an employee benefit company that offers all types of employee benefit administrative services on a national basis. By looking for the need, and then developing a customized solution, they have expanded their customer base to include companies of all sizes, as well as providing services to a number of insurance companies in the worksite insurance product arena.

They recognized that employers and insurance companies needed assistance in specialized areas of benefit administration, including Section 125 Plans, 401(k) Plans, Insurance Enrollment Processing and Billing Administration. After searching the marketplace for a software program that could handle these specialized needs, they elected to design and build their own. Today, that software system is the envy of the industry. Admitted perfectionists, Baker and Birdsong found that "paying their dues" meant building a superior software program over a period of years, which became the Benefit Administration System (BAS™). The unique combination of services available through BAS™ and excellence in customer service has led to national recognition for this company.

Now, thirteen years later, the two are celebrating unparalleled success at every level of operation. The company continues to expand, adding new clients quickly through references and strategic alliances with a few selected Insurance companies, and keeping current clients happy. "We recognized in the beginning that we would be our best sales people, and have never recruited a sales team. Our business is very much one of making your client happy enough to refer you to other companies needing the same stellar performance in benefit services. Our goal is to help our clients save money, offer their employees meaningful benefits, and communicate to those employees to ensure they have the information they need to make decisions to meet their family needs," says Baker.

A primary component in the building of this organization was the selection and development of a vice president of operations. This position rapidly took on importance in the areas of strategic planning, human resource development and training as new staff members joined the organization. Focusing on a team approach, the company has found that helping each other has also greatly helped their clients and improved customer service. The company currently operates two shifts, in order to be more readily available to human resource managers and employees on both coasts.

An electric energy permeates the halls of this organization. Staff members embrace corporate goals, consistently delivering on commitments made. Innovative concepts and processes are created, tested, and implemented by various teams. Victories are celebrated in each department and at corporate functions to honor these talented professionals.

Flexible work schedules, remote officing for workers with small children at home, Health Care Reimbursement accounts, Dependent Care Reimbursement accounts, part-time employment, both day and night shifts, remote accessibility to e-mail and network, and other benefits highlight the focus on both family and individual needs. The company found that many qualified workers had special needs due to family requirements, and has tried to meet those needs creatively.

The company serves clients nationally, which encouraged the development of expanded work hours to enable clients and their employees to call with questions or requests on their benefits program. Providing customized Section 125, insurance and 401(k) retirement plan administrative services to clients of all sizes has spurred the development of its own benefit structure, including flex time.

"What we have recognized over the years is that everybody is unique, with diverse needs and goals. We wanted to find a way to make every job as fulfilling as possible and help fit into personal schedules and preferences. Just as it has been important to offer the very best in benefit design and administration to our clients, we also wanted to offer the very best place for our employees," says Jeanne Baker, CEO. For instance, a key employee in the MIS department has had a total flex schedule for years. He prefers to work from around 9 A.M. to 2 P.M., then takes time for outdoor activities, and returns from approximately 5 or 6 P.M. on into the evening. Depending on the workload, each day's schedule may be different. But, overall, he averages at least forty hours per week.

As the company has expanded, it has made a special effort to expand the ability of workers to design a schedule that best fits their needs. By offering a two-shift approach, employees can select the hours that fit their family schedule, and share a workspace with another employee. Not only does the company provide the flexibility for employees, but also it makes best use of the computers, workspace, telephones, and office facility as it continues to grow.

What do we mean by being creative in offering services to employees as a benefit? Take the case of Jean Lemoin's high-tech public-relations firm, MCA, in Mountain View, California. The environment in MCA, as in many public-relations firms, can be hectic and stress producing. Lemoin, however, knew that something needed to be done to help lessen the anxiety. Her solution, after hearing what her employees really needed, Lemoin contracted with Katherine Russo of Corporate Concierge. Russo's job is to run errands for Lemoin's employees. At MCA, this means that Russo performs such tasks as taking employees' dogs for walks, picking up their prescriptions, buying gifts for special occasions, or going to the dry cleaners. Lemoin's employees are less stressed at work, because some of their menial errands are handled for them, and they needn't worry about having to leave work to "take care of something." An employee benefit they have has seen to this.

employee at no cost, or at a significant reduction from what might have been paid without the organization's support.

Services provided to employees may be such benefits as sponsored social and recreational events, employee assistance programs, credit unions, housing, tuition reimbursement, jury duty, uniforms, military pay, company-paid transportation and parking, free coffee, baby-sitting services or referrals, and even appliance repair services.[88] Companies can be as creative as they like in putting together their benefits program. The crucial point is to provide a package containing those benefits in which employees have expressed some interest and perceive some value in its offering.

AN INTEGRATIVE PERSPECTIVE ON EMPLOYEE BENEFITS

When an employer considers offering benefits to employees, one of the main considerations is to keep costs down. Traditionally employers attempted to do this by providing a list of benefits to their employees—whether employees wanted or needed any particular benefit, or used it at all. Rising costs, and a desire to let employees choose what they want, led employers to search for alternative measures of benefits administration. The leading alternative to address this concern was the implementation of **flexible benefits.**[89] Although flexible benefits offer greater choices to employees (and might have a "motivational" effect), we must understand that they are provided mainly to contain benefit

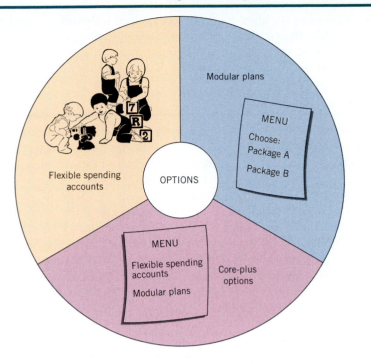

Exhibit 12-6
Flexible benefit programs.

costs.[90] The term *flexible benefits* refers to a system whereby employees are presented with a menu of benefits and asked to select, within monetary limits imposed, the employee benefits they desire.[91] Today, almost all major corporations in the United States offer flexible benefits. A number of types of flexible benefits exist. Specifically, three plans are popular: flexible spending accounts, modular plans, and core-plus options (see Exhibit 12-6).[92]

Flexible Spending Accounts

Flexible spending accounts, approved and operated under Section 125 of the Internal Revenue Code (IRC), are special types of flexible benefits that permit employees to set aside up to the dollar amount offered in the Plan to pay for particular services. For example, Abbott Laboratories has a flexible benefit plan that enables employees to pay for such items as health-care and dental premiums under premium accounts. Also, certain medical expenses (like deductibles, and dental and vision care under a medical reimbursement account); and dependent child-care expenses (up to $5000) under a dependent-care reimbursement account can be established.[93] By placing a specified amount into a spending account, the employee is permitted to pay for these services with monies not included in W-2 income. This can result in lower Federal, state, and social security tax rates for an employee, and can increase the amount of individual spending income. Such accounts also provide Social Security tax savings for the employer.

While tax benefits exist for employees, workers must understand that flexible spending accounts are heavily regulated. Each account established must operate independently. For instance, money set aside for dependent care expenses can be used only for that purpose. One cannot decide later to seek reimbursement from one account to pay for services where no account was established, or to pay for services from another account because all monies in the designated account have been withdrawn. Additionally, money that is deposited into these accounts must be spent during the period, or forfeited. Unused monies do not revert back to the employee in terms of a cash outlay; forfeited monies typically revert back to the company. This point must be clearly communicated to employees to avoid misconception of the plan requirements.

Modular Plans

The **modular plan** of flexible benefits is a system whereby employees choose a predesigned package of benefits. As opposed to selecting "cafeteria style," modular plans contain "a fixed combination of benefit plans put together to meet the needs of a particular segment of the employee population."[94] For example, suppose a company offers its employees two separate modules. Module 1 benefits consist of no dental or vision coverage, a life insurance policy at two times annual earnings, and HMO health-care insurance; this policy is provided to all employees at no cost to them. Module 2 benefits consist of dental and vision coverage, a life insurance policy of two times annual earnings, and traditional health insurance. This plan, however, requires a biweekly pre-tax payroll deduction of $57. While a choice does exist, it is limited to selecting either of the packages in its entirety.

Core-Plus Options Plans

A **core-plus options** flexible benefits plan exhibits more of a menu selection than the two programs just mentioned. Under this arrangement, employees typically are provided with coverage of core areas—typically medical coverage, life insurance at one-time annual earnings, minimal disability insurance, a 401(k) program, and standard time off from work with pay.[95] With these minimum benefits in place, not only are employees provided basic coverage from which they can build more extensive packages, the core-plus option helps to keep benefit costs relatively stable.

Under the core-plus plan, employees are given the opportunity to select other benefits. These additional benefits may range from more extensive coverage of the core plan to other benefits like spending accounts. Employees are generally given credits to purchase their additional benefits. These credits are often calculated according to an employee's tenure in the company, salary, and position held. As a rule of thumb, in first-time installations, the credits given to an employee equal the amount needed to purchase the identical plan in force before flexible benefits arrived; that is, no employee should be worse off. If the employee decides to select exactly what was previously offered, the employee will be able to purchase such benefits with no added out-of-pocket expenses (co-payments) other than what he or she had previously paid, with these payments now being made on a pre-tax basis.

SUMMARY

This summary relates to the Learning Objectives provided on p. 352.

After having read this chapter, you should know:

1. The linkage of benefits to motivation may not exist unless the benefits offered are tailored to the specific needs of the workers (their rewards). Traditional benefit administration, treating benefits as membership-based rewards, may not generate the increased productivity like that of flexible-benefit options.

2. Employers offer benefits to employees to attract

and retain them. Benefits are expected by today's workers, and as such, must be offered in such a way that they provide meaning and value to the employees.

3. Social Security is an insurance program funded by current employees to provide (1) a minimum level of retirement income, (2) disability income, and (3) survivor benefits. Unemployment compensation provides income continuation to employees who lose a job through no fault of their own. Unemployment compensation typically lasts for twenty-six weeks. Workers' compensation provides income continuation for employees who are hurt or disabled on the job. Workers' compensation also provides compensation for work-related deaths or permanent disabilities. All three are legally required benefits.

4. The three major types of health insurance benefits offered to employees are traditional, health maintenance organizations, and preferred provider organizations. The latter two are designed to provide a fixed out-of-pocket alternative to health-care coverage.

5. The most popular types of retirement benefits offered today are defined benefit pension plans, money purchase pension plans, profit-sharing plans, Social Security, individual retirement accounts, and 401(k)s. For special groups, however, 403(b)s, stock option programs, simplified employee pension plans, and Keogh plans may be used.

6. The Employment Retirement Income Security Act (ERISA) has had a significant effect on retirement programs. Its primary emphasis is to ensure that employees have a vested right to their retirement monies, to ensure that appropriate guidelines are followed in the event of a retirement plan termination, and to ensure that employees understand their benefits through the Summary Plan Description.

7. The primary reason for a company to provide a vacation benefit is to allow employees a break from work in which they can refresh/reenergize themselves.

8. Disability benefit programs are designed to ensure income replacement for employees in the event of a temporary or permanent disability arising from an injury or extended illness (typically originating off the job).

9. The term family-friendly benefits refers to a variety of benefits that are supportive of blending family and career. This may include on-site child care, flexible work schedules, dependent spending accounts, and part-time employment.

10. Flexible benefits programs come in a variety of packages. The most popular versions existing today are flexible spending accounts, modular plans, add-on plans, and core-plus options.

EXPERIENTIAL EXERCISE:
Employee Benefits

Each team member will be asked to call or visit two benefit specialists or administrators in two organizations and ask about their benefits and why they offer them, and if they motivate employees.

Next, find out their choice of health insurance options, pension programs, educational assistance, vacation benefits, disability insurance programs, family-friendly benefits, domestic partner benefits, flexible benefit option programs, and any other existing programs. Ask if they will share their plans, policies, or forms with permission to share with your team.

Next, record your findings, along with your team member's, on a comparison chart for the next meeting.

Share your findings and conclusions with your team, then prepare your team's recommendations.

WEB-WISE EXERCISES

Search and print findings of interest from the following sites:

Web Wise

Benefitslink
http://www.benefitslink.com/

Search, record Web address for future reference and for your team and print findings for the following organizations:

American Benefits Association

Families and Work Institute

National Council on Aging

Bureau of National Affairs

CASE APPLICATION:
Benefits Task Force

At the invitation of the new VP of human resources, Wanda Mayerling, you and six employees were asked to explore preferred benefits for the 653 employees of Universal Simulators Company, and to ensure the benefits offered were both competitive and innovative.

Wanda shared in the recent meeting, "What do I know about getting the children to school, or dealing with a sick child, or choosing between the school play and going out of town for five days? What I do know is that what is best depends on the individual, and to our best ability I want us to offer a package that reflects the needs of our employees—not some, all. Things have changed—a family is not necessarily Cleave, June, Wally, and the Beav anymore. If we are to attract, retain, and reward the best and brightest, we must accommodate their needs by benchmarking, learning, and developing a unique package. As a family-friendly company, our founder and board wants to be known as a world-class, cutting-edge company, but offering benefits that can meet the needs of USC's diverse work force is an ongoing challenge, and we need your help to lead this project.

The team's challenge is to identify specific concerns and problem areas and to propose solutions that can represent the most variation in terms of employees. In fact, we may need to hire a dependent-care program manager like Aetna or IBM or add work–family issues to the functions of a human resource staff member. And we should look into domestic partner benefits and expand ways to affirm family values as well, like offering parenting seminars after work or at lunch, or counseling and referral services. There's so much more we could do! Maybe convert empty space into a kitchen, game, and meeting room and movie theater as did Original Copy Center in Cleveland, or summer camps for children, or offer leaves for community service. Maybe use flexible dependent-care spending accounts to pay for child care and child-care referral services like *The Seattle Times*.

Stride Rite Corporation opened a combination childcare and elderly care center, and has estimated it saves $22,000 per employee by enabling it to keep highly skilled people and avoid the cost of retraining!

Your first objectives must be to learn about employee needs and concerns and about what supplemental health benefits, death and disability benefits, pension and retirement plans, time-off benefits, cafeteria plans, and other benefits are available.

Assignment

I would like to ask your team to develop a 20-minute presentation to educate and provide our executive management with an overview about the different types of plans and benefits for our first meeting.

At your second meeting present a 20-minute overview on HMOs and at the third meeting, worker's comp. We may even ask that you repeat the presentations to employees or videotape your sessions and distribute them to all locations. Our employees and managers need a better understanding of their benefits.

Meet as a team, and develop your presentations based upon your research.

Select your team leader, timekeeper, recorder, and facilitator, and let's get to work!

Be prepared for questions! In fact, I'll ask the first one now

Share your understanding of what your specific team objectives include:

1. Find out what issues are most important to employees:
2.
3.
4.

Wanda continued, "Recently I read that the top five ranked benefits were medical/health/dental insurance, vacations, retirement plan, sick leave, and holidays. Team, I would like each of you to rank your preferences of most valued 1 to 5 on the chart, and let's compare the six of you with national averages."

TESTING YOUR UNDERSTANDING

How well did you fulfill the learning objectives?
1. Employee benefits are important in today's organizations for all of these reasons except
   a. employees expect more than monetary rewards from their jobs.
   b. benefits packages are instrumental in recruiting the best workers for an organization.
   c. benefits packages increase employee productivity.
   d. benefits packages help to retain good workers in an organization.
   e. benefits packages are designed to meet the needs of a wide variety of workers.
2. Margaret worked for an electrical contracting organization for sixteen years. She quit her job when she moved out of state. Which of the following would provide the most information about her company retirement benefits?
   a. Social Security Administration Review
   b. COBRA
   c. Summary Plan Description
   d. Section 89 reports
   e. Pension Benefit Guaranty Corporation publications
3. Social Security, workers' compensation, and unemployment compensation are accurately compared by all of these statements except
   a. all programs are legally required.
   b. Social Security and workers' compensation are funded by employees and employers. Unemployment compensation is funded by employees and state government.
   c. Social Security and unemployment compensation provide monetary allocations to recipients. Workers' compensation may provide monetary allocation or payment for services.

d. Social Security is administered by the federal government. Workers' compensation and unemployment compensation are administered at the state level.

e. all three programs are designed to provide income protection or continuation.

4. Which statement best compares traditional health insurance, HMOs, and PPOs?

   a. PPOs try to combine the best features of the traditional and the HMO coverages.

   b. Most U.S. workers have PPO coverage. Fewest U.S. workers have traditional coverage.

   c. Traditional health insurance provides access to a qualified physician. HMOs and PPOs are usually staffed by physicians' assistants.

   d. Traditional coverage has no limit, or cap, on services provided. Both HMOs and PPOs have maximum benefit amounts.

   e. Traditional coverage usually has an annual deductible amount. HMOs and PPOs usually do not have a deductible.

5. Jason, a fifty-five-year-old engineer, works for a large manufacturing organization. Each year he contributes 10 percent of his earnings to an individual account and the company contributes an additional 6 percent. Michael has the option to choose whether the funds will be invested in stocks or bonds, and can change his choice every quarter. Projections are made as to probable retirement benefit levels from this account. What kind of retirement program does Michael have?

   a. Defined benefit plan

   b. 401 (k) plan

   c. Money purchase pension plan

   d. Capital accumulation program

   e. Individual Retirement Account

6. Barry, a plant manager, has worked for an electronic parts manufacturer for twenty years. Usually he takes his four weeks of vacation to go hunting in Alaska. This year, with three children in college, he wants to "sell" three weeks back to the company for additional income and take one week in September to help all the children move into their school dorms. Why would his human resources department advise against such action?

   a. There is no time to go through his files if he is not out of the office.

   b. Such a practice is against the law.

   c. Barry might suffer "burnout" without the rejuvenating effects of his vacation.

   d. It is too costly to allow people to have the additional salary.

   e. Such action would lower morale in the plant and damage future recruiting efforts.

7. Dana, director of employee benefits, wants to change the company's liberal sick leave policy. Currently, employees are entitled to four hours of paid sick leave for each month of service with the company. When employees leave or retire, unused sick leave is forfeited. Dana noticed that many employees are "sick" just before major holiday periods, such as Christmas or Independence Day, leaving critical areas of the company understaffed. Also, many employees are "sick" for a day or two after their annual vacations, creating scheduling problems for other employees who are then asked to rework their own vacation plans. Which of the following would be the best change for Dana's sick leave policy?

   a. Require employees to produce a physician's excuse for all sick leave taken.

   b. Designate time periods of before and after major holidays and before and after annual leave ineligible for sick leave. Any time off taken during those periods must be without pay and unexcused.

   c. Have someone on the human resources staff telephone to make sure employees are home, sick, when they say they are.

   d. Allow unused sick leave to accumulate. Fold it into retirement benefits to be credited and compensated as length of service.

   e. Cease to offer paid sick leave as a benefit.

8. Jackie, who earned $156,000 a year as vice president of marketing for a manufacturing firm, died in a plane crash on the way to an industry convention in Chicago. She had group term life insurance of four times her annual salary with a double indemnity provision, a $500,000 travel insurance policy, a $250,000 maximum short-term disability insurance plan, an additional purchased group life insurance plan of two times her annual salary (without double indemnity), and a $1,000,000 AD&D policy. How much money did Jackie's widower receive?

   a. $1,886,000

   b. $2,686,000

   c. $2,168,000

   d. $1,168,000

   e. $2,586,000

9. Dennis works for a company that provides HMO medical insurance, short-term disability, two-times life insurance, one week paid vacation, and a basic retirement plan to all employees. Dennis also has the option of purchasing $4,000 (amount calculated from 1 percent of salary, 3 years of service) worth of additional benefits from such areas as additional life or health insurance coverages, more retirement, childcare or elder-care accounts, tuition reimbursement, and more vacation. What kind of flexible spending plan is Dennis's company using?

   a. flexitime

   b. flexible spending accounts

   c. modular

    d. core-plus options

    e. none of the above

10. Which one of the following is not a family-friendly benefit?

    a. employee assistance programs

    b. dependent spending accounts

    c. part-time employment

    d. summer camp

    e. relocation programs

11. What is the major work-force demographics concern for benefits programs?

    a. The increased numbers of women in the work force mean more need for child care.

    b. The aging work force needs more health-care provision than earlier workers.

    c. In order to provide "something of value" for each worker, the diverse demographic needs must be considered.

    d. Retirement at an earlier age changes retirement needs.

    e. Legally mandated programs supersede all benefit options based on demographics.

12. What are vesting rights?

    a. After a certain length of service, employees have a right to a pension with a company when they reach retirement age, whether or not they still work for the company.

    b. After ten years of service, an employee may retire from a company with a certain percentage of retirement benefits.

    c. When the years of service plus an employee's age equal 70, the employee may retire, receiving 85 percent of retirement benefits.

    d. After twenty-five years of service, employees are entitled to stock options usually reserved for executives.

    e. After a certain length of service, employees have the right to continue their health-care coverage for three years if they leave the company.

13. Legally required employee benefits include

    a. Social Security, ERISA, and COBRA.

    b. Social Security, workers' compensation, and unemployment compensation.

    c. COBRA, workers' compensation, and unemployment compensation.

    d. Medicaid, workers' compensation, and COBRA.

    e. Social Security, Medicaid, and unemployment compensation.

14. A major difference between traditional health insurance and HMO coverage is

    a. medical/surgical expenses are covered only by traditional.

    b. mental health treatments are not covered under HMOs.

    c. preventive health care is covered only for HMOs.

    d. most HMOs have larger deductible amounts than traditional.

    e. HMOs are available only to single employees.

15. Why do companies offer paid vacations to employees?

    a. Increasingly, due to downsizing actions, companies are refusing to offer paid vacations.

    b. Most firms have to offer vacations to be competitive.

    c. Vacations are necessary due to globalization.

    d. Vacations provide a break so that employees can refresh themselves.

    e. Vacations allow time for supervisors to completely check the accuracy and completeness of an employee's files.

Endnotes

1. Based on the article by Tom Ehrenfeld, "Socially Responsible Entrepreneur of the Year: Friend of the Family," *Inc.* (December 1994), pp. 93–96.

2. For a more thorough coverage of this material, see David A. DeCenzo and Stephen J. Holoviak, *Employee Benefits* (Englewood Cliffs, N.J.: Prentice-Hall, 1991).

3. Robert McGarvey, "Something Extra," *Entrepreneur* (May 1995), p. 70.

4. Frederick Herzberg, *Work and the Nature of Man* (New York: World, 1966).

5. U.S. Bureau of the Census, *Statistical Abstracts of the United States: 1997* (Washington, D.C.: Government Printing Office, 1997), p. 377; and Commerce Clearing House, "Employees' Benefit Costs Averaged 40.2% of Payroll in 1992," *Human Resources Management: Ideas and Trends* (March 3, 1994), p. 36.

6. Ibid.

7. *Employee Benefits Journal*, Vol. 12, No. 2 (June 1987), p. 38.

8. BNA Datagraph, *BNA Bulletin to Management* (January 5, 1995), p. 4.

9. Kevin Rubens, "Changes in Russia: A Challenge for HR," *HRMagazine* (November 1995), p. 72.

10. This assumes that the insurance policy is part of a group term plan. Should it be a single policy, other than term insurance, or if the plan discriminates in favor of the more highly paid employees, then the entire benefit would be taxable.

11. As discussed in Chapter 3, government regulations had a major impact on the increases in employee benefits. It is equally important to note that management practices and labor unions also have affected benefit offerings.

12. See, for instance, Debra Kent, "Two Men and Their Babies," *Working Mother* (June 1995), pp. 24–27.

13. See, for instance, Robert W. Thompson, "Domestic Partner Benefits Catching On, Survey Finds," *HR News* (February 1997), p. 4; "Disney to Offer Insurance to Partners of Gay Workers," *The New York Times* (October 8, 1995), p. 2A; and Charles McCoy, "Texas County Reverses Course on Apple Plant," *The Wall Street Journal* (December 8, 1998), p. B-1.

14. Social Security here refers to FICA taxes, for Old Age, Survivors, and Disability Insurance (OASDI).

15. Ames Gross and Patricia Dyson, "The Iron Rice Bowl Cracks," *HRMagazine* (July 1996), pp. 84–88.

16. Ellen Hoffman, "The Real Problem with Social Security," *Money* (November 1997), p. 134.

17. Ibid., p. 356; and U.S. Bureau of the Census, *Statistical Abstracts of the United States: 1997* (Washington, D.C.: Government Printing Office, 1997), p. 434.

18. Based on the passage of the Omnibus Budget Reconciliation Act of 1993, the 2.9% Medicare portion no longer has a salary cap. Commerce Clearing House, "New Tax Law Will Require Review of Many HR Policies and Benefit Programs," *Human Resources Management: Ideas and Trends* (August 18, 1993), pp. 129–30.

19. "Public Confidence in the Social Security System," *Managers Handbook* (May 1997), p. 6.

20. Ibid. It's appropriate also to note that there are reductions in Social Security payments based on one's age and earnings. In 1999, individuals age 70 and older, receiving the maximum monthly Social Security, would receive $14,500 in total Social Security benefits. Their benefit would not be reduced for other earned income. Those 65 to 69, would lose $1.00 or every $3.00 of earned income. Those receiving Social Security who are under age 65 lose $1.00 for every $2.00 earned.

21. Louis S. Richman, "Why Baby-Boomers Won't Be Able to Retire," *Fortune* (September 4, 1995), p. 48.

22. Richard I. Henderson, *Compensation Management: Rewarding Performance,* 6th ed. (Englewood Cliffs, N.J.: Prentice-Hall, 1994), p. 87.

23. Ibid.

24. Ibid., p. 88. Wage bases for unemployment insurance vary. A number of states follow the federal $7,000 base, while others vary to a maximum of $22,700 in Hawaii. See Henderson, p. 88.

25. In 1992, President George Bush signed into law a bill extending the unemployment coverage from 26 weeks to 39 weeks for those experiencing long durations of unemployment brought about by the recession in the early 1990s. This extension expired July 4, 1992. However, on July 2, 1992, President Bush again extended the coverage for an additional 20 or 26 weeks, depending on the unemployment rates in each state. This extension expired on March 6, 1993. Those who exhausted the original 39 weeks, however, were not eligible for this extended coverage.

26. Although unemployment benefits are federally mandated, that does not mean that problems will not occur. Because of the tremendous layoffs occurring in the latter part of 1990 and early 1991, a number of states had depleted their unemployment funds. Accordingly, in such states as Connecticut, Massachusetts, Ohio, Michigan, Arkansas, West Virginia, and Missouri, their rates charged to employers increased (*The Wall Street Journal,* January 16, 1991, p. B-1).

27. Mark D. Fefer, "Taking Control of Your Workers' Comp Costs," *Fortune* (October 3, 1994), pp. 131–136.

28. "Paternity Leave in Norway–Use It or Lose It," *HRMagazine* (January 1996), p. 24.

29. Lenore Schiff, "Is Health Care a Job Killer," *Fortune* (April 6, 1992), p. 30.

30. "Not the Best of Times," *HR Focus* (February 1998), p. 8; and "Focus on–Ancillary Benefits," *Employee Benefit Plan Review* (November 1997), p. 20.

31. Point-of-service or network plans are often a variation of preferred provider organizations. The main distinction typically lies in the degree of choice permitted. For example, under a preferred provider, any physician who participates can be seen by a subscriber. In a point-of-service (POS) or network, the possible physicians may be more limited. Although there are some constraints placed on choosing a physician, they are not as great as those imposed by an HMO. See also "Moving to Managed Care," *HRMagazine* (January 1995), p. 20.

32. While Blue Cross and Blue Shield is the most widely known organization for traditional insurance, it is not the only one. Companies like Mutual of Omaha, New York Life, Aetna, and other commercial insurance companies all offer health-care coverage that models the BC/BS plan.

33. Jerry S. Rosenbloom and G. Victor Hallman, *Employee Benefit Planning,* 3d ed. (Englewood Cliffs, N.J.: Prentice-Hall, 1991), p. 80.

34. It is important to understand the difference between two terms that are widely used in Blue Shield contracts. These are non-pars and participating physicians. A non-par, or nonparticipating physician, will not accept Blue Shield payments as payment in full for services rendered. This means that any costs incurred above the repayment schedule set by the health insurer are the responsibility of the patient. *Participating physicians,* as the term implies, agree to accept Blue Shield payments as payments in full for services rendered.

35. Rosenbloom and Hallman, p. 85.

36. Stuart Gannes, "Strong Medicine for Health Bills," *Fortune* (April 13, 1987), p. 71.

37. "Managed Care Lowers Health Care Costs, But Which Plan Is Best," *HRMagazine* (May 1997), p. 26.

38. James C. Spee, "Addition by Subtraction," *HRMagazine* (March 1995), p. 41; and Joey J. Barber, "Lower Health Care Costs through Direct Contracting," *HRMagazine* (September 1995), pp. 66–67.

39. Rosenbloom and Hallman, p. 90.

40. It also should be noted that in some self-funding cases, organizations seek assistance from another company commonly referred to as a "Third Party Administrator (TPA)." The TPA's role is simply to process the health-care forms.

41. For employees who have been terminated or whose hours have been reduced, their coverage is for a period of 18 months (possibly extended to 29 months if qualifying dependents are covered). See Robert M. McCaffery, *Employee Benefit Programs: A Total Compensation Perspective,* 2d ed. (Boston, Mass.: PWS-Kent Publishing, 1992), p. 96.

42. The additional 11 months (19–29 months of coverage) were available to those who were disabled prior to receiving COBRA benefits. Under the Health Insurance Portability and Accountability Act of 1996, effective January 1, 1997, the 11 month extension is possible for any individual who becomes disabled within the first 60 days of COBRA coverage. See Percy Williams II, "Law Enhances Portability of Health Benefits," *HR News* (October 1996), pp. 4–5.

43. Leslie Wayne, "Pension Changes Raising Concerns," *New York Times* (August 29, 1994), pp. A-1; D-3.

44. Rodney N. Mara, "Communication of Benefits," in *Employee Benefits Handbook,* Fred K. Foulkes (ed.), (Boston, Mass.: Warren, Gorham, and Lamont, 1982), p. 6-2.

45. The Retirement Equity Act of 1984 and the Tax Reform Act of 1986 modified participation ages, minimum vesting age,

and vesting rights—requiring full vesting after five years, partial vesting after three years, and seven-year full vesting with plan years beginning after December 1, 1988. Those companies with a retirement plan year prior to that date were not required to go to the new lower vesting rules until December 1, 1989. It is also important to note, as will be discussed later in the chapter, that any monies contributed by employees toward their retirement are 100 percent vested immediately.

46. Portability of pension rights is a complex issue that goes beyond the scope of this book. However, depending on the company, employees may receive a permanent right to their monies, receiving a pension from the organization at retirement age, or be given a check that allows them to reinvest those monies on their own.

47. "Forewarning Rule," *The Wall Street Journal* (June 2, 1992), p. A-1.

48. Robert M. McCaffery, *Employee Benefit Programs: A Total Compensation Perspective* (Boston, Mass.: PWS-Kent Publishing, 1992), pp. 234, 246–47.

49. See, for instance, "Tell Employees: Summary Plan Descriptions," *Employee Benefit Plan Review* (May 1991), pp. 23–26.

50. The Bureau of National Affairs, "Pension Changes in Order," *Bulletin to Management,* No. 1795 (August 30, 1984), p. 1.

51. "Company Keeps Costs Steady While Long Service Employees Get Protection Through Floor Plan," *Employee Benefit Plan Review,* Vol. 42, No. 1 (July 1987), pp. 76–78.

52. McCaffery, p. 131.

53. Ibid., p. 142.

54. Profit-sharing plans require that there be profits before a contribution can be made. When there are no profits for the period, no contributions need to be made. The only partial exception is that contributions can be made in a year in which there are no profits if there are accumulated profits from prior years. However, should this occur, further restrictions apply.

55. Most companies offering matching contribution features to their 401(k) programs limit the amount of their contribution. Typically, their matching amount is set as one-half of the amount the employee contributes, with a 3 percent maximum. Thus, an employee setting aside 4 percent of his or her salary will have a 2 percent match, with up to 3 percent for a 6 percent deduction.

56. Elaine McShulskis, "Employee Benefit Specialists' New Priorities," *HRMagazine* (March 1996), p. 31.

57. Kate Walter, "Paid-Time-Off Leave Plans Experience Less Abuse," *HR News* (August 1995), p. 5.

58. Anita Bruzzese, "Workers Getting More Say in When, How They Take Time Off," *Carroll County Times* (July 23, 1993), p. B-5; and "Vacations Are Shorter in the U.S. and Japan than in Europe," *The Wall Street Journal* (June 2, 1992), p. A-1.

59. Bill Leonard, "The Employee's Favorite, The Employer's Quandary," *HRMagazine* (November 1994), p. 53.

60. Anita Bruzzese, "Workers Getting More Say in When, How They Take Time Off," *Carroll County Times* (July 23, 1993), p. B-5.

61. Rosenbloom and Hallman, p. 208.

62. Short-term disability programs may be provided through commercial carriers or through self-funding arrangements. The more popular of the two is purchased coverage.

63. Before we proceed, an important piece of federal legislation warrants mentioning. Based on the 1978 Pregnancy Disability Act, employers that offer short-term disability insurance to its employees must include pregnancy as part of the policy's coverage. This means that in whatever capacity employers "cover" other disabilities like an extended illness, the coverage for disability due to pregnancy must be the same (see Chapter 3).

64. The number of sick days offered to employees generally varies according to their position in the organization and their length of service. Many organizations require a waiting period, approximately six months, before sick leave kicks in.

65. Rochelle Sharpe, "Workplace Epidemic: Absenteeism for Third Year in a Row," *The Wall Street Journal* (February 27, 1996), p. A-1; and Elaine McShulskis, "Sick Leave Not Always for the Sick," *HRMagazine* (October 1996), p. 25.

66. Carl Quintanilla, "Calling in Sick? Some Airlines Pay Their Employees Not To," *The Wall Street Journal* (September 17, 1996), p. A-1.

67. Other employers are simply doing away with sick leave and are adding the time to vacation or personal days.

68. Commerce Clearing House, *Compensation* (May 1988), p. 2699.

69. Ibid.

70. The reason for the 70 to 80 percent of replacement income stems from the tax-free nature of some payments. (Payments from an employer LTD are generally taxable; the amount received from LTD based on employee paid premiums is not taxable income.) If long-term payments were not reduced, it is conceivable that an employee receiving LTD and government disability payments could have a greater income than when the employee was working. This logic defeats the purpose of the program.

71. Rosenbloom and Hallman, p. 222.

72. Some disability plans pay benefits for different periods if the disability is due to illness rather than injury.

73. Elaine McShulskis, "Voluntary Benefits Popular," *HRMagazine* (March 1997), p. 30.

74. Depending on company policy, there may be a time lag before a new employee's insurance policy takes effect. Waiting periods, when used, typically last about six months. Additionally, eligibility periods may be waived for management personnel.

75. U.S. Bureau of the Census, *Statistical Abstracts of the United States: 1997* (Washington, D.C.: Government Printing Office, 1997), p. 435.

76. Commerce Clearing House, Compensation (August 1990), p. 2605.

77. Allison Kindelan, "Dependent-Care Accounts Top Family-Friendly Benefits," *HR News* (April 1996), p. 14; Shu Shu Costa, "Babies Welcome," *Working Mother* (February 1996), p. 34; "Work-Life Initiatives Expanding at Leading Companies," *HR News* (June 1995), p. 15; and B. P. Noble, "Making a Case for Family Friendly Programs," *The New York Times* (May 2, 1993), p. F-25.

78. See, for example, Shirley Hand and Robert A. Zawacki, "Family-Friendly Benefits: More than a Frill," *HRMagazine* (October 1994), pp. 79–84; and Sharon Nelton, "A Flexible Style of Management," *Nation's Business* (December 1993), pp. 24–31.

79. Milton Moskowitz, "100 Best Companies for Working Mothers," *Working Mother* (October 1997), pp. 18–96; Sue Shel-

lenbarger, "A Tangible Commitment to Work-Family Issues," *The Wall Street Journal* (September 21, 1994), p. B-1; and Shirley Hand and Robert A. Zawacki, "Family-Friendly Benefits: More than a Frill," *HRMagazine* (October 1994), pp. 82–83.

80. We group together these two issues because of similarity. Their only difference lies in the age of the individual. Obviously, child care deals with the young, and elder care deals with caring for one's elderly dependents (e.g., parents).

81. For another perspective on child care and whether or not they are fair to "single" employees, see Robert McGarvey, "Singled Out," *Entrepreneur* (March 1998), pp. 80–83.

82. Richard Levine, "Childcare: Inching Up the Corporate Agenda," *Management Review,* Vol. 78, No. 1 (January 1989), pp. 43–47.

83. Douglas J. Petersen and Douglas Massengill, "Childcare Programs Benefit Employers, Too," *Personnel* (May 1988), pp. 58–62.

84. M. Galen, "Work & Family," *Business Week* (June 28, 1993), p20.

85. "Companies Team Up to Improve Quality of Their Employ-ees' Child-care Choices," *The Wall Street Journal* (October 17, 1991), p. B-1; see also Susan Gordon, "Helping Corporations Care," *Working Woman* (January 1993), p. 30.

86. Julia Lawlor, "Why Companies Should Care," *Working Woman* (June 1995), p. 38.

87. "Benefits: Get Ready for Elder Care," *Inc.* (September 1995), p. 101.

88. "Convenience Perks," *HRMagazine* (February 1995), p. 24.

89. For a thorough discussion of flexible benefits, the advantages and disadvantages, see DeCenzo and Holoviak, *Employee Benefits,* Chapter 11.

90. Christopher Caggiano, "Perks You Can Afford," *Inc.* (November 1997), p. 107.

91. Richard E. McDermott and Joan Ogden, "Five Ways to Improve Your Health Benefits Program," *HRMagazine* (August 1995), pp. 44–48.

92. Richard E. Johnson, "Flexible Benefit Plans," *Employee Benefits Journal,* Vol. 11, No. 3 (September 1986), pp. 3–6.

93. Johnson, p. 4.

94. Ibid, p. 4.

95. McCaffery, p. 197.

13. Employee Rights

LEARNING OBJECTIVES

After reading this chapter, you will be able to:

1. Explain the intent of the Privacy Act of 1974, and its effect on HRM.
2. Discuss the HRM implications of the Drug-Free Workplace Act of 1988, and the Polygraph Protection Act of 1988.
3. Describe the provisions of the Worker Adjustment and Retraining Notification Act of 1988.
4. Identify the pros and cons of employee drug testing.
5. Explain why honesty tests are used in hiring.
6. Discuss the implications of the employment-at-will doctrine.
7. Identify the four exceptions to the employment-at-will doctrine.
8. Define discipline and the contingency factors that determine the severity of discipline.
9. Describe the general guidelines for administering discipline.
10. Identify how employee counseling can be used to assist a poorly performing employee.

*B*ausch & Lomb, the Rochester, New York eye-wear company, made some major changes in the late 1990s that had a number of western Maryland citizens seeing red. A Bausch & Lomb plant in the area, makers of sunglass lenses, has been targeted for closure. As a result, approximately 600 jobs were lost.[1] Company representatives indicated that their decision to close the plant results from it being too expensive to maintain the current operation in the Maryland area. They have decided to shift the operations to plants in San Antonio, Texas, and Hong Kong.

Executives in companies like Bausch & Lomb have every right to run their business in the most effective manner. But what happens when decisions made adversely affect employees? For example, the Bausch & Lomb plant in western Maryland was closed after years of productive and quality work. The reason: the products made there could be made less expensively elsewhere.

Is Bausch & Lomb justified in its actions? Clearly, company officials have a right to manage their operations in the most profitable way they can. Moving to areas where employee pay is lower is one way to reduce costs. Therefore, from the "bottom line," these actions are warranted. Besides, it follows on the heels of the ousting of the company's chief executive, who watched profits fall from $171.4 million in 1992 to $31.1 million in a two-year period. Furthermore, management argued that it brought more to the relationship than the community gave back—specifically, high-paying jobs that allowed the community to grow and prosper—and that, in today's global economy, hometown loyalties cannot override economic considerations.

Bausch & Lomb's action created significant problems for employees and the surrounding community. That's because the company was the largest employer in the region. When the biggest employer in an area makes such a change, it not only affects employees who are laid off, it directly impacts other businesses. When income levels in a region drop significantly, less money is spent in the local economy. And when nothing was replacing this economic loss, problems arose. For instance, restaurants that opened and served a good portion of Bausch & Lomb employees have had to subsequently close because of a lack of patronage. Likewise, schools and other town-supported organizations face a similar fate as tax revenues drop significantly.

One reason for the company's actions related to how much employees were paid in the Maryland plant. When a company like Bausch & Lomb establishes an operation in the area, it does so to attract a skilled, dedicated, and committed work force. But Bausch & Lomb was also the primary employer in the region. As such, turnover was almost nonexistent. And pay levels of employees kept climbing upward. At the San Antonio plant, however, turnover was significant, and new employees were hired at lower wage rates than the person who left the job. As a result of the longevity, the average hourly wage rate in Maryland was about 33 percent higher than it was in Texas, and an even higher percentage when compared to Hong Kong. Although employees in the Maryland plant made more money than their counterparts in Texas and Hong Kong, they'd given the company something that other plants had not—highly recognized quality products. Over the years, this western Maryland plant had been recognized by several independent groups as producing some of the highest quality sunglass lenses in the world. In fact, employees have been awarded a prestigious international designation of quality, something few organizations anywhere in the world achieve. Additionally, this western Maryland plant received a productivity award from the U.S. government.

But all that was for naught. The fact remained: Bausch & Lomb had every legal right to do what it had done—irrespective of the effect it created on employees or the community.

INTRODUCTION

What once was an area where there was a thriving company—one typified by quality products—now has nearly become a ghost town. Shouldn't Bausch & Lomb employees have been rewarded for doing their jobs well and maintaining their loyalty to the company? Sure, there's a need for managers to make serious decisions—tough ones at that—without being questioned or even second-guessed. But were these employees of the western Maryland Bausch & Lomb plant treated fairly? Were their rights violated? Were Bausch & Lomb's actions ethical? It's answers to questions such as these that we will address in this chapter.

Employee rights has become one of the more important issues for human resource management to deal with. Individuals are guaranteed certain rights based on amendments to the U.S. Constitution. For instance, the Fourth Amendment prohibits illegal searches and seizures by the government or its agents. However, this does not mean that those outside the government, like businesses, cannot perform such an activity.[2] This has led to the question: Are employers all-powerful in this arena? The answer is no! In fact, in more and more situations—such as terminating an employee or maintaining health files on employees for insurance purposes—such organizational practices may be more constrained.[3] Consequently, various laws and Supreme Court rulings are establishing guidelines for employers dealing with employee privacy and other matters. Let's now turn to these laws.

EMPLOYMENT RIGHTS LEGISLATION AND THEIR HUMAN RESOURCE MANAGEMENT IMPLICATIONS

Over the past few decades, a number of federal laws have given specific protection to employees. These laws are the Privacy Act of 1974, the Drug-Free Work-Place Act of 1988, the Employee Polygraph Protection Act of 1988, and the Worker Adjustment and Retraining Notification Act of 1988.

The Privacy Act of 1974

When an organization begins the hiring process, it establishes a personnel file for that person—a file that is maintained throughout a person's employment. Any pertinent information, like the completed application, letters of recommendation, performance evaluations, or disciplinary warnings, are kept in the file. The contents of these files often were known only to those who had access to the files—often only managers and HRM personnel. The **Privacy Act of 1974** sought to change that imbalance of information. This act, while applicable to only federal government agencies, requires that an employee's personnel file be open for inspection. This means that employees are permitted to review their files periodically to ensure that the information contained within is accurate. The Privacy Act also gives these federal employees the right to review letters of recommendation written on their behalf.

Even though this act applies solely to the federal worker, it provided the impetus for state legislatures to pass similar laws governing employees of state- and private-sector enterprises. This legislation is often more comprehensive and includes protection regarding how employers disseminate information on past and current employees. For human resource management, a key question is: How should employees be given access to their files? Although the information contained within rightfully may be open for inspection, certain restrictions must be addressed. First, any information for which the employee has waived his or her right to review must be kept separate. For instance, job applicants often waive their right to see letters of recommendation written for them. When that happens, human resources is not obligated to make that information available to the employee. Second, an employee can't simply demand to immediately see his or her file; there is typically a twenty-four hour turnaround time. Consequently, organizations frequently establish special review procedures. For example, whether or not the employee can review the file alone or in the presence of an HRM representative is up to each organization. In either case, personnel files generally are not permitted to leave the HRM area. And although an individual may take notes about the file's contents, copying the file often is not permitted.

The increasing use of computers in human resource management has complicated the issue of file reviews. Because much of this information is now stored in computerized employee data systems, access has been further constrained. Yet although computerization of HRM files is a more complicated system, appropriate access to this information should not be any different than when using a paper file; employees still have a right to see the information about them, regardless of where it is kept. Gaining entry into computerized information, however, can be a more time-consuming process. Many times, such access requires certain security clearances to special screens—clearance that is not available to everyone. However, as technology continues to improve, HRM will be better able to implement procedures to give employees access, while simultaneously protecting the integrity of the system.

Companies are also being held accountable to the **Fair Credit Reporting Act of 1971,** an extension to the Privacy Act. In many organizations, the employment process includes a credit check on the applicant.[4] The purpose of such checks is to obtain information about the individual's "character, general reputation,"[5] and various other personal characteristics. Typically, companies can obtain this information by using two different approaches. The first is through a credit reporting agency, similar to the type that is used when you apply for a loan. In this instance, the employer is required to notify the individual that a credit report is being obtained. However, if an applicant is rejected based on information in the report, the individual must be provided a copy of the credit report, as well as a means for how to appeal the accuracy of the findings.[6] The second type of credit report is obtained through a third-party investigation. Under this arrangement, not only is one's credit checked, but people known to the applicant are interviewed regarding the applicant's lifestyle, spending habits, and character. For an organization to use this type of approach, the applicant must be informed of the process in writing, and as with the credit report, must be notified of the report's details if the information is used to negatively affect an employment decision. Keep in mind, however, that how the information is used must be job relevant. If, for example, an organization denies employment to an individual who once filed for bankruptcy and this information has no bearing on the individual's ability to do the job, the organization may be opening itself up to a challenge in the courts.

> **Credit report information used in employment decisions must be job relevant.**

The Drug-Free Workplace Act of 1988

The **Drug-Free Workplace Act of 1988** was passed to help keep the problem of substance abuse from entering the workplace. Under the act, government agencies, federal contractors, and those receiving federal funds ($25,000 or more) are required to actively pursue a drug-free environment. In addition, the act requires employees of companies regulated by the Department of Transportation (DOT) and the Nuclear Regulatory Commission who hold certain jobs to be subjected to drug tests.[7] For example, long-haul truck drivers, regulated by the DOT, are required to take drug tests.

For all organizations covered under this act, other stipulations are included. For example, the enterprise must establish its drug-free work environment policy and disseminate it to its employees. This policy must spell out what is expected of employees in terms of being substance free, and detail the penalties regarding infractions of the policy. In addition, the organization must provide substance-abuse awareness programs to its employees.

There's no doubt that this act has created difficulties for organizations. To comply with the act, they must obtain information about their employees. The whole issue of drug testing in today's companies is a major one, and we'll come back to its applications later in this chapter.

The Polygraph Protection Act of 1988

As a security specialist applicant for the Central Intelligence Agency (CIA), you are asked to submit to a polygraph test as a condition of employment. Unsure of what is going to transpire, you agree to be tested. During the examination, you are asked if you have ever smoked marijuana. You respond that you never have, but the polygraph records that you are not telling the truth. Because suspicion of substance use is grounds for disqualification from the job, you are removed from consideration. Can this organization use the polygraph information against you? In the case of a job involving security operations, it can!

However, the **Polygraph Protection Act of 1988**[8] prohibits employers in the private sector[9] from using polygraph tests (often referred to as lie-detector

NOTICE

EMPLOYEE POLYGRAPH PROTECTION ACT

The Employee Polygraph Protection Act prohibits most private employers from using lie detector tests either for pre-employment screening or during the course of employment.

Prohibitions

Employers are generally prohibited from requiring or requesting any employee or job applicant to take a lie detector test, and from discharging, disciplining, or discriminating against an employee or prospective employee for refusing to take a test or for exercising other rights under the act.

Exemptions*

The law does not apply to tests given by the federal government to certain private individuals engaged in national security-related activities.

The act permits *polygraph* (a kind of lie detector) tests to be administered in the private sector, subject to restrictions, to certain prospective employees of security service firms (armored car, alarm, and guard), and of pharmaceutical manufacturers, distributors and dispensers.

The act also permits polygraph testing, subject to restrictions, of certain employees of private firms who are reasonably suspected of involvement in a workplace incident (theft, embezzlement, etc.) that resulted in economic loss to the employer.

Examinee Rights

Where polygraph tests are permitted, they are subject to numerous strict standards concerning the conduct and length of the test. Examinees have a number of specific rights, including the right to a written notice before testing, the right to refuse or discontinue a test, and the right not to have test results disclosed to unauthorized persons.

Enforcement

The Department of Labor may bring court actions to restrain violations and assess civil penalties up to $10,000 against violators. Employees or job applicants may also bring their own court actions.

Additional Information

Additional information may be obtained, and complaints of violations may be filed, at local offices of the Wage and Hour Division, which are listed in the telephone directory under U.S. Government, Department of Labor, Employment Standards Administration.

The Law Requires Employers to Display This Poster Where Employees and Job Applicants Can Readily See It.

* The law does not preempt any provision of any state or local law or any collective bargaining agreement that is more restrictive with respect to lie detector tests.

Source: The U.S. Department of Labor, WH Publication 1462 (September 1988), Employment Standards Administration, Wage and Hour Division, Washington, D.C. 20210.

Exhibit 13-1

Polygraph protection notice.

tests) in all employment decisions. Based on the law, companies may no longer use these tests to screen all job applicants.[10] The act was passed because polygraphs were used inappropriately. In general, polygraph tests have been found to have little job-related value, and as such their effectiveness is questionable.[11] However, the Employee Polygraph Protection Act did not eliminate their use in organizations altogether. There are situations where the law permits their use, such as when there has been a theft in the organization, but this process is regulated, too. The polygraph cannot be used as a "witch-hunt." For example, suppose that there has been a theft in the organization. The Employee Polygraph Protection Act prohibits employers from testing all employees in an attempt to determine the guilty party. However, if an investigation into the theft points to a particular employee, then the employer can ask that employee to submit to a polygraph. Even in this case, however, the employee has the right to refuse to take a polygraph test without fear of retaliation from the employer. And in cases in which one does submit to the test, the employee must receive, in advance, a list of questions that will be asked. Furthermore, the employee has the right to challenge the results if he or she believes the test was inappropriately administered.[12] Exhibit 13-1 (previous page) contains the Department of Labor's Notice of Polygraph Testing explaining employee rights.

Worker Adjustment and Retraining Notification Act of 1988

In the mid-1990s, General Motors announced its plan to sell its car rental firm, National Car Rental Systems, to Vestar Equity Partners.[13] GM had been looking to divest itself of diversified activities in an effort to reinforce its automotive business. But, had GM been unable to find a buyer, and just decided to close the car rental business, could GM's management have immediately closed the business unit and terminated the 6,400 National employees without prior notification? No![14] Why? Because of the **Worker Adjustment and Retraining Notification (WARN) Act of 1988.**[15] Sometimes called the Plant Closing Bill, this act places specific requirements on employers considering significant changes in staffing levels. Under WARN, an organization employing one hundred or more individuals must notify workers sixty days in advance if it is going to close its facility or lay off fifty or more individuals. Should a company fail to provide this advance notice, it is subject to a penalty not to exceed "one day's pay and benefits to each employee for each day's notice that should have been given."[16]

Exhibit 13-2

Summary of laws affecting employee rights.

Law	Effect
Fair Credit Reporting Act	Requires employers to notify individuals that credit information is being gathered and may be used in the employment decision.
Privacy Act	Requires government agencies to make information in their personnel files available to employees.
Drug-Free Workplace Act	Requires government agencies, federal contractors, and those who receive government monies to take steps to ensure that their workplace is drug free.
Employee Polygraph Protection Act	Prohibits the use of lie-detector tests in screening all job applicants. Permits their use under certain circumstances.
Worker Adjustment and Retraining Notification Act	Requires employers with 100 or more employees contemplating closing a facility or laying off 50 or more employees to give 60 days' notice of the pending action.

However, the law does recognize that under certain circumstances, advance notice may be impossible. Assume, for example, a company is having financial difficulties and is seeking to raise money to keep the organization afloat. If these efforts fail and creditors foreclose on the company, no advance notice is required. For example, when Fair Lanes, Inc. (of bowling alley fame) was unable to meet its debt obligation, it filed for bankruptcy. Although filing for bankruptcy permitted the bowling alleys to remain open, had they closed immediately,[17] WARN would not have applied.

Plant closings, similar to the employee rights issues raised previously, continue to pose problems for human resource management. These laws have created specific guidelines for organizations to follow. None preclude the enterprise from doing what is necessary. Rather, the laws exist to ensure that whatever action the organization takes is done in such a way that employee rights are protected. A summary of these laws is presented in Exhibit 13-2.

Current Issues Regarding Employee Rights

Recently, emphasis has been placed on curtailing specific employer practices, as well as addressing what employees may rightfully expect from their organizations. These basic issues are drug testing, honesty tests, and employee monitoring.

Drug Testing   Previously in our discussion of the Drug-Free Workplace Act, we mentioned the legislation applicable to certain organizations. However, because of the severity of substance abuse in our organizations, many organizations not covered by this 1988 act have voluntarily begun a process of drug testing. Why? Let's look at some facts. It is estimated that approximately 25 percent of the U.S. work force may be abusing some substance (e.g., drugs or alcohol).[18] Forty percent of all on-the-job injuries and about half of all work-related deaths are attributed to substance abuse.[19] And if that weren't enough, it has been estimated that U.S. companies lose well over $111 billion and 75 million work days annually due to accidents—many attributable to substance abuse.[20]

As a result of the "numbers," many private employers, about 87 percent of major corporations[21] and 80 percent of smaller companies[22] began to implement programs to curb substance-related problems in their organizations.[23] For instance, Toys " Я " Us and Motorola test all current employees as well as job applicants.[24] In fact, walk into any Toys " Я " Us Store and you'll see prominently displayed at the entrance a sign that says something to the effect that "the employees of this store are drug free. Applicants who cannot pass a drug screening test should not apply." The intent of drug testing is to identify the abusers and either help them to overcome their problem (current employees) or not hire them in the first place (applicants). It is in this arena that many issues arise. For example, what happens if an individual refuses to take the drug test? What happens if the test is positive? Let's look at some possible answers.

A major concern for opponents of drug testing is how the process works and how the information will be used. **Drug testing** in today's organizations should be conducted to eliminate drugs in the workplace, not to catch those doing drugs.[25] For instance, drug testing may make better sense when there is "reasonable suspicion of substance abuse by an employee, or after an accident has occurred."[26] Although many might say that the same outcome is achieved, it's the process, and how employees view the process, that matters. At Mo-

Organizations like Toys " Я " Us remind all of us, applicants, current employees, and customers that the store supports a drug-free work environment.

NOTICE TO ALL JOB APPLICANTS:

OUR EMPLOYEES DON'T DO DRUGS.

IF YOU DO, DON'T APPLY. TOYS "Я" US. REQUIRES THAT YOU TAKE AND PASS A DRUG TEST AS A CONDITION OF EMPLOYMENT.

torola, individuals who refuse the drug test are terminated immediately.[27] Although this treatment appears harsh, the ill effect of employing a substance abuser is perceived as too great. But what if that person took the drug test and failed it? Many organizations place these individuals into a rehabilitation program, where they can get help—and the intent here is to help these workers. However, if they don't accept the help, or later fail another test, then they can be terminated.[28]

Applicants, on the other hand, present a different story. If an applicant tests positive for substance abuse, that applicant is generally no longer considered. The company's liability begins and ends there—they are not required to offer those applicants any help. But that needn't imply that applicants can't "straighten" out and try again. For example, the Red Lion Hotels and Inns organization requires all applicants to submit to a drug test. Should they test positive, their application is rejected; however, after a 90-day period, these individuals may reapply, as if nothing occurred previously.[29] It is recommended that employers conduct applicant drug testing only after a conditional job offer is made. That is, the job offer is contingent on the applicant passing a drug test. Why drug test at this stage? To properly administer the test, questions about one's health and medication record need to be addressed. Such questions before a conditional offer is made may be viewed as a violation of the Americans with Disabilities Act.[30]

From all indications, drug testing can work in achieving its goals of lessening the effect of drugs and alcohol on job-related activities like lower productivity, higher absenteeism, and job-related accidents.[31] Nonetheless, until individuals believe that the tests are administered properly and employees' dignity is respected, criticism of drug testing is likely to continue. There have been too many instances where the drug test gave a false reading or the specimen was improperly handled. It is estimated that many of the results may be false—that

Exhibit 13-3

Alternatives to body fluid testing.

Pupillary-Reaction Test

A trained professional can determine if a subject is under the influence of drugs or alcohol by examining the subject's eyes. The pupil will react differently to light (a flashlight is used) if the subject is under the influence of drugs. Follow-up tests by body fluid testings are usually needed.

Positive features: Noninvasive.

Negative features: Must be administered by a trained professional. Some medical conditions may give a false positive result. Follow-up tests are needed.

Hair Analysis

Hair samples are examined using radioimmunoassay, then confirmed by gas chromatography or mass spectrometry. The same techniques are used to test urine samples. Chemicals—drugs, legal or illegal—are left behind in hair follicles and provide a record of past drug use. Type of drug, frequency and duration of use can be determined. Because hair grows about half an inch per month, a relatively small sample can provide a long record of drug use.

Positive features: Accepted by courts in criminal trials. Detailed record of drug use. Cannot be avoided as easily as urinalysis. Less embarrassing than urinalysis.

Negative features: Highly invasive.

Video-based Eye–hand Coordination Test

One company has begun marketing a video-based test of eye–hand coordination. The test takes less than a minute to complete and is self-administered. The test determines only impairment and the employee is actually tested against their own normal performance. Lack of sleep, illness, stress, drugs, or alcohol could cause an employee to fail.

Positive features: Can be used immediately before employee begins work. Noninvasive. Does not make lifestyle judgments. Self-administered. Low cost.

Negative features: So far only implemented at test sites. Follow-up tests necessary.

SOURCE: Reprinted with permission of *HR Magazine,* published by the Society for Human Resource Management, Alexandria, VA: Michael R. Carroll and Christina Heavrin, "Before You Drug Test," *HR Magazine* (June 1990), p. 65.

is, attributed to legitimate medication or the food one eats.[32] To help with this concern, companies are moving toward more precise tests—ones that do not involve body fluids[33] (see Exhibit 13-3), and some that involve computers.[34]

As we move forward in drug-testing methodologies, the process should continue to improve. However, we must not forget the individual's rights—especially their privacy. Most employees recognize why companies must drug test, but expect to be treated humanely in the process; they also want safeguards built into the process to challenge false tests. And if there is a problem, many may want help, not punishment. For organizations to create this positive atmosphere, several steps must be addressed. This is where human resource management comes into play. HRM must issue its policies on substance abuse and communicate that message to every employee. That policy must state what is prohibited, under what conditions an individual will be tested, the consequences of failing the test, and how the process of testing will be handled.[35]

By making clear what is expected, as well as what the company intends to do, the emotional aspect of this process can be reduced.[36] Where such a policy exists, questions of legality and employee privacy issues are reduced.[37] Additionally, where drug testing is related to preventing accidents and actual job performance, tests have been shown to be more positively viewed.[38]

Honesty Tests How would you respond to the question: How often do you tell the truth?[39] All the time? Sorry, we can't hire you because everyone has stretched the truth at some point in his or her life. So you must be lying, and therefore not the honest employee we desire. Most of the time? Sorry again! We can't afford to hire someone who may not have the highest ethical standards. Sound like a Catch-22? Welcome to the world of **honesty tests.** Although polygraph testing has been significantly curtailed in the hiring process, employers have found another mechanism that supposedly provides similar information.[40]

> **Honesty tests focus on two areas—theft and drug abuse.**

Much of the intent of these tests is to get applicants to provide information about themselves that otherwise would be hard to obtain. These "integrity" tests tend to focus on two particular areas—theft and drug use.[41] But the tests are not simply indicators of what has happened; typically, they assess an applicant's past dishonest behavior and that individual's attitude toward dishonesty.[42] One would anticipate that applicants would try to answer these questions to avoid "being caught," or would even lie; however, research findings suggest otherwise. That is, individuals frequently perceive that "dishonesty is okay as long as you are truthful."[43] As such, applicants discuss questions in such a way that the tests do reveal the information intended. These tests frequently are designed with multiple questions covering similar topic areas, to assess consistency. If consistency in response is lacking, the test may indicate that an individual is being dishonest.[44]

Because of the effectiveness of these tests, coupled with their lower costs than those of other types of investigations, a number of companies have begun using them in their selection process. In fact, it was estimated that over 5,000 organizations are using some variation of honesty tests to screen applicants, testing some 5 million individuals each year.[45] Surprisingly, however, companies using these tests seldom reveal that they do. The large use of these tests has provoked questions about their validity and their potential for adverse impact. Research to date is promising.[46] Although instances have been recorded that indicate that individuals have been wrongly misclassified as dishonest,[47] other studies have indicated that they do not create an adverse impact against protected group members.[48] Based on the evidence, our conclusion is that these tests may be useful for providing more information about applicants, but should not be used as the sole criterion in the hiring decision.

Whistle-Blowing Over the past few years, more emphasis has been placed on companies being good corporate citizens. Incidents like the alleged misrepresentation by NBC regarding safety of GM pick-up trucks and the Space Shuttle Challenger disaster[49] have fueled interest in the area. One aspect of being responsible to the community at large is permitting employees to challenge management's practice without fear of retaliation. This challenge is often referred to as whistle-blowing.

Whistle-blowing occurs when an employee reports the organization to an outside agency for what the employee believes is an illegal or unethical practice. In the past, these employees were often subjected to severe punishment for doing what they believed was right.[50] For instance, several years ago, an employee in General Electric's nuclear fuel facility operation complained that "radioactive spills in the work setting were not properly cleaned up."[51] As the em-

Exhibit 13-4

Ten steps to an effective whistle-blowing policy.

1. Develop the policy in written form.
2. Seek input from top management in developing the policy, and obtain their approval for the finished work.
3. Communicate the policy to employees using multiple media. Inclusion in the employee handbook is not sufficient. Active communication efforts such as ethics training, departmental meetings and employee seminars will increase awareness of the policy and highlight the company's commitment to ethical behavior.
4. Provide a reporting procedure for employees that does not require them to go to their supervisor first. Instead, designate a specific office or individual to hear initial employee complaints. Streamline the process and cut the red tape. Make it easy for the employees to use the procedure.
5. Make it possible for employees to report anonymously, at least initially.
6. Guarantee employees who report suspected wrongdoing in good faith that they will be protected from retaliation from any member of the organization. Make this guarantee stick.
7. Develop a formal investigative process and communicate to employees exactly how their reports will be handled. Use this process to investigate all reported wrongdoings.
8. If the investigation reveals that the employee's suspicions are accurate, take prompt action to correct the wrongdoing. Employees will quickly lose confidence in the policy if disclosed wrongdoing is allowed to continue. Whatever the outcome of the investigation, communicate it quickly to the whistle-blowing employee.
9. Provide an appeals process for employees dissatisfied with the outcome of the initial investigation. Provide an advocate (probably from HRM) to assist the employee who wishes to appeal an unfavorable outcome.
10. Finally, a successful whistle-blowing policy requires more than a written procedure. It requires a commitment from the organization, from top management down. This commitment must be to create an ethical work environment.

SOURCE: Timothy R. Barrett and Daniel S. Cochran, "Making Room for the Whistleblower." *HR Magazine,* (January 1991), p. 59. Reprinted with permission of *HR Magazine,* published by the Society for Human Resource Management, Alexandria, Virginia.

ployee attempted to document her case, she was subjected to personnel actions by the company. The company believed that the employee, instead of leaving the "mess" for all to see, should have cleaned it up. This employee was ultimately terminated,[52] and unfortunately no federal law protected her.

Although federal legislation is lacking (except for a federal law passed during the Bush administration that covers public employees), state laws may be available in some jurisdictions. However, the extent of these laws, and how much protection they afford, differ greatly.[53] Nonetheless, many firms have voluntarily adopted policies to permit employees to identify problem areas.[54] The thrust of these policies is to have an established procedure whereby employees can safely raise these concerns and the company can take correct action. A suggested whistle-blower policy is presented in Exhibit 13-4.

Employee Monitoring and Workplace Security

Technology, enhanced in part by improvements in computers, has done some wonderful things in our work environment. It has allowed us to be more productive, to work smarter, not harder, and to bring about efficiencies in organizations that were not possible two decades ago. It has also provided us a means of **employee monitoring**—what some would call spying on our employees![55]

Employee Monitoring

If you worked for Nissan Motors in most of their many jobs, and used their e-mail system, how would you feel if your supervisor routinely read your computer messages (especially if in the past you've called your supervisor derogatory terms in e-mail messages to colleagues)? Or how would you feel as a loyal employee of the Boston Sheraton Hotel about you and a friend being secretly videotaped in the men's room at the hotel—even if the videotaping is designed to monitor behavior in hopes of ridding from the premises substance abusers and drug dealers. Technology today makes it possible, even easy, for companies to monitor their employees. And many do so in the hopes that it will help both you and them become more productive and more quality-oriented. The appropriate question for employee rights is, when does such employee snooping become unethical?

Just how pervasive is this practice of monitoring employees? Exact numbers are simply not known, although guestimates in the millions appear reasonable. For example, call most 800-customer-service numbers, like that of Gateway 2000, and you'll likely hear a message that calls are monitored for quality. Or recognize that networked computer stations can be monitored from a central location to assess "real time" productivity. Under such an arrangement, however, employers should issue an "employee monitoring" policy, which details what is monitored, when, and how the information is used. In such instances, employees appear more tolerant of being monitored. Yet, these same employees appear to exhibit more stress-related symptoms than employees who are not monitored.

Are employers overstepping the bounds of decency and respect for employees? Consider that it is almost kids' play to monitor cellular phone conversations or to intercept and copy fax transmissions. Or, take the case of Olivetti, which has employees wearing "smart badges." These identification devices can track the whereabouts of an employee. That can be helpful in having messages transferred to your location, but also means that Olivetti managers may know exactly your every move.

Sure, employee monitoring can help enhance performance and provide valuable feedback to both the employer and the employee. But at what point does the organization's need for that information violate an employee's right to privacy? What's your opinion?

SOURCE: Adapted from Lee Smith, "What the Boss Knows About You," *Fortune* (August 9, 1993), pp. 88–93.

Workplace security has become a critical issue for employers (see Ethical Decision in HRM). **Workplace security** can be defined as actions on behalf of an employer to ensure that the employer's interests are protected: that is, workplace security focuses on protecting the employer's property and its trade business.[56] Without a doubt, employers must protect themselves. Employee theft, revealing trade secrets to competition, or using the company's customer database for personal gain could be damaging to the company. But how far can this protection extend? Don't we need to consider employees' rights too? Obviously the answer is yes, but how is that balance created?

Consider what happened to Alana Shorts.[57] Arriving at work at Epson America one morning, Alana noticed her boss reading her electronic mail. Although company managers verbally stated that electronic mail messages were private, the company's written policy was different. It was her employer's contention that it owned the system and accordingly had the right to see what was going on. And they were right! In fact, employers can even film you in the restroom. But whatever employers deem fair game, they should explain for employees in terms of a company policy.[58]

Part of the problem here goes back to the balance of security. Abuses by some employees—for instance, employees using the company's computer system for gambling purposes, running their own businesses,[59] playing computer games or pursuing personal matters—have resulted in companies implementing a more "policing" role. This can extend, too, to Internet sites, ensuring that employees are not logging on to adult-oriented Web sites.

As employee-monitoring issues become more noticeable, keep a few things in mind. Employers, as long as they have a policy regarding how employees are monitored, will continue to check on employee behavior.[60] Specifically targeted for this monitoring are system computers, electronic mail, and the telephone.[61] In fact, it's estimated that more than 20 million employees have their computer files monitored each year."[62] In companies like Gateway, Continental Airlines, and UPS, employees are continually told that they may be monitored. Undoubtedly, the debate regarding the necessity of this action will continue. Nonetheless, only when employees understand what the company expects and how it will gather its information will their rights be safeguarded.[63]

Other Employee Rights Issues

Although we have addressed a number of employee rights issues, two additional concerns deserve discussion. These are the monitoring of office romances—sometimes called "legislating love"[64]—and AIDS testing. We'll leave this section also with a brief discussion of sexual orientation rights.

Legislating Love   **Legislating love** in our companies today is a direct result of potential discrimination or sexual harassment issues facing our organizations.[65] The workplace has long been a place to develop romantic interests; many individuals have met their mates or significant others through work or organizational contacts. But what happens when this organizational love reaches another plateau? What if your significant other is now your boss or has moved on to

---

AT&T

"Our attitude toward corporate romance is one of benign neglect," says corporate spokesperson Burke Stinson. The company, which is noted for its strong policy on sexual harassment, has never issued formal guidelines against dating, but it discourages direct supervisor–subordinate relationships, and forbids spouses from reporting to each other. "Until the 1980s," says Stinson, "all types of office romance were frowned upon. But the whole environment of corporate America has become a mini-*Love Boat*." Nationwide, there are an estimated 7,500 married couples at the company.

Prudential

After the Clarence Thomas Supreme Court nomination hearing, the company issued a memo to its employees restating its long-standing policy on sexual harassment and went on to warn that romantic relationships can "influence the quality of decisions and can potentially hurt other people."

"We certainly can't forbid dating," says Don Mann, the company's senior vice president of human resources. "Hundreds of couples met at the company, including the chairman and his wife. The main concern we have is about chain-of-command relationships. A transfer is the typical solution."

Du Pont

The company has one of the most extensive sexual-harassment prevention and education programs in the country, including a 24-hour hot line, seminars, and, when necessary, a team of harassment investigators. Dating, however, is allowed, provided that it's not a boss–subordinate relationship. In that case, one person is reassigned.

SOURCE: Ellen Rapp, "Legislating Love," *Working Woman* (February 1992), p. 61.

Exhibit 13-5

Selected companies: Policies on organizational romance.

work for a competitor? Most organizations typically find such situations unacceptable.[66] As a result, they try to avoid possible conflicts of interest that may arise. To do so, they have issued various guidelines on how—if at all—relationships at work may exist. Exhibit 13-5 lists the policies of several companies.

Some companies, on the other hand, like Mitchell Energy and Development, Interstate Bakeries, and Microsoft, are seeing this dilemma differently.[67] Top management in these organizations views office romance, and possible marriage between their employees, as having a positive effect on employee morale and productivity. For Bill Gates, the CEO of Microsoft, relationships were hard to start and maintain given his eighteen-hour workdays. If a legislating-love policy had existed, it might have prevented Gates from marrying his marketing executive, Melinda French, in January 1994. And for a company like DEC, permitting romantic relationships between employees has helped to foster their "company-centered family."[68]

AIDS Testing   We already know that under the Americans with Disabilities Act, an employer cannot discriminate in employment decisions against anyone who is HIV+ or has AIDS. However, more appropriate for employee rights, does a company have a right to know if an employee is HIV positive? The answer is, it depends. If the job requires certain types of contact with other individuals, such as a health-care provider performing invasive surgery, the answer may be yes.[69] In most other cases, it would be difficult to support a reason to know. Although companies have the right to require, and pay for, employees to take a physical exam upon being hired (usually for health insurance purposes), the more appropriate concern is what happens if the company finds out the employee is infected. Many companies appear to be grappling with this issue, particularly with regard to safeguarding employee confidentiality. IBM and Wells Fargo and Company are two organizations that have taken a leading role in this matter.[70] Both organizations have developed policies regarding how managers are to treat this information, specifically emphasizing the need to protect the privacy of the worker.[71]

Sexual Orientation Rights   When one considers the laws and court rulings presented in Chapter 3, one begins to appreciate what has occurred over the past few decades. Remember in Chapter 3, we mentioned that discrimination against an individual based on sexual orientation currently does not come under the jurisdiction of Title VII (although some state and local laws do exist). As a result, discriminating in hiring, firing or promoting on the basis of sexual orientation may exist. Some organizations have even gone a step further. For instance, Cracker Barrel is a retail chain known for its cheese products. If you walk around its stores, you will notice some very fine products. You should also know that no homosexuals work there, at least none who are open about their sexual preference.[72] Cracker Barrel management began questioning certain employees about their sexual preference. This action was based on a number of factors in response to an informal survey asking customers if they preferred not to patronize an establishment that hires homosexual workers (how they would know is uncertain). Some employees had a choice—lie and keep their jobs, turning their backs on their significant others, or tell the truth and be fired. Gay and lesbian groups have targeted Cracker Barrel and other "like" companies and have held rallies in support of employees—but federal law has not changed regarding sexual orientation in the workplace.

Workers at Lotus Development Corporation work hard at learning to accept one another. Here, straight and gay employees meet to discuss issues that effect their work relationship. Additionally, not only does Lotus offer sensitivity training to its employees, the company also provides employee benefits to same-sex partners.

Actions such as those witnessed at Cracker Barrel are not representative of all organizations. Companies like Apple, Disney, Lotus, and Du Pont have policies and programs in place that are "gay" friendly—like domestic partner benefits, and training programs designed to help employees accept one another.

THE ROLE OF THE EMPLOYMENT-AT-WILL DOCTRINE

Background

The concept of the **employment-at-will doctrine** is rooted in nineteenth-century common law, which permitted employers to discipline or discharge employees at their discretion. The premise behind this doctrine is to equalize the playing field. If employees can resign at any time they want, why shouldn't an employer have the same right?

Under the employment-at-will doctrine, an employer can dismiss an employee "for good cause, for no cause, or even for a cause morally wrong, without being guilty of a legal wrong."[73] Of course, even then, you can't fire on the basis of race, religion, sex, national origin, age, or disability.[74] Although this doctrine has existed for over one hundred years, the courts, labor unions, and legislation have attempted to lessen the use of this doctrine.[75] In these instances, jobs are being likened to private property. That is, individuals have a right to these jobs unless the organization has specified otherwise. Employees today are challenging the legality of their discharge more frequently. It is estimated that approximately 2 million workers are discharged each year, with about 10 percent of them being fired for reasons other than just cause.[76] When being fired without cause occurs, employees may seek the assistance of the courts to address their wrongful discharge.[77] All fifty states currently permit employees to sue their employers if they believe their termination was unjust.[78] At issue in these suits is that through some action on the part of the employer, exceptions to the employment-at-will doctrine exist.

Exceptions to the Doctrine

While employment-at-will thrives in contemporary organizations, there are four exceptions under which a wrongful discharge suit can be supported. These are through a contractual relationship, public policy violation, implied contracts, and a breach of good faith.[79] Let's take a closer look at these.

Contractual Relationship   A contractual relationship exists when employers and employees have a legal agreement regarding how employee issues are handled. Under such contractual arrangements, discharge may only occur if it is based on just cause. Inasmuch as a distinct definition of just cause does not exist, there are guidelines derived from labor arbitration of collective-bargaining relationships (we'll look at discipline in labor–management relationships in Chapter 16) under which just cause can be shown, as follows:

▶ Was there adequate warning of consequences of the worker's behavior?
▶ Are the rules reasonable and related to safe and efficient operations of the business?
▶ Before discipline was rendered, did a fair investigation of the violation occur?
▶ Did the investigation yield definite proof of worker activity and wrongdoing?
▶ Have similar occurrences, both prior and subsequent to this event, been handled the same and without discrimination?
▶ Was the penalty in line with the seriousness of the offense and in reason with the worker's past employment record?[80]

In addition to this contractual relationship, federal legislation may also play a key role. Discrimination laws such as those discussed in Chapter 3 may further constrain an employer's use of at-will terminations. For example, an organization cannot terminate an individual based on his or her age just because such action would save the company some money.

Public Policy Violation   Another exception to the employment-at-will doctrine is the **public policy violation.** Under this exception, an employee cannot be terminated for failing to obey an order from an employer that can be construed as an illegal activity. Additionally, should an employee refuse to offer a bribe to a public official to increase the likelihood of the organization obtaining a contract, that employee is protected. Furthermore, employers cannot retaliate against an employee for exercising his or her rights (like serving on a jury). Accordingly, employees cannot be justifiably discharged for exercising their rights in accordance with societal laws and statutes.

Implied Employment Contract   The third exception to the doctrine is the **implied employment contract.** An implied contract is any verbal or written statement made by members of the organization that suggests organizational guarantees or promises about continued employment.[81] These implied contracts, when they exist, typically take place during employment interviews or are included in an employee handbook.

One of the earlier cases reaffirming implied contracts was the case of *Toussaint* v. *Blue Cross and Blue Shield of Michigan*.[82] In this case, Toussaint claimed that he was improperly discharged, for unjust causes, by the organization. He asserted that he was told "he'd be with the company until age 65 as long as he did his job."[83] The employee's handbook also clearly reinforced this tenure with statements reflective of discharge for just cause. Even if just cause arose, the discharge could only occur after several disciplinary steps (we'll look at the topic of discipline in the next section) had occurred.[84] In this case, the court determined that the discharge was improper,[85] because permanence of his position was implied by the organization.

The issue of implied contracts is changing how human resources management operates in several of its functions. For instance, interviewers are increasingly cautious, avoiding anything that could conjure up a contract. Something as innocent as discussing an annual salary may cause problems, for such a comment implies at least twelve months on the job.[86] To avoid this, salaries are often communicated in terms of the amount of pay for each pay period. Many organizations, because management wants to maintain employment-at-will, have listed disclaimers such as, "This handbook is not a contract of employment," or "Employment in the organization is at the will of the employer," on the covers of their employee handbooks and manuals to reinforce their employment-at-will policy. Yet caution is warranted, as a supervisor's statements may override the printed words.

Breach of Good Faith   The final exception to the employment-at-will doctrine is the breach of good faith. Although this is the most difficult of the exceptions to prove, there are situations where an employer may breach a promise. In one noteworthy case, an individual employed over twenty-five years by the National Cash Register Company (NCR) was terminated shortly after completing a major deal with a customer.[87] The employee claimed that he was fired to eliminate NCR's liability to pay him his sales commission. In the case, the court ruled that this individual acted in good faith in selling the company's product and reasonably expected his commission. Although NCR had an employment-at-will arrangement with its employees, the court held that his dismissal, and their failure to pay commissions, was a breach of good faith.

DISCIPLINE AND EMPLOYEE RIGHTS

The exceptions to the employment-at-will doctrine mentioned above may be leading you to think that employers cannot terminate employees, or are significantly limited in their action. That's not the point of that discussion. Rather, where exceptions exist, there may be a requirement that such an employment action follow a specific process.[88] That process, and how it works are embedded in the topic we call discipline.

What Is Discipline?

The term **discipline** refers to a condition in the organization where employees conduct themselves in accordance with the organization's rules and

standards of acceptable behavior. For the most part, employees discipline themselves by conforming to what is considered proper behavior because they believe it is the reasonable thing to do. Once they are made aware of what is expected of them, and assuming they find these standards or rules to be
reasonable, they seek to meet those expectations.

But not all employees will accept the responsibility of self-discipline. There
are some employees who do not accept the norms of responsible employee behavior. These employees, then, require some degree of extrinsic disciplinary action. It is this need to impose extrinsic disciplinary action that we will address
in the following sections.

Factors to Consider When Disciplining

Before we review disciplinary guidelines, we should look at the major factors that need to be considered if we are to have fair and equitable disciplinary
practices. The following contingency factors can help us analyze a discipline
problem:[89]

▶ *Seriousness of the Problem.* How severe is the problem? As noted previously, dishonesty is usually considered a more serious infraction than reporting to work twenty minutes late.

▶ *Duration of the Problem.* Have there been other discipline problems in
the past, and over how long a time span? The violation does not take
place in a vacuum. A first occurrence is usually viewed differently than a
third or fourth offense.

▶ *Frequency and Nature of the Problem.* Is the current problem part of an
emerging or continuing pattern of disciplinary infractions? We are concerned with not only the duration but also the pattern of the problem.
Continual infractions may require a different type of discipline from that
applied to isolated instances of misconduct. They may also point out a
situation that demands far more severe discipline in order to prevent a
minor problem from becoming a major one.

▶ *Extenuating Factors.* Are there extenuating circumstances related to the
problem? The student who fails to turn in her term paper by the deadline
because of the death of her grandfather is likely to have her violation assessed more leniently than will her peer who missed the deadline because he overslept.

▶ *Degree of Socialization.* To what extent has management made an earlier
effort to educate the person causing the problem about the existing rules
and procedures and the consequences of violations? Discipline severity
must reflect the degree of knowledge that the violator holds of the organization's standards of acceptable behavior. In contrast to the previous
item, the new employee is less likely to have been socialized to these
standards than the twenty-year veteran. Additionally, the organization
that has formalized, written rules governing employee conduct is more
justified in aggressively enforcing violations of these rules than is the organization whose rules are informal or vague.

▶ *History of the Organization's Discipline Practices.* How have similar infractions been dealt with in the past within the department? Within the
entire organization? Has there been consistency in the application of discipline procedures? Equitable treatment of employees must take into

consideration precedents within the unit where the infraction occurs, as well as previous disciplinary actions taken in other units within the organization. Equity demands consistency against some relevant benchmark.

▶ *Management Backing*. If employees decide to take their case to a higher level in management, will you have reasonable evidence to justify your decision? Should the employee challenge your disciplinary action, it is important that you have the data to back up the necessity and equity of the action taken and that you feel confident that management will support your decision. No disciplinary action is likely to carry much weight if violators believe that they can challenge and successfully override their manager's decision.

How can these seven items help? Consider that there are many reasons for why we might discipline an employee. With little difficulty, we could list several dozen or more infractions that management might believe require disciplinary action. For simplicity's sake, we have classified the most frequent violations into four categories: attendance, on-the-job behaviors, dishonesty, and outside activities. We've listed them and potential infractions in Exhibit 13-6. However, these infractions may be minor or serious given the situation, or the industry in which one works. For example, while concealing defective work in a hand-tool assembly line may be viewed as minor, the same action in a aerospace manufacturing plant is more serious. Furthermore, recurrence and severity of the infraction will

Type of Problem	Infraction
Attendance	Tardiness
	Unexcused absence
	Leaving without permission
On-the-job Behaviors	Malicious destruction of organizational property
	Gross insubordination
	Carrying a concealed weapon
	Attacking another employee with intent to seriously harm
	Drunk on the job
	Sexually harassing another employee
	Failure to obey safety rules
	Defective work
	Sleeping on the job
	Failure to report accidents
	Loafing
	Gambling on the job
	Fighting
	Horseplay
Dishonesty	Stealing
	Deliberate falsification of employment record
	Clock-punching another's timecard
	Concealing defective work
	Subversive activity
Outside activities	Unauthorized strike activity
	Outside criminal activities
	Wage garnishment
	Working for a competing company

Exhibit 13-6

Specific disciplinary problems.

play a role. For instance, employees who experience their first minor offense might generally expect a minor reprimand. A second offense might result in a more stringent reprimand, and so forth. In contrast, the first occurrence of a serious offense might mean not being allowed to return to work, the length dependent on the circumstances surrounding the violation.

Disciplinary Guidelines

All human resource managers should be aware of disciplinary guidelines. In this section, we will briefly describe them.

> ▶ *Make Disciplinary Action Corrective Rather than Punitive.* The object of disciplinary action is not to deal out punishment.[90] The objective is to correct an employee's undesirable behavior. While punishment may be a necessary means to that end, one should never lose sight of the eventual objective.

> ▶ *Make Disciplinary Action Progressive.* Although the type of disciplinary action that is appropriate may vary depending on the situation, it is generally desirable for discipline to be progressive.[91] Only for the most serious violations will an employee be dismissed after a first offense. Typically, progressive disciplinary action begins with a verbal warning and proceeds through a written warning, suspension, and, only in the most serious cases, dismissal. More on this in a moment.

> ▶ *Follow the "Hot-stove" Rule.* Administering discipline can be viewed as analogous to touching a hot stove (therefore, the **hot-stove rule**).[92] While both are painful to the recipient, the analogy goes further. When you touch a hot stove, you get an immediate response; the burn you receive is instantaneous, leaving no question of cause and effect. You have ample warning; you know what happens if you touch a red-hot stove. Furthermore, the result is consistent: Every time you touch a hot stove, you get the same response—you get burned. Finally, the result is impersonal; regardless of who you are, if you touch a hot stove, you will get burned. The comparison between touching a hot stove and administering discipline should be apparent, but let us briefly expand on each of the four points in the analogy.

The impact of a disciplinary action will be reduced as the time between the infraction and the penalty's implementation lengthens. The more quickly the discipline follows the offense, the more likely it is that the employee will associate the discipline with the offense rather than with the manager imposing the discipline. As a result, it is best that the disciplinary process begin as soon as possible after the violation is noticed. Of course, this desire for immediacy should not result in undue haste. If all the facts are not in, managers may invoke a temporary suspension, pending a final decision in the case. The manager has an obligation to give advance warning prior to initiating formal disciplinary action. This means the employee must be aware of the organization's rules and accept its standards of behavior. Disciplinary action is more likely to be interpreted as fair by employees when there is clear warning that a given violation will lead to discipline and when it is known what that discipline will be.

Fair treatment of employees also demands that disciplinary action be consistent. When rule violations are enforced in an inconsistent manner, the rules lose

"Manager Should Be Prepared Before Disciplining Employees"

In a perfect world, there would be no disciplining, no policies or procedures to misinterpret or ignore.

Each employee would check his own work and contribute ways to cut costs, reduce waste and improve quality and service to both internal and external customers. Lunch hours would be held to agreed-upon limits, personal business and/or phone calls would not be conducted on company time or with company resources, equipment or personnel. Computers, equipment, managers, the company or "someone else" would not be blamed for work not completed or completed late or incorrectly.

Managers would involve, train and listen to employees, building teamwork through empowerment and trust.

In a perfect world.

In a slightly less perfect, but more exciting and challenging world, managers occasionally have to discipline employees. As a pleasurable managerial task, it ranks right after terminating someone.

Dealing with the effects of the mistakes and masking anger, resentment, disappointment and disgust to create these teaching moments can test even the most patient manager. The challenge is to keep employees focused on their behavior and how to correct or improve it, not on how they're being treated. Following these guidelines should help:

1. **Cool off, but don't wait too long.** Even though we would like to ignore the problem and hope that it might go away, don't kid yourself.

   Any problem has a tendency to escalate from a minor to a major issue. It's not worth it. Get comfortable with positively confronting situations, mutually identifying problems and agreeing on solutions and follow-up plans. Failing to address issues undermines your credibility and ability to do what it is you get paid to do: manage.

2. **Think before you speak.** Stay calm. It may be tempting to sound off, but how you handle it may be as important as the issue. Your goal should be to correct the situation, not to further impede the working relationship. You may wish to ask the employee to consider possible solutions and bring one or two to the meeting if appropriate.

3. **Always discipline in private, one on one.** Consider using a conference room, if added privacy is needed.

4. **Follow company disciplinary procedures to ensure fairness and consistency.** If in doubt, take the time to check the policy manual, boss or personnel officer first. If you don't, you may be the next person in line to be disciplined for not following procedures.

5. **Be prepared to hear a variety of both imaginative and worn-out excuses.** These can range from "I was stuck in traffic" to "Somebody made that up" to "The other department takes one-hour-45-minute lunches" to "Everybody else does it."

6. **Prepare in order to avoid nervousness.** No one likes to discipline, but it's part of the job. Before the meeting, think about objections or issues that may be raised. Rehearse in your mind, outline your comments—whatever it takes to resolve the issue in a win-win manner.

7. **Prepare by comparing the actual to the desired situation.** Then state what action is necessary, why it is necessary and its impact.

8. **Clarify expectations and contingencies for specific actions and timetables.** Make sure that the employee understands by asking for a summarization—something beyond just a grunt of agreement.

9. **Ask employees for feedback.** How can you best help or support them in making the necessary changes? What suggestions do they have? How can problems be prevented in the future?

Let it go. There is no need to ignore employees, stare at them or use any other of a variety of cruel and unusual—and immature—punishments.

Imagine an environment that tolerated no mistakes because it tolerated no risks, no changes, no tests. A less-than-perfect world looks good after all.

DR. CONNIE SITTERLY, CPCM

their impact. Morale will decline and employees will question the competence of management. Productivity will suffer as a result of employee insecurity and anxiety. All employees want to know the limits of permissible behavior, and they look to the actions of their managers for such feedback. If, for example, Barbara is reprimanded today for an action that she did last week, for which nothing was said, these limits become blurry. Similarly, if Bill and Marty are both goofing off at their desks and Bill is reprimanded while Marty is not, Bill is likely to question the fairness of the action. The point, then, is that discipline should be consistent. This need not result in treating everyone exactly alike, because that ignores the contingency factors we discussed earlier, but it does put the responsibility on management to clearly justify disciplinary actions that may appear inconsistent to employees (see Workplace Issues [previous page]).

The last guideline that flows from the hot-stove rule is: Keep the discipline impersonal. Penalties should be connected with a given violation, not with the personality of the violator. That is, discipline should be directed at what employees have done, not the employees themselves. As a manager, you should make it clear that you are avoiding personal judgments about the employee's character. You are penalizing the rule violation, not the individual, and all employees committing the violation can expect to be penalized. Furthermore, once the penalty has been imposed, you as manager must make every effort to forget the incident; you should attempt to treat the employee in the same manner as you did prior to the infraction.

Disciplinary Actions

As we briefly alluded to a few paragraphs ago, discipline generally follows a typical sequence of four steps: written verbal warning, written warning, suspension, and dismissal[93] (see Exhibit 13-7). Let's briefly review these four steps.

Written Verbal Warning   The mildest form of discipline is the written verbal warning. Yes, the term is correct. A **written verbal warning** is a temporary record of a reprimand that is then placed in the manager's file on the employee. This written verbal warning should state the purpose, date, and outcome of the interview with the employee. This, in fact, is what differentiates the written verbal warning from the verbal warning. Because of the need to document this step in the process, the verbal warning must be put into writing. The difference, however, is that this warning remains in the hands of the manager; that is, it is not forwarded to HRM for inclusion in the employee's personnel file.

The written verbal reprimand is best achieved if completed in a private and informal environment. The manager should begin by clearly informing the employee of the rule that has been violated and the problem that this infraction has caused. For instance, if the employee has been late several times, the manager would reiterate the organization's rule that employees are to be at their desks by 8:30 A.M., and then proceed to give specific evidence of how violation of this rule has resulted in an increase in workload for others and has lowered

Exhibit 13-7

The progressive discipline process.

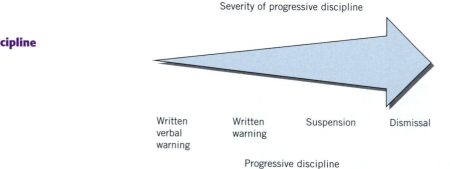

Severity of progressive discipline

Written verbal warning   Written warning   Suspension   Dismissal

Progressive discipline

departmental morale. After the problem has been made clear, the manager should then allow the employee to respond. Is he aware of the problem? Are there extenuating circumstances that justify his behavior? What does he plan to do to correct his behavior?

After the employee has been given the opportunity to make his case, the manager must determine if the employee has proposed an adequate solution to the problem. If this has not been done, the manager should direct the discussion toward helping the employee figure out ways to prevent the trouble from recurring. Once a solution has been agreed upon, the manager should ensure that the employee understands what, if any, follow-up action will be taken if the problem recurs.

If the written verbal warning is effective, further disciplinary action can be avoided. If the employee fails to improve, the manager will need to consider more severe action.

Written Warning   The second step in the progressive discipline process is the **written warning.** In effect, it is the first formal stage of the disciplinary procedure. This is because the written warning becomes part of the employee's official personnel file. This is achieved by not only giving the warning to the employee but sending a copy to HRM to be inserted in the employee's permanent record. In all other ways, however, the procedure concerning the writing of the warning is the same as the written verbal warning; that is, the employee is advised in private of the violation, its effects, and potential consequences of future violations. The only difference is that the discussion concludes with the employee being told that a formal written warning will be issued. Then the manager writes up the warning—stating the problem, the rule that has been violated, any acknowledgment by the employee to correct her behavior, and the consequences from a recurrence of the deviant behavior—and sends it to HRM.

Suspension   A **suspension** or layoff would be the next disciplinary step, usually taken only if the prior steps have been implemented without the desired outcome. Exceptions—where suspension is given without any prior verbal or written warning—occasionally occur if the infraction is of a serious nature.

A suspension may be for one day or several weeks; disciplinary layoffs in excess of a month are rare. Some organizations skip this step completely because it can have negative consequences for both the company and the employee. From the organization's perspective, a suspension means the loss of the employee for the layoff period. If the person has unique skills or is a vital part of a complex process, her loss during the suspension period can severely impact her department or the organization's performance if a suitable replacement cannot be located. From the employee's standpoint, a suspension can result in the employee returning in a more unpleasant and negative frame of mind than before the layoff.

Then why should management consider suspending employees as a disciplinary measure? The answer is that a short layoff is potentially a rude awakening to problem employees. It may convince them that management is serious and may move them to accept responsibility for following the organization's rules.

Dismissal   Management's ultimate disciplinary punishment is dismissing the problem employee. **Dismissal** should be used only for the most serious of-

Rich Cronin was the head of Nick-at-Nite and TV Land cable networks for Viacom. Planning to leave Viacom when his employment contract expired in June 1998 to head Fox Kids Broadcasting's Family Channel, Cronin let his employer know of his intention about six months early. But the reaction he received was not the one he expected. He was fired immediately. He has since filed claims that he was fired without cause.

fenses. Yet it may be the only feasible alternative when an employee's behavior seriously interferes with a department or the organization's operation.

A dismissal decision should be given long and hard consideration. For almost all individuals, being fired from a job is an emotional trauma. For employees who have been with the organization for many years, dismissal can make it difficult to obtain new employment or may require the individual to undergo extensive retraining. In addition, management should consider the possibility that a dismissed employee will take legal action to fight the decision. Recent court cases (remember the Mackenzie vs. Miller sexual harassment case cited in the last chapter?) indicate that juries are cautiously building a list of conditions under which employees may not be lawfully discharged.

Positive Discipline: Can It Work?

The concept of positive discipline was first reported at Union Carbide Corporation.[94] In its design, positive discipline attempts to integrate the disciplinary process with the performance management system. When problems arise, rather than promptly responding with a written verbal warning (punitive), positive discipline attempts to get the employee back on track by helping to "convince the individual to abide by company performance standards."[95] That is, in using positive discipline, attempts are made to reinforce the good work behaviors of the employee, while simultaneously emphasizing to the employee the problems created by the undesirable performance. The basis of positive discipline is presented in Exhibit 13-8.

Step 1: An Oral Reminder	Notice here that the word *warning* is removed. The **oral reminder,** supported by written documentation, serves as the initial formal phase of the process to identify to the employee what work problems he or she is having. This reminder is designed to identify what is causing the problem and attempts to correct it before it becomes larger.
Step 2: A Written Reminder	If the oral reminder was unsuccessful, a more formalized version is implemented. This **written reminder** once again reinforces what the problems are and what corrective action is necessary. Furthermore, specific timetables that the employee must accept and abide by, and the consequences for failing to comply, are often included.
Step 3: A Decision-making Leave	Here, employees are given a **decision-making leave**—time off from work, usually with pay—to think about what they are doing and whether or not they desire to continue work with the company: This "deciding day" is designed to allow the employee an opportunity to make a choice—correct the behavior, or face separation from the company.

Exhibit 13-8

Steps in positive discipline.

EMPLOYEE COUNSELING

Whenever an employee exhibits work behaviors that are inconsistent with the work environment (i.e., fighting, stealing, unexcused absences, and so forth) or is unable to perform his or her job satisfactorily, a manager must intervene. In many cases, this is done through a process called **employee counseling.** But before any intervention can begin, it is imperative for the manager to identify the problem. If as managers we realize that the performance problem is ability related, our emphasis becomes one of facilitating training and development efforts.[96] This type of intervention, then, is more closely aligned to mentoring or coaching (see Chapter 9). However, when the performance problem is desire-related, where the unwillingness is either voluntary or involuntary, employee counseling is the next logical approach.[97]

The Counseling Focus

Although **employee counseling** processes differ, some fundamental steps should be followed when counseling an employee. As a prerequisite, a manager must have good listening skills.[98] The purpose of employee counseling is to uncover the reason for the poor performance, a response that must be elicited from the employee. A manager who dominates the meeting by talking may dismiss the benefits of an effective counseling session.

In employee counseling, the manager must attack the inappropriate behavior, not the person. Although they appear difficult to separate, we must deal with only objective performance data. For instance, telling an employee he or she is a poor worker is only asking for emotions to run high and confrontation to arise. Instead, stating that he or she has been late four times this past month, which has caused a backlog of shipping receivables, is better understood and dealt with. In doing so, the manager is dealing with performance-related behaviors. Accordingly, the manager and the employee are in a better position to deal with the problem as adults.

In employee counseling, the manager must attack the inappropriate behaviors, not the person.

The manager must probe the employee to determine why the performance is not acceptable. It is important to note that the manager is not attempting to be a psychologist; he or she is only interested in the behaviors that affect performance. If the problem is personal, under no circumstances should the manager attempt to "fix" it. Rather, the well-informed manager, when recognizing a personal problem, will refer the employee to an appropriate place in or outside the organization (like the company's employee assistance program—we'll look at these in Chapter 14).[99] Irrespective of where the problem lies, the manager must get the employee to accept the problem. Until the employee has such an understanding, little hope exists for correcting the problem. When the employee accepts the problem, the manager should work with the employee to find ways to correct the problem. At this point, the manager may offer whatever assistance he or she can. Assistance aside, the employee must understand that it is his or her sole responsibility to make the change; failure to do so will only result in disciplinary procedures.

How to Counsel Employees

We offer the following nine steps that one should consider following when faced with a situation to counsel an employee.[100]

1. *Document all problem performance behaviors.* Document specific job behaviors, like absenteeism, lateness, and poor quality, in terms of dates, times, and what happened. This provides you with objective data.
2. *Deal with the employee objectively, fairly, and equitably.* Treat each employee similarly. That means that one should not be counseled for something that another person did, and nothing was mentioned. Issues discussed should focus on performance behaviors.
3. *Confront job performance issues only.* Your main focus is on those things that affect performance. Even though it may be a personal problem, you should not try to psychoanalyze the individual. Leave that to the trained specialists! You can, however, address how these behaviors are affecting the employee's job performance.
4. *Offer assistance to help the employee.* Just pointing the finger at an employee serves little useful purpose. If the employee could "fix" the problem alone, he or she probably would have. Help might be needed— yours and the organizations. Offer this assistance where possible.
5. *Expect the employee to resist the feedback and become defensive.* It is human nature to dislike constructive or negative feedback. Expect that the individual will be uncomfortable with the discussion. Make every effort, however, to keep the meeting calm such that the message can get across. Documentation, fairness, focusing on job behaviors, and offering assistance help to reduce this defensiveness.
6. *Get the employee to own up to the problem.* All things said, the problem is not yours; it's the employee's. The employee needs to take responsibility for his or her behavior, and begin to look for ways to correct the problems.
7. *Develop an action plan to correct performance.* Once the employee has taken responsibility for the problem, develop a plan of action designed to correct the problem. Be specific as to what the employee must do (e.g., what is expected and when it is expected), and what resources you are willing to commit to assist.

8. *Identify outcomes for failing to correct problems.* You're there to help, not carry a poor performer forever. You need to inform the employee about what the consequences will be if he or she does not follow the action plan.

9. *Monitor and control progress.* Evaluate the progress the employee is making. Provide frequent feedback on what you're observing. Reinforce good efforts.

SUMMARY

This summary relates to the Learning Objectives provided on p. 384.

After having read this chapter, you should know:

1. The intent of the Privacy Act of 1974 was to require government agencies to make available to employees information contained in their personnel files. Subsequent state laws have afforded the same ability to non-government agencies.

2. The implications of the Drug-Free Act of 1988 were to require government agencies, federal contractors, and those who receive more than $25,000 in government money to take various steps to ensure that their workplace is drug free. Non-government agencies with less than $25,000 in government grants are exempt from this law. The Polygraph Protection Act of 1988 prohibits the use of lie-detector tests in screening all job applicants. The act, however, does permit select use of polygraphs under specific circumstances.

3. The Worker Adjustment and Retraining Notification Act of 1988 requires employers with one hundred or more employees contemplating closing a facility or laying off fifty or more workers to provide sixty days' advance notice of the action.

4. Drug testing is a contemporary issue facing many organizations. Because of the problems associated with substance abuse in our society, and our organizations specifically, companies test employees. The costs in terms of lost productivity and the like support such action. On the other hand, however, comes the issue of privacy. Does the company truly have the right to know what employees do on their own time? Additionally, validity of drug tests as well as proper procedures are often cited as reasons for not testing.

5. Honesty testing in hiring has been used to capture the information now unavailable from polygraph in screening applicants. Many companies use these paper-and-pencil tests to obtain information on one's potential to steal from the company, as well as to determine if an employee has stolen before. Validity of honesty tests has some support, and their use as an additional selection device appears reasonable.

6. The employment-at-will doctrine permits employers to fire employees for any reason, justified or not. Although based on nineteenth-century common law, exceptions to employment-at-will have curtailed employers' use of the doctrine.

7. The four exceptions to the employment-at-will doctrine are contractual relationships, public policy violations, implied employment contracts, and a breach of good faith by the employer.

8. Discipline is a condition in the organization when employees conduct themselves in accordance with the organization's rules and standards of acceptable behavior. Whether discipline is imposed and how severe is the action chosen should reflect such contingencies as the seriousness of the problem, duration of the problem, frequency and nature of the problem, the employee's work history, extenuating circumstances, degree of orientation, history of the organization's discipline practices, implications for other employees, and management backing.

9. General guidelines in administering discipline include making disciplinary actions corrective, making disciplinary actions progressive, and following the hot-stove rule—be immediate, provide ample warning, be consistent, and be impersonal.

10. Employee counseling can be used to assist a poorly performing employee by helping the employee make behavior changes. It is an effort to correct performance declines, and to take corrective action before more serious disciplinary is taken.

EXPERIENTIAL EXERCISE: What If . . . ?

1. A co-worker, Bud, invites you to share a pizza for lunch on the shipping dock. After pizza, Bud lights a marijuana cigarette and asks if you would like your own or a share of his. Although you know that having or consuming drugs at the worksite is a violation of policy and law, you must decide whether to

   (a) inform Bud's supervisor, safety coordinator, or human resources manager of the incident

(b) tell Bud he shouldn't smoke dope at work and encourage Bud to seek help such as Employee Assistance Program in human resources department

(c) say nothing, excuse yourself, and hope that when Bud returns to the forklift his reflexes aren't slowed, mental powers and perceptions lessened, or that he becomes more forgetful and injures himself or someone else

(d) join Bud in prohibited behavior

(e) remember not to go to lunch with Bud again

(f) combination

(g) other

2. You are completing an honesty test for a potential employer. The question, "Have you ever knowingly stolen any item from an employer," is a tough one because you remember the time when you were working as a stocker in the grocery store and at break you and other stockers would eat pieces of fruit which did not meet quality requirements of store policy. You would:

▶ check yes, receiving a lower score
▶ check no, rationalizing fruit consumption as an employee benefit
▶ reconsider working for a company that asks such questions on tests
▶ other

3. A co-worker shares that she recently logged into the database, printed the customer mailing list, then sold it to various list subscribers for her "petty cash fund since she didn't get the raise increase she deserved." You:

▶ tell a human resources staff member
▶ tell other co-workers
▶ wish she hadn't told you and say nothing
▶ other

4. You know that a co-worker uses, sells, and distributes drugs to other co-workers. You

▶ say nothing to human resources because you fear retaliation from the dealer
▶ call the police
▶ leave an anonymous message
▶ tell security
▶ tell human resources
▶ other

WEB-WISE EXERCISES
Employee Rights

Explore and print findings about alcohol- and drug-related issues from the following site:

http://janweb.icdi.wvu.edu/kinder/. This site links to ADA resources. Includes sites regarding specific disabilities such as HIV/AIDS, hearing, visual and mobility impairment, as well as alcohol- and drug-related issues.

Search and print findings of interest from the following sites:

On-Line Journal of Ethics
http://condor.depaul.edu./ethics/ethg1.html

Human Resource Law Center
http://www.mleesmith.com/emp.html

HR News Online
http://www.shrm.org/hrnews/

CASE APPLICATION:
Almost Fatal Attraction

After Ally and Kevin met six months ago while working on their company process improvement team, they began having an affair although Kevin was married but separated. To complicate matters, Kevin was promoted to Ally's supervisor after they became involved. Kevin has decided to rebuild his relationship with his estranged wife and has told Ally he can no longer be involved with her. Because Kevin tries to avoid Ally, he provides her with less information or communication than she reasonably needs to do the job.

Ally continues to call Kevin at home, at work, sometimes twelve or more times a day, waits for him by his car when it's time to go home, and degrades him to her co-workers—his employees. Kevin is afraid that he will be terminated if he shares that he was involved with someone who directly reports to him, that management will think he can't handle the job if he complains about a woman who continues to want to be involved with him, that his employees will lose more respect for him, that Ally may escalate her pursuit.

The quality of Kevin's work is deteriorating, errors have increased, personality conflicts with co-workers have erupted, complaints from customers have surfaced due to his rude and abrupt attitude. The stress has taken its toll. Kevin has used up all his sick days with headaches or doctor's appointments, and now he needs more. Kevin asks you what he should do.

You suggest to Kevin that he:

1. share his concerns with the human resources manager and ask for her assistance
2. quit
3. transfer
4. confront Ally one more time
5. wait until she becomes interested in someone else
6. other

Kevin asks you what he should have done differently. Respond.

TESTING YOUR UNDERSTANDING

How well did you fulfill the learning objectives?

1. Dana is rewriting the section of the policies and procedures manual for her organization regarding employees' access to their employment history files. Which statement is most appropriate?
   a. No employee shall have access to any data in his or her file.
   b. Any employee may have access to any employee file data with supervisor approval.
   c. An employee may have access to his or her file with twenty-four-hour notice to personnel. The file must be reviewed in the human resources area.
   d. Any employee file may be requested by the employee. File contents will be mailed to the employee's official home address.
   e. Any employee may have access to his or her employee file with signatory approval of the immediate supervisor and one additional level of management.

2. The Fair Credit Reporting Act contains which provision?
   a. Job applicants must be informed in writing of third-party credit history investigations.
   b. Job applicants who have filed bankruptcy are guaranteed by a federal agency for seven years.
   c. Job applicants may refuse to submit to a credit check. Organizations must hire them anyway if all other relevant selection criteria are met.
   d. Standards of the act do not apply to female and minority applicants.
   e. Loan payment defaults must be removed from an employee's file in ninety days.

3. You are vice president of human resources in a federal security agency. Which procedure would be an appropriate pre-employment credit history practice?
   a. Do not tell the applicant of any credit history examinations that you intend to perform.
   b. Do not do any credit history evaluation. No one would apply if they had anything to hide.
   c. Ask the applicant for checking and savings account numbers.
   d. During the screening interview, have applicants sign a statement that informs them they will be subject to a third-party investigation to assess their character and general reputation. Secure names of individuals who may be contacted as personal references.
   e. Ask the candidate to complete a credit history form during the interview. Watch for stress reactions as the individual lists outstanding balances and monthly payment amounts. Ask probing questions if you notice any unusual responses.

4. A vice president of human resources for a large defense contractor has developed a drug-free workplace compliance policy that defines expected employee behaviors and states penalties for noncompliance. This policy should also include:
   a. providing substance-abuse awareness programs for all employees.
   b. requiring one hundred hours of community service work for all first-time offenders.
   c. sponsoring public service announcements on local television or radio stations about substance abuse.
   d. working with local school systems to prevent substance abuse in the schools.
   e. supplying an article in the company newsletter that identifies offenders.

5. An applicant was given a polygraph test to ascertain general levels of honesty when she applied for a job as a sales associate for a large department store. She "failed" the test and was subsequently removed from the applicant pool. What legal recourse, if any, does the individual have?
   a. She can notify the secretary of labor, who will enforce her right to work and require the organization to hire her.
   b. She can notify the secretary of labor, who may assess civil penalties up to $10,000 against the employer.
   c. She may file criminal action against the human resources professional who administered the test. If guilty, that person could be jailed for five years.
   d. The union will issue a walkout if she is employed.
   e. None.

6. As a corrections officer applicant, Jim was asked to submit to a routine polygraph test. He was shown the list of questions, and he agreed to take the test. When he said, "No," in response to a question about recreational drug usage, the machine indicated a lie. Jim was not hired because suspicion of drug use is grounds for dismissal for corrections officers. What recourse does he have?
   a. He can retake the test next month. Law stipulates that he must be given the questions thirty days prior to examination.
   b. He should be hired anyway if his drug test was negative.
   c. None. Corrections institutions may hire or not hire any job candidate at their discretion.
   d. None. The requirement for a security officer is reasonable.
   e. If Jim is a minority candidate, he can appeal the decision.

7. An employee has worked for twenty-two years at a twenty-employee branch of a large auto-parts chain. Business has been very bad lately, and there are rumors of consolidation, reorganization, even bankruptcy. What protection does this employee have under the Worker Adjustment and Retraining Notification Act?
   a. With over fifteen years' seniority, the employee cannot be laid off with less than six months' notice.
   b. No protection. This branch is too small for coverage under WARN.
   c. No protection. This industry is not covered by the Plant Closing Bill.
   d. The employee will be given sixty days' warning if this location closes.
   e. The employee will be given thirty days' warning, but only if the whole organization closes.

8. An accounts payable manager for a 250-employee graphics art manufacturer has been on the job for twenty-seven months. She went to work Monday morning to find the front door locked and a "THIS SPACE FOR LEASE" sign on the front door. She called her office from the local McDonald's and found that the telephone had been disconnected. What protection is given to this accounts payable manager under the Worker Adjustment and Retraining Notification Act?
   a. She is entitled to an amount equal to pay and benefits for up to sixty days.
   b. No protection. The company was too small for coverage.
   c. No protection. This industry was not covered.
   d. Her old firm must pay agency fees to have her placed with another organization.
   e. No protection. Managers are not covered by the law.

9. Honesty tests
   a. are only legal when they focus on drug use or theft.
   b. accept dishonesty as a valid behavior, as long as the respondent is truthful about that behavior.
   c. are typically designed to cover similar topic areas with multiple questions to assess consistency.
   d. provide information that is easily obtainable by other techniques.
   e. are permissible only after a person has been hired.

10. The original premise behind employment-at-will was
    a. if employers can fire whenever they want, employees should be able to quit whenever they want.
    b. if employers can hire whenever they want, employees should be able to quit whenever they want.
    c. if employers can schedule working hours, employees should be able to schedule their own vacations.
    d. if employees can quit whenever they want, employers should be able to fire whenever they want.
    e. if employees can request vacation leave, employers should be able to schedule working hours.

11. An employee in the software design department was fired for refusing use-licensed software provided to him by his supervisor. What type of wrongful discharge suit, if any, could he file?
    a. Breach of contractual relationship.
    b. Breach of good faith.
    c. Public policy violation.
    d. Breach of implied contract.
    e. There is no wrongful discharge in this case.

12. Robbie had been Carol's secretary for ten years. She often told him how valuable he was to her and that "as long as she was with the company, there would be a place for him." Carol got promoted from the Denver to the New York office last month. Robbie's employment was terminated because Carol's job was eliminated at the Denver site. What exception to the employment-at-will doctrine might Robbie use to support his claim of an illegal discharge?
    a. Breach of contractual relationship.
    b. Breach of implied contract.
    c. Public policy violation.
    d. Breach of good faith.
    e. There is no wrongful discharge in this case.

13. A manager of a fast-food franchise has learned that one of his employees, the night manager, has been stealing supplies. He called corporate to check with the human resources representative before beginning disciplinary procedures. What contingency factor is he considering?
    a. Nature and extent of the problem.
    b. Extenuating circumstances.
    c. History of organization's disciplinary procedures.
    d. Severity of the problem.
    e. Degree of socialization.

14. A longtime worker in a steel manufacturing plant no longer wears steel-toed shoes, an insulated work suit, hard hat, and safety glasses on the work floor, even though federal safety standards require such protective clothing. When his boss confronts him on the matter, he says that he has not had an accident in fifteen years on the job, and, therefore, has no need for such hot and heavy gear. What would be the next best step the manager should follow?
    a. Let the matter drop. The employee is successfully performing the duties of his job.
    b. Put a written warning of insubordination in the employee's file. Permit him to review the file

twenty-four hours after the document has been received by HRM.

c. Arrange an "accident" close enough to the employee to scare him into compliance.

d. Explain to the employee the legal requirements and the importance of his influence on less experienced workers, and tell him to conform to safety standards. Explain that further infractions will result in written documentation and could lead to his dismissal.

e. Hold a special safety training session for all steel workers, explaining the legal safety requirements, and the penalties for noncompliance.

15. Ben gambles at work. He runs a lucrative football pool for the accountants in Building A. Stephanie, his supervisor, has talked to him about the rules of the organization that prohibit gambling, and the consequences for such behavior that ultimately lead to dismissal. Stephanie filed a written warning with human resources after Ben resumed his activities for last year's Super Bowl. Now, at the start of a new football season, it is obvious that Ben is at it again. What should Stephanie do to administer progressive discipline?

a. Send Ben home for two days, without pay, to think about the seriousness of the gambling offense.

b. Fire Ben.

c. Give up. Let Ben run the pool as long as no one complains.

d. Talk to Ben, remind him of the consequences of gambling on the job.

e. Transfer Ben to an area of the company that is not likely to support his gambling activities.

16. If a manager follows the hot-stove rule of administering discipline, he will

a. be acting under the guidelines of the employment-at-will doctrine.

b. administer discipline that is immediate, forewarned, consistent, and impersonal.

c. administer discipline that is swift, painful, and deliberate.

d. administer discipline in hot anger, with large, visible consequences.

e. administer discipline in a folksy, supportive, parental, coaching sort of way.

Endnotes

1. Based on the story by Jay Hancock, "Made in the Shade No Longer," *The Sun: Business* (January 26, 1996), pp. E1, E2.

2. George D. Webster, "Privacy in the Work Place," *Association Management,* Vol. 43, No. 4 (November 1990), pp. 36–37.

3. See, for example, Stephanie Overman, "A Delicate Balance Protects Everyone's Rights," *HRMagazine,* Vol. 35, No. 1 (November 1990), pp. 36–37.

4. Kerry Hannon, "How to Pass the Secret Credit Test," *Working Woman* (July/August 1996), pp. 30–32.

5. Wayne F. Casio, *Applied Psychology in Personnel Management,* 4th ed. (Englewood Cliffs, N.J.: Prentice Hall, 1991), p. 37.

6. Jane Bryant, "Many Bosses Peeking at Workers' Credit Reports," *The Baltimore Sun* (March 24, 1997), p. 11c.

7. See, for example, Commerce Clearing House, *Government Implementation for the Drug-Free Workplace Act of 1988, Part 2* (Chicago: Commerce Clearing House, Inc., 1990), p. 17.

8. Public Law 100-347.

9. This act applies to all private sector organizations except those organizations the secretary of labor deems too small (e.g., family-owned businesses).

10. See, for example, Lois R. Wise and Steven J. Charuat, "Polygraph Testing in the Public Sector: The Status of State Legislation," *Public Personnel Management,* Vol. 19, No. 4 (Winter 1990), pp. 381–390.

11. However, in cases when they are job related (requiring someone who has fiduciary responsibilities in an organization), they may be used.

12. Commerce Clearing House, "Polygraph Testing," *Human Resource Management: Ideas and Trends,* No. 173 (July 12, 1988), p. 105.

13. Gabriella Stern and Jeffrey A. Tannenbaum, "GM Plans to Sell Car Rental Unit to Buyout Firm," *The Wall Street Journal* (September 23, 1994), p. A-3.

14. Of course, GM could do just that; if it did, however, it would be in violation of WARN, and subjected to the penalties imposed under the act.

15. Worker Adjustment and Retraining Notification Act, Public Law 100-379.

16. Commerce Clearing House, "Plant Closing," *Human Resources Management: Ideas and Trends,* No. 175 (August 9, 1988), p. 129.

17. Fair Lanes was able to keep operating by filing for Chapter 11 (bankruptcy) status. See Jay Hancock, "Fair Lanes Emerges from Bankruptcy," *The Baltimore Sun* (September 21, 1994), p. 8-C.

18. Donald M. Smith, "Workplace Drug Abuse: It's Deadly, It's Costly, It's Preventable," *National Petroleum News,* Vol. 83, No. 2 (February 1991), p. 28.

19. Kimberly A. Weber and Robin E. Shea, "Drug Testing: The Necessary Evil," *Bobbin,* Vol. 32, No. 12 (August 1991), p. 98.

20. "An Alternative to Drug Testing?" *Inc.* (April 1995), p. 112; Jim Carraher, "Progress Report: Drug Tests," *Security,* Vol. 28, No. 10 (October 1991), p. 40. See also Joseph G. Rosse, Deborah F. Crown, and Howard D. Feldman, "Alternative Solutions to the Workplace Drug Problem," *Journal of Employment Counseling,* Vol. 27, (June 1990), p. 60.

21. Commerce Clearing House, "Drug Testing, Basic Skills and AIDS Policy Benchmarks," *Human Resources Management: Ideas and Trends* (June 8, 1994), p. 97.

22. "And Whose Syringe Might This Be?" *Inc.* (August 1994), p. 104.

23. It is important to note that drug testing may be constrained by collective bargaining agreements, or state laws. See Er-

ica Gordon Sorohan, "Making Decisions About Drug Test-ing," *Training and Development* (May 1994), pp. 111–117.

24. "Motorola Aims High, So Motorolans Won't Be Getting High," *The Wall Street Journal* (June 26, 1990), p. A-19.

25. "Narc in a Can," *Executive Female* (November-December 1990), p. 24; and Edward J. Miller, "Investing in a Drug Free Workplace," *HRMagazine,* Vol. 36, No. 5 (May 1991), p. 48.

26. Jonathan A. Segal, "Urine or You're Out," *HRMagazine* (December 1994), pp. 33, 35.

27. "Motorola Aims High, So Motorolans Won't Be Getting High," p. A19.

28. Ibid., and "Narc in a Can," p. 24.

29. Leslee Jaquette, "Red Lion Pleased with Drug-Testing Pro-gram," *Hotel and Motel Management,* Vol. 206, No. 3 (Feb-ruary 25, 1991), p. 3.

30. Commerce Clearing House, "The ADA Changes the Rules," *Human Resources Management: Ideas and Trends* (July 11, 1994), p. 111.

31. J. Michael Walsh, "Is Workplace Drug-Testing Effective," *HR News* (April 1996), p. 5; and Jonathan A. Segal, "Urine or You're Out," *HRMagazine* (December 1994), pp. 30–38.

32. See, for example, Holtford Kent, MD, "*Urine Trouble* (Scottsdale, AZ: Vandalay Press, 1997).

33. For an interesting review of hair sampling, for example, see Pascal Kintz (ed.), *Drug Testing in Hair* (Boca Raton, FL: CRC Press, 1996).

34. "An Alternative to Drug Testing," *Inc.* (April 1995), p. 112.

35. Joseph G. Rosse, et al., p. 62.

36. Dianna L. Stone and Debra A. Kotch, "Individuals' Attitudes Toward Organizational Drug Testing Policies and Practices," *Journal of Applied Psychology,* Vol. 74, No. 3 (1989), p. 521.

37. Ibid., and Michael R. Carroll and Christina Heavrin, "Before You Drug Test," *HRMagazine* (June 1990), p. 64.

38. See, for example, Kevin R. Murphy, George C. Thornton III, and Kristin Prue, "Influence of Job Characteristics on the Acceptability of Employee Drug Testing," *Journal of Ap-plied Psychology,* Vol. 76, No. 3 (1991), pp. 447–453.

39. This question comes from an article citing actual questions on an honesty test. See Michael P. Cronin, "This Is a Test," *Inc.* (August 1993), p. 67.

40. Stephen Bennett, "Employee Testing: Truth or Conse-quence," *Progressive Grocer* (October 1990), p. 51.

41. Ibid.

42. Casio, p. 268.

43. Ed Bean, "More Firms Use Attitude Tests to Keep Thieves Off the Payroll," *The Wall Street Journal* (February 27, 1987), p. A-19.

44. Ibid.

45. Matthew Budman, "The Honest Business," *Across the Board* (November/December 1993), pp. 313–337.

46. See, for example, H. John Bernardin and Donna K. Cooke, "Validity of an Honesty Test in Predicting Theft Among Convenience Store Employees," *Academy of Management Journal,* Vol. 38, No. 5 (Fall 1993), pp. 1097–2108.

47. Ibid.

48. Casio, p. 268.

49. See, for instance, Janet P. Near and Marcia P. Miceli, "Effec-tive Wistle-Blowing," *Academy of Management Review,* Vol. 20, No. 3 (Summer 1995), pp. 679–708.

50. Hal Lancaster, "Workers Who Blow the Whistle on Bosses Often Pay a High Price," *The Wall Street Journal* (July 18,

1995), p. B-1; and "A Whistle-Blower Gets His Reward," *Business Week* (August 28, 1995), p. 38.

51. Commerce Clearing House, "Whistleblower Can Sue for Emotional Distress, Supreme Court Rules," *Human Re-sources Management: Ideas and Trends,* No. 223 (June 13, 1990), pp. 97–98.

52. Ibid.

53. Kenneth L. Sovereign, *Personnel Law,* 3rd ed. (Englewood Cliffs, N.J.: Prentice-Hall, 1994), p. 177.

54. Timothy R. Barnett and Daniel S. Cochran, "Making Room for the Whistleblower," *HRMagazine* (January 1991), p. 58.

55. James D. Vigneau, "To Catch a Thief . . . and Other Workplace Investigations," *HRMagazine* (January 1995), pp. 90–95.

56. See, for example, Michael F. Rosenblum, "Security v. Pri-vacy: An Emerging Employment Dilemma," *Employee Rela-tions Law Journal,* Vol. 17, No. 1 (Summer 1991), pp. 81–101.

57. Adapted from Glenn Rifkin, "Do Employees Have a Right to Electronic Privacy?" *The New York Times* (December 8, 1991), Sections 3–8.

58. Lee Smith, "What the Boss Knows About You," *Fortune* (August 9, 1993), p. 89.

59. Ibid.

60. Jeffrey A. Van Dorn, "Monitoring E-Mail? Better Have a Pol-icy," *HR News* (February 1996), p. 2; and Michael F. Ca-vanagh, "E-Mail, Workplace Privacy Policies Lag Need, Em-ployer Survey finds, *HR News* (February 1996), p. 2.

61. Michael Underhill, and Thomas A. Linthorst, "E-Mail in the Workplace" How Much is Private," *Society for Human Re-source Management: Legal Report* (Winter 1996), p. 1; Raju Narisetti, "E-Mail Snooping is OK in the Eyes of the Law," *The Wall Street Journal* (March 20, 1996), p. A-1; and Carl Quintanilla, "Employee Monitoring Accelerates as Technol-ogy Improves," *The Wall Street Journal* (June 11, 1996), p. A-1.

62. Dana Hawkins, "Who's Watching Now?" *U.S. News & World Report* (September 15, 1997), pp. 56–58; and Rochelle Sharpe, "Workers' Privacy Concerns Grow as Electronic Snooping, Urine Testing Increase," *The Wall Street Journal* (September 10, 1996), p. A-1.

63. See, for example, William L. Kandel, "Employee Dishonesty and Workplace Security: Precautions Against Prevention," *Employer Relations Law Journal,* Vol. 16, No. 2 (Autumn 1990), pp. 217–231.

64. Ellen Rapp, "Legislating Love," *Working Woman* (February 1992), p. 61.

65. See, for example, "Frisky Business," *Psychology Today* (March–April 1995), pp. 36–41, 70; and Alex Markels, "Employers' Dilemma: Whether to Regulate Romance," *The Wall Street Journal* (February 14, 1995), pp. B-1, B-13.

66. William C. Symonds, Steve Hamm, and Gail DeGeorge, "Sex on the Job," *Business Week* (February 16, 1998), pp. 30–31; and Jonathan A. Segal, "The World May Welcome Lovers," *HRMagazine* (June 1996), pp. 170–179.

67. Anne B. Fisher, "Getting Comfortable with Couples in the Workplace," *Fortune* (October 3, 1994), pp. 139–144.

68. Ibid., p. 142.

69. See, for example, Jonathan A. Segal, "A Need Not to Know," *HRMagazine,* Vol. 36, No. 10 (October 1991), pp. 85–90.

70. See Jennifer J. Koch, "Wells Fargo's and IBM's HIV Positive Policies Help Protect Employee Rights," *Personnel Journal,* Vol. 69, No. 4 (April 1990), pp. 40–51.

71. Ibid.

72. See, for example, Jack Hayes, "Cracker Barrel Comes Under Fire for Ousting Gays," *Nation's Restaurant News,* Vol. 25 (March 4, 1991), p. 1.

73. *Payne v. Western and Atlantic Railroad Co.,* 812 Tenn. 507 (1884). See also Marie Leonard, "Challenges to the Termination-at-Will Doctrine," *Personnel Administrator* (February 1983), p. 49. (Quoted from Lawrence E. Blades, *Columbia Law Review,* 67 [1967], 1405.)

74. Jane Easter Bahls, "Playing with Fire," *Entrepreneur* (October 1994), p. 66.

75. Commerce Clearing House, "Future of Employment-at-Will Uncertain, But Risk of Wrongful Discharge Suits Can Be Curtailed Now," *Human Resources Management: Ideas and Trends* (July 20, 1994), p. 119.

76. "Wrongful Discharge," *The Wall Street Journal* (September 10, 1991), p. A-1.

77. See, for instance, "Employees from Hell," *Inc.* (January 1995), p. 54.

78. Commerce Clearing House, *Topical Law Reports* (Chicago: Commerce Clearing House, 1989), p. 2773.

79. Michael J. Lotito, Esq., "State by State, the Rules of the Employment Relationship Are Changing," *Commerce Clearing House, Human Resources Management: Ideas and Trends,* No. 226 (July 25, 1990), p. 126.

80. Adapted from Carroll R. Daugherty, Enterprise Wire Co. 46 LA 359 (1966).

81. See, for example, Kenneth L. Sovereign, *Personnel Law,* 3rd ed. (Englewood Cliffs, N.J.: Prentice Hall, 1994), p. 178.

82. *Toussaint v. Blue Cross and Blue Shield of Michigan,* 408 Michigan, 529, 292 N.W. 2d 880 (1980).

83. Sovereign, p. 180.

84. Ibid.

85. Ibid., p. 179.

86. Ibid.

87. *Fortune v. National Cash Register,* 364 373 Massachusetts 91, 36 N.E. 2d 1251 (1977).

88. For another view of means of "reclaiming" employment-at-will practices, see Theresa Donahue Egler, "A Manager's Guide to Employment Contracts," *HR Magazine* (May 1996), pp. 28–33.

89. Wallace Wohlking, "Effective Discipline in Employee Relations," *Personnel Journal* (September 1975), pp. 491–492.

90. Martin Levy, "Discipline for Professional Employees," *Personnel Journal* (December 1990), pp. 27–28.

91. James G. Frierson, "How to Fire without Getting Burned," *Personnel* (September, 1990), p. 46.

92. Walter Kiechel, "How to Discipline in the Modern Age," *Fortune* (May 7, 1990), pp. 179–180.

93. It is true that two other disciplinary actions may be used— pay cuts or demotion—but they are rare. See, for example, John P. Kohl and David B. Stephens, "Is Demotion a Four Letter Word?" *Business Horizons* (March–April 1990), p. 75.

94. Chimezie A. B. Osigweh Yg, and William R. Hutchinson, "To Punish or Not to Punish? Managing Human Resources Through Positive Discipline," *Employee Relations* (March 1990), pp. 27–32.

95. Chimezie A. B. Osigweh Yg and William R. Hutchinson, "Positive Discipline," *Human Resource Management* (Fall 1989), p. 367.

96. Jerry Wisinski, "A Logical Approach to a Difficult Employee," *HR Focus* (January 1992), p. 9.

97. Ibid.

98. Gerald D. Cook, "Employee Counseling Session," *Supervision* (August 1989), p. 3.

99. See James Greiff, "When an Employee's Performance Slumps," *Nation's Business* (January 1989), pp. 44–45.

100. Adapted from Commerce Clearing House, "The Do's and Don't's of Confronting a Troubled Employee," *Topical Law Reports* (Chicago, IL: Commerce Clearing House, Inc., October 1990), pp. 4359–4360; Gerald D. Cook, "Employee Counseling Session, *Supervision* (August 1989), p. 3; and Andrew E. Schuartz, "Counseling the Marginal Performer," *Management Solutions* (March 1988), p. 30.

14. Safety and Health Programs

LEARNING OBJECTIVES

After reading this chapter, you will be able to:

1. Discuss the organizational effect of the Occupational Safety and Health Act.
2. List the Occupational Safety and Health Administration's (OSHA) enforcement priorities.
3. Explain what punitive actions OSHA can impose on an organization.
4. Describe what companies must do to comply with OSHA record-keeping requirements.
5. Identify three contemporary areas for which OSHA is setting standards.
6. Describe the leading causes of safety and health accidents.
7. Explain what companies can do to prevent workplace violence.
8. Define stress and the causes of burnout.
9. Explain how an organization can create a healthy work site.

For the past few decades, many people have been gambling on a dream. The thought of instant money—becoming a millionaire overnight—has enticed many individuals to play state lotteries. As these lotteries flourished, though, they required organizations to make them work. They had to hire employees to officiate over the lottery drawings, to ensure that they operate fairly, and to handle the required day-to-day business matters. At times, it took upwards of 100 employees to make this happen. Working for a state lottery agency, however, shouldn't be a gamble. Sure, anytime you put a group of employees together, disagreements and conflicts may arise. Still, no one possibly could have anticipated the events that occurred at the headquarters of the Connecticut State Lottery Office in Newington, Connecticut.[1]

The Connecticut State Lottery Office (CSL) was no different from any other organization. It had goals, hired employees to do a variety of duties, and provided an array of HRM functions to attract, motivate, and retain high perform-

No matter what an organization does to ensure employee safety, some events are just random. At the Connecticut State Lottery Agency, disgruntled employee Matthew Beck returned to work after a four-month stress leave. A few short days later, he shot three company officials before turning the gun on himself.

ers. One benefit of working for the CSL was a promising employee assistance program. Employees who had problems—work- or personal-related—could find help. The culture of the organization embodied giving employees the time needed to address their difficulties, and get that well-trained, effective employee back to work when possible. For years it has worked, and probably will work for years to come. Unfortunately, there's a blemish that will never be forgotten—at the hands of one employee, Matthew Beck.

Matthew Beck worked in the accounting office of CSL. For the major part of his tenure at the Lottery Agency, he had been a successful performer. Yet sometime in 1997, problems arose for Beck. He had been questioning his pay. He didn't feel that his boss or other CSL officials were adequately compensating him for all the extra hours he had worked. Beck challenged company officials, following policies and protocols as expected. He even had the support of his employees' association, who helped him in his dispute. But to no avail—as Beck was unsuccessful in his challenge. Upset over the decisions, Beck's behavior began to change. He was stressed, unhappy, and having difficulty concentrating on his job. Nothing his boss did could ease Beck's feeling that he was being wronged. Finally, these feelings overwhelmed Beck, and company officials decided that he needed a "stress-leave." For the next several months, Beck was away from work, with pay, to regain his composure and put this issue behind him. Four months later, he seemed fine, in good spirits, and ready to resume his job. And his boss welcomed him back to CSL.

For most of the week, everything appeared "normal." Beck was discharging his assigned duties, and everything about him appeared ordinary. What happened that frightful Friday, March 6, 1998, however, may never be explained. Beck arrived at work and headed to the executive offices. Inside the building, he produced a weapon and shot his boss and two other CSL officials. Hearing the commotion, and recognizing the threat to all employees, the president of CSL attempted to get everyone out of the building. Comfortable that he had removed employees from the immediate threat, the president ran from the building. In hot pursuit was Matthew Beck. With police officers arriving in the parking lot, the president tripped and fell to the ground. Immediately hovering over him was Beck—and in spite of pleas from the president not to kill him, Beck twice fired his 9-mm weapon. Moments later, another shot went off—a self-inflicted wound that ended the horror.

We all know that there are no guarantees in life. Yet going to work should not be a game of chance. That frightful day in March 1998 proved that things unexpectedly do transpire—as three CSL officials and Matthew Beck died at the scene.

INTRODUCTION

Organization officials have a legal responsibility, if not a moral one, to ensure that the workplace is free from unnecessary hazards and that conditions surrounding the workplace are not hazardous to employees' physical or mental health. Of course, accidents can and do occur, and the severity of these may astound you. There are approximately 45,000 reported work-related deaths[2] and 6.6 million injuries and illnesses each year in the United States, resulting in over 90 million days lost of productive time—costing U.S. companies more than $111 billion annually.[3] Heartless as it sounds, employers must be concerned about employees' health and safety if for no other reason than that accidents cost money.

From the turn of the century through the late 1960s, remarkable progress was made in reducing the rate and severity of job-related accidents and diseases. Yet the most significant piece of legislation in the area of employee health and safety was not enacted until 1970. This law is called the **Occupational Safety and Health Act.** Let's take an in-depth look at this law.

THE OCCUPATIONAL SAFETY AND HEALTH ACT

The passage of the Occupational Safety and Health Act (OSH Act) dramatically changed the role that HRM must play in ensuring that the physical working conditions meet adequate standards. What the Civil Rights Act did to alter the organization's commitment to affirmative action, the OSH Act has done to alter the organization's health and safety programs.

OSH Act legislation established comprehensive and specific health standards, authorized inspections to ensure the standards are met, empowered the Occupational Safety and Health Administration (OSHA) to police organizations' compliance, and required employers to keep records of illness and injuries, and to calculate accident ratios. The Act applies to almost every U.S. business engaged in interstate commerce, which means that 5 million workplaces employing approximately 64 million workers are covered. Those organizations not meeting the interstate commerce criteria of OSH Act are generally covered by state occupational safety and health laws.

The safety and health standards the OSH Act established are quite complex. Standards exist for such diverse conditions as noise levels, air impurities, physical protection equipment, the height of toilet partitions, and the correct size of ladders.[4] Furthermore, OSHA researches repetitive stress (or motion) injuries, problems associated with the eye strain that accompanies video display terminal use, and developing training and education programs for businesses.

The initial OSH Act standards took up 350 pages in the Federal Register, and some of the annual revisions and interpretations are equally extensive. Nev-

JOB SAFETY & HEALTH PROTECTION

Exhibit 14-1

Job safety and health Protection.

The Occupational Safety and Health Act of 1970 provides job safety and health protection for workers by promoting safe and healthful working conditions throughout the Nation. Provisions of the Act include the following:

Employers

All employers must furnish to employees employment and a place of employment free from recognized hazards that are causing or are likely to cause death or serious harm to employees. Employers must comply with occupational safety and health standards issued under the Act.

Employees

Employees must comply with all occupational safety and health standards, rules, regulations and orders issued under the Act that apply to their own actions and conduct on the job.

The Occupational Safety and Health Administration (OSHA) of the U.S. Department of Labor has the primary responsibility for administering the Act. OSHA issues occupational safety and health standards, and its Compliance Safety and Health Officers conduct jobsite inspections to help ensure compliance with the Act.

Inspection

The Act requires that a representative of the employer and a representative authorized by the employees be given an opportunity to accompany the OSHA inspector for the purpose of aiding the inspection.

Where there is no authorized employee representative, the OSHA Compliance Officer must consult with a reasonable number of employees concerning safety and health conditions in the workplace.

Complaint

Employees or their representatives have the right to file a complaint with the nearest OSHA office requesting an inspection if they believe unsafe or unhealthful conditions exist in their workplace. OSHA will withhold, on request, names of employees complaining.

The Act provides that employees may not be discharged or discriminated against in any way for filing safety and health complaints or for otherwise exercising their rights under the Act.

Employees who believe they have been discriminated against may file a complaint with their nearest OSHA office within 30 days of the alleged discriminatory action.

Citation

If upon inspection OSHA believes an employer has violated the Act, a citation alleging such violations will be issued to the employer. Each citation will specify a time period within which the alleged violation must be corrected.

The OSHA citation must be prominently displayed at or near the place of alleged violation for three days, or until it is corrected, whichever is later, to warn employees of dangers that may exist there.

Proposed Penalty

The Act provides for mandatory civil penalties against employers of up to $7,000 for each serious violation and for optional penalties of up to $7,000 for each nonserious violation. Penalties of up to $7,000 per day may be proposed for failure to correct violations within the proposed time period and for each day the violation continues beyond the prescribed abatement date. Also, any employer who willfully or repeatedly violates the Act may be assessed penalties of up to $70,000 for each such violation. A minimum penalty of $5,000 may be imposed for each willful violation. A violation of posting requirements can bring a penalty of up to $7,000.

There are also provisions for criminal penalties. Any willful violation resulting in the death of any employee, upon conviction, is punishable by a fine of up to $250,000 (or $500,000 if the employer

(Continued)

is a corporation), or by imprisonment for up to six months, or both. A second conviction of an employer doubles the possible term of imprisonment. Falsifying records, reports, or applications is punishable by a fine of $10,000 or up to six months in jail or both.

Voluntary Activity

While providing penalties for violations, the Act also encourages efforts by labor and management, before an OSHA inspection, to reduce workplace hazards voluntarily and to develop and improve safety and health programs in all workplaces and industries. OSHA's Voluntary Protection Programs recognize outstanding efforts of this nature.

OSHA has published Safety and Health Program Management Guidelines to assist employers in establishing or perfecting programs to prevent or control employee exposure to workplace hazards. There are many public and private organizations that can provide information and assistance in this effort, if requested. Also your local OSHA office can provide considerable help and advice on solving safety and health problems or can refer you to other sources for help such as training.

Consultation

Free assistance in identifying and correcting hazards and in improving safety and health management is available to employers, without citation or penalty, through OSHA-supported programs in each State. These programs are usually administered by the State Labor or Health department or a State university.

Posting Instructions

Employers in States operating OSHA ap-

proved State Plans should obtain and post the State's equivalent poster.

Under provisions of Title 29, Code of Federal Regulations, Part 1903.2(a)(1) employers must post this notice (or facsimile) in a conspicuous place where notices to employees are customarily posted.

More Information

Additional information and copies of the Act, specific OSHA safety and health standards, and other applicable regulations may be obtained from your employer or from the nearest OSHA Regional Office in the following locations:

Atlanta, GA (404) 347-3573
Boston, MA (617) 565-7164
Chicago, IL (312) 353-2220
Dallas, TX (214) 767-4731
Denver, CO (303) 844-3061
Kansas City, MO (816) 426-5861
New York, NY (212) 337-2378
Philadelphia, PA (215) 596-1201
San Francisco, CA (415) 744-6670
Seattle, WA (206) 442-5930

To report suspected fire hazards, imminent danger safety and health hazards in the workplace, or other job safety and health emergencies, such as toxic waste in the workplace, call OSHA's 24-hour hotline: 1-800-321-OSHA.

This information will be made available to sensory impaired individuals upon request. Voice phone: (202) 523-8615; TDD message referral phone: 1-800-326-2577.

Lynn Martin, Secretary of Labor, U.S. Department of Labor, Occupational Safety and Health Administration, Washington, D.C., 1992 (Reprinted) OSHA 2203 U.S. GOVERNMENT PRINTING OFFICE: 1992 0-320-762 QL 3

ertheless, employers are responsible for knowing these standards and ensuring that those that do apply to them are followed (see Exhibit 14-1).

OSHA Enforcement Priorities

Enforcement procedures of OSHA standards vary depending on the nature of the event and the organization. Typically, OSHA enforces the standards based on a five-item priority listing. These are, in descending priority: imminent danger; serious accidents that have occurred within the past forty-eight hours; a current employee complaint; inspections of target industries with a high injury ratio; and random inspections.

Imminent danger refers to a condition where an accident is about to occur. Although this is given top priority and acts as a preventive measure, imminent danger situations are hard to define. In fact, in some cases, the definition of imminent danger appears to be an accident in progress, and interpretation leaves much to the imagination. For example, suppose you were withdrawing cash at an ATM. As you remove your cash, you are grabbed by an individual who places a gun in your face and angrily demands your cash. Are you in imminent danger? Of course, most of us would say, absolutely! But, according to one interpretation of imminent danger, you may not be in "imminent" danger. That "state" would not exist until the "assailant" pulled the trigger of the weapon, and the bullet was rifling through the barrel. Tragically, by that time it is too late to worry about imminent danger. One's safety has already been threatened.

Being such, this has given rise to priority-two accidents—those that have led to *serious injuries* or death. Under the law, an organization must report these serious accidents to the Occupational Safety and Health Administration field office within forty-eight hours of occurrence. This permits the investigators to review the scene and try to determine the cause of the accident.

Priority three, *employee complaints,* is a major concern for any manager. If an employee sees a violation of the OSHA standards, that employee has the right to call OSHA and request an investigation. The worker may even refuse to work on the item in question until OSHA has investigated the complaint. This is especially true when there is a union. For instance, in some union contracts, workers may legally refuse to work if they believe they are in significant danger. Accordingly, they may stay off the job with pay until OSHA arrives and either finds the complaint invalid or cites the company and mandates compliance.[5]

Next in the priority of enforcement is the *inspection of targeted industries*. A few paragraphs ago, we stated that more than 5 million workplaces are covered under OSHA. To investigate each would require several hundred thousand full-time inspectors. OSHA, however, only employs about 1,200 inspectors who conduct about 70,000 inspections a year.[6] And its budget has been significantly cut in the past decade.[7] So, in order to have the largest effect, OSHA began to direct its attention to those industries with the highest injury rates–industries such as chemical processing, roofing and sheeting metal, meat processing, lumber and wood products, mobile homes and campers, and stevedoring. In addition, a new rule established in 1990 requires employers who handle hazardous waste (i.e., chemicals, medical waste) to follow strict operating procedures;[8] any employer who handles hazardous waste is required to monitor employee exposure, develop and communicate safety plans, and provide necessary protective equipment.[9]

The final OSHA priority is the random inspection. Originally, OSHA inspectors were authorized to enter any work area premise, without notice, to ensure that the workplace was in compliance. In 1978, however, the Supreme Court ruled in *Marshall v. Barlow's Inc.*[10] that employers are not required to let OSHA inspectors enter the premises unless the inspectors have search warrants. This decision, while not destroying OSHA's ability to conduct inspections, forces inspectors to justify their choice of inspection sites more rigorously. That is, rather than trying to oversee health and safety standards in all of their jurisdictions, OSHA inspectors often find it easier to justify their actions and obtain search warrants if they appear to be pursuing specific problem areas.[11]

But don't let the warrant requirement mislead you into a false sense of security. If needed, an OSHA inspector will obtain the necessary legal document. Attorneys who deal with OSHA suggest that companies cooperate rather than viewing this event as confrontational.[12] This cooperation focuses on permitting the inspection, but only after "agreeing to the exact facility and entity to be inspected as well as the scope of the inspection." [13] That's not to say, however, that you can keep inspectors from finding violations. Consider what happened at the electronics and refrigeration facility of Ford Motor Company.[14] On a routine inspection of the facility, in an area the company knew would be seen, an OSHA inspector witnessed unsafe equipment being used. Because the inspector determined that its use was condoned by management at the plant, the company was fined and paid $1.2 million for past violations. Finally, it is recommended that any information regarding the company's safety program be discussed with the OSHA inspector, emphasizing how the program is communicated to employees, and how it is enforced.[15]

Should an employer feel that the fine levied is unjust, or too harsh, the law permits the employer to file an appeal. This appeal is reviewed by the Occupational Safety and Health Review Commission, an independently operating safety and health board. Although this commission's decisions are generally final, employers may still appeal commission decisions through the federal courts.[16]

OSHA's Record-Keeping Requirements

To fulfill part of the requirements established under the Occupational Safety and Health Act, employers in industries listed in Exhibit 14-2 who have eleven or more employees must maintain safety and health records.[17] Organizations not listed in Exhibit 14-2, such as universities, still must comply with the law itself; their only exception is the reduction of time spent on maintaining safety records. The basis of record-keeping for the OSH Act is the completion of

Exhibit 14-2

Industries required to keep OSHA records.

Agriculture, forestry, and fishing

Oil and gas extraction

Construction

Manufacturing

Transportation and public utilities

Wholesale trade

Building materials and garden supplies

General merchandise and food stores

Hotels and other lodging places

Repair services

Amusement and recreational services

Health services

SOURCE: U.S. Department of Labor, Bureau of Labor Statistics, *A Brief Guide to Recordkeeping, Requirements for Occupational Injuries and Illness* (Washington, D.C.: Government Printing Office, June 1986), p. 1.

OSHA Form 200 (see Exhibit 14-3). On this form, employees must identify "when the occupational injury or illness occurred, to whom, the regular job of the injured or ill person at the time of injury or illness exposure, the department in which the person was employed, the kind of injury or illness, how much time was lost, and whether the case resulted in a fatality."[18] Employers are required to keep these safety records for five years.

In complying with OSHA record-keeping requirements, one issue arises for employers—that is, just what is a reportable accident or an illness? According to the Act, OSHA distinguishes between the two in the following ways. Any work-related illness (no matter how insignificant it may appear) must be reported on Form 200. Injuries, on the other hand, are reported only when they require medical treatment (besides first aid), involve loss of consciousness, restriction of work or motion, or transfer to another job.[19]

To help employers decide whether an incident should be recorded, OSHA offers a schematic diagram for organizations to follow (see Exhibit 14-4). By using this "decision tree," organizational members can decide if, in fact, an event should be recorded. Should that occur, the employer is responsible for recording it under one of three areas: fatality, lost workday cases, or neither fatality nor lost workdays.[20] Part of this information is then used to determine an organization's incident rate. An **incidence rate** reflects the "number of injuries, illnesses, or (lost) workdays related to a common exposure base rate of 100 full-time workers."[21] This rate is then used by OSHA for determining industries and organizations that are more susceptible to injury. Let's look at the incidence rate formula and use it in an example.

To determine the incident rate, the formula $(N/EH) \times 200,000$ is used,[22] where:

► N is the number of injuries and/or illnesses or lost workdays;
► EH is the total hours worked by all employees during the year; and,
► 200,000 is the base hour rate equivalent (100 workers $\times$ 40 hours per week $\times$ 50 weeks per year).

In using the formula and calculating an organization's accident rate, assume we have an organization with 1,800 employees that experienced 195 reported accidents over the past year. We would calculate the incidence rate as follows: $(195/3,600,000) \times 200,000$.[23] The incidence rate, then, is 10.8. What does that 10.8 represent? That depends on a number of factors. If the organization is in the meat-packing industry where the industry average incident rate is 36.6,[24] then they are doing well. If, however, they are in the petroleum manufacturing industry, where the industry incident rate is 4.8,[25] then a 10.8 indicates a major concern.

OSHA Punitive Actions

An OSHA inspector has the right to levy a fine against an organization for noncompliance. While levying the fine is more complicated than described here, if an organization does not bring a "red-flagged" item into compliance, it can be assessed a severe penalty. As originally passed in 1970, the maximum penalty was $10,000 per occurrence, per day. However, with the **Omnibus Budget Reconciliation Act of 1990,** that $10,000 penalty can increase to $70,000 if the violation is severe, willful, and repetitive.[26] Although in its first

Exhibit 14-3 OSHA Form 200.

Bureau of Labor Statistics
Log and Summary of Occupational
Injuries and Illnesses

| NOTE: | This form is required by Public Law 91-596 and must be kept in the establishment for *5 years.* Failure to maintain and post can result in the issuance of citations and assessment of penalties. *(See posting requirements on the other side of form.)* | | **RECORDABLE CASES:** You are required to record information about every occupational **death**; every nonfatal occupational **illness**; and those nonfatal occupational injuries which involve one or more of the following: loss of consciousness, restriction of work or motion, transfer to another job, or medical treatment (other than first aid) *(See definitions on the other side of form.)* |

Case or File Number	Date of Injury or Onset of Illness	Employee's Name	Occupation	Department	Description of Injury or Illness
Enter a nondupli-cating number which will facilitate com-parisons with supple-mentary records.	Enter Mo./day.	Enter first name or initial, middle initial, last name.	Enter regular job title, not activity employee was per-forming when injured or at onset of illness. In the absence of a formal title, enter a brief description of the employee's duties.	Enter department in which the employee is regularly employed or a description of normal workplace to which employee is assigned, even though temporarily working in another depart-ment at the time of injury or illness.	Enter a brief description of the injury or illness and indicate the part or parts of body affected. Typical entries for this column might be: Amputation of 1st joint right forefinger; Strain of lower back; Contact dermatitis on both hands; Electrocution--body.
(A)	(B)	(C)	(D)	(E)	(F)
					PREVIOUS PAGE TOTALS ⟶
					TOTALS (Instructions on other side of form.) ⟶

OSHA No. 200   ★U.S.GPO:1990-262-256/15419

Exhibit 14-3 OSHA Form 200. *(Continued)*

U.S. Department of Labor

Company Name

Establishment Name

Establishment Address

For Calendar Year 19 _____

Page ____ of ____

Form Approved
O.M.B. No. 1220-0029
See OMB Disclosure
Statement on reverse.

Extent of and Outcome of INJURY						Type, Extent of, and Outcome of ILLNESS													
Fatalities	Nonfatal Injuries					Type of Illness								Fatalities	Nonfatal Illnesses				
Injury Related	Injuries With Lost Workdays				Injuries Without Lost Workdays	CHECK Only One Column for Each Illness *(See other side of form for terminations or permanent transfers.)*								Illness Related	Illnesses With Lost Workdays				Illnesses Without Lost Workdays
Enter DATE of death. Mo./day/yr.	Enter a CHECK if injury involves days away from work, or days of restricted work activity, or both.	Enter a CHECK if injury involves days away from work.	Enter number of DAYS away from work.	Enter number of DAYS of restricted work activity.	Enter a CHECK if no entry was made in columns 1 or 2 but the injury is recordable as defined above.	Occupational skin diseases or disorders	Dust diseases of the lungs	Respiratory conditions due to toxic agents	Poisoning (systemic effects of toxic materials)	Disorders due to physical agents	Disorders associated with repeated trauma	All other occupational illnesses		Enter DATE of death. Mo./day/yr.	Enter a CHECK if illness involves days away from work, or days of restricted work activity, or both.	Enter a CHECK if illness involves days away from work.	Enter number of DAYS away from work.	Enter number of DAYS of restricted work activity.	Enter a CHECK if no entry was made in columns 8 or 9.
(1)	(2)	(3)	(4)	(5)	(6)	(a)	(b)	(c)	(d)	(e)	(f)	(g)	(7)	(8)	(9)	(10)	(11)	(12)	(13)

Certification of Annual Summary Totals By _____ Title _____ Date _____

OSHA No. 200   **POST ONLY THIS PORTION OF THE LAST PAGE NO LATER THAN FEBRUARY 1.**

Exhibit 14-4 Determining recordability of laser under OSHA.

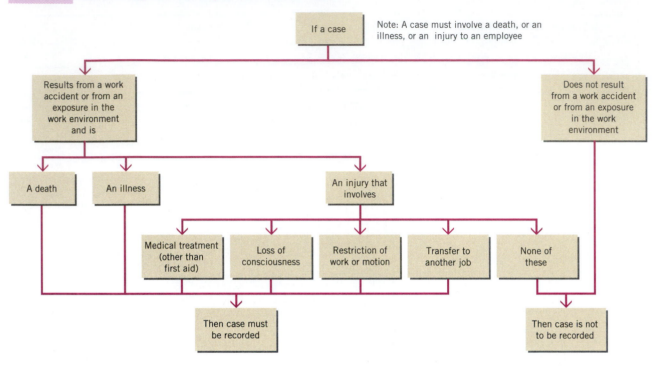

twenty years questions arose regarding the value of OSH Act to workers' health and safety,[27] such questions appear to be abating. Inroads have been made by the director of OSHA in redirecting OSHA's efforts. The agency has increased inspections and has been viewed as taking a tougher stance on workplace health and safety issues—and a number of companies have seen what that focus can mean. For example, the Budd Company was fined and paid $1.5 million for "843 willful violations."[28] But fines are not for safety violations alone. If a company fails to keep its OSH Act records properly, it, too, can be subjected to stiff penalties. For instance, the USX Corporation faced more than $7.3 million in fines, and Union Carbide more than $1.3 million, for failing to have adequate record-keeping procedures for the company's safety and health matters.[29]

Under the OSH Act, if an employee death occurs, executives can be criminally liable.

Under the OSH Act, if an employee death occurs, executives in the company can be criminally liable. For example, three executives at Pyro Mining were sentenced to prison and the company paid nearly $4 million in fines for the deaths of 10 miners.[30] Yet, most individuals have found the criminal penalties under the OSH Act somewhat limited—because of the death requirement. Accordingly, many state prosecutors are filing charges against company executives under general criminal statutes—and a few are having some success.[31]

OSHA: A Critique

Has the OSH Act worked? The answer is a qualified yes. In fact, the Act has had a direct and significant effect on almost every business organization in the United States. In some of the largest organizations, an additional administrator has been created who is solely responsible for safety. The impact of the OSH Act standards has made organizations more aware of health and safety. The standards may have been initially extreme in their specificity, and their red tape a nuisance, but that has been changing.[32]

What can we expect from OSHA over the next decade? Although its efforts will continue to concentrate on safety and health violations in organizations, OSHA is addressing problems associated with contemporary organizations, concentrating its efforts through the **National Institute for Occupational Safety and Health (NIOSH)** for researching, and in setting standards in such areas as blood-borne pathogens, and chemical process safety. Similarly, OSHA continues to explore motor vehicle safety, as well as focusing on fitting the work environment to the individual.[33]

Setting standards for blood-borne pathogens is designed to protect individuals, like medical personnel, from becoming infected with such diseases as AIDS[34] and hepatitis. In doing so, OSHA has established guidelines regarding protective equipment (like latex gloves, eye shields), and in cases where a vaccine is available, ensures that exposed workers have access to it.[35] Chemical processing standards reflect specific guidelines that must be adhered to when employees work with chemicals or other hazardous toxic substances. This requires companies to "perform hazardous analyses" and take any corrective action required.[36]

These concerns over chemical hazards led to a number of states passing *Right-to-Know Laws.* These laws helped identify hazardous chemicals in the workplace, required employers to inform employees of the chemicals they might be exposed to, the health risk associated with that exposure, and other policies guiding their use.[37] Although these state laws made progress in providing information regarding workplace toxins, there were variations among the

---

Each MSDS must contain:

_____ 1. Identity used on the label.
_____ 2. Chemical and common names of each hazardous ingredient (except as provided in 29 CFR 1910.1200(i)).
_____ 3. Physical and chemical characteristics of the hazardous chemical (such as vapor pressure or flashpoint).
_____ 4. The physical hazards of the hazardous chemical including the potential for fire, explosion and reactivity.
_____ 5. Health hazards of potential health risks, including signs and symptoms of exposure, and medical conditions aggravated by exposure.
_____ 6. Primary routes of entry.
_____ 7. OSHA, PEL, ACGIH TLV or other exposure limits.
_____ 8. Whether any ingredient is listed as a carcinogen by OSHA, NTP, or IARC.
_____ 9. Hygienic practices.
_____ 10. Procedures and precautions for safe handling.
_____ 11. Protective measures for repair and maintenance of contaminated equipment.
_____ 12. Spill and clean-up procedures.
_____ 13. Control measures such as engineering controls, work practices or personal protective equipment required such as gloves or goggles.
_____ 14. Emergency and first-aid procedures.
_____ 15. Date of MSDS preparation or revision.
_____ 16. Name, address and telephone number of responsible party, who can provide additional information on emergency procedures.

SOURCE: State of Maryland, Department of Licensing and Regulation Division of Labor and Industry.

Exhibit 14-5

Material Safety Data Sheet Checklist

Continuous keyboarding can lead to an illness referred to as "repetitive stress injury." OSHA has been investigating this occurrence hoping to influence work station designs that will reduce such injuries.

states—and some states didn't have these laws at all. Consequently, to provide some uniformity in protection, OSHA developed the **Hazard Communication Standard** in 1983.[38] This policy "requires employers to communicate chemical hazards to their employees by labeling containers, and by distributing data information (called Material Safety Data Sheets [see Exhibit 14-5]) provided by the manufacturer"[39] to the employees. In addition, employees exposed to various hazardous chemicals must be trained in their safe handling.[40] As enacted in 1983, this standard applied only to manufacturing industries. But by mid-1989, meeting the requirements of the Hazard Communication Standard became the responsibility of all industries.[41]

The third area, motor vehicle safety, reflects OSHA's interest in addressing the problems associated with workers who drive substantially as part of their job duties. This interest is due, in part, because approximately 36 percent of all worker deaths in any given year are attributed to motor vehicle accidents.[42] Accordingly, emphasis is placed on substance-abuse testing of drivers, safety equipment, and driver's education.

Finally, OSHA has been continuing its efforts in studying the proper design of the work environment such that it is conducive to productive work. Called *ergonomics,* OSHA has established an Internet Website (http//www.osha.gov/ergo) that helps organizations understand how ergonomics operates and how it can help. We'll come back to ergonomics later in this chapter.

JOB SAFETY PROGRAMS

If businesses are concerned with efficiency and profits, you may ask, why would they spend money to create conditions that exceed those required by law? The answer is the profit motive itself. The cost of accidents can be, and for many organizations is, a substantial additional cost of doing business. The direct cost of an accident to an employer shows itself in the organization's worker's compensation premium. This cost, as noted in the last chapter, is largely determined by the insured's accident history. Indirect costs, which generally far exceed direct costs, also must be borne by the employer. These include wages paid for time lost due to injury, damage to equipment and materials, personnel to investigate and report on accidents, and lost production due to work stoppages and personnel changeover. The impact of these indirect costs can be seen in statistics that describe the costs of accidents for American industry as a whole.[43]

In the early 1990s, workers' compensation premiums were costing U.S. employers almost $100 billion a year, an increase of almost 300 percent in a little under a decade.[44] Accidents cost employers additional billions of dollars in wages and lost production. The significance of this latter figure is emphasized when we note that this cost is approximately ten times greater than losses caused by strikes, an issue that historically has received much more attention. It's also interesting to note that on average, Japanese organizations have up to seven times fewer accidents in the workplace.[45] For Japanese firms, this has positively affected productivity.

Causes of Accidents

The cause of an accident can be generally classified as either human or environmental.[46] Human causes are directly attributable to human error brought about by carelessness, intoxication, daydreaming, inability to do the job, or other human deficiency. Environmental causes, in contrast, are attributable to the workplace and include the tools, equipment, physical plant, and general work environment. Both of these sources are important, but in terms of numbers, the human factor is responsible for the vast majority of accidents. No matter how much effort is made to create a work environment that is accident free, a low accident rate record can only be achieved by concentrating on the human element.

One of the main objectives of safety engineers is to scrutinize the work environment to locate sources of potential accidents. In addition to looking for such obvious factors as loose steps or carpets, oil on walkways, or a sharp protrusion on a piece of equipment at eye level, safety engineers will seek those that are less obvious. Standards established by OSHA provide an excellent reference to guide the search for potential hazards.

Preventative Measures

What traditional measures can we look to for preventing accidents? The answer lies in education, skill training, engineering, protection devices, and regulation enforcement. We have summarized these in Exhibit 14-6.

Ensuring Job Safety

One way HRM can be assured that rules and regulations are being enforced is to develop some type of feedback system. This can be provided by inspection of the work surroundings. HRM can rely on oral or written reports for information on enforcement. Another approach is to get firsthand information by periodically walking through the work areas to make observations. Ideally, safety personnel will rely on reports from supervisors on the floor and employ-

Exhibit 14-6

Accident prevention mechanisms.

Education	Create safety awareness by posting highly visible signs that proclaim safety slogans, placing articles on accident prevention in organization newsletters, or exhibiting a sign proclaiming the number of days the plant has operated without a lost-day accident.
Skills Training	Incorporate accident prevention measures into the learning process.
Engineering	Prevent accidents through both the design of the equipment and the design of the jobs themselves. This may also include eliminating those factors that promote operator fatigue, boredom, and daydreaming.
Protection	Provide protective equipment where necessary. This may include safety shoes, gloves, hard hats, safety glasses, and noise mufflers. Protection also includes performing preventative maintenance on machinery.
Regulation Enforcement	The best safety rules and regulations will be ineffective in reducing accidents if they are not enforced. Additionally, if such rules are not enforced, the employer may be liable for any injuries that occur.

ees in the work areas. These are then supported by the safety inspector's personal observations.

Although safety is everyone's responsibility, it should be part of the organization's culture.[47] Top management must show its commitment to safety by providing resources to purchase safety devices and maintaining equipment (see Meet Ann-Michele Bowlin). Furthermore, safety should become part of every employee's performance goals. As we mentioned in Chapter 10 on performance evaluations, if something isn't included, there's a tendency to diminish its importance. Holding employees accountable for safety issues by evaluating their performance sends the message that the company is serious about safety.

Another means of promoting safety is to empower the action. In organizations like General Electric, such employee groups are called *safety committees*.[48] Although chiefly prevalent in unionized settings, these committees serve a vital role in helping the company and its employees implement and maintain a good safety program.

Steps in Developing a Safety and Health Program

There are several steps that can be recommended for developing an organization's safety and health program.[49] Whether or not such programs are chiefly the responsibility of one individual, every supervisor must work to ensure that the work environment is safe for all employees.

▶ *Involve management and employees in the development of a safety and health plan.* If neither group can see the usefulness, and the benefit of such a plan, even the best plan will fail.

▶ *Hold someone accountable for implementing the plan.* Plans do not work by themselves. They need someone to champion the cause. This person must be given the resources to put the plan in place, but also must be held accountable for what it's intended to accomplish.

▶ *Determine the Safety and Health Requirements for Your Work Site.* Just as each individual is different, so, too, is each workplace. Understanding the specific needs of the facility will aid in determining what safety and health requirement will be necessary.

▶ *Assess what workplace hazards exist in the facility.* Identify the potential health and safety problems that may exist on the job. By understanding what exists, preventive measures can be determined.

ANN-MICHELE BOWLIN
Bowlin Engineering, Co.

Bob and Loene Bowlin founded Bowlin Engineering Co. in 1966 to design and build material handling systems for steel service centers and oil service companies. The offices were located in the basement of their new home in Fort Worth, Texas. Loene would cram a bottle of milk in her daughter Ann-Michele's mouth and answer "Good morning, Bowlin Engineering. How can I help you?" In 1969, son, Paul, joined the family and a new manufacturing facility was purchased in Saginaw, Texas. At 12, Ann-Michele was answering the phone and opening the mail while the office coordinator was on vacation. Paul at 13, was working in the plant—cleaning.

In 1982, the Bowlins founded Leland Southwest to manufacture stainless steel equipment for the commercial and institutional food processing industry. They purchased a building down the street from the Bowlin Engineering Co. facility and began their second manufacturing company. Throughout high school and college, Ann-Michele and Paul worked for either Leland Southwest or Bowlin Engineering during breaks. Both swore they would never, ever work for their parents after college. Famous last words.

In September 1992, Ann-Michele, after graduating from college and spending two and a half years in Japan, returned to join Leland Southwest. In December 1994, Paul graduated with a degree in mechanical engineering and joined Bowlin Engineering Co. Four Bowlins working together could have been chaos! However, with specific divi-

sions of labor—Paul in engineering and production, Ann-Michele in sales and finance, Loene managing human resources and Bob overseeing the big picture—it was at least a situation of controlled chaos.

The Bowlins' number one challenge in the late 1980s was how to blend two diverse companies with unrelated product lines into one central manufacturing facility. Since both design/build equipment developers were owned and operated by the same family, merging the two facilities made sense for a smoother, more efficient operation.

The equipment manufactured by both companies was highly regarded in each industry, and employees were proud of their respective products. Following the merger, expected efficiency improvements and reduced labor costs did not materialize. The problem? The employees wanted to build either the heavier material handling equipment or the smaller stainless food processing equipment—not both. Personnel resisted efforts for cross-training and competed for control of the corporate culture.

As a family-run organization, a new management approach was needed to create an atmosphere of cooperation, coordination, and communication in the merged facility. Management Training Specialists was retained to help bring together the two companies; the purpose was to establish goals, improve production efficiency, and increase employee participation and job satisfaction through the development of a comprehensive quality improvement plan.

A single mission statement was created which applied to both organizations. One policy and procedures man-

ual was developed from the two existing manuals that included performance standards and reviews, a comprehensive safety program and manual, an employee suggestion program and an incentive plan. To eliminate one of the sources of division, all employees were moved to the Leland Southwest payroll. Bowlin Engineering work was "outsourced" to Leland Southwest. This change was simple, but effective.

Communication increased through weekly production meetings with all staff members—the good things happening in both companies were lauded equally. In addition to the good, the production problems were also discussed in the production meetings, allowing both groups to assist the others in forming solutions. Teams were set up with members from both groups to solve company-wide issues from tooling to safety to customer service. The safety program with regularly scheduled safety meetings opened another outlet for communication and planning. In addition, the bonus plan was based on the joint success of the companies, which became one of the strongest incentives for everyone to cooperate. All of these measures slowly started bringing the group together.

And the results? Production efficiency has increased to allow for a 40 percent increase in sales over the past five years with no increase in production personnel. The number of employees with perfect attendance has doubled. Implementing error tracking procedures has allowed recurring problems to be resolved permanently. Our safety record is excellent—everyone is aware of the safety issues and takes pride in maintaining a safe work environment.

Now, when either company receives a significant order, everybody is enthusiastically involved. You can do anything on paper, but it means nothing without the support of the people involved.

—Ann-Michele Bowlin

▶ *Correct hazards that exist.* If certain hazards were identified in the investigation in the assessment, fix or eliminate them. This may mean decreasing the effect of the hazard, or controlling it through other means (e.g., protective clothing).

▶ *Train employees in safety and health techniques.* Make safety and health training mandatory for all employees. Employees should be instructed how to do their jobs in the safest manner, and understand that any protective equipment provided must be used.

▶ *Develop the mind-set in employees that the organization is to be kept hazard free.* Often employees are the first to witness problems. Establish a means for them to report their findings, including having emergency procedures in place, if necessary. Ensuring that preventive maintenance of equipment follows a recommended schedule can also prevent their breakdowns from becoming a hazard.

▶ *Continuously update and refine the safety and health program.* Once the program has been implemented, it must continuously be evaluated, and necessary changes must be made. Documenting the progress of the program is necessary for use in this analysis.

A Safety Issue: Workplace Violence

Inasmuch as there is growing concern for the job safety for our workers, a much greater emphasis today is being placed on the increasing violence that has erupted on the job.[50] No organization is immune from such happenstance, and the problem appears to be getting worse. Shootings at a local post office by a recently disciplined employee, an upset purchasing manager who stabs his boss because they disagreed over how some paperwork was to be completed, a disgruntled significant other enters the workplace and shoots his mate[51]—incidents like these have become all too prevalent. Consider the following statistics. Twenty employees are murdered each week while at work. Homicide has become the number-two cause of work-related death in the United States.[52] For women, it's the number-one cause of work-related death![53] In the United States, more than 1 million employees are attacked each year, and more than 6 million threatened with bodily harm.[54]

Homicide has become the number-two cause of work-related death. For women, it's the number-one reason!

Many individuals note that in U.S. cities, violent behaviors are spilling over into the workplace.[55] And we're talking about much more here than homicides committed during the commission of a crime—like those horrendous events happening to cab drivers or to clerks at retail stores.[56] Two factors have contributed greatly to this trend—domestic violence and disgruntled employees.[57] The issue for companies, then, is how to prevent the violence from occurring on the job—and to reduce their liability should an unfortunate event occur.[58]

Because the circumstances of each incident are different, a specific plan of action for companies to follow is difficult to detail. However, several suggestions can be made.[59] First, the organization must develop a plan to deal with the issue.[60] This may mean reviewing all corporate policies to ensure that they are not adversely affecting employees. In fact, in many of the cases where the violent individuals caused mayhem in an office setting, and didn't commit suicide, one common factor arose. That is, these employees were not treated with respect or dignity. They were laid off without any warning, or they perceived they were being treated too harshly in the discipline process. Sound HRM practices can help to ensure that respect and dignity exist for employees, even in the most difficult of issues like terminations.

Organizations must also train their supervisory personnel to identify troubled employees before the problem results in violence.[61] Employee assistance programs (EAPs) can be designed specifically to help these individuals. As we'll see shortly in our discussion of EAPs, rarely does an individual go from being happy, to committing some act of violence overnight! Furthermore, if supervisors are better able to spot the types of demonstrated behaviors that may lead to violence, then those who cannot be helped through the EAP can be removed from the organization before others are harmed. Organizations should also implement stronger security mechanisms. For example, many women who are killed at work, following a domestic dispute, die at the hands of someone who didn't belong on company premises. These individuals, as well as violence paraphernalia—guns, knives, etc.—must be kept from entering the facilities altogether.

Sadly, no matter how careful the organization is, and how much it attempts to prevent workplace violence, some will occur. In those cases, the organization must be prepared to deal with the situation.[62] As one researcher has stated, we need to "teach employees what to do when someone goes berserk,"[63] and we need to be prepared to offer whatever assistance we can to deal with the aftermath.

MAINTAINING A HEALTHY WORK ENVIRONMENT

Unhealthy work environments are a concern to us all. If workers cannot function properly at their jobs because of constant headaches, watering eyes, breathing difficulties, or fear of exposure to materials that may cause long-term health problems, productivity will decrease. Consequently, creating a healthy work environment not only is the proper thing to do, but it also benefits the employer. Often referred to as **sick buildings,** office environments that contain harmful airborne chemicals, asbestos, or indoor pollution (possibly caused by smoking) have forced employers to take drastic steps. For many, it has meant the removal of asbestos from their buildings. Because extended exposure to asbestos has been linked to lung cancer, companies are required by various federal agencies like the EPA to remove it altogether, or at least seal it so that it cannot escape into the air.

But asbestos is not the only culprit! Germs, fungi, and a variety of synthetic pollutants cause problems, too. For example, in the mid-1980s, employees at Eastman Kodak were experiencing symptoms of lung inflammation.[64] It took many months and several million dollars to locate the cause, and "cure" it. Kodak had to replace the entire germ-infested ventilation system.[65]

Although specific problems and their elimination go beyond the scope of this text, there are some suggestions for keeping the workplace healthy. These include:[66]

▶ *Making sure workers get enough fresh air.* The cost of providing it is peanuts compared with the expense of cleaning up a problem. One simple tactic: unsealing vents closed in overzealous efforts to conserve energy.

▶ *Avoiding suspect building materials and furnishings.* A general rule is that if it stinks, it's going to emit an odor. For instance, substitute tacks for smelly carpet glue, or natural wood for chemically treated plywood.

▶ *Testing new buildings for toxins before occupancy.* Failure to do so may lead to potential health problems. Most consultants say that letting a new building sit temporarily vacant allows the worst fumes to dissipate.

▶ *Providing a smoke-free environment.* If you don't want to ban smoking entirely, then establish an area for smokers that has its own ventilation system.

▶ *Keeping air ducts clean and dry.* Water in air ducts is a fertile breeding ground for fungi. Servicing the air ducts periodically can help eliminate the fungi before they cause harm.

▶ *Paying attention to workers' complaints.* Dates and particulars should be recorded by a designated employee. Because employees are often closest to the problems, they are a valuable source of information.

While the information presented above is important to follow, one in particular is noteworthy for us to explore a bit further. This is the smoke-free environment.

The Smoke-Free Environment

Should smoking be prohibited in a public place of business? Even, say, in a bar, where forbidding smoking could put the establishment out of business?[67] The dangers and health problems associated with smoking have been well documented—and this is translating into increased health insurance costs. For example, studies have shown that the premiums paid for insuring an employee who smokes cost up to $5,000 more than for one who doesn't.[68] Furthermore, smokers were found to be absent more than nonsmokers, to lose productivity due to smoke breaks, to damage property with cigarette burns, to require more routine maintenance (ash/butt cleanup),[69] and to create problems for other employees through secondhand smoke disorders. Recognized as a means to control these maladies associated with smoking, in conjunction with society's emphasis on wellness, smoke-free policies have appeared. In fact, about 53

As more and more organizations go "smoke-free," a major question arises. That is, what do the smokers do? In an organization such as this establishment, the answer is simple. They go outside to smoke. But that, too raises other issues, like lost productivity while employees are outside smoking, or clean-up of ashes and butts scattered on the ground.

Should Smokers Have Rights?

It has become well-documented that smoking can create health problems. Accordingly, health insurance premiums, as well as other premiums like life insurance, are significantly higher to those who "light-up." And in most cases, employers have passed these increased premium costs on to the worker. Companies have become more stringent in developing policies on smoking, and many have banned smoking on company premises altogether. Clearly, the smoker today is disadvantaged, but how far can that go?

Can an organization refuse to hire someone simply because they smoke? Depending on the organization, the requirement of the job, and the state in which one lives, they might! Even so, employers may take this one step further.

Companies may, in fact, be able to terminate an individual for smoking off the job—on an employee's own time. Do you believe companies have the right to dictate what you do outside of work? If an organization can take such action against employees for smoking, and justify it on the grounds that it creates a health problem, what about other things we do? Eating too much fatty food can create a health problem, so should we be susceptible to discipline for being caught eating a Big Mac? Some members of the medical community cite how one or two alcoholic drinks a day may in fact be therapeutic and prevent the onset of certain diseases. Yet, alcohol can be damaging to humans. Accordingly, should we be fired for having a glass of wine with dinner, or drinking a beer at a sporting event?

What do you think? How far should we permit regulating "wellness" in our organizations?

percent of U.S. companies have banned smoking altogether, while another 23 percent have smoking restricted to designated areas.[70]

Although many nonsmokers would agree that a total ban on smoking in the workplace is the most desirable, it may not be the most practical. For those employees who smoke, quitting immediately may be impossible. The nicotine addiction may prohibit a "cold-turkey" approach for the most ardent smoker. Accordingly, a total ban on smoking should be viewed as a phased-in approach.[71] For example, this gradual process may begin with the involvement of representative employees to determine what the organization's smoke-free goals and timetables should be. This means deciding if the organization will ban smoking altogether over a period of time; or if special areas will be designated as smoking rooms. If the latter is chosen, then these rooms must be properly ventilated to keep the smoke fumes from permeating other parts of the facility. For many companies, this option is quite expensive; Texas Instruments found the cost for constructing these rooms averages $70,000 each.[72]

Consequently, the organization needs to look at incentives for getting people not to smoke (see Ethical Decisions in HRM). As mentioned previously, health-care premiums—as well as life insurance policies—for smokers are significantly higher than for nonsmokers. Employers may decide to pay only the nonsmoking premium, and pass the additional premium costs on to the smokers. Companies also need to have in place various options for individuals to seek help. Through various assistance programs—like smoking cessation classes—the organization can show that it is making a deliberate commitment to eliminate the problems associated with smoking in the workplace.

Repetitive Stress Injuries

Whenever workers are subjected to a continuous motion like keyboarding, without proper work station design (seat and keyboard height adjustments), they run the risk of developing **repetitive stress injuries.** This phenomenon is referred to as **cumulative trauma disorders.** These disorders, which account for more than 60 percent of annual workplace illnesses from headaches, swollen feet, back pain, or nerve damage,[73] cost U.S. companies several billion dollars annually. The most frequent site of this disorder is in the wrist and is called **carpal tunnel syndrome,**[74] affecting more than 40,000 U.S. workers and costing companies more than $50 million annually in health-care claims.[75] Carpal tunnel has been found to be directly linked to office designs and the way that work is performed.[76]

One chief means of reducing the potential effects of cumulative trauma disorders for an organization is through the use of **ergonomics.**[77] Ergonomics involves fitting the work environment to the individual. Reality tells us that every employee is different—different shape, size, height, etc. Expecting each worker to adjust to "standard" office furnishings is just not practical. Instead, recognizing and acting on these differences, ergonomics looks at customizing the work environment such that it is not only conducive to productive work, but keeps the employee healthy.[78] For example, to reduce the likelihood of cumulative trauma disorders, Chevron purchased and installed ergonomically designed work stations.[79] Not only has the organization lessened the incidence of these disorders, they have also found that employees have become more productive. As one of Chevron's legal support service members stated, "It costs us about $1,000 per employee [for ergonomically designed adjustable desk add-ons]. . . but our employees are more productive because they don't have backaches, headaches, and don't complain as much." [80]

When we speak of ergonomics, we are primarily addressing two main areas: the "office environment and office furniture." [81] Organizations are reviewing their office settings, their work environment, and their space utilization in an effort to provide more productive atmospheres. This means that new furniture is being purchased—furniture that is designed to reduce back strain and fatigue. Properly designed and fitted office equipment, like Chevron's adjustable desk add-on for a keyboard stand, can also help reduce repetitive stress injuries. Furthermore, they are using colors, like the mauves and grays, that are more pleasing to the eye, and experimenting with lighting brightness as a means of lessening employee exposure to harmful eyestrain associated with today's video display terminals.

STRESS

Stress is a dynamic condition in which an individual is confronted with an opportunity, constraint, or demand related to what he or she desires, and for which the outcome is perceived to be both uncertain and important.[82] This definition is complicated, so let us look at it more closely. Stress can manifest itself in both a positive and a negative way. Stress is said to be positive when the situation offers an opportunity for one to gain something; for example, the "psyching-up" that an athlete goes through can be stressful, but this can lead to maximum performance. It is when constraints or demands are placed on us that stress can become negative. Let us explore these two features—*constraints* and *demands.*

Constraints are barriers that keep us from doing what we desire. Purchasing a sports utility vehicle (SUV) may be your desire, but if you cannot afford the $30,000 price, you are constrained from purchasing it. Accordingly, constraints inhibit you in ways that take control of a situation out of your hands. If you cannot afford the SUV, you cannot get it. Demands, on the other hand, may cause you to give up something you desire. If you wish to go to a movie with friends on Tuesday night but have a major examination Wednesday, the examination may take precedence. Thus, demands preoccupy your time and force you to shift priorities.

Constraints and demands can lead to potential stress. When they are coupled with uncertainty about the outcome and importance of the outcome, potential stress becomes actual stress.[83] Regardless of the situation, if you remove the uncertainty or the importance, you remove stress. For instance, you may have been constrained from purchasing the SUV because of your budget, but if you just won one in McDonald's Monopoly game, the uncertainty element is significantly reduced. Furthermore, if you are auditing a class for no grade, the importance of the major examination is also reduced. However, when constraints or demands have an effect on an important event and the outcome is unknown, pressure is added—pressure resulting in stress.

While we are not attempting to minimize stress in people's lives, it is important to recognize that both good and bad personal factors may cause stress. Of course, when you consider the changes, like restructuring, that are occurring in U.S. companies, it is little wonder that stress is so rampant in today's companies. Just how rampant? A Northwestern National Life Insurance study reported that more than 60 percent of the workers surveyed experienced significant job stress—[84] resulting in more than $150 billion in lost time and productivity.[85] And stress on the job knows no boundaries.

In Japan, worker stress has been identified in 70 percent of the workers by a Fukoku Life Insurance Company study.[86] In fact, in Japan there is a concept called **karoshi,** which means death from overworking—employees who die after working more than 3000 hours the previous year. Over 2300 individuals died in 1996, having karoshi listed as their cause of death.[87] Many Japanese employees literally work themselves to death—with one in six Japanese employees working more than 3,100 hours annually.[88] Employees in Germany and Britain, too, have suffered the ill effects of stress—costing their organizations more than DM 100 billion and £7 billion ($65 billion and $11.4 billion USD, respectively).[89]

The Symptoms of Stress

What signs indicate that an employee's stress level might be too high? There are three general ways that stress reveals itself. These include physiological, psychological, and behavioral symptoms.

Most of the early interest over stress focused heavily on health-related, or the *physiological* concerns.[90] This was attributed to the realization that high stress levels result in changes in metabolism, increased heart and breathing rates, increased blood pressure, headaches, and increased risk of heart attacks. Because detecting many of these requires the skills of trained medical personnel, their immediate and direct relevance to HRM is negligible.

Of greater importance to HRM are psychological and behavioral symptoms of stress. It's these things that can be witnessed in the person. The *psychological symptoms* can be seen as increased tension and anxiety, boredom, and procrastination—which can all lead to productivity decreases. So too, can the *behaviorally related symptoms*—changes in eating habits, increased smoking or substance consumption, rapid speech, or sleep disorders.

Work-Related Stress

Work-related stress is brought about by both organizational and individual factors. As shown in Exhibit 14-7, these in turn are influenced by individual differences. That is, not all people in similar situations experience similar levels of stress.

Organizational Factors   There is no shortage of factors within the organization that can cause stress. Pressures to avoid errors or complete tasks in a limited time period, a demanding supervisor, and unpleasant co-workers are a few examples. The discussion that follows organizes stress factors into five categories: task, role, and interpersonal demands; organization structure; and organizational leadership.[91]

Task demands are factors related to an employee's job. They include the design of the person's job (autonomy, task variety, degree of automation), working conditions, and the physical work layout. Work quotas can put pressure on employees when their "outcomes" are perceived as excessive. The more interdependence between a employee's tasks and the tasks of others, the more potential stress there is. Autonomy, on the other hand, tends to lessen stress. Jobs where temperatures, noise, or other working conditions are dangerous or undesirable can increase anxiety. So, too, can working in an overcrowded room or in a visible location where interruptions are constant.

Role demands relate to pressures placed on an employee as a function of the particular role he or she plays in the organization. **Role conflicts** create expectations that may be hard to reconcile or satisfy. **Role overload** is experienced when the employee is expected to do more than time permits. **Role ambiguity** is created when role expectations are not clearly understood and the employee is not sure what he or she is to do.

Interpersonal demands are pressures created by other employees. Lack of social support from colleagues and poor interpersonal relationships can cause considerable stress, especially among employees with a high social need.

Organization structure can increase stress. Excessive rules and an employee's lack of opportunity to participate in decisions that affect him or her are examples of structural variables that might be potential sources of stress.

Organizational leadership represents the supervisory style of the organization's company officials. Some officials create a culture characterized by tension,

Exhibit 14-7

Potential sources of stress and their consequences.

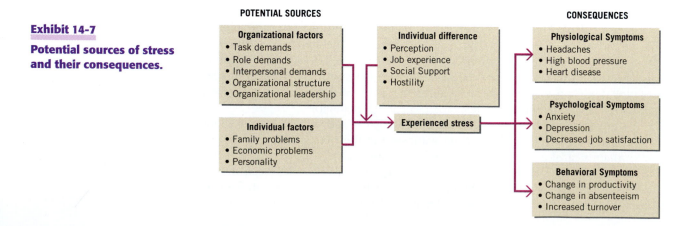

fear, and anxiety. They establish unrealistic pressures to perform in the short run, impose excessively tight controls, and routinely fire employees who don't measure up. This style of leadership flows down through the organization to affect all employees.

Individual Factors　The typical employee works about fifty hours a week. The experiences and problems that they encounter in those other 118 non-work hours each week, however, can and often do spill over to the job.[92] Our other category, then, encompasses factors in the employee's personal life. Primarily, these factors are *family issues, personal economic problems, and inherent personality characteristics.*

National surveys consistently show that people hold family and personal relationships dear. Marital difficulties, the breaking off of a relationship, discipline troubles with children, and relatives with serious illnesses are examples of relationship problems that create stress for employees and that aren't left at the front door when they arrive at work.

Economic problems created by individuals overextending their financial resources is another set of personal troubles that can create stress for employees and distract their attention from their work. Regardless of income level (people who make $90,000 a year seem to have as much trouble handling their finances as those who earn $23,000), some people are poor money handlers or have wants that always seem to exceed their earning capacity.

Recent studies have found that stress symptoms reported prior to beginning a job don't change much from that reported nine months later. This has led to the conclusion that some people may have an inherent tendency to accentuate negative aspects of the world in general. If true, then a significant individual factor influencing stress is a person's basic disposition. That is, stress symptoms expressed on the job may actually originate in the person's personality.

Stress Plus Stress Equals More Stress

A fact that tends to be overlooked when stress factors are reviewed individually is that stress is an additive phenomenon. Stress builds up. Each new and persistent stressor adds to an individual's stress level. A single stressor may seem relatively unimportant in and of itself, but if it is added to an already high level of stress, it can be "the straw that breaks the camel's back."

Individual Differences　Some people thrive on stressful situations, while others are overwhelmed by them. What is it that differentiates people in terms of their ability to handle stress? Four individual difference factors have been found to be important: perception, experience, social support, and hostility.

One person's fear that he'll lose his job because his company is laying off personnel may be perceived by another as an opportunity to get a large severance allowance and start his own business. Similarly, what one employee perceives as an efficient and challenging work environment may be viewed as threatening and demanding by others. So stress potential doesn't lie in objective conditions. Rather, it lies in an employee's perception and interpretation of those conditions.

Experience is said to be a great teacher. It can also be a great stress reducer. Think back to your first date or your first few days in college. For most of us, the uncertainty and newness of these situations created stress. But as we gained experience, that stress disappeared or at least significantly decreased. The same phenomenon seems to apply to work situations. Why? One explanation is the process of selective withdrawal. Voluntary turnover is more probable among people who experience more stress. Therefore, people who remain with the organization longer are those with more stress-resistant traits, or those who are more resistant to the stress characteristics of their organization. A second explanation is that people eventually develop coping mechanisms to deal with stress. Because this takes time, senior members of the organization are more likely to be fully adapted and experience less stress.

There is increasing evidence that social support—that is, collegial relationships with co-workers and supervisors—can buffer the impact of stress. The logic underlying this conclusion is that social support acts as a palliative, lessening the negative effects of even high-stress jobs.

For much of the 1970s and 1980s, a great deal of attention was directed at what became known as **Type A behavior.** It was frequently seen as the primary individual difference factor in explaining who would be affected by stress. Type A behavior is characterized by feelings of a chronic sense of time urgency and by an excessive competitive drive. Type A's try to do more and more in less and less time. The opposite of Type A is **Type B behavior.** Type B's never suffer from time urgency or impatience. Until quite recently, it was believed that Type A's were more likely to experience stress on and off the job. A closer analysis of the evidence, however, has produced new conclusions. It has been found that only the hostility and anger associated with Type A behavior is actually associated with the negative effects of stress. The chronically angry, suspicious, and mistrustful person is the one at risk of stressing out.

Reducing Stress

Reducing stress is one thing that presents a dilemma for HRM. Some stress in organizations is absolutely necessary. Without it, there's no energy in people. Accordingly, whenever one considers stress reduction, what is at issue is reducing its dysfunctional aspects.

One of the first means of reducing stress is to make sure that employees are properly matched to their jobs—and that they understand the extent of their "authority." Furthermore, by letting employees know precisely what is expected of them, role conflict and ambiguity can be reduced. Redesigning jobs can also help ease work overload-related stressors. Employees should also have some input in those things that affect them. Their involvement and participation have been found to lessen stress.[93]

HRM must also recognize that no matter what they do to eliminate organizational stressors, some employees will still be "stressed-out." They simply have little or no control over the personal factors. Moreover, HRM faces an ethical issue when it is personal factors that are causing stress. That is, just how far can HRM intrude on an employee's personal life?

Chronic Stress: Burnout

Worker burnout is costing U.S. industry billions of dollars. One estimate revealed that almost $20 billion is lost each year due to burnout and its related implications.[94] Burnout is a multifaceted phenomenon, the byproduct of both personal variables and organization variables. It can be defined as a function of three concerns: "chronic emotional stress with (a) emotional and/or physical exhaustion, (b) lowered job productivity, and (c) dehumanizing of jobs."[95] Note that none of the three concerns includes long-term boredom. While boredom is often referred to as burnout, it is not!

Causes and Symptoms of Burnout The factors contributing to burnout can be identified as follows: organization characteristics, perceptions of organization, perceptions of role, individual characteristics, and outcomes.[96] Exhibit 14-8 summarizes these variables. While these variables can lead to burnout, their presence does not guarantee that burnout will occur. Much of that outcome is contingent on the individual's capability to work under and handle stress. Because of this contingency, stressful conditions result in a two-phased outcome—the first level being the stress itself, and the second level being the problems that arise from the manifestation of this stress.[97]

Reducing Burnout Recognizing that stress is a fact of life and must be channeled properly, organizations must establish procedures for reducing these stress levels before workers burn out.[98] Although no clear-cut remedies are available, four techniques have been proposed: These include:

1. *Identification*. This is the analysis of the incidence, prevalence, and characteristics of burnout in individuals, work groups, subunits, or organizations.
2. *Prevention*. Attempts should be made to prevent the burnout process before it begins.
3. *Mediation*. This involves procedures for slowing, halting, or reversing the burnout process.
4. *Remediation*. Techniques are needed for individuals who are already burned out or are rapidly approaching the end stages of this process.[99]

The key point here is that accurate identification is made and then, and only then, is a program tailored to meet that need. Because of the costs associated with burnout, many companies are implementing a full array of programs—like employee assistance programs—to help alleviate the problem. Many of these programs are designed to do two things: increase productivity and make the job more pleasant for the worker.

Exhibit 14-8 Variables found to be significantly related to burnout.

Organization Characteristics	Perceptions of Organization	Perceptions of Role	Individual Characteristics	Outcomes
Caseload	Leadership	Autonomy	Family/friends support	Satisfaction
Formalization	Communication	Job involvement	Sex	Turnover
Turnover rate	Staff support	Being supervised	Age	
Staff size	Peers	Work pressure	Tenure	
	Clarity	Feedback	Ego level	
	Rules and procedures	Accomplishment		
	Innovation	Meaningfulness		
	Administrative support			

SOURCE: Baron Perlman and E. Alan Hartman, "Burnout: Summary and Future Research," *Human Relations*, Vol. 25, No. 4 (1982), p. 294.

THE EMPLOYEE ASSISTANCE PROGRAM

No matter what kind of organization or industry one works in, one thing is certain. At times, employees will have personal problems. Whether that problem is job stress, legal, marital, financial, or health-related,[100] one commonality exists: If an employee experiences a personal problem, sooner or later it will manifest itself at the workplace in terms of lowered productivity, increased absenteeism, or turnover (behavioral symptoms of stress).[101] To help employees deal with these personal problems, more and more companies are implementing **employee assistance programs (EAPs).**[102]

A Brief History

EAPs as they exist today are extensions of programs that had their birth in U.S. companies in the 1940s. Companies like Du Pont, Standard Oil, and Kodak recognized that a number of their employees were experiencing problems with alcohol.[103] To help these employees, formalized programs were implemented on the company's site to educate these workers on the dangers of alcohol and to help them overcome their "addiction."[104] The premise behind these programs, which still holds today, is getting a productive employee back on the job as swiftly as possible. Let's examine this for a moment.

Throughout this text thus far, we have discussed the various aspects of HRM designed to create an environment where an employee can be productive. Emphasis was placed on finding the right employees to "fit" jobs, training them to do the job, then giving them a variety of opportunities to excel. All of this takes considerable time and money. We know it takes considerable time for employees to become fully productive—a process that requires the company to make an investment in its people. As with any investment, the company expects an adequate return. Now, how does this relate to EAPs?

Suppose you have a worker, Robin, who has been with you for a number of years. Robin has been a solid performer for several years, but lately something has happened. You notice Robin's performance declining. The quality of Robin's work is diminishing, she has been late three times in the past five weeks, and rumor has it that Robin is having marital problems. You could, and would, have every right to discipline Robin according to the organization's discipline process. But it is doubtful discipline alone would help. Consequently, after a period of time, you may end up firing Robin. You've now lost a once good performer, and must fill the position with another—a process that may take eighteen months to finally achieve the productivity level Robin had. However, instead of firing Robin, you decide to refer this individual to the organization's EAP. This confidential program[105] works with Robin to determine the cause(s) of the problems, and seeks to help this employee overcome them. Although meeting more frequently at first with the EAP counselor, you notice that after a short period of time, Robin is back on the job—performance improving. And after four months, Robin is performing at the level prior to the problem getting out of hand. In this scenario, you now have your fully productive employee back in four months, as opposed to possibly eighteen months had you fired and replaced Robin. As for the return on investment, it is estimated that U.S. companies spend almost $1 billion each year on EAP programs.[106] For most, studies suggest that these companies save up to $5.00 for every EAP dollar spent.[107] That, for most of us, is a significant return on investment!

EAPs Today

Since their early focus on alcoholic employees, EAPs have ventured into new areas. One of the most notable areas is the use of EAPs to help control rising health insurance premiums, especially in the areas of "mental health and substance abuse services."[108] For example, at the Campbell's Soup Company, the company's EAP program is the first stop for individuals seeking psychiatric or substance-abuse help. By doing this, Campbell's was able to trim insurance claims by 28 percent.[109] These cost savings accrue from such measures as managing "inpatient length of stays, outpatient treatment days, disability days, and stress-related claims."[110]

No matter how beneficial EAPs may be to an organization, one aspect cannot be taken for granted: employee participation. EAPs must be perceived as being worthwhile to the employee. Employees must see the EAP as an operation that is designed to help them deal with such problems as "alcohol and chemical dependency, emotional problems, stress, pre-retirement planning, marital problems, careers, finances, legal matters, or termination."[111] In addition, EAPs are becoming more involved in helping employees who have AIDS, as well as counseling employees on cultural diversity issues.[112] For employees to accept EAPs, a few criteria must exist. These are "familiarity with the program, and the perception of the trustworthiness and opportunity for personal atten-

Richard Hoffman, Chief Operating Officer at Alamco, the Clarksburg, West Virginia oil and gas company encourages his employees to lead a healthy life. What's interesting about Alamco's plan is that employees receive incentives for "healthy" behavior. For instance, blood cholesterol levels below 150 during one's annual physical examination earn the employee $100; blood pressure below 135/85 provides a $50 incentive. Hoffman, too, gives employee spouses incentive money too, at 50 percent the employee rate. All told, employees earn about $19,000 each year. Why do this? There are a number of reasons. First, Hoffman believes in it. Moreover, his company has not had health insurance premiums raised in the past five years. Additionally, morale is higher, absenteeism is down, and his employees are healthier.

tion." [113] Accordingly, there must be extensive information given to employees regarding how the EAP works, how employees can use its services, and how confidentiality is guaranteed. [114] Furthermore, supervisors must be properly trained to recognize changes in employee behaviors and to refer them to the EAP in a confidential manner. And with the AIDS issue, confidentiality has become of even greater importance. [115]

Although EAPs can help employees when problems arise, companies have given much support to finding ways to eliminate some factors that may lead to personal problems. In doing so, some organizations such as the Adolph Coors Company have promoted wellness programs. [116]

Wellness Programs

When we mention **wellness programs** in any organization, we are talking about any type of program that is designed to keep employees healthy. These programs are varied and may focus on such things as smoking cessation, weight control, stress management, [117] physical fitness, nutrition education, high blood-pressure control, violence protection, work team problem intervention, [118] etc. Wellness programs are designed to help cut employer health costs, [119] and to lower absenteeism and turnover by preventing health-related problems. [120] For instance, it is estimated that over a ten-year period, the Adolph Coors Company saved almost $2 million in decreased medical premium payments, reduced sick leave, and increased productivity. [121] For Coors, that represents a greater than $6.00 return for every $1.00 spent on wellness. [122] Although savings like those achieved at Coors are not often calculated, there is evidence that the effects on health-care premiums and productivity are positive. [123] However, such results may not occur in all wellness programs. [124]

> The Adolph Coors Company receives a $6.00 return on investment for every $1.00 spent on employee wellness programs.]

It is interesting to note that, similar to EAPs, wellness programs don't work unless employees view them as having some value. Unfortunately for wellness, the numbers across the United States are not as promising. It is estimated that only about 20 percent of employees who have access to these programs actually use them. [125] To help combat this low turnout, a number of key criteria must exist. [126] First of all, there must be top management support—without their support in terms of resources, and in personally using the programs, the wrong message may be sent to employees. Second, there appears to be a need to have the programs serve the family as well as the employees themselves. This not only provides an atmosphere where families can "get healthy together," it also reduces possible medical costs for the dependents. And finally comes the issue of employee input. If programs are designed without considering employees' needs, even the best ones may fail. Organizations need to invite participation by asking employees what they'd use if available. Although many organization members know that exercise is beneficial, few initially addressed how to get employees involved. But after finding out that employees would like such things as on-site exercise facilities or aerobics, organizations were able to begin appropriate program development. [127] For example, at AT&T in Kansas City and New Jersey, an on-site fitness facility is made available to all employees. [128] In addition to the regular exercise equipment and aerobics, AT&T also offers T'ai-chi, the Chinese meditative art that exercises all muscle groups. [129]

As wellness programs continue to expand in corporate America, the question regarding top management support is still crucial, but questions about that support being present are lessening. Why? Because in finding out how to get senior executives involved, it was discovered that they, too, wanted a place to go for exercise. Many of these executives, as one of their perks, are provided with a membership in a health club; executives at such companies as Merrill Lynch, Revlon, and Tenneco enjoy such memberships as a means of maintaining their physical fitness.[130] Whether it is executives or support staff participation, wellness or EAPs, U.S. organizations appear to be continuing their efforts to support a healthy work environment. The companies reap a good return on their investments; programs such as EAP and wellness have proven to be win–win opportunities for all involved.

INTERNATIONAL SAFETY AND HEALTH

It is important to know the safety and health environments of each country in which an organization operates.[131] Generally, corporations in western Europe, Canada, Japan, and the United States put great emphasis on the health and welfare of their employees. However, most businesses in less-developed countries have limited resources and thus cannot establish awareness or protection programs.

Most countries have laws and regulatory agencies that protect workers from hazardous work environments. It is important for American firms to learn the often complex regulations that exist, as well as the cultural expectations of the local labor force. Manufacturers, in particular, where there are myriad potentially hazardous situations, must design and establish facilities that meet the expectations of the local employees—not necessarily those of Americans.

International Health Issues

For corporations preparing to send executives on overseas assignments, a few basic health-related items appear on every checklist. These include:

▶ *An Up-to-date Health Certificate*. Often called a "shot book," this is the individual's record of vaccinations against infectious diseases such as cholera, typhoid, and smallpox. Each country has its own vaccination requirements for entry inside its borders, but in addition, the U.S. Department of State Traveler Advisories "hotline" provides alerts to specific problems with diseases or regions within a country. For example, in 1991, cholera was a serious health concern in Peru and certain parts of other South American countries.

▶ *A General First Aid Kit*. This should include all over-the-counter medications such as aspirin, cold and cough remedies, and so on that the employee or family members would usually take at home, but that might not be available at the overseas drugstore. In addition, any prescription drugs should be packed in twice the quantity expected to be used. In case of an accidental dunking, overheating, or other problem, it is wise to pack the two supplies of drugs separately. It also is advisable to know the generic name—not the U.S. trade name—of any prescription drug. Finally, include special items such as disinfectant solutions to treat fresh fruit or vegetables, and water purifying tablets, as the sanitation system of the host country warrants.

▶ *Emergency Plans.* Upon arrival at the foreign destination, employees should check out the local medical and dental facilities; and plan on what care can be expected in the host country. This might include evacuation of a sick or injured employee or family member to another city or even another country. For example, expatriates in China often prefer to go to Hong Kong even for regular medical checkups. It is always wise to take along copies of all family members' medical and dental records.

International Safety Issues

Safety for the employee has become increasingly an issue of security, both while traveling and after arrival. Again, the U.S. Department of State provides travel alerts and cautions on its "hotline."[132]

But safety precautions begin before the overseas journey.[133] While it may be a matter of status and comfort to fly first class, experience with skyjacks has shown that it is safer to fly economy class. The goal is to blend into the crowd as much as possible, even if the corporation is willing to pay for greater luxury. Many corporations offer some of the following advice for traveling executives: blending in includes wearing low-key, appropriate clothing, not carrying obviously expensive luggage, avoiding luggage tags with titles like "vice president," and, if possible, traveling in small groups. Upon arrival at the airport, it is advisable to check in at the airline's ticket counter immediately and go through security checkpoints to wait in the less public gate area. The wisdom of this advice was confirmed in Rome, Athens, and other airport bombings.

Once the expatriate family has landed, the goal remains to blend in. These individuals must acquire some local "savvy" as quickly as possible; in addition to learning the language, they also must adapt to the local customs and try to dress in the same style as the local people.

Foremost on many individuals' minds when they go abroad is security. Many corporations now provide electronic safety systems, floodlights, and the like for home and office, as well as bodyguards or armed chauffeurs—but individual alertness is the key factor. It is suggested that kidnappers select their potential targets by seeking someone who is valuable to either a government or corporation, with lots of family money or a wealthy sponsor, and where there is opportunity to plan and execute the kidnaping. This last criterion means it is important to avoid set routines for local travel and other behaviors. The employee should take different routes between home and office, and the children should vary their paths to school. The family food shopping should be done at varying times each day, or in different markets, if possible. These and other precautions, as well as a constant awareness of one's surroundings, are important for every family member.

SUMMARY

This summary relates to the Learning Objectives provided on p. 418.
After having read this chapter, you should know:

1. The Occupational Safety and Health Act (OSHA) outlines comprehensive and specific safety and health standards.

2. OSHA has an established five-step priority enforcement process consisting of imminent danger, serious accidents, employee complaints, inspection of targeted industries, and random inspections.

3. OSHA can fine an organization up to a maximum penalty of $70,000 if the violation is severe, willful,

and repetitive. For violations not meeting those criteria, the maximum fine is $7,000. OSHA may, at its discretion, seek criminal or civil charges against an organization's management if they willfully violate health and safety regulations.

4. Companies in selected industries must complete OSHA Form 200 to record accidents, injuries, and illnesses that are job related. This information is then used to calculate the organization's incident rate.

5. OSHA is setting standards to protect workers exposed to blood-borne pathogens, chemicals and other work-related toxins, and is setting standards for motor vehicle safety.

6. The leading causes of accidents are human or environmental factors.

7. A company can help prevent workplace violence by ensuring that its policies are not adversely affecting employees, by developing a plan to deal with the issue, and by training its managers in identifying troubled employees.

8. Stress is a dynamic condition in which an individual is confronted with an opportunity, constraint, or demand for which the outcome is perceived as important and uncertain. Burnout is caused by a combination of emotional and/or physical exhaustion, lower job productivity, or dehumanizing jobs.

9. Creating a healthy work site involves removing any harmful substance, like asbestos, germs, fungi, cigarette smoke, and so forth, thus limiting employee exposure.

10. Employee assistance and wellness programs are designed to offer employees a variety of services that will help them to become mentally and physically healthy, which in turn helps to contain the organization's health-care costs.

EXPERIENTIAL EXERCISE:
Ensuring Workplace Safety

Role Play

Your team may wish to role play this case for the class, then discuss what the supervisor should do and how he should respond.

Billy Jo Rhea has been a machinist for Linco Tool and Die, a manufacturer of engine parts for large motors, for sixteen years. Lately more of Billy Jo's parts have been rejected for errors; he seems preoccupied with outside matters—leaving early, asking to take days beyond sick days allowed. He has missed work three days in two weeks, and Charlie, his supervisor, wondered if he smelled alcohol on his breath after lunch yesterday. Charlie hasn't said anything yet; he doesn't want to invade his privacy. He thinks Billy Jo may just be going through a

tough time, because he has been cooperative, positive, highly productive, and rarely sick or absent in the past.

Besides, it has been difficult in the last month because a major shipment has required overtime, and all machinists have been asked to work 80–95 hours a week until the shipment is complete.

At lunch you overhear an argument between Billy Jo and a co-worker Terry, each blaming the other for a part being rejected by Quality Assurance. Billy Jo threatens him to "stay out of his way and his area" and "the next time they'll settle it outside," poking him in the chest with his finger as he states it. Billy Jo then slams a $250.00 gauge down on the floor, shouts profanities, and adds, "I don't care if the part falls off or if this place burns to the ground anymore; I've about had all I can take of you and this place! You know my wife left me for my best friend last week, left me with a two year old by myself to raise, and my other kid got expelled for possession. It just doesn't much matter to me what you think; so I'd leave me alone if I were you!"

Charlie heads for the human resource office, unsure of how to proceed.

Class Discussion

What should Charlie do?
What advice would you give Charlie as the human resource manager?
How should Charlie respond to the immediate situation?
How can you apply the assessment questions regarding violence to enable Charlie and other supervisors to handle future situations more effectively?

WEB-WISE EXERCISES

Search and compare the information available in the following site:

Occupational Safety and Health Administration (OSHA) http://www.osha.gov/, which is the home page of the major monitor of the safety and health of U.S. workers and workplace with the information available in your text. http://www.osha.gov

National Association of Manufacturers
http://www.nam.org/NAM

Manufacturing Systems http://www.manufacturing systems.com. This magazine focuses on manufacturing information systems, as well as links to other sites.

Code of Federal Regulations
http://www.access.gpo.gov/nara/cfr/index.html

CASE APPLICATION:
Repetitive Motion Disorder

Jan Breedlow is a data entry clerk at Linco Tool and Die. Two weeks ago she visited her doctor for pain in her right hand. The doctor diagnosed her pain as carpal tunnel syndrome. He provided a note for Jan's supervisor, placed two splints on her hand, and advised Jan to discuss switching jobs or tasks with her supervisor due to extensive damage to her hand.

One week later Jan returned to the doctor, and the doctor said, "Jan your body is going to win—you must consider another type of activity at work or your wrist will not heal." Although Jan believes that there is no other job at Linco and that her supervisor will not be sympathetic, she knows she must discuss the alternatives to fifty hours of typing a week. When Jan returns to work, her supervisor, Betty, asks, "Well, Jan, was that a nice break? We left your work for you, though, and I hope you'll stay until it's finished, even if working in that vise might get a little uncomfortable!"

Jan responds, "Betty, that wasn't a break. Laying awake at night with my hand aching is not a break. My doctor advised that I not type for two weeks, to change activities, and to discuss with you how I might change tasks to let it heal as well as it can."

Betty replies, "You know Jan, we'd all like variety. Every data clerk here has carpal tunnel; so do I; what's new? I can't rotate tasks or change activities for you—there are no other activities. Data entry is just the same job you've held for twelve years, and the only one you'll probably ever hold here. The only one who can decide if you can do the job is you. I can't do you any favors; it wouldn't be fair to the others since they complain of carpal tunnel too. You either enter your data and keep up, or find a job someplace else. That's what they pay us for. Understand?"

Jan understands. She takes two pain pills, and begins typing, hurting physically and emotionally, and wonders if she should talk to someone in personnel.

Discussion Questions

If you were the personnel manager at Linco Tools:

1. What would you suggest to Jan?
2. What would you advise Betty?
3. What are the implications of this incident for Linco's human resource manager to better prepare and inform Betty and other supervisors in the future and to more fairly and appropriately deal with employees?

TESTING YOUR UNDERSTANDING

How well did you fulfill the learning objectives?

1. OSHA legislation did all of the following except
   a. established comprehensive and specific health standards.
   b. authorized inspections to ensure the standards are met.
   c. required employers to keep records of illnesses and injuries.
   d. required employers to calculate hospitalization and medical treatment costs for job-related injury and illness.
   e. required employers to calculate accident ratios.

2. If OSHA wants to inspect your facility, you should do all of the following except
   a. discuss the company's safety program with the OSHA inspector.
   b. agree with OSHA, before the inspection, on the exact facility and entity to be inspected.
   c. insist on seeing the search warrant.
   d. tell the OSHA representative how safety programs are communicated to employees.
   e. explain to the OSHA representative how safety programs are enforced.

3. An OSHA safety inspector is scheduled to inspect a meat-processing plant the day after tomorrow. All of the following could preempt that inspection except
   a. A complaint from an automotive distributor.
   b. A complaint from a sawmill.
   c. A serious accident at a chemical plant.
   d. A serious accident at a shipyard.
   e. A refusal to allow entry without a search warrant by an electronics firm.

4. Last month, the OSHA inspector in a chicken-processing plant "red-flagged" a production area for an old and faulty water boiler. Yesterday, the boiler exploded, injuring thirty-one workers. There were no fatalities, and all but two of the twenty-seven workers who were sent to the hospital were treated and released the same day. The two hospitalized employees are expected to return to work within sixty days. What OSHA penalty can this firm expect?
   a. No penalty. A report would not be filed without a fatality.
   b. The firm will be fined at least $70,000 for failing to fix the boiler.
   c. The shift supervisor will be imprisoned for the total amount of time the injured workers are hospitalized.
   d. No penalty. This minor incident would result in only a report being filed.
   e. The plant would be closed.

5. All of the following are accurate statements about the current status and impact of OSHA except
   a. OSHA has refocused its energy from enforcing the intent of the law to stipulating the law.
   b. many unions argue that OSHA enforcement efforts have not been extensive enough.
   c. in some large organizations, an additional administrative position has been created with a sole responsibility of safety.
   d. OSHA standards have become more realistic in recent years.
   e. in the last few years, OSHA standards have focused more on health than on safety.

6. A chemical engineer for a pharmaceutical plant was blinded when a pipe he was adjusting cracked and spewed hot vapor into his face. He wasn't wearing safety glasses or a hard hat, although both were specified for the job he was doing. The employee's report indicated that he knew about the safety equipment, but that for the last five years, had gotten along quite well without the cumbersome gear. What means of preventing accidents was not being used effectively in this situation?
   a. Education.
   b. Skills training.
   c. Engineering.
   d. Protection.
   e. Regulation enforcement.

7. In academic life, the year that tenure is decided for a professor is usually a very stressful one. The tenure decision means that a professor can either stay at that university until retirement or must leave that university within a year to find employment elsewhere. Bob, an untenured assistant professor, cut a "deal" with the provost and the dean, two key decision makers in his tenure process, well in advance of the decision. Bob was not stressed during his tenure decision year due to the lack of which stress contributor?
   a. Constraints.
   b. Demands.
   c. Outcome importance.
   d. Outcome uncertainty.
   e. Burnout.

8. Why do companies use EAPs?
   a. Two years of treatment usually return up to 80 percent of employees to the workforce. Costs of hiring and training new employees amount to over four years' salary.
   b. Studies suggest that $5.00 is saved for each EAP dollar spent.
   c. EAPs are more popular with employees than traditional health insurance coverage.
   d. Title VII compliance requires either EAP or wellness programs. EAPs are cheaper.

   e. EAPs are required in most health insurance packages.

9. Which one of the following is not a recommended measure for preventing workplace violence?
   a. Have police agencies from the local area frequently visit the office facility.
   b. Train supervisors to identify troubled employees and refer them for help.
   c. Install security measures such as guards and electronic detection equipment.
   d. Establish an employee assistance program.
   e. Instruct employees on what to do if someone becomes violent.

10. Which statement applies to OSHA's "random inspection" level of enforcement?
    a. OSHA may inspect any facility, at any time, without warning.
    b. Employers are not required to admit OSHA inspectors without a search warrant.
    c. OSHA is so understaffed that they never conduct "random inspections."
    d. Employers in noncritical industries are notified at the start of each month if they are to be potentially investigated by OSHA during that month.
    e. Any organization that has had a legitimate OSHA complaint filed against it is subject to "random inspections" of the facility at any time during the next five years.

11. Which of the following statements best describes OSHA's enforcement mechanisms?
    a. Fines can be levied for noncompliance, up to $70,000 per violation, if the violation is severe, willful, and repetitive.
    b. Top company officials have been convicted of manslaughter.
    c. Government contracts have been canceled with noncompliant firms.
    d. Firms with repeated violations are required to keep, at their own expense, an OSHA inspector on site at all times.
    e. Fines up to $100,000 per violation can be levied against firms that do not comply with record-keeping requirements.

12. Indirect costs of accidents that must be borne by the employer include all of the following except
    a. wages paid for time lost due to injury.
    b. damage to equipment and material.
    c. the workers' compensation premium.
    d. personnel to investigate and report accidents.
    e. lost production due to stoppages and change-overs.

13. Burnout is defined as a function of all of these concerns except
    a. dehumanizing of jobs.
    b. boredom.

c. emotional exhaustion.

d. physical exhaustion.

e. lowered job productivity.

14. Which of the following would qualify as smoke-free environments?

    a. Smoking is prohibited in portions of the employee cafeteria.

    b Smoking is prohibited in meetings, conferences, and training sessions.

    c. Smoking is prohibited in all areas of the building except private offices.

    d. Smoking is prohibited on all company premises.

    e. All of these would qualify as a smoke-free environment.

15. Which of the following is a basic health-related item that would appear on a checklist for expatriates?

    a. Take along a shot-book with a record of all current immunizations.

    b. Be immunized for all communicable diseases, whether or not they are reported in the designated foreign country, before traveling.

    c. Pack at least three separate sets of all prescription medicine to take along.

    d. Copy down the brand names of all over-the-counter drugs you frequently use. Packaging will probably be different overseas, and you may not recognize the item.

    e. Schedule a physical examination in the foreign country as soon as possible after your arrival.

Endnotes

1. This opening vignette is based on the Associated Press article "Connecticut Lottery Office Swept Clean of Traces of Gunman," *The Sun* (March 11, 1998), p. 9A.

2. U.S. Department of Commerce, Bureau of the Census, *Statistical Abstracts of the United States: 1997* (Washington, D.C.: Government Printing Office, 1994), p. 437.

3. Leon Rubis, "1995 Drop in Workplace Injuries Includes Repetitive Motion Cases," *HR News* (April 1997), p. 9; and Elizabeth Sheley, "Preventing Repetitive Motion Injuries," *HRMagazine* (October 1995), p. 57.

4. See, for example, Elaine McShulskis, "Protect Employees from Hazardous Noise Levels," *HRMagazine* (April 1997), p. 22.

5. In the case of the Supreme Court case of *Whirlpool Corporation* v. *Marshall* [445 U.S. 1(1980)], employees may refuse to work if they perceive doing so can cause serious injury. This case has weakened termination for insubordination when the refusal stems from a safety or health issue. This refusal was further clarified in *Gateway Coal* v. *the United Mine Workers* [94 S. Ct. 641(1981)], where a three-part test was developed. This was where (1) the refusal is reasonable; (2) the employee was unsuccessful in getting the problem fixed; and (3) normal organizational channels to address the problem haven't worked.

6. Horace A. Thompson III, "Negotiate with the Inspectors— Then Let Them In," *Human Resources Management: Ideas and Trends* (Chicago: Commerce Clearing House, April 18, 1990), p. 72.

7. Stephen Barlas, "Safety Last?" *Entrepreneur* (October 1995), p. 100.

8. Jerome Mansfield, "OSHA Rule 1910.120: A Rule to Live By," *Professional Safety* (May 1990), p. 38.

9. Ibid., pp. 39–40.

10. *Marshall* v. *Barlow, Inc.,* 436 U.S., 307 (1978).

11. "Federal Court Upholds OSHA Warrant Procedure," *HR News* (April 1995), p. 19.

12. Thompson III, p. 72.

13. Peter J. Sheridan, "How to Handle an OSHA Inspection," *Occupational Hazards* (September 1991), p. 132.

14. Adapted from Myron I. Peskin and Francis J. McGrath, "Industrial Safety: Who Is Responsible and Who Benefits?" *Business Horizons* (May–June 1992), p. 62.

15. Vic H. Henry, "Make Sure You Know Your Legal Rights When OSHA Arrives at Your Facility," *Occupational Health and Safety* (January 1992), p. 18.

16. State of Maryland, *Occupational Safety and Health Regulations* (Baltimore, Md.: Division of Labor and Industry, 1993), pp. 25–39; and U.S. Department of Labor, Occupational Safety and Health Administration, *All About OSHA* (Washington, D.C.: Government Printing Office, 1985).

17. The material in this section is adapted from U.S. Department of Labor, Bureau of Labor Statistics, *A Brief Guide to Recordkeeping Requirements for Occupational Injuries and Illnesses* (Washington, D.C.: Government Printing Office, June 1986), pp. 1–19.

18. Ibid., p. 3.

19. Ibid., p. 9.

20. Ibid., p. 12.

21. Ibid., p. 15.

22. Ibid.

23. The number 3,600,000 is determined as follows: 1,800 employees, working 40 hour weeks, for 50 weeks a year [1,800 × 40 × 50].

24. *Statistical Abstract of the United States* (1997), p. 437.

25. Ibid, p. 438.

26. See Stephen C. Yohay, "Safety and Health Regulation Intensified," *Employee Relations Law Journal* (Autumn 1991), pp. 323–334; and "OSHA Trends," *Human Resources Management: Ideas and Trends* (Chicago: Commerce Clearing House, Inc., January 23, 1991), p. 14. For willful violation the minimum penalty is $5,000; other fines levied for violations other than willful and repetitive carry with them a $7,000 maximum.

27. John W. Ruser and Robert S. Smith, "Reestimating OSHA's Effects: Has the Data Changed?" *Journal of Human Resources* (Spring 1991), p. 212; see also, Bradlee Thompson, "OSHA Bounces Back," *Training* (January 1991), pp. 45–53.

28. Colleen Johnson, "Concern over Safety Shows up on Companies' Bottom Line: Directory of Safety Consultants," *Business Insurance* (September 10, 1990), p. 36.

29. Susan B. Garland, "A New Chief Has OSHA Growling Again," *Business Week: Industrial/Technology Edition* (August 20, 1990), p. 57; and Robert Reid, "OSHA Warns Industry: Big Fines Are Here to Stay," *Occupational Hazards* (May 1988), p. 87.

30. "Three Men Receive Sentences, Fines in Mine Explosion," *The Wall Street Journal* (June 13, 1996), p. A-4; and Stephen G. Minter, "Courts Give Criminal Prosecution a Green Light," *Occupational Hazards* (December 1989), p. 41. The prosecution and fines in the Pyro Mining case stemmed from a situation where company officials allegedly lied to inspectors and failed to adhere to safety procedures. In all, 15 employees of Pyro Mining pleaded guilty, with only three executives receiving prison terms up to 18-months.

31. Jeffrey M. Rosin, "A New Twist in Enforcement Efforts," *HRMagazine* (May 1997), pp. 128–134.

32. Howard Banks, "The Agenda for Labor Law Reform," *Forbes* (January 16, 1995), p. 37.

33. Bill Leonard, "OSHA Launches Ergonomics Page on the World Wide Web," *HRMagazine* (June 1997), p. 10; and Gregg Labar, "OSHA in 1992: Standards Are Job One," *Occupational Hazards* (December 1991), p. 31.

34. Rhonda West and Art Durity, "Does My Company Need to Worry about AIDS?" *Personnel* (April 1991), p. 5.

35. "Procedures for Bloodborne Disease Standards Outlined," *Human Resource Management: Ideas and Trends* (Chicago: Commerce Clearing House, Inc., April 15, 1992), p. 62.

36. Gregg Labar, "OSHA in 1992: Standards Are Job One," *Occupational Hazards* (December 1991), p. 31.

37. See, for example, Matthew M. Carmel and Michael F. Dolan, "An Introduction to Employee Right-to-Know Laws," *Personnel Journal* (September 1984), pp. 117–121.

38. "Hazard Communication Standard," *Human Resources Management: Ideas and Trends* (Chicago: Commerce Clearing House, Inc., March 7, 1990), p. 45.

39. Ibid.

40. Neville C. Tompkins, "Labor-Supported Committees Advocate Workers Right to Understand an MSDS," *Occupational Health and Safety* (July 1991), p. 23.

41. Ibid.

42. Garland, p. 57.

43. *Statistical Abstracts of the United States* (1997), p. 435–436.

44. Mark D. Fefer, "What to Do about Worker's Comp," *Fortune* (June 29, 1992), p. 80.

45. "Falling Behind: The U.S. Is Losing the Job Safety War to Japan, Too," *The Wall Street Journal* (May 16, 1992), p. A-1.

46. See Peskin and McGrath, pp. 66–69.

47. Ibid.

48. Ibid., p. 67.

49. Adapted from *Maryland Occupational Safety and Health, Developing a Workplace Safety and Health Program* (Baltimore: Maryland Occupational Safety and Health Agency, 1993), pp. 5–16.

50. Jonathan A. Segal, "When Norman Bates and Baby Jane Act Out at Work," *HRMagazine* (February 1996), p. 31.

51. Anastasia Toufexis, "Workers Who Fight Firing with Fire," *Time* (April 25, 1994), p. 35–36; and *L.A. Times* (April 9, 1994), p. A-31.

52. John K. Sage, "Attack on Violence," *Industry Week* (February 15, 1997), p. 16. See also Douglas Harbrecht, "Talk About Murder, Inc.," *Business Week* (July 11, 1994), p. 8.

53. Ibid.; Anne M. O'Leary-Kelly, Ricky W. Griffin, and David J. Glew, "Organization-Motivated Aggression: A Research Framework," *Academy of Management Review*, Vol. 21, No. 1 (February 1996), p. 225; and Tom Dunkel, "Danger Zone," *Working Woman* (August 1994), pp. 39–40.

54. "Self-Defense," *Entrepreneur* (March 1997), p. 38; and "Vehicle Accidents, Homicide Led 1993 Workplace Deaths," *HR News* (September 1994), p. 3.

55. Brett Pulley, "Crime Becomes Occupational Hazard of Deliverers," *The Wall Street Journal* (March 7, 1994), p. B-1; and John D. Thompson, "Employers Should Take Measures to Minimize Potential for Workplace Violence," *Commerce Clearing House: Ideas and Trends* (December 20, 1993), pp. 201–203; 208.

56. Linda Micco, "Night Retailers Take Stock of Workers' Safety," *HRMagazine* (June 1997), p. 79.

57. Joseph A. Kinney, "When domestic Violence Strikes the Workplace," *HRMagazine* (August 1995), pp. 74–78; and John D. Thompson, "Employers Should Take Measures to Minimize Potential for Workplace Violence," *Commerce Clearing House: Ideas and Trends* (December 20, 1993), pp. 201–203; 208.

58. Edward Felsenthal, "Potentially Violent Employees Present Bosses with a Catch-22," *The Wall Street Journal* (April 5, 1995), pp. B-1; B-5.

59. Ibid.

60. "Workplace Security: Preventing On-the-Job Violence," *Inc.* (June 1996), p. 116.

61. See, for example, Kate Walter, "Are Your Employees on the Brink," *HRMagazine* (June 1997), pp. 57–63; Malcolm P. Coco, Jr., "The New War Zone: The Workplace," *SAM Advanced Management Journal* (Winter 1997), pp. 15–20; Jacquelin Lynn, "Striking Back," *Entrepreneur* (June 1995), p. 56; Dennis L. Johnson, John G. Kurutz, and John B. Kiehlbauch, "Scenario for Supervisors," *HRMagazine* (February 1995), p. 63; and Commerce Clearing House, "Workplace Violence: Strategies Start with Awareness," *Human Resources Management: Ideas and Trends* (July 11, 1994), p. 109.

62. John K. Sage, Attach on Violence," *Industry Week* (February 17, 1997), p. 18; Rudy M. Yandrick, "Long-Term Follow-Up Urged After Workplace Disasters," *HR News* (December 1996), p. 6; and Kathleen Menda, "Defusing Workplace Violence," *HRMagazine* (October 1994), p. 113.

63. Harbrecht, p. 8.

64. Faye Rice, "Do You Work in a Sick Building," *Fortune* (July 2, 1990), p. 88.

65. Ibid.

66. Faye Rice, "Do You Work in a Sick Building?" p. 88.

67. See for example, Stephanie Barlow, "Up In Smoke," *Entrepreneur* (August 1994), pp. 126–131.

68. Ibid., p. 130.

69. Jim Collison, "Work Place Smoking Policies: Questions and Answers," *Personnel Journal* (April 1988), p. 80.

70. "Smoke-Free Workplaces Prevalent," *HRMagazine* (June 1996), p. 18; and "U.S. Employers Crack Down on Workplace Smoking But Few Provide Help," *Manpower Argus* (July 1997), p. 8.

71. Rudy M. Yandrick, "More Smokers Prohibit Smoking," *HRMagazine* (July 1994), pp. 68–69.

72. Ibid., p. 71.

73. Leon Rubis, "1995 Drop in Workplace Injuries Includes Repetitive Motion Cases," *HR News* (April 1997), p. 9; and "Office Workers' Barking Dog Syndrome," *Business Week* (July 31, 1995), p. 8.

74. See, for example, Linda Himelstein, "The Asbestos Case of the 1990s?" *Business Week* (January 16, 1995), pp. 82–83;

and Frank Swoboda, "U.S. Acts to Reduce Repetitive Motion Injuries," *Washington Post* (August 31, 1990), p. A-4.

75. "Carpal Tunnel Syndrome and U.S. Workforce," *Manpower Argus* (October 1996), p. 11.

76. Michael A. Verespej, "Ergonomics: Taming the Repetitive Motion Monster," *Industry Week* (October 7, 1991), p. 26.

77. Dominic Bencivenga, "The Economics of Ergonomics: Finding the Right Fit," *HRMagazine* (August 1996), pp. 68–75; and Linda Thornburg, "Workplace Ergonomics Makes Economic Sense," *HRMagazine* (October 1994), pp. 58–60.

78. Robina A. Gangemi, "Ergonomics: Reducing Workplace Injuries," *Inc.* (July 1996), p. 92.

79. J. A. Savage, "Stuck Between a VDT and a Hard Place," *Computerworld* (May 13, 1991), p. 63

80. Ibid.

81. Ibid.

82. Adapted from Randall S. Schuler, "Definition and Conceptualization of Stress in Organizations," *Organizational Behavior and Human Performance* (April 1980), p. 189.

83. Ibid., p. 191.

84. "Workplace Stress Is Rampant, Especially with the Recession," *The Wall Street Journal* (May 5, 1992), p. A-1.

85. Kate Lynch, "Humor Can Beat Stress," *Industry Week* (May 4, 1998), p. 55.

86. This information is adapted from a newswire report by Mari Yamaguchi as cited in "Stress in Japanese Business," *Audio Human Resource Report,* Vol. 2, No. 2 (March 1991), pp. 6–7.

87. "Work-Related Deaths Are on the Rise in Japan," *Manpower Argus* (April 1997), p. 11.

88. "Huge Payout by Japanese Firm for 'Karoshi'," *Manpower Argus* (September 1996), p. 8.

89. "Stress on the Job in Germany," and "Workplace Stress Is Biggest Health Hazard in Britain," *Manpower Argus* (February 1997), p. 7.

90. See, for instance, John Schaubroeck and Deryl E. Merritt, "Divergent Effects of Job Control on Coping with Work Stressors: The Key Role of Self-Efficacy," *Academy of Management Journal,* Vol. 40, No. 3 (June 1997), pp. 738–754.

91. Also see John H. Harris and Lucy A. Arendt, "Stress Reduction and the Small Business: Increasing Employee and Customer, Satisfaction," *SAM Advanced Management Journal* (Winter 1997), pp. 27–34.

92. For an interesting overview of this topic, see Victoria J. Doby and Robert D. Caplan, "Organizational Stress as Threat to Reputation: Effects on Anxiety at Work and at Home," *Academy of Management Journal,* Vol. 38, No. 4 (September 1995), pp. 1105–1123.

93. A. A. Brott, "New Approaches to Job Stress," *Nation's Business,* May 1994, pp. 81–82; and C. J. Bacher, "Workers Take Leave of Job Stress," *Personnel Journal,* January 1995, pp. 38–48.

94. Sal Marine, "The Stress Epidemic," *Industry Week* (April 7, 1997), p. 14.

95. Ibid., p. 293.

96. Ibid.; see also Patti Watts, "Are Your Employees Burnout Proof?" *Personnel* (September 1990), pp. 12–14; and Philip J. Dewe, "Applying the Concepts of Appraisal to Work Stresses: Some Explanatory Analysis," *Human Relations* (February 1992), pp. 114–115.

97. Donald F. Parker and Thomas A. DeCotiis, "Organizational Determinants of Job Stress," *Organizational Behavior and Human Performance,* 32 (1983), p. 166.

98. John M. Kelly, "Getting a Grip on Stress," *HRMagazine* (February 1997), pp. 51–54.

99. Whiton Stuart Paine, *Job Stress and Burnout* (Beverly Hills, Calif.: Sage, 1982), p. 19.

100. Stuart Feldman, "Today's EAPs Make the Grade," *Personnel* (February 1991), p. 3.

101. Kevin J. Williams and George M. Alliger, "Role Stressors, Mood Spillover, and Perceptions of Work-Family Conflict in Employed Parents," *Academy of Management Journal,* Vol. 37, No. 4 (1994), p. 837.

102. Ibid.

103. Valla Howell, "The Groggy Beginnings of EAPs," *JEMS* (November 1988), p. 43.

104. Ibid.

105. Employee rights legislation mandates that any activity in an EAP remains confidential. This means records of who is visiting the EAP, the problems, and intervention, must be maintained separately from other personnel records. See Robert J. Noble, "Matter of Confidentiality," *Personnel* (February 1991), p. 11.

106. Feldman, p. 3.

107. See George Nicholas, "How to Make Employee Assistance Programs More Productive," *Supervision* (July 1991), pp. 3–6; and "EAPs to the Rescue," *Employee Benefit Plan Review* (February 1991), pp. 26–27.

108. "EAPs Evolve to Health Plan Gatekeeper," *Employee Benefit Plan Review* (February 1992), p. 18.

109. Edward Stetzer, "Bringing Sanity to Mental Health Costs," *Business and Health* (February 1992), p. 72.

110. See Meg Bryant, "Testing EAPs for Coordination," *Business and Health* (August 1991), pp. 20–24.

111. Diane Kirrane, "EAPs: Dawning of a New Age," *HRMagazine* (January 1990), pp. 30–34.

112. John S, McClenahen, "Working with AIDS," *Industry Week* (November 17, 1997), pp. 51–52; and Deborah Shalowitz, "Employee Assistance Plan Trends," *Business Insurance* (June 24, 1991), p. 24.

113. Michael M. Harris and Mary L. Fennell, "Perceptions of an Employee Assistance Program and Employees' Willingness to Participate," *Journal of Applied Behavioral Science,* Vol. 24, No. 4 (1988), p. 423.

114. See, for instance, Joan Hamilton, "Can Company Counselors Help You Cope?" *Business Week* (November 14, 1994), p. 141.

115. See Cynthia E. Griffin, "Crisis Control," *Entrepreneur* (August 1995), pp. 128–135.

116. Shari Caudron, "The Wellness Payoff," *Personnel Journal* (July 1990), p. 55.

117. Stephanie L. Hyland, "Health Care Benefits Show Cost-Containment Strategies," *Monthly Labor Review* (February 1992), p. 42.

118. Rudy M. Yandrick, "EAPs Explore Boundaries of Evolving Profession," *HR News* (August 1995), p. 1; and Therese R. Welter, "Wellness Programs: Not a Cure-All," *Industry Week* (February 15, 1988), p. 42.

119. Scott Campbell, "Better Than the Company Gym." *HRMagazine* (June 1995), pp. 108–110; and Harry Harrington, "Retiree Wellness Plan Cuts Health Costs," *Personnel Journal* (August 1990), p. 60.

120. Leah Ingram, "Many Healthy Returns," *Entrepreneur* (September 1994), p. 84.

121. Caudron, p. 56.

122. Ibid.

123. John E. Riedel and Andrea Frank, "Corporate Health Promotion: Marketing Studies Show Who Buys and Who Succeeds," *Employee Benefits Journal,* Vol. 15, No. 2 (June 1990), p. 29.

124. See Kenneth J. Smith, George S. Everly, Jr., and G. Timothy Haight, "An Empirical Analysis of the Impact of a Corporate Health Promotion Intervention on Reported Sick Leave Absenteeism," *Benefits Quarterly,* Vol. 6, No. 1 (1990), pp. 37–45.

125. James W. Busbin and David P. Campbell, "Employee Wellness Programs: A Strategy for Increasing Participation," *Journal of Health Care Marketing,* Vol. 10, No. 4 (December 1990), p. 22.

126. Adapted from Caudron, pp. 57-58.

127. David E. Upton, "When Health Is Money," *Northwest Airlines World Traveler* (May 1992), p. 34.

128. Lucia Landon, "Pump Up Your Employees," *HRMagazine* (May 1990), p. 35.

129. Ibid., p. 46.

130. See Faye Rice, "How Execs Get Fit," *Fortune* (October 22, 1990), pp. 144–152.

131. Timothy Pasquarelli, "Dealing with Discomfort and Danger," *HRMagazine* (October 1996), pp. 104–110.

132. U.S. Department of State, *Traveler's Telephone Advisory Line* (January 12, 1990 and February 27, 1990).

133. Rudy M. Yandrick, "EAPs Help Expatriates Adjust and Thrive," *HR News* (January 1995), p. B7.

15. Effective HRM Communications

LEARNING OBJECTIVES

After reading this chapter, you will be able to:

1. Explain how communication serves as the foundation for HRM activities.
2. Identify the legally required communications with respect to benefit administration and safety and health.
3. Describe the purpose of HRM communications programs.
4. Discuss how corporate culture is affected by effective communication.
5. State the role of the chief executive officer promoting communications programs.
6. Specify what information employees should receive under an effective communications program.
7. Describe the purpose of the employee handbook.
8. Explain what information should be included in an employee handbook.
9. List four popular communication methods used in organizations.
10. Discuss the critical components of an effective suggestion program.

*E*mployee handbooks have the potential to provide a wealth of information to employees—information that is important to them and is critical to their employment. Simultaneously, however, the handbook can also provide specific information that "protects" the organization from claims being made against it at a later date. This documentation, then, almost creates the necessity that handbooks be thorough, detailed, and "legally cleared." For Carol Ruprecht, International Sales Manager of the Fountain Valley, California, Kingston Technologies, nothing could be further from the truth.[1]

Several years ago Kingston's management recognized the need to have in place an accurate and technically correct employee handbook. To achieve that goal, they hired a consultant to develop the manual and submit it to the company in camera-ready format for duplication and binding. Several weeks later, the company got just what it wanted. The handbook was done—another project completed. Or so the company thought! Ruprecht later recognized that the finished product was poor. In fact, she "never expected anybody would be offended by it. But it contained all this legal butt-covering language—which made it seem as if the company didn't trust [employees]." Employees hated the manual, which got the attention of the founders of the organization.

Kingston Technologies operated as a wholesome company. Its president's philosophy is to build trust and loyalty with every member of the company. The president wanted to make that statement on the first day of hiring, yet the thing new employees left with that first day, the handbook, created just the opposite view. Consequently, the handbook had to be redone—not by outsiders, but by an individual in the organization, like Carol, who understood the philosophical underpinnings of Kingston.

Kingston's new employee handbook has been a big success. Ruprecht has met her goal of providing the information that employees need, but this time in a simple and straightforward manner. Each of the twenty pages of the handbook addresses important questions employees may have, and embellishes on the company's philosophies—courtesy, compassion, modesty, and honesty. As far as handbooks go, you can't get much better than this!

INTRODUCTION

For fourteen chapters, we have been discussing a variety of HRM activities. Inherent in all of these activities is one common thread—effective **communication.** Although we may not have elaborated specifically on how HRM involves itself in the communication process, we have addressed its needs on several occasions. For example, in Chapter 2 the discussion of worker diversity identified the need for better communications with employees, especially those who do not speak the native language.[2] Communications in work-force diversity also means letting these individuals know that they are welcome in the corporation and that the company will make every attempt to provide them equal opportunity in the organization.[3]

We also addressed the need to communicate with respect to the recruiting and selection process (in terms of understanding what the job entails, and realistic job previews), in orientation (acclimating employees to HRM activities and policies), and training (understanding how to do the job). Yet probably the most critical HRM activities emphasizing communications came in the discussion of motivation, performance evaluations, benefits, and safety and health. In motivation, we discussed the need to be able to communicate the relationship that exists between one's efforts and individual goal attainment. In that discussion we highlighted the need for performance goals to be communicated—goals that will, when met, facilitate achieving organization-wide objectives. Specificity for doing so was discussed in performance evaluations, and how the interaction between an employee and manager can affect performance outcomes. When these outcomes are positive, individuals should be rewarded; when they are not positive, effort must be expended to correct the problem. For that, we introduced employee counseling, which relies heavily on effective communications.

For benefits and safety and health, we discussed not only the importance of informing employees of the benefits offered them, and availability of EAP and wellness programs, but the legal issues of providing certain information. That is, with respect to benefits, HRM is responsible for providing each employee with a Summary Plan Description, which describes in understandable terms employee rights under ERISA, their pension plan requirements, and updated benefits accumulations.[4] Likewise, OSHA, under its Hazard Communication Standard, requires employers to notify employees of potential dangers and protective measures when exposed to workplace hazardous chemicals or toxins.

As we move into the twenty-first century, we recognize that our companies will be different. Factors like global competition and technology enhancements are making company officials rethink how they are organized. We've witnessed extensive delayering, mergers, and acquisitions in the past. When such events occur, employee stress levels increase. One way of allaying such stress is to reduce the uncertainty that surrounds the situation—in our terms, effective communications.[5]

We know the years ahead will continue to witness change in our companies.[6] Our movement toward leaner structures, continuous improvement, employee involvement, and work teams will work best if effective communication exists.[7] And where good communications programs are operating, benefits accrue to the company. For instance, one study credits communications with "better work relations; greater trust between employees and managers; greater employee satisfaction, and leading to lower turnover rates."[8] And with our diverse work force, this means communicating in different languages to ensure that the message is understood by all employees.

HRM COMMUNICATIONS PROGRAMS

Achieving the goals effective communications can offer is not easy. It doesn't happen by itself. Rather, it evolves after careful thought, implementation, and evaluation. For much of that, we rely on HRM. Although we've highlighted many of these items throughout the text, there are still a few that warrant exposure. Specifically, in this chapter we want to focus on HRM's role in the communications process, look at the purpose of employee handbooks and newsletters, and close with a discussion of suggestion systems/complaint procedures that exist in companies. Let's now turn our attention to the specifics surrounding effective HRM communications programs.

The Purpose

Human resource management communications programs are designed to keep employees abreast of what is happening in the organization, and knowledgeable of the policies and procedures affecting them.[9] Whereas public relations departments are created to keep the public informed of what an organization does, HRM communications focus on the internal constituents—the employees.[10] As we mentioned in Chapter 1, regarding the role of the employee relations department in the maintenance function, communication programs serve as a basis for increasing employee loyalty and commitment.[11] How? By building into the corporate culture a systematic means through which information is free-flowing, timely, and accurate, employees are better able to perceive that the organization values them.[12] Such a system builds trust and openness among organizational members, even assisting the sharing of "bad news."[13]

For example, at Georgia Power Company, company executives were able to use communications effectively to stave off any further deterioration of the company's operations.[14] Georgia Power had been experiencing several crises during the latter part of the 1980s. Failure to act on these problems, like profitability and customer service, may have led to significant changes in the organization and the employees' lives. Instead, Georgia Power's top management decided to take the issue to the employees. By empowering its nine-person communications department to get employees motivated to achieve the company's objectives, several programs were implemented. One program involved calling employees at home to determine if they knew corporate goals; those who did were received a cash rewarded. Various other communications programs were also instituted, again to reinforce what the company was about. As a result of these efforts, Georgia Power's employees had helped turn the company around in just a few short years—while simultaneously indicating that employee morale was at its highest level in years.[15]

HRM communications has the ability to bring about many positive changes in an organization. This process, by whatever means it exists, should stay focused on keeping employees informed, thereby setting the stage for enhancing

> **HRM communications programs are designed to keep employees informed of organizational events, and knowledgeable of the policies affecting them.**

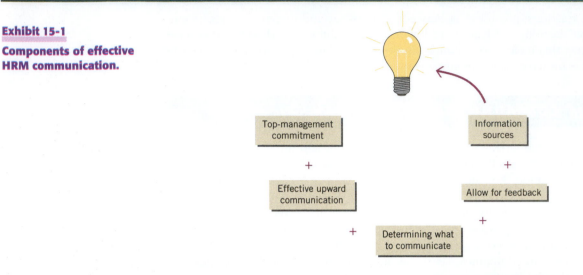

employee satisfaction. For employees at Hewlett-Packard, that is what has been happening. Because of the efforts of its managers to enhance communications with employees, Hewlett-Packard has witnessed more employee job satisfaction and a higher quality of work life for its organization members.[16] And at Challenger Electrical Equipment Corporation in Allentown, Pennsylvania, it took a union organizing campaign before company managers realized that employees were dissatisfied with the information they had (or hadn't) been getting.[17] With these in mind, let's look at some fundamental requirements for an effective HRM communications program (see Exhibit 15-1).

Guidelines for Supporting Communications Programs

Building effective HRM communications programs involves a few fundamental elements. These include top management commitment, effective upward communication, determining what is to be communicated, allowing for feedback, and information sources. Let's look at each of these.

Top Management Commitment   Before any organization can develop and implement an internal organizational communications program it must have the backing, support, and "blessing" of the CEO.[18] Any activity designed to facilitate work environments must be seen by employees as being endorsed by the company's top management. In doing so, these programs are given priority and are viewed as significant components of the corporate culture.[19] Just as it is critical for employees to see top management supporting communications, so, too, is it for them to see communications effectively operating at all levels—that is, effective communications does not just imply that top management sends information down throughout the company. It also implies that information flows upward as well, and laterally to other areas in the organization.

Effective Upward Communication   The upward flow of communication is particularly noteworthy because it is often the employees, the ones closest to the work, who may have vital information that top management should know. For instance, let's take a situation that occurs in HRM.[20] We've witnessed this changing field and recognize its ever-changing nature. Legislation at any level—

federal, state, or local—may add new HRM requirements for the organization. Unless top management is made aware of the implications of these requirements—like knowing how to ensure that sexual harassment charges are thoroughly investigated—severe repercussions could occur. Thus, that information must filter up in the company.

A similar point could easily be made for any part of an organization. And in keeping with the spirit of employee empowerment, as employees are more involved in making decisions that affect them, that information must be communicated "up the ladder." Furthermore, it's important for top management to monitor the pulse of the organization regarding how employees view working for the company. Whether that information is obtained from walking around the premises, through formal employee suggestions, or through employee satisfaction/morale surveys, such information is crucial. In fact, on the latter point, with the advent of technology, some of the employee satisfaction measures can be captured in almost "real time." At IBM, such surveys are "on-line," making it easier for the employee to use, more expedient in its analysis, and more timely for company use.[21]

Determining What to Communicate   At the extreme, if every piece of information that exists in our organizations were communicated, no work would ever get done; people would be spending their entire days on information overload. Employees, while wanting to be informed, are not concerned with every piece of information, like who just retired, was promoted, or what community group was given a donation yesterday.[22] Rather, employees need pertinent information—addressing those things employees should know to do their jobs. This typically includes where the business is going (strategic goals),[23] current sales/service/production outcomes, new product or service lines, and human resource policy changes.[24]

The Whole Story

Effective communications in organizations is built on the premise that appropriate and accurate information must be conveyed. Organization members should be afforded the respect and dignity that factual information can deliver. But at what point is it best to withhold information from employees?

We've addressed a so-what test—if it really matters to individuals, the information should be conveyed. But reality tells us that even factual information can, at times, be difficult to deliver, and may best be withheld for a number of reasons. For example, confidentiality is a must in matters that affect employees personally. Assume, then, that you have just been informed by one of your employees that he has Hodgkin's lymphoma, a treatable form of lymph-node cancer. Consequently, he may be absent frequently at times, especially during his chemotherapy treatments. Yet, he does-

n't anticipate his attendance to be a problem, nor will it directly affect his work. After all, some of his duties involve direct computer work, so he can work at home and forward the data electronically to the appropriate people.

On several occasions, the employee has either called in sick or has had to leave early because he felt ill. Your employees are beginning to suspect something is wrong, and have come to you to find out what is wrong. There are even rumors going around that the employee might be HIV-positive, and that is causing quite a stir. You simply, and politely, decline to discuss the issue about an employee with other individuals. However, a number of your employees think that you are giving this employee preferential treatment. You know if they only knew what was going on they'd understand, but you can't disclose the nature of the illness. On the other hand, continued "favoritism" will surely be a disruptive force in your department. You are stumped. What do you do? Should employees be given the whole story? What's your opinion?

Should HRM make it a priority to immediately communicate the health insurance premium changes to its employees? Following the what-if, so-what test, they should. Such a change will affect each of these employees' paychecks. Accordingly, delaying the announcement might have negative consequences.

One means of determining what to communicate is through a "what-if, so-what" test. When deciding the priority of the information to be shared, HR managers should ask themselves what if this information is not shared (see Ethical Decisions in HRM). Will employees be able to do their jobs as well as if it were shared? Will they be disadvantaged in some way by not knowing? If the answers are no, then that may not be a priority item. And then, the so-what test. Will employees care about the information? Will they see it as an overload of meaningless information? If they may, then that, too, is not priority information. That's not to say this information may never be exchanged; it only means that it's not important for employees to get the information immediately.

To illustrate these decision guidelines, let's consider we have two pieces of information to share. One item is that the company's health insurance premiums are significantly changing—which means that employees' payroll deductions for health insurance premiums will increase nearly 25 percent. Would this meet our what-if, so-what test? What if we didn't communicate this in a timely fashion? Would the employees be affected? You bet! When they received their first paycheck with the new deductions taken out, you'd have some inquisitive, if not upset employees. And as we discussed in terms of individual goals being met for motivation purposes, such a change matters, thus passing the so-what test. But contrast a benefit–cost change with information regarding the company officials installing a security system to protect the organization's computer files. Will employees be adversely affected if the information is delayed a day or a week? Probably not! But this delaying of information must be considered on an individual basis—that is, while many employees may not need the immediate information on security mechanisms, certain areas of the company, like management information systems and systems maintenance, would find it a necessity. Accordingly, they would need the information immediately.

Allow for Feedback   We cannot assume that our communication efforts are achieving their goals. Consequently, we must develop into the system a means of assessing the flow of information, and for fostering employee feedback. How that information is generated may differ from organization to organization. For some, it may be a casual word-of-mouth assessment. Others may use employee surveys to capture the data, or provide a suggestion box where comments can be given. For others, there is a formalized and systematic communications audit program.[25]

Irrespective of how that information is gathered, employees must be involved. Otherwise, not only will measurement of the effectiveness of the communications program be difficult,[26] but you may also give the perception that employee commitment is unnecessary.

Information Sources   HRM communications should serve as a conduit in promoting effective communications throughout the organization. Although HRM plays an important role in bringing this to fruition, they are not the only, or the main, source of information. For that, we have to turn to one's immediate supervisor.[27] If successful programs can be linked to the immediate supervisor, then HRM must ensure that these individuals are trained in how to communicate properly. Even our health insurance premium change cited a few paragraphs ago, if implemented, would likely result in a number of questions for one's supervisor. Thus, HRM must make every effort to empower these supervisors with accurate data to deal with the "frontline" questions. From an HRM point of view, where is information best conveyed? Although the sources for this information may be varied, there is one medium that is central to providing information to employees: the employee handbook.

A GUIDE FOR EMPLOYEES: THE EMPLOYEE HANDBOOK

During the orientation of new employees, we inform them of a number of important facts regarding employment in the organization. But we must recognize that stating this information once isn't enough. There's often too much for the employee to absorb, especially during the excitement of the first day on the job. Consequently, a permanent reference guide is needed. This reference guide for employees is called the employee handbook.

The Purpose of an Employee Handbook

An **employee handbook** is a tool that, when developed properly, serves both employees and the employer. For employees, a well-designed handbook provides a central information source that conveys such useful information as "what the company is about, its history, and employee benefits."[28] The handbook, then, gives employees an opportunity to learn about the company, and what the company provides for them—in a way that permits each employee an opportunity to understand the information at his or her own pace.[29] By having this resource available, questions that may arise over such benefits as vacation accrual, matching contributions, vesting, etc. can be more easily answered. Serving as an easy reference guide, the employee handbook can be used by employees whenever it is warranted.[30] Beyond just being a source of information, employee handbooks also generate some other benefits. Where they exist, it has been found that they assist in creating an atmosphere in which employees become more productive members of the organization, and increase their commitment and loyalty to the organization.[31] By being thorough in its coverage, an employee handbook will address various HRM policies and work rules, which set the parameters within which employees are expected to perform.[32] For example, the handbook may express information on discipline and discharge procedures and a means of redressing disciplinary action should the employee feel that it was administered unfairly. The handbook, then, serves to ensure that any HRM policy will be fair, equitable, and consistently applied.[33]

Employers, too, can benefit from using an employee handbook. In addition to any benefits accrued from having a more committed and loyal work force, handbooks can also be used in the recruiting effort.[34] Remember, we advocated the use of realistic job previews for helping to "sell" recruits on the organization; a well-written employee handbook, shown to an applicant, can be useful in providing some of the necessary information an applicant may be seeking. Although employee handbooks are designed to "educate, inform, and guide" employees in the organization,[35] a word of caution is in order. In Chapter 13, in our discussion of employee rights and employment-at-will, we addressed the issue of implied contracts. Recall that an implied contract is anything expressed, verbally or in writing, that may be perceived by the individual to mean that she or he can't be terminated. For example, telling an employee that as long as her performance is satisfactory, she will have a job until retirement, could be construed as an implied contract. Over the years, the courts have ruled that various statements made in employee handbooks may be binding on the company.[36] To prevent this from occurring, many legal advocates and HRM researchers recommend a careful choice of words in the handbook, and a disclaimer.[37] We have reproduced a disclaimer from one business in Exhibit 15-2.

Before we move into the specific components of a handbook, there is one other important aspect for management to consider. That is, an employee handbook is of little use if employees don't read it. To facilitate that goal, we recommend that, first of all, the handbook should be pertinent to employees' needs.[38] Providing information that is viewed as unnecessary, or having a handbook that contains unclear wording or excessive verbiage,[39] may diminish meeting this goal. Consequently, employers should, through feedback mechanisms, assess how employees perceive the usefulness of employee handbook information, gather their input, and make modifications where necessary.[40] HRM should not assume that once developed and disseminated to employees, the employee handbook is final. Rather, it should be viewed as something to be updated and refined on a continuous basis. Employers often find that using some sort of loose-leaf binder system more readily allows for corrections/updates/additions.[41]

As a second requirement, it is recommended that the handbook be well organized to make it easy to find the needed information.[42] Just as this book has a

> The employee handbook serves to ensure that any HRM policy is fair and equitable, and consistently applied.

Exhibit 15-2

A sample employee handbook disclaimer.

This handbook is not a contract, expressed or implied, guaranteeing employment for any specific duration. Although [the company] hopes that your employment relationship with us will be long-term, either you or the company may terminate this relationship at any time, for any reason, with or without cause of notice.

A well-designed, well-written employee handbook should convey such information as:

1. **What the organization expects from its employees.** Employees need to be informed of company policies. This includes such items as work hours, employee conduct, performance evaluations, disciplinary process, moonlighting, vacations, holiday, and sick and personal leave usage.
2. **What the employee can expect from the organization.** What benefits does the employee receive? These should be detailed enough such that the employee fully understands the "fringes" of the job. The company's HRM policies regarding salary increases, promotions, and so on, also need to be conveyed.
3. **The history of the organization.** The history section provides an opportunity to help employees understand where the organization has been, and where it is heading. This section also includes the philosophy/culture of the organization.
4. **A glossary section.** Words have different meanings to different people, and may differ depending on the context used. To eliminate confusion, the terms used in the handbook should be defined.

SOURCE: Adapted from "The (Handbook) Handbook: A Guide to Writing the Perfect Manual for Employees You Care About," *Inc.* (November 1993), pp. 60–61.

Exhibit 15-3

Suggested do's for an employee handbook.

table of contents and an index to help you find specific information more quickly, so too should the employee handbook. HRM must remember that the handbook will be helpful to employees, and it must do whatever possible to make it easy to use. To assist in achieving this goal, we have summarized some "Do's" for employee handbooks in Exhibit 15-3.

Contents of an Employee Handbook

Although there are no right or wrong ways of putting together the contents of an employee handbook, there is a recommended format.[43] As a means of facilitating this discussion, we will present an outline from an actual employee handbook (see Exhibit 15-4). Let's look at these components.

Introductory Comments   In this section, the company conveys various introductory information to the employees. Carroll Tree Service begins by having its top management send a letter of greetings to the employees, welcoming them into the organization. The purpose of this letter is to describe to employees what the company is about, its mission and goals. Furthermore, the company conveys to its employees the corporate value of customer satisfaction, and how by achieving that goal the firm can provide those things that employees may desire (e.g., job security, pay increases, better benefits).

These introductory remarks also tell new employees that they are valuable assets to the organization. By making employees feel important, and letting them know the roles they play and what the company will do to help them grow as employees, the organization fosters an environment where effective worker performance and loyalty and commitment can be realized.

There is often a final component to this introductory section, that is, a brief history of the organization. Although not all employees will value this information, it does provide them with a better understanding of how the company progressed to its current state.[44]

Exhibit 15-4
Sample employee handbook table of contents.

(Effective February 1998—Carroll Tree Service)

What You Should Know This section is designed to inform all employees of the rules and policies regarding employment in the company. Those items of importance to employees, such as attendance, work hours, and so forth, are presented so that there is no misunderstanding by employees. For example, in this company, specific information regarding the length of one's lunch period, paydays, work hours, and how employees will be evaluated is laid out in such clear terms that confusion is avoided.

In Chapter 12, on performance appraisals, we discussed the need for managers to explicitly state what is required of employees. If, for example, you expect employees on the job by 8 A.M., tell them so, and hold employees accountable for being on time. The handbook, then, reinforces those work behaviors a company expects of its employees.

Your Benefits   No matter how much value we place on the introductory re-marks of any employee handbook, the section on employee benefits is proba-bly the most widely read and perceived most important by employees. This sec-tion should thoroughly explain the benefits employees receive, when they are eligible (if not immediately), and what, if any, costs the employee might incur. As we explained in Chapter 14 on employee benefits, although these benefits are membership-based, they are important to keep employee morale high. Therefore, we must make every effort to convey the full slate of benefits to em-ployees in such a manner that they know what they have, and how they can use them.

Your Responsibility and Safety Procedures   Just as employers are respon-sible for creating a safe and healthy workplace, workers must also do their part. Accordingly, this section of Carroll Tree's handbook provides information re-garding company policies on reporting accidents, alcohol and substance abuse, and personal conduct, among others, explained in such terms that employees know what compliance requires. Furthermore, failure to comply with these policies and subsequent outcomes is thoroughly explained.

Other Vehicles for Employee Communications

In the spirit of finding various ways to ensure that communication takes place, there are a number of other means available besides the employee hand-book. The following sections discuss the four most popular means: bulletin boards, company newsletters, company-wide meetings, and electronic media. Of course, which one works best for any group of employees will depend on such factors as what the employees prefer, the organization culture, and the em-ployees' access to technology.

Bulletin Boards

A **bulletin board** in any organization serves several purposes in communi-cating with employees. Bulletin boards are generally centrally located in the or-ganization where a majority of employees will have exposure to it. For many, these bulletin boards are found near company cafeterias (if they exist), or by the main entrance.

The information posted on a bulletin board will vary among organizations. Job postings, upcoming company-sponsored events, new HRM policies, and the like may be posted in this highly visible location to help "get the information out." Furthermore, if employees know that important information is placed on these boards, they will be more inclined to examine them periodically. Bulletin boards also can be used for activities other than employer-related business. For instance, some organizations permit employees to post information for other employees to see—like advertising personal belongings for sale, or promoting a charitable event an employee is associated with. Although the information employees place on the bulletin board is given great latitude, most organiza-tions require such information to have HRM approval before it is posted. By fol-lowing this procedure, inappropriate or offensive information can be eliminated before any problems arise.

Company Newsletter

The **company newsletter** or newspaper is designed to provide sound internal communication to employees regarding important information they need to know, activities happening in the organization, and anything else of interest.[45] Just as a town's daily newspaper discusses current events, sports, and human-interest stories, so too should the company newsletter. Company newsletters provide employees with a permanent record they can keep and refer to at some future time. Furthermore, some information, like technical and detailed information, may be better communicated in this written format.

While there is no definitive design for company newsletters, they should focus attention on activities of concern to employees of the company, problems the company may be experiencing, successes the company has enjoyed, updates on newsworthy company items (such as company-sponsored sporting events and United Way campaigns), and stories about employees (those receiving awards, recognition, retiring, etc.). Company newsletters also can be enhanced with sections devoted to questions raised by employees and answered by someone in management, and by having employees writing articles.[46] Finally, those organizations that have effective newsletters have found that they have improved employee morale.[47]

Company-Wide Meetings

Every so often, there is a need to inform all employees at once in a face-to-face encounter. Should an organization be facing a merger, going into a new product line, or changing its culture, for example, it may be useful for the CEO to address all employees en masse. In doing so, the CEO can add emphasis to this new direction, while simultaneously answering questions and addressing concerns.

One of the most notable uses of this "town meeting" was the company-wide session held by former GM Chairman Robert Stemple. Faced with pending layoffs and restructuring, Stemple, through electronic hook-ups, was able to send his message to all GM employees at once, wherever the plant was located. The success of this method has been periodically repeated at GM.

In addition to opening up the channels of communications for employees, **company-wide meetings** permit all employees to have the same information at once. This, for many operations, reduces the grapevine rumors that may occur, especially when the company is facing difficult times.[48]

The Electronic Media

Technology has served organizational communications well. Whether it be the Internet, an Intranet (similar to the Internet but confined solely to an organization's network), an interactive video, or having access to e-mail, technology is enhancing the effectiveness of communications.[49] And this technology is no more noteworthy than in HRM.

Whenever a company wishes to provide employees with up-to-date, even real-time information regarding their pay and benefits, nothing serves that purpose better than the **electronic media.** For AT&T and IBM, this has meant developing an in-house television station.[50] Through their television stations, these companies are able to send information faster and with less chance of distraction. At Levi Strauss, the company has greatly expanded the use of personal computers to assist employees in getting up-to-date information on their compensation packages.[51] Through the system called Oliver, employees can access their records to gain information on such topics as "compensation, disability insurance, health care, pension employee investment plans, and survivor benefits." [52] Workers also can use this system to "obtain financial projections regarding future income and retirement benefits, as well as getting information on upcoming training and development workshops." [53] Through computers, flexible benefits programs can also be better implemented, giving employees opportunities to examine what is offered to find what will best serve them.[54] Such computerized systems can be used to provide employees with personalized benefits statements.[55] Not only do these statements provide employees information on their selections, they also reinforce the "hidden pay" they are receiving.[56]

COMMUNICATIONS AND THE OFF-SITE EMPLOYEE

Communications in many of today's organizations no longer follow the traditional downward or upward flows so typical of hierarchical organizations. Instead, as our work changes, as well as our work force, communication mechanisms, too, must adapt. As we described in Chapter 2, the trend today is the movement to the off-site worker. Worker needs, coupled with technology advancements, have enabled some workers to work at home. How, then, can effective communications be fostered with off-site employees? The answer typically lies in the technology that has become routine today—facsimile (fax) machines, the Internet, and e-mail (see Exhibit 15-5).

With the use of home computer systems, employees can remain in close contact with their employers, even though they are miles away. For instance,

One means of informing employees is through the use of telecommunications. Here, these employees at Sprint are exposed to information broadcast on the company's Intranet. Moreover, employees have a moderator who is available to answer questions regarding the message being sent.

Exhibit 15-5

Electronic mail.

Source: Scott Adams, United Feature Syndicate, Inc., 12/11/95. Used with permission.

modems can be used to receive and transmit data to main-frame computers at a company location. Data downloaded to an employee can be properly manipulated, and sent back to the organization in its final form. Where electronic wires won't do, fax machines can send documents in hard copy formats almost instantaneously to anywhere in the world. E-mail allows written messages to be sent between parties that have computers that are linked together with an appropriate software. They are fast, cheap, and permit the reader to retrieve the message at his or her convenience. And let's not forget the old standby, the telephone. It has been around for decades and is still an effective way to communicate with employees.

We know that communication to our employees is important, in whatever form, but there still remains one final aspect to be addressed: Is there a mechanism in the organization that allows employees to raise their concerns? In the next section, we'll briefly look at employee complaint and suggestion systems.

MECHANISMS FOR EFFECTIVE UPWARD COMMUNICATIONS

Any communications system operating in an organization will only be effective if it permits information to flow upward. For HRM, enabling this process revolves around two central themes—complaint procedures and a suggestion system.[57]

The Complaint Procedure

An organization's **complaint procedure** is designed to permit employees to question actions that have occurred in the company, and to seek the company's assistance in correcting the problem (see Meet Ray Gameson). For example, if the employee feels her boss has inappropriately evaluated her performance, or believes the behavior of the boss to be counterproductive, a complaint process allows for that information to be heard. Typically under the direction of employee-relations specialists, complaints are investigated, and decisions regarding the validity of the alleged wrongdoings are made.

Complaint procedures implemented in nonunionized organizations are called by a variety of titles. Irrespective of their names, most follow a set pattern; that is, given the structure of HRM laid out in Chapter 1, a nonunionized complaint procedure may consist of the following:

RAY GAMESON
Sr. Vice President Human Resources
Pilgrim's Pride Corporation

Since his promotion to Senior Vice President of Human Resources at Pilgrim's Pride Corporation, Gameson has focused on enhancing the *company/employee relationship.* Giving the over ten thousand employees, called Partners, a process by which they can challenge management decisions has helped. The process, called the Dispute Resolution Procedure, offers Partners a forum in which they can air their differences without fear of reprisal. Partners are encouraged to first try to solve problems with their immediate supervisor. If that is unsuccessful, or for some reason it is not practical to address the issue with the supervisor, the Partner is directed up the organizational structure by no more than two levels to seek a resolution. If the Partner is not satisfied after meeting with these managers, he/she may take the problem to the Partner Review Committee.

Each location has a Partner Review Committee. The committee has five voting members; three hourly Partners and two members of management. A representative from human resources acts as facilitator and advisor on personnel policy issues, but has no vote. Committee members are carefully selected. Three years of company service is a requirement, as well as having a satisfactory work history. At one-year intervals, members are rotated on and off the committee. New members come from the plant floor as well as offices, and are a reflection of the company's *ethnic* diversity. Prospective committee members observe for some time before they are officially on the team.

Initiated in March, 1994, the procedure has been utilized regularly to solve employment-related issues before they escalate or are taken outside the company. The committee's decision is final and never has management overruled a committee decision. Just having the committee in place has an influence on management actions. No manager is an *island;* any disciplinary decision may eventually be evaluated by the committee, and no one wants a bad decision publicized.

Another Pilgrim's Pride program that has paid big dividends in employee relations is their Chaplaincy service called "Pilgrim's Cares." For this service, Pilgrims contracts with Marketplace Ministries, Inc., of Dallas, Texas, a nationwide EAP provider. Fifty-six full-time Chaplains are assigned to aid and comfort Partners and their family members in times of need. These Chaplains are available to any Pilgrim's Pride Partner or family member 24 hours a day, 365 days a year. These interdenominational Chaplains visit work sites daily and maintain an off-site office for confidential conversations. Nothing told to a Chaplain is revealed to management of Pilgrim's Pride unless the Partner specifically requests it. Since its inception in 1990, Pilgrim's Chaplains have logged over 35,000 work site visits, performed over 100 marriages, conducted over 100 funerals and participated in thousands of formal and informal consultations.

Not only a benefit of Pilgrim's Partners and their families; the chaplaincy service has proved to be valuable to management as well. Without breaking confidentiality, the Chaplains let management know what the issues are that affect their Partners on and off the job. Management decisions are often made as the result of feedback from the Chaplains. Pilgrims realizes that problems in one's personal life roll over to the job and it is impossible to give 100 percent at work when one's personal problems seem unmanageable. The Chaplains are an ever present helping hand and one of Pilgrim's Pride's most valued benefits.

Through these two programs, Pilgrim's Pride has done a lot to bridge the gap that often exists between management and the rest of the organization. The results are win–win all the way for Pilgrim's Pride and the Pilgrim's Pride Partners.

Step 1: Employee–supervisor. This is generally regarded as the initial step to resolve an employee problem. Here, the employee tries to address the issue with her supervisor, seeking some resolution. If the issue is resolved here, nothing further need be done. Accordingly, this is considered an informal step in the process. Furthermore, depending on the problem, this step may be skipped altogether, should the employee fear retaliation from the supervisor.

Step 2: Employee–employer relations. Not getting the satisfaction desired in Step 1, the employee then proceeds to file the complaint with the employee-relations representative. As part of his or her job, the ER representative investigates the matter, including gathering information from both par-

Handling Warring Workers Takes Calm Understanding

In a perfect workplace there would be no conflict, just happy people with no hidden agendas, no difference in opinion, values, work ethic, wants or needs. No finger pointing, blaming, misunderstanding or gossiping would occur. No one would question or criticize their boss, co-workers, company, decisions or changes, just happy little workers exceeding expectations. Noncommunicative, hostile, negative, judgmental, uncooperative people would always work somewhere else, not in your company.

In our dreams. How many job descriptions have you ever read that made "getting along" or "service" a requirement? Attitude may show up on the performance appraisal, but it's hard to change attitudes once or twice a year. Why shouldn't "getting along" be a job requirement? Maybe "adult behavior" won't likely be added to the next revised performance appraisal, but we can emphasize the importance of maintaining acceptable standards of cooperation and civility to reduce some conflict.

When conflicts affect performance, morale or teamwork, they are no longer just the problems of those involved; they become the manager's problem too. As uncomfortable as such squabbling or politicking makes us, well, conflict resolution is a tough job, but somebody has got to do it. Conflict is normal; it's inevitable. How many courses did you take in school that helped you deal with conflict or even address feelings? Psychology 101 or Introductory Sociology isn't enough.

Now more than any time in history we must not only get along with our fellow employees, we must work in the most collaborative, professional manner possible to achieve more, with fewer people and resources. Survival in this competitive environment demands unparalleled service, innovation and quality achieved through teamwork and communication. It means putting the goals, issues and needs of our employing organizations above our own agendas; getting along with people that we may not even like, understand or respect; focusing on what we get paid to do; achieving the goals and objectives of our organization in the most responsive, professional manner possible. We're paid not just to deliver on time, error-free goods and services, we're also paid to respect differences, to not allow our emotions to get in the way of what's best for the company, to honor a fellow employee's self-respect and dignity, even when we differ in values, methods or purpose.

It's hard not to lose our tempers at times, to address a person's behavior and not their personality, to seek win/win resolutions when we find it difficult to find points of agreement, especially when we know we're right, and of course, they're wrong. Most of us could stand to learn or improve our conflict resolution skills. If we must deal with feuding co-workers, let's try one or more of the following suggestions:

1. Let them vent. Listen to each party separately without taking sides until you have both perceptions and all the facts. Just listen. You may find it helpful to ask each to write their perception of the situation down and give it to you before you meet with them to compare perceptions of both parties involved. We have worked with clients whose written descriptions of the same situation were so different it was hard to imagine it could have occurred at the same company.

2. Separate them, if needed or possible, initially from meetings or projects to allow cool-down time and to minimize damage.

3. Ask them for their perception or description of the situation, what they think, how they feel, what impact the current situation has on them, their projects, department, etc. Ask who, what, when, where, why and how questions. For example, what they think is the cause, who is affected or contributes to the situation, when it occurs, how often, why it occurred, etc. Most importantly, involve the parties in the resolution, ask them what they think could resolve it, what they are willing to do to bring the resolution about. Then hold them accountable for following through the resolution.

4. Not through. Create a teaching moment on how to improve or prevent the situation from occurring. If others need to be included in sharing the resolution, do so, without blaming name calling. Consider it a growth opportunity.

5. Reinforce and recognize the positive efforts of the parties as they improve the situation. Nothing stays the same, and this conflict may be that golden opportunity to shake the status quo, to build rapport and ultimately morale, relations, and end results. Understanding breeds acceptance and confidence, not only to feuding parties, but to those of us who foster such resolutions.

DR. CONNIE SITTERLY, CPCM

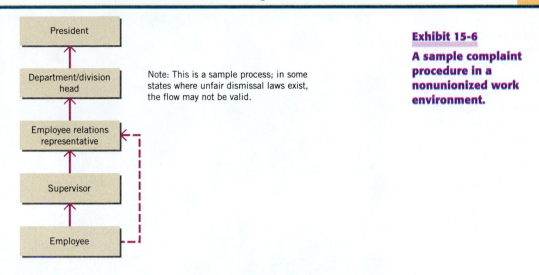

Note: This is a sample process; in some states where unfair dismissal laws exist, the flow may not be valid.

Exhibit 15-6

A sample complaint procedure in a nonunionized work environment.

ties, and makes a recommendation for resolution. Although this is the first formal step, the employee may continue upward, should the recommended solution be unsatisfactory to the employee.

Step 3: Employee–department head. If employee relations fails to correct the problem, or if the employee wishes to further exercise her rights, the next step in the complaint procedure is to meet with the manager of the area. Once again, an investigation will take place and a decision rendered. It is important to note, however, that if employee relations found no validity in the individual's charge, they are not responsible for providing continued assistance to the employee.

Step 4: Employee–president. The final step in the process involves taking the issue to the president. Generally, although employee rights may be protected under various state laws, the president's decision is final.

Inasmuch as this is a generic portrayal of a complaint process, it is important to recognize that this serves as the foundation of an internal complaint procedure. We have graphically portrayed these steps in Exhibit 15-6. Keep in mind that in actuality, more levels of management could be included in the picture. In either case, however, employees must be notified that this is how the company will resolve employee complaints. And this communication should occur initially during orientation, appear in employee handbooks, and be posted throughout the company.

Finally, we mentioned that this process is generally useful in nonunionized settings. Why not in a unionized company? The answer to that question lies in the various labor laws that are unique to labor–management relationships. Although there is a complaint procedure, called a grievance procedure, its uniqueness requires us to discuss it as part of the "Collective Bargaining Process" (Chapter 16).

The Suggestion Program

Similar to the complaint procedure, a **suggestion program** is designed to allow employees opportunities to tell management what it is doing inefficiently and what the company should do from an employee's point of view. That is,

How do organizations like the Dana Company promote innovation, creativity, and enhanced productivity? Many of them have found employee suggestion programs quite useful. Whether formalized like they are at Dana, or handled informally, most suggestion programs provide a financial reward for employees who nominate cost-saving ideas.

Suggestion programs give employees the chance to tell management what they are doing right, and what they are doing wrong.

suggestion programs give employees the chance to tell management "what they are doing right, and what they are doing wrong." [58] In many companies, in conjunction with continuous improvement processes and employee involvement, management welcomes such suggestions.[59] In fact, as we discussed in Chapter 12, companies such as Lincoln Electric, and those that use plans such as Scanlon or IMPROSHARE, actually provide cash rewards to employees for suggestions that are implemented. The same holds true at the Dana Company, where more than 650,000 suggestions are received each year from its 45,000 employees. And more than 70 percent of the suggestions are accepted—saving the company hundreds of thousands of dollars.[60]

Although employees value the "reward," the most important aspect of a suggestion program is for individuals to witness management action.[61] That is, whether the suggestion is useful or not, employers must recognize employees submitting suggestions and inform them of their outcome. Even if the idea wasn't appropriate for the company, employees still should be told what management's decision was. Failure to do so will more than likely decrease employees' willingness to make suggestions. And if the suggestion is good, in the spirit of employee communication, not only reward them, but recognize their input in the company's next newsletter!

SUMMARY

This summary relates to the Learning Objectives provided on p. 456.

After reading this chapter, you should know:

1. Effective communication surrounds the effective operations in HRM activities in that it enables understanding to occur between the organization and its

employees, assists in recruiting and selection, and specifies what activities must be performed to successfully perform one's job. Effective communication also implies keeping employees informed of happenings in the organization.

2. Communications in benefits administration and

health and safety is mandated by law. In benefits administration, employers must provide employees with a summary plan description. In health and safety, employees must be given information concerning exposure to hazardous and toxic materials.

3. Human resources management communication programs are designed to keep current employees abreast of events occurring in the organization, including the various policies and procedures that affect them.

4. Effective communications can affect corporate culture in that open, frank discussions indicate a culture where employees are valued.

5. The CEO of an organization is the one individual responsible for setting the foundation from which the culture is built. If this individual promotes and practices open communications, then that activity will filter down through the company.

6. A communication program should, at the minimum, inform employees what is expected of them, what they can expect from the company, and what the various personnel policies are.

7. The employee handbook is a tool that provides one central source of organizational information for employees regarding the company and its HRM policies.

8. Although employee handbooks differ, most include introductory comments about the organization, information about what employees need to know about the workplace, their benefits, and employee responsibility.

9. Four popular means of communication program vehicles include bulletin boards, company newsletters, company-wide meetings, and electronic media (such as e-mail, Internet, and Intranet).

10. A critical component of an organizational suggestion program is the recognition that employees' suggestions will be heard. Failure to pay attention to employees' suggestions may decrease the value of the program to them.

EXPERIENTIAL EXERCISE
On-Site Visits

Individual, team, or class visit

1. Visit two manufacturing plants or organizations with over 50 employees and read and compare their bulletin boards and observe items posted on their walls. Discuss what you learned about the culture as well as how the walls and boards were used for employee communication.

2. Do you see suggestion forms?

3. What types of communication examples do you see?

4. Do the communications seem updated and written for employees?

5. What do the communications reveal about the culture of the company?

6. Do you see photographs of employees or employee teams on the walls?

7. Read the federal and state posters on the wall.

8. Are the communications available in languages besides English?

9. Are managers and supervisors accessible to employees?

10. Does the communication seem more formal or informal?

Prepare a one-page (minimum) report of your impressions to share with your team and class.

WEB-WISE EXERCISES

Watch live audio, video, and multimedia clips of press conferences and corporate presentations from the CNBC/Dow Jones (Business Video) Web site www.cnbc-dowjones.com.

CASE APPLICATION:
Suggestions

During a training session, "Quality Improvement," the trainer asked if there was a formal suggestion. A participant, Donnie Williams, who was a machinist with the 50-year-old manufacturer, replied no, but it sounded like a good idea. The machinist, as a result of the training, formed a suggestion benchmarking team to visit different organizations and discuss the process, types of forms and tracking systems used, and their challenges in communicating the status as well as their successes. Six months later, a suggestion system was proposed to the organization's executive committee, comprised of managers and union representatives who agreed to implement the proposed system with some changes. It was approved without standards for accountabilities, or support of management. Some suggestions pended for over six months, and a few for over a year! The 22 suggestions that were followed through implementation saved over $100,000 for the company and points were awarded.

Comments from some managers included:

"But can we really afford pizza?"
"I don't have time—ask somebody else."
"I haven't had time to calculate if the figures are right."
"I thought of that some time ago."
"That's too much money to give someone for a suggestion."

"Why should someone get paid or points for gifts for making a suggestion?"

Comments from some employees included:

"What good will it do, I've told them before"

"My supervisor will take the credit"

"My supervisor wouldn't approve it because he wouldn't want anyone to know how we're doing it now"

"These things come and go"

Questions

1. What type of standards or accountabilities or support from management could be helpful to ensure that suggestions are followed-up in a consistent, timely manner?

2. What happens when someone makes a suggestion and they do not hear a timely decision?

3. How would you respond to the comments from managers if you were on the suggestion team?

4. How would you respond to the comments from employees if you were on the suggestion team?

5. How could the suggestions be followed-up to ensure the supervisor was the first to review and implement if possible, but that the president was also aware of all suggestions?

6. If you were a human resource manager, would you implement a suggestion system? Why or why not? Describe.

TESTING YOUR UNDERSTANDING

How well did you fulfill the learning objectives?

1. Effective communication is an important contributor to successful work-force diversity because
   a. it lets minority workers know that the company will make every attempt to provide them equal opportunity in the organization.
   b. it ensures realistic job previews.
   c. it helps employees understand how to do their jobs.
   d. it helps employees understand the relationship between their efforts and individual goal attainment.
   e. it helps to increase positive outcomes for interactions between managers and their employees.

2. Human resource management communications programs are designed to
   a. keep employees knowledgeable about policies and procedures affecting customers.
   b. keep customers informed about policies and programs designed to increase service.
   c. keep employees knowledgeable about policies and programs affecting them.
   d. keep customers informed about policies and programs affecting employees.

e. improve interactions between employees and their managers.

3. How does HRM communication affect corporate culture?
   a. HRM communications do not affect corporate culture.
   b. HRM communications can be used to state corporate culture effectively.
   c. HRM communications often replace corporate culture in large, hierarchical organizations.
   d. A free-flowing, timely, and accurate HRM communications system can help to build trust.
   e. A free-flowing, timely, and accurate HRM communications system can help to improve productivity.

4. A CEO of a 300-employee electronics manufacturer had just been convinced by her vice president of human resources that an "open door" management policy would help to improve worker morale. Agreeing to the idea, how can she best show support for this program?
   a. Support can be shown by "opening" her own door to employees.
   b. Support can be shown by making a video to endorse the program to be shown to all employees.
   c. Support can be shown by announcing the program herself, over the company address system.
   d. Support can be shown by writing a column endorsing the new system for the next issue of the company newsletter.
   e. Support can be shown by feigning ignorance of the new program.

5. Why is upward communication important in empowered organizations?
   a. Upward communication is the definition of an empowered work force.
   b. Empowered employees make more decisions about how to do their work. These decisions need to be communicated to top management.
   c. Workers feel empowered when they can communicate with top management.
   d. There is no upward communication in empowered organizations. Top management has been removed, and most decisions are made by individuals closest to the problem.
   e. Customer information and satisfaction are top priorities in an empowered organization.

6. A well-written employee handbook will provide all of these benefits to the organization except
   a. create an atmosphere in which employees become more productive.
   b. create an atmosphere in which employee commitment is increased.
   c. create a sense of security for employees.
   d. provide an implied employment contract.
   e. provide a source of information for many employee work-related questions.

7. A small, family-run electronics firm has just been acquired by an aggressive transnational organization. What is the best way to inform employees?
   a. employee handbook
   b. bulletin board
   c. company-wide meeting
   d. company newsletter
   e. electronic media

8. If you have a complaint about the grade you receive in this course, who should you go to first?
   a. the professor
   b. the department chairperson who is the "boss" of the professor
   c. the dean of the school in which the professor teaches
   d. your academic advisor
   e. another professor

9. Compare suggestion programs and complaint processes.
   a. Suggestion programs are found only in union shops. Complaint processes are found only in nonunion shops.
   b. Both suggestion programs and complaint processes allow the upward flow of information in an organization.
   c. Suggestion programs allow employees to tell management what it is doing right. Complaint processes allow employees to tell management what it is doing wrong.
   d. Suggestion programs target individual performance. Complaint processes target group performance.
   e. Suggestion program events are initiated by managers. Complaint process events are initiated by employees.

10. Effective communication is an important contributor to the recruiting and selection process because
    a. it lets minority workers know that the company will make every attempt to provide them equal opportunity in the organization.
    b. it helps to increase positive outcomes for interactions between managers and their employees.
    c. it helps employees understand how to do their jobs.
    d. it helps employees understand the relationship between their efforts and individual goal attainment.
    e. it ensures realistic job previews.

11. The Summary Plan Description is all of the following except
    a. a presentation of ERISA rights.
    b. a presentation of OSHA requirements.
    c. information about pensions.
    d. a statement of updated benefits accumulations.
    e. required by law.

12. Diane has just been promoted to director of HRM communications. She is writing a mission statement for her department. What item should be included?

a. departmental reason for its existence and what services it will provide to the organization.
b. organizational policies and programs for retirement options and financial planning.
c. organizational efforts to assist in improving interactions between employees and their managers.
d. departmental issues regarding benefits and services provided to employees.
e. organizational policies and programs regarding achieving excellence in customer services.

13. If new HRM communications programs are endorsed by top management,
    a. they are bound to fail.
    b. they are viewed as significant components of corporate culture.
    c. they are more slowly accepted by the rest of the organization.
    d. they are viewed with suspicion by the rest of the organization.
    e. they replace the authority of the top management.

14. All of the following questions are appropriate for managers to use in determining how to filter information to their employees except
    a. Will my employees be able to do their jobs as well if this information is not shared?
    b. Will my employees be disadvantaged in some way by not knowing this information?
    c. Will employees care about the information?
    d. Will my employees think badly of me for telling them?
    e. Will my employees view this information as information overload?

15. Employee handbooks should convey all of this information except
    a. specific wage and salary information.
    b. what the company expects of its employees.
    c. what the company history is.
    d. why individuals would want to work for the company.
    e. what the company's mission is.

16. There has been a lot of confusion lately about the corporate policy on sexual harassment. One of the human resource managers is willing to write a question and answer column to deal with the subject. What is the best way to share this column?
    a. employee handbook
    b. bulletin board
    c. company newsletter
    d. company-wide meeting
    e. electronic media

Endnotes

1. "The (Handbook) Handbook: A Guide to Writing the Perfect Manual for Employees You Care About," *Inc.* (November 1993), pp. 63–64.

2. Jean-Anne Jordan, "Clear Speaking Improves Career Prospects," *HRMagazine* (June 1996), p. 75.

3. Mary V. Williams, "Managing Work-Place Diversity: The Wave of the '90s," *Communication World* (January 1990), p. 16.

4. See "Tell Employees: Summary Plan Descriptions," *Employee Benefit Plan Review* (May 1991), pp. 23–26.

5. William Briggs, "Taking Control after a Crisis," *HRMagazine* (March 1990), p. 60.

6. Michelle Neely Martinez, "Break the Bad Attitude Habit," *HRMagazine* (July 1997), p. 55; and Thomas A. Stewart, "The Search for the Organization of Tomorrow," *Fortune* (May 18, 1992), pp. 91–92.

7. Karen M. Kroll, "By the Books," *Industry Week* (July 21, 1997), pp. 47–50.

8. Elizabeth Coleman, "Communication: A Precursor for the New Industrial Environment," *Work and People* (March 1991), pp. 17–21.

9. Richard G. Charlton, "The Decade of the Employee," *Public Relations Journal* (January 1990), p. 26.

10. Ibid. and Martha Finney, "Will Fiery Headlines Make Your Firm's Morale Go Up in Smoke," *HRMagazine* (July 1997), p. 95.

11. Julie Foehrenback and Steve Goldfarb, "Employee Communication in the '90s: Great(er) Expectation," *Communication World* (May–June 1990), pp. 101–106.

12. Alvie L. Smith, "Bridging the Gap between Employees and Management," *Public Relations Journal* (November 1990), p. 20.

13. Jerry Beilinson, "Communicating Bad News," *Personnel* (January 1991), p. 15.

14. Leslie Lamkin and Emily W. Carmain, "Crisis in Communications at Georgia Power," *Personnel Journal* (January 1991), p. 35.

15. Ibid., p. 36.

16. See Brad Whitworth, "Proof at Last," *Communication World* (December 1990), pp. 28–31.

17. Commerce Clearing House, "Challenger Meets Employee Communication Challenge with Merit Plan," *Human Resources Management: Ideas and Trends* (April 13, 1994), p. 61.

18. James V. O'Connor, "Building Internal Communications," *Public Relations Journal* (June 1990), p. 29.

19. See Pamela K. Cook, "Employee Communications in the United States: What Works, and Why," *Benefits and Compensation International* (June 1991), pp. 2–5.

20. Adapted from David K. Lindo, "They're Supposed to Know," *Supervisor* (March 1992), pp. 14–17.

21. Walter H. Read, "Gathering Opinion On-Line," *HRMagazine* (January 1991), pp. 51–52.

22. David N. Bateman, "Communications," *Human Resource Management: Ideas and Trends* (Chicago: Commerce Clearing House, Inc., July 26, 1988), p. 128.

23. Smith.

24. Bateman.

25. McKeand, p.26.

26. Bateman.

27. Whitworth, p. 28.

28. Randal G. Hesser, *Nation's Business* (December 1989), p. 50.

29. Roderick Wilkinson, "All-Purpose Employee Handbook," *Supervision* (January 1992), p. 5.

30. Lori Block, "Texas Utility Effort Shines among Benefit Handbooks," *Business Insurance* (November 18, 1991), p. 63.

31. Ibid.

32. See, for example, Robert J. Nobile, "Leaving No Doubt About Employee Leaves," *Personnel* (May 1990), pp. 54–60.

33. Ibid.

34. Ibid.

35. Paula Cohen and Robert J. Nobile, "Confessions of a Handbook Writer, Say It Legally," *Personnel* (May 1991), p. 9.

36. See Randall G. Hesser, "Watch Your Language," *Small Business Reports* (July 1991), pp. 45–49.

37. See Cohen and Nobile; Elliot H. Shaller, "Avoiding the Pitfalls in Hiring, Firing," *Nation's Business* (February 1991), pp. 51–54; and Pamela R. Johnson and Susan Gardner, "Legal Pitfalls of Employee Handbooks," *Advanced Management Journal* (Spring 1989), pp. 42–46.

38. Wilkinson.

39. Marilyn Melia, "Mergers, New Laws Spur Rewrites of Employee Handbooks," *Savings Institutions* (April 1992), p. 47.

40. See Bruce G. Posner, "The Best Little Handbook in Texas," *Inc.* (February 1989), pp. 84–88.

41. Ibid., p. 6.

42. Cohen and Nobile.

43. This format is adapted from the compilation of data presented in Commerce Clearing House, "What Should Be in the Handbook?" *Topical Law Reports* (Chicago: Commerce Clearing House, Inc., October 1990), pp. 5451–5476.

44. Donna Fenn, "Communication: Tell It Like It Was," *Inc.* (January 1995), p. 95.

45. See Linda Lee Brubaker, "Six Secrets for a Great Employee Newsletter," *Management Review* (January 1990), pp. 47–50.

46. Art Durity, "Confessions of a Newsletter Editor," *Personnel* (May 1991), p. 7; see also Brubaker.

47. Betty Sosnin, "Corporate Newsletters Improve Employee Morale," *HRMagazine* (June 1996), pp. 106–110.

48. Suellyn McMillian, "Squelching the Rumor Mill," *Personnel Journal* (October 1991), pp. 95–101.

49. See, for example, Martha I. Finney, "Harness the Power Within," *HRMagazine* (January 1997), pp. 69–71.

50. Karen Matthes, "Corporate Television Catches Employees' Eyes," *Personnel* (May 1991), p. 3.

51. Jennifer J. Laabs, "Oliver: A Twist on Communications," *Personnel Journal* (September 1991), p. 79.

52. Ibid.

53. Ibid., p. 81.

54. See, for example, Peter D. Bergh, "Ten Steps for Communicating Flex Benefits," *HRMagazine* (April 1991), p. 47.

55. Gayle Potter, "Personalized Benefits Statements," *HRMagazine* (May 1991), p. 23.

56. Ibid., p. 25.

57. Denis Detzel, "Their Employees Tend to Report That Management Listens to 'Problems and Complaints,'" in *Human Resources Management: Ideas and Trends* (Chicago: Commerce Clearing House, Inc., February 21, 1990), p. 39.

58. Ibid.

59. See, for example, Phyllis Kane, "Two-Way Communication Fosters Greater Commitment," *HRMagazine* (October 1996), pp. 50–52; and Pamela Bloch-Flynn and Kenneth Vlach, "Employee Awareness Paves the Way for Quality," *HRMagazine* (July 1994), p. 78.

60. Richard Teitelbaum, "How to Harness Gray Matter," *Fortune* (June 9, 1997), p. 168.

61. Ibid., p. 58.

16. Labor Relations and Collective Bargaining

LEARNING OBJECTIVES

After reading this chapter, you will be able to:

1. Define what is meant by the term *unions.*

2. Discuss what effect the Wagner and the Taft-Hartley Acts had on labor–management relations.

3. Identify the significance of Executive Orders 10988 and 11491, and the Civil Service Reform Act of 1978.

4. Describe the union organizing process.

5. Describe the components of collective bargaining.

6. Identify the steps in the collective bargaining process.

7. Explain the various types of union security arrangements.

8. Describe the role of a grievance procedure in collective bargaining.

9. Identify the various impasse resolution techniques.

10. Discuss how sunshine laws affect public sector collective bargaining.

One of the fundamental issues in labor–management relationships is that both sides will come to the bargaining table and negotiate. In fact, some labor laws mandate this, as they require both unions and management to negotiate in good faith. Good-faith bargaining requires both sides to willingly work toward a settlement. That is, their efforts must be viewed as having a positive influence on the process—toward the ultimate goal of reaching an agreement. But good-faith bargaining does not guarantee that this agreement will be reached. On the contrary, serious disagreements do arise at times, resulting in negotiations breaking off. That's all part of the process—and it's precisely what occurred between United Parcel Service (UPS) and the Teamsters Union.[1]

These UPS employees cheer after hearing that their negotiations have ended in a "victory" for them. They will have more full-time jobs created, higher wages, and for the first time in nearly two decades, have witnessed public support for their strike.

Since the mid-1960s, UPS has been a leading company involved in moving ground parcels from one location to another. In fact, during their first decade of existence, UPS had little to no competition—only the U.S. Postal System handled similar activities. Undoubtedly, given the service problems associated with the Post Office, coupled with the ability of UPS to ensure delivery, the company grew. But with this growth came competition. Companies like RPS soon found that there was plenty of money to make in this industry. And then Federal Express entered the picture with their guaranteed overnight service, which significantly changed how companies like UPS, RPS, or FedEx function. Yet in spite of stiff competition, UPS has held its ground. As mail-order businesses flourished, their number one choice for delivery was often UPS.

Maintaining their competitive advantage has for the past two decades been a major concern for UPS management. The company employs more than 250,000 individuals. More than 185,000 of these employees are members of the Teamsters Union. Over the years, in negotiations with UPS management, the Teamsters Union has reached agreement which made working for UPS one of the more coveted jobs in the industry. Full-time employees, typically the drivers, earned upwards of $20.00 per hour. Part-time employees earned about $10.00 per hour. In addition, both groups of employees enjoyed excellent health and pension benefits. So what's the issue at UPS? In the negotiations that started in early 1997, the primary focus became the part-time employees.

Although UPS has created more than 40,000 unionized jobs since 1993, more than 80 percent of them were part-time employees. But part-time at UPS has become somewhat of a misnomer. Many of the part-time employees work more than 30 hours per week. And although they do receive health and pension benefits, many just simply cannot move into full-time positions and nearly double their income. UPS, however, has justified the use of part-timers from several perspectives. First, most of the part-timers are under age 25, many of whom are attending college and working at UPS to pay for their education. Second, FedEx has a nonunionized work force that earns 30 to 50 percent less per hour than UPS employees.

During contract negotiations, both sides held steady. UPS was willing to increase wages, but wanted to control the administration of the unionized employees' pension program. They were also willing to add 1000 new full-time positions and pledged to convert 10,000 current part-time positions over the next several years. The Teamsters, however, saw things differently. While they agreed that wages should increase, they were unbending on moving the pension program from their "multi-employer" pension to one for just "UPS" workers. Furthermore, the Teamsters wanted the company immediately to create 10,000 new full-time positions. After months of hard negotiations and many collective bargaining tactics, negotiations finally broke off on August 3, 1997. At 12:01 A.M., 185,000 unionized UPS employees went out on strike. And while the company's 75,000 management and nonunionized personnel attempted to keep the company operating, less than 5 percent of the daily 12 million packages were delivered. As a result, UPS and much of the ground parcel delivery in the United States was brought to a halt. Compounding this, too, was a strikingly supportive position of the Teamsters by the general public. After years of hearing about record corporate profits, downsizing, out-sourcing, and contingent workers, the public supported this strike. This fact alone was something that unions had not witnessed in the past few decades. And make no mistake about it, it had a tremendous effect on these negotiations. By all accounts, if one has to declare a winner in these negotiations, the Teamsters and unionization in general won. In fact, the deal signed and ratified by the workers included converting 10,000 part-time jobs to full-time at twice the part-timers' hourly wage. Wages for full-timers will increase 15 percent over the next five years—35 percent increase for part-timers during the same period. And the pension program remains as it was before negotiations began.

There's no doubt that the negotiations between the Teamsters and UPS may have a major effect on unions and collective bargaining in the years ahead. Only time will tell whether such a visible "win" will help unions organize more workers or give unions more public support to strike.

INTRODUCTION

A **union** is an organization of workers, acting collectively, seeking to promote and protect its mutual interests through collective bargaining. However, before we can examine the activities surrounding the collective bargaining process, it is important to have an understanding of the laws that govern the labor–management process, what unions are and how employees unionize. While it is true that just over 14 percent of the private sector work force is unionized,[2] the successes and failures of organized labor's activities affect most segments of the work force in two important ways. First, since major industries in the United States—such as automobile, steel, and electrical manufacturers, as well as all branches of transportation—are unionized, unions have a major ef-

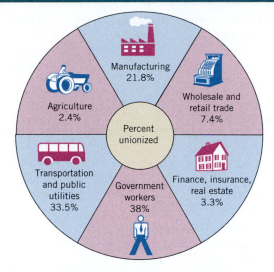

Exhibit 16-1

Union membership by industry concentrations.

fect on some of the important sectors of the economy (see Exhibit 16-1). Second, gains made by unions oftentimes spill over into other nonunionized sectors of the economy.[3] So, the wages, hours, and working conditions of nonunion employees at a Linden, New Jersey, lumber yard may be affected by collective bargaining between the United Auto Workers and General Motors at one of the latter's North American assembly plants.

For many managers, HRM practices in a unionized organization consist chiefly of following procedures and policies laid out in the labor contract. This labor contract was agreed to by both management and the labor union, stipulating, among other things, the wage rate, the hours of work, and the terms and conditions of employment for those covered by the negotiated agreement. Decisions about how to select and compensate employees,[4] employee benefits offered, procedures for overtime, etc. are no longer unilateral prerogatives of management for jobs that fall under the unions' jurisdiction. Such decisions are generally made at the time the labor contract is negotiated.

The concept of labor relations, and the collective bargaining process, may mean different things to different individuals depending on their experience, background, and so on. One means of providing some focus in these areas is to have an understanding of why people join unions, and the laws that serve as the foundation of labor–management relationships.

WHY DO EMPLOYEES JOIN UNIONS?

The reasons individuals join unions are as diverse as the people themselves. Just what are they seeking to gain when they join a union? The answer to this question varies with the individual and the union contract, but the following captures the most common reasons.

Higher Wages and Benefits

There are power and strength in numbers. As a result, unions sometimes are able to obtain higher wages and benefit packages for their members than employees would be able to negotiate individually. One or two employees walking off the job over a wage dispute is unlikely to significantly affect most businesses, but hundreds of workers going out on strike can temporarily disrupt or even close down a company. Additionally, professional bargainers employed by the union may be able to negotiate more skillfully than any individual could on his or her own behalf.

Greater Job Security

Unions provide its members with a sense of independence from management's power to arbitrarily hire, promote, or fire. The collective bargaining contract will stipulate rules that apply to all members, thus providing fairer and more uniform treatment. For example, after a lengthy strike involving the Teamsters Union and the Giant Food Company, an agreement was reached between the parties that guarantees Teamsters' union members lifelong job security—regardless of external factors effecting the company.

Influence Work Rules

Where a union exists, workers are provided with an opportunity to participate in determining the conditions under which they work, and an effective channel through which they can protest conditions they believe are unfair. Therefore, a union is not only a representative of the worker but also provides rules that define channels in which complaints and concerns of workers can be registered. Grievance procedures and rights to third-party arbitration of disputes are examples of practices that are typically defined and regulated as a result of union efforts.

Compulsory Membership

Many labor agreements contain statements that are commonly referred to as *union security clauses*. When one considers the importance of security arrangements to unions—importance brought about in terms of numbers and guaranteed income—it is no wonder that such emphasis is placed on achieving a union security arrangement that best suits their goals. Such arrangements range from compulsory membership in the union to giving employees the freedom in choosing to join the union.[5] The various types of union security arrangements—the union shop, the agency shop, and the right-to-work shop, as well as some special provisions under the realm of union security arrangements—are briefly discussed below and summarized in Exhibit 16-2.

The most powerful relationship legally available (except in right-to-work states[6]) to a union is a **union shop.** This arrangement stipulates that employers, while free to hire whomever they choose, may retain only union members. That is, all employees hired into positions covered under the terms of a collective-bargaining agreement must, after a specified probationary period of typically thirty to sixty days, join the union or forfeit their jobs.[7]

An agreement that requires nonunion employees to pay the union a sum of money equal to union fees and dues as a condition of continuing employment is referred to as an **agency shop.** This arrangement was designed as a compromise between the union's desire to eliminate the "free rider" and management's desire to make union membership voluntary. In such a case, if for whatever reason workers decide not to join the union (e.g., religious beliefs, values, etc.),

Under a union shop arrangement, all employees in the bargaining unit must join the union, or forfeit their jobs.

Union Shop	The strongest of the union security arrangements. Union shops make union membership compulsory. After a given period of time, typically 30 days, a new employee must join the union, or be terminated. A union shop guarantees the union that dues paying members will become part of the union. In a right-to-work state, union shops are illegal.
Agency Shop	The second strongest union security arrangement, the agency shop, gives workers the option of joining the union or not. As such, membership is not compulsory. However, because the "gains" that are made at negotiations will benefit those not joining the union, all workers in the unit must pay union dues. However, Supreme Court decisions dictate that those individuals not members of the union, who still pay dues, have the right to have their monies used solely for collective-bargaining purposes. Like the union shop, the agency shop, too, is illegal in a right-to-work state.
Open Shop	The weakest form of a union security arrangement is the open shop. In an open shop, workers are free to join a union. If they do, they must stay in the union for the duration of the contract—and pay their dues. Those who do not wish to join the union are not required to do so—and thus pay no dues. In an open-shop arrangement, there is an escape clause at the expiration (typically two weeks) in which an individual may "quit" the union. The open shop is based on the premise of freedom of choice, and is the only union security arrangement permitted under right-to-work legislation.
Maintenance of Membership	Because unions need to be able to administer their operations, in an open shop, once someone joins the union, they must maintain their union affiliation, and pay their dues, for the duration of the contract. At the end of the contract, an escape period exists in which those desiring to leave the union may do so.
Dues Checkoff	Dues checkoff involves the employer deducting union dues directly from a union member's paycheck. Under this provision, the employer collects the union dues and forwards a check to the union treasurer. Generally management does not charge an administrative fee for this service.

Exhibit 16-2

Union security and related provisions.

they still must pay dues. Because workers will receive the benefits negotiated by the union, they must pay their fair share. However, a 1988 Supreme Court ruling upheld union members' claims that although they are forced to pay union dues, those dues must be specifically used for collective bargaining purposes only—not for political lobbying.[8] In early 1992, President George Bush extended the same rights to federal-sector employees when he signed into law Executive Order 12800.[9] Moreover, several states have adopted the Paycheck Protection Act which requires unions "to get permission from each member before using a penny of his or her dues for political purposes."[10] In Washington State, the effect of this Act was quite evident as political use of union dues dropped from 40,000 in 1992 to 82 in 1996.[11]

The least desirable form of union security from a union perspective is the **open shop.** This is an arrangement in which joining a union is totally voluntary. Those who do not join are not required to pay union dues or any associated fees. For workers who do join, there is typically a **maintenance of membership** clause in the existing contract that dictates certain provisions. Specifically, a maintenance of membership agreement states that should employees join the union, they are compelled to remain in the union for the duration of the existing contract. When the contract expires, most maintenance of membership agreements provide an escape clause—a short interval of time, usually ten days to two weeks—in which employees may choose to withdraw their membership from the union without penalty.

What makes these workers join a union, and then strike when an agreement cannot be reached in contract negotiations? Research tells us it's to get higher wages and benefits, to achieve greater job security, to influence work rules, and to have compulsory membership. Furthermore, when employees are upset with their management, they, too, are likely to seek union representation.

A provision that often exists in union security arrangements is a process called the **dues checkoff.** A dues checkoff occurs when the employer withholds union dues from the members' paychecks. Similar to other pay withholdings, the employer collects the dues money and sends it to the union. There are a number of reasons why employers provide this service, and a reason why the union would permit them to do so. Collecting dues takes time, so a dues checkoff reduces the "downtime" by eliminating the need for the shop steward to go around to collect dues. Furthermore, recognizing that union dues are the primary source of income for the union, having knowledge of how much money there is in the union treasury can provide management with some insight as to whether or not a union is financially strong enough to endure a strike.[12] Given these facts, why would a union agree to such a procedure? Simply, the answer lies in guaranteed revenues! By letting management deduct dues from a member's paycheck, the union is assured of receiving their monies. Excuses from members that they don't have their money, or will pay next week, are eliminated!

Being Upset with Management

In spite of the reasons why employees join a union, there appears to be one common factor—management, especially the first-line supervisor. If employees are upset with the way their supervisor handles problems, upset over how a co-worker has been disciplined, etc., they are likely to seek help from a union. In fact, it is reasonable to believe that when employees vote to unionize, it's often a vote against their immediate supervisor rather than a vote in support of a particular union.

LABOR LEGISLATION

The legal framework for labor–management relationships has played a crucial role in its development. In this section, therefore, major developments in labor law will be discussed. An exhaustive analysis of these laws and their legal and practical repercussions is not possible within the scope of this book.[13] However, we'll focus our discussion on two important laws that have shaped much of the labor relations process. We'll then briefly summarize other laws that have helped shape labor–management activities.

The Wagner Act

The National Labor Relations Act of 1934, commonly referred to as the **Wagner Act,** is the basic "bill of rights" for unions. This law guarantees workers the right to organize and join unions, to bargain collectively, and to act in concert to pursue their objectives. In terms of labor relations, the Wagner Act specifically requires employers to bargain in good faith over mandatory bargaining issues—wages, hours, and terms and conditions of employment.

The Wagner Act is cited as shifting the pendulum of power to favor unions for the first time in U.S. labor history. This was achieved, in part, through the establishment of the **National Labor Relations Board (NLRB).** This administrative body, consisting of five members appointed by the president,[14] was given the responsibility for determining appropriate bargaining units, conducting elections to determine union representation, and preventing or correcting employer actions that can lead to unfair labor practice charges. The NLRB, however, has only remedial and no punitive powers.

Unfair labor practices (Section 8[a]) include any employer tactics that:

▶ Interfere with, restrain, or coerce employees in the exercise of the rights to join unions and to bargain collectively:

▶ dominate or interfere with the formation or administration of any labor organization; discriminate against anyone because of union activity;

▶ discharge or otherwise discriminate against any employee because he or she filed or gave testimony under the Act;

▶ and refuse to bargain collectively with the representatives chosen by the employees.[15]

While the Wagner Act provided the legal recognition of unions as legitimate interest groups in American society, many employers opposed its purposes. Some employers, too, failed to live up to the requirements of its provisions. That's because employers recognized that the Wagner Act didn't provide protection for them from unfair union labor practices. Thus, the belief that the balance of power had swung too far to labor's side, and the public outcry stemming from post-World War II strikes, led to the passage of the Taft-Hartley Act (Labor–Management Relations Act) in 1947.

The Taft-Hartley Act

The major purpose of the **Taft-Hartley Act** was to amend the Wagner Act by addressing employers' concerns in terms of specifying unfair union labor practices. Under Section 8(b), Taft-Hartley states that it is an unfair labor practice for unions to:

- ▶ restrain or coerce employees in joining the union, or coerce the employer in selecting bargaining or grievance representatives;
- ▶ discriminate against an employee to whom union membership has been denied, or to cause an employer to discriminate against an employee;
- ▶ refuse to bargain collectively;
- ▶ engage in strikes and boycotts for purposes deemed illegal by the Act;
- ▶ charge excessive or discriminatory fees or dues under union-shop contracts;
- ▶ and obtain compensation for services not performed or not to be performed.[16]

In addition, Taft-Hartley declared illegal one type of union security arrangement: the *closed shop*. Until Taft-Hartley's passage, the closed shop was dominant in labor contracts. The closed shop was an arrangement where a union "controlled" the source of labor. Under this arrangement, an individual would join the union, be trained by the union, and sent to work for an employer by the union. In essence, the union acted as the clearing house of employees. When an employer needed a number of employees—for whatever duration— the employer would contact the union and request that these employees start work. When the job was completed, and the employees were no longer needed on the job by the employer, they were sent back to the union.

By declaring the closed shop illegal, Taft-Hartley began to shift the pendulum of power away from unions. Furthermore, in doing so, the Act enabled states to enact laws that would further reduce compulsory union membership. Taft-Hartley also included provisions that forbade secondary boycotts,[17] and gave the president of the United States the power to issue an eighty-day cooling-off period when labor–management disputes affect national security. A **secondary boycott** occurs when a union strikes against Employer A (a primary and legal strike), and then strikes and pickets against Employer B (an employer against which the union has no complaint) because of a relationship that exists between Employers A and B, such as Employer B handling goods made by Employer A. Taft-Hartley also set forth procedures for workers to decertify, or vote out, their union representatives.

Whereas the Wagner Act required only employers to bargain in good faith, Taft-Hartley imposed the same obligation on unions. Although the negotiation process is described later in this chapter, it is important to understand what is meant by the term "bargaining in good faith." This does not mean that the parties must reach agreement, but rather that they must come to the bargaining table ready, willing, and able to meet and deal, open to proposals made by the other party, and with the intent to reach a mutually acceptable agreement.

Realizing that unions and employers might not reach agreement and that work stoppages might occur, Taft-Hartley also created the **Federal Mediation and Conciliation Service (FMCS)** as an independent agency separate from the Department of Labor. The FMCS's mission is to send a trained representative to negotiations to "prevent or minimize interruptions of commerce . . . and to help the parties to settle their dispute through conciliation and mediation."[18] Both employer and union have the responsibility to notify the FMCS when other attempts to settle the dispute have failed or contract expiration is pending.

An FMCS mediator is not empowered to force parties to reach an agreement, but he or she can use persuasion and other means of diplomacy to help them reach their own resolution of differences. Finally, a fact worth noting was the amendment in 1974 to extend coverage to the health-care industry. This health-care amendment now affords Taft-Hartley coverage to profit and nonprofit hospitals, as well as "special provisions for the health care industry, both profit and nonprofit, as to bargaining notice requirements and the right to picket or strike." [19]

Other Laws Affecting Labor–Management Relations

While the Wagner and Taft-Hartley Acts were the most important laws influencing labor–management relationships in the United States, there are some other items that are pertinent to our discussion. Specifically, these are the Railway Labor Act, the Landrum-Griffin Act, Executive Orders 10988 and 11491; the Racketeer Influenced and Corrupting Organizations Act of 1970; and the Civil Service Reform Act of 1978. Let's briefly review the notable aspects of these laws.

The Railway Labor Act of 1926

The **Railway Labor Act** provided the initial impetus for widespread collective bargaining in the United States.[20] Although the Act covers only the transportation industry, it was important because workers in these industries were guaranteed the right to organize, bargain collectively with employers, and establish dispute settlement procedures in the event that an agreement was not reached at the bargaining table. This dispute settlement procedure allows congressional and presidential intercession in the event of an impasse.

Landrum-Griffin Act of 1959

The **Landrum-Griffin Act of 1959** (Labor and Management Reporting and Disclosure Act) was passed to address the public outcry over misuse of union funds and corruption in the labor movement. This Act, like Taft-Hartley, was an amendment to the Wagner Act.[21]

The thrust of the Landrum-Griffin Act is to monitor internal union activity by making officials and those affiliated with unions (e.g., union members, trustees, etc.) accountable for union funds, elections, and other business and representational matters. Restrictions are also placed on trusteeships imposed by national or international unions; and conduct during a union election is regulated. Much of this act is part of an ongoing effort to prevent corrupt practices and to keep organized crime from gaining control of the labor movement. The mechanisms used to achieve this goal are requirements for annual filing by unions as organizations and by individuals employed by unions, reports regarding administrative matters to the Department of Labor—reports such as their "adoption of constitutions and by-laws, administrative policies, and finances." [22] This information, filed under forms L-M 2 or L-M 3[23] with the Department of Labor, is available to the public. Furthermore, Landrum-Griffin included a provision that allowed all members of a union to vote irrespective of their race, sex, national origin, and so forth. This provision gave union members certain rights that would not be available to the general public for another five years until the passage of the Civil Rights Act of 1964. Landrum-Griffin also required that all who voted on union matters would do so in a secret ballot, especially when the vote concerned the election of union officers.

Executive Orders 10988 and 11491   Both of these executive orders deal specifically with labor legislation in the federal sector.[24] In 1962, President Kennedy issued Executive Order 10988, which permitted, for the first time, federal government employees the right to join unions. The order required agency heads to bargain in good faith, defined unfair labor practices, and specified the code of conduct to which labor organizations in the public sector must adhere. Strikes, however, were prohibited.[25]

While this executive order was effective in granting organizing rights to federal employees, areas for improvement were identified. This was especially true regarding the need for a centralized agency to oversee federal labor relations activities. To address these deficiencies, President Richard Nixon issued Executive Order 11491 in 1969. The objectives of this executive order were to make federal labor relations more like those in the private sector and to standardize procedures among federal agencies. This order gave the assistant secretary of labor the authority to determine appropriate bargaining units, oversee recognition procedures, rule on unfair labor practices, and enforce standards of conduct on labor relations. It also established the Federal Labor Relations Council (FLRC) to supervise the implementation of Executive Order 11491 provisions, handle appeals from decisions of the assistant secretary of labor, and rule on questionable issues.

Both of these executive orders served a vital purpose in promoting federal sector unionization. However, if a subsequent administration ever decided not to permit federal sector unionization, a president would only have had to revoke a prior executive order. To eliminate this possibility, and to remove federal sector labor relations from direct control of a president, Congress passed the Civil Service Reform Act.

Racketeering Influenced and Corrupt Organizations Act (RICO) of 1970

Although this act has far-reaching tentacles, the Racketeering Influenced and Corrupt Organizations Act (RICO) serves a vital purpose in labor relations. RICO's primary emphasis with respect to labor unions is to eliminate any influence exerted on unions by members of organized crime.[26] That is, it is a violation of RICO if "payments or loans are made to employee representatives, labor organizations, or officers and employees of labor organizations," [27] where such action occurs in the form of "bribery, kickbacks, or extortion." [28] Over the past decade, RICO has been used to oust a number of labor officials in the Teamsters union who were alleged to have organized crime ties.[29]

Civil Service Reform Act of 1978   Title VII of the **Civil Service Reform Act** established the Federal Labor Relations Authority (FLRA) as an independent agency within the executive branch to carry out the major functions previously performed by the FLRC. The FLRA was given the authority to decide, subject to external review by courts and administrative bodies,[30] union election and unfair labor practice disputes, appeals from arbitration awards, and to provide leadership in establishing policies and guidance. An additional feature of this act is a broad-scope grievance procedure that can be limited only by the negotiators. Under Executive Order 11491, binding arbitration had been optional. While the Civil Service Reform Act of 1978 contains many provisions similar to those of the Wagner Act, two important differences exist. First, in the private sector, the scope of bargaining includes wages and benefits, and mandatory subjects of bargaining. In the federal sector, wages and benefits are not negotiable—they are set by Congress. Additionally, the Reform Act prohibits negotiations over union security arrangements.

HOW ARE EMPLOYEES UNIONIZED?

Employees are unionized after an extensive, and sometimes lengthy process called the *organizing campaign*. Exhibit 16-3 contains a simple model of how the process typically flows in the private sector. Let's look at these elements.

Efforts to organize a group of employees may begin by employee representatives requesting a union to visit the employees' organization and solicit members, the union itself might initiate the membership drive, or in some cases, unions are using the Internet to promote their benefits to workers.[31] Regardless of "how," as established by the NLRB, the union must secure signed **authorization cards** from at least 30 percent of the employees it wishes to represent. Employees who sign the cards indicate that they wish the particular union to be their representative in negotiating with the employer.

Although a minimum of 30 percent of the potential union members must sign the authorization card prior to an election, unions are seldom interested in bringing to vote situations in which they merely meet the NLRB minimum. Why? The answer is simply a matter of mathematics and business: to become the certified bargaining unit, the union must be accepted by a majority of those eligible voting workers.[32] Acceptance in this case is determined by a secret-ballot election. This election held by the NLRB, called a **representation certification (RC),** can occur only once in a twelve-month period; thus, the more signatures on the authorization cards, the greater the chances for a victory. How great? Research into union authorization card signatures suggests the following: when more than 75 percent of the eligible workers sign the authorization card, the union has a 60 percent chance of winning the election; when the signatures total between 60 and 75 percent, the chances of winning drop to 50–50. And when the minimum is achieved (30 percent), unions have only an 8 percent chance of winning a certification election.[33]

Why the significant drop in numbers? Even when a sizable proportion of the workers sign authorization cards, the victory is by no means guaranteed. Management often is not passive during the organization drive. Although there

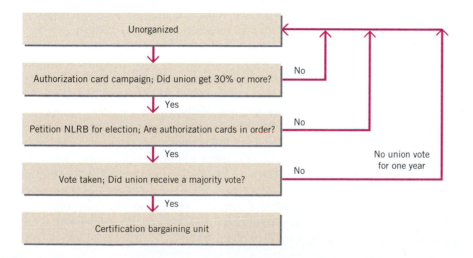

Exhibit 16-3
Union organizing process.

are laws governing what management can and cannot do, management of the organization may attempt to persuade the potential members to vote no. Union organizers realize that some initial signers might be persuaded to vote no, and thus unions usually require a much higher percentage of authorization cards so they can increase their odds of obtaining a majority. When that majority vote is received, the NLRB certifies the union and recognizes it as the exclusive bargaining unit. Irrespective of whether the individual in the certified bargaining union voted for or against the union, each worker is covered by the negotiated contract and must abide by its governance. Once a union has been certified, is it there for life? Certainly not. On some occasions, union members may become so dissatisfied with the union's actions in representing them that they may want to turn to another union or return to their nonunion status. In either case, the rank-and-file members petition the NLRB to conduct a **representation decertification (RD).** Once again, if a majority of the members vote the union out, it is gone. However, once the election has been held, no other action can occur for another twelve-month period. This grace period protects the employer from employees decertifying one union today and certifying another tomorrow.

Finally, and even more rare than an RD, is a representation decertification initiated by management, or RM. The guidelines for the RM are the same as for the RD, except that it is the employer who is leading the drive. Although RDs and RMs are ways of decertifying unions, it should be pointed out that most labor agreements bar the use of either decertification election during the term of the contract.

Organizing drives may be unsuccessful, but when they do achieve their goal to become the exclusive bargaining agent, the next step is to negotiate the contract. In the next section, we'll look at the specific issues surrounding collective bargaining.

COLLECTIVE BARGAINING

The term **collective bargaining** typically refers to the negotiation, administration, and interpretation of a written agreement between two parties that covers a specific period of time. This agreement, or contract, lays out in specific terms the conditions of employment; that is, what is expected of employees and what limits there are in management's authority. In the following discussion, we will take a somewhat larger perspective—we will also consider the organizing, certification, and preparation efforts that precede actual negotiation.

Most of us only hear or read about collective bargaining when a contract is about to expire or when negotiations break down. When a railroad contract is about to expire, we may be aware that collective bargaining exists in the transportation industry. Similarly, teachers' strikes in New Orleans, workers striking General Motors at the Buick Plant in Flint, Michigan,[34] or baseball players striking against major league baseball owners remind us that organized labor deals with management collectively. In fact, collective-bargaining agreements cover about half of all state and local government employees and one-ninth of employees in the private sector. The wages, hours, and working conditions of these unionized employees are negotiated for periods of usually two or three years at a time. Only when these contracts expire and management and the union are unable to agree on a new contract are most of us aware that collective bargaining is a very important part of HRM.

The Objective and Scope of Collective Bargaining

The objective of collective bargaining is to agree on an acceptable contract—acceptable to management, union representatives, and the union membership. But what is covered in this contract? The final agreement will reflect the problems of the particular workplace and industry in which the contract is negotiated.[35]

Irrespective of the specific issues contained in various labor contracts, four issues appear consistently throughout all labor contracts. Three of the four are mandatory bargaining issues, which means that management and the union must negotiate in good faith over these issues. These mandatory issues were defined by the Wagner Act as wages, hours, and terms and conditions of employment. The fourth issue covered in almost all labor contracts is the grievance procedure, which is designed to permit the adjudication of complaints. Before we progress further into collective bargaining, let's inspect our cast of characters.

Collective-Bargaining Participants

Collective bargaining was described as an activity that takes place between two parties. In this context, the two parties are labor and management. But who represents these two groups? Given our previous discussion, would it be erroneous to add a third party—the government?

Management's representation in collective-bargaining talks tends to depend on the size of the organization. In a small firm, for instance, bargaining is probably done by the president. Since small firms frequently have no specialist who deals only with HRM issues, the president of the company often handles this. In larger organizations, there is usually a sophisticated HRM department with full-time industrial relations experts. In such cases, we can expect management to be represented by the senior manager for industrial relations, corporate executives, and company lawyers—with support provided by legal and economic specialists in wage and salary administration, labor law, benefits, and so forth.

On the union side, we typically expect to see a bargaining team made up of an officer of the local union, local shop stewards, and some representation from the international/national union.[36] Again, as with management, representation is modified to reflect the size of the bargaining unit. If negotiations involve a contract that will cover 50,000 employees at company locations throughout the United States, the team will be dominated by international/national union officers, with a strong supporting cast of economic and legal experts employed by the union. In a small firm or for local negotiations covering special issues at the plant level for a nationwide organization, bargaining representatives for the union might be the local officers and a few specially elected committee members.

Watching over these two sides is a third party—government. In addition to providing the rules under which management and labor bargain, government provides a watchful eye on the two parties to ensure the rules are followed, and it stands ready to intervene if an agreement on acceptable terms cannot be reached, or if the impasse undermines the nation's well-being.

Are there any more participants? No, for the most part, with one exception—financial institutions.[37] Most people are unaware of the presence of the financial institutions' role in collective bargaining. Although not directly involved in negotiations, these "banks" set limits on the cost of the contract. Exceeding that amount may cause the banks to call in the loans that had been made to the company. This results in placing a ceiling on what management can spend. While we can show that there are more groups involved in collective bargaining, our discussion will focus on labor and management. After all, it is the labor and management teams that buckle down and hammer out the contract.

The Collective-Bargaining Process

Let's now consider the actual collective-bargaining process. Exhibit 16-4 contains a simple model of how the process typically flows in the private sector—which includes preparing to negotiate, actual negotiations, and administering the contract after it has been ratified.

Preparing to Negotiate   Once a union has been certified as the bargaining unit, both union and management begin the ongoing activity of preparing for negotiations. We refer to this as an "ongoing" activity because ideally it should begin as soon as the previous contract is agreed upon or union certification is achieved. Realistically, it probably begins anywhere from one to six months before the current contract expires. We can consider the preparation for negotiation as composed of three activities: fact gathering, goal setting, and strategy development.

Information is acquired from both internal and external sources. Internal data include grievance and accident records; employee performance reports; overtime figures; and reports on transfers, turnover, and absenteeism. External information should include statistics on the current economy, both at local and national levels; economic forecasts for the short and intermediate terms; copies of recently negotiated contracts by the adversary union to determine what issues the union considers important; data on the communities in which the company operates—cost of living; changes in cost of living, terms of recently negotiated labor contracts, and statistics on the labor market; and industry labor statistics to see what terms other organizations, employing similar types of personnel, are negotiating.

With homework done, information in hand, and tentative goals established, both union and management must put together the most difficult part of the bargaining preparation activities—a strategy for negotiations. This includes assessing the other "side's" power and specific tactics.

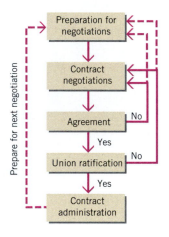

Exhibit 16-4

The collective-bargaining process.

Negotiating at the Bargaining Table   Negotiation customarily begins with the union delivering to management a list of "demands." By presenting many demands, the union creates significant room for trading in later stages of the negotiation; it also disguises the union's real position, leaving management to determine which demands are adamantly sought, which are moderately sought, and which the union is prepared to quickly abandon. A long list of demands, too, often fulfills the internal political needs of the union. By seeming to back numerous wishes of the union's members, union administrators appear to be satisfying the needs of the many factions within the membership.

While both union and management representatives may publicly accentuate their differences, the real negotiations typically go on behind closed doors. Each party tries to assess the relative priorities of the other's demands, and each begins to combine proposals into viable packages. What takes place, then, is the attempt to get management's highest offer to approximate the lowest demands that the union is willing to accept. Hence, negotiation is a form of compromise. When an oral agreement is achieved, it is converted into a written contract. Negotiation finally concludes with the union representatives submitting the contract for ratification or approval from rank and file members. Unless the rank and file members vote to approve the contract, negotiations must resume. That's precisely what happened when Federal Express and the Air Line Pilots Association representing FedEx pilots saw their long-negotiated agreement rejected by the pilots—even though union leadership supported the agreement.[38]

Contract Administration   Once a contract is agreed upon and ratified, it must be administered. In terms of contract administration, four stages must be carried out. These are: (1) getting the information agreed to out to all union members and management personnel; (2) implementing the contract; (3) interpreting the contract and grievance resolution; and (4) monitoring activities during the contract period.[39]

In terms of providing information to all concerned, both parties must ensure that changes in contract language are spelled out. For example, the most obvious would be hourly rate changes; HRM must make sure its payroll system is adjusted to the new rates as set in the contract. But it goes beyond just pay: Changes in work rules, hours, and the like must be communicated. If both sides agree to mandatory overtime, something that was not in existence before, all must be informed of how it will work. Neither the union nor the company can simply hand a copy of the contract to each organization member and expect it to be understood. It will be necessary to hold meetings to explain the new terms of the agreement.

The next stage of contract administration is ensuring that the agreement is implemented. All communicated changes now take effect, and both sides are expected to comply with the contract terms. One concept to recognize during this phase is something called *management rights*. Typically, management is guaranteed the right to allocate organizational resources in the most efficient manner; to create reasonable rules; to hire, promote, transfer, and discharge employees; to determine work methods and assign work; to create, eliminate, and classify jobs; to lay off employees when necessary; to close or relocate facilities with a sixty-day notice; and to institute technological changes. Of course, good HRM practices suggest that whether the contract requires it or not, management would be wise to notify the union of major decisions that will influence its membership.

Probably the most important element of contract administration relates to spelling out a procedure for handling contractual disputes.[40] Almost all collective-bargaining agreements contain formal procedures to be used in resolving grievances of the interpretation and application of the contract. These contracts have provisions for resolving specific, formally initiated grievances by employees concerning dissatisfaction with job-related issues.[41]

Grievance procedures are typically designed to resolve grievances as quickly as possible and at the lowest level possible in the organization (see Exhibit 16-5). The first step almost always has the employee attempt to resolve the grievance with his or her immediate supervisor.[42] If it cannot be resolved at this stage, it is typically discussed with the union steward and the supervisor. Failure at this stage usually brings in the individuals from the organization's industrial

Exhibit 16-5

A sample grievance procedure.

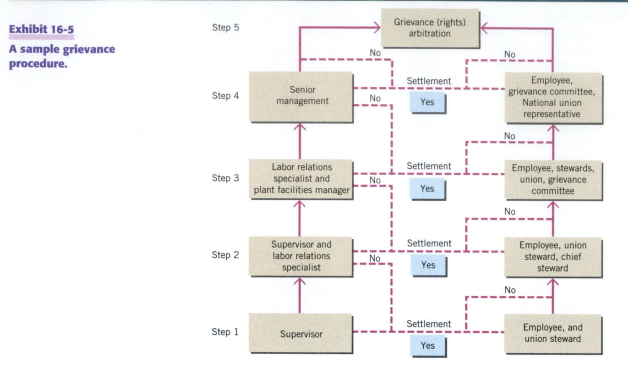

relations department and the chief union steward. If the grievance still cannot be resolved, the complaint passes to the facilities' manager, who discusses it typically with the union grievance committee. Unsuccessful efforts at this level give way to the organization's senior management and typically a representative from the national union. Finally, if those efforts are unsuccessful in resolving the grievance, the final step is for it to go to arbitration—called **grievance (rights) arbitration.**

In practice, we find that 98 percent of all collective-bargaining agreements provide for grievance (rights) arbitration as the final step to an impasse.[43] Of course, in small organizations these five steps described tend to be condensed, possibly moving from discussing the grievance with the union steward to taking the grievance directly to the organization's senior executive or owner, and then to arbitration, if necessary.

Finally, in our discussion of preparation for negotiations, we stated that both company and union need to gather various data. One of the most bountiful databases for both sides is information kept on a current contract. By monitoring activities, company and union can assess how effective the current contract was, when problem areas or conflicts arose, and what changes might need to be made in subsequent negotiations.

When Agreement Cannot Be Reached

Although the goal of contract negotiations is to achieve an agreement that is acceptable to all concerned parties, sometimes that goal is not achieved. Negotiations do break down, and an impasse occurs. Sometimes these events are triggered by internal issues in the union, the desire to strike against the company, the company's desire to lock out the union, or its knowledge that striking workers can be replaced. Let's explore some of these areas.

Strikes versus Lockouts   There are only two possible preliminary outcomes from negotiations. First, and obviously preferable, is agreement. The other alternative, when no viable solution can be found to the parties' differences, is a strike or a lockout.

There are several types of strikes. The most relevant to contract negotiations is the economic strike. An **economic strike** occurs when the two parties cannot reach a satisfactory agreement before the contract expires. When that deadline passes, the union leadership will typically instruct its members not to work—thus leaving their jobs.[44] Although in today's legal climate, replacement workers can be hired, no disciplinary action can be taken against workers who participate in economic strike activities [see Ethical Decisions in HRM].

Another form of strike is the **wildcat strike.** A wildcat strike generally occurs when workers walk off the job because of something management has done. For example, if a union employee is disciplined for failure to call in sick according to provisions of the contract, fellow union members may walk off the job to demonstrate their dissatisfaction with management action. It is important to note that these strikes happen while a contract is in force—an agreement that usually prohibits such union activity. Consequently, wildcat strikers can be severely disciplined or terminated. In the past, the most powerful weapon unions in the private sector had was the economic strike. By striking, the union was, in essence, withholding labor from the employer, thus causing the em-

The Striker Replacement Dilemma

Inherent in collective-bargaining negotiations is an opportunity for either side to generate a power base that may sway negotiations in their favor. For example, when labor shortages exist, or when inventories are in short supply, a strike by the union could have serious ramifications for the company. Likewise, when the situation is reversed, management has the upper hand and could easily lock out the union to achieve its negotiation's goals. In fact, both the Wagner and Taft–Hartley Acts saw to it that the playing field was to be as fair as possible, by requiring both sides to negotiate in good faith, and permit impasses if they should be warranted.

For decades, this scenario played itself out over and over again. Timing of a contract's expiration proved critical for both sides. For example, in the coal industry, having a contract expire just before the winter months—when coal is needed in greater supply for heating and electricity—worked to the union's advantage, unless the coal companies stockpiled enough coal to carry them through a lengthy winter strike. This game, although serious to both sides, never appeared to be anything more than bargaining strategy; one that could show how serious both sides were. And even though a Supreme Court case from 1938, *NLRB* v. *MacKay*

Radio, gave employers the right to hire replacement workers for those engaged in an economic strike, seldom was that used. In fact, often to settle a strike, and for the organization to get back its skilled work force, one stipulation would be that all replacement workers be "let go."

But in the early 1980s, that began to change. When President Ronald Reagan fired striking air-traffic controllers and hired their replacements, businesses began to realize the weapon they had at their disposal. As their union-busting attempts materialized, some organizations, like Caterpillar, the National Football League, and John Deere, realized that using replacement workers could be to their advantage. The union members either came back to work on management's terms, or they simply lost their jobs. Period.

Undoubtedly, in any strike situation, management has the right to keep its doors open and to keep producing what it sells. Often that may mean using supervisory personnel in place of striking workers, or in some cases, bringing in replacements. But does a law that permits replacement workers undermine the intent of national labor law? Does it create an unfair advantage for management in that it could play hardball just to break the union? Should a striker replacement bill (which would prevent permanent replacement workers from being hired) be passed? Should striking workers' jobs be protected while they exercise their rights under the Wagner Act? What's your opinion?

One "weapon" unions have to display their dissatisfaction with not reaching an agreement with management during contract negotiation is the economic strike. These State of Oregon employees show their solidarity and displeasure with the state government negotiators.

ployer financial hardships. For instance, U.S. organizations lost more than 4.8 million workdays to strike activity in 1996.[45]

Today, however, the strike weapon is questioned.[46] Strikes are not only expensive, but public sentiment supporting their use by unions is not very strong. And management hasn't been sitting by idly, for today it is more inclined to replace striking workers.[47] Although strikes fell to a near record low in 1995 and 1996,[48] worker dissatisfaction with some management practices may increase strike activity in the years ahead.

In contemporary times, we have also witnessed an increase in management's use of the lockout. A **lockout,** as the name implies, occurs when the organization denies unionized workers access to their jobs during an impasse. A lockout, in some cases, is management's predecessor to hiring replacement workers. In others, it's management's effort to protect their facilities and machinery, and other employees at the work site.

In either case, the strategy is the same. Both sides are attempting to apply economic pressure on their "opponent" in an effort to sway negotiations in their direction. And when they work, negotiations are said to reach an impasse. When that happens, impasse resolution techniques are designed to help.

Impasse Resolution Techniques   When labor and management in the private sector cannot reach a satisfactory agreement themselves, they may need the assistance of an objective third-party individual. This assistance comes in the form of *conciliation* and *mediation, fact-finding,* or *interest arbitration.*

Conciliation and mediation are two very closely related impasse resolution techniques. Both are techniques whereby a neutral third party attempts to get labor and management to resolve their differences. Under conciliation, however, the role of the third party is to keep the negotiations ongoing. In other words, this individual is a go-between—advocating a voluntary means through which both sides can continue negotiating. Mediation, on the other hand, goes one step further. The mediator attempts to pull together the common ground that exists and make settlement recommendations for overcoming the barriers that exist between the two sides. A mediator's suggestions, however, are only advisory. That means that the suggestions are not binding on either party.

Fact-finding is a technique whereby a neutral third-party individual conducts a hearing to gather evidence from both labor and management. The fact-finder then renders a decision as to how he or she views an appropriate settlement. Similar to mediation, the fact-finder's recommendations are only suggestions—they, too, are not binding on either party.

The final impasse resolution technique is called **interest arbitration.** Under interest arbitration, generally a panel of three individuals—one neutral and one each from the union and management—hears testimony from both sides. After the hearing, the panel renders a decision on how to settle the current contract negotiation dispute. If all three members of the panel are unanimous in their decision, that decision may be binding on both parties.

With respect to public-sector impasse resolution techniques, some notable differences do exist. For instance, in many states that do permit public-sector employee strikes, some form of arbitration is typically required. The decisions rendered through arbitration are binding on both parties. Moreover, in the public sector, a particular form of arbitration is witnessed. Called *final-offer arbitration,* both sides present their recommendations, and the arbitrator is required to select one party's offer in its entirety over the other. There is no attempt in final-offer arbitration to seek compromise.

CRITICAL ISSUES FOR UNIONS TODAY

As the percentage of the unionized work force has declined throughout the past few decades, several questions arise. Why has union membership declined? Can labor and management find a way to work together more harmoniously? Is public sector unionization different than in the private sector? And where are unions likely to focus their attention in the next decade? In this section, we'll look at these issues.

Union Membership: Where Have the Members Gone?

The birth of unionization in the United States can be traced back to the late 1700s. Although there was labor strife for about 200 years, it was not until the passage of the Wagner Act in 1935 that we began to witness significant union gains. In fact, by the early 1940s, union membership in the United States reached its pinnacle of approximately 36 percent of the work force.[49] Since that time, however, there's been nothing more than a steady decline (see Exhibit 16-6). What accounted for this phenomenon? There is no single answer to this question. However, major contributing factors can be identified.

In the early to mid-1970s, many unionized workers, especially in the private sector, were able to join the ranks of the middle class as a result of their unions' success at the bargaining table. This often meant that they were more concerned with taxes than with ideological and social issues or with support for legislation that favored the union movement. Furthermore, the private-sector labor movement had difficulty accepting into its ranks public and federal sector workers, women, African Americans, and the rising tide of immigrants.

Exhibit 16-6

Trends in union membership.

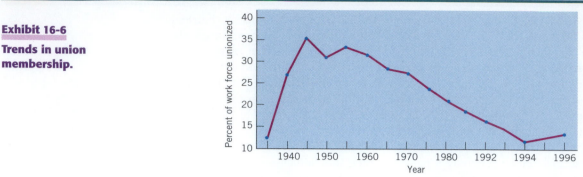

Exhibit 16-6

Trends in union membership.

The 1970s was also the decade in which predictions about the post-industrial age came to pass and manufacturing was replaced by service as the dominant industry in the American economy. As a consequence, the most rapid growth in employment was in wholesale and retail trade, service industries including high technology, and white-collar jobs. These are areas where unions either had not previously focused organizing efforts or were largely unsuccessful for a variety of reasons.

Double-digit inflation, beginning in the mid-1970s, was also a factor. High rates of inflation resulted in the first massive layoffs in both the private and public sectors, which radically diminished the financial resources of numerous unions to represent members and to engage in organizing and political activities. Additionally, the emergence of global competition caught much of American business by surprise. The primary response was to try to restore their financial positions by demanding concessions from workers (concession bargaining) and/or by reducing the work force. Both of these responses have had an enormous effect on the unions at the workplace. Fueled by these pressures, the latter half of the 1970s ushered in the strongest antiunion movement since the post-World War II era. And "out-sourcing"[50] of production and assembly operations to foreign countries such as the Pacific Rim, Mexico, Brazil, Hong Kong, Taiwan, and parts of Africa was another means that originated in the late 1970s.

The 1980s and early 1990s witnessed an even more dramatic decline in union membership and power. Massive layoffs had ripped through the ranks of such unions as the United Automobile Workers (UAW), the United Steelworkers of America (USWA), the United Mine Workers (UMW), the Rubber Workers, and the Communications Workers, so that their numbers were significantly less than at the beginning of the decade. The cumulative effects of factors identified in the 1970s had even harsher consequences during the next fifteen years. Union busting and avoidance were no longer sideline issues for management consultants, but were a thriving and lucrative enterprise in their own right. Worker replacement became a management weapon. If the union would not accept management's "best" offer, the company simply hired new workers to replace those on strike. The 1980s also witnessed a legislative sentiment that began to turn against unions. In such an environment, the role of the strike also took on new meaning. The transition began in 1981, when nationwide attention focused on President Ronald Reagan's firing of illegally striking air-traffic controllers. Important here was the message this action sent to employers across the country: the strike is no longer a union weapon, but rather a management weapon to push workers out of their jobs in an effort to bust the union and/or to gain concessions from workers that they might not otherwise have given.[51]

The picture for unions in the 1990s was just as bleak. Union avoidance and busting tactics, delayering of corporate America, de-jobbed organizations, technology advancements, the contingent work force, replacement workers, etc. all contributed to a continual decline in membership. From its heyday of almost 36 percent in the early 1940s to its current 14 percent in 1997, unions appear not to be the force they once were. But don't count unions down and out. Unions are changing some of their organizing tactics and, as we witnessed with the UPS negotiations, public sentiment might be changing to support and sympathize with union causes. Unions have also posted some major victories, like reversing Nynex plans to lay off more than 22,000 workers.[52] Unions have also found that "recruiting" members in the service sectors—with a fair amount of success in Las Vegas—has been rewarding.[53]

Labor–Management Cooperation

Historically, the relationship between labor and management was built on conflict. The interests of labor and management were seen basically at odds— each treating the other as the opposition. But times have somewhat changed. Management has become increasingly aware that successful efforts to increase productivity, improve quality, and lower costs require employee involvement and commitment. Similarly, some labor unions have come to recognize that they can help their members more by cooperating with management rather than fighting them.[54]

Unfortunately, current U.S. labor laws, passed in an era of mistrust and antagonism between labor and management, may have become a barrier to both parties cooperative partners. As a case in point, the National Labor Relations Act was passed to encourage collective bargaining and to balance worker's power against that of management.[55] That legislation also sought to eliminate the then widespread practice of firms setting up company unions for the sole purpose of undermining efforts of outside unions organizing their employees. So the law prohibits employers from creating or supporting a "labor organization." Ironically, labor laws—like the National Labor Relations Act—may have also presented a minor roadblock in management and labor cooperation. For instance, the National Labor Relations Board ruled in the Electromation Inc. case that it was an unfair labor practice for the employer to set up employee committees in "order to impose its own unilateral form of bargaining on employees."[56] Furthermore, Electromation's actions were also viewed as a means of thwarting a Teamsters Union organizing campaign which began in its Elkhart, Indiana plant. What the Electromation case, and a few others have indicated, was that companies must ensure that their quality circle programs, quality of work life, and other employee involvement programs are legal under federal labor laws.[57]

Although this issue has been the subject of Congressional debate,[58] the current legal environment doesn't prohibit employee-involvement programs in the United States. Rather, to comply with the law, management is required to give its employee-involvement programs independence. That is, when such programs become dominated by management, they're likely to be interpreted as groups that perform some functions of labor unions but are controlled by management. What kinds of actions would indicate that an employee-involvement program is *not* dominated by management? Some examples mighty include choosing program members through secret ballot elections, giving program members wide latitude in deciding what issues to deal with, permitting mem-

Meet

LINDA CHAVEZ-THOMPSON
Executive Vice President, AFL-CIO

When President Bill Clinton formed the nation's first advisory board of the Initiative on Race in 1997, he appointed AFL-CIO Executive Vice President Linda Chavez-Thompson to the seven-member panel. Chavez-Thompson is the only labor representative and the only Latino board member. A recent interview highlights her ideals.

Question: What is the goal of the Initiative on Race?

Chavez-Thompson: We are trying to put a face on the issue of diversity, to show what America must do to deal with the issue of race. I firmly believe the keys are education and economics. Economics cuts across race. If you look at people of color who belong to unions, they earn better pay. And when you earn more, you can turn yourself around and do things for yourself that government is now doing. Most people of color live in cities where there are poor facilities and services and a decaying infrastructure. There is little tax base, so the city cannot pay for the same quality schools and facilities that are available in the suburbs. That would not be the case if workers were earning a living wage and could afford a decent education for their children or buy a home and revive the economy in their towns. But despite all our progress, people of color still are hurt by stagnant wages and the decline in good-paying

manufacturing jobs that affect working people of every background.

Yet, better wages alone are not the answer. We need to find ways to deal with the issues of education and social division. In education, we have to look at how we can give children of every race a good education that will give them a leg up. Last December, I conducted a hearing at an elementary school in Virginia where there are 900 students who speak more than 20 languages. We wanted to know how educators bridge the language gap and successfully teach those students.

Q: You are the only labor representative on the board. How does your role as an advocate for working families inform the discussions?

Chavez-Thompson: I believe one of the reasons the president appointed me is that, as a labor leader, I believe many of the causes—and cures—of inequality of all kinds can be found in the workplace. Working in the Texas cotton fields as a girl and organizing workers throughout the Southwest as an adult, I saw injustices against blacks, Hispanics and women. That's why I hope our advisory board, through our national discussion, will address the issues of jobs and paychecks. The Rev. Martin Luther King Jr. declared that it wasn't enough to be able to sit at a lunch counter if you couldn't afford the price of a hamburger—and he gave his life supporting the struggle of Memphis sanitation workers to organize a union. Dr. King understood that working people of all backgrounds can win a greater measure of justice when they organize.

Some of the most important civil rights struggles are being waged by working Americans who are organizing to join unions and gain a better life. For workers in the strawberry fields of California, the clothing and textile mills of the South and the hospitals and nursing homes of the Northeast and Midwest, the challenges to their human dignity are as stark as during the civil rights struggles of the 1960s.

I also believe that the labor movement is one of the few institutions that can build bridges across the barriers of race, culture and class. The AFL-CIO is preparing a *Practical Guide to Improving Race Relations, Equality and Opportunity in the Workplace* that will focus on the best practices of unions and management to fight discrimination. The Federation also will sponsor forums around the country to highlight how workers and managers have joined together to improve race relations and fight discrimination.

Q: The public perception is that the Initiative does not have a focus and is not accomplishing anything. Is that the case?

Chavez-Thompson: That's the perception that the media has portrayed. From the beginning, the media decided that the advisory board would not accomplish anything—and every news story repeats that theme. We are trying to gather good information about programs that have successfully overcome problems of race in schools, workplaces and neighborhoods. We have gathered more than 200 specific suggestions for improving race relations from across the country. In December, we had a great discussion with some top educators, including former Education Secretary William Bennett, about handling diversity at the elementary and secondary school levels.

bers to meet apart from management, and specifying that program members are not susceptible to dissolution by management whim. The key theme labor laws appear to be conveying is that where employee-involvement programs are introduced, members must have the power to make decisions and act independent of management.

Public-Sector Unionization

Unionizing government employees, either in the federal sector or in state, county, and municipal jurisdictions, has proven to be very lucrative for unions.[59] Significant gains have been made in these sectors, as unions increased membership from 11 percent in 1970 to 45 percent in 1996.[60] But labor relations in the government sector is not identical to its counterpart in the private sector.[61] For example, in the federal sector, wages are nonnegotiable. Likewise, compulsory membership in unions is prohibited. At the state, county, and local levels, laws must be passed to grant employees in any jurisdiction the right to unionize—and more importantly, the right to strike.[62] Yet, probably the most notable difference lies in determining "who's the boss."

In a private company, management is the employer. This, however, is not the case in government sectors. Instead, a president, a governor, mayor, county executive, etc. is responsible for the government's budget. These are elected officials, who have fiduciary responsibilities to their citizenry. Who, then, "owns" the government? Of course, it's the people. Accordingly, unionized employees in the public sector are actually negotiating against themselves as taxpayers. And even if some agreement is reached, the negotiated contract cannot be binding, even though the unions members support it, until some legislative body has approved it.

Finally, because these negotiations are a concern to the general public, citizens have the right to know what is going on. This is handled through what are called **sunshine laws.**[63] The intent of these laws is to require the parties in public-sector labor relations to make public their negotiations; that is, contract negotiations are open to the public. This freedom of information is based on the premise that the public-sector negotiations directly affect all taxpayers, and thus, they should have direct information regarding what is occurring. However, while information is important, sunshine laws have been questioned by labor relations personnel. Their contention is, for those who do not understand what happens in negotiations, what the public may see or hear during open negotiations may ultimately differ from the final contract. As such, the public may gain a false sense of negotiation outcomes.

Unionizing the Nontraditional Employee

The strength of unionization in years past resided in the manufacturing industries of the U.S. economy. Steel, tires, automobiles, and transportation were major industries that dominated every aspect of American life—and the world. In each of these industries, there was a common element. That thread was the presence of unions. Over the past few decades, however, the United States has changed gears. While once a manufacturing giant, the United States has become a service economy. Unfortunately for unions, the service sector previously had not been one of their targeted areas for organizing employees. But that, too, is changing, as survival for unions depends on their reaching out and fulfilling the

Traditional union strongholds included the manufacturing industries. Yet, as they've declined, unions have attempted to unionize nontraditional workers. In Cleveland, for example, this has meant having more focused organizing campaigns—such as organizing school teachers.

needs of the nontraditional employee. Who are these groups? *Nontraditional employees* could be classified as anyone who is not in the manufacturing and related industries. Such people include government workers, nurses, secretaries, professional and technical employees, and even some management members.[64] Let's demonstrate this growth by looking at one of these groups of service workers—health-care professionals.

Union activities in the health-care field could logically be argued as nothing new for unions. After all, many a hospital's maintenance staffs have been associated with unions of employee associations for many years. What's different, however, is that unions are not confining their organizing efforts simply to these workers. Rather, they are focusing their sights on nurses, administrative employees, lab technicians, and even those working in private doctor's offices.[65] In fact, more than 4,000 RC elections have been held in the past several years in an attempt to unionize these workers. That's about one-third of all NLRB elections held in the same time period. And unions, like the Teamsters, won about 55 percent of these elections—much better than the success ratio of "winning" in the private sector as a whole.[66] Consequently, unions are tasting some success!

As the world of work continues to radically evolve, it is safe to assume that unions will target an even broader group of employees. The same things that unions "sold" fifty years ago to get people interested in the union cause— wages, benefits, job security, and having a say in how employees are treated at work—are the same things that concern employees as we enter the new millennium.[67] Restructuring, delayering, and the de-jobbing of corporate America has forced affected workers to pay closer attention to what the unions promise. For the health-care professionals who voted to be represented by unions, this has resulted in more job security, and wages and benefits 10 to 15 percent above their nonunion counterparts.[68]

Is history repeating itself? Only time will tell. But remember, the decline in union membership—especially in the traditional industries in the 1970s—was brought about, in part, by people achieving their middle-class status. As organi-

Union survival depends on their reaching out and fulfilling the needs of nontraditional employees.

zational changes threaten this social class rank, there is every reason to believe that workers will present a unified, mutual front to the employer.[69] In some cases, that is best achieved through union activities.

INTERNATIONAL LABOR RELATIONS

Labor relations practices, and the percent of the work force unionized, are different in every country (see Exhibit 16.7). Nowhere is employee representation exactly like that in the United States. In almost every case, the relationships among management, employees, and unions (or other administrative bodies) are the result of long histories. The business approach to unionism, or emphasizing economic objectives, is uniquely American. In Europe, Latin America, and elsewhere, unions have often evolved out of a class struggle, resulting in labor as a political party. The Japanese Confederation of Shipbuilding and Engineering Workers' Union only recently began dropping its "class struggle" rhetoric and slogans to pursue a "partnership" with management.[70] The basic difference in perspective sometimes makes it difficult for U.S. expatriates to understand how the labor relations process works because even the same term may have very different meanings. For example, in the United States, "collective bargaining" implies negotiations between a labor union and management. In Sweden and Germany, it refers to negotiations between the employers' organization and a trade union for the entire industry.[71] Furthermore, arbitration in the United States usually refers to the settlement of individual contractual disputes, while in Australia arbitration is part of the contract bargaining process.

Not only does each country have a different history of unionism, each government has its own view of its role in the labor relations process. This role is often reflected in the types and nature of the regulations in force. While the U.S. government generally takes a "hands-off" approach toward intervention in labor–management matters, the Australian government, to which the labor movement has very strong ties, is inclined to be more involved. Thus, not only must the multinational corporate industrial relations office be familiar with the separate laws of each country, it also must be familiar with the environment in which those statutes are implemented. Understanding international labor relations is vital to an organization's strategic planning. Unions affect wage levels, which in turn affect competitiveness in both labor and product markets. Unions and labor laws may limit employment-level flexibility through security clauses that tightly control layoffs and terminations (or redundancies). This is especially

Country	Percent of Employees Unionized
Sweden	81%
Great Britain	39%
Italy	34%
Germany	32%
Japan	26%
United States	14%
Spain	11%
France	10%

SOURCE: "European News in Brief," *Facts on File* (Chicago: Rand McNally Corporation, 1993; 1997).

Exhibit 16-7

Unionization around the world

true in such countries as England, France, Germany, Japan, and Australia, where various laws place severe restrictions on employers.

Differing Perspectives Toward Labor Relations

If labor relations can affect the strategic planning initiatives of an organization, it is necessary to consider the issue of headquarters' involvement in host-country international union relations. The organization must assess if the labor relations function should be controlled globally from the parent country, or if it would be more advantageous for each host country to administer its own operation. There is no simple means of making this assessment; frequently, the decision reflects the relationship of the product market at home to that of the overseas product market. For instance, when domestic sales are larger than those overseas, the organization is more likely to regard the foreign office as an extension of the domestic operations. This is true for many U.S. multinational organizations because the home market is so vast. Thus, American firms have been more inclined to keep labor relations centrally located at corporate headquarters. Many European countries, by contrast, have small home markets with comparatively larger international operations; thus, they are more inclined to adapt to host-country standards and have the labor relations function decentralized.

Another divergence among multinational companies in their labor relations is the national attitude toward unions. Generally, American multinational corporations view unions negatively at home and try to avoid unionization of the work force. Europeans, on the other hand, have had greater experience with unions, are accustomed to a larger proportion of the work force being unionized, and are more accepting of the unionization of their own workers.[72] In Japan, as in other parts of Asia, unions are often closely identified with an organization.[73]

The European Community

The European Community brings together a dozen or more individual labor relations systems. For both the member nations and other countries doing business in Europe, like the United States and Japan, it is important to understand the dynamics of what will necessarily be a dramatically changing labor environment.[74]

Legislation about workers' rights is continually developing,[75] which has far-ranging implications for all employers. While the French and Germans lean toward strong worker representation in labor policy, reflecting their cultural histories, the United Kingdom and Denmark oppose it. Many basic questions remain to be answered with the implementation of the free trade of labor across national boundaries. For example, with the increase in production that accompanies the opening of this market, workers and their union representatives are going to want their fair share. And what is this fair share? For starters, European unions want a maternity package that provides 80 percent of salary for a fourteen-week period. They are also seeking premium pay for night work, full benefits for workers who are employed more than eight hours a week, participation on companies' boards of directors, and an increase in the minimum wage level to two-thirds of each country's average manufacturing wage.[76] Some of these inducements will be difficult to obtain, but companies doing business overseas must be aware of what is happening in pending labor legislation, and fully understand and comply with the host country's laws and customs.

SUMMARY

This summary relates to the Learning Objectives provided on p. 480.

After having read this chapter, you should know:

1. A union is an organization of workers, acting collectively, seeking to promote and protect their mutual interests through collective bargaining.

2. The Wagner (National Labor Relations) Act of 1935 and the Taft-Hartley (Labor–Management Relations) Act of 1947 represent the most direct legislation affecting collective bargaining. The Wagner Act gave unions the freedom to exist and identified employer unfair labor practices. Taft-Hartley balanced the power between uniforms and management by identifying union unfair labor practices.

3. Executive Orders 10988 and 11491 paved the way for labor relations to exist in the federal sector. Additionally, Executive Order 11491 made federal labor relations similar to its private-sector counterpart. The Civil Service Reform Act of 1978 removed federal sector labor relations from under the jurisdiction of the president and established a forum for its continued operation.

4. The union organizing process officially begins with the completion of an authorization. If the required percentage of potential union members show their intent to vote on a union by signing the authorization card, the NLRB will hold an election. If 50 percent plus one of those voting vote for the union, then the union is certified to be the bargaining unit.

5. Collective bargaining typically refers to the negotiation, administration, and interpretation of a written agreement between two parties that covers a specific period of time.

6. The collective-bargaining process is comprised of the following steps: preparation for negotiation, negotiation, and contract administration.

7. The various union security arrangements are the closed shop (made illegal by the Taft-Hartley Act); the union shop, which requires compulsory union membership; the agency shop, which requires compulsory union dues; and the open shop, which enforces workers' freedom of choice to select union membership or not.

8. The role of the grievance procedure is to provide a formal mechanism in labor contracts for resolving issues over the interpretation and application of a contract.

9. The most popular impasse resolution techniques include mediation (a neutral third party informally attempts to get the parties to reach an agreement); fact-finding (a neutral third party conducts a hearing to gather evidence from both sides); and interest arbitration (a panel of individuals hears testimony from both sides and renders a decision).

10. Sunshine laws require parties in the public sector to make their collective bargaining negotiations open to the public.

EXPERIENTIAL EXERCISE:
Getting A Union Perspective

Identify and visit the offices of two local unions to interview union officers or representatives using any of the questions that follow.

1. What are some of the benefits of union membership?
2. How are unions striving to save jobs?
3. What are some examples of companies that have good union–management relationships, and how do they achieve good relationships? What criteria are used to determine what constitutes good relationships from a union perspective?
4. Although union membership is reported to have declined in the last decades, why does it still serve a purpose in some organizations for 2000 and beyond?
5. Can you describe your role and responsibilities as a union leader?

WEB-WISE EXERCISES

Assignment

Search and print findings of interest from the following sites:

American Arbitration Association
http://www.adr.org/
Employee Relations and Labor Law
Labor Policy Association
www.1pa.org
Institute of Industrial Relations
:violet.berkeley.edu
Institute of Collective Bargaining
.www.ilr.cornell.edu
Industrial & Labor Relations Link
.www.uwm.edu:80

HR HEADQUARTERS http://www.hrq.com/ Collects information regarding human resources management issues regarding labor relations, unions, employee involvement, collective bargaining, or grievances.

AFL-CIO http://www.aflcio.org/ This is a major labor federation site. Many U.S. labor unions are members of the AFL-CIO.

Compare recent decisions with labor relations issues using information available from the following three sites:

1. National Labor Relations Board (NLRB) http://www.doc.gov:80/nlrb/homepg.html, which provides continuous updates of NLRB decisions.
2. U.S. Department of Labor http://www.dol.gov/, which provides links to several department agencies under the Department of Labor supervision.
3. Cornell University School of Industrial and Labor Relations http://www.ilr.cornell.edu/, which provides an extensive collection of resources on labor and human resources, including government reports, databases, as well as Cornell publications and journals.

CASE APPLICATION:
Employee Involvement: It Makes Cents (but Common Cents Isn't Always Common Practice)

Background

In a union 50-year-old manufacturing plant, employment involvement is negotiated by the union in their new contract.

The union appoints a union EI coordinator to establish the processes and mechanisms to involve employees.

To date, training for employees has been minimal to nonexistent, no suggestions or recognition system has been in place, and job descriptions have not been updated or established for managers or employees in decades.

The company's primary customer, responsible for over 60 percent of their revenues, or $30 million, has placed the company on "probation" due to poor quality, including late or defective parts.

Stockholders are complaining about less than a 4 percent return on their investment.

Management blames employees, and employees blame management. Engineers blame programmers who blame machinists who blame programmers who blame engineers who blame. . . . Employees speak of "the wall" between the shop and the offices.

Managers are rarely seen on the shop floor because

they are striving through management meetings to identify ways to cut costs and reduce scrap and defective parts, costing millions. Management spends millions on upgrading needed equipment and technology, paints the plant, reorganizes the offices, and terminates some managers.

Many employees feel that they are not respected or listened to and that their ideas or suggestions are not acted upon.

Employee involvement, through the union, develops a suggestion system, but becomes frustrated when managers "don't have time . . . or they'll look at them when they do have time." One manager wonders how they will afford pizza.

Overtime continues to "just get the parts out the door" with employees working 89–90 hours a week, week after week.

Some employees, including some members, believe "it's just another program, they'll never change, it won't make any difference, just a paycheck, wait and see, management doesn't care."

Employee involvement contracts a training/consulting company to develop twenty customized training programs for employees and trains employees to present the programs, through a "train the trainer" certification program.

Two years and several management changes later, management requires employees to complete two courses. Management also asks that two of the twenty courses approved on quality improvement and change be shortened to two hours.

The union employee involvement team does not feel supported, believes the employees could help turn the company around, understands that the process will take time, but wonders why what would seem common sense is not common practice.

Part One: Instructions

Based on the information provided, you and your class team are invited to suggest how the union could gain management's and members' support for EI efforts to help the company achieve its goals and thereby help ensure jobs of its members.

Respond by contributing at least four ideas to your team, then discussing each team member's suggestions, and compiling a list of ten suggestions.

Part Two: Questions

1. If EI makes common sense, why would a company's management such as the one described not support EI?
2. What types of beliefs or values would the managers described likely hold and what actions, reactions, impact, or consequences are likely, as a result, to the company and themselves?

3. What types of beliefs or values would the nonsupportive employees described likely hold and what actions, reactions, impact, or consequences are likely, as a result, to the company and themselves?

4. What types of beliefs or values would the EI leaders and trainers described likely hold and what actions, reactions, impact, or consequences are likely, as a result, to the company and themselves?

4. What would you predict for the company and employees in the future if their current trend continues?

TESTING YOUR UNDERSTANDING

How well did you fulfill the learning objectives?

1. How do activities differ for human resource professionals in an organization that is unionized, and one that is not?
   a. Where a union exists, human resource professionals' responsibilities often consist mainly of following procedures and policies laid out in the labor contract. In a nonunion setting, human resource professionals are involved in a range of activities from planning through implementation of procedures and policies.
   b. In a union setting, human resource professionals spend most of their time in deciding wage rates. Where a union does not represent workers, human resource professionals are involved in a range of activities from planning through implementation of the whole array of human resource procedures and policies.
   c. Where a union represents workers, human resource professionals have setting and monitoring the hours of work as their primary responsibility. Where they don't, human resource professionals are involved in a range of activities from planning through implementation of the whole array of human resource procedures and policies.
   d. In a union setting, human resource professionals are responsible only for selecting and monitoring employee benefits packages, primarily health-care options. In a nonunion setting, human resource professionals are involved in a range of activities from planning through implementation of the whole array of human resource procedures and policies.
   e. There is no difference between the two.

2. The Wagner Act required employers to bargain in good faith over mandatory bargaining issues of all of the following except
   a. wages.
   b. working hours.
   c. medical benefits.
   d. terms of work.
   e. conditions of work.

3. Provisions of the Taft-Hartley Act include all of the following except
   a. management must bargain in good faith.
   b. unions must bargain in good faith.
   c. closed shops were declared illegal.
   d. unions could not obtain compensation for services not performed.
   e. the president of the United States can issue an eighty-day cooling off period if national security is involved.

4. What effect do sunshine laws have on labor–management relations?
   a. All labor relations contract negotiations, public and private sector, are required to be open to the public.
   b. Sunshine laws are based on the premise that taxpayers have a right to know how their money is being spent.
   c. Sunshine laws assist in getting negotiations completed more quickly because the public is aware of the events occurring in negotiations.
   d. Sunshine laws adversely affect negotiations in that negotiations must stop periodically to allow for reporters to interview the negotiators.
   e. Sunshine laws permit unions to exist in the public sector.

5. Why are union activities important to the rest of the work force?
   a. Unions affect important sectors of the U.S. economy.
   b. They are not important to the rest of the work force.
   c. Unions are instrumental in achieving successful globalization.
   d. Unions lead the way in empowering the work force.
   e. Unions are one of the most innovative forces in the U.S. economy.

6. Provisions of the Landrum-Griffin Act include all of the following except
   a. secret ballots were used for union elections.
   b. union officials were made accountable for union funds.
   c. management was restrained from filing injunctions.
   d. restrictions were placed on trusteeships.
   e. conduct during elections was regulated.

7. In the past decade, which legislation has been used to oust a number of labor officials in the Teamsters Union who were alleged to have organized crime ties?
   a. Civil Service Reform Act.
   b. Landrum-Griffin Act.
   c. Racketeering Influenced and Corrupt Organizations Act.

    d. Executive Order 10988.

    e. Executive Order 11491.

8. Issues that appear consistently throughout labor contracts are all of the following except

    a. wages.

    b. hours.

    c. grievance procedure.

    d. terms and conditions of employment.

    e. technology transfer.

9. Government is involved in labor negotiations in all of the following ways except

    a. to intervene if an impasse undermines the nation's well-being.

    b. to provide financial backing for the negotiators.

    c. to provide the rules under which labor and management bargain.

    d. to provide a watchful eye on the two parties to make sure the rules are followed.

    e. to intervene if an agreement on acceptable terms cannot be reached.

10. Union contract negotiation

    a. is the attempt to get management's highest offer to approximate the lowest demands that the union is willing to accept.

    b. is conducted in public.

    c. begins with a written formal agreement and proceeds to verbal discussions of final details.

    d. is increasingly accompanied by union strikes.

    e. is most successful when a lockout results.

11. Erica works for a company that has a union. She has refused, on religious grounds, to join the union. She must choose between forfeiting her job and paying a sum of money equal to union dues to the union to continue her employment. Erica works in a(n)

    a. closed shop.

    b. union shop.

    c. agency shop.

    d. open shop.

    e. right-to-work shop.

12. A union security arrangement is

    a. a means to ensure some consistency in income.

    b. a way to keep the press out of union negotiation meetings.

    c. designed to prevent access of organized crime to union files.

    d. a cooperative venture between workers and managers.

    e. part of the health and safety provisions in most new union contracts.

13. Mark was hired last week as a fry cook at a fast-food restaurant. After he successfully completes his thirty-day probationary period, he must either join the union or forfeit his job. John is working in a(n)

    a. closed shop.

    b. union shop.

    c. agency shop.

    d. open shop.

    e. right-to-work shop.

14. A secretaries' union has been trying to negotiate a new contract with management for ninety days. The old contract expires in two weeks. To resolve the contract negotiation disputes, a third party has been hired to gather evidence from both the secretaries and the managers and present the findings to both parties. The recommendation will not be binding on either party. What kind of impasse resolution technique is being used?

    a. lockout

    b. grievance arbitration

    c. fact-finding

    d. interest arbitration

    e. mediation

Endnotes

1. Information for this opening vignette is based on Paul Magnusson, Nicole Harris, Linda Himelstein, Bill Vlasic, and Wendy Zellner, "A Wake-Up Call for Business," *Business Week* (September 1, 1997), pp. 28–29; Matthew Miller, "Packaging the Strike," *U.S. News & World Report* (September 1, 1997), pp. 44–46; Aaron Bernstein and Nicole Harris, "This Package Is a Heavy One for the Teamsters," *Business Week* (August 25, 1997), pp. 40–41; and Aaron Bernstein, "At UPS, Part-Time Work Is a Full-Time Issue," *Business Week* (June 16, 1997), pp. 88–92.

2. "Union Organizing Fails to Stanch Loss of Membership," *The Sun* (March 22, 1998), p. 5-A, and Department of Labor, *Statistical Abstracts of the United States, 1997* (Washington, D.C.: GPO), p. 441.

3. Robert Kornfeld, "The Effects of Union Membership on Wages and Employee Benefits: The Case of Australia," *Industrial and Labor Relations Review* (October 1993), p. 114.

4. Marianne J. Koch and Greg Hundley, "The Effects of Unionism on Recruitment and Selection Methods," *Industrial Relations* (July 1997), p. 349.

5. Readers should recognize that although the closed shop (compulsory union membership before one is hired) was declared illegal by the Taft-Hartley Act, a modified form still exists today. That quasi-closed shop arrangement is called the *hiring hall* and is found predominantly in the construction and printing industries. However, a hiring hall is not a form of union security because it must assist all members despite their union affiliation. Additionally, the hiring hall must establish procedures for referrals that are nondiscriminatory. See Bruce Feldecker, *Labor Guide to Labor Law,* 3d ed. (Englewood Cliffs, N.J.: Prentice-Hall, 1990), pp. 319–323.

6. Currently, 21 of 50 states are right-to-work states. These include Alabama, Arizona, Arkansas, Florida, Georgia, Idaho, Iowa, Kansas, Louisiana, Mississippi, Nebraska, Nevada, North Carolina, North Dakota, South Carolina, South Dakota, Tennessee, Texas, Utah, Virginia, and Wyoming. [*Statistical Abstracts of the United States, 1997,* p. 441.]

7. There are, however, exceptions to this in the construction industry.

8. *Communication Workers of America* v. *Beck,* U.S. Supreme Court, 109LC (1988).

9. Commerce Clearing House, *Human Resources Management: Ideas and Trends* (April 29, 1992), p. 70.

10. "The AFL-CIO's Dues Blues: Democracy Strikes Unions," *Fortune* (April 13, 1998), p. 36.

11. Ibid.

12. Aaron Bernstein and David Griesing, "Baseball's Strike Talk Turns Serious," *Business Week* (June 27, 1994), p. 34.

13. For a comprehensive review of labor laws, see Bruce Feldacker, *Labor Law Guide to Labor Law,* 3d ed. (Englewood Cliffs, N.J.: Prentice-Hall, 1990).

14. As passed in 1947, the NLRB administrative body originally consisted of three members. It was expanded to five members with the passage of Taft-Hartley in 1947.

15. Commerce Clearing House, p. 1521.

16. Ibid.

17. See Commerce Clearing House, *Labor Law Course,* p. 1524.

18. Commerce Clearing House, *Labor Law Course,* p. 7054

19. Bruce Feldacker, Labor Law Guide to Labor Law, 3d ed., p. 5. For a more in-depth look at unionization in the hospital sector, see Edmund R. Becker and Jonathon S. Rakich, "Hospital Union Election Activity, 1974–1975," in *Health Care Financing,* Vol. 9, No. 3 (Spring 1988), pp. 59–66.

20. The Railway Labor Act created the National Mediation Board, which works on matters of recognition, dispute resolution, and unfair labor practices in the railroad and airline industries only. The National Railroad Adjustment Board was also part of the Railway Labor Act, and this body arbitrated disputes between railroads and unions.

21. It is also important to note that the Wagner Act was also amended in 1974 with the Health Care Amendments. This amendment brought both nonprofit hospitals and health care organizations under the jurisdiction of the Wagner Act.

22. Commerce Clearing House, p. 1524.

23. L-M 2 reports are required of unions that have revenues of $100,000 or more. L-M 3 reports are required of unions that have less than $100,000 in revenues.

24. It must be noted that when one discusses government labor relations, two categories emerge. One is the federal sector, the other the public sector. In a brief discussion of government labor relations, the focus is on the federal sector due to its federal legislation. However, one must realize that state or municipal statutes do define practices for labor–management relationships for state, county, and municipal workers (typically police officers, fire fighters, and teachers). Because these laws differ in the many jurisdictions, it goes beyond the scope of this text to attempt to clarify each jurisdiction's laws.

25. Although government employees often face a no-strike clause, with the exception of the Air Traffic Controllers case, such restrictions are generally ineffective. Working to rules, "blue flues" and recorded sanitation, nursing, and teacher strikes across this country support the contention that a no-strike clause is weak.

26. United States Code Annotated, *Title 18, Section 1961* (St. Paul, Minn.: West Publishing, 1984), p. 6.

27. Ibid., p. 228.

28. United States Code Annotated, *Title 29, Section 186* (St. Paul, Minn.: West Publishing, 1978), p. 17.

29. See, for example, "The Liberation of the Teamsters," *National Review* (March 30, 1992), p. 35; and "Breaking the Teamsters," *Newsweek* (June 22, 1987), p. 43.

30. Only pure grievance awards can be solely determined by the FLRA. See Joseph R. Gordon and Joyce M. Najita, "Judicial Response to Public-Sector Arbitration," in Aaron et al., op. cit., p. 247.

31. Mark A. Spognardi and Ruth Hill Bro, "Organizing Through Cyberspace: Electronic Communications and the National Labor Relations Act," *Employee Relations Law Journal* (Spring, 1998), pp. 141–151.

32. Elections may not be the only means of unionizing. In cases where a company has refused to recognize a union because of a past unfair labor practice, the NLRB may certify a union without a vote.

33. Jim Wimberly, "Union Elections," *Commerce Clearing House, Human Resources Management: Ideas and Trends* (February 15, 1990), p. 35.

34. "Rumble in Buick City," *Business Week* (October 10, 1994), p. 42.

35. D. C. Bok and J. T. Dunlop, "Collective Bargaining in the United States: An Overview," in W. Clay Hammer and Frank L. Schmidt (eds.), *Contemporary Problems in Personnel* (Chicago: St. Clair Press, 1977), p. 383.

36. An international union, in this context, refers to a national union in the United States that has local unions in Canada.

37. If we take into account public-sector collective bargaining, then we have another exception—the public. The tax-paying voting public can influence elected officials to act in certain ways during negotiations.

38. Nicole Harris, "Flying into a Rage," *Business Week* (April 27, 1998), p. 119.

39. Mollie H. Bowers and David A. DeCenzo, *Essentials of Labor Relations* (Englewood Cliffs, N.J.: Prentice-Hall, 1992), p. 101.

40. For a thorough explanation of the grievance procedure, see ibid., pp. 109–114.

41. Michael R. Carroll and Christina Heavrin, *Collective Bargaining and Labor Relations* (New York: Merrill/Macmillan Publishing, 1991), pp. 310–311.

42. Adapted from Stephen P. Robbins and David A. DeCenzo, *Supervision Today,* 2nd ed. (Upper Saddle River, N.J.: Prentice-Hall, 1998), p. 557.

43. Ibid., p. 316.

44. To be accurate, a strike vote is generally held at the local union level in which the members authorize their union leadership to call the strike.

45. U.S. Department of Labor, *Statistical Abstracts of the United States, 1997* (Washington, D.C., GPO, 1997), p. 439, and "Unions-Arise—With New Tricks," *Time* (June 13, 1994), p. 56.

46. See Michael A. Verespej, "Wounded and Weaponless," *Industry Week* (September 16, 1996), p. 46; and Jim Stern, "Unions Rethinking Role of the Strike," *Washington Post* (March 18, 1990), p. H-3.

47. "The Strike Weapon Remains Highly Troublesome for Unions," *The Wall Street Journal* (February 26, 1991), p. A-1.

48. U.S. Bureau of the Census, *Statistical Abstracts of the United States, 1997*), p. 439; "Unions and Strikers: A Huge Nonproblem," *Fortune* (May 31, 1994), pp. 175–176; and "Unions Arise—With New Tricks," p. 56.

49. "Why Labor Keeps Losing," *Fortune* (July 11, 1994), p. 178.

50. See Philip A. Miscimarra and Kenneth D. Schwartz, "Frozen in Time—The NLRB, Outsourcing, and Management Rights," *Journal of Labor Research* (Fall 1997), pp. 561–580. Outsourcing refers to a situation where work is taken away from unionized workers in a company and given to nonunionized employees in a separate location.

51. "Why Labor Keeps Losing," *Fortune* (July 11, 1994), p. 178; and John David, "U.S. Labor Movement Cornered," *The Charleston Gazette* (June 21, 1989), p. 6-A. It is also interesting to point out that President Clinton lifted the ban on hiring air traffic controllers who had been fired by President Reagan. Any air traffic controller fired by Reagan was not eligible to work again for the Federal Aviation Administration—the agency that hires air controllers. The removal of the ban came on August 12, 1993.

52. George J. Church, "Unions Arise—With New Tricks," *Time* (June 13, 1994).

53. Vivienne Walt, "Labor's Big Net," *U.S. News & World Report,* (February 9, 1998), pp. 52–53; and Aaron Bernstein, "Sweeney's Blitz," *Business Week* (February 17, 1997), p. 56.

54. Timothy J. Loney, "TQM and Labor-Management Cooperation—A Noble Experiment for the Public Sector," *International Journal of Public Administration* (October 1996), p. 1845; and Bill Vlasic, "The Saginaw Solution," *Business Week* (July 15, 1996), pp. 78–80.

55. "Teamwork for Employees and Managers (TEAM) Act," *HR Legislative Fact Sheet* (June 1996), pp. 28–29; and Randall Hanson, Rebecca I. Porterfield, and Kathleen Ames, "Employee Empowerment at Risk: Effects of Recent NLRB Rulings," *Academy of Management Executive,* Vol. 9, No. 2 (1995), pp. 45–56.

56. Betty Southard Murphy, Wayne E. Barlow, and D. Diane Hatch, "NLRB Decides Labor-Management Committees Case," *Personnel Journal* (February 1993), p. 20.

57. Ibid. and "Team Act," *The Journal for Quality and Participation* (January/February 1998), p. 7.

58. Legislation, called the "Teamwork For Employees and Managers (TEAM) Act," has been proposed in both the House of Representatives and the Senate. The Act, as proposed, was designed to "permit employers and employees to establish and maintain employee involvement programs—including various approaches to problem-solving, communication enhancement, productivity improvement programs." In May 1996, the Act was passed in the House and sent to the Senate for approval. By a vote of 53 to 46, the Senate approved the Act in principal but did not agree to some of its language. ["Teamwork for Employees and Managers (TEAM) Act." *HR Legislative Fact Sheet* (June 1996), pp. 28–29.]

59. See, for example, Leo Troy, "Why Labor Unions Are Declining," *Journal of Commerce and Commercial* (August 1994), p. 6A; and S. Overman, "The Union Pitch Has Changed," *HRMagazine* (December 1991), pp. 44–46.

60. "The U.S. Public Sector," *IRS Employment Review* (March 1997), p. E-8.

61. Adapted from Molly H. Bowers and David A. DeCenzo, *Essentials of Labor Relations* (Englewood Cliffs, N.J.: Prentice-Hall, 1992), pp. 138–144.

62. Victor G. Devinatz, "Testing the Johnston 'Public Sector Union Strike' Hypotheses: A Qualitative Analysis," *Journal of Collective Negotiations in the Public Sector,* Vol. 26, No. 2 (1997), pp. 99–112.

63. Sunshine laws exist in eleven states: Alaska, California, Delaware, Florida, Idaho, Iowa, Minnesota, Texas, Ohio, Vermont, and Wisconsin. In addition, Indiana, Kansas, Maryland, Montana, and Tennessee have laws regarding the openness of the collective bargaining process. From B. V. H. Schneider, "Public Sector Labor Legislation—An Evolutionary Analysis," p. 219.

64. "Why White-Collar Staff Join Unions," *IRS Employment Trends* (August 1994), pp. 2–3.

65. See, for example, Clyde Scott and Christopher M. Lowery, "Union Election Activity in the Health Care Industry," *Health Care Management Review* (Winter 1994), pp. 18–28.

66. Ibid.

67. *IRS Employment Trends*, p. 3.

68. Clyde Scott and Christopher M. Lowery, "Union Election Activity in the Health Care Industry," *Health Care Management Review* (Winter 1994), p. 22.

69. *IRS Employment Trends*, p. 3.

70. "Japan Report," *The Wall Street Journal* (April 23, 1991), p. A-1.

71. See, for example, Peter J. Dowling and Randall S. Schuler, *International Dimensions of Human Resource Management* (Boston: PWS-Kent Publishing, 1990), pp. 138–157.

72. David Woodruff, "The German Worker Is Making a Sacrifice," *Business Week* (July 28, 1997), pp. 46–47.

73. See Robert E. Cole and Donald R. Deskins, Jr., "Racial Factors in Site Location and Employment Patterns of Japanese Auto Firms in America," *California Management Review* (1988), pp. 9–22.

74. See, for example, Peter Dowling, Randall S. Schuler, and Denice E. Welch, *International Dimensions of Human Resource Management,* 2d. ed. (Belmont, Calif.: Wadsworth, 1994), pp. 201–203.

75. Brooks Tigner, "The Looming Crunch," in M. Mendenhall and G. Oddou (eds.), *Readings and Cases in International Human Resource Management* (Boston: PWS-Kent Publishing, 1991), pp. 412–417.

76. "Workers Want Their Piece of Europe Inc.," *Business Week* (October 29, 1990), p. 46.

Appendix
Getting into the
Organization?

In Chapters 6 and 7, we introduced you to the recruiting and selection processes. When recruiters make a decision to hire employees, information is often sent out announcing the job. Seeing that announcement, and feeling like there's a potential match between what you can offer and what the organization wants, you need to throw your hat into the "hiring ring."

One of the more stressful situations you will face happens when you apply for a job. This occurs because generally there are no specific guidelines to follow to guarantee you success. However, several tips can be offered that may increase your chances of finding employment. Even though getting a job interview should be one of your major goals in the hiring process, being offered an interview opportunity requires hard work. You should view getting a job as your job at the moment.[1]

Competition for most jobs today is fierce. As such, you can't wait until the last minute to enter the job market. Your job hunt must start well in advance of when you plan to start work. So for seniors in college who plan to graduate in May, for instance, we suggest your job search begin sometime around the previous September. Why is starting in the Fall helpful? There are two advantages. First, it shows that you are taking an interest in your career and that you are planning. You're not waiting until the last minute to begin, and this reflects favorably on you. Second, starting in the fall coincides with many companies' recruiting cycles. If you wait until March to begin the process, some job openings are likely to already have been filled. For specific information regarding the company recruiting cycles in your area, visit your college's career development center.

Some On-Line Job Sites

Over the past few years, there has been a proliferation of Web sites that provide job searchers with information regarding job openings. Listed below are some of the more popular sites that have been shown to help individuals in their job searches.[2] As you begin your job search, we recommend you "surf" some of these Web sites for valuable and useful information.

Site:	*Web Address:*
America's Job Bank	*http://www.ajb.dni.us*
Boldface Jobs	*http://www.boldfacejobs.com/*
Career Resource Center	*http://www.careers.org/*
Career Path	*http://careerpath.com*
CareerMosaic	*http://www.careermosaic.com*
Careers and Jobs	*http://www.startbere.com/jobs/*
Emory Colossal List	*http://wwwemory.edu/CAREER/Links.html*
Federal Jobs	*http://fedworld.gov//jobs/jobsearch/html*
High Tech Careers	*http://bitechcareer.com/bitech*
JobWeb	*http://jobweb.org*
NationJob Network	*http://www.nationjob.com*
Online Career Center	*http://www.careers.org*
The Riley Guide	*http://www.jobtrack.com/jobguide*
The Monster Board	*http://www.monster.com*

Preparing the Resume

All job applicants need to have information circulating that reflects positively on their strengths. That information needs to be sent to prospective employers in a format that is understandable and consistent with the organization's hiring practices. In most instances, this is done through the résumé.

No matter who you are or where you are in your career, you need a current résumé. Your résumé is typically the only information source that a recruiter will use in determining whether to grant you an interview. Therefore, your résumé must be a sales tool; it must give key information that supports your candidacy, highlights your strengths, and differentiates you from other job applicants. An example of the type of information that should be included is shown in Exhibit A-1. Notice, too, that volunteer experience this individual has is noted on the resume. Anything that distinguishes you from other applicants should be included. It shows that you are well rounded, committed to your community, and willing to "help" others.

It is important to pinpoint a few key themes regarding résumés that may seem like common sense but are frequently ignored. First, your résumé must be printed on a quality printer—or at the very least, professionally typed. The style of font should be easy to read (e.g., Courier or Times New Roman type fonts). Avoid any style that may be hard on the eyes, such as a script or italics font. A recruiter who must review 100 or more résumés a day is not going to look favorably at difficult-to-read résumés. So use an easy-to-read font and make the recruiter's job easier.

It is also important to note that many companies today are using computer scanners to make the first pass through résumés. They scan each résumé for specific information like key job elements, experience, work history, education, or technical expertise.[3] The use of scanners, then, has created two important aspects for résumé writing.[4] The computer matches key words in a job description. Thus, in creating a résumé, typical job description phraseology should be used. Secondly (and this goes back to the issue of font type), the font used should be easily read by the scanner. If it can't, your résumé may be put in the rejection file.

RÉSUMÉ OF:	**DANA BROWN** **1690 West Road** **Charlotte, NC 56013**
CAREER OBJECTIVE:	Seeking employment in an investment firm that provides a challenging opportunity to combine exceptional interpersonal and computer skills.
EDUCATION:	**Pembroke Community College** A.A., Business Administration (May 1996) **Wake Forest University** B.S., Finance (May 1999)
EXPERIENCE: 12/97 to present	**Wake Forest University** Campus Bookstore, Assistant Bookkeeper *Primary Duties:* Responsible for the coordinating book purchases with academic departments; placing orders with publishers; invoicing, receiving inventory, pricing, and stocking shelves. Supervised four student employees. Managed annual budget of $25,000.
9/94 to 9/96	**Pembroke Community College** Student Assistant, Business Administration *Primary duties:* Responsible for routine administrative matters in an academic department—including answering phones, word processing faculty materials, and answering student questions.
10/91 to 6/94	**High Point High School** Yearbook Staff *Primary Duties:* Responsible for coordinating marketing efforts in local community. Involved in fund raising through contacts with community organizations.
SPECIAL SKILLS:	Experienced in Microsoft Excel and Word, Netscape, D-Base, and powerpoint presentations software. Fluent in speaking and writing Spanish. Certified in CPR.
SERVICE ACTIVITIES:	Vice-president, Student Government Association Volunteer, Meals-On-Wheels Volunteer, United Way
REFERENCES:	Available on request.

Exhibit A-1
A Sample Résumé

Your résumé should be copied on good quality white or off-white paper (no off-the-wall colors). There are certain types of jobs—like a creative artist position—where this suggestion may be inappropriate. But these are the exceptions. You can't go wrong using a 20-bond-weight paper that has some cotton content (about 20 percent). By all means, don't send standard duplicating paper—it may look as if you are mass-mailing résumés [even if you are].

Our last point regarding résumés relates to proofreading. Because the résumé is the only representation of you the recruiter has, a sloppy résumé can be deadly. If it contains misspelled words or is grammatically incorrect, your chances for an interview will be significantly reduced. Proofread your résumé, and if possible, let others proofread it too.

In addition to your résumé, you need a cover letter. Your cover letter should contain information that tells the recruiter why you should be considered for the job. You need to describe why you'd be a good job candidate. This means having a cover letter that highlights your greatest strengths and indicates how these strengths can be useful to the company. Your cover letter should also contain some information citing why the organization getting your résumé is of interest to you. Cover letters should be carefully tailored to each specific organization. This shows that you've taken some time and given some thought to the job you're applying for.

Cover letters must be addressed to a real name. Don't send anything out "To Whom It May concern—" such letters tell the recruiter that you are on a fishing expedition, mass mailing résumés in hopes that some positive response is generated. This technique seldom works in job hunting. You may not always have the recruiter's name and title, but with some work you can get it. Telephone the company in question and ask for it; most receptionists in an Employment office will give out the recruiter's name and title. If you just can't get a name, go to the reference section of a library (you may also find this information on the Internet) and locate a copy of a publication like the Standard and Poor's Register Manual, or Moody's. These publications usually list the names and titles of officers in the organization. If everything else fails, send your résumé to one of the officers, preferably the officer in charge of employment or administration, or even to the president of the organization.

Like the résumé, the cover letter should be flawless. Proofread this as carefully as you do the résumé. Finally, sign each cover letter individually.

Excelling at the Interview

Once you've made it through the initial screening process, you're likely to be called in for an interview. Interviews play a critical role in determining whether you will get the job. Up to now, all the recruiter has seen is your well-polished cover letter and résumé. Remember, however, what was said in Chapter 6 regarding hiring. Few individuals, if anyone, get a job without an interview. No matter how qualified you are for a position, if you perform poorly in the interview, you're not likely to be hired!

The reason interviews are so popular is that they help the recruiter determine if you are a "good fit" for the organization, in terms of your level of motivation and interpersonal skills.[5] Popularity aside, however, how interviews are conducted can be problematic. We presented a summary of the research conducted on interviews in Chapter 7 (see pages 201–202). While interviewer mistakes or bias shouldn't be part of your interview, it's important for you to understand that they may exist. Why is this knowledge important? If you know how the interviewer may react in the hiring process, it can help you to avoid making a costly mistake.

Additionally, many of the biases that may exist in the interview may be overcome through a technique called *impression management*. Impression management refers to attempts to project an image that will result in achieving a favorable outcome.[6] For example, if you can say or do something that is viewed favorably by the interviewer, then you may create a more favorable impression of yourself. Take a situation where you find out in the early moments of the interview that your interviewer values workers who are capable of balancing work and personal responsibilities. Making statements of being an individual who likes to work hard, but also reserves time to spend with family and friends, may result in creating a positive impression. You need to understand, too, that interviewers generally have short and inaccurate memories.[7] Research has shown that most only remember about half of what you say. While taking notes can help them remember more, what they remember most will be those impressions you make—both favorable and unfavorable.[8] Given this background information on interviews and interviewers, what can you do to increase your chances of excelling in the interview?

First, do some homework. Go to your library—or do a search for the company in the Internet—and get as much information as possible on the organization. Develop a solid grounding in the company, its history, markets, financial situation—and the industry in which it competes.

The night before the interview, get a good night's rest. Eat a good breakfast to build your energy level, as the day's events will be grueling. As you prepare for the interview, keep in mind that your appearance is going to be the first impression you make. Dress appropriately. Even though appearance generally is not supposed to enter into the hiring decision, incorrect attire can result in a negative impression. In fact, one study suggests that 80 percent of the interviewer's perception of you in the interview comes from his or her initial perception of you, based primarily on your appearance and body language.[9] Therefore, dress appropriately and be meticulous in your attire. In getting to the interview location, arrive early—about 30 minutes ahead of your scheduled interview. It is better for you to wait than to have to contend with something unexpected, like a traffic jam, that could make you late. Arriving early also gives you an opportunity to survey the office environment and possibly gather some clues about the organization. You should use any clues you can pick up to increase your chances of making a favorable impression.

As you meet the recruiter, give him or her a firm handshake. Make good eye contact and maintain it throughout the interview. Remember, your body language may be giving away secrets about you that you don't want an interviewer to pick up. Sit erect and maintain good posture. At this point, you are probably as nervous as you have ever been. While this is natural, try your best to relax. Recruiters know that you'll be anxious, and a good one will try to put you at ease. Being prepared for an interview can also help build confidence and reduce the nervousness. You can start building that confidence by reviewing a set of questions most frequently asked by interviewers. You can usually get a copy of these from the career center at your college. More important, however, since you may be asked these questions, you should have developed responses beforehand. But let's add a word of caution here. The best advice is to be yourself. Don't go into an interview with a prepared text and recite it from memory. Have an idea of what you would like to say, but don't rely on verbatim responses. Experienced interviewers will see through this "over-preparedness" and downgrade their evaluation of you.

You should also try to go through several "practice" interviews if possible. Universities often have career days on campus, when recruiters from companies are on-site to interview students. Take advantage of them. Even if the job does not fit what you want, the process will at least serve to help you become more skilled at dealing with interviews. You can also practice with family, friends, career counselors, student groups to which you belong, or your faculty advisor.

When the interview ends, thank the interviewer for his or her time, and for giving you this opportunity to talk about your qualifications. But don't think that "selling" yourself has stopped there. As soon as you get home, send a thank you letter to the recruiter for taking the time to interview you and giving you the opportunity to discuss your job candidacy. You'd be amazed at how many people fail to do this! This little act of courtesy has a positive effect—use it to your advantage.

And from both of us, good luck in your job search!

Endnotes

1. See, for instance, Robyn D. Clarke, "Getting a Job! . . . After College," *Black Enterprise* (February 1998), pp. 135–138.

2. Information for these Web addresses has been provided from Laurel Touby, "Finding a Job Online," *Working Mother* (April 1998), p. 20; "Careers: *WWW.Getajobyoulazybum.org*," *Men's Health* (April 1997), p. 58; Mike Frost, HR Cyberspace," *HRMagazine* (April 1997, pp. 34–35; and Bronwyn Fryer, "Job Hunting, the Electronic Way," *Working Woman* (March 1995), pp. 59; 78.

3. See, for example, Julia Lawlor, "Scanning Resumes: The Impersonal Touch," *USA Today* (October 7, 1991), p. 7B.

4. T. Mullins, "How to Land a Job," *Psychology Today* (September/October 1994), pp. 12–13.

5. For a discussion on fit and its appropriateness to the interviewing process, see "The Right Fit," *Small Business Reports* (April 1993), p. 28.

6. For a more detailed discussion of impression management, see A. L. Kristof and C. K. Stevens, "Applicant Impression Management Tactics: Effects on Interviewer Evaluations and Interview Outcomes," Moore (ed.), *Academy of Management Best Papers Proceedings,* D. P. (August 14–17, 1994), pp. 127–131.

7. Reported in R. E. Carlson, P. W. Thayer, E. C. Mayfield, and D. A. Peterson, "Improvements in the Selection Interview," *Personnel Journal* (April 1971), p. 272.

8. R. L. Dipboye, *Selection Interviews: Process Perspectives* (Cincinnati, Ohio: South-Western Publishing, 1992), p. 201.

9. K. Schabacker, "Tips on Making a Great First Impression," *Working Woman* (February 1992), p. 55.

Answers to Testing Your Understanding

Chapter 1
1. b
2. d
3. e
4. d
5. a
6. b
7. a
8. c
9. b
10. a
11. c
12. a
13. d
14. d
15. d
16. a
17. b
18. a

Chapter 2
1. e
2. b
3. b
4. e
5. c
6. d
7. c
8. a
9. e
10. d
11. c
12. e
13. b
14. d

Chapter 3
1. b
2. c
3. a
4. a
5. a
6. b
7. b
8. d
9. c
10. d
11. c

Chapter 4
1. c
2. a
3. d
4. a
5. b
6. d
7. b
8. a
9. c
10. d

Chapter 5
1. c
2. d
3. d
4. a
5. d
6. b
7. c
8. c
9. b
10. d
11. e
12. d

Chapter 6
1. d
2. d
3. e
4. c
5. a
6. e
7. b
8. b
9. a
10. a
11. d
12. b
13. d
14. c

Chapter 7
1. d
2. b
3. b
4. a
5. d
6. c
7. e
8. c
9. a
10. e
11. c
12. d
13. b
14. c

Chapter 8
1. d
2. c
3. d
4. b
5. d

6. d
7. c
8. b
9. a
10. d
11. c
12. d
13. a
14. c

Chapter 9
1. e
2. c
3. a
4. d
5. c
6. d
7. c
8. a
9. b
10. a
11. c
12. d

Chapter 10
1. a
2. e
3. b
4. e
5. b
6. c
7. a
8. b
9. b
10. e
11. e
12. b
13. c

14. c
15. b

Chapter 11
1. e
2. c
3. b
4. e
5. c
6. a
7. e
8. d
9. a
10. b
11. c
12. a
13. b
14. e
15. d
16. c

Chapter 12
1. e
2. c
3. d
4. c

5. d
6. a
7. b
8. a
9. c
10. b
11. d
12. a
13. e
14. a
15. d

Chapter 13
1. c
2. c
3. b
4. a
5. b
6. c
7. d
8. b
9. d
10. a
11. c
12. a
13. b

14. c
15. d

Chapter 14
1. d
2. c
3. e
4. b
5. a
6. e
7. d
8. b
9. a
10. b
11. a
12. c
13. b
14. d
15. a

Chapter 15
1. a
2. c
3. d
4. a
5. b

6. d
7. c
8. a
9. b
10. e
11. b
12. a
13. b
14. d

Chapter 16
1. a
2. c
3. a
4. b
5. a
6. c
7. c
8. e
9. b
10. a
11. c
12. a
13. b
14. c

Glossary

(Number in parentheses indicates chapter in which term first appeared)

Absolute Standards (10) Measuring an employee's performance against some established standards.

Accept Errors (6) Accepting candidates who would later prove to be poor performers.

Adjective Rating Scales (10) A performance appraisal method that lists a number of traits and a range of performance for each.

Adverse (Disparate) Impact (3) A consequence of an employment practice that results in a greater rejection rate for a minority group than it does for the majority group in the occupation.

Adverse (Disparate) Treatment (3) An employment situation where protected group members receive different treatment than other employees in matters like performance evaluations, promotions, etc.

Adverse Selection (12) A situation in flexible benefits administration where those in greatest need of a particular benefit choose that benefit more often than the average employee.

Advertisements (6) Materials communicating to the general public that a position in a company is open.

Affirmative Action (3) A practice in organizations that goes beyond discontinuance of discriminatory practices, including actively seeking, hiring, and promoting minority group members and women.

Age Discrimination in Employment Act (3) Passed in 1967 and amended in 1978 and 1986, this act prohibits arbitrary age discrimination, particularly among those over age 40.

Agency Shop (16) A type of union security arrangement whereby employees must pay union dues to the certified bargaining unit even if they choose not to join the union.

Albermarle Paper Company v. Moody (3) Supreme Court case that clarified the requirements for using and validating tests in selection processes.

Americans with Disabilities Act of 1990 (3) Extends EEO coverage to include most forms of disability, requires employers to make reasonable accommodations, and eliminates post-job-offer medical exams.

Apathy (4) Significant dysfunction tension resulting in no effort being made.

Application Form (6) Company-specific employment forms used to generate specific information the company wants.

Apprenticeship (8) A time—typically two to five years—when an individual is considering to be training to learn a skill.

Assessment Centers (7) A facility where performance simulation tests are administered. These are made up of a series of exercises and are used for selection, development, and performance appraisals.

Attitude Survey (8) Questionnaires used to elicit responses from employees regarding how they feel about their jobs, work groups, supervisors, and the organization.

Attribution Theory (10) A theory of performance evaluation based on the perception of who is in control of an employee's performance.

Attrition (5) A process whereby the jobs of incumbents who leave for any reason will not be filled.

Authorization Card (16) A card signed by prospective union members indicating that they are interested in having a union election held at their work site.

Autonomy (4) The freedom and independence involved in doing one's job.

Baby Boomers (2) Those individuals born between 1946 and 1964.

Baby Busters (2) Those individuals born in 1965 and years after. Often referred to as "generation Xers."

Background Investigation (6) The process of verifying information job candidates provide.

Behavioral Symptoms (14) Symptoms of stress characterized by decreased productivity, increased absenteeism and turnover, and increased smoking and alcohol/substance consumption.

Behaviorally Anchored Rating Scales (BARS) (10) A performance appraisal technique that generates critical incidents and develops behavioral dimensions of performance. The evaluator appraises behaviors rather than traits.

Blind-box Ad (6) An advertisement in which there is no identification of the advertising organization.

Blue Cross (12) A health insurer concerned with the hospital side of health insurance.

Blue Shield (12) A health insurer concerned with the provider side of health insurance.

Broad-banding (11) Paying employees at preset levels based on the level of competencies they possess.

Bulletin Board (15) A means a company uses to post information of interest to its employees.

Burnout (14) Chronic and long-term stress.

Career (9) The sequence of positions that a person has held over his or her life.

Career Counseling (9) Assisting employees in setting directions and identifying areas of professional growth.

Career Development (9) A process designed to assist workers in managing their careers.

Career Stages (9) An individual's career moves through five stages: exploration, establishment, mid-career, late-career, and decline.

Central Tendency (11) The tendency of a rater to give average ratings.

Change Agent (8) Individuals responsible for fostering the change effort, and assisting employees in adapting to the changes.

Checklist Appraisal (10) A performance appraisal type in which a rater checks off those attributes of an employee that apply.

Civil Service Reform Act (16) Replaced Executive Order 11491 as the basic law governing labor relations for federal employees.

Civil Rights Acts of 1991 (3) Employment discrimination law that nullified selected Supreme Court decisions. Reinstated burden of proof by the employer, and allowed for punitive and compensatory damage through jury trials.

Civil Rights Act of 1866 (3) Federal law that prohibited discrimination based on race.

Classification Method (11) Method of job evaluation that focuses on creating common job grades based on skills, knowledge, and abilities.

Clayton Act (16) Labor legislation that attempted to limit the use of injunctions against union activities.

Coaching (8) A development activity in which a manager takes an active role in guiding another manager.

Collective Bargaining (16) The negotiation, administration, and interpretation of a written agreement between two parties, at least one of which represents a group that is acting collectively, that covers a specific period of time.

College Placements (6) An external search process focusing recruiting efforts on a college campus.

Communication (15) The transference of meaning and understanding.

Communications Programs (1) HRM programs designed to provide information to employees.

Company Newsletter (15) A means of providing information for employees in a specific recurring periodical.

Company-wide Meetings (15) Frequently held meetings used to inform employees of various company issues.

Comparable Worth (3) Equal pay for similar jobs, jobs similar in skills, responsibility, working conditions, and effort.

Compensation Administration (11) The process of managing a company's compensation program.

Competency-based Compensation Programs (11) Organizational pay system that rewards skills, knowledge, and behaviors.

Complaint Procedure (15) A formalized procedure in an organization through which an employee seeks resolution of a work problem.

Comprehensive Interviews (6) A selection device in which in-depth information about a candidate can be obtained.

Comprehensive Selection (6) Applying all steps in the selection process before rendering a decision about a job candidate.

Concurrent Validity (6) Validating tests by using current employees as the study group.

Consolidated Omnibus Budget Reconciliation Act (12) Provides for the continuation of employee benefits for a period up to three years after an employee leaves a job.

Constraints on Recruiting Efforts (6) Factors that can affect maximizing outcomes in recruiting.

Construct Validity (6) The degree to which a particular trait is related to successful performance on the job (e.g., IQ tests).

Content Validity (6) The degree to which the content of the test, as a sample, represents all the situations that could have been included (e.g., a typing test for a clerk typist).

Contingent Work Force (2) The part-time, temporary, and contract workers used by organizations to fill peak staffing needs, or perform work unable to be done by core employees.

Continuous Process Improvement (2) A total quality management concept whereby workers continue toward 100 percent effectiveness on the job.

Contract Administration (16) Implementing, interpreting, and monitoring the negotiated agreement between labor and management.

Controlling (1) A management function concerned with monitoring activities.

Core employees (2) An organization's full-time employee population.

Core-plus Plans (12) A flexible benefits program whereby employees are provided core benefit coverage and then are permitted to buy additional benefits from a menu.

Correlation Coefficients (6) A statistical procedure showing the strength of the relationship between one's test score and job performance.

Cost/Benefit Analysis (8) Evaluating an activity where costs are known, but where the standard by which these costs must be measured is ambiguous.

Criterion-related Validity (6) The degree to which a particular selection device accurately predicts the important elements of work behavior (e.g., the relationship between a test score and job performance).

Critical Incident Appraisal (10) A performance appraisal method that focuses on the key behaviors that make the difference between doing a job effectively or ineffectively.

Cultural Environments (2) The attitudes and perspectives shared by individuals from specific countries that shape their behavior and how they view the world.

Culture (8) The rules, jargon, customs, and other traditions that clarify acceptable and unacceptable behavior in an organization.

Cumulative Trauma Disorder (14) An occupational injury that occurs from repetitively performing similar physical movements.

Cut Score (6) A point at which applicants scoring below that point are rejected.

Decentralized Work Sites (2) Work sites that exist away from an organization's facilities.

Decline Phase (9) The final stage in one's career, usually marked by retirement.

Defined Benefit (12) A type of retirement program whereby a retiring employee receives a fixed amount of retirement income based on some average earnings over a period of time.

Defined Contribution Plans (12) A retirement plan whereby an employer only agrees to contribute to employees' retirement funds. The amount contributed is not fixed.

Delegation (2) A management activity in which activi-

ties are assigned to individuals at lower levels in the organization.

Deprivation (4) A state of having an unfulfilled need.

Diary Method (5) A job analysis method requiring job incumbents to record their daily activities.

Dictionary of Occupational Titles (5) A government publication that lists more than 30,000 jobs.

Differential Validity (6) A special type of validation whereby a cut score is lower due to bias in the test.

Discipline (13) A condition in the organization when employees conduct themselves in accordance with the organization's rules and standards of acceptable behavior.

Dismissal (13) A disciplinary action that results in the termination of an employee.

Distributive Bargaining (16) A competitive, confrontational bargaining strategy.

Documentation (10) Used as a record of the performance appraisal process outcomes.

Downsizing (2) An activity in an organization aimed at creating greater efficiency by eliminating certain jobs.

Drug Testing (13) The process of testing applicants/ employees to determine if they are using illicit drugs.

Drug-free Workplace Act (13) Requires specific government-related groups to ensure that their workplace is drug free.

Dual-career Couples (9) A situation in which both husband and wife have distinct careers outside the home.

Dues Checkoff (16) Employer withholding of union dues from union members' paychecks.

Dysfunctional Tension (14) Tension that leads to negative stress.

E-mail (15) An electronic device that allows for messages to be left for another party.

Early Retirement (5) A downsizing effort whereby employees close to retirement are given some incentive to leave the company earlier than expected.

Economic Strike (16) An impasse that results from labor and management's ability to agree on the wages, hours, terms, and conditions of a "new" contract.

Effort (4) Outward action of individuals directed toward some goal.

Effort–performance Relationship (4) The likelihood that putting forth the effort will lead to successful performance on the job.

Electronic Media (15) Any technological device that enhances communications.

Employee Assistance Programs (EAPS) (14) Specific programs designed to help employees with personal problems.

Employee Benefits (12) Membership-based, nonfinancial rewards offered to attract and keep employees.

Employee Counseling (8) A process whereby employees are guided in overcoming performance problems.

Employee Development (8) Future-oriented training, focusing on the personal growth of the employee.

Employee Handbook (15) A booklet describing the important aspects of employment an employee needs to know.

Employee Leasing (6) Hiring "temporary" employees for long periods of time.

Employee Monitoring (13) An activity whereby the company is able to keep informed of its employees' activities.

Employee Referrals (6) A recommendation from a current employee regarding a job applicant.

Employee Retirement Income Security Act (12) Law passed in 1974 designed to protect employee retirement benefits.

Employee Rights (13) A collective term dealing with varied employee protection practices in an organization.

Employee Training (8) Present-oriented training, focusing on individuals' current jobs.

Employment Legislation (1) Laws that directly affect the hiring, firing, and promotion of individuals.

Employment Tests (7) Any selection examination that is designed to determine if an applicant is qualified for the job.

Employment-at-Will (13) Nineteenth-century common law that permitted employers to discipline or discharge employees at their discretion.

Empowering (2) Affording employees more delegation, participative management, work teams, goal setting, and training.

Encounter Stage (8) The socialization stage where individuals confront the possible dichotomy between their organizational expectations and reality.

Environmental Influences (1) Those factors outside the organization that directly affect HRM operations.

Equal Employment Opportunity Commission (3) The arm of the federal government empowered to handle discrimination in employment cases.

Equal Pay Act (11) Passed in 1963, this act requires equal pay for equal work.

Ergonomics (14) The process of matching the work environment to the individual.

Essay Appraisal (10) A performance appraisal method whereby an appraiser writes a narrative about the employee.

Establishment Phase (9) A career stage in which one begins to search for work. It includes getting one's first job.

Executive Order 10988 (16) Affirmed the right of federal employees to join unions and granted restricted bargaining rights to these employees.

Executive Order 11491 (16) Designed to make federal labor relations more like those in the private sector. Also established the Federal Labor Relations Council.

Expatriates (6) Individuals who work in a country in which they are not citizens of that country.

Exploration Phase (9) A career stage that usually ends in one's mid-twenties as one makes the transition from school to work.

External Dimension (9) The objective progression of steps through a given occupation.

Extinction (9) The elimination of any reinforcement that maintains behavior.

Extrinsic Rewards (11) Rewards one gets from the employer, usually money, a promotion, or benefits.

Fact-finder (16) A neutral third-party individual who conducts a hearing to gather evidence and testimony from the parties regarding the differences between them.

Factor Comparison Method (11) A method of job analysis in which job factors are compared to determine the worth of the job.

Fair Credit Reporting Act (13) Requires an employer to notify job candidates of its intent to check into their credit.

Fair Labor Standards Act (11) Passed in 1938, this act established laws outlining minimum wage, overtime pay, and maximum hour requirements for most U.S. workers.

Family and Medical Leave Act (3) Federal legislation that provides employees up to twelve weeks of unpaid leave each year to care for family members, or for their own medical reasons.

Family-Friendly Benefits (12) Flexible benefits that are supportive of caring for one's family.

Family-Friendly Organization (5) Organizations that provide benefits that support employees' caring for their families.

Federal Mediation and Conciliation Service (16) A government agency that assists labor and management in settling their disputes.

Feedback (4) Knowledge of results.

Flexible Benefits (12) A benefits program in which employees are permitted to pick benefits that most meet their needs.

Flexible Spending Accounts (12) Special benefits accounts that allow the employee to set aside money on a pretax basis to pay for certain benefits.

Flextime (4) A scheduling system in which employees are required to work a number of hours per week but are free, within limits, to vary the hours of work.

Forced-choice Appraisal (10) A type of performance appraisal method in which the rater must choose between two specific statements about an employee's work behavior.

4/5ths Rule (3) A rough indicator of discrimination, this rule requires that the number of minority members that a company hires must be at least 80 percent of the majority members in the population hired.

401(k)s (12)   Tax code section that permits employees to set aside a part of their salary for retirement on a pretax basis.

Functional Tension (4)   Positive tension that creates the energy for an individual to act.

Glass Ceiling (3)   The invisible barrier that blocks females and minorities from ascending into upper levels of an organization.

Global Village (2)   The production and marketing of goods and services worldwide.

Golden Parachute (11)   A protection plan for executives in the event that they are severed from the organization.

Graphology (13)   Handwriting analysis.

Grievance Procedures (16)   A complaint-resolving process contained in union contracts.

Grievance (Rights) Arbitration (16)   Specialized steps followed for handling contractual disputes arising from a collective-bargaining agreement.

Griggs v. Duke Power (3)   Landmark Supreme Court decision stating that tests must fairly measure the knowledge or skills required for a job.

Group Interview Method (5)   Meeting with a number of employees to collectively determine what their jobs entail.

Group Order Ranking (10)   A relative standard of performance characterized as placing employees into a particular classification, such as the "top one-fifth."

Halo Error (10)   The tendency to let our assessment of an individual on one trait influence our evaluation of that person on other specific traits.

Hawthorne Studies (1)   A series of studies that provided new insights into group behavior.

Hazard Communication Standard (14)   Requires organizations to communicate to its employees hazardous chemicals they may encounter on the job and how to deal with them safely.

Health Insurance (12)   An employee benefit designed to provide coverage in the event of an injury or illness.

Health Maintenance Act (12)   Established the requirement that companies offering traditional health insurance to its employees must also offer alternative health-care options.

Health Maintenance Organization (12)   Provides comprehensive health services for a flat fee.

Holland Vocational Preferences (9)   An individual occupational personality as it relates to vocational themes.

Honesty Tests (13)   A specialized paper-and-pencil test designed to assess one's honesty.

Host-country national (6)   Hiring a citizen from the host country to perform certain jobs in the global village.

Hot-stove Rule (13)   Discipline should be immediate, provide ample warning, be consistent, and be impersonal.

Human Resource Inventory (5)   Describes the skills that are available within the organization.

Human Resource Management System (5)   A computerized system that assists in the processing of HRM information.

Human Resource Planning (5)   The process of linking human resource planning efforts to the company's strategic direction.

Imminent Danger (14)   A condition where an accident is about to occur.

Impasse (16)   A situation where labor and management cannot reach a satisfactory agreement.

Implied Employment Contract (13)   Any organizational guarantee or promise about job security.

Impression Management (7)   Influencing performance evaluations by portraying an image that is desired by the appraiser.

IMPROSHARE (11)   A special type of incentive plan using a specific mathematical formula for determining employee bonuses.

Incident Rate (14)   Number of injuries, illnesses, or lost workdays as it relates to a common base of 100 full-time employees.

Independent Contractors (6)   Temporary employees offering specialized services to an organization.

Individual Interview Method (5)   Meeting with an employee to determine what his or her job entails.

Individual Needs (4)   A basic want or desire.

Individual Performance–Organizational Goal Relationship (4)   The likelihood that successful performance on the job will lead to the attainment of organizational goals.

Individual Ranking (10)   Ranking employees' performance from highest to lowest.

Initial Screening (6)   The first step in the selection process whereby inquiries about a job are screened.

Integrative Bargaining (16)   A cooperative strategy in which a common goal is the focus of negotiations.

Interactive Videos (8)   Videos that permit the user to make changes/selections.

Interest Arbitration (16)   An impasse resolution technique used to settle contract negotiation disputes.

Internal Search (6)   A promotion-from-within concept.

Interview (7)   A selection method that involves a face-to-face meeting with the candidate.

Intrinsic Rewards (11)   Rewards one receives from the job itself, such as pride in one's work, a feeling of accomplishment, or being part of a team.

Job Analysis (5)   Provides information about jobs currently being done and the knowledge, skills, and abilities that individuals need to perform the jobs adequately.

Job Characteristics Model (4)   A framework for analyzing and designing jobs. JCM identifies five primary job characteristics and their interrelationship.

Job Description (5) A written statement of what the job-holder does, how it is done, and why it is done.

Job Enrichment (4) The process of expanding the depth of the job by allowing employees to do more planning and controlling of their work.

Job Evaluation (5) Specifies the relative value of each job in the organization.

Job Instruction Training (8) A systematic approach to on-the-job training consisting of four basic steps.

Job Rotation (8) Moving employees horizontally or vertically to expand their skills, knowledge, or abilities.

Job Specifications (5) Statements indicating the minimal acceptable qualifications incumbents must possess to successfully perform the essential elements of their jobs.

Jungian Personality Typology (9) Four dimensions of personality matched to work environments.

Karoshi (14) A Japanese term meaning death from overworking.

Labor and Management Reporting and Disclosure Act (16) (See Landrum-Griffin Act.)

Labor-Management Relations Act (16) Also known as the Taft-Hartley Act, it constrained the powers of unions.

Landrum-Griffin Act (16) Also known as the Labor and Management Reporting and Disclosure Act, this legislation protected union members from possible wrongdoing on the part of their unions. Its thrust was to require all unions to disclose their financial statements.

Late-career Phase (9) A career stage in which individuals are no longer learning about their jobs, nor is it expected that they should be trying to outdo levels of performance from previous years.

Layoffs (5) Removing workers from an organization on a temporary or permanent basis.

Leading (1) A management function concerned with directing the work of others.

Learning Curve (8) Depicts the rate of learning.

Legally Required Benefits (12) Employee benefits that are required by law.

Legislating Love (13) Company guidelines on how personal relationships may exist at work.

Leniency Error (10) A means by which performance appraisal can be distorted by evaluating employees against one's own value system.

Local union (16) Provides the grass-roots support for union members in day-to-day labor–management relations.

Lockout (16) A situation in labor–management negotiations whereby management prevents union members from returning to work.

Management (1) The process of efficiently getting activities completed with and through other people.

Management by Objectives (MBO) (10) A performance appraisal method that includes mutual objective setting and evaluation based on the attainment of the specific objectives.

Management Rights (16) Items that are not part of contract negotiations, such as how to run the company, or how much to charge for products.

Management Thought (1) Early theories of management that promoted today's HRM operations.

Marshall v. Barlow, Inc. (14) Supreme Court case that stated an employer could refuse an OSHA inspection unless OSHA had a search warrant to enter the premises.

Mature Workers (2) Those workers born before 1946.

McDonnell-Douglas Corp. v. Green (3) A four-part test used to determine if discrimination has occurred.

Medical/Physical Examination (6) An examination indicating an applicant is physically fit for essential job performance.

Membership-based Rewards (11) Rewards that go to all employees regardless of performance.

Mentoring or Coaching (8) Actively guiding another individual.

Merit Pay (11) An increase in one's pay, usually given on an annual basis.

Metamorphosis Stage (8) The socialization stage whereby the new employee must work out inconsistencies discovered during the encounter stage.

Mid-career Phase (9) A career stage marked by a continuous improvement in performance, leveling off in performance, or the beginning of deterioration of performance.

Mission Statement (5) The reason an organization is in business.

Modular Plans (12) A flexible benefit system whereby employees choose a pre-designed package of benefits.

Motivating Potential Score (4) A predictive index suggesting the motivation potential of a job.

Motivation (4) The willingness to do something, conditioned by the action's ability to satisfy some need.

National Institute for Occupational Safety and Health (NIOSH) (14) The government agency that researches and sets OSHA standards.

National/International Union (16) A federation of local unions.

National Labor Relations Act (16) Legislation giving employees the right to form and join unions and to engage in collective bargaining. (Also known as the Wagner Act.)

National Labor Relations Board (16) Established to administer and interpret the Wagner Act, the NLRB has primary responsibility for conducting union representation elections.

Negative Reinforcement (8) An unpleasant reward.

NLRB v. *Bildisco & Bildisco* (16) Upheld the premise that a company could file for bankruptcy to have a labor contract nullified.

Norms (8) Tells group members what they ought or ought not do in certain circumstances.

Norris–LaGuardia Act (16) Labor law act that set the stage for permitting individuals full freedom to designate a representative of their choosing to negotiate terms and conditions of employment.

Observation Method (5) A job analysis technique in which data are gathered by watching employees work.

Occupational Safety and Health Act (14) Set standards to ensure safe and healthful working conditions and provided stiff penalties for violators.

Office of Federal Contract Compliance Programs (3) The government office that administers the provisions of Executive Order 11246.

Omnibus Budget Reconciliation Act of 1990 (14) Law that increased OSHA penalties from $10,000 to $70,000 for a severe, willful, and repetitive OSHA violation.

Open Shop (16) Employees are free to choose whether or not to join the union, and those who do not are not required to pay union dues.

Operant Conditioning (8) A type of conditioning in which behavior leads to a reward or prevents punishment.

Organizational Development (8) The part of HRM that deals with facilitating systemwide change in the organization.

Organizational Goals (4) Meeting company objectives.

Organizational Goal–Individual Goal Relationship (4) The expectation that achieving organizational goals will lead to the attainment of individual goals.

Organizing (1) A management function that deals with what jobs are to be done, by whom, where decisions are to be made, and the grouping of employees.

Orientation (8) The activities involved in introducing new employees to the organization and their work units.

Outdoor Training (8) Specialized training that occurs outdoors that focuses on building self-confidence and teamwork.

Outplacement (5) A process whereby an organization assists employees, especially those being severed from the organization, in obtaining employment.

Paired Comparison (10) Ranking individuals' performance by counting the number of times any one individual is the preferred member when compared with all other employees.

Participative Management (2) A management concept giving employees more control over the day-to-day activities on their job.

Pay-for-performance (4) Rewarding employees based on their performance.

Peer Evaluations (10) A performance evaluation situation in which coworkers provide input into the employee's performance.

Peer Orientation (8) Coworker assistance in orienting new employees.

Pension Benefit Guaranty Corporation (12) The organization that lays claim to corporate assets to pay or fund inadequate pension programs.

Performance (4) Effective and efficient work, which also considers personnel data such as measures of accidents, turnover, absence, and tardiness.

Performance Appraisal Process (10) A formal process in an organization whereby each employee is evaluated to determine how he or she is performing.

Performance-based Rewards (11) Rewards exemplified by the use of commissions, piecework pay plans, incentive systems, group bonuses, or other forms of merit pay.

Performance Simulation Tests (7) Work sampling and assessment centers focusing on actual job activities.

Perquisites (11) Attractive benefits, over and above a regular salary, granted to executives ("perks").

Physiological Symptoms (14) Characteristics of stress that manifest themselves as increased heart and breathing rates, higher blood pressure, and headaches.

Piecework Plans (11) A compensation plan whereby employees are typically paid for the number of units they actually produce.

Planning (1) A management function focusing on setting organizational goals and objectives.

Plant Closing Bill (13) Also known as WARN, requires employers to give sixty days' advanced notice of pending plant closings or major layoff.

Plant-wide Incentives (11) An incentive system that rewards all members of the plant based on how well the entire group performed.

Plateauing (9) A condition of stagnating in one's current job.

Point Method (11) Breaking down jobs based on identifiable criteria and the degree to which these criteria exist on the job.

Polygraph Protection Act (13) Prohibits the use of lie detectors in screening all job applicants. Often referred to as a "lie-detector" test.

Position Analysis Questionnaire (5) A job analysis technique that rates jobs on 194 elements in six activity categories.

Positive Reinforcement (8) Providing a pleasant response to an individual's actions.

Post-Training Performance Method (8) Evaluating training programs based on how well employees can perform their jobs after they have received the training.

Pre–Post-Training Performance Method (8) Evaluating training programs based the difference in performance before and after one receives training.

Pre–Post-Training Performance with Control Group (8) Evaluating training by comparing pre- and post-training results with individuals who did not receive the training.

Prearrival Stage (8) The socialization process stage that recognizes individuals arrive in an organization with a set of organizational values, attitudes, and expectations.

Predictive Validity (6) Validating tests by using prospective applicants as the study group.

Preferred Provider Organizations (12) Organization that requires using specific physicians and health-care facilities to contain the rising costs of health care.

Pregnancy Discrimination Act (3) Law prohibiting discrimination based on pregnancy.

Privacy Act (13) Requires federal government agencies to make available information in an individual's personnel file.

Professional Organizations (6) A source of job applicants where placement facilities at regional conferences and national conferences usually occur.

Programmed Instruction (8) Material is learned in a highly organized, logical sequence, that requires the individual to respond.

Protected Group Member (3) Any individual who is afforded protection under employment discrimination laws.

Psychological Symptoms (14) Characteristics of stress that manifest themselves as tension, anxiety, irritability, boredom, and procrastination.

Public Policy Violation (13) Prohibiting the termination of an employee for refusing to obey an order the employee considered illegal.

Punishment (13) Penalizing an employee for undesirable behaviors.

Railway Labor Act (16) Provided the initial impetus to widespread collective bargaining.

Ranking Method (11) Rating employees from highest to lowest.

Realistic Job Preview (7) A selection device that allows job candidates to learn negative as well as positive information about the job and organization.

Reduced Work Hours (5) A downsizing concept whereby employees work fewer than forty hours and are paid accordingly.

Reengineering (2) Radical, quantum change in an organization.

Reject Errors (6) Rejecting candidates who would later perform successfully.

Relative Standards (10) Evaluating an employee's performance by comparing the employee with other employees.

Reliability (6) A selection device's consistency of measurement.

Repetitive Motion Disorder (14) Injuries sustained by continuous and repetitive movements of the hand.

Replacement Charts (5) HRM organizational charts indicating positions that may become vacant in the near future and the individuals who may fill the vacancy.

Representation Certification (16) The election process whereby union members vote in a union as their representative.

Representation Decertification (16) The election process whereby union members vote out their union as their representative.

Restricted Policy (3) An HRM policy that results in the exclusion of a class of individuals.

Reverse Discrimination (3) A claim made by white males that minority candidates are given preferential treatment in employment decisions.

Rightsizing (5) Linking employee needs to organizational strategy.

Roles (8) Behaviors that job incumbents are expected to display.

Scanlon Plan (11) An organization-wide incentive program focusing on cooperation between management and employees through sharing problems, goals, and ideas.

Scientific Management (1) A set of principles designed to enhance worker productivity.

Selection Process (6) The process of selecting the best candidate for the job.

Sexual Harassment (3) Anything of a sexual nature where it results in a condition of employment, an employment consequence, or creates a hostile or offensive environment.

Shared Services (1) Sharing HRM activities among geographically dispersed divisions.

Sick Building (14) An unhealthy work environment.

Similarity Error (10) Evaluating employees based on the way an evaluator perceives himself or herself.

Simulations (8) Any artificial environment that attempts to closely mirror an actual condition.

Situational Interview (7) Structured interview where questions relate directly to actual work activities.

Skill Deficiencies (2) The lacking of basic abilities to perform many of today's jobs.

Skill Variety (4) A situation in which jobs require a number of skills.

Smoke-Free Environment (14) A work environment where smoking is significantly reduced or eliminated.

Smoke-Free Policies (14) Organization policies that reduce or prohibit smoking on company premises.

Social Learning Theory (8) Theory of learning that views learning occurring through observation and direct experience.

Social Security (12) Retirement, disability, and survivor benefits, paid by the government to aged, former members of the labor force, the disabled, or their survivors.

Socialization (8)   A process of adaption that takes place as individuals attempt to learn the values and norms of work roles.

Span of Control (2)   The number of employees a supervisor can effectively and efficiently direct.

Strategic Goals (5)   Organization-wide goals setting direction for the next five to twenty years.

Stress (14)   A dynamic condition in which an individual is confronted with an opportunity, constraint, or demand related to what he or she desires and for which the outcome is perceived to be both uncertain and important.

Stress Interview (7)   An interview designed to see how the applicants handle themselves under pressure.

Stressors (14)   Something that causes stress in an individual.

Structured Interviews (7)   An interview in which there are fixed questions that are presented to every applicant.

Structured Questionnaire Method (5)   A specifically designed questionnaire on which employees rate tasks they perform on their jobs.

Succession Planning (5)   An executive inventory report indicating which individuals are ready to move into higher positions in the company.

Suggestion Program (15)   A process whereby employees have the opportunity to tell management how they perceive the organization is doing.

Summary Plan Description (12)   An ERISA requirement of explaining to employees their pension program and rights.

Sunshine Laws (16)   Laws that exist in some states that mandate that labor–management negotiations be open to the public.

Suspension (13)   A period of time off from work as a result of a disciplinary process.

Taft-Hartley Act (16)   See Labor-Management Relations Act.

Task Identity (4)   A situation in which a worker completes all phases of a job.

Task Significance (4)   A situation in which the employee has a substantial impact on the lives of other employees.

Team-Based Rewards (11)   Rewards based on how well the team performed.

Technical Conference Method (5)   A job analysis technique that involves extensive input from the employee's supervisor.

Temporary Employees (6)   Employees hired for a limited time to perform a specific job.

360-Degree Appraisal (10)   Performance appraisal process in which supervisors, peers, employees, customers, and the like evaluate the individual.

Title VII (3)   The most prominent piece of legislation regarding HRM, it states that it is illegal to discriminate against individuals based on race, religion, color, sex, or national origin.

Total Quality Management (2)   A continuous process improvement.

Unemployment Compensation (12)   Program designed to provide employees with some income continuation during periods of involuntary unemployment.

Union (16)   Organization of workers, acting collectively, seeking to protect and promote their mutual interests through collective bargaining.

Union Avoidance (16)   A company tactic of providing to employees those things unions would provide without employees having to join the union,.

Union Busting (16)   A company tactic designed to eliminate the union that represents the company's employees.

Union Security Arrangements (16)   Labor contract provisions designed to attract and retain dues-paying union members.

Union Shop (16)   Employers can hire nonunion workers, but they must become dues-paying members within a prescribed period of time.

Upward Appraisals (10)   An employee appraisal process whereby employees evaluate their supervisors.

Validity (6)   The proven relationship of a selection device to some relevant criterion.

Validity Generalization (6)   Statistically corrected test that is valid across many job categories.

Values (6)   Basic convictions about what is right or wrong, good or bad, desirable or not.

Vesting Rights (12)   The permanent right to pension benefits.

Virtual Reality (8)   A process whereby the work environment is simulated by sending messages to the brain.

Vocational Rehabilitation Act (3)   This act extended to the physically and mentally disabled the same protection afforded racial minorities and women.

Wage Curve (11)   The result of the plotting of points of established pay grades against wage base rates to identify the general pattern of wages and find individuals whose wages are out of line.

Wage Structure (11)   A pay scale showing ranges of pay within each grade.

Wage Surveys (11)   Used to gather factual data on pay practices among firms and companies within specific communities.

Wagner Act (16)   Also known as the National Labor Relations Act of 1935, this act gave employees the legitimate right to form and join unions and to engage in collective bargaining.

Walk-ins (6) Unsolicited applicants.

Weighted Application Form (7) A special type of application form where relevant applicant information is used to determine the likelihood of job success.

Wellness Program (14) Organizational programs designed to keep employees healthy.

Whistle-blowing (11) A situation in which an employee notifies authorities of wrongdoing in an organization.

Wildcat Strike (16) An unauthorized and illegal strike that occurs during the terms of an existing contract.

Work-Force Diversity (2) The varied personal characteristics that make the work force heterogeneous.

Work Sampling (7) A selection device requiring the job applicant to actually perform a small segment of the job.

Work Sharing (7) A work concept whereby two or more individuals share one full-time job with the remaining time spent on individual pursuits.

Work Teams (2) Formal work groups made up of inter-

dependent individuals who are responsible for attainment of a specific goal.

Worker Adjustment and Retraining Notification Act (13) Federal law requiring employers to give sixty days' notice of pending plant closing or major layoff.

Workers' Compensation (12) Payment to workers or their heirs for death or permanent or total disability that resulted from job-related activities.

Workplace Security (13) A situation in which employers protect their property and trade business.

Written Tests (7) An organizational selection tool designed to indicate whether an applicant will be successful on the job if hired.

Written Verbal Warning (7) The first formal step in the disciplinary process.

Written Warning (13) First formal step of the disciplinary process.

Yellow-dog Contract (16) An agreement whereby employees state that they are not now, nor will they be in the future, union members.

Name Index

Subject and Organization Index

Photo Credits

Chapter 1
Page 3: Gabe Palmer/The Stock Market. Page 7: Lee Angle Photography, courtesy Nancy Howell. Page 13: ©Ted Rice. Page 21: ©Sergio Dorantes.

Chapter 2
Page 31: ©Mark Richardson/Contact Press Images. Page 35: Courtesy Patricia Gallup. Page 36: ©Pablo Bartholomew/Gamma Liaison. Page 44: ©Brenda Priddy. Page 52: ©Kenneth Jarecke/Contact Press Images.

Chapter 3
Page 64: ©Doug Hoke. Page 68: Courtesy Colgate-Palmolive Company. Page 72: ©Scott Braman. Page 78: Courtesy Ingrid Knox. Page 79: ©Jeffrey Lowe. Page 87: ©Eduardo Citrinblum.

Chapter 4
Page 99: Courtesy Fact Media International. Page 105: SuperStock, Inc. Page 110: Courtesy of BB Sams. Page 115: ©Michael A. Schwarz. Page 117: Dilbert reprinted by permission of United Feature Syndicate, Inc. Page 120: B. Seitz/Photo Researchers.

Chapter 5
Page 129: ©Simon Griffiths. Page 135: Najlah Feanny/SABA. Page 148: Mark Lewis/Gamma Liaison.

Chapter 6
Page 155: ©Erik Freeland/U.S. News & World Report. Page 164: Terry Vine/Tony Stone Images/New York, Inc. Page 167: Courtesy CLAM Associates. Page 171: ©Steve Niedorf/The Image Bank.

Chapter 7
Page 191: Lucas Abreu/The Image Bank. Page 196: ©Mark Newman/PhotoEdit. Page 203: ©Bruce Ayers/Tony Stome Images/New York, Inc. Page 208: ©1997 Mark Parisi/Atlantic Feature. Page 210: Courtesy Motherwear, Inc.

Chapter 8
Page 219: Courtesy Marriott International. Page 226: Courtesy Bo Pilgrim. Page 235: Charles Gupton. Page 240: ©Charlie Archambault/U.S. News & World Report. Page 244: Andy Washnik.

Chapter 9
Page 253: ©Louise Gubb/The Image Works. Page 257: ©Peter Gregoire. Page 261: Courtesy American Business Women's Association. Page 264: Courtesy The Home Depot. Page 274: ©Michelle McDonald.

Chapter 10
Page 285: ©Andrew Brusso. Page 291: Jeff Smith/The Image Bank. Page 304: Dan Bosler/Tony Stone Images/New York, Inc. Page 309: Courtesy David Blackwell. Page 312: ©Sergio Dorantes/Sygma.

Chapter 11
Page 321: Wendy Carr, courtesy Tom Warner. Page 327: Courtesy Connie Sitterly. Page 335: ©Chris Usher. Page 339: Courtesy Saturn Corporation. Page 343: ©John Abbott.

Chapter 12
Page 353: Courtesy Work/Family Directions. Page 360: Matthew McVay/SABA. Page 369: ©Mark Katzman/Ferguson Katzman Photography. Page 373 (left): Courtesy Jeanne Baker. Page 373 (right): Courtesy Robin Birdsong. Page 374: ©Eric Millette.

Chapter 13
Page 385: Dilip Mehta/Contact Press Images/PNI. Page 392: Courtesy Toys R Us. Page 399: ©Max Aguilera-Hellweg. Page 408: ©Steve Boljonis.

Chapter 14
Page 419: Steve Miller/AP/Wide World Photos. Page 430: ©Lara Jo Regan/SABA. Page 433: Courtesy Bob and Ann Bowlin. Page 436: ©Jason Grow/SABA. Page 445: ©Terry Clark.

Chapter 15
Page 457: ©Chuck Potter Photography. Page 462: Bard Martin/The Image Bank. Page 469: Courtesy Sprint. Page 470: Dilbert reprinted by permission of United Feature Syndicate, Inc. Page 471: Courtesy Ray Gameson. Page 474: Courtesy Dana Corporation.

Chapter 16
Page 481: ©Ron Haviv/SABA. Page 486: Jim Callaway. Page 498: ©Bette Lee/Impact Visuals. Page 502: Bill Burke/Impact Visuals. Page 504: Jim Callaway.